The Earthscan Reader in Sustainable Consumption

The Earthscan Reader in Sustainable Consumption

Edited by

Tim Jackson

EARTHSCAN

London • Sterling, VA

First published by Earthscan in the UK and USA in 2006

ISBN-10:   1-84407-165-0   paperback
ISBN-13:   978-1-84407-165-4   paperback
ISBN-10:   1-84407-164-2   hardback
ISBN-13:   978-1-84407-164-7   hardback

Typeset by Composition and Design Services
Printed and bound in the UK by TJ International, Padstow, Cornwall
Cover design by Andrew Corbett

For a full list of publications please contact:
Earthscan
8–12 Camden High Street
London, NW1 0JH, UK
Tel: +44 (0)20 7387 8558
Fax: +44 (0)20 7387 8998
E-mail: earthinfo@earthscan.co.uk
Web: www.earthscan.co.uk

22883 Quicksilver Drive, Sterling, VA 20166-2012, USA

Earthscan is an imprint of James and James (Science Publishers) Ltd and publishes in association with the International Institute for Environment and Development

A catalogue record for this book is available from the British Library

Library of Congress Cataloging-in-Publication Data

The Earthscan reader in sustainable consumption / edited by Tim Jackson.
    p. cm.
  ISBN-13: 978-1-84407-164-7 (pbk.)
  ISBN-10: 1-84407-164-2 (pbk.)
  ISBN-13: 978-1-84407-165-4
  ISBN-10: 1-84407-165-0
  1. Consumption (Economics)--Environmental aspects. 2. Consumption (Economics)--Moral and ethical aspects. 3. Voluntary simplicity movement. I. Jackson, Tim, 1957-
  HB820.E17 2006
  339.4'7--dc22

                            2006020116

Contents

Part 1   Framing Sustainable Consumption

Part 2   Resisting Consumerism

Part 3   Resisting Simplicity

Part 4   Reframing Sustainable Consumption

List of Boxes, Figures and Tables

Boxes

Figures

Tables

List of Acronyms and Abbreviations

BTU	British thermal unit
CES	consumer expenditure survey
CFC	chlorofluorocarbon
CO_2	carbon dioxide
CSD	Commission on Sustainable Development (United Nations)
Defra	Department for Environment, Food and Rural Affairs (UK)
DETR	Department for Environment, Transport and the Regions (UK, 1997–2001)
DOE	Department of the Environment
DTI	Department of Trade and Industry (UK)
EAP	Energy Analysis Program (University of Groningen)
ESRC	Economic and Social Research Council
FoE	Friends of the Earth
GAP	Global Action Plan
GDP	gross domestic product
GHG	greenhouse gas
HEI	household environmental impact
IIED	International Institute of Environment and Development
IOA	input–output analysis
IPCC	International Panel on Climate Change
IPP	integrated product policies (the Netherlands)
ISO	International Standards Organization
LCA	life-cycle assessment
NCC	National Consumer Council (UK)
NDP	net domestic product
NEPP	Netherlands Environmental Policy Plan
NGO	non-governmental organization
NIDO	National Initiative for Sustainable Development (the Netherlands)
NO_x	nitrogen oxide
OCSC	Oxford Commission on Sustainable Consumption
OECD	Organisation for Economic Co-operation and Development
OPEC	Organization of the Petroleum Exporting Countries
SAM	social accounting matrix
SDC	Sustainable Development Commission
SO_2	sulphur dioxide
UN	United Nations

UNCED   United Nations Conference on Environment and Development
UNDESA   United Nations Department of Economic and Social Affairs
UNDP   United Nations Development Programme
UNEP   United Nations Environment Programme
VROM   Ministry of Housing, Spatial Planning and the Environment (the Nether-
          lands)
WCED   World Commission on Environment and Development
          (the Brundtland Commission)
WSSD   World Summit on Sustainable Development

List of Sources

Chapter 1 Jackson, T. (2006) 'Readings in sustainable consumption', original material for this book
Copyright © Tim Jackson, 2006.

Chapter 2 United Nations Development Programme (1998) 'Consumption from a human development perspective', Chapter 2 in *Human Development Report 1998*, Oxford University Press, Oxford, pp38–45
Copyright © United Nations Development Programme, 1998. Reproduced with permission of Oxford University Press, Inc.

Chapter 3 Robins, N. and Roberts, S. (1998) 'Making sense of sustainable consumption', *Development*, vol 41, no 1, pp28–36
Copyright © Palgrave Macmillan, 1998. Reproduced with permission.

Chapter 4 Princen, T. (2002) 'Consumption and its externalities: Where economy meets ecology', Chapter 2 in T. Princen, M. Maniates and K. Concha (eds) *Confronting Consumption*, MIT Press, Cambridge, MA, pp23–42
Copyright © MIT Press, 2002. Reproduced with permission.

Chapter 5 Moll, H. C., Noorman, K., Kok, R., Engström, R., Throne-Hoist, H. and Clark, C. (2005) 'Pursuing more sustainable consumption by analysing household metabolism in European countries and cities', *Journal of Industrial Ecology*, vol 9, no 1–2, pp253–269
Copyright © MIT Press, 2002. Reproduced with permission.

Chapter 6 Hertwich, E. G. (2006) 'Accounting for sustainable consumption: A review of studies of the environmental impacts of households', original material for this book
Copyright © Edgar Hertwich, 2006.

Chapter 7 Jackson, T. (2006) 'Challenges for sustainable consumption policy', adapted by the author from Chapter 8 of P. Vass (ed) *CRI Regulatory Review 2004/2005*, Centre for the Study of Regulated Industries, Bath, pp143–169
Copyright © Tim Jackson, 2006.

Chapter 8 Durning, P. (1992) 'The dubious rewards of consumption', originally titled 'The dubious rewards of consumerism' as Chapter 3 of *How Much is Enough?*, Worldwatch Institute, Boston, MA, pp37–48
Copyright © Worldwatch Institute, www.worldwatch.org, 1992. Reproduced with permission.

Chapter 9 Hirsch, F. (1977) 'The new commodity fetishism', Chapter 6 in *Social Limits to Growth*, Routledge, London, pp84–94
Copyright © Routledge, 1977. Reproduced with permission.

Chapter 10 Kotlowitz, A. (1999) 'False connections', Chapter 5 in R. Rosenblatt (ed) *Consuming Desires: Consumption, Culture and the Pursuit of Happiness*, Island Press, Washington, DC, pp65–72
Copyright © Island Press, 1999. Reproduced with permission.

Chapter 11 Elgin, D. (1981) 'Living more simply', Chapter 5 in *Voluntary Simplicity: Towards a Way of Life that is Outwardly Simple, Inwardly Rich*, William Morrow, New York, pp143–160
Copyright © Duane Elgin, 1981. Reproduced with permission of HarperCollins Publishers.

Chapter 12 Etzioni, A. (1998) 'Voluntary simplicity: Characterization, select psychological implications and societal consequences', *Journal of Economic Psychology*, vol 19, no 5, pp619–643
Copyright © Journal of Economic Psychology, 1998. Reproduced with permission.

Chapter 13 Schor, J. (1998) 'Learning Diderot's lesson: Stopping the upward creep of desire', Chapter 6 in *The Overspent American: Upscaling, Downshifting and the New Consumer*, Basic Books, New York, pp145–167
Copyright © Juliet Schor, 1998. Reproduced with permission of Basic Books, a member of Perseus Books, LLC.

Chapter 14 Martens, S. and Spaargaren, G. (2005) 'The politics of sustainable consumption: The case of the Netherlands', *Sustainability: Science, Practice and Policy*, vol 1, no 1, pp29–42
Copyright © Susan Martens and Gert Spaargaren, 2005. Reproduced with permission.

Chapter 15 Miller, D. (2001) 'The poverty of morality', *Journal of Consumer Culture*, vol 1, no 2, pp225–243
Copyright © Sage Publications, 2001. Reproduced with permission.

Chapter 16 Douglas, M. (1976) 'Relative poverty – relative communication', in A. Halsey (ed) *Traditions of Social Policy*, Basil Blackwell, Oxford, pp197–215
Copyright © Blackwell Publishing, 1976. Reproduced with permission.

Acknowledgements

I am profoundly grateful to all those who have contributed advice, insights and suggestions during the compilation of this volume. I owe a particular debt of gratitude to Glenn Johnstone for helping negotiate permissions from various publishers and to Hamish Ironside, Michael Fell, Rob West and the rest of the Earthscan team for their patience and support throughout the process. The work was supported in part by a fellowship from the Economic and Social Research Council (ESRC) under the Sustainable Technologies Programme (RES-332-27-0001).

Readings in Sustainable Consumption

Tim Jackson

Introduction

At one level, the subject matter of this book is very straightforward: the consumption patterns that characterize modern Western society are unsustainable. They rely too heavily on finite resources and they generate unacceptable environmental impacts.

They are also unfair. The richest nations enjoy the benefits of material affluence, while the poorest still suffer from inadequate access even to the basic necessities of life. To make matters worse, the poorest sometimes bear more than their fair share of environmental impacts from the consumption patterns of the richest – an uncomfortable kind of 'double whammy'.

Inequities in the present are compounded by our debts to the future. In many cases, the worst impacts from activities today will only transpire later on. The running down of finite resources may not matter much until they are gone. The pollution of pristine environments may not bother us unduly until the soil is toxic or the water unsafe. The worst of the changes to our climate may not materialize for another 50 years. It may be decades before the social wounds from a divided world come home to roost. But none of this diminishes our responsibility for the effect consumption today might have on well-being tomorrow.

Perhaps surprisingly, there is also evidence to suggest that consumer society may have failed even in its own terms. After a certain point, material wealth has not delivered consistent improvements in well-being, even for those who benefit from its cornucopia of modern goods and services. Having more stuff doesn't always make us happy. Material aspirations don't necessarily deliver well-being. And a society dedicated to materialist values sometimes undermines the conditions on which well-being depends.

These are some of the contentions that have given rise to the emerging discourse on 'sustainable consumption'.

The discourse is a fascinating one for all sorts of reasons. In the first place, it requires policy to engage in areas it has traditionally been far from comfortable engaging in: the values, expectations and aspirations of ordinary people. It forces us to confront not just the hidden driving forces of human behaviour but the limitations on our goals and intentions – the place where agency stops and social structure begins. In addition, the whole discourse embodies a profoundly ethical dimension in which rights and responsibilities are deeply entwined, in which both present and future generations are implicated. Finally, it turns out that sustainable consumption can only really be understood or evaluated in the context of much older and deeper debates about consumption, consumer behaviour and consumerism itself.

In short, sustainable consumption has emerged as one of the most challenging and vital policy debates of our time. The discourse around sustainable consumption has become a place where it is possible (perhaps even necessary) to address not just the technological and economic questions about the human appropriation of environmental resources, but deeper and broader questions about the nature of the 'good life' and the course of human progress.

So much for grand claims. It is also entirely possible to pin down sustainable consumption as a historical discourse, emerging out of a very specific set of institutional and policy processes. In the next couple of sections, I provide a very brief overview of these processes and discuss questions of definition and scope.

In spite of the simple premise with which I opened this chapter, making sense of the burgeoning literature on sustainable consumption is far from easy. This volume is an attempt to negotiate a number of different complexities. It gathers together a variety of different kinds of writing: some older, some more recent; some already published, some written or adapted specifically for this anthology; some academic, some almost journalistic in nature; each dealing with different aspects of the wider debate.

Choosing from the vast available literature has been challenging. In a later part of this opening chapter I describe a little of my rationale for making the selections I have. I also attempt to link the contributions to each other and to wider trends and debates. Neither of these efforts is likely to be entirely satisfactory. This book could have been twice the size and still not covered the territory. And if it had waited any longer before going to the publisher, it would have been different again; the field is growing so rapidly. In the couple of years since I started this project, both academic and policy interests in sustainable consumption have burgeoned massively. What has been left out from what follows will dwarf what has been included.

All the same, I hope this reader will provide an introduction to the debate, an insight into its historicity, and something in the way of a route map through at least a part of the rugged terrain that is sustainable consumption.[1]

A Brief History of Sustainable Consumption

The terminology is recent. But the concern with resource consumption is scarcely new. Those with a bent for history might happily trace its origins to (at least) the second or third century BC.[2] Early modern critics of the level of consumption in industrial society date from the mid-19th century and include Henry Thoreau, William Morris and Thorstein Veblen.[3] Over-consumption of resources first registered in the international policy arena in 1949.[4] The issue was placed firmly on the policy map at the United Nations Conference on the Human Environment in Stockholm in 1972.

In the same year, the Club of Rome published its influential treatise on *The Limits to Growth* (Meadows et al, 1972). Falling commodity prices and new discoveries undermined many of the authors' worst predictions about resource scarcity. But the relevance of consumption patterns to pressing environmental problems (climate change is the most obvious and relevant example) proved a more robust element of the Club of Rome critique, and by the late 1980s, consumption had become a vital aspect of the debate about sustainable development (WCED, 1987).

The term sustainable consumption itself can be dated more or less precisely to Agenda 21 – the main policy document to emerge from the Rio Earth Summit in 1992. Chapter 4 of Agenda 21 was entitled 'Changing Consumption Patterns'. It argued that 'the major cause of the continued deterioration of the global environment is the unsustainable pattern of consumption and production, particularly in industrialized countries'. Agenda 21 (1992, 4.3–4.13) called in particular for action:

a. To promote patterns of consumption and production that reduce environmental stress and will meet the basic needs of humanity;
b. To develop a better understanding of the role of consumption and how to bring about more sustainable consumption patterns.

In effect, the Rio Conference provided a far-reaching mandate for examining, questioning and revising consumption patterns – and, by implication, consumer behaviours, values, expectations and lifestyles.

This mandate was taken up with some enthusiasm during the mid-1990s by the international policy community. In 1994, the Norwegian government hosted a roundtable on sustainable consumption in Oslo involving business, non-governmental organization (NGO) and government representatives (Ofstad, 1994). The United Nations Commission on Sustainable Development (CSD) launched an international work programme on changing production and consumption patterns in 1995. At the 'Rio Plus 5' conference in 1997, governments had identified sustainable consumption as an 'overriding issue' and a 'cross-cutting theme' in the sustainable development debate.

By the late 1990s, initiatives on sustainable consumption were in full flood. The 1998 *Human Development Report* focused explicitly on the topic of consumption (UNDP 1998; see also Chapter 2 in this book). In the same year, the Norwegian government organized a further workshop in Kabelvåg. One of the outcomes of that workshop was the launching of the United Nations Environment Programme's (UNEP's) Sustainable Consumption Network (SC.net) which has continued to provide a rich source of information on policy initiatives in the area and marked the emergence of UNEP as a 'lead' international agency – along with the United Nations Department of Economic and Social Affairs (UNDESA) – in sustainable consumption and production. By the time the World Summit on Sustainable Development (WSSD) convened in Johannesburg in 2002, 'changing consumption and production patterns' had been identified as one of three 'overarching objectives' for sustainable development (UN, 2002a).

Chapter 3 of the Johannesburg Plan of Implementation (UN, 2002b) called for the development of 'a 10-year framework of programmes in support of regional and national initiatives to accelerate a shift towards sustainable consumption and production'. The so-called 'Marrakech process' – led by UNEP and UNDESA – includes regular regional and global meetings, supported by informal expert task forces and roundtables to promote progress in the area. It has spawned an extensive international effort on a range of different aspects of sustainable consumption. Examples of recent initiatives include the launch of the UNEP/Wuppertal Institute Collaborating Centre on Sustainable Consumption and Production; the setting up of a series of International Task Forces (for example on sustainable procurement, education for sustainable consumption and sustainable lifestyles); and the publication of a number of reports on marketing sustainable consumption and sustainable lifestyles (UNEP, 2005a, 2005b, 2005c).

Defining Sustainable Consumption

This decade of initiatives placed the language of sustainable consumption firmly on the policy agenda. But agreement on what sustainable consumption is or should be about proved more difficult to negotiate.[5] The broad idea had been defined around a kind of double negative. Agenda 21 and a great deal of other early environmental literature had identified the *unsustainability* of existing patterns of consumption and production. Sustainable consumption was, in a very broad sense, born out of the idea that this unsustainability had to be reversed. In other words, the aim was to arrive (somehow) at patterns of consumption that are *not unsustainable* in the way that previous patterns of consumption have been.

Within this broad consensus, however, a variety of different definitions (Box 1.1) have been adopted by different institutions. Several points are worth noting about this range of definitions. The first is that they each take different positions on the extent to which sustainable consumption involves changes in consumer behaviours and lifestyles. Some definitions are quite explicit that the domain of interest is consumer needs and aspirations and the constraints imposed on these by environmental limits. Other definitions clearly favour an approach that concentrates on production processes and consumer products, suggesting that the route to sustainable consumption lies mainly in the more efficient production of more sustainable products. Others seem, almost deliberately, to conflate these two issues.

A second, related point of variation between the definitions in Box 1.1 lies in the extent to which the different positions imply consuming more efficiently, consuming more responsibly or quite simply consuming less. While some definitions insist that sustainable consumption implies consuming less, others assert that it means consuming differently, and in particular consuming more efficiently, and that it categorically does not mean consuming less.

The dominant institutional consensus has tended to settle for a position which is closer to this latter kind of definition (consume efficiently) than it is to the former (change lifestyles). A case in point was the Plan of Implementation signed at the Johannesburg Summit in 2002 (UN, 2002b). Far from cementing the focus on lifestyle issues implicit in Agenda 21, the Plan appeared to retreat from the idea of lifestyle change altogether. Instead, the focus was placed firmly on improvements in technology and the supply of more eco-efficient products, services and infrastructures.

Essentially, this institutional view is one in which sustainable consumption means (more) consumption of more sustainable products. This is to be achieved primarily through improvements in the efficiency with which resources are converted into eco-

---

Box 1.1 *Defining sustainable consumption*

The use of goods and services that respond to basic needs and bring a better quality of life, while minimizing the use of natural resources, toxic materials and emissions of waste and pollutants over the lifecycle, so as not to jeopardize the needs of future generations. (Ofstad, 1994)

The special focus of sustainable consumption is on the economic activity of choosing, using, and disposing of goods and services and how this can be changed to bring social and environmental benefit. (IIED, 1998)

Sustainable consumption means we have to use resources to meet our basic needs and not use resources in excess of what we need. (Participant definition, Kabelvåg, IIED, 1998)

Sustainable consumption is not about consuming less, it is about consuming differently, consuming efficiently, and having an improved quality of life. (UNEP, 1999)

Sustainable consumption is consumption that supports the ability of current and future generations to meet their material and other needs, without causing irreversible damage to the environment or loss of function in natural systems. (OCSC, 2000)

Sustainable consumption is an umbrella term that brings together a number of key issues, such as meeting needs, enhancing quality of life, improving efficiency, minimizing waste, taking a lifecycle perspective and taking into account the equity dimension; integrating these component parts in the central question of how to provide the same or better services to meet the basic requirements of life and the aspiration for improvement, for both current and future generations, while continually reducing environmental damage and the risk to human health. (UNEP, 2001)

Sustainable consumption and production is continuous economic and social progress that respects the limits of the Earth's ecosystems, and meets the needs and aspirations of everyone for a better quality of life, now and for future generations to come. (DTI, 2003a)

Sustainable consumption is a balancing act. It is about consuming in such a way as to protect the environment, use natural resources wisely and promote quality of life now, while not spoiling the lives of future consumers. (NCC, 2003)

Sources: DTI (2003a); IIED (1998); NCC (2003); OCSC (2000); Ofstad (1994); UNEP (1999); UNEP (2001).

---

nomic goods. It is a position typified by a speech given by the former UK Trade and Industry Secretary, Patricia Hewitt, in 2003 (DTI, 2003b) in which she argued that:

> There is nothing wrong with rising consumption, indeed it is to be welcomed as symptomatic of rising living standards in our communities. And it is quite right that the poorest in the world aspire to escape poverty and enjoy those standards. But we need to make

sure the products and services we consume are designed not to harm our environment. We can enjoy more comfort, more enjoyment and more security without automatically increasing harmful and costly impacts on the environment. But it requires a re-thinking of business models to make more productive use of natural resources.

Reasons for this institutional retreat from the thorny issues of consumer behaviour and lifestyles are not particularly hard to find. The area of lifestyle choice has often been regarded as too subjective, too ideological, too value laden, or simply too intractable to be amenable to policy intervention. In particular, addressing it appears to involve questioning some fundamental assumptions about the way modern society functions. Intervening in consumer behaviour would contradict the much-vaunted 'sovereignty' of consumer choice. Reducing consumption appears to threaten a variety of vested interests and undermine the key structural role that consumption plays in economic growth. Finally, arguments to reduce consumption appear to undermine legitimate efforts by poorer countries to improve their quality of life.

Nonetheless, the fall-back position is also problematic for a number of reasons. In particular, the concentration on efficiency and productivity tends to obscure important questions about the *scale* of resource consumption patterns. In fact, it would be entirely possible, under this framing of the problem, to have a growing number of ethical and green consumers buying more and more 'sustainable' products produced by increasingly 'efficient' production processes, and yet for the absolute scale of resource consumption – and the associated environmental impacts – to continue to grow.

One of the many confusing tensions underlying this debate is the question of what, precisely, is being or should be (or should not be) consumed in the consumer society. There is an important (although not always very clearly articulated) difference between material resource consumption and economic consumption. Material resource consumption – with its attendant implications for resource scarcity and environmental degradation – has been the principal focus of many of the policy debates on sustainable development. But economic consumers do not only buy and consume material resources. In fact, so-called 'final consumers' (households, for example) rarely buy materials per se at all. Rather they consume a variety of goods and services, which employ a variety of different kinds of material inputs and give rise to a range of different material and environmental impacts. Resources are consumed in the course of economic consumption; but the two processes are not identical or even congruent. Some forms of resource consumption take place outside of the economic framework. Some forms of economic consumption involve virtually no resource consumption at all.

This lack of congruence is, in one sense, precisely what has allowed the institutional position on sustainable consumption to retain a degree of credibility. So long as the decoupling of economic expenditure from material resources occurs faster than the growth in economic consumption, then surely it should be possible to preserve the sanctity of economic growth and at the same time achieve important environmental goals? This position is problematic, however, in the face of historical evidence. There is little doubt that economic consumption has historically relied heavily on the consumption of material resources; that improvements in resource productivity have generally been offset by increases in scale; and that the goods and services that people actually buy continue to be inherently material in nature. Simplistic appeals to reduce material consumption while maintaining economic growth risk charges of naivety or even disingenuousness.

Sustainable Consumption: A Debate within a Debate

Almost inevitably, policy-makers have been brought back to the idea that engaging in the complex terrain of lifestyle and behavioural change is going to be essential to make progress on sustainable consumption. Quite recently, and somewhat hesitantly, policy-makers have begun to engage with the question of how and whether it might be possible to intervene in consumption patterns and to influence people's behaviours and lifestyles.

The effort of the international agencies (UNEP, 2003, 2005a) has focused mainly on the benefits achievable through marketing, trying to communicate better to people the advantages of buying more sustainable products. But one of the International Task Forces convened under the Marrakech Process by the Swedish government is looking more broadly at the question of sustainable lifestyles. The role of the Task Force is to 'engage, exemplify, enable and encourage relevant stakeholders to work on sustainable lifestyles by assembling results and good examples from ongoing work' (Ministry of Sustainable Development, 2005).

The UK, for example, has taken a (perhaps surprising) lead in this area. In 2003, in the wake of the Johannesburg Summit, the UK government was among the first to launch a national strategy on sustainable consumption and production (DTI, 2003a). This strategy initiated a continuing and wide-ranging process of consultation, evidence review and deliberation that has already had significant impact on UK policy. Among the activities fostered under this umbrella were the UK Round Table on Sustainable Consumption established in 2004, the initiation in 2005 of a new 'evidence base' on sustainable consumption and production to be developed over the next five years, a set of public engagement activities on sustainable living and a sustainable consumption action plan launched in 2006 (Defra, 2005; SDC/NCC 2006).

At the heart of these initiatives is the idea that lifestyle change is not only desirable but essential if key sustainability goals are to be met. This is particularly true for far-reaching emission reduction targets such as those required for climate change mitigation, as British Prime Minister Tony Blair has recently pointed out (HMG, 2006):

> Making the shift to a more sustainable lifestyle is one of the most important challenges for the 21st century. The reality of climate change brings home to us the consequences of not facing up to these challenges.

Lifestyle change is fast becoming a kind of 'holy grail' for environmental and social policy. How can we persuade people to behave in more environmentally and socially responsible ways? How can we shift people's transport modes, appliance choices, eating habits, social drinking, leisure practices, holiday plans, lifestyle expectations (and so on) in such a way as to reduce the damaging impact on the environment and on other people? How can we encourage 'sustainable living' and discourage unsustainable living? These questions lie at the heart of the emerging policy debate. But they also pose some searching questions about the underlying nature of consumption itself and about the driving forces behind modern lifestyles.

In fact, the emerging debate about sustainable consumption cannot be understood in isolation from older debates about consumer behaviour, consumer society and consumerism. These wider debates have an extraordinary pedigree reaching back to classical philosophy and encompassing the critical social theory of the 19th and early 20th century, the consumer psychology and 'motivation research' of the early post-war years, the 'ecological humanism' of the 1960s and 1970s, the anthropology and social philosophy of the 1970s and 1980s, and the sociology of modernity, popularized in the 1990s.

Each of these different strands of thought was asking slightly different questions about consumer behaviour. The motivation researchers wanted to find out the best way to design and market products that people would buy; the critical social theorists and the humanists were alarmed at the ecological and social impacts of rampant materialism; the anthropologists and the sociologists were out to understand modernity, and reflect on the kind of society we had become. In spite of these differences, they all had something to say about consumption and about consumerism, and as such what they said is relevant to an understanding of the sustainable consumption debate.

There is a sense, therefore, in which the debate on sustainable consumption, even if this fact is not always recognized by its protagonists, is a debate within a debate, a literature within a literature. Little wonder that it has proved so hard to agree upon! It is beyond the scope of this chapter to provide a detailed overview of this broader literature. I have tried to capture a flavour of it in the chapters selected for this book. More extensive accounts can be found in a variety of places.[6] In the following section, I reflect briefly on some of the key dimensions of that wider debate.

Consumption: The 'Vanguard of History'

Our consumption patterns offer a complex, yet telling picture of the kind of society we have become and of our relationship to material goods. The evidence on consumer behaviour suggests that consumer goods and services play a huge variety of different roles in our lives. Among these roles we must include at least: the satisfaction of functional needs, the construction of identity, the pursuit of status and social distinction, the maintenance of social cohesion, social and/or sexual selection, negotiation of the boundary between the sacred and the profane, and the pursuit of personal and collective meaning. This diversity of roles is what led Gabriel and Lang (1995) to refer to the modern consumer as 'unmanageable' and inspired Miller (1995) to talk about consumption as the 'vanguard of history'. Getting to grips with such complexity is challenging. But several key issues emerge.

One of these issues is the nature of the relationship between consumption and human well-being. In some simple sense, consumption can be seen as an attempt to provide for individual and collective well-being. This is the view encoded a little more precisely in conventional economics. Consumer goods and services are to be seen, in this view, as a proxy for the well-being that people derive from them. Since the sum of consumption expenditures is equivalent (under certain conditions) to the value placed by consumers on the goods they consume then – according to the conventional argument – the national income (or gross domestic product – GDP) can be taken as some kind of 'proxy' for the well-being derived from our consumption activities.[7] And since the GDP rose more or less consistently over the last 50 years in most Western countries, the comforting logic of this view suggests that rising levels of consumption have been pretty successful in delivering an increasing standard of living and, by proxy, improving our collective well-being over recent decades.[8]

But this equation of economic growth with increasing quality of life has come under considerable scrutiny over the last few decades, from a number of different quarters and for a variety of different reasons.[9] Not least among these is the realization that conventional measures of economic progress fail to account for the depletion of natural resources, and for the environmental and social impacts of consumption and production.[10] In addition, this conventional view is faced with what is perhaps the most striking ambivalence involved in understanding modern lifestyles: the so-called 'life-satisfaction paradox'.

This phenomenon is illustrated in Figure 1.1. When Inglehart and Klingemann (2000) plotted data on life satisfaction and happiness against data on national income they found a strong correlation between the two only at low incomes. Across most developed countries, however, the correlation between increased income and reported well-being is weak at best. And for countries with average incomes in excess of US$15,000, there is very little correlation at all between income and happiness. Data across time are equally striking. Incomes in the UK (for example) have almost doubled since the early 1970s. Yet reported life satisfaction over the same period has scarcely changed at all (e.g. Jackson, 2006, Figure 2). A recent survey for the BBC found that the proportion reporting themselves 'very happy' in the UK had fallen from 52 per cent in 1957 to 36 per cent today (BBC, 2006).

If rising consumption is supposed to deliver increasing levels of well-being, these data on stagnant 'life-satisfaction' levels pose a series of uncomfortable questions for modern society. Why is life satisfaction not improving in line with higher incomes? Is economic growth delivering improved well-being or not? What exactly is the relationship between consumption and well-being?

Explanations for the life-satisfaction paradox have been sought in a variety of different places.[11] Some authors highlight the fact that relative income has a bigger effect on individual well-being than absolute levels of income. If my income rises relative to those around me I am likely to become happier. If everyone else's income rises at the same rate as my own, I am less likely to report higher life satisfaction. Moreover, if my increase in income causes envy in those around me, my increased satisfaction is likely to be offset by dissatisfaction in others, so that aggregate life satisfaction across the nation may not change at all.

Some commentators point to the impact of 'hedonic adaptation'. As I get richer, I simply become more accustomed to the pleasure of the goods and services my new income affords me. And if I want to maintain the same level of happiness, I must achieve ever-higher levels of income in the future just to stay in the same place.

Humanistic psychologists (and some ecologists and philosophers) have argued that the entire project of income growth rests on a misunderstanding of human nature. Far

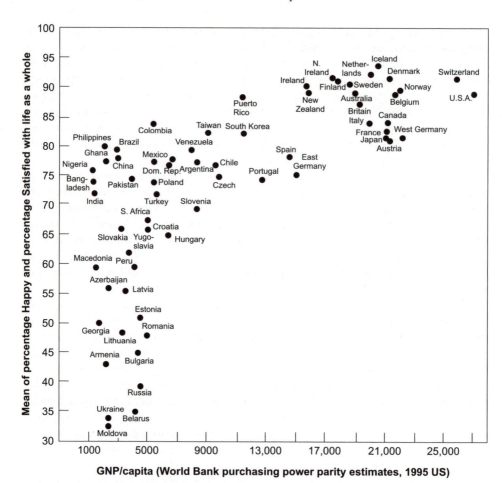

Source: Inglehart and Klingemann (2000).

Figure 1.1 *Subjective well-being and per capita incomes*

from making us happier, according to this critique, the pursuit of material things damages us psychologically and socially. Beyond the satisfaction of our basic material needs for housing, clothing and nutrition, the pursuit of material consumption merely serves to entrench us in unproductive status competition, disrupts our work–life balance and distracts us from those things that offer meaning and purpose to our lives.[12]

Others have suggested a different – but equally radical – explanation for the paradox. In a recent attempt to construct an international index of quality of life, *The Economist*'s Intelligence Unit suggested the explanation for the paradox was that 'there are factors associated with modernization that, in part, offset its positive impact'. They (*The Economist*, 2004) argue that:

Concomitant breakdown of traditional institutions is manifested in the decline of religiosity and of trade unions; a marked rise in various social pathologies (crime, and drug and alcohol addiction); a decline in political participation and of trust in public authority; and the erosion of the institutions of family and marriage.

The point about these changes – which have occurred hand in hand with the rise in incomes and the expansion of individual choice – is not that income growth is irrelevant to individual quality of life; all the evidence suggests the contrary. Rather it is that the pursuit of income growth appears to have undermined some of the conditions (family, friendship, community) on which we know that people's long-term well-being depends.

If any of this kind of critique is right, consumer society appears to be seriously adrift – not just in terms of its impacts on the environment, but even in terms of its own pursuit of well-being. As Paul Wachtel comments in *The Poverty of Affluence*, the 'consumer way of life is deeply flawed, both psychologically and ecologically'. We might perhaps be tempted to put up with a little environmental degradation if it was the only way of increasing human well-being. But damaging the environment and at the same time failing to deliver consistent improvements in well-being is potentially tragic. Consumer society, in this view, appears to be in the grip of a kind of social pathology.

But this critique also raises a glaring question: why, if consumerism fails to satisfy, are we driven to continue – indeed to increase – our levels of material consumption?

One answer to this question is to be found in modern theories of evolutionary psychology, which suggests that consumer behaviour is conditioned in part at least by sexual and social competition.[13] The idea that consumption has something to do with sexual desire is borne out by sociological research and clearly resonates with the common wisdom of advertising executives (Belk et al, 2003). Among the consumption trends predicted by this approach are display and status-seeking behaviours. Such behaviours have been the focus of sociological discourses on consumption for well over a century. Veblen's (1899) notion of *conspicuous consumption*, and Hirsch's (1977, chapter 6 reprinted as Chapter 9 in this reader) concept of *positional goods* both highlight the importance of material goods in social comparison and positioning. Hirsch also points to the dynamic nature of this kind of consumption. We must run faster and faster to stay in the same place, because our competitors are also engaged in the race. Evolutionary psychology appears to offer some legitimation for this behaviour. But social critics argue that it remains pathological.[14]

Some recent work suggests that display and status-seeking aspects of consumer behaviour may have been overemphasized. Ordinary, every-day consumption, argue some authors, is not particularly oriented towards display. Rather it is about convenience, habit, practice, and individual responses to social and institutional norms (Gronow and Warde, 2001; Shove, 2003). Far from being willing partners in the process of consumerism, consumers are seen as being 'locked-in' to a process of unsustainable consumption over which they have very little individual control. This perspective identifies a vital role for government in shifting the institutional architecture of consumer 'lock-in' (Sanne, 2002).

In spite of these reservations, there is one underlying feature of consumption which has much wider connotations than its application to status-seeking behaviours. This is the insight that consumer goods play vital symbolic roles in our lives. Drawing inspiration from anthropology and social philosophy, this idea also has a popular resonance.

From wedding dresses to sports cars, from children's toys to the colours of our favourite team, material goods convey important signals about our lives, our social standing and our allegiances. We value goods not just for what they can do, but for what they represent to us and to others.[15]

The explanatory uses of this hypothesis are diverse. One of its applications lies in understanding the role of commodities in constructing and maintaining personal identity. The symbolic properties of goods allow us to see material possessions as part of our 'extended self' (Belk, 1988). Some authors see the continual construction and reconstruction of identity through consumption as a defining feature of modernity (Baumann, 1998; Giddens, 1991).

However, the symbolic importance of commodities is not confined to matters of personal identity. Goods also communicate belongingness, affiliation, group identity, allegiance to particular ideals, distance from certain other ideals. Douglas and Isherwood drew attention to the role of goods in providing 'marking services' – social rituals that serve to embed the individual within their social group.[16]

This view provides one of the clearest messages that simplistic appeals to forgo consumption will not work. In a society in which goods provide vitally important sources of social information, giving them up is not an option. But it also points up the existence of a kind of tension that runs through the literature on consumption and haunts the debate on sustainable consumption. Most simply put, this tension revolves around the question of whether current levels and patterns of consumption are or are not 'good for us'.

The simplistic equation of increasing consumption with improved well-being is clearly problematic. Some argue that the scale of consumption in modern society is out of proportion to our material needs and that we could reduce consumption considerably without threatening the quality of our lives. But the evidence on symbolic consumption confuses this claim, by pointing to the key social and psychological roles that material goods play in our lives. On one perspective, material goods provide consumers with the freedom to choose the best way of pursuing the 'good life' according to individual tastes and preferences. On another perspective modern consumer society is locked into a kind of 'social pathology' – driven to consume by a mixture of greed, social norms and the overwhelming power of modern institutions.

This latter position is interesting in particular because it seems to suggest a kind of 'double dividend' associated with sustainable consumption. If the consumer way of life is 'deeply flawed' then the possibility appears to remain that we could live better by consuming less, and reduce our impact on the environment at the same time.[17] But how realistic is this perspective? Is it really consistent with fundamental understandings about consumer behaviour and human motivation? Or is it simply a delusion based on utopian understandings of human nature?

Readings in Sustainable Consumption

None of these questions is easy to answer. Yet, at one level, the tension inherent here emerges as one of the most fundamental and intriguing aspects of the debate about sustainable consumption. It is evident in one form or another in just about every contribution I have selected for this reader, and appears to me so fundamental to sustainable consumption that I have deliberately framed the structure of this volume to reflect the dialectical nature of it.

The 24 substantive contributions to the Reader are divided in what follows into four distinct parts. Part 1 (*Framing Sustainable Consumption*) is composed mainly of papers that deal directly with the concept of sustainable consumption as it has been articulated in the recent policy debates. Different contributions summarize the key influences on and components of the debate. Some of the papers discuss institutional and grass-roots initiatives in the area. Others explore the kinds of tools we need to account for the environmental impacts of consumption. Some deal with the challenges posed to policy by consumption. Part 1 is deliberately historical in its scope. It attempts to pick out some influential contributions from various points over the last decade or so. It cannot be exhaustive, but is meant to be representative of the early positions taken in the debate.

Part 2 of the Reader (*Resisting Consumerism*) provides a variety of critical perspectives on consumerism. It sets out clearly one of the principal contentions within the sustainable consumption debate: the idea that conventional notions of consumer society are failing us. Far from offering us a better quality of life, according to this critique, they compromise our well-being and destroy important social and public goods. Contributions within Part 2 include a variety of recent and historical critiques and an overview of the literature on 'downshifting', 'voluntary simplicity' and ethical consumerism.

As we have already noted, resistance to consumerism has itself not gone unchallenged. Part 3 (*Resisting Simplicity*) draws together some of this counter-challenge. It highlights some of the complexity associated with consumer motivations and behaviours and some of the oversimplification inherent in the critique of consumerism. The contributions in Part 3 provide the basis for a more robust understanding of the constraints associated with changing people's behaviour. They also offer some salutary lessons for simplistic notions of lifestyle change.

Part 4 of the Reader (*Reframing Sustainable Consumption*) moves towards a sophisticated understanding of the demands of sustainable consumption, incorporating key insights from the sociology, psychology and anthropology of consumption. Selected contributions in this section call in one way or another for a move beyond moralistic critiques of consumerism. They point to ways in which it might be possible to incorporate a more sophisticated understanding of consumer motivations into the sustainable consumption debate.

In the following paragraphs I summarize briefly my rationale for selecting each of the different contributions to the Reader and summarize the relevance of these contributions to the wider debate.

Part 1: Framing Sustainable Consumption

During the 1990s, the debate about sustainable consumption was characterized by a series of institutional 'position documents'. One of the most sophisticated of these was the 1998 Human Development Report, published by the United Nations Development Programme, from which **Chapter 2** is taken. Almost a decade later, this document remains a sophisticated summary of the relationship between consumption and human development, drawing carefully from sociological, anthropological and environmental understandings of the issue. For this reason, it still serves as a perfect introduction to the themes in this volume. An added bonus in Chapter 2 is the commentary from John Kenneth Galbraith, author of *The Affluent Society*.

Some part of the explosion of interest in sustainable consumption was due to the campaigns spearheaded by NGOs. The International Institute for Environment and Development was at the vanguard of attempts to forge a consensus on the issues following the Rio Earth Summit in 1992. Nick Robins and Sarah Roberts' 1998 paper (**Chapter 3**) reflects on the dialogues around consumption that characterized the early 1990s. It also provides a good overview of several grass-roots movements for 'alternative consumption' and lifestyle change that emerged during that period.

The problem of consumerism had never been very far from the minds of US environmentalists – as some contributions in Part 2 of this book demonstrate. But the terminology of sustainable consumption (like that of sustainable development) seemed to have more resonance in Europe, in the years following the Rio conference, than it did in the US. A systematic attempt to articulate an approach to environmental policy in the US that took account of the question of consumption had to wait until 2002, the year of the Johannesburg conference. In that year, Tom Princen and his colleagues published their landmark book *Confronting Consumption*, from which **Chapter 4** has been extracted. Princen's main concern was to put consumption on the policy map. But he also offers here some potentially useful ways of dividing up the territory, pointing in particular to several interpretative layers in understanding 'excess' consumption. Of particular interest to the themes in this book is his characterization of 'misconsumption': consumption which results in net losses to the consumer.

As Princen and his colleagues pointed out, confronting consumption places a number of new demands on policy-makers. One of these is to establish, with some degree of precision, which resources are consumed where, by which activities and by which sets of people. In fact, this kind of analysis pre-dates the recent discourse on sustainable consumption. It had been emerging gradually over earlier decades in the fields of energy analysis, resource flow analysis and environmental input–output analysis. A full treatment of these subjects could easily be the subject of a separate anthology. In this volume I have chosen to represent this burgeoning literature – which has received a considerable boost from the dialogues around consumption – by selecting two recent (2005) contributions to the literature.

In **Chapter 5**, Henri Moll and his colleagues describe the work pioneered in the Netherlands using the University of Groningen's Energy Analysis Program (EAP) which models the direct and the indirect energy associated with household consumption. The paper describes the recent application of the EAP to four case study countries: the Netherlands, Norway, Sweden and the UK.

For the second of the two contributions exploring how to account for the impacts of modern consumption, I asked Edgar Hertwich to write a synthesis paper based on his extensive (2005) review of studies analysing household environmental impact. **Chapter 6** suggests that, for the most part, these studies confirm the emerging importance of environmental input–output analysis and life-cycle analysis as essential tools in understanding and quantifying the material flows and environmental impacts associated with different household activities. The chapter also highlights some of the limitations of this kind of study and points towards future research needs.

The first decade of sustainable consumption was characterized by a flurry of research and institutional interest, but very little in the way of concrete policy initiatives. As this situation begins to change, **Chapter 7** explores the dimensions of the challenge facing policy-makers in their task. Among those challenges is the extent to which policy interventions on consumption are believed to contravene the concept of 'consumer sovereignty'. In this chapter, drawn from my own work for the Sustainable Development Research Network, I suggest that modern government may have backed itself into an unrealistic corner with the rhetoric of 'hands-off' governance, and propose a very specific conception of policy as a mediator and 'co-creator' of the culture of consumption. I argue that this view of policy opens out a much more creative vista for policy intervention than has hitherto been acknowledged.

Part 2: Resisting Consumerism

Although the US may have lagged behind in adopting the terminology of sustainable consumption, North American writers have certainly not been slow in offering critiques of consumer society, as several of the contributions in this section demonstrate. In 1992, when Alan Durning wrote a short, readable monograph for the WorldWatch Institute called *How Much Is Enough?* he was still able to refer to consumption as 'the neglected god in the trinity of issues the world must address' – the other two being population and technology. The publication of that book helped put the issue of consumption firmly on the map. Its strength – and the reason for its subsequent popularity – lies partly in its readability and partly in the historical and philosophical breadth Durning brought to bear in his arguments against consumerism. It is not a particularly academic piece, but it has made a lasting impression on the environmental debate. **Chapter 8** (drawn from that 1992 book) remains a telling exposition of the thesis that consumer society is failing us: not just environmentally but socially and psychologically as well.

Critiques of consumerism were by no means new to the 1990s. A vigorous 'counter-culture' had already emerged in the literature of the 1960s and 1970s. Jean Baudrillard, Erich Fromm, John Kenneth Galbraith, Ivan Illich, Herbert Marcuse, Abraham Maslow, Vance Packard, Tibor Scitovsky: these were among the authors who offered critical perspectives on late 20th-century consumer society. I have chosen to represent that literature through an excerpt from Fred Hirsch's 1977 book on the *Social Limits to Growth*. Made famous for its exposition of the role of 'positional goods' – goods whose value lies in their ability to position us among our social peers – this carefully argued book also demonstrated how the positional economy (perhaps ironically) tends to erode sociability and lead to increasingly commoditized lives. In **Chapter 9**, Hirsch revisits Marx's idea of 'commodity fetishism', illustrating the pernicious results of commoditization through examples – including the commercialization of sex – that are as salient today as they were 30 years ago.

One of the accusations thrown at consumer society by the critical literature of the 20th century was that of 'falseness'. From Marx to Marcuse and from Veblen to Scitovsky, commentators accused the modern economy of generating a whole set of 'false needs' and 'pseudo-satisfiers'. (The same idea was inherent in Rousseau's much earlier critique of civilization.) I could have chosen any number of academic excerpts to illustrate this element of the critique. But in the end, I settled on Alex Kotlowitz's wonderful exploration of fashion distortions on the streets of New York – a chapter from Roger Rosenblatt's 1999 book *Consuming Desires*. **Chapter 10** is a very anecdotal – semi-journalistic – slice of social anthropology with which to try and capture a complex and contentious argument. But there's something both entertaining and compelling about Kotlowitz's short essay.

If critiques of consumerism were rife during the second half of the 20th century, so too were dreams of escaping it. These visions revolved mostly around the persuasive – if problematic – hypothesis that it might be possible to live better by consuming less. This was the premise of a wide variety of experiments in 'simple living' that emerged in Western societies during the late 1970s and early 1980s. Driven as much by desires to escape the 'rat race' and improve personal quality of life as by concerns about global equity and the environment, these initiatives found common ground beneath the umbrella term 'voluntary simplicity'. In **Chapter 11**, taken from Elgin's eponymous 1981 book, the advantages of voluntary simplicity are cashed out in terms of sufficiency, aestheticism, authenticity and compassion – the very things lamented by the counter-culture as casualties of consumer society.

The discourse around voluntary simplicity may have arisen as an element in counter-culture. But like many cultural discourses it has become over time an object of academic scrutiny in its own right. The last decade has seen a proliferation of research interest in the subjects of voluntary simplicity, ethical consumption and 'alternative' lifestyles. **Chapter 12** is reproduced from a 1998 paper by the US sociologist Amitai Etzioni. It serves both as an exemplar of the emerging academic interest in simplicity and as an excellent overview of the subject matter itself. Of particular interest is Etzioni's attempt to tease out the environmental and social benefits of a (hypothetical!) mass movement towards simplicity.

The final selection in Part 2 is taken from Juliet Schor's seminal 1998 treatise against the consumer society, *The Overspent American*. The starting point for **Chapter 13** is a delightful 18th-century essay by the French philosopher Diderot lamenting the casting out of his favourite dressing gown. This tale is the source of what sociologists now call the Diderot effect: a vicious cycle of continual replacement of old with new that tends to accelerate material consumption. But Schor's object is not entirely lamentation. On the contrary, the principal aim of this chapter is to set out nine clear principles for escaping from the endless cycle of work and spend which – according to Schor – characterizes modern living.

Part 3: Resisting Simplicity

The movement towards simplicity has been, at best, a marginal development in Western nations and, as Etzioni recognizes, has piggy-backed to some extent on affluence. Susan Martens and Gert Spargaaren are clearly sceptical of what they call 'demodernization' as a route to sustainable consumption. In **Chapter 14**, first published as a journal article in 2005, they analyse the emergence of sustainable consumption policy in the Netherlands. It is salutary to note that Dutch policy attempts to foster 'ecologically adjusted behaviour' can be traced to the early 1970s; and that in spite of the early start, progress towards the goal has been painfully slow. But the authors go further than this, suggesting that simplicity will lead to questionable environmental and social outcomes. Whether or not they are right about this, it is clearly important to find a strategy that will operate in the mainstream, and not purely at the margins, of modern society. In pursuit of this aim, Martens and Spargaaren highlight two important aspects of the debate. The first is a framing of consumption itself in terms of a wide variety of 'social practices' in different 'consumption domains'. The second is the importance of engaging the 'citizen–consumer' in initiatives for change. Both these ideas emerge again strongly from contributions in Part 4 of this volume.

Critiques of consumerism – such as those exemplified in Part 2 of this book – have often adopted an overtly moral stance, railing against the individualistic and materialistic nature of consumer society. But this moral stance has not itself gone unchallenged. Daniel Miller has written extensively on the social anthropology of consumption. In **Chapter 15**, taken from an article first published in 2001, he brings an insightful and biting critique to bear. Miller accuses the counter-culture of a variety of crimes, including demonizing consumers, serving the causes of discrimination and espousing a too-thin concept of morality. But this is not pro-capitalist backlash. It is a genuinely progressive attempt to place social issues – poverty, inequality, injustice – at the heart of the consumption debate and promote an empathetic understanding of the social dilemmas faced by the modern consumer.

Anthropologist Mary Douglas has had interesting, surprising and sometimes downright irreverent things to say about consumption throughout her long and distinguished career. From her much-cited book with Baron Isherwood, *The World of Goods*, to her insightful essay 'In defence of shopping' she has provoked and challenged those thinking about consumption to engage in a more sophisticated debate about the social uses of goods. Like Miller, she laments what she has seen as the unsophisticated 'moralizing' inherent in the critique of consumption. For this reader, I have selected a slightly less well-known piece, originally published in 1976. **Chapter 16** remains for me one of the clearest and strongest statements of Douglas's rather persuasive case. My own debt to her thinking should be obvious from the final chapter of this book.

Juliet Schor (Chapter 13) condemns the work and spend culture. But why exactly is it, when we are so much more affluent than we were even three decades ago, that we continue to work rather than reap the rewards of productivity in increased leisure and more time spent with our families? What is it that keeps the consumer economy going in spite of all its much-vaunted failings? This is the question addressed by Kjell Arne Brekke and Rich Howarth's contribution to this reader. **Chapter 17** has been adapted for this volume at my request from some of their other writing – in particular their 2002 book *Social Identity and Material Goods*. They come up with two candidate answers to the question of 'over-consumption', one based on conventional economic theory and the other based on Mary Douglas's hypothesis about the use of goods in signalling identity (Chapter 16). In both models, it turns out, consumers would continue to work equally hard regardless of how much consumption this provides. But the second model provides a better explanation of the real world, in the authors' view. It also leads to rather different policy implications.

There's no doubt that anthropologists, on the whole, have preferred to understand rather than condemn the consumer culture. Grant McCracken is no exception. His work has been a careful and lively exploration of the subtle dynamics of our relationship to material goods. In **Chapter 18**, excerpted from his classic 1990 book *Culture and*

Consumption, he pushes the boundary of the 'goods as communication' hypothesis to suggest that, far from leading to ignoble ends, the 'evocative power of things' can serve to express our highest hopes and preserve our noblest ideals from the withering light of day. It is a possibility that I explore further in Chapter 25 of this book.

Sociologist Colin Campbell is best known for his detailed historical exploration of the relationship between the rise of consumer society and the ethic of Romanticism. Once again, his work is in part an example of social science coming to the defence of consumerism against the social critique of the counter-culture. At the heart of his argument – exemplified by the 1994 journal article reprinted as **Chapter 19** – is the idea that a new form of 'hedonism' inhabits modern society. Eschewing the accusations of 'falseness' which pervade the critical viewpoints gathered together in Part 2, Campbell insists like McCracken that consumerism is a way of allowing people to pursue their highest aspirations in modern society. It's an intriguing argument and its implications are substantial. In particular, Campbell suggests that intervening in consumerism involves far more than tinkering at the edges of our lives. In essence, he claims, this kind of change implies 'no minor adjustment to our way of life, but the transformation of our civilization'. It's a sentiment that some at least of those represented in Part 2 might agree with.

Part 4: Reframing Sustainable Consumption

Compelling though the social defence of consumerism might be in humanistic terms, it falls a long way short of addressing the fundamental challenge of sustainable consumption: that current patterns of resource consumption are environmentally unsustainable and socially inequitable. And concentrating purely on efficiency, as Elizabeth Shove points out in **Chapter 20**, has consistently failed to 'square the circle'. Something more sophisticated is needed, something informed by social theory, but which recognizes the reality and importance of social and environmental limits. In one way or another each of the contributions in the final Part of the Reader acknowledges this challenge.

Shove's work has consistently focused on the part that technical, institutional and social structures play in defining patterns of resource consumption. In this contribution, drawn from a 2004 journal paper, she explores further the view of consumption as a set of social practices, introduced in Chapter 14 by Martens and Spargaaren. In some earlier writing, this view has led her to be sceptical of the role of policy in fostering change. In this paper, by contrast, and it's one of the reasons I like it, she highlights the plurality of intervention possibilities opened up by a social practices perspective.

Like Shove, Kersty Hobson (**Chapter 21**) is sceptical of the discourse around efficiency. She is particularly critical of the concept of 'rationalization' of behaviour that characterized the first decade in the institutional debate on sustainable consumption. In Hobson's case, however, the scepticism revolves around the fact that efficiency just doesn't mean that much to ordinary people. Drawing on qualitative evidence from participants in a programme of lifestyle change called Action at Home, she shows how the 'rationalization' of lifestyles tends to alienate people and act as an impediment to change, precisely because it neglects the pressing social concerns that shape and guide people's lives. In contrast, according to Hobson, it is the discourse of social justice which holds the key to opening up 'spaces of hope' in which people feel motivated to lead more sustainable lifestyles.

Chapter 22 was adapted at my request from a paper published by the Oxford Commission on Sustainable Consumption in 2000. The Oxford Commission was one of the many initiatives on sustainable consumption to emerge in the decade following Rio and engaged extensively with the international debate. In this paper, Laurie Michaelis explores the ethical underpinnings of the consumer society. Like Campbell (Chapter 19) and others, he highlights the combination of Romantic and Enlightenment thought that characterizes modern ethical thinking. Unlike Campbell, however, Michaelis refuses to take these underpinnings for granted. Turning the sociological argument on its head, he suggests that if our current ethics got us into this mess, then a different ethic is needed to get us out of it. He points in particular to the role that egalitarian, community-based narratives might play in fostering new visions of the 'good life'.

In Chapter 16 Mary Douglas identified the aims of consumers with the creation and maintenance of the social world. But what is the nature of that social world? And what kind of impact do different kinds of social organization have on our consumption patterns? Would different kinds of social organization favour different kinds of sustainable consumption? Cultural Theory – another brainchild of Douglas and her colleagues – suggests that they would. Karl Dake and Michael Thompson (a student of Douglas) explore the question empirically in **Chapter 23**. It is a fascinating exploration of five distinct kinds of consumption associated with Cultural Theory's five distinct approaches to social organization. Often cited, but difficult to obtain, I have reproduced this 1999 article here partly out of fondness for its quirkiness. At the same time, I think it offers another example of the possibility of approaching the goal of sustainable consumption from a sophisticated social scientific perspective.

The psychologist Mihalyi Csikszentmihalyi is best known for his work on 'flow': a state of mind in which people achieve a high level of psychic fulfilment. In **Chapter 24** – reproduced from a journal article published in 2000 – he uses the concept of flow to revisit the possibility that consuming less might lead to a higher quality of life. Specifically, he explores a differentiation among human activities according to two separate factors: (1) their potential to induce flow and (2) their reliance on the consumption of finite resources. Like other authors included in this volume, Csikszentmihalyi suggests that some at least of the high-consuming activities lead to low levels of satisfaction, while some very low-consuming activities have a high potential to induce flow. It is a powerful hypothesis reminiscent of some of the arguments in the simplicity debate in Part 2. Its sophistication lies in the attempt to map social-psychological variables quite precisely on to material impacts, marrying social science to physical science in a way that has considerable potential for understanding how to approach sustainable consumption.

Choosing one's own contribution to an anthology of this kind is especially difficult. Justifying it is probably impossible! Various suggestions were made by those who generously provided me with editorial advice in this project. In the end, I selected two specific contributions. One of these (Chapter 7) was an exploration of the challenges faced by sustainable consumption policy. The second contribution is a very different kind of piece. **Chapter 25** represents my best – or at least most recent – effort to frame the problem of sustainable consumption in a broader social and cultural context.

At one level, it can be seen as my own attempt to navigate the tension that underlies the contributions to this reader. It is neither an adequate summary of those contributions nor a convincing answer to the questions they raise. But it does articulate some of the psychological and cultural ground rules on which social change must be predicated. In doing so, I have tried to find a place where critiques of consumerism and critiques of simplicity might meet; and to articulate a vision of change that evades the charges of naivety and moralism. Whether or not I have succeeded I leave the reader to decide.

Live Better by Consuming Less?

Where do these contributions leave the 'double dividend' hypothesis? What do the arguments and counter-arguments tell us about the potential for sustainable consumption? How should we construe the idea that it is possible to live better by consuming less? Should it simply be abandoned as an unrealistic reading of a much more complex situation? Or is there still room for manoeuvre in negotiating a less materialistic society, capable of delivering improved well-being?

The arguments against simplicity are, at first sight, damaging. In particular, if material artefacts play vitally important roles in relation to social interactions, for example through 'marking services' and these marking services play such vital roles in maintaining information networks and protecting our resilience to social shocks, then it becomes extremely problematic for any set of people to suggest to another set of people – or to society at large – that their needs might be better served by forgoing the benefits of material artefacts. Indeed it would appear to be a clear recipe for exploitation of one social group by another. Unfortunately, however, we are driven at the same time away from the possibility that we might seek dematerialization of these social and cultural needs.

On the other hand, it seems to me that a more sophisticated approach does offer some promising insights for sustainable consumption. At the very least, the social anthropology of consumer behaviour does not preclude the possibility of negotiating or renegotiating the conditions and the means under which 'marking services', for example, are exchanged. Moreover, the insight that a certain amount of consumer behaviour is dedicated to an (ultimately flawed) pursuit of meaning opens up the tantalizing possibility of devising some other, more successful and less ecologically damaging strategy for creating and maintaining personal and cultural meaning.

This is not in any sense a simple task, nor one that can easily be pursued by any given individual or set of individuals. On the contrary, it is a fundamentally social and cultural project, which will require sophisticated policy interventions at many different levels. Nonetheless, it remains a very real possibility that we could collectively devise a society in which it is possible to live better (or at least as well as we have done in the affluent West) by consuming less; in which the riches of one section of the population do not contribute to the poverty of the rest; in which improving our own quality of life is not achieved at the expense of those living in the future; and in which learning to live within these limits allows us to become, in some sense, more human. That, at least, is my hope for sustainable consumption.

Notes

1   A companion volume is planned for the future, which will gather together a similar collection of papers around the related concept of 'sustainable production'.
2   See, for example, Bloch (1950).
3   See, for example, Morris (1891); Thoreau (1854); Veblen (1899).
4   This was the year when the newly formed United Nations held an international Scientific Conference on the Conservation and Use of Resources.
5   For a fuller discussion, see Manoochehri (2002).
6   See, for example, Bocock (1993); Crocker and Linden (1998); Gabriel and Lang (1995); Miller (1995); Reisch and Røpke (2004).
7   In fact, a seminal paper in welfare economics (Weitzman, 1976) showed that the net domestic product (NDP) is a better proxy than gross domestic product (GDP), because it accounts for the depreciation of (human-made) capital. But the adjustment from this refinement is relatively small.
8   This phrase was used until very recently as one of four overarching objectives in the government's sustainable development strategy (DETR, 1999).
9   Most specifically, a critique of this conventional view lies at the heart of the concept of sustainable development and has been coded more or less explicitly into both the 1999 and the 2005 Sustainable Development Strategies (Defra, 2005). See also DETR (1999).
10 For a fuller discussion of some of these issues see Jackson (2002b, 2004).
11 For more detailed discussions of this issue see, for example, NEF (2004); Layard (2005); *The Economist* (2004).
12 See, for example, Csikszentmihalyi (2000, reprinted as Chapter 24 in this reader); de Boton (2004); Kasser (2002); Wachtel (1983).
13 For an overview of this literature and its relevance to consumption see Jackson (2002a); see also Wright (1994); Tooby and Cosmides (1990).
14 See also Fromm (1976); Scitovsky (1976).
15 For a more extensive discussion of this point see Chapters 16 and 25 in this reader.
16 See, for example, Douglas and Isherwood (1979).
17 I have explored this specific question in some depth in Jackson (2005).

References

Agenda 21 (1992) *Agenda 21*, report on United Nations Conference on Environment and Development, Rio de Janeiro, Brazil, 3–14 June, available at www.un.org/esa/sustdev/documents/agenda21/english/Agenda21.pdf
Baumann, Z. (1998) *Work, Consumerism and the New Poor*, Open University Press, Milton Keynes
BBC (2006) 'Happiness survey', available at http://news.bbc.co.uk/nol/shared/bsp/hi/pdfs/29_03_06_happiness_gfkpoll.pdf
Belk, R. (1988) 'Possessions and the extended self', *Journal of Consumer Research*, vol 15, pp139–168
Belk, R., Ger, G. and Askegaard, S. (2003) 'The fire of desire: A multi-sited inquiry into consumer passion', *Journal of Consumer Research*, vol 30, pp326–351
Bloch, J. (1950) *Les Inscriptions d'Asoka*, Belles Lettres, Paris
Bocock, R. (1993) *Consumption*, Routledge, London

Crocker, D. A. and Linden, T. (eds) (1998) *The Ethics of Consumption*, Rowman and Littlefield, New York

Csikszentmihalyi, M. (2000) 'The costs and benefits of consuming', *Journal of Consumer Research*, vol 27, pp267–272 (reprinted as Chapter 24 in this reader)

de Boton, A. (2004) *Status Anxiety*, Oxford University Press, Oxford

Defra (Department for Environment, Food and Rural Affairs) (2005) *Securing the Future – Developing UK Sustainable Development Strategy*, The Stationery Office, London

DETR (Department for Environment, Transport and the Regions) (1999) *Towards a Better Quality of Life: A Strategy for Sustainable Development for the United Kingdom*, The Stationery Office, London

Douglas, M. and Isherwood, B. (1979) *The World of Goods – Towards an Anthropology of Consumption*, Routledge, London and New York

DTI (2003a) *Changing Patterns – UK Government Framework for Sustainable Consumption and Production*, Department of Trade and Industry, London

DTI (2003b) Speech to the Green Alliance Environment Forum, Right Hon Patricia Hewitt, Department of Trade and Industry, available at www.dti.gov.uk/ministers/speeches/hewitt140703.html

The Economist (2004) 'The Economist Intelligence Unit's quality of life index', *Economist Online*, December 2004, available at www.economist.com/media/pdf/QUALITY_OF_LIFE.pdf

Fromm, E. (1976) *To Have or to Be?* Jonathon Cape, London

Gabriel, T. and Lang, T. (1995) *The Unmanageable Consumer*, Routledge, London

Giddens, A. (1991) *Modernity and Self-Identity: Self and Society in the Late Modern Age*, Polity Press, Cambridge

Gronow, J. and Warde, A. (2001) *Ordinary Consumption*, Routledge, London

Hirsch, F. (1977) *Social Limits to Growth* (rev edn 1995), Routledge, London (chapter 6 of *Social Limits to Growth* is reproduced as Chapter 9 in this reader)

IIED (1998) *Consumption in a Sustainable World*, Report of the Workshop Held in Kabelvåg, Norway, 2–4 June 1998, Ministry of the Environment, Oslo, and International Institute of Environment and Development, London

Inglehart, R. and Klingemann, H-D. (2000) *Genes, Culture and Happiness*, MIT Press, Boston, MA

Jackson, T. (2002a) 'Evolutionary psychology in ecological economics: Consilience, consumption and contentment', *Ecological Economics*, vol 41, no 2, pp289–303

Jackson, T. (2002b) 'Quality of life, sustainability and economic growth', in T. Fitzpatrick and M. Cahill (eds) *Environment and Welfare*, Palgrave Macmillan, London

Jackson, T. (2004) *Chasing Progress: Beyond Measuring Economic Growth*, New Economics Foundation, London

Jackson, T. (2005) 'Live better by consuming less? Is there a double dividend in sustainable consumption?', *Journal of Industrial Ecology*, vol 9, nos 1–2, pp19–36

Jackson, T. (2006) 'Sustainable consumption and lifestyle change', in A. Lewis (ed) *Cambridge Handbook of Psychology and Economic Behaviour*, Cambridge University Press, Cambridge, UK

Kasser, T. (2002) *The High Price of Materialism*, MIT Press, Cambridge, MA

Layard, R. (2005) *Happiness – Lessons from a New Science*, Allen Lane, London

Manoochehri, J. (2002) 'Post-Rio sustainable consumption: Establishing coherence and a common platform', *Development*, vol 45, no 3, pp51–57

Meadows, D. H., Meadows, D. L., Randers, J. and Behrens III, W. W. (1972) *The Limits to Growth: A Report to the Club of Rome*, Signet, New York

Miller, D. (1995) *Acknowledging Consumption*, Routledge, London

Ministry of Sustainable Development (2005) 'Memorandum, 25th August 2005', International Task Force on Sustainable Lifestyles, Ministry of Sustainable Development, Stockholm, available at www.uneptie.org/pc/sustain/resources/MTF/Sweden%20TF%20Sust.Lifestyles. pdf

Morris, W. (1891) *News from Nowhere; or an Epoch of Rest: Being Some Chapters from a Utopian Romance* (reprinted 1970), Routledge, London

NCC (2003) *Green Choice: What Choice?* Summary of NCC research into consumer attitudes to sustainable consumption. National Consumer Council, London

NEF (2004) *A Wellbeing Manifesto for a Flourishing Society*, New Economics Foundation, London

OCSC (2000) *Report on the Second Session of the Oxford Commission on Sustainable Consumption*, OCSC 2.8, Oxford Centre for the Environment, Ethics and Society, Oxford

Ofstad, S. (ed) (1994) *Symposium: Sustainable Consumption*, Ministry of Environment, Oslo

Reisch, L. and Røpke, I. (2004) *The Ecological Economics of Consumption*, Edward Elgar, Cheltenham

Sanne, C. (2002) 'Willing consumers – or locked in? Policies for a sustainable consumption', *Ecological Economics*, vol 42, pp273–287

Scitovsky, T. (1976) *The Joyless Economy*, Oxford University Press, Oxford

SDC/NCC (2006) *I Will if You Will: Towards Sustainable Consumption*, Report of the Sustainable Consumption Round Table, SDC/NCC, London

Shove, E. (2003) *Comfort, Cleanliness and Convenience: The Social Organisation of Normality*, Berg, Oxford

Thoreau, H. (1854) *Walden (and Resistance to Civil Government)* (reprinted 1992), W. W. Norton, New York

Tooby, J. and Cosmides, L. (1990) 'The past explains the present: Emotional adaptations and the structure of ancestral environments', *Ethology and Sociobiology*, vol 11, pp375–421

UN (2002a) *Johannesburg Declaration*, United Nations, New York

UN (2002b) *Johannesburg Plan of Implementation*, United Nations, New York

UNDP (1998) *Human Development Report 1998*, Oxford University Press, Oxford and New York

UNEP (1999) 'Changing consumption patterns', *Industry and Environment*, vol 22, no 4, special issue, October–December 1999

UNEP (2001) *Consumption Opportunities: Strategies for Change*, United Nations Environment Programme, Paris

UNEP (2003) 'Shopping for a Better World', UNEP Press Release, 2 June, UNEP, Paris

UNEP (2005a) *Talk the Walk? Advancing Sustainable Lifestyles through Marketing and Communications*, UNEP/UN Global Compact/Utopies, Paris

UNEP (2005b) *Communicating Sustainability: How to Produce Effective Public Campaigns*, UNEP DtIE/Futerra, Paris

UNEP (2005c) *Marrakech Task Forces*, UNEP, Paris, available at www.uneptie.org/pc/sustain/10year/taskforce.htm

Veblen, T. (1899) *The Theory of the Leisure Class* (reprinted Great Minds Series 1998), Prometheus Books, London

Veenhoven, R. (2004) *States of Nations, World Database of Happiness*: www1.eur.nl/fsw/happiness

Wachtel, P. (1983) *The Poverty of Affluence – A Psychological Portrait of the American Way of Life*, The Free Press, New York

WCED (1987) *Our Common Future. The Report of the World Commission on Environment and Development* (the 'Brundtland Commission'), Oxford University Press, Oxford

Weitzman, M. (1976) 'On the welfare significance of the national product in a dynamic economy', *Quarterly Journal of Economics*, vol 90, pp156–162

Wright, R. (1994) *The Moral Animal – Why we Are the Way we Are: The New Science of Evolutionary Psychology*, Abacus, London

Part 1

Framing Sustainable Consumption

2

Consumption from a Human Development Perspective

United Nations Development Programme

Consumption of goods and services is a constant activity in daily life – yet it is not the ultimate end of the lives that people lead. We consume for a purpose, or for various purposes simultaneously. Thus the role of consumption in human lives cannot be comprehended without some understanding of the ends that are pursued through consumption activities. Our ends are enormously diverse, ranging from nourishment to amusement, from living long to living well, from isolated self-fulfilment to inter active socialization.

Concepts of Consumption

The human development perspective focuses on the many different ways in which consumption of goods and services affects people's lives. From such a people's perspective, consumption is a means to human development. Its significance lies in enlarging people's capabilities to live long and to live well. Consumption opens opportunities without which a person would be left in human poverty:

- Food, shelter, water, sanitation, medical care and clothing are necessary for leading a long and healthy life.
- Schooling and access to information through books, radio, newspapers – and, increasingly, electronic networks – are necessary to acquire language, literacy, numeracy and up-to-date information.
- Transport and energy are critical inputs to all these things and virtually all other human activity. There is growing evidence that lack of mobility and access lie at the heart of economic and social disempowerment of women.

Consumption is also a means of participating in the life of a community, for goods are the words of a social language. As Marcel Mauss pointed out in his classic work *The Gift* (Mauss, 1925), we offer gifts to express sentiments and to establish a need for reciprocity, cementing a relationship between giver and receiver. Furthermore, communities each have standards of dress, food, housing, transport and communications, without which a person would be excluded from full participation in society.

Goods and services from

Figure 2.1 *Consumption inputs for human development*

From the human development perspective, consideration is not limited to material consumption by individuals using their personal incomes; this approach would capture only a fraction of the goods and services that contribute to human development. Equally important in the life of a community are many collective and non-material goods and services supplied through public provisioning, such as social security, health care, education and transport. The human development approach goes further still, embracing consumption that lies outside the monetized economy: goods and services supplied through unpaid work – especially by women – and those supplied from the natural resources of the environmental commons. When all these are taken into account, a far broader perspective is gained of a community's consumption levels and patterns (Figure 2.1).

Consumption clearly contributes to human development when it enlarges the capabilities of people without adversely affecting the well-being of others, when it is as fair to future generations as to the present ones, when it respects the carrying capacity of the planet and when it encourages the emergence of lively and creative communities.

Yet even though consumption is critical for some human development advances, it is not always necessary. A family does not have to own many possessions to respect the rights of each of its members. A nation does not have to be affluent to treat men and women equally. Artistic creativity – in literature, dance, music and many other modes of expression – can flourish even with minimal material resources, so long as people enjoy freedom of expression, freedom of thought and freedom of time.

At the foundation of human development is the principle of the universalism of life claims, acknowledging the life claims of everyone – women, men and children – without discrimination. It demands a world where consumption is such that all have enough to eat, no child goes without education, no human being is denied health care, and all people can develop their potential capabilities to the full extent. The human development perspective values human life for itself. It does not value people merely because they can produce material goods, important though that might be. Nor does it value one person's life more than another's.

The principle of universalism demands both intragenerational and intergenerational equity. Sustainable development may sometimes be interpreted carelessly to mean that the present level and pattern of development and consumption should be sustained for future generations as well. This is clearly wrong. The inequities of today are so great that sustaining the present patterns of development and consumption would mean perpetuating similar inequities for future generations. Development and consumption patterns that perpetuate today's inequities are neither sustainable nor worth sustaining.

It is from this perspective of the universalism of life claims – as reflected in many declarations and covenants, starting with the Universal Declaration of Human Rights – that we need to explore the linkages between consumption and human development. Addressing consumption shortfalls is of fundamental importance. If every member of society – woman, man and child – must be able to consume a minimum amount of goods and services essential for ensuring the development of their capabilities and for enjoying a decent standard of living, then high priority must be given to eliminating those shortfalls that perpetuate human deprivations.

This human development perspective on consumption draws on diverse disciplines and ideas put forward by many key thinkers (Box 2.1).

Box 2.1 *Consumption hypotheses: From Veblen to Sen*

Veblen
Thorstein Veblen (1899) initiated the study of consumption as a social phenomenon and of the way individual tastes are influenced by others. Veblen clarified the two major means by which the relatively small leisure class extended its influence over society through its tastes. First, refined or cultivated taste became associated with distance from the world of work; objects suggesting practical necessity could be dismissed as cheap. Second, the process of emulation, by which each group seeks to copy those above itself, extended conspicuous consumption and upper-class standards throughout society.

Weber
Max Weber introduced the notion of a 'status group' sharing a common lifestyle (Gerth and Mills, 1946). This provided a wider framework for analysing class and social differentiation, incorporating criteria based on consumption patterns rather than just property ownership and incomes.

Mauss
Marcel Mauss (1925) saw reciprocity in exchange and consumption of goods as the social glue binding individuals and communities to one another.

Keynes
John Maynard Keynes (1936) mainly looked at consumption from a macro-economic perspective. He saw aggregate consumption expenditures as important components of national income. Keynes argued that with rises in income, consumption would also increase, but not as fast. When income rises, the marginal propensity to consume would go down as consumer needs are satisfied. Keynes regarded effective demand by the consumer as the principal vehicle of economic growth.

Samuelson
The impossibility of observing and measuring the utility of consumption was an awkward feature of neo-classical theory from the start. Economists sought to escape this

embarrassment by showing that the theory could still be derived without actually measuring utility, Paul Samuelson's revealed preference hypothesis (1938) is a classic example of this thinking. Samuelson believed that no utility function, cardinal or ordinal, was required; it was enough for consumers to reveal their preferences through their purchases in the market-place.

Duesenberry
The issue of copying the neighbours in consumption behaviour – keeping up with the Joneses – was taken up by James Duesenberry in the late 1940s. The notion is that individual' preferences are influenced by the consumption preferences of admired neighbours, so they try to keep up. The relative income hypothesis of Duesenberry (1949) provides the analytical framework for this view. Duesenberry considered the major determinant of consumption to be relative income – not absolute income, as proposed by Keynes.

Scitovsky
Tibor Scitovsky (1976) distinguishes between comfort and stimulation and emphasizes in particular the role of culture in generating durable pleasure from stimulation. He emphasizes the need for acquiring 'the consumption skills that will give us access to society's accumulated stock of past novelty and so enable us to supplement at will and almost without limit the currently available flow of novelty as a source of stimulation'.

Douglas
Mary Douglas describes consumption of goods as a medium of communication particularly central to the establishment of people's personal identity and social standing (Douglas and Isherwood, 1979).

Sen
Amartya Sen (1985) focuses not on the ownership of commodities but on the uses to which they can be put in extending people's capabilities. Commodities are important for enriching human lives, but their effectiveness depends on personal characteristics and social circumstances, variations in which contribute to inequalities in a society.

Source: Human Development Report Office

In economics, the focus is typically on consumption of final goods and services. Mainstream economics tends to concentrate at the micro-economic level on individual utility and satisfaction derived from consumption and at the macro-economic level on the generation and use of national income. The alternative activity to consumption is savings, which is related to deferred consumption. Many economists differentiate between consumption of necessities, which are required to meet basic human needs, and consumption of luxuries, which go beyond that.

In sociology and anthropology, consumption activities are analysed in the con text of social relations and institutions. People's consumption decisions are influenced by their social commitments – that is, the social class to which they belong, the social norms within that class and the relationships that they have with others. Following from this, consumption is a means for social communication, and without it one becomes socially non-interacting. For example, apart from meeting the biological need of hunger, sharing a meal is a form of collective participation.

In environmental studies, the focus with regard to consumption is on the level and depletion of natural resources. Natural resources are categorized as renewables, such as water, wood and fish, or non-renewables, such as metals and minerals. Consumption entails depleting both kinds of natural capital. In addition, what is consumed is ultimately disposed of – creating waste and pollution problems.

For philosophers, social commentators and theologians, concern with consumption relates to the tension between the values embodied in materialism and those of simpler lifestyles. Major world religions have commented on materialism, giving guidance to their followers (Box 2.2).

Given the contrasting approaches taken to consumption, each of these fields of study debates very different issues. Economics discusses utility maximization, optimiza-

---

Box 2.2 *Revolt against consumer materialism in religion*

Restraint in consumption has been recognized as a virtue throughout the ages by many religions, as is reflected in their texts and teachings:

In Hinduism
'When you have the golden gift of contentment, you have everything.'

In Islam
'It is difficult for a man laden with riches to climb the steep path that leads to bliss.'

'Riches are not from an abundance of worldly goods, but from a contented mind.'

In Taoism
'He who knows he has enough is rich.'

'To take all one wants is never as good as to stop when one should.'

In Christianity
'Watch out! Be on your guard against all kinds of greed: a man's life does not consist in the abundance of his possessions.'

In Confucianism
'Excess and deficiency are equally at fault.'

In Buddhism
'By the thirst for riches, the foolish man destroys himself as if he were his own enemy.'

'Whoever in this world overcomes his selfish cravings, his sorrow falls away from him like drops of water from a lotus flower.'

Source: Parthasarathi (1997)

tion of aggregate demand and present versus deferred consumption. Issues in sociology and anthropology include how consumption is used for group identity, inclusion and exclusion, since objects are given symbolic meaning. There is increasing interest in the interaction of local and global cultures in developing societies through the consumption of goods and services. In the environmental field the debate is over the problems of natural resource scarcity and environmental unsustainability.

These are diverse perspectives on consumption, focused on contrasting issues. But they are not necessarily conflicting – in fact, they complement one another. This chapter uses the understanding generated by all the perspectives to explore the impact of consumption on human lives from many angles.

Factors Affecting Consumption Options

Individual consumers are assumed to be in the best position to judge their own needs and preferences and to make their own choices. It is fair to presume that people know what they are seeking and have reasons for their preferences when they opt for one consumption pattern over another. Even when a person may not be all that well informed, the idea that another person could judge her decisions better than she can is not, as a general rule, easy to accept.

Before being able to make any such decisions, however, the consumer must at least be presented with choices. Yet millions of people face too narrow a range of consumption options, which prevents them from enlarging their capabilities. The existing distribution of consumption options points to serious shortfalls affecting people in every society who lack access to a range of essential goods and services. They may not be able to get enough food, may lack health care services or may have little access to transport beyond their own feet. There are many factors causing these constraints on consumption options. Income is not the only one. Other factors include the availability and infrastructure of essential goods and services, time use, information, social barriers and the household setting.

Income

Income is an important means of widening the range of consumption options, especially as economies around the world become increasingly monetized. Income gives people the ability to buy diverse, nutritious foods instead of eating only their own crops, to pay for motorized transport instead of walking, to pay for health care and education for their families, to pay for water from a tap instead of walking for many hours to collect it from a well.

The increasing dependence of much consumption on private income means that changes in income have a dominant influence on changes in consumption. When incomes rise steadily – as they have in most industrial countries over the past few decades – consumption rises for most of the population. But for the same reason, when incomes decline, consumption also falls sharply, with devastating consequences for human well-being.

Availability and infrastructure of essential goods and services

Consumption options depend on the range of goods and services available – from the market and state provisioning, from home production and common resources. Many of the most basic essential goods and services – water, sanitation, education, health care, transport and electricity – cannot be provided without an infrastructure, without laying down water pipes, drains and electricity cables, without establishing a school or health centre, without building roads for vehicles. Money is of little use if there is no health dispensary within miles for buying medicine, no school that children can reach, no way to get electricity in the home.

Traditionally, these services have been provided first by the community and then by the state. As markets develop and technology improves, the services increasingly are being provided by the private sector in areas where profit can be made. In less profitable areas community organizations are stepping in to raise funds and provide for their needs themselves. Yet it is still the state that must ensure that, by whatever means, access is available to all – rural as well as urban, poor as well as rich.

Even as markets increasingly take over services previously supplied by the state, there is complementarity between public and private goods. Privately owned cars and buses need well-maintained roads to run effectively. Private companies supplying water services still expect the state to provide the underlying infrastructure. And despite the growth of private schools, there must also be state schools for those who cannot afford to pay the fees, A balance must be maintained between public and private goods. Yet in many countries and regions there is now a large and unhealthy imbalance, leading to great social inequity. This was the forceful thesis presented by John Kenneth Galbraith in his seminal work *The Affluent Society* about 40 years ago (Galbraith, 1958). Galbraith revisits the scene now and finds that 'the contrast between needed public services and affluent private consumption has become much greater' in those 40 years (Box 2.3).

Time use

Opportunities to consume can be severely limited by lack of time. Women in Africa and Asia spend many hours a day meeting the household's needs for energy and water, and have no time left for education, better health care or community activities, Similarly, overworked labourers may receive an adequate wage, but they often work long hours and are denied the opportunity of regular leave. Women frequently face a triple constraint that severely affects their consumption choices. Not only is much of their work unpaid, but their domestic obligations on top of their responsibilities for bearing and raising children leave them with little time to do much else. And families in the industrial world find that their over-busy lifestyles prevent them from enjoying leisure time activities, despite their high incomes. Even though the choice to work long hours is often voluntary, many workers also face pressure to do so. And they may be motivated by a perception of 'need' for money that can only be met by working so many hours that they end up with little time and opportunity to use the money they earn.

Box 2.3 *On the continuing influence of affluence*
John Kenneth Galbraith

It is now 40 years and something more since I surveyed the scene in the economically advanced countries, especially the US, and wrote *The Affluent Society.* The book had a satisfying reception, and I am here asked about its latter-day relevance. That should not be asked of any author, but the mistake having been made, I happily respond. The central argument in the book was that in the economically advanced countries, and especially in the US, there has been a highly uneven rate of social development. Privately produced goods and services for use and consumption are abundantly available. So available are they, indeed, that a large expenditure on talented advertising and salesmanship is needed to persuade people to want what is produced. Consumer sovereignty, once governed by the need for food and shelter, is now the highly contrived consumption of an infinite variety of goods and service.

That, however, is in what has come to be called the private sector. There is no such abundance in the services available from the state. Social services, health care, education – especially education – public housing for the needful, even food, along with action to protect life and the environment, are all in short supply. Damage to the environment is the most visible result of this abundant production of goods and services. In a passage that was much quoted, and which I thought myself at the time was perhaps too extravagant, I told of the family that took its modern, highly styled, tailfinned automobile out for a holiday. They went through streets and countryside made hideous by commercial activity and commercial art. They spent their evening in a public park replete with refuse and disorder and dined on delicately packaged food from an expensive portable refrigerator.

So it seemed 40 years ago: in the time that has since elapsed the contrast between needed public services and affluent private consumption has become much greater. Every day the press, radio and television proclaim the abundant production of goods and the need for more money for education, public works and the desolate condition of the poor in the great cities. Clearly affluence in the advanced countries is still a highly unequal thing.

All this, were I writing now, I would still emphasize. I would especially stress the continuing unhappy position of the poor. This, if anything, is more evident than it was 40 years ago. Then in the US it was the problem of southern plantation agriculture and the hills and hollows of the rural Appalachian Plateau. Now it is the highly visible problem of the great metropolis.

There is another contrast. Were I writing now, I would give emphasis to the depressing difference in well-being as between the affluent world and the less fortunate countries – mainly the post-colonial world. The rich countries have their rich and poor. The world has its rich and poor nations. When I wrote *The Affluent Society,* I was becoming more strongly aware of this difference on the world scene and had started at Harvard one of the first courses on the problems in the poor countries. I went on to spend a part of my life in India, one of the most diversely interesting of the post-colonial lands. There has been a developing concern with these problems; alas the progress has not kept pace with the rhetoric.

The problem is not economics; it goes back to a far deeper part of human nature. As people become fortunate in their personal well-being, and as countries become similarly fortunate, there is a common tendency to ignore the poor. Or to develop some rationalization for the good fortune of the fortunate. Responsibility is assigned to the poor themselves. Given their personal disposition and moral tone, they are meant to be poor. Poverty is both inevitable and in some measure deserved. The fortunate individuals and fortunate countries enjoy their well-being without the burden of conscience, without a troublesome sense of responsibility. This is something I did not recognize writing 40 years ago; it is a habit of mind to which I would now attribute major responsibility.

This is not, of course, the full story. After the Second World War decolonization, a greatly civilized and admirable step, nonetheless left a number of countries without effective self-government. Nothing is so important for economic development and the human condition as stable, reliable, competent and honest government. This in important parts of the world is still lacking. Nothing is so accepted in our time as respect for sovereignty; nothing, on occasion, so protects disorder, poverty and hardship. Here I am not suggesting an independent role for any one country and certainly not for the US. I do believe we need a much stronger role for international action, including, needless to say, the United Nations. We need to have a much larger sense of common responsibility for those suffering from the weakness, corruption, disorder and cruelty of bad government or none at all. Sovereignty, though it has something dose to religious status in modern political thought, must not protect human despair. This may not be a popular point; popularity is not always a test of needed intelligence.

So I take leave of my work of 40 years ago. I am not entirely dissatisfied with it but I do not exaggerate its role. Books may be of some service to human understanding and action in their time. There remains always the possibility, even the probability, that they do more for the self-esteem of the author than for the fate of the world.

Information

Information is the key to raising awareness of the range of consumption options available and enabling the consumer to decide which choices are best. Without information, there is no way of knowing what goods and services are available in the market, and what services are being provided by the state and are, by right, available to all. Advertising and public information campaigns play an important role in this respect. As with all things, a balance is required. Commercial information needs to be complemented by public education to make consumers aware of both the benefits and the potential drawbacks of the choices they face. As products become more sophisticated – especially foods, medicines and chemical-based goods – information on how to use them correctly is essential for protecting the health of the consumer and of others.

Social barriers

Income cannot always remove barriers to access to opportunities. This is particularly so when considerations of gender, class, caste or ethnicity limit people's freedom to consume the goods and services they want. For example, people belonging to certain ethnic groups might be denied equal access to education, employment and other basic social services by the state, regardless of how much they earn. Women often face social barriers. In Afghanistan today they are denied the opportunity to pursue formal education and to participate in many economic activities.

The household – decision-making and upbringing

Much analysis of consumer decision-making assumes that the person making the decision is the one who will directly benefit from the consumption. This is far from the truth in many cases. A great deal of house hold consumption decision-making is in the hands of one person – often the mother or the father of the family. Although this may lead to good outcomes, it can also be a source of inequity within the family – with girls being given less chance to get an education than boys, and women being overworked. Sometimes the father controls the money for his own use, not for the family's benefit.

Household values have a wider effect on the consumption options of individual members. The education and upbringing given to children early in life play a critical part in establishing their ability to make good use of the options available for living a full and fulfilling life. The remarkable expansion and diversification in consumption options have made it more difficult for consumers to make informed choices. People are sometimes unaware of the con sequences of their decisions. If an infant is not fed adequately, if a child is not sent to school, if an adolescent is not made aware of reproductive health care, if a youth is not given the opportunity to develop a sense of community, they will not have the same ability as others to make choices that maximize their best interests and those of the community.

Consumption and the Links with Human Development

There is a complex chain of links between consumption and human development. Those links can be strong, creating positive impacts for many people. But the links can also break down, producing some negative impacts – on the consumer and on others, near and far.

Impacts on the consumer

As consumption levels have risen over the past few decades, there have been many positive and previously unimagined impacts on the lives of millions of people. Increased consumption of nutritious food by the undernourished has reduced hunger and improved health. Improved access to medicines and the introduction of new drugs have reduced morbidity and mortality. Massive improvements in transport have greatly increased people's mobility – leading to opportunities for employment and social interaction. The technology revolution in information and telecommunications has made it possible for people living in remote areas to interact with others all over the world – for example, enabling health workers in remote villages to call for emergency help. The impressive advances in refrigeration and packaging technology have greatly improved people's access to nutritious and convenient foods. The increasing availability of such goods and services has transformed the quality of people's lives all over the world.

Yet consumption can sometimes have harmful effects on consumers, Drinking water that is not clean causes disease and can even be fatal. Using cow dung and wood as a cooking fuel produces a smoke that can cause lung disease. Travelling in over-crowded buses or in poorly maintained cars can lead to fatal road accidents. Foods can be contaminated – through poor household hygiene or through substandard produc-tion. Electrical products may be faulty and unsafe to use, and toys can contain small parts that cause babies to choke. Although intended to promote health, medicines can be extremely dangerous if they are contaminated, if they are past the expiry date or if instructions are not provided or are not followed. When consumed in large quantities, some foods are unhealthy, causing obesity, heart disease and cancer. And consumers can become addicted to drugs, alcohol or gambling, to the point at which their judgement, health, self-respect and social standing are impaired.

Impacts on others

Although consumption decisions are made by individuals, they have impacts on oth-ers – not only at the household level but in the community and even globally. These impacts – or 'externalities' – can be positive or negative.

Positive externalities abound and make an important contribution to human devel-opment. Ownership of a telephone by one person in a village can bring information to all. Educating a woman not only opens opportunities to her but also has positive bene-fits for the health of her family. Vaccinating someone against an infectious disease reduces the health risks for others. A beautiful garden can be enjoyed by all passers-by. And the stronger are community ties, the more opportunities there are for those positive impacts to be spread to others.

Consumption can also have negative effects on other people, breaking the links with human development. These impacts occur both locally and globally, through the environment and through society.

Impacts on others through the environment

Each person's consumption is linked, mainly through production and disposal proc-esses, with environmental impacts that can ultimately cover the globe:

* Use of non-renewable resources (metals, minerals and fossil fuels) depletes their stocks and future availability.
* Intensive use and abuse of renewable resources (soil, water, wood and fish) degrades their condition and increases scarcity for present and future generations.
* Emissions of pollutants create unhealthy local conditions: cigarette smoke fills a room and traffic fumes hang over a city, harming the health of all around.

- Generation of pollution and waste beyond the Earth's capacity to absorb them causes critical changes in the temperature and acidity of the Earth, affecting the future of all.

Impacts on others through social inequality and exclusion

The consumption of some goods and services is linked, through production processes, to circumstances that are exploitative of workers. This occurs particularly in poorly regulated markets where the state fails to intervene and protect the rights of workers and small producers. Consumption can also have a negative impact on society when it is used for social rivalry. Pressure to consume 'status goods' can be high, leading to debt and the sacrifice of essential goods for the household. Failure to consume a symbolic brand of goods can lead to social exclusion. Lack of access to the technology – especially transport and communications – widely used in the community can exclude individuals from effective participation.

***

The links between consumption and human development are clearly neither automatic nor always positive. The report from which this chapter has been reprinted (UNDP, 1998) focuses on the question of how and why those links break down. How can they be restored and maintained? What policy actions should be taken? And by whom? This chapter has outlined a conceptual framework within which the links between consumption and human development can be explored.

References

Douglas, M. and Isherwood, B. (1979) *The World of Goods: Towards an Anthropology of Consumption*, Basic Books, New York

Duesenberry, J. S. (1949) *Income, saving and the Theory of Consumer Behaviour*, Harvard University Press, Cambridge, MA

Galbraith, J. K. (1958) *The Affluent Society*, Houghton Mifflin, Boston, MA

Gerth, H. H. and Mills, C. W. (1946) *From Max Weber: Essays in Sociology*, Galaxy Books, New York

Keynes, J. M. (1936) *The General Theory of Employment, Interest and Money*, Macmillan, London

Mauss, M. (1925) 'Essai sur le don: Forme et raison de l'échange dans les sociétés archaïques', *L'Année sociologique*, nouvelle série, vol I (1923–1924), pp30–186. English edition (1954, tr. Ian Cunnison) titled *The Gift* published by Cohen and West, London

Parthasarathi, P. (1997) 'Religion and consumption', unpublished background paper

Samuelson, P. A. (1938) 'A note on the pure theory of consumer behavior', *Economica*, vol 5

Scitovsky, T. (1976) *The Joyless Economy*, Oxford University Press, Oxford

Sen, A. (1985) *Commodities and Capabilities*, North-Holland, Amsterdam

UNDP (United Nations Development Programme) (1998) *Human Development Report 1998*, Oxford University Press, Oxford

Veblen, T. (1899) *The Theory of the Leisure Class: An Economic Study in the Evolution of Institutions*, Macmillan, New York

3

Making Sense of Sustainable Consumption

Nick Robins and Sarah Roberts

Putting Consumption on the Agenda

Sustainable consumption has come of age as a global priority. The 1992 Earth Summit recognized that unsustainable patterns of consumption and production, particularly in the industrialized North, were not only the major cause of global environmental deterioration, but also of aggravated poverty and social exclusion. The North accepted responsibility for 'taking the lead' in developing new concepts of wealth and property less dependent on the Earth's finite resources, despite opposition from the US that 'the American way of life is not up for negotiation'.

Five years on, the policy consensus has deepened. The European Union has signed on to the goal of achieving fourfold gains in environmental efficiency over the coming decades, with the longer-term aim of a 90 per cent reduction in environmental burden, directly taking up the call for the Factor 4 and Factor 10 improvements proposed by Germany's Wuppertal Institut. And despite the unwillingness of Southern governments to acknowledge the unsustainable consumption in their midst, the 'Rio Plus 5' event in June 1997 placed sustainable consumption and production as one of the twin pillars of the wider goal of sustainable development – the other being the eradication of world poverty.

The motor behind these potentially profound shifts in policy has been a diverse set of pressures from civil society, ranging from individual action to reject over-packaged goods, through community initiatives to buy organic food and organized campaigns on transport and energy use. Governments and corporations have generally been reluctant to tackle questions of personal choice and consumption, and have shied away from addressing the underlying social, economic and technological patterns that determine demand and its impacts. It is civil action which first pushed the issue into public consciousness and then on to national and international policy agendas, prompting governments and businesses to start examining how demand can serve sustainable development.

Take waste as an example. Environmental and consumer campaigns against one-way and over-packaged goods have been instrumental in both raising recycling rates and forcing the implementation of new waste management regulations. Extended producer responsibility, introduced in Germany in the 1990s after concerted environmental campaigning and now spreading across the EU and America, marks a significant development, shifting responsibility for waste management from the end-user and the public sector on to those who can influence the amount of waste that is ultimately generated, notably producers and retailers.

Yet, sustainable consumption is still a technocratic term with little popular resonance and distinctly different meanings. Part of the problem lies in a fog of imprecision that clouds the consumption debate. Environmentalists use the word to describe resource use. Economists, however, use it to describe total spending on goods and services. This leads to inevitable and somewhat pointless disputes, such as when environmentalists call for reduced consumption (meaning a cut in resource use) which economists interpret as taking away people's income. Over the years, a compromise position has emerged which views consumption as the economic activity of purchasing and using goods and services, which, if it is to be made sustainable in the sense defined by the Brundtland Commission, has to both regenerate natural capital and meet needs, particularly those of the poor.[1] In this way, sustainable consumption can be seen not as a goal in itself, but as a means to an array of different ends. For individuals and households, consumption is one way of fulfilling material needs and cultural aspirations; for producers, consumption is a necessary step to serve end-users; and for the public sector, consumption is the means to provide collective services, such as education, health and security.

Looking across the wide range of civil actions under the sustainable consumption umbrella, it is clear that there is only a vague sense of a common vision uniting often disparate initiatives; there is certainly no 'movement' for sustainable consumption. And out in the real world, only marginal progress has been made either in reducing environmental stress or in improving the quality of life since the Earth Summit. What is now required is a re-evaluation of the goals, strategies and tactics of civil action in six critical areas: ethics; lifestyles; markets; communities; patterns; and global link ages.

Facing Up to the Ethical Crisis

Civil action to change consumption is nothing new. Throughout history, consumption patterns have been subject to ethical control and critique, usually sanctioned by religious injunctions to renounce the use of certain materials, foods, drinks or luxury practices. In the secular consumer economies of North America, Europe and East Asia, concern for the environment has largely replaced religion as the principal ethical response to consumption. As Elizabeth Dowdswell, Executive Director of the UN Environment Programme, has observed: 'Ultimately, sustainable consumption is not a scientific or a technical question. It really is first and foremost a question of values.' This ethical dimension to sustainable development was underlined in the 1992 *Caring for the Earth* strategy adopted by the World Conservation Union, the UN Environment Programme and the World Wide Fund for Nature in 1992. This proposed an 'ethic for living sustainably', designed to stimulate changes in attitude and behaviour, so that people did not seek fulfilment 'solely (or even largely) through indefinite growth in their personal level of consumption' (IUCN, UNEP, WWF, 1992). The ethical dimension is one of the main reasons that governments and businesses have been so wary about the consumption debate, either feeling that it is outside their domain, or in the case of some businesses, that it threatens their very raison d'être.

What is new is the global scale of consumption. Simple arithmetic tells us that 'it is simply impossible for the world as a whole to sustain a Western level of consumption for all', as Gro Harlem Brundtland noted in 1994. Sustainable consumption effectively restates Immanuel Kant's 200-year-old categorical imperative – 'What would happen if everyone acted like this?' – for an environmentally constrained world. Over 60 per cent of Americans polled in a recent survey accepted that the global environment would be destroyed if the South consumed as much as they do (Merck Family Fund, 1995).

Changing Lifestyles through Creative Campaigning

This stress on the ethical dimension to sustainable consumption should not be confused with the preference for 'simpler lifestyles' expressed by the affluent in every generation, which George Orwell so mercilessly caricatured in the 1930s. Experience suggests that 'voluntary simplicity' – seen in its latest guise as 'downshifting' – remains a positional good for a small minority who have the resources to resist pressures for greater consumption (Elgin, 1981; Ghazi, 1996). In Norway, for example, 'The Future in Our Hands' movement was launched in the 1970s with the goal of pioneering reduced consumption and simpler lifestyles. Original members were deliberately chosen from 'the great and the good', who committed themselves to simpler lifestyles, even though they had above-average incomes. Research comparing actual consumption patterns of these pioneers with the average population revealed that they had a higher proportion of cars and dishwashers and lived in larger houses or flats (Strandbakken, 1995).

A perennial barrier to traditional efforts aimed at changing lifestyles has been the focus on giving up and losing out. Sustainable consumption is associated with 'hairshirtism'. As the UK Advisory Council on Business and the Environment put it, 'a sustainable future conjures up negative impressions – colder, darker and offering less choice and comfort' (Advisory Committee on Business and the Environment, 1997). While it is certainly true that a sustainable world would require large reductions in resource use and pollution by the world's affluent, this message can be more alienating than empowering, particularly for those in the North who live on low incomes. One way of tackling this negative image is through the range of anticonsumerism initiatives, aiming to stimulate people to ask 'how much is enough?' through humour, theatre, art and subversive advertising (see Box 3.1).

One focal point for international campaigns is the annual 'Buy Nothing Day' in November, which has seen Dutch activists occupying a shopping centre dressed as stressed-out rodents, urging people to leave the rat race, while in the UK, shopping-free zones were created in malls complete with comfy sofas, and a group of silver-suited aliens visited Manchester to try and understand the strange things that humans do, such as paying huge premiums for brands of footwear.[2] What helps to get some of the anticonsumerism campaigns across so strongly is their use of humour and the aspirational nature of the message – anticonsumerism is not just about cutting shopping, but it is also about creating a future that is more enjoyable to live in.

Box 3.1 *Challenging the creation of desire: Adbusters*

In 1997, Adbusters, the Vancouver-based 'Journal of the Mental Environment', described sustainable consumption as 'meme of the year' for 1996. 'For the first time in the history of capitalism,' it declared, 'consumption itself became a frequent topic of discussion even in the mainstream press' (Adbusters, 1997). With its skilful refinements of well-known advertising images – introducing Joe Chemo alongside Joe Camel – Adbusters is challenging the creation of desire for polluting and unhealthy products through advertising and marketing:

We will take on the archetypal mind-polluters – Marlboro, Budweiser, Benetton, McDonalds, Coke, Calvin Klein – and beat them at their own game.

We will uncool their billion-dollar images with uncommercials on TV, subvertisements in magazines and anti-ads right next to theirs in the urban landscape.

We will take control of the role that tobacco, alcohol, fashion, cosmetics and fast-food corporations play in our lives.

We will hold their marketing strategies up to public scrutiny and set new agendas in their industries.

We will culture jam the pop-culture marketeers – MTV, Time-Warner, Sony – and bring their image factories to a sudden shuddering halt.

On the rubble of the old media culture, we will build a new one with a non-commercial heart and soul.

Using the Market as a Lever for Positive Action

Alongside urging lifestyle change, environment, development and community groups have long attempted to harness consumer power for sustainable development, championing boycotts of damaging products and promoting alternatives. Recently, efforts have moved from blocking the negative to using the market as a lever for positive action, and the forest products sector provides important insights into this shift.

For over a decade, high profile campaigns have been waged to highlight global deforestation, particularly in tropical rainforests, with the aim of pressuring governments to introduce effective regulation. Campaigners urged individuals and institutions in industrialized countries to cut their consumption of wood-based products and boycott tropical timber in particular. In Europe, environmental campaigns have certainly been one factor in the recent decline in the import of tropical timber. But when it became clear that regulation could not deliver sustainable forestry quickly enough, the focus shifted to the market-place. One example is the establishment of the Forestry Stewardship Council, set up by a global coalition of environmental and social interest groups. The FSC has developed principles and criteria for sustainable forest management, which producers can use to certify their products on a voluntary basis. Simultaneously, in a

---

Box 3.2 *The Tagua Initiative: Buying buttons in the US supports sustainability in Ecuador*

The Tagua Initiative is the result of a partnership between the communities of the Comuna Rio Santiago-Cayapas in Ecuador, Conservation International (CI), a North American NGO whose mission is to conserve biodiversity, and CIDESA, an Ecuadorean community development organization. The Initiative is based in a forested area of high biodiversity and extreme poverty where tagua palms grow naturally. For over a hundred years, nuts from this palm have been used as a raw material for button-making but demand has declined steadily in the face of plastic substitutes. CI and CIDESA have been working to develop national and international markets for tagua nuts by working with button manufacturers and distributors and putting renowned garment manufacturers such as Gap, Banana Republic and DKNY in touch with distributors. Since 1990 over 70 million tagua buttons have been sold, with a whole sale value of US$5 million, sustaining 3000 jobs and creating incentives for biodiversity conservation.

Sustainable timber: European demand aids producers in the Pacific
Forests are being exploited at a wholly unsustainable rate in the Solomon Islands as foreign timber companies buy up communal logging rights. Communities were finding the incentives offered difficult to resist in a country with few employment options and services until NGOs in the Solomons and Europe began working together to develop trade in timber which would offer communities long-term sustainable livelihoods while maintaining the forest resource. Several NGOs are working with producer groups in the Solomons to develop sustainable management systems for the forests and gain FSC certification. The timber that they produce is being sold through alternative trading organizations in Europe, where there is high awareness of the impacts of unsustainable logging and willingness from individual and institutional consumers to seek out alternatives and in some cases, pay a premium for wood products that are guaranteed as coming from a sustainable source.

Source: Robins and Roberts, 1996

---

number of countries the FSC has formed buyers' groups of companies who pledge to phase out all non-FSC certified wood producers by a certain date. The FSC is thus using business concerns about reputation, risk management and customer loyalty to develop a new market in sustainable timber. Interestingly, one of the most fervent business supporters of the FSC in the UK is B&Q, a do-it-yourself chain targeted in the 1980s by environmental groups for allegedly selling unsustainable timber. This strategy has already opened up opportunities for disadvantaged forest communities in the South to achieve a measure of security in the global market-place and gain financial and environmental improvements (see Box 3.2).

Focusing on Community Action

Many gains can be achieved through the focus on the supermarket as the arena for achieving sustainable consumption. But it is insufficient. There is an important collective aspect to consumption as well. Consumption is an economy-wide activity: for example, over one-quarter of industrialized countries' national income is still spent in 'collective consumption'. As more attention is given to providing services and not products, to leasing rather than purchasing goods, then a community dimension to consumption becomes increasingly important. Alongside the supermarket, other communal institutions such as libraries are emerging as an important arena for sustainable consumption, where needs are met fairly and environmental pressures minimized through sharing rather than purchasing resources. In the UK, one local community recently took dramatic action to try to prevent their local authority from closing down their library: 200 protesters took out their quota of 10 books each, emptying the library in the process. They are still waiting to hear if their library will remain open (*Independent,* 8 October 1997, p8).

Consumption patterns are also created, changed and passed on in a social context. Focusing on the individual alone can often be an ineffective way of changing habits. A range of community-based initiatives have emerged to provide a supportive social framework within which individuals can rethink and change their lifestyles. Internationally, the most well-established programme is the Global Action Plan (GAP), an NGO initiative operating in more than 12 countries. GAP has found that the traditional approaches to lifestyle change of offering information and modest incentives were 'grossly inadequate in changing deeply ingrained behaviour patterns' (Global Action Plan, 1995). GAP's response has been to design the Household EcoTeam programme which provides people with a structured approach that supports them in changing their habits. A similar approach is taken by the Norwegian Environmental Home Guard organization which looks to change the consumption patterns of ordinary people by taking an optimistic solution-oriented approach, using simple and direct language, including humour, and linking action with cultural activities, such as theatre, music and sports. In Senegal, Enda Tiers Monde has launched an 'alternative consumption' campaign to relink consumption with the struggle against poverty, drawing on its practical experience with sanitation and waste management in low-income settlements inRufisque. The campaign is targeted on identifying and spreading the 'front-line technologies' that the poor require to meet their daily requirements. It also attempts to suggest some new models of consumption and to combat the process of import substitution for local products, partly by reinvesting local products with a sense of quality (Gaye, 1997; Gaye and Diallo, 1997).

Knitting the Pattern

Yet the success of these and other community initiatives at changing underlying patterns of consumption is poor. The Norwegian Environmental Home Guard has identified a range of obstacles to practical progress, including poor systems for waste separation, collection and recycling of materials; inadequate environmental information on products; low priority given to durable products; low cost of waste disposal; the failure to include the cost of waste management in disposable products; and increased advertising through direct mail (Norwegian Environmental Home Guard, 1994). All of these obstacles are part of the overall patterns of consumption that ultimately determine the sustainability of millions of purchasing choices.

Today's consumption patterns, values, behaviour and technologies, have all coevolved over the last century on the back of cheap fossil fuels, which has forced 'a wedge between cultural evolution and the biosphere' (Norgaard, 1994). Furthermore, these consumption patterns are driven by a range of social, economic and technological pressures, described almost 40 years ago by Vance Packard, as leading to 'a force-fed society with a vested interest in prodigality and with no end in sight to the need for ever-greater and wasteful consumption'. Packard's proposals for reform have a certain sense of déjà vu for those engaged in civil action today to change consumption, ranging from the ethical (e.g. restoring pride in prudence), through the regulatory (e.g. introducing quality labelling of products) to the distributive (e.g. tackling the unmet real needs of urban renewal, education, health, old age support and development assistance).

The real value added of the sustainable consumption debate since Rio is its emphasis on rethinking the *patterns* of consumption. This focuses attention on to the overall determinants of demand, which either enable or constrain individuals and institutions from contributing to sustainability, rather than simply looking to personal action. These determinants include income levels and distribution, demographic trends (including age and gender), and cultural norms and habits, as well as technological innovation, producer interests and physical infrastructure. Many of these patterns are deeply rooted and costly to overturn. The private and public costs that have been sunk into the automobile-dominated land-use patterns of North America over the past half-century provide a telling example: 'The US has invested the bulk of its capital development since World War II in an increasingly centrifugal fashion. We cannot declare this obsolete without bankrupting the country' (Stemlieb and Hughes, 1982). Here and elsewhere, sustainability is a problem of economic design, not of individual morality.

To date, the favoured policy response from governments has been to support eco-efficiency as a strategy for separating consumption growth from environmental impacts. This places the emphasis on technological innovation to update the capital stock in ways that radically reduce resource use and pollution per unit of consumption. While there are certainly opportunities for substantial eco-efficiency gains, these will not be realized under current market conditions. Initial estimates by the Organisation for Economic Co-operation and Development (OECD) suggest that annual energy efficiency gains would have to grow threefold if industrialized countries were to achieve Factor 4 savings over the next 30 years. In fact, the only area where OECD countries have achieved a substantial improvement in eco-efficiency – the reduction in airborne heavy metals – has been the result of concerted regulatory action to constrain and ban polluting emissions.

The limitations of the voluntary eco-efficiency strategy are many. There is still a lack of trustworthy information on the environmental performance of different goods, a challenge which eco-labelling only partially addresses. Market prices do not include environmental costs, so that green goods are still expected to be sold at a premium, rather than being cheaper than polluting products. Inherited stocks of energy, housing and transport infrastructures lock individuals and institutions into environmentally damaging practices over which they have little control. There is also no guarantee that efficiency gains will compensate for continuing pressures caused by volume growth, or that the resources released by efficiency improvements will be used for sustainable ends.

To date, the vast majority of civil action has focused on changing individual behaviour. But if it is to be successful, efforts will also have to focus on the aspects of consumption that the individual has very little control over. Transport is an obvious example, but even in sectors where consumers seem to have a high degree of control, such as over paper use, on digging deeper it becomes clear that most of these products (e.g. 85 per cent in the US) are not bought by the final consumers but form intermediate inputs into other products (Robins and Roberts, 1996).

Upshifting and Downshifting in a Global Economy

While governments are increasingly recognizing the importance of values, they remain uneasy with the central ethical entry point into the sustainable consumption debate: the notion of need. As the OECD Environment Directorate has recognized, this means constructing 'a wider vision of welfare in which the satisfaction of needs, rather than consumption per se, is the aim' (OECD, 1997). For Consumers International, need is 'the crux of the matter', both defining what it is that people really need and what is the most Earth-saving way to meet that need (Consumers International, 1993). Sustainable consumption combines traditional development concerns with basic needs such as shelter, primary health care and food security with the issue of aspirations for a better quality of life – or as the Brundtland Commission put it, 'lifestyles within the bounds of the ecologically possible and to which all can reasonably aspire' (World Commission on Environment and Development, 1987). But at least 1 billion people, living mostly in Africa and South Asia, are still 'underconsumers', with wholly inadequate access to the goods and services to meet their basic food, water, shelter and sanitation needs (Durning, 1992).

The planetary consequences of consumption in one country for distant people, far-off lands and future generations mean that the rich in the industrialized world – along with the rich within the developing world – can no longer insulate their practices from international scrutiny. The consumption patterns pioneered by the industrialized world are not only unsustainable because of their direct impacts, but also because they provide the model emulated by the emerging economies in their current phase of 'upshifting', powerfully supported by the trade and investment strategies of international corporations. 'Downshifting' by an affluent fringe of Northern households simply does not address the scale of the crisis.

William Greider describes this unprecedented collective dilemma as follows: 'If industrial growth proceeds according to its accepted patterns, everyone is imperiled. Yet if industrialization is not allowed to proceed, a majority of the world's citizens are consigned to a permanent second-class status, deprived of the industrial artefacts that enhance life's comforts' (Greider, 1997). The result is that 'the world has entered new ground, a place where people have never been before. They will have no choice but to think anew.'

Perhaps the best example of such new thinking has come from Friends of the Earth's (FoE's) 'fair shares' vision of sustainable consumption. Looking ahead to 2010 and beyond, FoE has projected a way that all the world's 7 billion people can meet their needs and live a high-quality life within environmental constraints by allocating each person an equal right to consume resources. Because the industrialized world currently consumes far more than their per capita allocation of resources, significant reductions in current resource use and pollution levels would be required (Friends of the Earth Europe, 1996). The link between needs and environmental limits is perhaps strongest in the case of agricultural land, where the Friends of the Earth Netherlands has estimated that placing a priority on meeting food security needs would require a reduction in the current Dutch land use of 45 per cent by 2010 – in effect cutting meat consumption from about 180kg per person per annum to about 60kg (Milieudefensie, 1992). Internationally, Friends of the Earth has stressed the importance of a global bargain to underpin such changes, and has worked with partner organizations in Indonesia, India, Ghana, Senegal, Nigeria, Uruguay, Brazil and Georgia. In the run-up to the 'Rio Plus 5' meeting, Friends of the Earth acknowledged that such a bargain remained distant, adding that: 'This stalemate can only be broken when a sustainable consumption policy exists that takes account of the reality of ecological limits and the wishes of the inhabitants and governments from both the industrialized and developing countries' (Milieudefensie, 1997).

Japan's rapid transition to consumer affluence gives it a special role in the uncertain shift from a 'mass consumption/mass disposal' economy to one of sustainable consumption. The Japanese government has started to explore what could be learned from the resource wisdom of Old Japan, which was based on principles such as 'utilize resources with gratitude' and 'use what you need in an appropriate quantity' (Environmental Agency, Government of Japan, 1994). A recent survey of consumer awareness and behaviour has revealed that women over the age of 40 are Japan's environmental leaders, prompting calls for ways in which these women can pass on traditional values to younger generations caught in consumerism (National Institute for Environmental Studies and Sumitomo, Life Research Institute). This stress on values is also marked in the ECO ASIA initiative launched by the government of Japan to draw up a long-term perspective for sustainable development for the Asia-Pacific region up to 2025. ECO ASIA found that there was a common Asia-Pacific 'eco-consciousness', based on features such as frugal traditional lifestyles and a stress on coexistence with nature, which has often been threatened by the arrival of mass consumption. Even so, the patterns of consumption that have emerged are generally more energy efficient, with a more equitable and less excessive calorie consumption than in Europe and North America. For the future, ECO ASIA called on each country to 'rediscover those elements in its traditional way of life that are suited to conserving the environment' and to work together to deepen the Asia-Pacific 'eco-consciousness' (Environmental Agency, Government of Japan, 1994). Emil Salim, Indonesia's former Environment Minister, goes further, calling for a South–North 'ethical transfer' so that 'the South enhances further its environmental ethics and pulls the North along on this path' (Salim, 1994).

Has Sustainable Consumption a Future?

If it has taken over a century for today's patterns of consumption to evolve and achieve their global reach, then action to change them for sustainable development will have to be

Table 3.1 *Trends in civil action for sustainable consumption*

Traditional	Emerging
1 Lifestyles: voluntary simplicity	1 Lifestyles: social justice
2 Markets: boycotting the bad	2 Markets: promoting the positive
3 Communities: household by household	3 Communities: collective facilities for consumption
4 Patterns: stress on personal morality	4 Patterns: understanding the drivers of demand
5 Global responsibility: North first	5 Global responsibility: common action

at least as long term. It is civil society that has so far set the terms of the consumption debate and dragged it into public consciousness and on to the international stage. There have been many practical achievements and civil action is now evolving away from its traditional, often reactive approach to a more proactive agenda (see Table 3.1). There is a new focus on social justice and not just voluntary simplicity for the rich. New commercial relationships are being forged between progressive producers, NGOs and retailers, bringing a convergence of the 'fair trade' and 'sustainable production' movements. Beyond the market-place, there is action to sustain or generate communal facilities for waste management and other services. And there are efforts to generate new thinking about the global responsibilities of consumption behaviour, such as the eco-space campaign.

Yet for all this, fears remain that continuing consumption growth will bring the global economy crashing into a brick wall of environmental limits long before the end of the 21st century. The 'China Syndrome' of a billion or more new consumers adopting OECD standards of living lurks beneath the surface of the sustainable consumption debate. The critical question is whether sustainable consumption can shift from being a 'North first' concern to an issue of common concern for the international community. Central to this will be whether environment, development and consumer groups can unite around an agenda of quality of life for all.

Notes

1 The 1994 Oslo Symposium hosted by Norway's Ministry of the Environment produced a working definition of sustainable consumption as 'the use of services and related products which respond to basic need and bring a better quality of life, while minimizing the use of natural resources and toxic materials so as not to jeopardize the needs of future generations'.
2 These campaigns are described in Enough Anticonsumerism Campaign (1997).

References

Adbusters (1997) *Journal of the Mental Environment*, spring, Vancouver
Advisory Committee on Business and the Environment (1997) *Seventh Progress Report to and Response from the President of the Board of Trade and the Secretary of State for the Environment*, Department of the Environment. London

Consumers International (1993) *Beyond the Year 2000: The Transition to Sustainable Consumption*, Consumers International, London

Durning, A. (1992) *How Much Is Enough?*, Earthscan, London

Elgin, D. (1981) *Voluntary Simplicity*, William Morrow and Co, New York

Enough Anticonsumerism Campaign (1997) *Never Enough? A Critical Look at Consumerism, Poverty and the Planet*, Enough, Manchester, available at www.enough.org.uk/

Environmental Agency, Government of Japan (1994) *Search for Environmentally Friendly Lifestyle*, October, Environmental Agency, Tokyo

Friends of the Earth Europe (1996) *Sustainable Europe*, Friends of the Earth Europe, Brussels

Gaye, M. (1997) *Consuming in Another Way*, Enda Tiers Monde, Dakar

Gaye, M. and Diallo, F. (1997) 'Community participation in the management of the urban environment in Rufisque (Senegal)', *Environment and Urbanisation,* April, International Institute of Environment and Development, London

Ghazi, P. (1996) *Get a Life!*, William Morrow and Co, New York

Global Action Plan (1995) *America Puts its House in Order... Household by Household*, Woodstock, New York

Greider, W. (1997) *One World, Ready or Not*, Simon and Schuster, New York

IUCN (World Conservation Union), UNEP (United Nations Environment Programme) and WWF (World Wide Fund for Nature) (1992) *Caring for the Earth*, IUCN/UNEP/WWF Gland, Switzerland, available at http://coombs.anu.edu.au/~vern/caring/caring.html

Merck Family Fund (1995) *Yearning for Balance*, prepared by The Harwood Group for the Merck Family Fund, Takoma Park, MD, available at www.iisd.ca/consume/harwood.html

Milieudefensie (1992) *Action Plan Sustainable Netherlands*, Milieudefensie, Amsterdam

Milieudefensie (1997) *Sustainable Consumption: A Global Perspective*, Milieudefensie, Amsterdam

Norgaard, R. (1994) *Development Betrayed,* Routledge, London

Norwegian Environmental Home Guard (1994) *Turning Spectators into Participants*, Norwegian Environmental Home Guard, Oslo

OECD (Organisation for Economic Co-operation and Development) (1997) *Sustainable Consumption and Production*, OECD, Paris

Robins, N. and Roberts, S. (1996) *Rethinking Paper Consumption*, International Institute of Environment and Development, London

Salim, E. (1994) *Symposium: Sustainable Consumption*, Ministry of Environment, Oslo

Stemlieb, G. and Hughes, J. (1982) *Energy Constraints and Development Patterns in the 1980s*, Rutgers University, New Brunswick, NJ

Strandbakken, P. (1995) 'The challenge of sustainable consumption', in E. Sto (ed) *Sustainable Consumption*, National Institute for Consumer Research, Oslo

World Commission on Environment and Development (1987) *Our Common Future*, Oxford University Press, Oxford

4

Consumption and Its Externalities: Where Economy Meets Ecology

Thomas Princen

Analytic and policy approaches to environmental problems can be roughly grouped into two categories. There are those that take current resource-use practices as given and look for marginal improvements. And there are those that presume current practices are unsustainable, possibly catastrophic if pursued to their logical conclusions, and that look for alternative forms of social organization. Research within the economic strands of social science disciplines such as political science, sociology and anthropology has been preponderantly in the first category, what might be termed *environmental improvement*. Pollution control, environmental movements and environmental organizations are common topics.

At the same time that social science has focused on environmental improvement, those who chart biophysical trends say marginal change is not enough. Every time a 'state of the environment' report comes out, authors across the ideological spectrum call for a fundamental shift in how humans relate to the natural world. Some call for global citizenship, others for spiritual awakening. But nearly all call for a drastic overhaul of the economic system, a system that is inherently and uncontrollably expansionist, that depends on ever-increasing throughput of material and energy, and that risks life-support systems for humans and other species. And then the best prescriptions these analysts, who are not students of human behaviour for the most part, come up with are changes in taxes – classic marginal tinkering.

If the social sciences are going to make a contribution commensurate with the severity of biophysical trends, it must do better than analyse environmental improvement measures. Social scientists must develop analytic tools for the analyst (biophysical and social alike) and an effective vocabulary for the policy-maker and activist that allow, indeed encourage, an escape from well-worn prescriptions that result in marginal change at best.

The difficulty in conducting such a transformative research agenda, I submit, lies in two facts. One is the reluctance or inability of social scientists to ground their theorizing in the biophysical, a problem I only touch on here.[1] A second is the fact that the economic strands of the various disciplines focus on *production*. Economic sociology concerns itself with issues of labour and management, economic history with the rise of industrialism, economic anthropology with subsistence provisioning, and political economy with the political effects of increasing trade, finance and development. *Con-*

sumption is nearly invisible. These strands of research adopt the position of the dominant social discipline – economics – and accept consumption as a black box, as simply what people do at the end point of material provisioning, as the reason for all the 'real stuff' of economic activity, that is, production. The economy produces goods and goods are good so more goods must be better. There is little reason to investigate consumption, except to estimate demand functions. Consumers, after all, will only purchase what is good for them and producers, as a result, will only produce what consumers are willing to pay for.

When the prevailing social concern was insufficient production, shortages of food and shelter for a growing population, inadequate investment and risk taking, this stress on production was understandable (Leach, 1993). It is also understandable when natural resource abundance and unending waste-sink capacity, at home or abroad, could be safely assumed. But today, such an ecologically 'empty world' cannot be reasonably assumed. Humans are stressing ecosystem services and causing irreversible declines around the world, on land and water and in the atmosphere. What is more, the contemporary economic system is stressing societies at the in dividual, family, community and national levels. The biophysical and social trends are unsustainable and cannot be corrected through more tinkering – that is, more environmental improvement.

Under these conditions, one must ask if the exclusive focus on production might itself contribute to abuse of resources, to the neglect of serious environmental change, especially change entailing irreversibilities and the diminution of ecosystem services, and to societal stress. One must at least ask if the predilection for *environmental improvement* might obscure – indeed, help drive – serious environmental change and do so by promoting *production,* since enhanced production, however implicit, is the over-riding normative goal of the economic strands of the social sciences.

This chapter is an attempt to point in an alternative direction, what I term the *consumption angle.* The task is straightforward in the initial stages of conceptualizing: reject the production angle, adopt its polar opposite, the consumption angle, and play out its implications. The result is to show how the consumption angle raises questions outside the production angle. The first step, however, is to play out the nature of the production angle and its associated 'environmental improvement' approach and show how they neglect throughput and irreversibility issues.

Before proceeding, however, it is worth noting that, although such initial conceptualization is, in many ways, straightforward, the more operational it becomes the trickier it gets, as will be evident in the hypothetical example at the end of this chapter. This trickiness, I suspect, is not due so much to the difficulties of constructing an alternative logic, one grounded in the biophysical, as it is to the hegemony of the production angle. When the idea of production as the core of economic activity is pervasive, problems in the economy (like ecosystem decline and community deterioration) are logically construed as production problems – problems to be solved with more or better production. If more, even better, production makes only marginal improvements, if it increases risk or material throughput (Daly, 1996), it only postpones the day of reckoning. Contradictions mount and risks proliferate. The challenge is to push beyond the production angle, to chart an analytic perspective that at once eschews the production orientation and raises difficult questions about excess resource use.

The Production Angle

The coincidence of a production angle on economic matters and an 'improvement' perspective on environmental matters is not accidental. When economic activity or, most broadly, humans' material provisioning, is preponderantly production oriented, the only logical way to deal with problems of production – for example, pollution or deforestation – is to 'produce better'. If automobiles are polluting, manufacturers produce catalytic converters. If they are consuming too much gasoline, manufacturers produce more efficient engines. If traffic is congested, planners produce more roadway and traffic signals. If suburban growth exceeds population growth, 'smart growth' is pursued. If flooding destroys property, engineers build better levees. If aquifers are being drawn down, agriculturalists sink deeper wells. If a fish stock is being depleted, distributors develop markets for 'trash species'. If slash piles left after a logging operation create visual blemishes or a fire hazard, processors make particle board out of the slash.

In all these examples, the operation is 'improved,' made more efficient, or the impacts are softened. But the fundamental problem is skirted or displaced in time or space. Pollutants cannot exceed absorptive capacity. Suburban growth is still growth – that is, the conversion of farmland to residential and commercial use while previously used land is left abandoned and degraded. Aquifers are still 'mined' unless their extraction rate is below their regeneration rate. Aquatic systems are still disrupted, possibly irreversibly, if one species after another is fished out. And so on.

What is more, the production angle pervades all sectors of modern industrial society, not just the industrial. Consider the position of a major environmental NGO in the US, the Natural Resources Defense Council, with respect to gas guzzling, private transportation trends and the National Petroleum Reserve in Alaska: 'It is time to ask what kind of energy policy this country really needs. Sport-utility vehicles (SUVs) are getting as little as 12 miles to the gallon. By making small improvements in the fuel economy of SUVs and other light trucks, we could save ten to forty times the estimated oil holdings of the *entire* reserve' (Adams, 1999).

The prevalence of the production angle on economic and environmental issues and the inadequacy of this perspective for dealing with 'full-world', ecologically constrained conditions, suggest the need for an alternative perspective. The tack taken here is to develop a perspective centred on production's apparent flip side, consumption. This perspective maintains the focus on economic issues – that is, on the appropriation of resources for human benefit. To do so, I characterize two approaches. One is to retain the prevailing production–consumption, supply–demand dichotomy where consumption is largely wrapped up in the black box of consumer sovereignty. Certainly extensive study has been carried out on consumption within micro-economics (consumer theory) and marketing, and, in recent years, growing literatures have emerged in sociology, anthropology and social history (Leach, 1993; Miller, 1995; Wilk, 1998). What has been missing in these lines of work, though, is explicit analysis of the *externalities of consumption*. How do decisions of consumers, individually and collectively, contribute to the displacement of costs in space and time? How do personal lives change as expression, identity and status shift to purchasing and display? How does the polity change as democracy is increasingly defined as a vote in the market-place?[2] In addition to the neglect of externalities, these literatures have largely ignored the role of power, whether it be the power some actors marshal over consumers or the power, potential or realized, consumers marshal to counter existing practices. Consumption all too often is treated as a passive process, indeed, merely a natural result of 'real economics', namely, production and its variants of growth, investment, trade and innovation.

The second approach to developing the consumption angle is to flip the production angle entirely around, to stand it on its head and construe all economic activity as 'consuming', as using up, as degrading. This approach pushes the analytic gaze to the opposite extreme from that of the prevailing production angle where goods are good and more goods are better. As will be seen, this approach lends itself to an *ecological conception* of economic activity, where consideration of environmental impact is not just an add-on but is integral to the analysis. Goods may be good but cautious consuming is better.[3]

Consumption as Product Use

Consumption as the necessary complement to production is eating the apple, burning the log, wearing the socks. Research on consumption and its externalities must examine such decisions and influences for their biophysical impacts. A conventional starting point is the decision to purchase. From the prevailing production angle, especially that of retailing, whatever happens after purchase is of little concern unless the consumer's anticipation of subsequent decisions affects the purchase decision. But from an environmental impact perspective, the critical decision is a combination of purchase and product-use decisions, where, in some cases, major purchases drive resource use (Stern et al, 1997) and, in others, the patterns of use are most important (Nordman, 1995).

Disaggregating the relative impacts of purchase and use decisions is certainly critical to the consumption and environment agenda. But a more extensive approach would be to go beyond product to consider the non-purchase decision. That is, individuals consume to meet needs. Sometimes those needs can only be met with purchased items – say, grain, electric power and high-technology equipment. But many other needs can be obtained through productive effort, individually or collectively. Fresh produce can be purchased at a grocery store or grown at home. Personal transportation can entail driving to work or walking (or at least walking part-way). Community members can raise funds to purchase playground equipment and pay to have it installed, or they can collect materials and build it themselves. If one has a need for musical experience, one can buy an album or call a few musician friends over for a jam session. In each of these examples, *a priori*, one cannot know for sure which activity has the least environmental impact. But an initial and plausible operating assumption is that the commercial, purchased choices are more a part of the current trends: *ever-increasing throughput*.

Little if any research has been done on people's choices *not* to purchase or to seek less consumptive, less material-intensive means of satisfying a need. The reason may be obvious: it is very hard to get an analytic or empirical handle on an act that entails not doing something. But my hunch (and it can only be a hunch, given the state of knowledge on this kind of question) is that this gap exists in large part because the question is out of, or contrary to, the dominant belief system where value is presumed to inhere in market transactions. A consumption perspective that is more expansive, that recognizes that individuals actually meet their needs with non-commercial or relatively non-material means, makes *the non-purchase decision a critical focus of enquiry.*

Research that retains the consumption–production dichotomy, then, must address product use, not just purchase. What is more, both post-purchase decisions and non-purchase decisions must be included in the analysis. At least two empirical questions arise. One, under what conditions do individuals switch from purchasing a high-environmental-impact item to a relatively low-impact item, when impact is evaluated not just in production but in the use of the product itself? This question might fit existing research programmes, including those of energy use (Cleveland et al, 1984; Schipper, 1997), household metabolism (Noorman and Schoot Uiterkamp, 1998), industrial ecology (Keoleian and Menerey, 1994; Graedel and Allenby, 1995), and market research (Richins, 1994; Ahuvia and Wong, 1997; Ger, 1997). Two, and this may well be the most difficult yet most important question, under what conditions do individuals opt for a *non-commercial or relatively non-material response to meet a need?* Research does exist on intrinsic satisfaction as it relates to conservation behaviour (De Young, 1990–1991), subjective well-being (Inglehart and Abramson, 1994; Andrews and Withey, 1976), and work and leisure (Scitovsky, 1992; Schor, 1997). Much of this research could be extended to consumption patterns and their environmental impacts.

Conducting such research within the framework of the supply–demand, producer–consumer dichotomy is important, as noted, because production has been the dominant focus not only in economics but in the economic strands of other disciplines. It may also be the safest research tack, given the hegemony of the economistic belief system. Unpacking the demand function for environmental impacts can enrich existing research traditions and inform policy-making, and do so without challenging the underlying assumptions. But for those seeking a more transformative approach to environmental problems, an approach that goes beyond 'environmental improvement', the prevailing dichotomy is probably more of a hindrance than an aid. It tends to constrain the analysis to market functioning (and malfunctioning) where 'the environment' is merely an externality.

A more radical approach – one that challenges this dichotomy and its propensity to relegate consumption to a black box or to the marginal status of emotion or personal values – is to treat all resource use as consuming and ask what risks are entailed in patterns of resource acquisition, processing and distribution. This approach is more consistent with the ecological economics perspective where human economic activity is seen as an open subset of a finite and closed biophysical system (Costanza, 1991; Daly and Townsend, 1993). Consuming is that part of human activity that 'uses up' material, energy and other valued things.

Consumption as 'Using Up'

A definition of consumption that transcends the supply–demand dichotomy would start with biophysical conditions and their intersection with human behaviour. That intersection, following from systems theory, has many attributes but key is ecological feedback: signals from the biophysical system that are picked up and reacted to by individuals and groups in the social system (Kay, 1991; Ulanowicz, 1997; Costanza et al, 2001). At its most basic and general level, the human behaviour that intersects with the biophysical realm can be termed *material provisioning* – that is, the appropriation of material and energy for survival and reproduction.

Material provisioning

All human activity can be divided among overlapping sets of behaviour that include reproduction, defence, social interaction, identity formation and material provisioning. Three broad categories of material provisioning are hunting/gathering, cultivating and manufacturing. The question then is, what aspects of each category of material provisioning are best construed as consumption? Alternatively, if the activities encompassed by hunting/gathering, cultivating and manufacturing are each construed as consumption rather than as production, what insights are gained? Answering this first requires a general definition of consumption itself.

Consumption, according to *The American Heritage Dictionary of the English Language,* is to expend or use up, to degrade or destroy. Thermodynamically, it is to increase entropy. Biologically, it is capturing usable material and energy to enhance survival and reproduction and, ultimately, to pass on one's genes. Socially, it is using up material and energy to enhance personal standing, group identity and autonomy.

Hunting/gathering

A defining characteristic of consuming behaviour, therefore, is that it is the feature of material provisioning that permanently degrades material and energy and serves some purpose to the individual or to the group. Within hunting/gathering, consumption begins when the deer is shot or the apple is picked and ends when the user has fully expended the material and energy in that deer or apple. It is important to stress that, in hunting/gathering, the consumption act is only the appropriation *of the item* and its ingestion. The one deer and the one apple is permanently degraded, not the deer herd or species and not the apple tree or species. This level of consumption is the most fundamental biologically and, indeed, is integral to all life. When some argue that consumption is 'natural', they are right – at this level.

Cultivation

In cultivation, one begins to see both the extension of consumption beyond single items and the external effects of consumption. Consumption in cultivation begins when a forest is cleared or a grassland ploughed. It ends when the crop is harvested and the wood burned or the bread eaten. What is expended – used up or degraded – is not just the wood fibre or seed of individual plants. Rather, it is, first and foremost, the ecosystem that preceded the cultivation and, second, the cultivated plants that no longer function within integrated ecosystems. Cultivation may be conventionally thought of as production – that is, as adding value. But from the consumption angle, a perspective grounded in the biophysical, cultivation is a set of degrading behaviours – clearing, breeding, harvesting and ingesting.[4]

Manufacturing

Whereas cultivation involves rearranging extant plants and animals, manufacturing, quite literally, is making things by hand. It is applying human labour and ingenuity to create wholly new substances. Ecologically, it draws on more than the available soil and water and associated ecosystems. In particular, manufacturing extends consumption beyond the direct use of individual organisms and ecosystems to the use of energy sources and waste sinks. Converting a log into lumber and then furniture entails an expenditure of low-entropy fuel and the disposal of waste material and heat. From the production angle, this is value added. But from the consumption angle, it is using up secondary resources (energy and waste-sink capacities) to amplify and accelerate the use of primary resources (forests, grasslands, fisheries and so on). Consuming here may entail permanent and unavoidable depletion, as with fossil fuels, or a temporary draw-down with the possibility of regeneration, as with soil buffering.

Both cultivation and manufacturing risk permanent degeneration in ecosystem functioning. But manufacturing is generally more risky due to the separation of activity from primary resources. High technology and global finance are extreme examples where so-called 'wealth creation' is far removed, some would argue completely removed, from a natural-resource base. The consumption angle directs attention to the heightened risks of such distanced material provisioning (Dryzek, 1987).

In sum, an ecologically grounded definition of consumption takes as a starting point human material provisioning and the draw on ecosystem services. It is distinguished from definitions that begin with market behaviour and ask what purchasers do in the aggregate, and from definitions that start with social stratification and ask how consumption patterns establish hierarchy or identity. The potential of such an ecological definition is to escape the confines of both limits-to-growth and economistic frameworks that tend *to* prescribe top-down, centralized correctives for errant (i.e. overconsuming) human behaviour. An ecological approach to consumption directs attention to ecological risk and the myriad ways clever humans have of displacing the true costs of their material provisioning. The next step in conceptualizing the consumption–environment nexus is to specify what excessive or maladaptive consumption is. In particular, it is to ask how a given act of consumption (e.g. eating the apple, converting the forest, manufacturing the chair) can be interpreted or judged. I start with the broad biophysical context in which consuming behaviour can be interpreted as 'natural' or 'background' and then consider both ecological and social definitions of degradative consumption, what I call *over-consumption* and *misconsumption*.

Excess Consumption: Three Interpretive Layers

A strictly ecological interpretation takes consumption as perfectly 'natural'. To survive, all organisms must consume – that is, degrade resources. This interpretation of a given consumption act is *background consumption*. It refers to the normal, biological functioning of all organisms, humans included. Every act of background consumption by an individual alters the environment, the total environmental impact being a function of aggregate consumption of the population. Individuals consume to meet a variety of needs – physical and psychological, both of which contribute to the ability of the individual to survive and reproduce.

From this limited, *a*social, *non*-ethical interpretation of consumption, all consumption patterns and consequences are natural, including population explosions and crashes and irreversibilities caused by the expansion of one species at the expense of other species. If, however, the interpretation is modified to include *human concern* for population crashes, species extinctions, permanent diminution of ecosystem functioning, diminished reproductive and developmental potential of individuals, and other irreversible effects, then 'problematic consumption' becomes relevant. Two interpretive layers are *over-consumption* and *misconsumption.*

Over-consumption is the level or quality of consumption that undermines a species' own life-support system and for which individuals and collectivities have choices in their consuming patterns. Over-consumption is an aggregate-level concept. With instances of over-consumption, individual behaviour may be perfectly sensible, conforming either to the evolutionary dictates of fitness or to the economically productive dictates of rational decision-making. Collective, social behaviour may appear sensible, too, as when increased consumption is needed in an advanced industrial economy to stimulate productive capacity and compete in international markets. But eventually the collective outcome from over-consuming is catastrophe for the population or the species. From a thermodynamic and ecological perspective, this is the problem of *excessive throughput* (Boulding, 1993; Daly, 1993; Georgescu-Roegen, 1993). The population or species has commanded more of the regenerative capacity of natural resources and more of the assimilative capacity of waste sinks than the relevant ecosystems can support. And it is an *ethical* problem because it inheres only in populations or species that can reflect on their collective existence. What is more, for humans it becomes a *political* problem when the trends are towards collapse, power differences influence impacts, and those impacts generate conflict.

The second interpretive layer within problematic consumption is *misconsumption,* which concerns individual behaviour. The problem here is that the individual consumes in a way that undermines his or her own well-being even if there are no aggregate effects on the population or species. Put differently, the long-term effect of an individual's consumption pattern is either suboptimal or a net loss to that individual. It may or may not, however, undermine collective survival. Such consumption can occur along several dimensions.

Physiologically, humans misconsume when they eat too much in a sitting or over a lifetime or when they become addicted to a drug. The long-term burden overwhelms the immediate gratification. Psychologically, humans misconsume when, for example, they fall into the advertiser's trap of 'perpetual dissatisfaction'. They purchase an item that provides fleeting satisfaction, resulting in yet another purchase. Economically, humans misconsume when they overwork – that is, engage in onerous work beyond what can be compensated with additional income. With more income and less time, they attempt to compensate by using the additional income, which is to say, by consuming.

Ecologically, humans misconsume when an increment of increased resource use harms that resource or related resources and humans who depend on the resource. In the short term, if one builds a house on a steep, erosion-prone slope, the construction itself increases the likelihood of massive erosion and the destruction of one's consumption item, the house. In the longer term, if one uses leaded house-paint, one's children or grandchildren are more likely to have developmental problems.

Misconsumption, then, refers to individual resource-using acts that result in net losses for the individual. They are not 'rational' or sensible in any of several senses – psychological, economic or healthwise. And, once again, they may or may not add up to aggregate, ecological decline. The question that critically defines the consumption and environment research agenda at this, the individual level, is, what forms of individual misconsumption lead to collective over-consumption? Put differently, when is over-consumption not simply a problem of excessive throughput – that is, a problem of too many people or too much economic activity – and when is it a question of the inability of individuals to meet their needs in a given social context? When, in other words, do individuals simultaneously wreak harm on themselves *and* on the environment through their consumption patterns?

These questions are important because they point towards potential interventions that make sense at both levels and without requiring evolutionarily novel human behaviour such as global citizenship (Low and Heinen, 1993) or authoritarian command structures (De Young, 1996). These questions point toward win-win, 'no-regrets' policies that simultaneously produce improved human welfare and reduced ecological risk to humans' life-support system. A critical area of research, therefore, is the intersection of misconsumption and over-consumption where individuals and society together can potentially benefit from improved consumption patterns. This may offer the greatest, and certainly the easiest, opportunities for interventions. But a second area is at least as important yet more vexing. This is consumption patterns that involve individually satisfying behaviour with net benefits to the individual and, say, to that individual's kin, yet net harms to others. This is unavoidably a distributional question and, hence, a moral and political issue. Below I explore part of this moral and political dimension by considering how producers must exercise restraint and resistance when demand is overwhelming.

A Simple Application

To grasp how a critique of the production angle and a preliminary ecological conceptualization of a consumption angle may be operationalized in a research-and-action agenda, imagine that a resource is stressed, say, more timber is being harvested in a watershed than the forest ecosystem can regenerate. What is more, the primary reason is demand. Consumers want more of the timber than the ecosystem can bear and they can pay a sufficiently high price or marshal enough coercion to compel high production.[5] Imagine further that the forest users – that is, those who decide harvest rates and management techniques – are responding entirely to this demand, managing the forest and choosing harvest rates and practices that best fit that demand. As demand increases, they increase the harvest rate in the short term and, for the longer term, plant, say, fast-growing species. Their entire enterprise is production oriented and demand driven. More demand, expressed either through higher prices or increased orders or both, compels more production. The only question forest users and others ask is, how can demand be anticipated and then met? Consequently, the timber owner tries to improve harvesting methods to get more usable logs off each acre and the mill owner tries to improve milling to get more sellable board feet out of each log. Builders and retailers develop new construction methods to get more square feet of building or more pieces of furniture out of a load of lumber. And all step up production with more labour and more hours of operation. To deal with the loss of the forest, government officials and activists might require replanting or mandate a set-aside to preserve a portion of the forest. They might require buffer strips along streams to reduce siltation and beauty strips along roadways to reduce aesthetic loss.

All these production-oriented measures fall within the realm of 'environmental improvement'. For a given level of harvest they generate more usable product or less environmental damage. But the harvest is, indeed, *given* – that is, given by demand, by some combination of human need and desire and agents to supply (or stoke) that demand. And all via a supply of money that exists completely outside of ecological carrying capacity. Such production-oriented measures may be able to accommodate more of the demand or ameliorate the environmental effects. But when demand continues to increase and then exceed supply (in an ecological sense), the real issue regarding over-harvesting is, indeed, the demand, not the supply. Better forest management practices, less wood waste, more efficient milling, lower transportation costs, rehabilitation, and set-asides will have little effect on the excessiveness of the demand.[6] Use of the forest may appear to be a production issue, but when over-harvesting is the concern, it is really a consumption issue. For both analytic and behaviour-change reasons, it should be investigated from the consumption angle.

Before doing so, it is important to point out that the production angle starts with a set of conditions that, in contemporary industrial society, are taken as the base-line, the starting point from which all else progresses. What is more, this base-line is unecological. If policy-makers want to increase employment, the central banker stimulates demand through the money supply and interest rates. Financial signals start in the capital city, work their way through planners, designers, and builders to retailers and processors and, eventually, in this case, to the timber owner, who hires more workers and develops new technologies to cut more trees. The financial stimulus occurs as if ecological constraints are irrelevant. Indeed, the financial signal exists completely independent of signals from the ecosystems that must adjust.

Signals from elsewhere in the commodity chain operate similarly. If members of the wood-products industry want to capture market share in rot-resistant timber, say, they convince municipalities to mandate pressure-treated timber in outdoor applications. What were once trash species become highly marketable and demand rises. Production again increases, and all as if there were no ecological constraint, as if ecosystems were mere *inputs* to the economy, not a *foundation* of the economy.

The production angle is, thus, inherently unecological. If countervailing biophysical signals happen to work their way from the forest to the timber owner to processors, distributors, and retailers (let alone to money-supply managers), they are overwhelmed by the presumption of net benefits from more production: producers produce goods, goods are good, more goods are better. Consumers benefit as revealed by their willingness to pay. (Note how the notion of consumer sovereignty is integral to the production angle.) But as many have argued, economic growth, conventionally defined and measured, can be 'uneconomic', even on its own terms, let alone on ecological terms. It can lead to net harm, especially when ecosystem services, family and community integrity, and future generations are taken into account (Ayres, 1996; Daly, 1996; Scitovsky, 1992; Hirsch, 1995).

If the production angle is inherently unecological, if it naturally overwhelms feedback that would otherwise reveal long-term net harm, then the consumption angle, if it has analytic and policy utility, ought to do just the opposite. It should direct analytic attention to what is lost, to what risks are incurred when, in this example, the harvest rate exceeds the regenerative rate of the forest ecosystem. Following the framework outlined above, I begin the consumption angle within the production–consumption, supply–demand dichotomy, then shift to material activity up and down the chain of resource-use decisions.

Within the production–consumption dichotomy, the first observation is that the production-oriented measures do not solve the problem of over-harvesting. They mitigate the damage or extend the time until the forest is completely cut over. When resource-use decisions are largely governed by agents and managers and consumers highly removed from the forest itself, the problem is not inefficiencies or lack of political will or greed. The problem is not inefficient use of logs and lumber or the political difficulties of creating parks and buffer strips. Indeed, the problem is not the intricacies of meeting ever-increasing demand, satisfying customers, stockholders and workers. Rather, the problem is the demand itself, the array of signals and incentives coming from actors highly distanced from ecological constraint.

A consumption perspective therefore asks about the *nature of the demand,* what is otherwise forbidden territory in the production angle where consumers are sovereign. The consumption angle asks whether the increasing demand is simply a matter of a growing population in need, say, of shelter; whether the prices paid by buyers reflect full costs, social and ecological (however measured); whether consumption is facilitated, maybe subsidized, by low-cost transportation infrastructure or easy credit;[7] whether the benefits of new products are highlighted while the drawbacks are shaded; whether retailers launched a new line of luxury furniture or builders doubled the average house size (yet again). It asks whether consumers have the option of choosing less wood-intensive means of meeting the same needs. What is more, the consumption angle raises questions of non-purchase. Is some segment of the population for going purchase of the product and, if so, is it because of income, availability, information or alternative means of meeting the same needs? In other words, is non-purchase a meaningful option and, if so, does the increasing demand truly reflect a net social-welfare gain, the implicit as sumption in the production angle?

Shifting to consumption as 'using up', a comprehensive analysis would examine each decision node from initial extraction to ultimate use and disposal. Here I focus on processing and initial extraction. From the production angle, a mill owner 'produces' lumber from logs. Equally logically, yet from the consumption angle, the mill owner *consumes* logs from the timber owner's forest. That is, what is used up is a log and its alternative uses. The log is irretrievably converted to one item – lumber – never to be used for veneer or paper or larger-dimension lumber.

Applying the same logic to the timber owner and the forest, what is used up, it would appear at first glance, is trees. Each tree cut is irreversibly removed, its ability to photosynthesize and provide habitat for other plants and animals, completely elimi-nated. But at some rate and extent of harvest, more than single trees' capacity to put on cellulose is consumed. Each tree constitutes a node in a complex system. As some trees fall to the axe (or to wind or insects), the system, being adaptive and resilient, adjusts. But as more trees fall, a threshold is passed and the integrity of the system is compro-mised. At this level of harvest, the system itself and all the species it entails and ecosys-tem services it provides are, indeed, consumed – that is, used up. Efficient production, erosion control, and preserves (unless on a system scale) do nothing to alter this ultimate effect of ever-increasing harvest. They may postpone the threshold or soften its impact, but the forest ecosystem is still consumed.

From this analytic perspective, all decision-makers along the chain from extraction to end use are 'consumers'. As such, they and policy-makers and citizens who condition their choices logically must ask what is 'used up', what services are put at risk, what features of the primary resource – the forest ecosystem (not the trees) – are being elimi-nated. Moreover, to ask these questions is unavoidably to ask about long-term effects. If the ecosystem is degraded, will there always be another? Do the benefits accrued by each actor along the material chain accumulate so as to unambiguously over-ride the risk or loss of the ecosystem (especially if such a judgement is made in an open, well-informed forum rather than in the market)? Are future generations likely to recognize and accept the value of the trade-off: more human capital (timber and furniture and their associ-ated technologies) for less natural capital?

These are questions of long-term sustainable resource use, not environmental improvement. They take high-integrity ecosystems as given, indeed necessary, not the social organization for resource use and economic expansion that happens to be hegem-onic at this historical juncture. But I should stress that these questions derive logically from the consumption angle, not from the arbitrary or ideologically derived positions of those who 'value nature' or who profess concern for future generations. These questions come from turning the dominant perspective on its head and asking not what goods are produced (and presuming that all such goods consumed are 'good'), but what services, *what forms of social and natural capital, are consumed.* Just as the production angle pre-sumes goods are good and more goods are better, in the consumption angle, *life-support systems are presumed fragile and critical irreversibilities possible.* 'Cautious consuming' is not only prudent but rational. In addition, not only do these questions derive logically from the consumption angle, whether emphasizing the demand side or viewing all eco-nomic activity as consuming, the perspective itself is at least as logical as the production angle. In fact, although the production angle may be the most logical in an 'empty-world', frontier economy, in a 'full world', in an ecologically constrained economy, the consumption angle can be judged more logical. It does, after all, draw attention to eco-system functioning as an integral part of the analysis, not as an add-on, not as an 'exter-nality', the prevailing approach in the production angle.

Finally, I should add that instances do exist where production-oriented measures are eschewed by resource users. Under some conditions timber owners, fishers, and others will deliberately limit output (McGoodwin, 1990; Colchester and Lohman, 1993; Alcorn and Toledo, 1995). Such measures entail behaviours by producers that tend to be ignored, if not suppressed, when a production perspective is dominant. Two such behaviours that derive logically from the consumption angle are *restraint* and *resistance.*

If forest users have a strong interest in their own long-term economic security and if they depend on the forest, it is sensible to avoid or modulate demand-driven harvest decisions. When demand is low, these forest users would harvest little and invest little. But they would also shift to different forest uses, from timber harvesting only, say, to hunting and fishing and tourism, as well as to non-forest means of making a living.[8] Multiple use, therefore, makes sense as a survival strategy for the user, as a means of ensuring long-term economic security, not just as public policy. If demand is high, they would increase the harvest rates only to a point. Beyond that point, a point determined not by short-term economic opportunity but by a sense of ecological limits, by a risk-averse approach to complex natural systems and to the users' own economic security, they would logically *restrain* their harvests so as not to jeopardize future use and those other uses. What is more, if demand is so intrusive, so overwhelming via temptingly high prices or coercion (force or law), then a second behaviour would logically be *resistance.* Users would develop organizational, legal, or, if necessary, coercive means of their own to resist the intrusion, limit their harvest, and thus maintain the resource over the long term.[9]

Again, the problem here may appear to be one of production – that is, harvest rates. But it is really one of *consumption* vis-à-vis production. The foci of conventional production analysis – issues of investment, management, extraction, pricing, processing, distributing – tend not to ask questions about restraint and resistance among producers. Quite the contrary, the productive enterprise is precisely one of opening markets, lowering prices, gaining efficiencies and capturing market share – in short, increasing production. It is a process that sees the *addition* of value, not the *subtraction* of value, not the *risks* to multiple uses or to residents' economic security or to the long-term viability of the supporting ecosystem.

In sum, this simple application suggests that a consumption angle on resource-use problems – especially problems of ecological overuse – compels examination of decisions among extractors and processors that tend not to get asked from a conventional production perspective. Among these decisions are those associated with the general behaviours of restraint, that is, self-limiting behaviour, and of resistance to destructive intrusions. Comparing cases where restraint and resistance are prominent with those in which they are not and applying indices of sustainable practice would be a useful research direction.

Conclusion

By making consumption more visible analytically, certain activities be come more prominent. From a production angle, the simple-living movement, home power and local currencies are trivial instances of protest; they are of little political or economic consequence. From a consumption angle, however, they are concrete expressions of concern and resistance. They represent a sense that too much of what is important in day-to-day life is lost through the lens of ever more production meeting the (presumably) insatiable desires of people as consumers. These cases not only give meaning to consumption, but they give meaning to economic activity as being more than that which ascribes value only to what is produced and sold in the open market and that assigns people the role of consumer, not producer and certainly not citizen. If simple living, home power and local currencies are trivial by conventional (read, production) measures, they are not trivial representations of the widespread discontent with consumerist society.

In short, the consumption angle is a means of 'rethinking how humans relate to nature'. It is a way to, in effect, wipe the slate clean with respect to how analysts, policy-makers, and citizens understand social organization for resource use. It puts aside, or goes back to the origins of, the neo-classical economic model and asks what model would have been most useful *given* ecological constraint, *given* the lack of unending frontiers and infinite waste sinks, and *given* the inability to find a technical substitute for everything from petroleum to the ozone layer. The consumption angle not only allows for consideration of 'full-world', ecologically constrained conditions, but places ecosystem functioning up front and central. It does so by generating questions that ask what is consumed, what is put at risk, what is lost. And it does so without restricting the questions to consumer products or even industrial inputs but by going all the way back up the decision chain to organisms and ecosystems and biogeochemical processes. It also does so by drawing attention to behaviours and movements that otherwise tend to escape those who hold the production angle sacrosanct: restraint and resistance with respect to ever-increasing demand, simple living, home power and local currencies with respect to lifestyle and economic life. Finally, the consumption angle lends itself to explicit assignment of responsibility for excess throughput. This stands in marked contrast to the production angle, where actors routinely escape responsibility via distanced commerce and the black box of consumer sovereignty.

Notes

1   Economics, curiously enough, is the only discipline that has spawned efforts (albeit well out of the mainstream discipline) at biophysical grounding. See, for example, Boulding (1993); Daly (1993); and Georgescu-Roegen (1993). For attempts within an institutionalist tradition, see Costanza et al (2001) and Princen (1998).

2   This neglect of the externalities of consumption does have its exceptions. Within economics, see Daly (1996) and Schor (1997). Within anthropology, see Rappoport (1994).

3   For an extended critique of the production perspective, including that adopted by many environmentalists, as well as an explanation of why to pursue a research agenda on consumption and environment engenders resistance, see Princen (1999).

4   To characterize cultivation as degrading is not to judge it as wrong. I use 'degrade' primarily in the thermodynamic sense of increased entropy, but also in the ecological sense of decreased autonomous functioning over long periods of time. Thus, a corn field may generate more calories than its grassland predecessor, but it does so only with continuous external inputs. It likely operates at a net energy loss and without the resilience of a less 'productive' yet self-organizing system.

Also, this treatment is not to suggest that there is no value in cultivation. The consumption angle on cultivation merely directs analytic attention to *degradation* and *irreversibility* in a way that the prevailing perspective – the production angle – does not do, or does so only as an add-on where value added is the focus and environmental impacts are unfortunate side effects that can be cleaned up if actors have the funds, the interest and the political will.

5   This scenario, although highly simplified to make the argument, is not unlike that which occurred in the great cutovers of North America (see Cronon, 1991) or that are occurring currently in South America and Southeast Asia (see Peluso, 1993).

6   More efficient use of a tree may appear to be a logical response to increasing demand. Certainly, getting more usable wood per tree would, all else being equal, accommodate at least some of the excess demand. But, in general, such efficiency always makes sense, regardless of demand. The issue raised here is what a producer must do outside of production efficiencies to deal with excess demand and still ensure long-term production from the resource.

7   For evidence of the role credit plays in creating excess demand for commodities, see Gale (1998).

8   Some evidence does exist that extractors who attempt to maximize their long-term economic security, rather than respond to extant demand, pursue strategies of diversified production. When either demand or the resource declines, they shift to other pursuits. Fishers in the Norwegian Arctic and many independent farmers follow this model (see Jentoft and Kristoffersen, 1989; McGoodwin, 1990; Clunies-Ross and Hildyard, 1992). To my knowledge, however, no systematic research has been done on such work strategies and their impact on natural resources.

9   Empirical support for restraint does exist, especially in the common property literature. See Ostrom (1990); Bromley (1992); and Acheson and Wilson (1996). Other instances in private property are beginning to develop (for example, the cases being developed by the MacArthur Foundation's Sustainable Forestry programme). On resistance, see Gadgil and Guha (1992) and Peluso (1993).

References

Acheson, J. M. and Wilson, J. A. (1996) 'Order out of chaos: The case of parametric fisheries management', *American Anthropologist,* vol 98, no 3, September 1996, pp579–594

Adams, J. H. (1999) 'Oilgate in the Arctic: Message from the president', *Amicus Journal,* vol 20, no 4, winter, p2

Ahuvia, A. and Wong, N. (1997) 'Three types of materialism: Their relationship and origin', Paper presented to University of Michigan Business School, Ann Arbor, 13 April

Alcorn, J. B. and Toledo, V. M. (1995) 'The role of tenurial shells in ecological sustainability: Property rights and natural resource management in Mexico', in S. Hanna and M. Munasinghe (eds) *Property Rights in a Social and Ecological Context: Case Studies and Design Applications,* Beijer International Institute of Ecological Economics and the World Bank, Washington, DC

Andrews, F. and Withey, S. (1976) *Social Indicators of Well-Being: American Perceptions of Life Quality,* Plenum, New York

Ayres, R. U. (1996) 'Limits to the growth paradigm', *Ecological Economics,* vol 19, no 2, November, pp117–134

Boulding, K. E. (1993) 'Spaceship Earth', in H. E. Daly and K. N. Townsend (eds) *Valuing the Earth: Economics, Ecology, Ethics,* MIT Press, Cambridge, MA

Bromley, D. W. (ed) (1992) *Making the Commons Work: Theory, Practice, and Policy,* Institute for Contemporary Studies Press, San Francisco

Cleveland, C., Costanza, J., Hall, C. and Kaufman, R. (1984) 'Energy and the US economy: A biophysical perspective', *Science,* vol 225, no 4665, 31 August, pp890–897

Clunies-Ross, T. and Hildyard, N. (1992) 'The politics of industrial agriculture', *The Ecologist,* vol 22, no 2, March/April, pp65–71

Colchester, M. and Lohman, L. (eds) (1993) *The Struggle for Land and the Fate of the Forests,* Zed Books, London

Costanza, R. (ed) (1991) *Ecological Economics: The Science and Management of Sustainability,* Columbia University Press, New York

Costanza, R., Low, B. S., Ostrom, E. and Wilson, J. (eds) (2001) *Institutions, Ecosystems, and Sustainability,* Lewis, Boca Raton, FL

Cronon, W. (1991) *Nature's Metropolis: Chicago and the Great West,* Norton, New York

Daly, H. E. (1993) 'Steady-state economy', in H. E. Daly and K. N. Townsend (eds) *Valuing the Earth: Economics, Ecology, Ethics,* MIT Press, Cambridge, MA

Daly, H. E. (1996) *Beyond Growth: The Economics of Sustainable Development,* Beacon Press, Boston

Daly, H. E. and Townsend, K. N. (eds) (1993) *Valuing the Earth: Economics, Ecology, Ethics,* MIT Press, Cambridge, MA

De Young, R. (1990–1991) 'Some psychological aspects of living lightly: Desired lifestyle patterns and conservation behavior', *Journal of Environment Systems,* vol 20, no 3, pp215–227

De Young, R. (1996) 'Some psychological aspects of reduced consumption behavior: The role of intrinsic satisfaction and competence motivation', *Environment and Behavior,* vol 28, no 3, May, pp358–409

Dryzek, J. S. (1987) *Rational Ecology: Environment and Political Economy,* Blackwell, New York

Gadgil, M. and Guha, R. (1992) *This Fissured Land: An Ecological History of India,* University of California Press, Berkeley, CA

Georgescu-Roegen, N. (1993) 'Energy and economic myths', in Daly, H. E. and Townsend, K. N. (eds) *Valuing the Earth: Economics, Ecology, Ethics,* MIT Press, Cambridge, MA

Gale, F. (1998) *The Tropical Timber Trade Regime,* Macmillan, Basingstoke, UK, and St Martin's Press, New York

Ger, G. (1997) 'Human development and humane consumption: Well-being beyond the "good life"', *Journal of Public Policy and Marketing,* vol 16, no 1, spring, pp110–125

Graedel, T. E. and Allenby, B. R. (1995) *Industrial Ecology,* Prentice Hall, Englewood Cliffs, NJ

Hirsh, F. (1995 [1976]) *Social Limits to Growth,* Harvard University Press, Cambridge, MA

Inglehart, R. and Abramson, P. (1994) 'Economic security and value change', *American Political Science Review,* vol 88, no 2, June, pp336–354

Jentoft, S. and Kristoffersen, T. (1989) 'Fishermen's co-management: The case of the Lofoten fishery', *Human Organization,* vol 48, no 4, winter, pp355–365

Kay, J. J. (1991) 'A nonequilibrium thermodynamic framework for discussing ecosystem integrity', *Environmental Management,* vol 15, no 4, pp483–495

Keoleian, G. A. and Menerey, D. (1994) 'Sustainable development by design: Review of life cycle design and related approaches', *Journal of the Air and Waste Management Association,* vol 44, no 5, pp645–668

Leach, W. (1993) *Land of Desire: Merchants, Power, and the Rise of a New American Culture,* Pantheon Books, New York

Low, B. S. and Heinen, J. T. (1993) 'Population, resources and environment: Implications of human behavioral ecology for conservation', *Population and Environment,* vol 15, no 1, September, pp7–41

McGoodwin, J. R. (1990) *Crisis in the World's Fisheries: People, Problems, and Policies,* Stanford University Press, Stanford, CA

Miller, D. (ed) (1995) *Acknowledging Consumption: A Review of New Studies,* Routledge, London

Noorman, K. J. and Schoot Uiterkamp, T. (eds) (1998) *Green Households? Domestic Consumers, Environment, and Sustainability,* Earthscan, London

Nordman, B. (1995) 'Celebrating consumption', Paper presented to Lawrence Berkeley Laboratory, Berkeley, CA, available at www.eetd.LBL.gOv/EA/Buildings/BNordman/C/consmain.html

Ostrom, E. (1990) *Governing the Commons: The Evolution of Institutions for Collective Action,* Cambridge University Press, Cambridge, UK

Peluso, N. (1993) 'Coercing conservation: The politics of state resource control', in R. Lipshcutz and K. Conca (eds) *The State and Social Power in Global Environmental Politics,* Columbia University Press, New York

Princen, T. (1998) 'From property regime to international regime: An ecosystem perspective', *Global Governance,* vol 4, no 4, October–November, pp395–413

Princen, T. (1999) 'Consumption and environment: Some conceptual issues', *Ecological Economics,* vol 31, no 3, December, pp347–363

Rappoport, R. (1994) 'Disorders of our own: A conclusion', in S. Forman (ed) *Diagnosing America: Anthropology and Public Engagement,* University of Michigan Press, Ann Arbor, MI

Richins, M. L. (1994) 'Valuing things: The public and private meanings of possessions', *Journal of Consumer Research,* vol 21, pp504–521

Schipper, L. J. (1997) 'Carbon emissions from travel in the OECD countries', in P. Stern, T. Dietz, V. W. Ruttan, R. Socolow and J. L. Sweeney (eds) *Environmentally Significant Consumption: Research Directions,* National Academy Press, Washington, DC

Schor, J. (1997) 'A new economic critique of consumer society', in D. Crocker and T. Linden (eds) *Ethics of Consumption: The Good Life, Justice and Global Stew,* Rowman and Littlefield, Lanham, MD

Scitovsky, T. (1992 [1976]) *The Joyless Economy: The Psychology of Human Satisfaction,* Oxford University Press, Oxford

Stern, P., Dietz, T., Ruttan, V. W., Socolow, R. and Sweeney, J. L. (eds) (1997) *Environmentally Significant Consumption: Research Directions,* National Academy Press, Washington, DC

Ulanowicz, R. E. (1997) *Ecology: The Ascendent Perspective,* Columbia University Press, New York

Wilk, R. (1998) 'Emulation, imitation and global consumerism', *Organization and Environment,* vol 11, no 3, September, pp314–333

5

Pursuing More Sustainable Consumption by Analysing Household Metabolism in European Countries and Cities

Henri C. Moll, Klaasjan Noorman, Rixt Kok, Rebecka Engström, Harold Throne-Holst and Charlotte Clark

Introduction

The last decades have witnessed an enormous growth in production and consumption levels. Related to this production and consumption, environmental decay is occurring everywhere around the globe. The World Summit on Sustainable Development in Johannesburg (WSSD, 2002, Chapter III, point 14) found that:

> Fundamental changes in the way societies produce and consume are indispensable for achieving global sustainable development. All countries should promote sustainable consumption and production patterns, with the developed countries taking the lead and with all countries benefiting from the process... Governments, relevant international organizations, the private sector and all major groups should play an active role in changing unsustainable consumption and production patterns.

Quantification of the environmental load related to consumption is required to facilitate this process.

In the 1970s an approach to modelling the total energy use due to a household's consumption was developed by Bullard and Herendeen (see Bullard and Herendeen, 1975; Herendeen and Tanaka, 1976; Bullard et al, 1978). This approach takes into account both direct energy use, such as heating and motor fuel, and the indirect energy use required to produce the products and services consumed by a household. This approach was further extended in the Netherlands by Biesiot and Moll (1995) and by Vringer and Blok (1995). They analysed the Netherlands household energy requirements of 1990 in detail, using data on energy use in the Dutch economy and on Dutch household expenditures. Studies have also been performed to determine the energy requirements and/or the carbon dioxide (CO_2) emissions related to household consumption in several other countries (Lenzen, 1998; Munksgaard et al, 2000; Kim, 2002; Reinders et al, 2003; Pachauri, 2004; Bin and Dowlatabadi, 2005; Cohen et al, 2005).

In these studies, energy use (and the related greenhouse gas emissions) has been chosen as the most significant proxy indicator of environmental load.

All of these studies have demonstrated that the contribution of household consumption to the environmental load of the economy is substantial. The environmental load is partially caused by energy use within households, but a substantial remaining part of the environmental load is attributed to the consumption of goods and services by households. In total 70–80 per cent of national energy use and greenhouse gas emissions may be related either to household activities directly or to activities required to deliver goods and services to households and to manage the waste flows generated by households.

These findings generate new research questions:

- What are the determining factors that may explain the environmental load due to household consumption?
- Which parts of household consumption patterns may be susceptible to environmentally relevant changes, and in what ways can the environmental load of consumption be diminished by changes at other levels?
- What advice can be given to individual households, to the government, and to the economic and institutional actors at each level of society to effect change in household consumption patterns toward a sustainable direction?

These questions are discussed and elaborated in the studies mentioned above, mostly at the level of a single country and using broad categories to describe household consumption. So the answers to these questions provided by these previous studies have a preliminary or incomplete status. In this article we present a cross-national comparison of the average household energy requirements of the Netherlands, the UK, Norway, and Sweden, and we analyse in greater detail within these countries the household energy requirements of some cities and of some household groups.[1] Our results, produced in the ToolSust project,[2] are useful in elaborating these three research questions.

First we present a framework for identifying the main determinants of the environmental load of households, and then we develop approaches for recognizing the triggers for diminishing this environmental load. The potential consequences of following this methodology to perform this research are discussed, and findings relevant to these research questions are presented. Finally, we derive some conclusions about the determining factors and about the potential for change, and we discuss how this research may contribute to the development of sustainable consumption patterns.

Conceptual Approach: Depicting the Household Energy Metabolism

The 'industrial metabolism' concept refers to the flows of natural resources entering the production side of the economy and the flows of goods and services – to be consumed and/or exported – and of wastes and emissions to the environment leaving the production sectors. Seen from the consumer perspective, the consumption of goods and services can be linked to patterns of inputs and outputs of the economy and, thus, to the associated environmental effects of economic activities. Because the major part of consumer activities takes place within households, households rather than individual consumers determine a large part of resource consumption. The 'household metabolism' concept refers both to the demand for resources (the direct flows of resources through households) and to the indirect requirements for resources – the flows of resources occurring elsewhere to accomplish household consumption (e.g. in mining, the production of materials, the construction of houses, the manufacturing of goods and the handling of waste) (see Noorman and Schoot Uiterkamp, 1998).

In Figure 5.1 these energy flows are presented, relating the use of natural resources to consumption in households. Natural resources are extracted out of the environmental system and converted to energy carriers supplied directly to the households and to the production sectors supplying the households. The disposal of goods by the households also has effects on the indirect energy use by households. In this figure, two intermediate levels also are discerned between the environmental system and the households. National conditions mainly determine the energy supply system and factors related to the production of goods and services in the economic sectors. The city infrastructure partly determines the travel behaviour of households and also influences the local energy supply to households.

Direct household energy consumption – energy that is literally consumed in households (electricity, natural gas, etc.) or via car fuels – composes a fraction of the national energy consumption (about 35 per cent). Indirect energy flows, on the other hand, are

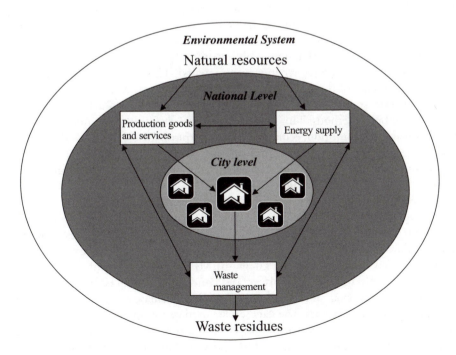

Figure 5.1 *System description of household energy metabolism*

very substantial. The indirect energy consumption of households is equal to the energy directly used for producing and distributing consumer goods and services and for handling consumer waste. The direct and indirect energy requirements are calculated as primary energy values. Primary energy use refers to the energy content of the resources required to deliver the final energy to be used (in forms such as electricity, motor oil and heat) to the production sectors and to the households.

The total household energy requirement is calculated as the sum of the direct and indirect energy requirements. So the total household energy requirements are determined largely by the household spending pattern. This approach reflects the interdependency between industrial metabolism and household metabolism (see Figure 5.1). Changes in the production processes of consumer items have a significant impact on the indirect household energy use, and changes in consumption patterns have effects on the structure of the production side of the economy.

This system description implies that determinants of the total household energy requirements may occur at several levels: the national level, the city level and the household level. How relevant these levels are to understanding and to changing consumption patterns in the direction of sustain ability is further researched in this article.

Methodological Approach: Hybrid Energy Analysis of Household Consumption

The method we used, based on the household energy metabolism concept, projects the energy requirements in production, distribution, consumption and waste processing for household consumption on household budget items. This analysis generates insights into the relationship between household spending patterns and the effects thereof (counted as direct and indirect energy requirements). This method, which assesses the energy requirements of budget items, is outlined in Figure 5.2. In a hybrid approach, elements of process analysis and input–output analysis are combined, building on the advantages of both methods. This approach requires statistical data concerning energy production and consumption, economic input–output matrices, household budget surveys, and goods and services price information. This method had been outlined by Bullard and colleagues (1978) and has been elaborated by Van Engelenburg and colleagues (1991) and Wilting (1996).

The combination of sector production data and energy data delivers data on the direct energy intensities of the various production sectors. Energy intensities are defined as the energy requirements divided by the monetary value (added), expressed in megajoules per Euro (MJ/Euro).[3] Process analysis is also used to determine the energy requirements (expressed in megajoules per kilogram [MJ/kg])[4] of a range of (over 100) basic materials frequently used in the delivery and consumption of goods and services. The input–output energy analysis methodology is used to calculate the indirect energy intensities of the production sectors. The data sets are used in a simplified life-cycle assessment (LCA) of goods and services corresponding to the items included in the household budget surveys. The LCA results are calculated by and stored in a software program called the Energy Analysis Program (EAP) and its related database (Wilting et al, 1999).

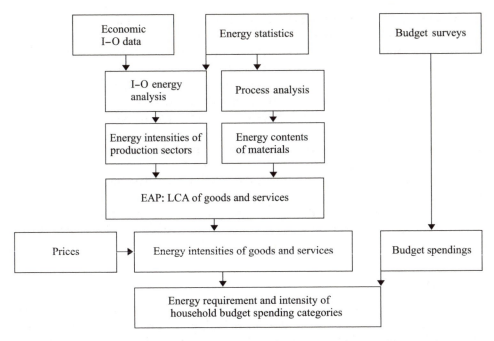

Note: I–O = input–output; EAP = Energy Analysis Program; LCA = life-cycle assessment.

Figure 5.2 *Flow chart of the method for calculating energy parameters of budget spending categories (budget items)*

For a detailed description of the EAP methodology and calculations schemes we refer to work by Wilting (1996).

The EAP databases

The EAP approach uses the following databases:

- energy requirements for basic materials;
- energy intensities of economic sectors;
- energy requirements of modes of transport;
- energy intensities of trade and services sectors; and
- energy requirements for waste processing.

Energy requirements for basic materials, transport modes and waste processing are derived from a variety of studies presenting process descriptions, energy statistics and LCAs.

The energy intensities of the production, trade and service sectors were calculated using country-specific energy data and economic data in the format of input–output tables.

The following economic data were used:

- an input–output table with intermediate deliveries, total production value, and net value added in basic prices;
- an input–output table with competitive and (where available) non-competitive imports (competitive imports are imported commodities that are also produced domestically, whereas non-competitive imports are not produced domestically);
- a data table of energy prices paid by the producing sectors; and
- a data table of the consumption of fixed capital (depreciation of capital goods).

In addition to economic data, the following energy data were used:

- energy consumption data per sector, categorized per fuel type; and
- energy data describing the losses in energy transformation processes (e.g. refining oil, generating electricity) determining the ratio between primary energy use and final energy use, expressed in the so-called energy requirement for energy (ERE) value.

EAP analyses

Once the EAP databases were available, EAP was used to calculate the energy intensities of products (i.e. budget items). The selection of budget items was based on the structure of the available household budget surveys. A separate EAP analysis has to be carried out to calculate the energy intensity of each consumer item. For these EAP analyses, different types of information are needed:

- price information (i.e. consumer price of the product, including value-added tax);
- composition of the product (i.e. type and amount of the basic goods, and type and amount of packaging materials);
- origin of the product (i.e. name of the manufacturer, names of the wholesale and retail traders, and transport distances); and
- how the consumer product is treated after it is used (i.e. waste processing, including recycling).

With the help of these data, EAP calculates the energy intensity of each budget item. Dutch EAP analyses were used as a default in many cases where country-specific information was not available. The total energy requirement of the house holds was calculated by combining the information on energy intensities of the budget items with the expenditure data from the household budget survey.

The household energy requirements for the Netherlands were calculated following this approach for the year 1990 (Biesiot and Moll, 1995) and 1996 (Kok et al, 2001). In the ToolSust project, for three other countries – the UK, Sweden and Norway – EAP country-specific databases were developed for the first time. Also, country-specific EAP analyses were performed of all of the items in each country's budget survey. The Dutch EAP database and Dutch budget items analyses served as a starting point, but as far as possible country-specific data were applied. Also, some methodological adjustments were made on the EAP approach in order to make it applicable in other European countries. The processes used to develop country-specific databases and analyses are found in

Clark and colleagues (2003), Carlsson-Kanyama and colleagues (2002) and Throne-Holst and colleagues (2002).

Evaluation of Determinants for the Total Household Energy Requirement

As mentioned earlier, the total household energy requirement is determined by various factors related to the different levels – the national level, the city level and the household level. Assessing the relevance of these factors is important for the identification of the triggers for changing household consumption patterns in a sustainable direction.

Comparative analysis is necessary to measure the importance of these factors. For a full evaluation, comparisons are required between countries to examine the determinants related to the national level, comparisons are required within countries between national data and data from specific cities to examine locally determined factors, and comparisons are required between household groups within a country to examine the role of household characteristics.

The results of the ToolSust project enable us to make some of these comparisons, indicating the most relevant determining factors as well as the levels at which these factors may be influenced. Here we present some results grouped around the comparisons made at the national level, the city level and the household level.

Comparisons of household energy metabolism between countries

Household consumption patterns and the household metabolism of the Netherlands, the UK, Sweden, and Norway are compared here. See Kok and colleagues (2003) for the comparative results and Falkena and colleagues (2003), Clark and colleagues (2003), Carlsson-Kanyama and colleagues (2002) and Throne-Holst and colleagues (2002) for country-specific results.

Figure 5.3 shows the total expenditures of households and the division of the expenditures over budget categories. The total expenditure per household in Norway is the highest, with 27,900 Euro per year, followed by the UK with 25,500 Euro per year; the lowest are the Netherlands and Sweden with 21,400 and 20,300 Euro per year respectively. When looking at the relative importance of the different budget categories, the most important similarities (and differences) between the countries are the following:

- low expenditures on the aggregate of direct energy categories (motor fuel, solid and liquid fuels, electricity, district heating, and natural gas), ranging from 7 to 10 per cent;
- high expenditures on the food category in all countries, ranging from 18 to 21 per cent;
- high expenditures on the house category in all countries, ranging from 15 to 23 per cent;
- high expenditures on the transport category (excluding motor fuels), ranging from 10 to 20 per cent (transport expenditures generally are relatively high in countries with high total expenditures, and are by far the highest in Norway);

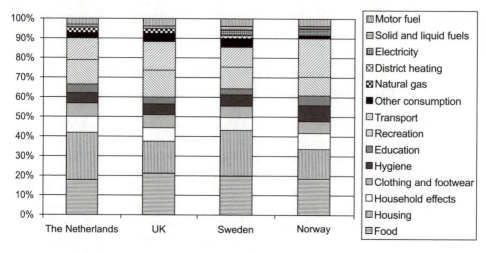

Figure 5.3 *Division of expenditures per budget category for an average household in the different countries*

- high expenditures on the recreation category, ranging from 9 to 14 per cent (recreation expenditures in the UK and the Netherlands are relatively higher than in Sweden and Norway); and
- expenditures on other categories are relatively low and do not differ substantially between the different countries.

The first part of the total household energy requirement is the direct energy portion. The primary and final direct energy use of households in the various countries are given in Figure 5.4. The primary household energy use is relatively low in Norway and is relatively high in the UK. For the final demand, though, the differences between the countries are small. So the differences between the countries in primary energy use by households are mainly caused by differences in the energy supply. The use of hydropower in Norway explains relatively low primary energy use, although the final energy use is high. For the UK the low efficiency due to the large shares of coal for electricity production explains high primary energy use. Comparing the division of the final energy demand, we observe a very high share of electricity in Norway and a high share of natural gas in the Netherlands. In the Netherlands the share for motor fuel is low compared to the other countries.

Figure 5.5 shows the total indirect energy requirement per household and the relative shares of the indirect budget categories for the countries. The indirect energy requirement is the highest in the UK, closely followed by Norway. The indirect energy requirements for Sweden and especially for the Netherlands are much lower. With regard to the division of indirect energy over the budget categories, we observe some striking similarities and some differences:

- The food category has the highest indirect energy requirement in all countries, ranging from 26 to 32 per cent of the total indirect energy requirement.

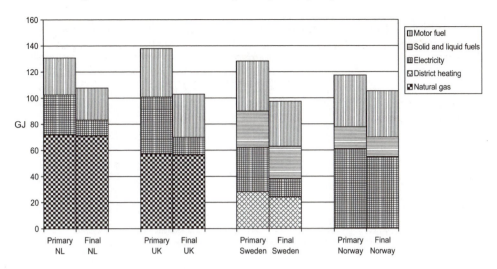

Note: One gigajoule (GJ) = 10^9 joules (J, SI) $\approx 2.39 \times 10^5$ kilocalories (kcal) $\approx 9.48 \times 10^5$ British thermal units (BTU).

Figure 5.4 *Primary and final annual energy requirements in the different countries*

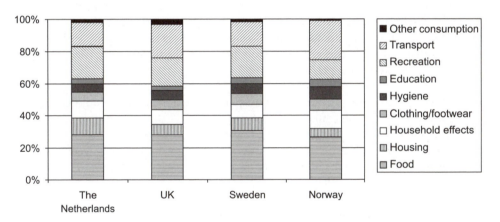

Figure 5.5 *Division of indirect energy requirements over the budget categories in the different countries*

- The transport and recreation categories are important in each country. Of these categories, transport has the highest energy requirement in Norway and in the UK, and recreation has the highest energy requirement in the Netherlands, followed closely by the UK and Sweden.
- The housing category has a low share of the indirect energy requirement (at most 10 per cent), although the expenditures for housing are high (see Figure 5.3).
- Other indirect budget categories have a minor share in the indirect household energy requirement.

Table 5.1 *Indirect energy intensities of the different budget categories*

Category	The Netherlands MJ/Euro	UK MJ/Euro	Sweden MJ/Euro	Norway MJ/Euro
Food	9.4	9.9	10.4	8.9
Housing	2.4	2.8	2.5	2.2
Household effects	7.7	9.0	8.8	8.8
Clothing and footwear	4.8	7.6	8.6	7.1
Hygiene	5.6	7.5	8.0	6.8
Education	5.3	6.9	8.2	5.9
Recreation	9.5	9.2	12.4	8.5
Transport	8.0	10.5	10.5	7.9
Other consumption	2.4	5.1	1.9	6.2
Total indirect energy intensity	6.4	8.0	7.8	7.1

Note: One megajoule (MJ) = 10^6 joules (J, SI) ≈ 239 kilocalories (kcal) ≈ 948 British thermal units (BTU).

Differences between the countries with regard to the average indirect household energy requirements are partly explained by differences in the amounts of money spent. The differences of indirect energy intensities deliver an other part of the explanation. In Table 5.1 the energy intensities of the indirect budget categories and the total average indirect energy intensities are given for all countries. These figures clarify earlier-stated observations about the indirect energy requirements for the budget categories. The table demonstrates the following general pattern:

- The energy intensities of the food, transport, recreation and household effects categories are high for all countries.
- Other indirect budget categories have low energy intensities.
- On average the indirect energy intensity is highest in the UK, followed closely by Sweden. Norway is in the middle, and the Netherlands has the lowest figures for the indirect intensities.

The total energy requirements of the countries are shown in Figure 5.6. The important role of indirect energy requirements is demonstrated by this graph. The total energy requirement is highest for the UK and lowest for the Netherlands, just as for the indirect energy requirement portion alone.

Although expenditures on direct energy have only a minor share in the total household expenditures, direct energy use is responsible for a large share of the total energy requirement. Direct and indirect household energy requirements are roughly of the same order of magnitude. Some summarizing results are presented in Table 5.2. This table shows that the share of direct energy use in the Netherlands and in Sweden is around 50 per cent, whereas the share in the UK and in Norway is around 40 per cent.

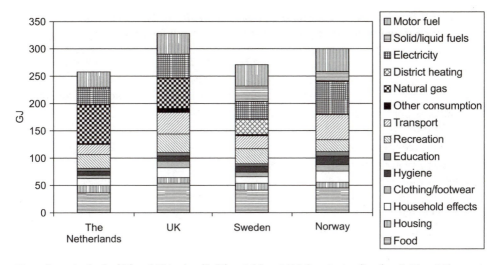

Note: One gigajoule (Gj) = 10^9 joules (J, SI) ≈ 2.39 × 10^5 kilocalories (kcal) ≈ 9.48 × 10^5 British thermal units (BTU).

Figure 5.6 *Total annual energy requirements and energy requirement per budget category for an average household in the different countries*

Table 5.2 *Overview of the annual household metabolism results for the four countries*

	The Netherlands	UK	Sweden	Norway
Expenditure (1000 Euro)	21.4	25.4	20.3	27.9
Total energy requirement per household (GJ)	257	327	271	298
Total energy requirement per person (GJ)	112	135	123	130
Average total energy intensity (MJ/Euro)	12.0	12.9	13.3	10.7
Average indirect energy intensity (MJ/Euro)	6.4	8.0	7.8	7.1
Share of direct energy use (%)	51	42	47	40

Note: One megajoule (Mj) = 10^6 joules (J, SI) ≈ 239 kilocalories (kcal) ≈ 948 British thermal units (BTU). One gigajoule (GJ) = 10^9 joules.

Comparisons of household energy metabolism within countries

Household consumption patterns and household metabolism are compared here within two countries, juxtaposing the national averages of the Netherlands and Sweden with the city averages of Groningen (a Dutch city) and Stockholm (the capital of Sweden).

In Table 5.3 results are given with regard to average household expenditures, household size, total energy requirement per household and per person, indirect energy requirement per household, the share of direct energy, and the total and indirect intensities of consumption.

The expenditures per household are lower in the city of Groningen than the national average for the Netherlands, but the expenditures per person in the city of Groningen

Table 5.3 *Overview of household metabolism results for the Netherlands (on a national and a city level) and for Sweden (on a national and a city level)*

	The Netherlands		Sweden	
	National average	City of Groningen	National average	City of Stockholm
Expenditures per household (in 1000 Euro/year)	21.4	14.1	20.3	20.9
Household size (persons)	2.3	1.5	2.2	1.8
Total energy requirement per household (GJ/year)	257	168	271	246
Total energy requirement per person (GJ/year)	112	111	123	137
Indirect energy requirement per household (GJ/year)	126	83	142	151
Share of direct energy requirement (%)	51	50	47	39
Average indirect energy intensity (MJ/Euro)	6.4	6.4	7.8	7.7
Average total energy intensity (MJ/Euro)	12.0	11.9	13.3	11.8

Note: One megajoule (MJ) = 10^6 joules (J, SI) ≈ 239 kilocalories (kcal) ≈ 948 British thermal units (BTU). One gigajoule (GJ) = 10^9 joules.

are the same as for the Netherlands. For the total energy requirement, the same pattern may be observed. Although the energy requirements per person are the same, differences are found in the direct energy requirement, as follows:

- Motor fuel use is lower in the city of Groningen, explained by the low car possession rate in the city.
- Notwithstanding the smaller average size of the houses in the city of Groningen, natural gas use is higher in the city, mainly explained by climatic differences in the Netherlands.

The expenditures per household are a little bit higher in Stockholm than the average for Sweden, but the household energy requirement in Stockholm is lower than on average in Sweden. Due to the lower average number of persons per household in Stockholm, the total energy requirement per person in Stockholm is higher than on average in Sweden. For all indirect categories the energy requirements per person in Stockholm are higher than for Sweden, the energy requirement for heating and appliances is approximately the same, and the energy use for motor fuel is considerably lower in Stockholm.

Comparisons of household energy metabolism within countries at the level of consumer groups with different household characteristics

The dependence of household consumption patterns and household metabolism on the income variable, the household size variable and the household composition variable is analysed here for two countries: the Netherlands and the UK.

In Tables 5.4 and 5.5 some results are given for the relationship between total household energy requirement and income for the Netherlands and for the UK, respectively. A strong rising trend is observed in total energy requirements with increased income, although the relationship is not proportional (e.g. for the Netherlands the income ratio between the fourth and the first quarter is almost 3, whereas this ratio for energy requirements is about 2.5). For all individual budget categories, the energy requirements increase with income as well. The shares of the household total energy requirement for each of the budget categories are shown for the different income classes in Figure 5.7. In the Netherlands the shares for the categories of transport and recreation increase with income, whereas the shares for electricity and natural gas decrease with income. In the UK we see the same pattern, but the share of the food category also decreases. The share

Table 5.4 *Overview of the results for households of different income groups in the Netherlands*

	First quarter	Second quarter	Third quarter	Fourth quarter
Total indirect energy intensity (MJ/Euro)	5.6	6.0	6.3	6.5
Total energy intensity (MJ/Euro)	13.4	12.7	12.2	11.5
Share of direct energy use (%)	62	57	53	48
Total energy requirement per household (GJ/year)	141	204	263	347

Note: Four income classes; the first quarter refers to the lowest 25% income class, and the fourth quarter refers to the highest 25% income class. One megajoule (MJ) = 10^6 joules (J, SI) ≈ 239 kilocalories (kcal) ≈ 948 British thermal units (BTU). One gigajoule (GJ) = 10^9 joules.

Table 5.5 *Overview of the results for households of different income groups in the UK*

	First quintile	Second quintile	Third quintile	Fourth quintile	Fifth quintile
Total indirect energy intensity (MJ/Euro)	7.8	7.9	7.9	8.2	8.2
Total energy intensity (MJ/Euro)	15.1	13.8	12.8	12.3	11.6
Share of direct energy use (%)	53	47	43	38	33
Total energy requirement per household (GJ/year)	142	218	297	401	579

Note: Five income classes; the first quintile refers to the lowest 20% income class, and the fifth quintile refers to the highest 20% income class. One megajoule (MJ) = 10^6 joules (J, SI) ≈ 239 kilocalories (kcal) ≈ 948 British thermal units (BTU). One gigajoule (GJ) = 10^9 joules.

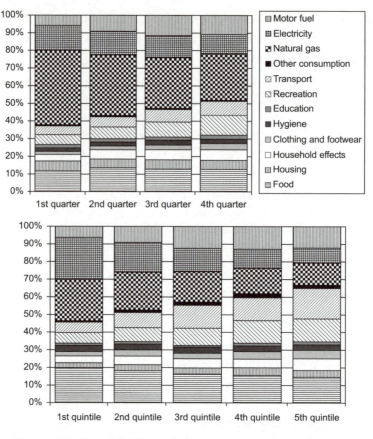

Figure 5.7 *Share of different budget categories in total annual energy requirements for households from different income groups in the Netherlands (top) and the UK (bottom)*

of direct energy use decreases with income from 62 to 48 per cent in the Netherlands and from 53 to 33 per cent in the UK. The decreasing share of direct energy explains the fact that the total energy intensity decreases with higher income. The average energy intensity of the indirect categories, on the other hand, increases with higher income. In both countries the increasing indirect energy intensity is mainly due to the heavily increasing categories of recreation and transport.

Table 5.6 shows the total energy requirements of households in the Netherlands for various household sizes. The energy requirements (just like the expenditure level) increase with growing household size. The average household size of a 3+ person household is 3.9 persons. Table 5.6 demonstrates that the total energy requirement per person for different household sizes decreases substantially with rising household size, especially for the 3+ person households. The share of direct energy use decreases slightly with rising house hold size. It turns out that the total energy intensity is the same for all households. The in direct energy intensity, however, is highest for the largest households, implying a more energy-intensive spending pattern.

Table 5.6 *Overview of results for households in the region of Groningen with various household sizes*

	One person	Two persons	Three or more persons
Total indirect energy intensity (MJ/Euro)	5.8	6.4	6.7
Total energy intensity (MJ/Euro)	13.2	13.2	13.1
Share of direct energy use (%)	59	55	53
Total energy requirement per household (GJ/year)	146	258	320
Total energy requirement per person (GJ/year)	146	129	82

Note: One megajoule (MJ) = 10 joules (J, SI) ≈ 239 kilocalories (kcal) ≈ 948 British thermal units (BTU). One gigajoule (GJ) = 10^9 joules.

Figure 5.8 shows the total energy requirements of households in the UK with different household characteristics, and in Table 5.7 some quantitative findings are given. Between these households three characteristics can be identified: income, household size and family phase. For the latter the distinction is relevant between pensioner households, households without children and households with children. For the income variable, the pattern as discussed above is valid, although the other characteristics may alter that pattern remarkably. For the household size variable, the total energy requirement per household shows an increasing trend, as is also seen in the Netherlands when the three different family phases are considered case by case. The comparisons of all types together bring in additional factors (such as age). Single households have a higher energy requirement than one-pensioner households, as is also the case for two-adult households compared to two-pensioner households. Furthermore, households with one adult and children have an energy requirement much lower than that for two-adult households and a bit lower than that for two-pensioner households.

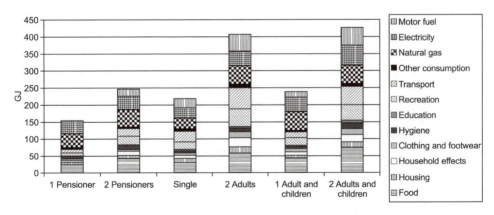

Note: One gigajoule (GJ) = 10^9 joules (J, SI) ≈ 2.39 × 10^5 kilocalories (kcal) ≈ 9.48 × 10^5 British thermal units (BTU)

Figure 5.8 *Total annual energy requirements and energy requirement per budget category for households with different characteristics in the UK*

Table 5.7 *Overview of results for different household types in the UK*

	One Pensioner	Two Pensioners	Single	Two adults	One adult and children	Two adults and children
Total energy intensity (MJ/Euro)	14.4	14.4	11.9	12.1	14.1	12.1
Total indirect energy intensity (MJ/Euro)	7.7	8.7	7.5	8.3	7.9	7.9
Share of direct energy use (%)	51	45	41	36	48	39
Total energy requirement per household (GJ)	150	246	217	406	237	426
Household size (persons)	1.0	2.0	1.0	2.0	2.8[a]	3.8[a]
Total energy requirement per person (GJ)	150	123	217	203	85	112

Note: One megajoule (MJ) = 10^6 joules (J, SI) $\approx$ 239 kilocalories (kcal) $\approx$ 948 British thermal units (BTU). One gigajoule (GJ) = 10^9 joules.
[a] Data on household sizes of these samples were not available. The household size is based on the fact that the average number of children in the UK is 1.8.

For each family phase, a few specific features are identified. Pensioner households have relatively low energy requirements for the categories of transport, recreation and motor fuels, but have a high energy requirement for gas and electricity, explained by the relatively large amount of time spent at home and by relatively low in comes. For single and two-adult households, energy requirements for food, gas and electricity are relatively low and energy requirements for recreation, transport and motor fuels are relatively high. Households with children have relatively high energy requirements for food. The two types of households with children have large differences. Households with two adults and children have relatively high energy requirements for recreation, transport and motor fuel, whereas households with one adult and children have high energy requirements for gas and electricity. For the latter, this again can be explained by the large amount of time spent at home and the low expenditures.

The energy requirement per person decreases with increasing household size for pensioner households. For single and two-adult households the energy requirement per person is approximately the same. For households with children the energy requirement per person is the lowest compared to the other households, and the figures for households with one adult and children are lower than those for two adults and children.

Discussion and Conclusions

The results for the four countries are strikingly similar. In all countries and for all household types, heating, electricity, food, transport and recreation are the most important categories with regard to energy requirements. Apparently in these wealthy (north-) western European countries, consumption patterns and the resulting energy requirements are similar, but important differences do exist. Discussing these differences, we try to identify determinants that may explain the environmental load due to household consumption.

The three main determinants of the differences in average household energy requirements between countries are the efficiency of electricity generation, the average levels of household expenditures and the average indirect energy intensities. We learn from this analysis that reducing energy use in the economic sectors and especially in the electricity production sector is an important strategy.

The main determinant of the differences in average household energy requirements within countries is the average expenditure level of the household. We also observe, however, that in urban areas direct energy use, especially for motor fuels, is lower than in the corresponding national average data. This suggests that on the city level some triggers exist to decrease direct energy requirements: a traffic and transportation system that includes cycling and public transport, and a compact city structure in which local recreational facilities are available.

The quantitative differences between households with different characteristics (income, size of household and so on) are mostly explained by the level of household expenditure. Other determinants are relevant as well. For a low-income household, the share of the household budget used for heating and electricity is high (together around 50 per cent of the total energy requirement) and the share for motor fuel, transport and recreation is low (together less than 20 per cent). For a high-income household, the share for heating and electricity is low (together 25–35 per cent) and the share for motor fuel, transport and recreation is high (together 30–40 per cent). Comparing households of differing size, we observe a remarkable difference with regard to the average energy requirement per person. A small household demonstrates a relatively high energy requirement per person. Similar results were found by Vringer and Blok (1995) and by Pachauri (2004).

The results presented in this chapter were generated by a specific method. This method enables us to study factors at the national level, at the local level and at the household level together in a consistent methodological framework. Here we discuss briefly the most important source of uncertainty influencing the significance of these results (see Kok et al, 2003 for a full discussion of uncertainties with regard to these results).

The Dutch EAP model was modified for application in other countries. For this purpose, databases describing other countries should be constructed and also country-specific analyses of products (i.e. budget items) should be performed. As much as possible, country-specific data were used for these modifications. We were not able, though, to fully replace the complete Dutch data set. Assessing this source of uncertainty, we conclude that the quantitative figures related to in direct energy use in the countries other than the Netherlands have a considerable margin of error. Because different assumptions have been made for each country, caution is required in comparing the absolute results describing the indirect energy use of these countries. Even so, the results do allow comparative conclusions within countries to be made to a fairly high level of certainty, and are therefore useful for our purposes. This is because the main uncertainties work in the same direction for all household types. So the conclusions about the determinants presented above are not affected by these sources of uncertainty.

The most important determinant explaining household energy requirements is the average level of household expenditure (or income). This was also found in other studies – in the Netherlands by Vringer and Blok (1995), in India by Pachauri (2004) and in Brazil by Cohen and colleagues (2005). But it would be socially and politically very difficult to reduce expenditures in order to achieve reductions in the environmental load. Other determinants are identified at the various system levels that are more susceptible to change and may serve better than those at the expenditure level as trigger points to affect decreases in the environmental load of production and consumption patterns. The relevant factors to affect change are as follows:

- At the (inter)national level, the structure of the economy and the structure and efficiency of the energy supply system determine the prices of goods and services and the energy intensity of consumer items.
- At the city level, the physical structure (such as the transport and energy infrastructure), the way in which buildings, houses and other facilities are situated, the quality of the public transport system and the (thermal) quality of dwellings all influence direct household energy requirements.
- At the level of individual households, the division of the budget among different consumption items and categories and the use of direct energy determine to a high extent the household energy requirements.

The identification of these determining factors is helpful for governmental, economic and institutional actors in designing approaches and policies aiming at a decrease in the environmental load of household consumption. The consistent set of data describing production and consumption developed by the EAP is also useful in the following ways for the practical implementation of more sustainable production and consumption patterns. The calculated energy requirements and energy intensities of different consumption categories and more than 300 consumption items can offer help in daily environmentally motivated decision-making about consumption. In several projects in the Netherlands such data were used fruitfully (for a discussion and evaluation of Dutch 'sustainable consumption' projects, see Moll and Groot-Marcus, 2002). In the ToolSust project these data were used in workshops with consumers, stakeholders and governmental authorities to design images of everyday life in the future city (Carlsson-Kanyama et al, 2003).

This chapter presents an analysis of average household energy requirements results. Such results are important for general communication with citizens, but are of limited use in addressing change in a specific household (Nonhebel and Moll, 2001).

Finally, we would like to stress that the average household does not exist, so options based on average results have a general value but will not optimally fit the change potential of each individual household. Reasoning further along this line, one should advocate personalized energy advice to households addressing their consumption pattern. In a recent project (Wiersma et al, 2003) this approach was used experimentally for households in Groningen in a computer-aided information and feedback experiment. Based on the answers given to a questionnaire – filled in online – the direct and indirect energy use of the household of the participants was evaluated, and targeted advice about energy savings was provided instantly to the participants. Some months later a behavioural change was determined and the effects on direct and indirect energy were calculated and communicated to the participants. The evaluation of this experiment showed promising results: an average reduction in both the direct and indirect household energy requirements of more than 5 per cent realized during the half-year. The EAP approach was used in this experiment to predict the effect of energy-saving options and to evaluate the results of behavioural change.

Notes

1   For an analysis of household energy requirements in Sweden, see Carlsson-Kanyama et al (2005).
2   The ToolSust project – with the full name 'The Involvement of Stakeholders to Develop and Implement Tools for Sustainable Households in the City of Tomorrow' – was developed within the fifth framework programme of the EU, as a part of Energy, Environment and Sustainable Development, Key action 4: City of Tomorrow and Cultural Heritage; 4.1.2: Improving the Quality of Urban Life. An important objective of this project is the development of tools to measure the impact of consumption and to develop approaches to direct consumption toward sustainability.
3   One megajoule (MJ) = 10^6 joules (J, SI) $\approx$ 239 kilocalories (kcal) $\approx$ 948 British thermal units (BTU).
4   One kilogram (kg, SI) $\approx$ 2.204 pounds (lbs).

References

Biesiot, W. and Moll, H. C. (1995) *Reduction of CO_2 Emissions by Lifestyle Changes: Final Report to the NRP Global Air Pollution and Global Change*, Research report no 80, IVEM, Groningen

Bin, S. and Dowlatabadi, H. (2005) 'Consumer lifestyle approach to US energy use and the related CO_2 emissions', *Energy Policy*, vol 33, no 2, pp197–208

Bullard, C. W. and Herendeen, R. A. (1975) 'The energy cost of goods and services', *Energy Policy*, vol 3, no 4, pp268–278

Bullard, C. W., Penner, P. S. and Pilati, D. A. (1978) 'Net energy analysis: Handbook for combining process and input–output analysis', *Resources and Energy*, vol 1, no 3, pp267–313

Carlsson-Kanyama, A., Dreborg, K.-H., Eenkhoorn, R., Engström, R., Falkena, H. J., Gatersleben, B., Hendriksson, G., Kok, R., Moll, H. C., Padovan, D., Rigoni, F., Stø, E., Throne-Holst, H., Tite, L. and Vittersø, G. (2003) *Images of Everyday Life in the Future Sustainable City: Experiences of Back-casting with Stakeholders in Five European Cities*, FMS report 182, Environmental Strategies Research Group, Stockholm

Carlsson-Kanyama, A., Engström, R. and Kok, R. (2005) 'Indirect and direct energy requirements of city households in Sweden: Options for reduction, lessons from modeling', *Journal of Industrial Ecology*, vol 9, no 1–2, pp221–235

Carlsson-Kanyama, A., Karlsson, R., Moll, H. C. and Kok, R. (2002) *Household Metabolism in the Five Cities: Swedish National Report – Stockholm*, FMS report 177, Environmental Strategies Research Group, Stockholm

Clark, C., Gatersleben, B., Moll, H. C. and Kok, R. (2003) *Household Metabolism in the Five Cities: UK National Report – Guildford*, Department of Psychology, University of Surrey, Guildford, UK

Cohen, C., Lenzen, M. and Schaeffer, R. (2005) 'Energy requirements of households in Brazil', *Energy Policy*, vol 33, no 4, pp555–562

Falkena, H. J., Moll, H. C., Noorman, K. J., Kok, R. and Benders, R. M. J. (2003) *Household Metabolism in Groningen: Dutch National Report – Groningen*, Research report no 109, IVEM, Groningen

Herendeen, R. and Tanaka, J. (1976) 'Energy costs of living', *Energy*, vol 1, no 2, pp165–178

Kim, J. H. (2002) 'Changes in consumption patterns and environmental degradation in Korea', *Structural Change and Economic Dynamics*, vol 13, no 1, pp1–48

Kok, R., Benders, R. M. J. and Moll, H. C. (2001) *Energie-Intensiteiten van de Nederlandse Consumptieve Bestedingen anno 1996* [*Energy Intensities of Dutch Consumption Items in 1996*], Research report no 105, IVEM, Groningen

Kok, R., Falkena, H. J., Benders, R. M. J., Moll, H. C. and Noorman, K. J. (2003) *Household Metabolism in European Cities and Countries: Comparing and Evaluating the Results of the Cities Fredrikstad (Norway), Groningen (The Netherlands), Guildford (UK) and Stockholm (Sweden)*, Research report no 110, IVEM, Groningen

Lenzen, M. (1998) 'Primary energy and greenhouse gases embodied in Australian final consumption: An input–output analysis', *Energy Policy*, vol 26, no 6, pp495–506

Moll, H. C. and Groot-Marcus, A. (2002) 'Households past, present and opportunities for change', in Kok, M., Vermeulen, W., Faaij, A. and de Jager, D. (eds) *Global Warming and Social Innovation: The Challenge of a Climate Neutral Society*, Earthscan, London

Munksgaard, J., Pedersen, K. A. and Wien, M. (2000) 'Impact of household consumption on CO_2 emissions', *Energy Economics*, vol 22, no 4, pp423–440

Nonhebel, S. and Moll, H. C. (2001) *Evaluation of Options for Reduction of Greenhouse Gas Emissions by Changes in Household Consumption Patterns: Final Report to the NRP of the Green-House Project*, Research report no 106, IVEM, Groningen

Noorman, K. J. and Schoot Uiterkamp, T. (1998) *Green Households? Domestic Consumers, Environment and Sustainability*, Earthscan, London

Pachauri, S. (2004) 'An analysis of cross-sectional variations in total household energy requirements in India using micro survey data', *Energy Policy*, vol 32, no 15, pp1723–1735

Reinders, A. H. M. E., Vringer, K. and Blok, K. (2003) 'The direct and indirect energy requirements of households in the European Union', *Energy Policy*, vol 31, no 2, pp139–153

Throne-Holst, H., Stø, E., Kok, R. and Moll, H. C. (2002) *Household Metabolism in the Five Cities: Norwegian National Report – Fredrikstad*, SIFO project report no 9-2002, National Institute for Consumer Research, Lysaker

Van Engelenburg, B. C. W., van Rossum, T. F. M., Blok, K., Biesiot, W. and Wilting, H. C. (1991) *Energiegebruik en Huishoudelijke Consumptie*, Department of Science, Technology and Society, Utrecht University, and Center for Energy and Environmental Studies, University of Groningen, Utrecht, the Netherlands

Vringer, K. and Blok, K. (1995) 'The direct and indirect energy requirements of households in the Netherlands', *Energy Policy*, vol 23, no 10, pp893–910

Wiersma, G., Noorman, K. J., Kok, R., Benders, R. M. J., Moll, H. C., Abrahamse, W., Steg, L. and van der Valk, M. (2003) *Netwerken met Energie* [*Changing Energy Consumption with an Internet Tool*], KNN, Groningen, the Netherlands

Wilting, H. C. (1996) *An Energy Perspective on Economic Activities*, PhD thesis, University of Groningen, Groningen, the Netherlands

Wilting, H. C, Benders, R. M. J., Biesiot, W., Louwers, M. and Moll, H. C. (1999) *EAP Energy Analysis Program Manual, Version 3.0*, Research report no 98, IVEM, University of Groningen

WSSD (World Summit on Sustainable Development) (2002) *Report of the World Summit on Sustainable Development, Johannesburg, South Africa, 26 August–4 September*, United Nations, New York, p13, available at http://daccessdds.un.org/doc/UNDOC/GEN/N02/636/93/PDF/N0263693.pdf?OpenElement (accessed 16 May 2006)

Accounting for Sustainable Consumption: A Review of Studies of the Environmental Impacts of Households

Edgar G. Hertwich

Introduction

The 2002 World Summit on Sustainable Development (WSSD) in Johannesburg recognized that it is necessary to 'chang[e] unsustainable patterns of consumption and production' and called for a comprehensive set of programmes focusing on sustainable consumption and production. The 'Plan of Implementation', the main document to emerge from the WSSD, called for 'fundamental changes in the way societies produce and consume' (UNGA, 2002, §13). The Summit also resolved to 'encourage and promote the development of a 10-year framework of programmes in support of regional and national initiatives to accelerate the shift towards sustainable consumption and production ...' (UNGA, 2002, §14).

A prerequisite for sustainable consumption policy is the ability to assess the patterns of consumption that exist at the moment or will emerge in the future, and to account for the environmental impacts of those consumption patterns. Developing a consistent and comprehensive set of tools to achieve this is a priority. Interestingly, the Plan of Implementation argued that this task should be approached through the use of life-cycle assessment (LCA). LCA has proven useful in the context of sustainable production. LCA, narrowly defined, has been little used in sustainable consumption. Questions that one needs to answer when addressing sustainable consumption – who causes how much of which impact and how can consumption patterns be changed to reduce these impacts – certainly require an analysis that extends beyond traditional LCA.

What is clear, however, is that a systematic way of accounting for consumption patterns (and their impacts) is needed. A quantification of the environmental impacts of household consumption can tell us the magnitude of these impacts. It can identify which activities contribute most to the total, and whether a shift in consumption patterns contributes to reducing or increasing these impacts. We can compare various households and populations and identify underlying factors which determine the magnitude of these impacts. We can decompose the development over time to find out how changes in consumption patterns affect the environmental impacts and whether technology is able to offset the increases in consumption and population. An evaluation of the effectiveness of consumer initiatives or policy measures may also require a quantification of impacts, before and after. The use of quantitative analyses of the environmental impacts of consumption presents interesting opportunities that have only recently begun to emerge and are not yet well understood by policy-makers.

This chapter introduces some of the methods used in the literature to assess household environmental impacts. It discusses in particular the emerging case studies that use environmental input–output analysis to analyse consumption patterns. It systematically explores different assessment purposes and study designs, and reviews assessments conducted in different countries. Based on a more extended journal publication (Hertwich, 2005a), the chapter describes how such analyses have been used for a variety of purposes in the area of sustainable consumption: to inform policy-making, to select areas of action, to identify which lifestyles are more sustainable, to advise consumers and to evaluate the effectiveness of sustainable consumption measures.

Current research tends to be mostly descriptive, whereas sustainable consumption policy also requires some strategic analysis, including scenario analysis and backcasting, as a way of addressing changes in both technologies and consumption patterns. This chapter reviews some attempts to provide these more sophisticated analyses and outlines some of the outstanding conceptual and methodological issues that still need to be addressed.

Assessing Household Environmental Impacts

Household environmental impact (HEI) assessment commonly distinguishes between emissions or resource use caused by households directly, for example through driving a car, and those 'indirect' emissions or resource use required to produce the goods and services consumed, for example the emissions of the car factory, and of the refinery supplying the fuel. Statistical offices regularly conduct consumer expenditure surveys, which provide information on what households consume. Energy consumption and travel surveys are sometimes used as additional sources of information. Direct 'impacts' are derived using statistical estimates, engineering calculations and measurement. The calculation of indirect impacts requires a modelling of the production process, including the quantification of all inputs required to produce a specific good and of the emissions and resource use associated with these inputs. Such a modelling is usually based either on economic input–output analysis, product life-cycle assessment or a hybrid between the two.

Life-cycle assessment (LCA) is commonly based on process engineering models of production processes or the collection of data on physical inputs, outputs and emissions from companies. Given the highly interlinked character of our economy, a wide range of products and production processes have been assessed and, for industrialized countries, data on these processes are available from commercial LCA databases. LCAs are often incomplete, as they are not able to trace all inputs to production (Lenzen, 2001a). There is much less knowledge on services and their associated environmental impacts. In LCAs of physical products, the input of services from engineering design to marketing are often not included, because they are considered unimportant.

Input–output analysis (IOA) is the basis for the national accounts and describes the flow of goods between different sectors of a (national) economy (Leontief, 1986). Input–output tables are collected by national statistical offices, often in five-year intervals. All economic activity is recorded. HEI assessment requires modelling of the upstream impacts of all the products consumed by a household and usually relies at least in part and often exclusively on data from input–output analysis to describe production processes (Bullard and Herendeen, 1975).

It is possible in principle to describe both the LCA and the IOA approach through a set of simultaneous linear equations, written in matrix form as:

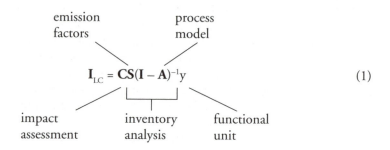

$$\mathbf{I}_{LC} = \mathbf{CS}(\mathbf{I} - \mathbf{A})^{-1}y \tag{1}$$

where $\mathbf{I}_{LC}$ is the life-cycle impact, expressed as a vector of impact indicators for different impact categories; y is the vector representing the functional unit; $(\mathbf{I} - \mathbf{A})^{-1}$ (sometimes called the Leontief inverse) represents the matrix of production, use and disposal processes that contributes to the product life cycle; $\mathbf{S}$ represents the table of emissions factors per unit process; and $\mathbf{C}$ the table of characterization factors per impact category.

Although all attributional models can be represented in this generalized notation, one should note that there are significant differences between IOA economics-based models and engineering-based LCA models. Input–output analysis presents the trade among industry sectors, while LCA presents the flow of specific, physical products among various production, use and disposal processes. LCA is therefore very technology-specific and can resolve differences, for example among different alloys of steel or different colours of paint. Input–output analysis, on the other hand, deals better with non-physical inputs like 'overhead', it can calculate value added and employment, and it has a more complete coverage of the economy. The two approaches can also be combined, and such a hybrid approach is often used in HEI assessments (Suh et al, 2004). Table 6.1 provides an overview of the different modelling approaches.

Most studies of household environmental impacts have used input–output tables, but some have used hybrid analysis or process analysis. Consumption data come from consumer expenditure surveys, which provide expenditure for different income groups, age classes, household sizes, urban/rural areas and so on. It is, hence, both easy and insightful to analyse how these distinctions affect the total impact of households. There is also a growing interest in the application of life-cycle approaches for scenario development, backcasting and the evaluation of sustainable consumption policies and measures. While such study designs in themselves are interesting and deserving of a more detailed elaboration because of their challenging combination of IOA, LCA and consumer research, I will focus on the requirements of such studies on HEI assessment.

Table 6.1 *Overview of related analysis/modelling methods*

Method	Summary of analysis used	Source
Process LCA	'Classical' life-cycle assessment; calculation of environmental impacts based on a physical description of the processes involved in a product life cycle	ISO, 1997; Baumann and Tillman, 2004
Input–output LCA, environmentally extended input–output analysis	Use of input–output tables and emissions per industry to calculate upstream environmental impacts.	Hendrickson et al, 1998
Hybrid input–output analysis, energy input–output analysis	Input–output analysis in which some commodity flows (usually electricity, fuels) are expressed in physical units (kWh, GJ, kg) instead of monetary units.	Casler and Wilbur, 1984
Hybrid life-cycle assessment	A combination of input–output LCA and process LCA. Commonly the input–output tables are not altered, but used for some processes in a process LCA. In principle, there is duplicate information, since the information in the process LCA is, on a higher level of aggregation, also included in the input–output analysis.	Suh et al, 2004
Social accounting matrix (SAM)	Extension of an input–output table which also includes the monetary flow through households and the government. Households earn income from labour and capital and spend it on consumption. SAMs are 'closed' in the sense that there is no net monetary flow outside the SAM.	Duchin, 1998
Structural decomposition analysis	An approach that can be used to analyse the change over time in the environmental impact as a function of changes in variables on the right-hand side of Equation 1, including changes in the structure (composition) of economic activity.	de Haan, 2001
Eco-efficiency vector (E2 vector)	Graphical analysis of impact per value (or cost), which can be used to compare alternatives and evaluate the rebound effect. The analysis of impact can be based on LCA, IOA or a combination.	Goedkoop and Spriensma, 1999; Hertwich, 2005b

In the next section, I highlight interesting findings from path-breaking studies, review the collective results from the bulk of the studies on HEIs. In the following section, I address some of the limitations of existing studies and highlight some future research needs.

Review of Studies

In most developed countries, household consumption is the most important final demand category, both in terms of expenditure and in terms of total energy use or CO_2 emissions. In developing countries, exports dominate if there is a lot of export-oriented heavy industry. Public consumption is usually less energy intensive. There are different practices for treating capital investment: either as a final demand or as an input to production. In some developing countries investment in infrastructure can be important. In Australia in 1994, 59 per cent of the CO_2 emissions were associated with private final consumption, 10 per cent with public final consumption, and 31 per cent with export. As much as 81 per cent of the CO_2 emissions occurred in Australia, while 19 per cent were embodied in the imports, if imports are assumed to have the same pollution intensity as domestic production (Lenzen, 1998). For Norway, exports account for a full 65 per cent of domestic CO_2 emissions, household consumption accounts for 19 per cent, government consumption for 4 per cent, and trade and transport margins for 9 per cent. Using realistic pollution intensities of Norway's seven most important trade partners, imports account for 56 per cent of the CO_2 emissions due to Norwegian final consumption. Of the CO_2 emissions embodied in imports, 36 per cent goes directly to domestic final consumption, 29 per cent is in intermediate input used for domestic final consumption, and 35 per cent goes to the production of products for export (Peters et al, 2004). Part of public expenditure is directly consumed by households, such as health care and education, and can be assigned to households. Mäenpää (2005) proposes a classification scheme with which he assigns 64 per cent of Finland's government expenditure (14 per cent of GDP) to household consumption. One-quarter of household consumption is hence financed by the government.

Household environmental impact analysis started with Herendeen and Bullard (Bullard and Herendeen, 1975; Herendeen, 1978; Herendeen and Tanaka, 1976), who presented the calculations of direct and indirect energy consumption. They used national input–output models with data on the energy consumption of different industry sectors and the direct consumption by households. The household expenditure for different items came from consumer expenditure surveys. The results show that shelter (heating/cooling plus construction), mobility and food are the most important consumption categories in both the US and Norway, a result that has been reproduced by many subsequent studies. This early investigation already included an analysis of the variation of energy consumption with household income. Direct energy consumption flattens out with rising income, while indirect energy consumption continues to rise. As a result, a large share of the total 'energy cost of living' for poor households is related to the combustions of fuels in the household, while for rich people two-thirds of these energy costs are related to the purchase of goods. The increase of household energy consumption with a doubling of income varies between 67 per cent for India in 1993–1994 (Pachauri, 2004) and 90 per cent for Denmark in 1995 (Wier et al, 2001; Hertwich and Ornetzeder, 2005).

Most analyses of household environmental impact focus on the energy consumption and/or CO_2 emissions caused by different household consumption activities. Figure 6.1 presents an overview of the average per capita energy use and CO_2 emissions from different studies. As the figure indicates, there are large differences both in absolute values and in the share of the various activities among countries. There are also significant changes across time. The highest values of both per capita annual energy use and CO_2 emission can be found in the US. The CO_2 numbers for Australia include non-combustion CO_2 emissions and other greenhouse gases, and land use plays an important role. This explains why the emissions are almost as high as for the US, but Australians' energy consumption is less than half as high. The carbon intensity of energy supply varies significantly among the nations and explains why the CO_2 emissions vary more than the energy consumption. The share of household direct energy use (mostly for heating, cooling and warm water) and the building itself ('other shelter') is generally between 40 and 50 per cent. The share of food varies between 7 per cent (the US in 1997) and 22 per cent (India in 1993–1994) and shows a clear, inverse relationship with the total energy use. The share of mobility varies between 8 per cent (India) and 36 per cent (the US). Mobility also varies significantly inside Europe, where the Nordic countries and the UK have significantly larger shares (20–30 per cent) than Germany and the Netherlands (12–18 per cent).

The results in Figure 6.1 were collected from various studies. The underlying studies and the presented results are not fully comparable. There are differences in the methods, in the nomenclature for the activities, in the activities included in the assessment, in how capital is treated, and in the indicators used to express environmental impacts. These differences can have a substantial influence on the result, as a comparison of the two estimates for Japan shows. The activity classification and part of the data presented in Figure 6.1 is based on Wier et al (2001). For other countries, I had to make some assumption in aggregating finer classifications or contact the authors of studies to request underlying numbers.

Table 6.2 presents an overview of the characteristics of different studies, including aim, methods and assumptions. The overview focuses on studies that use input–output analysis or hybrid LCA for the analysis of upstream emissions. I have found only two attempts of modelling HEI using process LCA. Rønning et al (1999) calculate the CO_2 emission of the average Norwegian; they are able to account for only half of the emissions. Frischknecht et al (2002) investigate the most important consumption categories in Switzerland, but not the entire household consumption. In the input–output models used by most analysts, products are commonly represented by the output of domestic industry sectors. There are usually 50–400 sectors in an input–output table. This resolution is sufficient for aggregate analysis of the type presented in Figure 6.1, but it does not capture differences in product qualities or consumer preferences. Vringer and Blok (1995, 2000) and Wilting (1996; Wilting and Biesiot, 1998) therefore developed a more detailed hybrid model in which process analysis, in physical units, is combined with input–output analysis, in monetary units, to better represent the direct and indirect household energy consumption. They found, for example, that in the Netherlands cut flowers account for an unexpectedly large portion of the indirect energy consumption, because of the high energy intensity of their production.

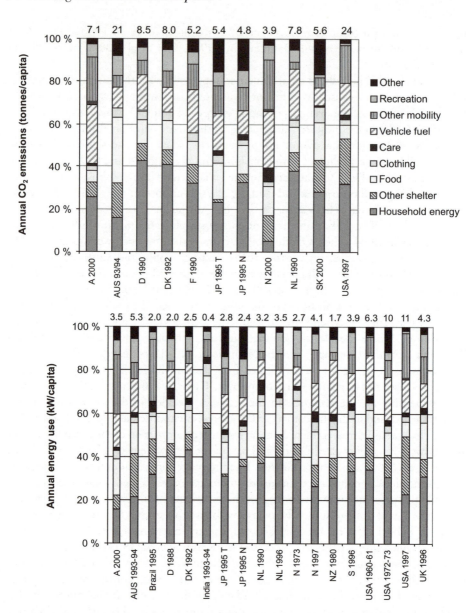

Sources: Austria: Hertwich and Ornetzeder (2005); Australia: Lenzen (1998); Brazil: Cohen et al (2005); Germany, France and the Netherlands 1990: Weber and Perrels (2000); India: Pachauri and Spreng (2002); Japan T: Takase et al (2005); Japan N: Nansai (personal communication); New Zealand: Peet et al (1985); Norway, the Netherlands, Sweden and the UK 1996/1997: Moll et al (2005); Norway 2000: Peters and Hertwich (2005); Slovakia: Korytarova and Hubacek (2005); US: Herendeen and Tanaka (1976), Herendeen et al (1981), Bin and Dowlatabadi (2005).

Figure 6.1 *Comparison of annual per capita CO_2 emissions and energy use according to household activity*

Table 6.2 *The characteristics of published household environmental impact assessments*

Country	Year	Source	Content	Methods
Australia	1993/1994	Lenzen (1998)	Energy and greenhouse gas (GHG) requirements by activity of households differentiated by geography, demography, and income.	IOA with 45 commodities in combination with consumer expenditure survey (CES) and physical data for direct energy use. Domestic intensities for import, steady-state assumption for capital.
Brazil	1995/1996	Cohen et al (2005)	Energy use by activity of households differentiated according to income. Expenditure elasticity of energy by activity and for different regions.	Energy IOA with 80 commodities and 43 sectors, in combination with CES.
Denmark	1966–1992	Munksgaard et al (2000)	Structural decomposition of indirect household CO_2 requirements to measure the effect of changes in consumption level and structure, energy technology and mix at the household and industry level, and economic structure.	Structural decomposition analysis of indirect HEI determined by IOA (117 sectors, 66 commodities) and detailed energy model with 30 energy carriers.
Denmark	1995	Wieretal (2001)	CO_2 and energy requirements by activity and energy type of households differentiated by income, urban/rural. Determination of income/expenditure and household size elasticities.	Multivariate regression analysis of HEI determined by IOA (130 sectors, 92 commodities) and detailed energy model with 30 energy carriers.
Germany, France, the Netherlands	1990	Weber and Perrels (2000)	Scenarios for CO_2, sulphur dioxide (SO_2), nitrogen oxides (NO_x) in 2000 and 2010 based on different demographic and technological developments.	Hybrid IOA with detailed consideration of household technology, energy and transport.
India	1993–1994	Pachauri (2004), Pachauri and Spreng (2002)	Energy use by activity of households differentiated according to income, household size, urban/rural. Significant determining factors of household energy use. Influence of changes in consumption level and structure, economic structure and population size.	Energy IOA with 99 sectors and 15 fuels including informal energy, combined with CES. Multivariate statistical analysis and structural decomposition analysis.

Table 6.2 *continued*

Country	Year	Source	Content	Methods
Japan	1960–1990	Morioka and Yoshida (1995,1997)	Development of household CO_2 as a function of demographic changes, household type, economic development for 1960, 1970, 1980 and 1990, with scenarios for 2010 and evaluation of conservation measures. Comparison with UK in 1990.	IOA with 112 sectors, in combination with information on household energy equipment, demographic and socio-economic variables from CES. Domestic intensities for import.
Japan	1995	Takase et al (2005)	CO_2 emissions and landfill consumption by households and scenarios for behaviour changes in transportation and diets.	IOA model with a detailed, physical treatment of waste sectors, with 80 goods and 36 types of waste.
Japan	1995	Based on Nansai et al (2003)	CO_2 and energy by industry sector and household fuel.	IOA with 300 sectors, final demand from IOA.
New Zealand	1974–1980	Peet et al (1985)	Development of household energy use over time, as a function of income and household size, and by household activity.	Energy IOA with data from 1971, 19 commodities, CES for every year, direct household energy use.
The Netherlands	1990	Vringer and Blok (1995)	Energy use by activity of households differentiated according to income, household size, urban/rural, age.	Hybrid energy analysis model based on a detailed technology description of critical activities. Multivariate analysis with expression of variation among households.
The Netherlands	2000	Nijdam et al (2005)	Environmental load of households expressed in Eco-Indicator (Goedkoop and Spriensma, 1999) by activity, type of impact and world region in which the load occurs.	Inter-regional IOA of the world economy with 30 sectors for Organisation for Economic Co-operation and Development (OECD) and non-OECD and 105 sectors for the Netherlands.

Country	Year	Source	Content	Methods
Norway	1973	Herendeen (1978)	Energy use by activity of households differentiated according to income.	Energy IOA with 55 sectors in combination with CES; US intensities for import. No consideration of capital. (Potentially of relevance for housing).
Norway	1997/ 2000	Peters et al (2004), Hertwich et al (2002)	CO_2, SO_2 and NO_x emissions by activity of households, with a focus on methodological issues regarding the treatment of import and exports.	IOA with 49 sectors, steady-state assumption for capital, trade data and emissions intensities for four important trading partners.
Norway, Sweden, the Netherlands, UK	1996/ 1997	Moll et al (2005)	Cross-national comparison of household energy use by activity, comparison aimed at specific cities, differentiation by income.	Hybrid energy analysis model based on a detailed technology description of critical activities, CES, national IOA table for Sweden.
Sidney	1998/ 1999	Lenzen et al (2004)	Geographical and socio-economic influencing factors of household energy use in different subdivisions.	Multivariate regression analysis of household energy use determined with IOA (135 sectors). Structural path analysis.
US	1963	Bullard and Herendeen (1975), Herendeen and Tanaka (1976)	Energy use by activity of households differentiated according to income, household size, urban/rural.	Energy IOA with 357 sectors in combination with CES; domestic intensities for trade, no consideration of capital.
US	1997	Bin and Dowlatabadi (2005)	Energy and CO_2 requirements by household activity.	IOA with 485 commodities, CES with 70 expenditure categories, combined with residential energy-use data (four energy commodities).

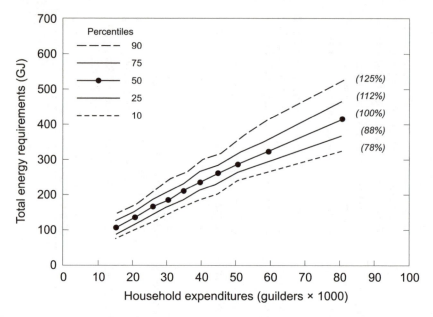

Source: Vringer and Blok (1995)

Figure 6.2 *Total household energy requirements v. household expenditures based on the Dutch consumer expenditure survey from 1990*

Vringer and Blok (1995) conducted a detailed statistical analysis of household energy consumption based on the Dutch consumer expenditure survey. They found that the level of consumer expenditure accounted for much of the variance in per capita energy consumption, as indicated in Figure 6.2.

Figure 6.2 indicates the variation of energy use at different household income levels through specific percentiles. The numbers in parenthesis include the level of energy use at this percentile as a multiple of the median. A doubling of expenditure leads to an 80 per cent increase in energy use. Other significant explanatory variables were the number of household members, car ownership, and the location in urban or rural areas. In general, singles consume more energy per capita than larger families, urban households consume less than rural or suburban households, and the ownership of a first and second car leads to increases in energy consumption, all assuming the same expenditure level. While these items were not found to be sufficient to explain all the variance, no other items were identified to be significant explanatory variables. The hybrid energy analysis model has been used in a number of other studies, including adaptation to other countries (Alfredsson, 2004; Biesiot and Noorman, 1999; Carlsson-Kanyama et al, 2005; Moll et al, 2005; Reinders et al, 2003). These studies indicate that an adjustment for price differences is crucial and that otherwise results strongly depend on expenditure levels and climatic variables, but that these factors are not sufficient to explain all the variance.

Model Limitations and Future Research Needs

There are a number of important limitations with the present analyses. First, there are very few studies considering impacts other than energy consumption and CO_2 emissions. Weber and Perrels (2000) include NO_x, which is also a combustion-related pollutant, in their calculations. Mäenpää (2005) includes aggregate material flows and the LCA impact categories acidifying emissions, eutrophication and photochemical oxidant creation.

Second, most studies use domestic emissions intensities for imported products. A notable exception to both limitations is the work by Nijdam and colleagues (Nijdam et al 2005; Goedkoop et al 2002), which for the Netherlands includes imports from OECD Europe, other OECD countries, and the rest of the world, modelled in a 30 by 30 input–output model for each of the three exporting regions. Their model also includes data on many types of pollutants and resource uses. It shows that imports are more important than what would be estimated based on domestic emissions intensities, a result that also holds for Norway (Peters and Hertwich, 2006). While there are limitations in the low resolution and the uncertainty in the data, especially for developing countries, this study (Nijdam et al, 2005) points out the direction in which this field needs to develop to provide a richer and more reliable picture of the environmental pressures caused by household consumption.

Third, the studies all assume the same energy intensity per unit expenditure in a specific product category. Hence they do not systematically address what might be called luxury consumption: the purchase of handmade chairs or designer watches, for example, which potentially have a lower intensity per unit expenditure than mass-produced chairs or watches. This may cause a systematic flaw, as Vringer and Blok (1995) already note.

Fourth, the capital used to produce goods is often not accounted for at all, because capital expenditures are treated as a final demand category in national accounts. Lenzen (2001b) takes the capital expenditure of that year as the capital required to produce the goods produced in the same year, in effect assuming a steady-state economy. While better than not accounting for capital, this approach is not entirely satisfying, because capital expenditure varies annually, and a given year may not contain investment in new aluminium factories or automobile plants.

Finally, many input–output studies do not include the emissions connected to aviation and ocean transport, because the consumption of so-called 'bunker fuels' is commonly not included in the national environmental accounts and these emissions are not accounted for under the Kyoto Protocol.

A better analysis of the impacts of consumption is clearly needed. This analysis needs to cover more pollutants and realistically reflect production conditions in a global economy. Research is needed to determine the degree of resolution (i.e. product specificity) that is required for different purposes. While it is in general clear that a combination of traditional process LCA and input–output analysis can provide results that are both specific and cover the complete product range, it remains an open methodological question of how to best integrate the two tools. Depending on the purpose of the analysis, different processes will require a detailed modelling through process analysis. These basic modelling questions need to be solved to improve the quality of the models.

Available process LCA data has not yet been fully utilized, although this situation is usually better in projects that focus on selected consumption categories. For food, for example, extensive process data have been used (Carlsson-Kanyama et al, 2003; Gerbens-Leenes and Nonhebel, 2002; Jungbluth, 2000). There are further significant challenges to develop inventory data for different impacts, to model global value chains, and to understand the uncertainty in the models. There is a need for more empirical research and a systematic evaluation of regional and inter-country variability, for example for food and leisure. The improvement of the modelling tools and the underlying data should occur in parallel with the development of new research approaches and applications.

Most research to date has focused on empirical investigations of the environmental impacts of existing consumption patterns. To formulate an effective sustainable consumption policy and to stimulate effective action, more strategic analysis is needed. This analysis should identify promising courses of action, evaluate specific activities and measures to see which ones should be implemented, and provide feedback about measures that have been taken. Scenarios play an important role in environmental policy, because they allow us to scope out possible future developments and evaluate alternative courses of action. This is powerfully illustrated by the emissions scenarios developed for the International Panel on Climate Change (IPCC, 2000). Duchin (1998; Duchin and Hubacek, 2003) has proposed to use a social accounting matrix (SAM) to construct scenarios about consumption. SAM is an extension of input–output tables that includes earnings and expenditures by different household types, including transfers between household types. It offers the advantage of including consumption in a consistent manner, but it has, to my knowledge, not yet been used in the manner proposed by Duchin. In their work on Germany, France and the Netherlands, Weber and Perrels (2000) develop the following scenarios: stagnation, business as usual, sustainable technology and sustainable consumption. Of these scenarios, stagnation is the worst, whereas sustainable consumption and sustainable technology offer the largest emissions reductions, with certain differences among countries. Hubacek and Sun (2001, 2005) develop input–output-based scenarios for land use and water consumption and show significant regional shortages of both land and water. Alfredsson (2002, 2004) investigates the environmental benefit of Swedish households adopting green lifestyles. Most of these scenarios, however, work from a micro-perspective: emissions and resource use coefficients are either not changed or are changed in accordance to trends. Wilting (1996; Wilting and Biesiot, 1998) develop a scenario for Dutch household energy use in 2015, while Rood et al (2003) evaluate the effect of increased consumer expenditure in 2030 assuming both constant and 1 per cent per annum increasing energy efficiencies. Hubacek and Sun (2001) go furthest in evaluating the effect of the scenarios for household consumption on the larger economy, including changes in resource use. Duchin (2005) presents a proposal for developing scenarios for US food production and consumption that describes how such an analysis could yield interesting insights and provides preliminary figures based on a literature survey. On the macro level, Duchin and Lange (1994) have investigated whether the Brundtland Commission's (WCED, 1987) goals for sustainable development can be reached through the means suggested, focusing specifically on CO_2, NO_x and SO_2. The answer was negative.

Historical rates of change can be used to inform scenario modelling about likely rates of change. Structural decomposition analysis is a method that can be used to study changes in a desired variable over time and attribute it to changes in underlying variables, such as changes in population, spending level, composition and technology. Munksgaard et al (2000) present a structural decomposition analysis for HEI for the period 1966–1992. Most of the growth in CO_2 emissions can be attributed to the overall growth in consumer expenditure, but increased energy efficiency in both the energy supply sector and other industry has offset some of this growth. Kim (2002) presents a decomposition of household CO_2 and SO_2 emissions for South Korea, and Pachauri and Spreng (2002) apply the technique to energy use in India. Another approach to inform scenario modelling is through the identification of distinct behaviour patterns of specific cohorts and subsequent modelling of underlying demographic and socioeconomic developments (Büttner and Grübler, 1995; Morioka and Yoshida, 1995; O'Neill and Chen, 2002).

The development and evaluation of different scenarios is interesting not only as it offers an opportunity to look at likely developments, but also because it allows a comparison of how alternative courses of action would play out in terms of emissions. Emissions targets can be defined, and the steps required to achieve these targets given expected developments in population, wealth, household size and other variables can be defined, for example through backcasting. Implications for different industry sectors and political constituencies can be evaluated.

A further area in which IOA models can be used to inform policy is in the analysis of the so-called 'rebound effect', which has been suggested as a reason for the failure of energy efficiency measures to deliver reduced energy demand. In the policy debate, the general notion of the rebound effect is that a technical or policy measure produces secondary effects which at least in part offset the initial, positive effect of the primary measure, so that the measure is less effective in achieving the primary policy goal. The rebound effect is often understood as the behavioural response to a technical improvement. The behavioural response, for economists, covers changes in purchasing behaviour as a result of changes in market prices. The discussion addresses both cost reductions as a result of improvements in technical energy efficiency (Khazzoom, 1987) and economy-wide effects (Brookes, 1978). Greening et al (2000) distinguish between the following effects: pure price effect, income effect, secondary effects on the cost of producing other products, effects on the fuel supply (and the market power of Organization of the Petroleum Exporting Countries, OPEC) and transformational effects.

Numerous empirical studies have focused on price and income effects (Hertwich, 2005a). Greening et al (2000) present a survey of studies in the US which indicates that the rebound effect is somewhere between 0 (for white goods) and 50 per cent (for space cooling), but typically less then 30 per cent (space heating, lighting, automotive transport). Schipper and Grubb (2000) review studies covering 80–90 per cent of energy use in OECD countries and find that the rebound is of the order of 5–15 per cent. They also review the issue of economy-wide effects and find no evidence for substantial macro effects.

Interestingly, the discussion of the rebound effect in energy economics focuses on reductions in the price of energy services as a result of energy efficiency measures, and the effect this has on demand. As Binswanger (2001) has pointed out, the cost of an energy service also includes capital costs and time spent on the part of the consumer. Discussions of a time rebound have recently appeared in the sustainable consumption literature (Hofstetter and Madjar, 2003; Jalas, 2002, 2005). This effect results when the time-saving due to technical progress leads to increased consumption. For example, transportation research has shown that faster transport implies that people expand their radius of action but keep total travel time approximately constant.

Discussion and Policy Implications

It is clear that HEI analysis – based either on IOA or on hybrid IOA–LCA techniques – is a useful tool for identifying the activities and purchases that cause the largest overall environmental impacts. It also provides a measure of the impact per unit of expenditure. This analysis can hence be used to identify promising measures for sustainable consumption policy and develop suggestions for consumer action. In the 'Consumer's guide to effective environmental choices', Brower and Leon (1999) present recommendations to consumers based on an analysis of what environmental impacts are associated with which products and household activities. They used impact intensities calculated using IOA. Similar recommendations are derived from ecological footprint calculations (Wackernagel and Rees, 1996). On-line or downloadable calculators for environmental impacts, such as CO_2 emissions, have also been tried as a tool to raise awareness and inform consumer choices, and ideas exist to further customize the assessments so that they can more effectively guide consumer action (Fukushima and Hirao, 2004).

Hannon and colleagues (Hannon, 1974; Hannon et al, 1978) first developed methods to evaluate the impact of changes in expenditure patterns on aggregate energy use during the energy crises of the 1970s. These analyses included an assessment of the effect on employment, including the shift in employment among different occupations. Several studies evaluate the effects of different household expenditure options on the overall HEI (Alfredsson, 2002; Biesiot and Noorman, 1999; Lenzen and Dey, 2002; Morioka and Yoshida, 1995; Takase et al, 2005). The straightforward modelling approach is prospective: what is likely to happen when consumers shift their consumption from xxx to yyy, assuming that the cost savings are used like the average expenditure (Alfredsson, 2002; Lenzen and Dey, 2002; Morioka and Yoshida, 1995; Takase et al, 2005). Biesiot and Noorman (1999) evaluate the effect of specific shifts in spending on the overall HEI, using observed differences in the consumer expenditure of households. Their calculations are based on observed consumer behaviour. Gatersleben et al (2002) show that pro-environmental attitudes do not necessarily correspond to a lower household energy consumption. Some evaluations of the acceptability of energy-saving measures also take into account life-cycle energy use (Gatersleben, 2001; Poortinga et al, 2003).

Another interesting option is the evaluation of sustainable consumption policy measures that are being or have been implemented. Longitudinal or intervention studies may be the best ways to evaluate the effect of a measure, because it follows the same set of people and observes changes in their behaviour. While other study designs usually assume fixed expenditure, such a study can get around this questionable assumption. I have not found any study where such a design is fully implemented. The closest is Fritsche and colleagues (Fritsche, 2002; Brohmann et al, 2002), who were guided through and followed up the conversion of two German military bases into housing developments by an LCA-type evaluation. This project is very interesting and should stimulate more research of this type. A more careful study design – taking into consideration how people behaved before they moved into their new flats and including a complete HEI assessment – would be desirable. A case control study of a car-free housing project in Vienna illustrates an approach to evaluating an example of sustainable consumption when there are no data on consumption prior to the measure being introduced (Hertwich and Ornetzeder, 2005).

Last but not least, HEI modelling should inform sustainable development policy not only through empirical assessments of the current situation and projections of probable future developments, but also through an evaluation of how sustainable development could be achieved through a combination of possible technological, social and economic changes, and what this implies for both consumers and industries. A systematic extension in this direction can go further than energy analysis has gone: changes or differences in consumer expenditure can be observed in panel studies of sustainable consumption measures; income elasticities and cohort effects can be measured and used in scenario analysis.

In summary, this chapter has described how HEI assessment methods can be used to conduct prospective and expost evaluation of sustainable consumption and production measures. The methods described in this paper have been used for some of the research questions outlined. Other research designs have not yet been tested. The indications are, however, that quantitative HEI modelling needs to be combined with economic and sociological investigations to be useful as a tool for sustainable consumption. While the development of a further method and data collection is advisable, efforts should focus on developing and testing new research designs that are directly relevant to policy-making.

Acknowledgement

This work was carried out as part of the FESCOLA project financed by the European Union's 6th framework programme through grant NMP2-ct-2003-505281. The ideas described here have been developed while the author was at the International Institute of Applied Systems Analysis in Austria and have been presented at the United Nations Environment Programme (UNEP)/Society of Non-Traditional Technology (SNTT) Sustainable Consumption workshop, 5–6 March 2004 at Leeds University, UK. Input data were provided by Keisuke Nansai, Koji Takase and Glen Peters. Helpful feedback by Mitch Small, Glen Peters, Katarina Korytarova, and four anonymous reviewers is acknowledged.

References

Alfredsson, E. (2002) 'Green consumption: Energy use and carbon dioxide emissions', *Social and Economic Geography*, University of Umeå, Umeå, Sweden, p200

Alfredsson, E. C. (2004) '"Green" consumption – No solution for climate change', *Energy*, vol 29, pp513–524

Baumann, H. and Tillman, A.-M. (2004) *The Hitch Hiker's Guide to LCA*, Studentlitteratur, Lund, Sweden

Biesiot, W. and Noorman, K. J. (1999) 'Energy requirements of household consumption: A case study of The Netherlands', *Ecological Economics*, vol 28, pp367–383

Bin, S. and Dowlatabadi, H. (2005) 'Consumer lifestyle approach to US energy use and the related CO_2 emissions', *Energy Policy*, vol 33, pp197–208

Binswanger, M. (2001) 'Technological progress and sustainable development: What about the rebound effect?' *Ecological Economics*, vol 36, pp119–132

Brohmann, R., Fritsche, U., Hartard, S., Schmied, M., Schmitt, C., Schoenfelder, C., Schuett, N., Roos, W., Stahl, H., Timpe, C. and Wiegmann, K. (2002) *Sustainable Districts on Urban Areas: Material Flow Analyses as an Instrument for Evaluation – End Report* (German), Oeko-Institut (Institute for Applied Ecology e.V.), Frieburg, Germany

Brookes, L. G. (1978) 'Energy policy, the energy price fallacy and the role of nuclear energy in the UK', *Energy Policy*, vol 6, pp94–106

Brower, M. and Leon, W. (1999) *The Consumer's Guide to Effective Environmental Choices*, Three Rivers Press, New York

Bullard III, C. W. and Herendeen, R. A. (1975) 'Energy impact of consumption decisions', *Proceedings of the IEEE*, vol 63, pp484–493

Büttner, T. and Grübler, A. (1995) 'The birth of a green generation – Generational dynamics of resource consumption patterns', *Technological Forecasting Social Change*, vol 50, pp113–134

Carlsson-Kanyama, A., Ekstrom, M. P. and Shanahan, H. (2003) 'Food and life cycle energy inputs: Consequences of diet and ways to increase efficiency', *Ecological Economics*, vol 44, pp293–307

Carlsson-Kanyama, A., Engström, R. and Kok, R. (2005) 'Indirect and direct energy requirements of city households in Sweden: Options for reduction, lessons from modeling', *Journal of Industrial Ecology*, vol 9, pp221–236

Casler, S. D. and Wilbur, S. (1984) 'Energy input–output analysis', *Resources and Energy*, vol 6, 187–201

Cohen, C., Lenzen, M. and Schaeffer, R. (2005) 'Energy requirements of households in Brazil', *Energy Policy.*, vol 33, pp555–562

de Haan, M. (2001) 'A structural decomposition analysis of pollution in the Netherlands', *Economic Systems Research*, vol 13, pp181–196

Duchin, F. (1998) *Structural Economics: Measuring Changes in Technology, Lifestyles, and the Environment*, Island Press, Washington, DC

Duchin, F. (2005) 'The sustainable consumption of food: A framework for analyzing scenarios about changes in diets', *Journal of Industrial Ecology*, vol 9, pp99–114

Duchin, F. and Hubacek, K. (2003) 'Linking social expenditures to household lifestyles: The social accounting matrix', *Futures*, vol 35, pp61–74

Duchin, F. and Lange, G.-M. (1994) *The Future of the Environment: Ecological Economics and Technological Change*, Oxford University Press, New York

Frischknecht, R., Jungbluth, N. and Nauser, M. (2002) *Embodied Greenhouse Gas Emissions in Switzerland: A Case Study for the Trade with Products from the Energy and Food Sector*, ESU Services, Ulster (CH)

Fritsche, U. R. (2002) 'Nachhaltige Stadtteile – die Rolle des Warenkorbs der Konsumenten', in G. Scherhorn and C. Weber (eds) *Nachhaltiger Konsum: Auf dem Weg zur gesellschaftlichen Verankerung*, Ökonom Verlag, Munich, pp335–342

Fukushima, Y. and Hirao, M. (2004) '"EcoLife" as a navigator for consumers', in *The Third International Workshop on Sustainable Consumption*, Society for Non-Traditional Technology, Tokyo, pp113–120

Gatersleben, B. (2001) 'Sustainable household consumption and quality of life: The acceptability of sustainable consumption patterns and consumer policy strategies', *International Journal for Environmental Policy*, vol 15, pp200–216

Gatersleben, B., Steg, L. and Vlek, C. (2002) 'Measurement and determinants of environmentally significant consumer behavior', *Environmental Behaviour*, vol 34, pp335–362

Gerbens-Leenes, P. W. and Nonhebel, S. (2002) 'Consumption patterns and their effects on land required for food', *Ecological Economics*, vol 42, pp185–199

Goedkoop, M. and Spriensma, R. (1999) *The Eco-indicator 99*, Pré Consultants, Amersfoort, the Netherlands

Goedkoop, M. J., van Halen, C. J. G., te Riele, H. R. M. and Rommens, P. J. M. (1999) *Product Service Systems: Ecological and Economic Basics*, Pré Consultants, Amersfoort, the Netherlands

Goedkoop, M. J., Madsen, J., Nijdam, D. S. and Wilting, H. C. (2002) 'Environmental load from private Dutch consumption', in E. Hertwich (ed) *Life-cycle Approaches to Sustainable Consumption – Workshop Proceedings*, International Institute for Applied Systems Analysis, Laxenburg, Austria, pp38–47

Greening, L., Green, D. and Difiglio, C. (2000) 'Energy efficiency and consumption – the rebound effect – a survey', *Energy Policy*, vol 28, pp389–401

Hannon, B. (1974) 'Options for energy conservation', *Technology Review*, vol 76, pp24–31

Hannon, B., Stein, R. G., Segal, B. Z. and Serber, D. (1978) 'Energy and labor in construction sector', *Science*, vol 202, pp837–847

Hendrickson, C., Horvath, A., Joshi, S., and Lave, L. (1998) 'Economic input–output models for environmental life-cycle assessment', *Environmental Science and Technology*, vol 32, pp184A–191A

Herendeen, R. A. (1978) 'Total energy cost of household consumption in Norway, 1973', *Energy*, vol 3, pp615–630

Herendeen, R. A. and Tanaka, J. (1976) 'Energy cost of living', *Energy*, vol 1, pp165–178

Herendeen, R. A., Ford, C. and Hannon, B. (1981) 'Energy cost of living, 1972–1973', *Energy*, vol 6, pp1433–1450

Hertwich, E. G. (2005a) 'Lifecycle approaches to sustainable consumption: A critical review', *Environmental Science and Technology*, vol 39, pp4673–4684

Hertwich, E. G. (2005b) 'Consumption and the rebound effect: An industrial ecology perspective', *Journal of Industrial Ecology*, vol 9, pp85–98

Hertwich, E. G. and Ornetzeder, M. (2005) 'The environmental benefit of car-free housing: A case in Vienna', in E. G. Hertwich, T. Briceno, P. Hofstetter and A. Inaba (eds) *Sustainable Consumption: The Contribution of Research*, Industrial Ecology Program, Norwegian University of Science and Technology, Oslo, vol 2005/1, pp161–170

Hertwich, E. G., Erlandsen, K., Sørensen, K., Aasness, J. and Hubacek, K. (2002) 'Pollution embodied in Norway's import and export and its relevance for the environmental profile of households', in E. Hertwich (ed) *Life-cycle Approaches to Sustainable Consumption – Workshop Proceedings*, International Institute for Applied Systems Analysis, Laxenburg, Austria, pp63–72

Hofstetter, P. and Madjar, M. (2003) *Linking Change in Happiness, Time-Use, Sustainable Consumption, and Environmental Impacts; An Attempt to Understand Time-Rebound Effects*, Consultrix, Zurich

Hubacek, K. and Sun, L. (2001) 'A scenario analysis of China's land use and land cover change: Incorporating biophysical information into input–output modeling', *Structural Change and Economic Dynamics*, vol 12, pp367–397

Hubacek, K. and Sun, L. (2005) 'Changes in China's economy and society and its effects on water use: A scenario analysis', *Journal of Industrial Ecology*, vol 9, pp187–200

IPCC (2000) *Mitigation of Climate Change: Special Report on Emissions Scenarios*, Cambridge University Press, Cambridge

ISO (1997) *ISO 14040: Environmental management: Life cycle Assessment – Principles and Framework*, International Standards Organization, Geneva, Switzerland

Jalas, M. (2002) 'A time use perspective on the materials intensity of consumption', *Ecological Economics*, vol 41, pp109–123

Jalas, M. (2005) 'The everyday life-context of increasing energy demands: Time use survey data in a decomposition analysis', *Journal of Industrial Ecology*, vol 9

Jungbluth, N. (2000) *Environmental Impact of Nutrition: Evaluation of Product Criteria Based on a Modularly Ecological Balance* (German), dissertation.de, Berlin

Khazzoom, J. D. (1987) 'Energy saving resulting from the adoption of more efficient appliances', *Energy Journal*, vol 8, pp85–89

Kim, J.-H. (2002) 'Changes in consumption patterns and environmental degradation in Korea', *Structural Change and Economic Dynamics*, vol 13, pp1–48

Korytarova, K. and Hubacek, K. (2005) 'CO_2 emissions from consumption in a transition economy: The case of Slovakia', in E. G. Hertwich, T. Briceno, P. Hofstetter and A. Inaba (eds) *Sustainable Consumption: The Contribution of Research*, Industrial Ecology Program, Norwegian University of Science and Technology, Oslo, vol 2005/1, pp79–87

Lenzen, M. (1998) 'Energy and greenhouse gas cost of living for Australia during 1993/94', *Energy*, vol 23, pp497–516

Lenzen, M. (2001a) 'Errors in conventional and input–output-based life-cycle inventories', *Journal of Industrial Ecology*, vol 4, pp127–148

Lenzen, M. (2001b) 'A generalised input–output multiplier calculus for Australia', *Economic Systems Research*, vol 13, pp65–92

Lenzen, M. and Dey, C. J. (2002) 'Economic, energy and greenhouse emissions impacts of some consumer choice, technology and government outlay options', *Energy Economics*, vol 24, pp377–403

Lenzen, M., Dey, C. and Foran, B. (2004) 'Energy requirements of Sydney households', *Ecological Economics*, vol 49, pp375–399

Leontief, W. W. (1986) *Input–Output Economics*, Oxford University Press, New York

Mäenpää, I. (2005) 'Analysis of environmental impacts of consumption in Finland', in E. G. Hertwich, T. Briceno, P. Hofstetter and A. Inaba (eds) *Sustainable Consumption: The Contribution of Research*, Industrial Ecology Program, Norwegian University of Science and Technology, Trondheim, Norway, pp1–21, www.indecol.ntnu.no

Moll, H. C., Noorman, K. J., Kok, R., Engström, R., Throne-Holst, H. and Clark, C. (2005) 'Bringing about more sustainable consumption patterns: Analyzing and evaluating the household metabolism in European countries and cities', *Journal of Industrial Ecology*, vol 9, pp259–276

Morioka, T. and Yoshida, N. (1995) 'Comparison of carbon dioxide emission patterns due to consumers' expenditure in UK and Japan', *Journal of Global Environmental Engineering*, vol 1, pp59–78

Morioka, T. and Yoshida, N. (1997) 'Carbon dioxide emission patterns due to consumers' expenditure in life stages and life styles', *Journal of Environmental Systems and Engineering*, Japan Society of Civil Engineers, vol 559, pp91–101

Munksgaard, J., Pedersen, K. A. and Wier, M. (2000) 'Impact of household consumption on CO_2 emissions', *Energy Economics*, vol 22, pp423–440

Nansai, K., Moriguchi, Y. and Tohno, S. (2003) 'Compilation and application of Japanese inventories for energy consumption and air pollutant emissions using input–output tables', *Environmental Science and Technology*, vol 37, pp2005–2015

Nijdam, D. S., Wilting, H. C., Goedkoop, M. J. and Madsen, J. (2005) 'Environmental load from Dutch private consumption: How much pollution is exported?' *Journal of Industrial Ecology*, vol 9, pp147–168

O'Neill, B. C. and Chen, B. (2002) 'Demographic determinants of household energy use in the United States', in W. Lutz, A. Prskawetz, and W. C. Sanderson (eds) *Population and Environment: Methods of Analysis, Supplement to Population and Development Review*, vol 28, pp53–88

Pachauri, S. (2004) 'An analysis of cross-sectional variations in total household energy requirements in India using micro survey data', *Energy Policy*, vol 32, pp1723–1735

Pachauri, S. and Spreng, D. (2002) 'Direct and indirect energy requirements of households in India', *Energy Policy*, vol 30, pp511–523

Peet, N. J., Carter, A. J. and Baines, J. T. (1985) 'Energy in the New Zealand household, 1974–1980', *Energy*, vol 10, pp1197–1208

Peters, G. and Hertwich, E. G. (2005) 'Pollution embodied in Norwegian consumption', in E. G. Hertwich, T. Briceno, P. Hofstetter and A. Inaba (eds) *Sustainable Consumption: The Contribution of Research*, Industrial Ecology Program, Norwegian University of Science and Technology, Oslo, vol 2005/1, pp22–38

Peters, G. P. and Hertwich, E. G. (2006) 'The importance of import for household environmental impacts', *Journal of Industrial Ecology*, vol 10, no 3, pp89–109

Peters, G., Briceno, T. and Hertwich, E. G. (2004) *Pollution Embodied in Norwegian Consumption*, Industrial Ecology Program, Norwegian University of Science and Technology, Oslo

Poortinga, W., Steg, L., Vlek, C. and Wiersma, G. (2003) 'Household preferences for energy-saving measures: A conjoint analysis', *Journal of Economic Psychology*, vol 24, pp49–64

Reinders, A., Vringer, K. and Blok, K. (2003) 'The direct and indirect energy requirement of households in the European Union' *Energy Policy*, vol 31, pp139–153

Rønning, A., Magnussen, K. and Modahl, I. S. (1999) *A Life over 365 Days: CO_2 Balance and Human Life-Cycle*, Østfold Research, Fredrikstad, Norway

Rood, G. A., Ros, J. P. M., Drissen, E. and Vringer, K. (2003) 'A structure of models for future projections of environmental pressure due to consumption', *Journal of Cleaner Production*, vol 11, pp491–498

Schipper, L. and Grubb, M. (2000) 'On the rebound? Feedback between energy intensities and energy uses in IEA countries', *Energy Policy*, vol 28, pp367–388

Suh, S., Lenzen, M., Treloar, G. J., Hondo, H., Horvath, A., Huppes, G., Jolliet, O., Klann, U., Krewitt, W., Moriguchi, Y., Munksgaard, J. and Norris, G. (2004) 'System boundary selection in life-cycle inventories using hybrid approaches', *Environmental Science and Technology*, vol 38, pp657–664

Takase, K., Kondo, Y. and Washizu, A. (2005) 'An analysis of sustainable consumption by the waste input–output model', *Journal of Industrial Ecology*, vol 9, pp201–220

UNGA (United Nations General Assembly) (2002) *World Summit on Sustainable Development: Plan of Implementation*, United Nations Division for Sustainable Development, New York

Vringer, K. and Blok, K. (1995) 'The direct and indirect energy requirements of households in the Netherlands', *Energy Policy*, vol 23, pp893–910

Vringer, K. and Blok, K. (2000) 'Long-term trends in direct and indirect household energy intensities: A factor in dematerialization?' *Energy Policy*, vol 28, pp713–727

Wackernagel, M. and Rees, W. (1996) *Our Ecological Footprint*, New Society Publishers, Philadelphia

WCED (1987) *Our Common Future. The Report of the World Commission on Environment and Development* (the 'Brundtland Commission'), Oxford University Press, Oxford

Weber, C. and Perrels, A. (2000) 'Modelling lifestyle effects on energy demand and related emissions', *Energy Policy*, vol 28, pp549–566

Wier, M., Lenzen, M., Munksgaard, J. and Smed, S. (2001) 'Effects of household consumption patterns on CO_2 requirements', *Economic Systems Research*, vol 13, pp259–274

Wilting, H. C. (1996) *An Energy Perspective on Economic Activities*, Groningen University, Groningen, the Netherlands

Wilting, H. C. and Biesiot, W. (1998) 'Household energy requirements' in K. J. Noorman and T. S. Uiterkamp (eds) *Green Households?*, Earthscan, London, pp64–81

7

Challenges for Sustainable Consumption Policy

Tim Jackson

Introduction

Consumer behaviour is key to the impact that society has on the environment.[1] The actions that people take and the choices we make – to consume certain products and services or to live in certain ways rather than others – all have direct and indirect impacts on the environment, on other people's lives and on our own personal and collective well-being. But to what extent is it possible, or even desirable, for governments to intervene in people's lifestyles and behaviours?

Among the most firmly held *desiderata* of modern liberal society is the notion of individual freedom of choice. It seems almost sacrilegious for government to assume influence over the complex mix of personal preference, social expectation and cultural norm which, taken together, constitute 'consumer choice'. Yet this is precisely what the new environmental and social agenda of 'sustainable consumption' appears to demand of us.

To take just one example, the target to reduce carbon emissions by 60 per cent before 2050 is central to the UK government's climate change policy. But there is an increasing recognition that changes in technology and increases in resource productivity will be insufficient to deliver such targets. Shifts in the scale and pattern of consumption are also likely to be essential. Achieving the latter relies on being able to influence not only the efficiency of industry, the performance of business and the design of products, but also the expectations, choices, behaviours and lifestyles of consumers.

Moreover, meeting such 'deep' reduction targets will require more than slight shifts in people's marginal preferences for energy-efficient light bulbs. Policy will need to influence behaviours and practices in a number of different arenas including: supply tariff choices, purchases of energy-using appliances, energy-consuming practices in the home (personal hygiene, laundry, food preparation, etc.), demands for mobility and access (for both work-related and recreational reasons), food consumption behaviours, engagement in recycling and re-use of products, material product choices, home-buying, patterns of use of domestic space, choice of leisure pursuits, demand for public services and so on.

In short, it appears that in order to accomplish its own declared environmental and social goals, government now finds itself forced to engage in a terrain which, if the rhetoric of the last two or three decades is to be believed, is not the terrain of govern-ment at all.

This brief review aims to elucidate the challenge with which policy-makers are now confronted. It examines first of all the existing basis for conventional policy-making on matters of private choice. It then critiques the underlying basis for this model. In the process, it attempts to show more clearly the nature of the apparent impasse with which pro-environmental and pro-social policy-making is faced. This challenge will require a committed effort by policy-makers if key environmental or social goals are not to be abandoned as unattainable.

In the final analysis, however, it emerges not so much that government can and should intervene more proactively to regulate cultures of consumption, but that they are already, in some sense, co-creators of the cultures of consumption they now seek to change. This chapter argues that this is a much more useful and empowering perspective from which to design policy than continued adherence to misleading notions of hands-off governance and consumer sovereignty.

'Correcting Market Failure': The Conventional Policy Response

Conventional responses to issues of consumer policy tend to be based on a particular model of the way that choices are made.[2] This 'rational choice' model contends that consumers make decisions by calculating the individual costs and benefits of different courses of action and then choosing the option that maximizes their expected net ben-efits. If it is cheaper for me to travel from A to B by train than by car, I will usually choose to go by train. If it is more costly and time-consuming for me to recycle my household waste than to throw it in the trash, I will tend to do the latter.

There is a familiar and appealing logic to this model. Faced with two clear choices, different in cost but equal in all other respects, it is in my own self-interest to choose the less expensive one. From this perspective, the role of policy appears to be straightfor-ward, namely to ensure that the market allows people to make efficient choices about their own actions.

For the most part, this has been seen as the need to correct for 'market failures' (Figure 7.1). These failures occur, for example, if consumers have insufficient informa-tion to make proper choices. Policy should therefore seek to improve access to informa-tion. In addition, private decisions do not always take account of 'externalized' social and environmental costs. Policy intervention is therefore needed to 'internalize' these external costs and make them more 'visible' to private choice.

These two policy options are clearly important. Market failures do exist and correct-ing for them is vital. In particular, it is plain that a failure to account for the value of public goods and services will lead to these being undervalued and overexploited. At the same time, sadly, the evidence does not support unconditional optimism in relation to either of these policy options – at least by themselves. In fact, the history of information and advertising campaigns to promote sustainable behavioural change is littered with failures. In one extreme case, a Californian utility spent more money on advertising the

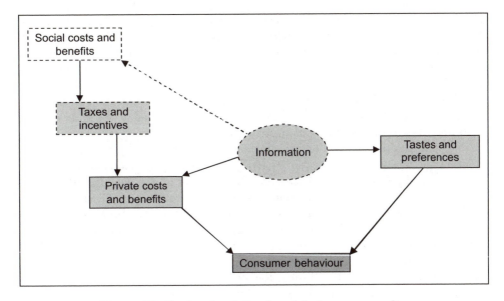

Figure 7.1 *The 'market failure' model of consumer policy*

benefits of home insulation than it would have cost to actually install insulation in the target population.[3]

The fiscal approach has also faced limited success in encouraging long-term pro-environmental behaviour changes. Although there is evidence to suggest that price differentials (for example) are sometimes successful in persuading people to shift between different fuels, there is much less convincing evidence of the success of economic strategies in improving energy efficiency overall or in shifting behaviours more generally. Examples of pro-environmental interventions which offer both private benefits to individual consumers are legion. Yet it is well known that people still tend not to take up these options. A variety of different obstacles and barriers are blamed for this.[4]

McKenzie-Mohr (2000) argues that the failure of such campaigns to foster sustainable behaviours is partly the result of a failure to understand the sheer difficulty associated with changing behaviours. As a review of the Residential Conservation Service – an early energy conservation initiative in the US – once concluded, most such efforts tend to overlook 'the rich mixture of cultural practices, social interactions, and human feelings that influence the behaviour of individuals, social groups and institutions' (Stern and Aronson, 1984).

Beyond 'Market Failure': Consumer Policy in the Real World

A part of the problem with the existing policy model rests with the underlying rational choice basis. Although it may not yet have filtered down to the level of policy or political rhetoric, the critique of rational choice theory is long established. Consumer actions are not always as straightforward as the rational choice model suggests. We do not always deliberate carefully over costs and benefits. We do not always act in our own self-interest. Individual choice is continually tempered by social constraints. Sometimes we just do not deliberate at all, acting through instinct, emotion, moral conviction or habit, rather than reason.

This is one of the most intractable of the paradoxes haunting modern lifestyles. Modern society celebrates choice and personal opportunity; and at the same time we often find ourselves locked into rather predictable patterns of living, working and consuming. The idea that modern society, and consumerism specifically, operates as a kind of 'iron cage' binding us into certain material dependencies and patterns of behaviour has a long pedigree in the social sciences.[5] Recent work in sociology has revived this traditional theme as a way of better understanding real consumer behaviours.

These sociologists have argued that too much emphasis has been placed on the conspicuous aspects of modern consumer lifestyles and that a great deal of consumption in fact takes place *inconspicuously* as a part of the everyday decision-making of millions of ordinary individuals. 'Ordinary' consumption, argue these authors, is not oriented particularly towards individual display. Rather it is about convenience, habit, practice, and individual responses to social norms and institutional contexts over which the individual has little control.[6]

To take one simple and relevant example, the fuel consumption associated with heating our home is determined (among other things) by the available fuel supply, the efficiency of the conversion devices, the effectiveness of thermal insulation in the dwelling and the level of thermal comfort programmed into our thermostats. These factors in their turn are constrained by the historical development of the fuel supply and appliance industries, the institutional design of the energy services market, the social norms associated with personal convenience and thermal comfort, and our own individual responses to those norms.

The evolution of social and institutional norms is itself complex, often involving incremental changes over long historical periods. Typically, at the point of everyday decision, the ordinary consumer will have little or no control over much of this decision architecture.[7]

This message tends to be borne out by empirical studies of consumer attitudes and behaviours. The National Consumer Council, for example, has published a number of studies looking at people's attitudes towards and access to sustainable lifestyle options. They concluded that, for the most part, consumers find their options curtailed by a variety of factors including time constraints, economic disincentives and the absence or inaccessibility of more sustainable choices (Holdsworth, 2003, 2005; Klein, 2003). This is particularly true of low-income households – for whom restrictions in choice are already onerous. Similar results have been found in other studies (Brook Lyndhurst, 2004; Darnton, 2004).

The matter of habit

At the heart of this concept of 'ordinary consumption' lies the issue of habit. The important role that habit plays in our lives has been acknowledged for some time.[8] It is also one of the most difficult issues for policy-makers. Rational choice models assume that behaviour is based on cognitive deliberation. But many of our everyday actions are carried out with very little conscious thought at all. Rather, we relegate routine decisions to the realm of semi-conscious automaticity. At best, we use a variety of mental short cuts – what the sociologist Anthony Giddens has called 'practical consciousness' – to simplify routine choice in our lives. How often, for example, do we ponder where to throw our waste paper, whether or not to drive to work, or even which brands to buy in the supermarket?

For the most part, we use a variety of mental 'short cuts' – habits, cues, heuristics – to reduce the effort required to make routine choices. It is often only when circumstances disrupt our routines – when someone moves the waste bin in the kitchen, say – that conscious deliberation enters the picture. Now I have to think twice about what I am doing and search consciously for the bin. I may find myself reaching instinctively for the old location, even several weeks later.

This example illustrates both the good and the bad aspects of habitual behaviour. On the one hand, habit makes it possible to function efficiently and frees up the conscious mind for more important tasks – like writing (or reading) articles on sustainable consumption. In an increasingly hectic world, this is a useful ability. But the process of habituation makes our everyday behaviours less visible to conscious deliberation, less amenable to policy intervention, and more difficult to change when they are no longer appropriate.

It is important for policy-makers engaging with behavioural change to find ways of addressing the problem of habitual behaviour. This looks challenging. But like many social and psychological processes, habit formation has its own rules and dynamics. For instance, a vital ingredient for changing habits is to 'unfreeze' existing behaviour – to raise the behaviour from the level of 'practical' to 'discursive' consciousness. This process is known to be most effective when it is carried out within a supportive community.

Morals and norms

Our everyday behaviour is guided by two kinds of social norms.[9] 'Descriptive norms' teach us how most people around us behave. They allow us to moderate our own behaviour without too much cognitive effort. I know what kind of clothes to wear and when to put out my recycling partly by observing continually what others around me do. 'Injunctive norms' alert us to what is sanctioned or punished in society. Driving outside the speed limit, polluting the water supply and (perhaps) failing to separate our recyclables from the rubbish are all examples of behaviours which carry varying degrees of moral sanction.

In both cases, there is lot at stake. Our ability to observe social norms influences the way we are perceived in our peer group and is important to our personal success. My ability to find a mate, keep my friends and stay in a good job are all mediated by my success in following social norms. Descriptive and injunctive norms can sometimes point in opposite directions. Most people agree that breaking the speed limit is wrong; but many people do it. The same is true for other unsustainable behaviours.

Pro-environmental behaviours are not always motivated by altruistic concerns. Some can be motivated entirely by self-serving interests. But a part of the case for pro-environmental behaviour is a moral one. The environmental impacts of my actions here today are as likely (or perhaps more likely) to fall on other people at some other time and place as they are to fall directly on me. Understanding moral action is therefore crucial.

Rational choice theories struggle to elucidate moral behaviours because of underlying assumptions about individuality and self-interest. But useful models do exist. Schwartz's (1977) 'Norm Activation' theory suggests that my intention to behave in pro-social ways is higher when (a) I am aware of the consequences of my actions and (b) I assume responsibility for them. If I am aware of the consequences of fuel consumption for the problem of climate change and prepared to accept that I have some responsibility for my own fuel-consuming behaviour, then I am more likely to develop a personal norm to reduce my fuel consumption.

These insights reinforce the idea that awareness plays an important role in pro-environmental behaviour. But they also indicate that awareness is not enough. Mechanisms for promoting responsibility (commitments, quotas, targets, for example) are also vital. At one level, pro-environmental behavioural change can be thought of as a transition in social norms. Better understanding of the evolution of social norms can only enhance environmental policy.

Sociality and self

We are fundamentally social creatures. We learn by example and model our behaviours on those we see around us. We learn most effectively from those who are attractive to us or influential for us, or from people who are simply 'like us'. Sometimes we learn by counter-example. And we learn not to trust people who tell us one thing and do another.

Some social theories go further and suggest that our behaviours, our attitudes and even our concepts of self are (at best) socially constructed and (at worst) helplessly mired in a complex 'social logic'.[10] Social identity theory, for example, regards key aspects of our behaviour as being motivated by the particular social groups that we belong to.[11] Certain behaviours are more or less ruled in or ruled out for me, simply because I perceive myself as belonging to a particular social group.

The roots of these 'normal behaviours' have very little to do with individual choice. Individual change is often not feasible and usually insufficient. Interventions based on the rational choice model simply miss the vital role of the social context within which individual action is embedded.

The dimensions of consumer action

A grand unified theory of human behaviour is probably impossible and may not be particularly useful. But a pragmatic synthesis is an essential starting point for policy design. Triandis's (1977) early theory of interpersonal behaviour (Figure 7.2) provides a good illustration of such a synthesis. A more complicated social-psychological model along the same lines has been developed by Bagozzi and his colleagues (Bagozzi et al, 2002).

In summary, this kind of integrated view suggests that my behaviour in any particular situation is a function partly of my attitudes and intentions, partly of my habitual responses, and partly of the situational constraints and conditions under which I oper-

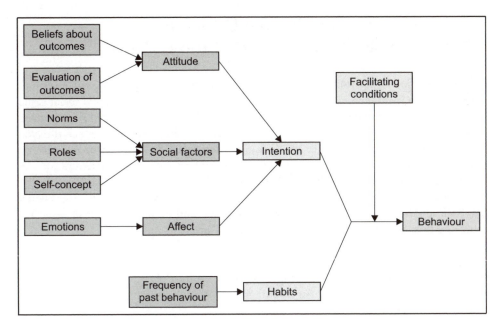

Source: Triandis (1977)

Figure 7.2 *Triandis's theory of interpersonal behaviour*

ate. My intentions in their turn are influenced by social, normative and affective factors as well as by rational deliberations. I am neither fully deliberative nor fully automatic in this view. I am neither fully autonomous nor entirely social. My behaviours are influenced by my moral beliefs, but the impact of these is moderated both by my emotional drives and my cognitive limitations.

At one level, the lessons from all this are salutary. Looking at consumer behaviour through a social and psychological lens reveals a complex and outwardly hostile landscape that appears to defy conventional policy intervention. Consumer behaviours and motivations are complex and deeply entrenched in conventions and institutions. Social norms and expectations appear to follow their own evolutionary logics, immune to individual control. Social learning is powerful but not particularly malleable. Public service persuasion is confounded both by strong commercial interests and by the sheer information density of modern society.

The rhetoric of consumer sovereignty is inaccurate and unhelpful here because it regards choice as entirely individualistic and because it fails to unravel the social and psychological influences on people's behaviour. But short of mandating particular behaviours and prohibiting others – an avenue that government has been reluctant to pursue – it is difficult at first sight to see what progress can be made in this intractable terrain.

At the same time the urgency of addressing the task remains undiminished. So how should policy-makers go forward from this point? What options are available to them for addressing these key issues? And what kind of framework should we use to think about policy interventions, beyond the limited perspective of rational choice?

Framing the Question:
Policy Options in Cultural Context

At its broadest level, the problem of motivating sustainable consumption – or of encouraging pro-environmental changes – is a particular manifestation of a perennial social issue. As Gardner and Stern (2002), Ophuls (1973, 1977), Daly and Cobb (1989) and others have pointed out, it is essentially the problem of ensuring that behaviours which threaten the well-being of the social group are discouraged and that those which promote long-term well-being are encouraged. In one sense, it is quite precisely the problem of societal governance, of coordinating individual behaviour for the common good.

Ophuls (1973) suggested that, from time immemorial, there have only ever been a few basic methods – written about by philosophers and employed by societies – for achieving this. Specifically, the four 'solution types' are:

- government laws, regulations and incentives;
- programmes of education to change people's attitudes;
- small group/community management; and
- moral, religious and/or ethical appeals.

Different societies and different writers at different times have tended to favour specific options or combinations of options. Hobbes, for example, championed the first approach, while Rousseau favoured the third. As we have already noted, conventional policy prescriptions in our society tend to favour the first two options. Or, to be more precise, we tend to favour a specific configuration of the first two solutions, one in which the balance of government intervention is focused on fiscal incentives designed to internalize social and environmental externalities and providing information to ensure that people make informed or 'rational' individual choices. Quite why our society should favour this set of options is slightly puzzling at first. Some insights into the ascendancy or otherwise of specific solution types can, however, be gained from an understanding of cultural theory (Figure 7.3).

Cultural theory suggests four distinct forms of social organization, with associated 'cultural types' and related assumptions about the appropriate form of governance. Modern societies can best be categorized within this framework as low-group, low-grid[12] societies, that is lying in the lower left-hand quadrant of Figure 7.3. The guiding principles for social organization in such societies favour the rights of the individual over the rights of the group and place a premium on social mobility. Governance is 'light' in this cultural worldview. Competition, open access to markets, and equality of opportunity are all prized. Regulation, hierarchy and social insulations are eschewed. This is the entrepreneurial, individualistic society. And its models of governance are precisely those that conform to a particular combination of the first two solution types.

Although cultural theory does not exactly explain how we came to be such a society, it does do two things. First, it highlights that this form of social organization is only one of a number of possible different forms. Second, it suggests that since the world is inhabited by a variety of cultural types, a single over-riding form of social organization is never likely to be entirely successful.

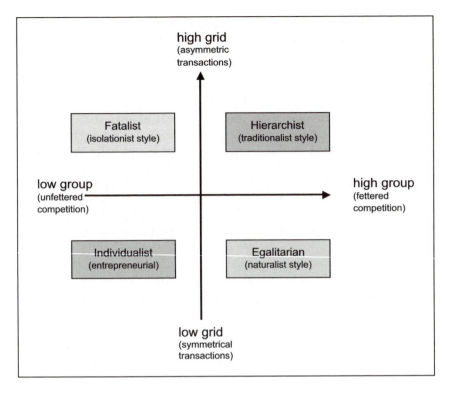

Figure 7.3 *Cultural theory's typology of social organization and cultural type*

From the perspective of this review, we might also offer here another hypothesis. Namely, that the forms of governance familiar to the individualistic/entrepreneurial society are never, by themselves, going to be sufficient to achieve sustainable development. The complexity of human behaviour and the enormity of the challenge of achieving pro-environmental behavioural change mean that we can no longer afford to restrict policy options to the particular combination of solution types conventionally attributed to low-group, low-grid societies. Thinking outside the familiar policy options is going to be vital.

The option that stands out perhaps most obviously as lying outside the conventional policy menu is the third: small group or community management. In organizational terms, according to Gardner and Stern (2002), what makes community management systems work is a combination of participatory decision-making, monitoring, social norms and community sanctions. Interestingly, sanctions are not the most important element in compliance. Rather, the effectiveness of group management comes from the internalization of the group's interest by individuals in the group.

This happens for several reasons. In the first place, people have participated in creating them. In the second place, they can see the value of these norms for themselves in preserving and protecting the interests of the local community and themselves as members of that community. In addition, these group norms become a part of the shared meaning of the community and contribute to the social well-being of the group, not just through the protection of resources, but through the development of trust, collaboration and social cohesion. Sanctions may be necessary to protect the group from those tempted to violate the collective good for individual interests, but the main reason people accept and act on social norms is that doing so cements social relations, signals membership of the group, and contributes to a sense of shared meaning in their lives.

It is clear of course that, as a form of social organization, local management of communal resources is less common today than it was 100, 50 or even 25 years ago. Powerful social and economic forces have intensified trade, eroded community boundaries, distanced cause from effect and undermined some of the basis for local governance. These trends have been supported by ideological transitions that prioritize social mobility, the globalization of commerce and culture, and uniformity of political form. From a cultural theory perspective, community management belongs in a completely different quadrant (specifically the lower right – and to some extent the upper right side of Figure 7.3) from the entrepreneurial, individualistic cultural form that characterizes modern society.

In the final analysis, no single solution type, on its own, is likely to be effective in delivering pro-environmental behaviour change. Effective policies for motivating sustainable consumption are going to need to explore the untapped potential for governance within each perspective. But given the critical importance of social processes in consumer behaviour alluded to earlier in this paper, the scope for exploring the 'forgotten strategy' – namely community management – from among Gardner and Stern's solution types deserves renewed consideration.

Policy as a 'Co-creator' of the Culture of Consumption

The conclusion to be drawn from this is not that fiscal incentives and information campaigns are irrelevant or inappropriate as policy options to facilitate lifestyle change. People are sometimes self-interested. They often do make 'rational' self-interested decisions. Their choices are swayed by cost. Adjusting prices to incorporate negative or positive externalities is therefore a legitimate avenue through which to promote pro-environmental or pro-social behaviour and to discourage antisocial or environmentally damaging behaviour. Providing accessible and appropriate information to facilitate pro-environmental choice is also a key avenue for policy.

But the evidence does suggest very strongly that these measures are insufficient on their own to facilitate pro-environmental behaviour change of the kind and scale required to meet existing environmental challenges. And, as such, this evidence base provides a critique of the model of governance in which the role of policy is confined mainly to providing information and internalizing externalities. In the language of cultural theory, the individualistic/entrepreneurial cultural form is insufficient to deliver sustainable consumption. It simply fails to reflect the complexity and social embeddedness of human behaviours.

Moreover, there is evidence that this model of governance is nothing more than an 'ideal form', supported by a set of rather unrealistic assumptions about human behaviour and the role of the state. In a sense, the 'hands-off' rhetoric of modern governance is nothing more than an ideological discourse. The reality is that policy intervenes continually in people's behaviour. It intervenes directly – through taxes, incentives and the regulatory framework. More importantly, it intervenes indirectly through its extensive influence over the social and institutional context within which individual behaviours are negotiated.

This view of the state – as a continual mediator and 'co-creator' of the social and institutional context – opens out a range of vital avenues for policy intervention in pursuit of behavioural change. The complex terrain of human behaviour, as viewed in a social, psychological and cultural context, is not a place devoid of possibilities for state influence. Rather it is one in which there are numerous possibilities at multiple levels for motivating pro-environmental behaviours and encouraging sustainable consumption. The following paragraphs outline some of these possibilities very briefly.

Facilitating conditions

Time and again, the evidence suggests that external situational factors (also referred to in the literature as facilitating conditions or contextual factors) are a key influence on the uptake of pro-environmental behaviours. Such conditions include the provision of recycling facilities, access to energy-efficient lights and appliances, the availability of public transport services and so on. The adequacy of such facilities and services, equality of access to them, and reliability and consistency in their standards of operation are all vital ingredients in encouraging pro-environmental choice. Inadequate or unequal access, unreliability, and inconsistencies between pro-environmental goods and services and people's lifestyles and expectations: all these factors are known to reduce the effectiveness and uptake of pro-environmental behaviours.

Institutional context

At a broader level, the set of rules, regulations and operating conditions – defining the context within which choice is negotiated – is another key intermediary between policy and public behaviour. For example, the market conditions – established by government – under which energy supplies are generated, distributed and supplied has a profound impact on the kinds of energy generation that are preferred and the extent to which energy efficiency is or is not cost-effective for consumers. These conditions could either foster or sabotage the viability of renewable energy, energy efficiency, energy service companies and so on.

Government also has a vital role in negotiating the institutional context in which business and consumers operate through the setting of legislation, regulations and standards. In particular, it is clear that:

- *Product standards* could make vital differences between durability and obsolescence, between efficiency and waste, between recyclability and landfill.
- *Building standards* could further improve or simply hinder the efficiency of the UK building stock.
- *Trading standards* might either foster or prevent excessive or addictive consumption and play a key role in the success or failure of sustainable consumption patterns.

- *Media standards* play a vital role in influencing the wider social and cultural context of consumer attitudes, motivations and desires.
- *Marketing standards* could either encourage or inhibit unscrupulous or inappropriate selling, advertising and marketing practices.[13]

Social and cultural context

Government plays a significant role in the social and cultural context within which consumers act. Nor is state influence simply confined to regulation, information and tax setting. These activities are obviously important, both as direct and as indirect influences on consumer behaviour. But there is more at stake here. A part of the indirect influence of state policy is symbolic. Evidence from social anthropology suggests that people respond quite explicitly to the symbolic meanings of things.[14] Responses to government interventions and public policy messages are no different in this respect.

Government policies and practices send important signals to consumers about institutional goals and national priorities. They indicate in sometimes subtle but very powerful ways the kinds of behaviours that are rewarded in society, the kinds of attitudes that are valued, the goals and aspirations that are regarded as appropriate, what success means and the worldview under which consumers are expected to act. Policy signals have a major influence on social norms, ethical codes and cultural expectations.

In particular, the consistency or inconsistency of government actions can have a profound effect on the success or viability of pro-environmental messages and interventions. A good deal of ethnographic evidence on consumer behaviour suggests that people mistrust and ignore pro-environmental exhortation if it appears inconsistent with policy messages coming from elsewhere in government, or is seen to be at odds with the behaviour of central government, local authorities, private companies and the behaviours of other key social actors.[15]

In short, it is not enough to expect that individuals can be exhorted to behave in certain ways. Consumers are social beings, enmeshed in a complex institutional and cultural logic. The architecture of this social logic plays a vital role in facilitating or inhibiting what is socially possible. Government policy must be aware of its own role in this context, and seek to act accordingly.

Business practices

Consumers are also employees. As employees, people are immersed daily in a certain set of behaviours, values and logics. In particular, they are exposed to a variety of environmentally significant practices. Does the company behave in an environmentally responsible manner? Do they recycle? Are their procurement practices sustainable? Do they operate a sustainable transport policy? The answers to these questions can have a significant influence on consumers – both as employees and as householders.

In the first place, there is evidence to suggest that behaving in certain ways in one context can have a knock-on effect in another context. If I am encouraged to recycle at work, it is more likely that I will attempt to recycle at home. This spillover is thought to occur in two distinct ways. On the one hand, I gain a familiarization with the actual practice of recycling. I learn, for example, that wastes can be separated, that quality grading of wastes is important and that appropriate siting receptacles can facilitate sorting. On the other hand, I am encouraged to think of myself in a particular way and this changed self-concept has an influence on my domestic behaviour.

Sadly, the evidence appears to suggest that sustainable consumption at work often lags behind sustainable consumption in the home.[16] This means not only that business practices are less sustainable than they ought to be, but also that a unique opportunity for influencing and supporting domestic behaviours is lost. There is even a danger that failure to encourage pro-environmental behaviours at work can significantly reduce the incentive for consumers to act responsibly at home. Through its influence on business, government policy can seek to redress this balance.

Community-based social change

This chapter has highlighted the social dimensions of consumer behaviour. Time and again, the evidence points to the influence of social norms, expectations and identification processes on human action. These social processes can present significant impediments to pro-environmental consumer behaviour. But they can also be powerful forces for pro-environmental and pro-social change.

The previous section drew attention to the community management of social resources and the role of internalized group norms in promoting the common good. The evidence is unequivocal that consumer behaviours are socially negotiated. Changing behaviour cannot be conceived as the processes of encouraging change at the individual level; pro-environmental behavioural change has to be a social process.

Government can play a key role in these processes: by recognizing the importance of social norms in behaviour change policies; by initiating, promoting and supporting community-led initiatives for social change; by supporting the community management of social resources; and by designing effective community-based social marketing strategies.

Leading by example

Finally, evidence suggests a clear role for government in leading by example. Clear environmental management initiatives and strong sustainable procurement programmes in both the public sector and within public–private partnerships can have a robust influence on sustainable consumption in a variety of ways.

There are at least four good reasons for government to practise what it preaches on sustainable consumption. First, public sector consumption constitutes a significant proportion of total consumption. Second, procurement practices can play a key role in stimulating markets for sustainable products and services. Third, the process of changing behaviour across Whitehall (and more widely across public services) would provide invaluable lessons to policy-makers about what is involved.

Finally, government policies and practices send important signals to people about public priorities, and social and cultural preferences. Unfavourable or inconsistent policy signals can undermine the best efforts of government to motivate sustainable consumption.

Concluding Remarks

In summary, it is clear that achieving sustainable changes in people's everyday behaviours and practices demands a sophisticated policy approach, responsive to the social complexity of modern lifestyles. Overcoming lock-in and facilitating alternative avenues of social conversation will be vital. A concerted strategy will be needed to make behaviour change easy for people. This must include:

- ensuring that incentive structures and institutional rules favour more sustainable behaviours;
- enabling access to pro-environmental (and pro-social) lifestyle choices;
- engaging people in initiatives to help themselves; and
- exemplifying the desired changes within government's own policies and practices.

Most importantly, the evidence suggests that policy plays a vital role in shaping the social context within which we live and act. Governments influence and co-create the culture of consumption in a variety of ways. In some cases this influence proceeds through specific interventions – such as the imposition of regulatory and fiscal structures. In other cases it proceeds through the absence of such interventions. Most often it is a complex combination of the ways in which government does intervene, and the ways in which it chooses not to intervene.

For example, the way in which the energy market was liberalized in the UK (and in other countries) offers consumers a remarkable choice of energy suppliers who compete vigorously for custom on the basis of the lowest unit price. The same liberalization process has actively impeded the development of energy service companies, and occasionally hindered robust and fair mechanisms for choosing green electricity or improving domestic energy efficiency.

Or to take an example from another field, government regulation of complementary health is reducing some of the alternatives available to consumers, while its failure to regulate so-called 'stealth marketing' techniques,[17] leaves consumers open to a variety of ethically dubious strategies for selling more conventional pharmaceuticals. In similar vein, the UK government have seen fit to ban cigarette advertising, and yet it leaves unregulated the advertising of products that threaten the success of its own carbon emission targets.

Selective policy intervention has an enormous influence on the institutional and social context of lifestyles. The long-standing failure of successive UK governments to reduce inequalities in the distribution of incomes has the effect of increasing competitive social pressures, and reducing affiliative, cooperative and social behaviours. Successive deregulation of retail and trade has eroded the cultural space previously afforded by religious and social practices.

This view of the state – as a continual mediator and 'co-creator' of the social and institutional context – opens out a range of vital avenues for policy intervention in pursuit of behavioural change. The complex terrain of human behaviour, as viewed in a social, psychological and cultural context, is not a place devoid of possibilities for state influence. Rather it is one in which there are numerous possibilities (Figure 7.4), at multiple levels, for motivating pro-environmental behaviours and encouraging more sustainable lifestyles.[18]

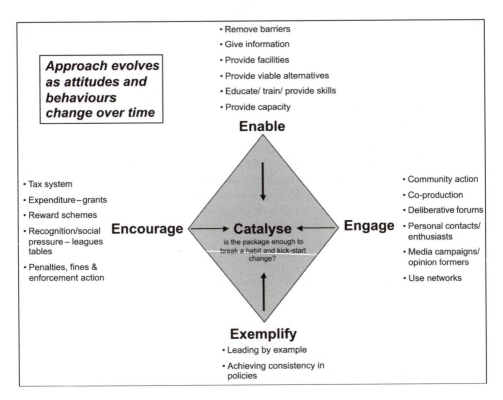

Source: Defra (2005, p26)

Figure 7.4 *A new model for behaviour change policy*

Changing the culture of consumption is difficult. The evidence is unequivocal in that respect. Overcoming problems of consumer lock-in, unfreezing old habits and forming new ones, understanding the complexity of the social logic in which individual behaviours are embedded: all of these are prerequisites for successful initiatives designed to deliver pro-environmental and pro-social behavioural change.

But in spite of all appearances, this complex terrain is not intractable to policy intervention. The evidence suggests that policy plays a vital role in shaping the social context within which we act. Governments are not just innocent bystanders in the negotiation of consumer choice. They influence and co-create the culture of consumption in a variety of ways.

As this chapter has attempted to demonstrate, a genuine understanding of the social and institutional context of consumer action opens out a much more creative vista for policy innovation than has hitherto been recognized. Expanding on these opportunities is the new challenge for sustainable consumption policy.

Notes

1 This chapter is adapted by the author for this reader from a paper originally entitled *Can we (should we) regulate cultures of consumption?*, chapter 8 in the CRI Regulatory Review 2004/2005 (CRI, 2005); it also draws heavily on Jackson (2005a).

2 For a more extensive review of the rational choice model, its implications and limitations, see Jackson (2005a).

3 Cited in McKenzie-Mohr (2000).

4 See, for example, Sorrell et al (2000).

5 Most obviously, of course, in Weber's concept of the 'iron cage' as a mixture of alienation, bureaucracy and constraints on personal creativity that inhabit the modern capitalist system (Weber, 1930). For more recent discussions of this theme see, for example, Ritzer (2001).

6 See, for example, Gronow and Warde (2001).

7 For a fuller discussion of these issues see, for example, Shove (2003); Guy and Shove (2000).

8 See, for example, Tversky and Kahneman (1974); Kahneman (1973); Camic (1986).

9 See, for example, Cialdini et al (1990).

10 For a more detailed discussion of this point see Chapter 25 in this reader. See also: Baudrillard (1970); Mead (1934).

11 See, for example, Tajfel (1982).

12 The 'grid' categorization was coined by anthropologists to distinguish societies according to the degree of 'insulation' between different social classes. Low-grid societies are characterized by fewer formal class relations and high degrees of social mobility.

13 The importance of marketing and media standards becomes increasingly clear when one considers the vast asymmetry of resources between commercial advertising and public service interests. For a more detailed discussion of this issue see also: Jackson (2004, 2005a).

14 For a fuller discussion of this see Jackson (2005b).

15 See, for example, Klein (2003); RRF (2004).

16 See, for example, KPMG (2004)

17 These are new kinds of communication strategies that attempt to 'fly beneath the consumer's radar' and influence their buying behaviours without the consumer being aware that they are subject to persuasion. See, for example, Kaikati and Kaikati (2004).

18 For more detailed analyses of the possibilities see: Jackson (2005a); also Halpern et al (2003); Defra (2005, Chapter 2). In the wake of the new Sustainable Development Strategy, behavioural change is now the subject of an ongoing cross-departmental working group in the UK government.

References

Bagozzi, R., Gürnao-Canli, Z. and Priester, J. (2002) *The Social Psychology of Consumer Behaviour*, Open University Press, Milton Keynes

Baudrillard, J. (1970) *The Consumer Society: Myths and Structures* (reprinted 1998), Sage Publications, London

Brook Lyndhurst (2004) *Bad Habits and Hard Choices: In Search of Sustainable Lifestyles*, Brook Lyndhurst Ltd, London

Camic, C. (1986) 'The matter of habit', *American Journal of Sociology*, vol 91, no 5, pp1039–1087

Cialdini, R., Reno, R. and Kallgren, C. (1990) 'A focus theory of normative conduct: Recycling the concept of norms to littering in public places', *Journal of Personality and Social Psychology*, vol 58, pp749–758

CRI (2005) *CRI Regulatory Review 2004/2005*, Centre for the Study of Regulated Industries, Bath

Daly, H. and Cobb, J. (1989) *For the Common Good*, Island Press, Washington, DC

Darnton, A. (2004) *The Impact of Sustainable Development on Public Behaviour*, Report 1 of Desk Research commissioned by COI on behalf of Defra, available at www.sustainable-development.gov.uk/documents/publications/desk-research1.pdf

Defra (Department for Environment, Food and Rural Affairs) (2005) *Securing the Future – Developing UK Sustainable Development Strategy*, The Stationery Office, London

Gardner, G. and Stern, P. (2002) *Environmental Problems and Human Behaviour* (2nd edn), Pearson, Boston, MA

Gronow, J. and Warde, A. (2001) *Ordinary Consumption*, Routledge, London

Guy, S. and Shove, E. (2000) *A Sociology of Energy, Buildings and the Environment: Constructing Knowledge, Designing Practice*, Routledge, London

Halpern, D., Bates, C. and Beales, G. (2003) *Personal Responsibility and Behaviour Change*, Strategic Audit Paper, Cabinet Office Strategy Unit, London

Holdsworth, M. (2003) *Green Choice: What Choice? Summary of NCC Research into Consumer Attitudes to Sustainable Consumption*, National Consumer Council, London

Holdsworth, M. (2005) *16 Pain-free Ways to Help Save the Planet*, National Consumer Council, London

Jackson, T. (2004) 'Consuming paradise? Unsustainable consumption in social-psychological and cultural context', in K. Hubacek, A. Inaba and S. Stagl (eds) *Driving Forces of and Barriers to Sustainable Consumption*, Proceedings of an International Conference, University of Leeds, 5–6 March 2004 (reprinted in a revised form as Chapter 25 in this volume)

Jackson, T. (2005a) *Motivating Sustainable Consumption – A Review of Evidence on Consumer Behaviour and Behavioural Change*, SDRN/Policy Studies Institute, London

Jackson, T. (2005b) 'Live better by consuming less? Is there a "double dividend" in sustainable consumption?' *Journal of Industrial Ecology*, vol 9, nos 1–2, pp19–36

Kahneman, D. (1973) *Attention and Effort*, Prentice-Hall, Englewood Cliffs, NJ

Kaikati, A. and Kaikati, J. (2004) 'Stealth marketing: How to reach consumers surreptitiously', *California Management Review*, vol 46, no 4, pp6–22

Klein, G. (2003) *Life Lines: The NCC's Agenda for Affordable Energy, Water and Telephone Services*, National Consumer Council, London

KPMG (2004) 'Recycling at home more popular than at work', results of a YouGov survey for KPMG, Business Europe article available at www.businesseurope.com/newsfeed/document?id=BEP1_News_0000065961

McKenzie-Mohr, D. (2000) 'Promoting sustainable behavior: An introduction to community-based social marketing', *Journal of Social Issues*, vol 56, no 3, pp543–554

Mead, G. (1934) *Mind, Self, and Society*, University of Chicago Press, Chicago

Ophuls, W. (1973) 'Leviathan or oblivion?', in H. Daly (ed) *Towards a Steady State Economy*, W. H. Freeman and Co, San Francisco

Ophuls, W. (1977) *Ecology and the Politics of Scarcity: Prologue to a Political Theory of the Steady State*, W. H. Freeman and Co, San Francisco

Ritzer, G. (2001) *Explorations in the Sociology of Consumption*, Sage, London

RRF (2004) *Household Waste Behaviour in London, Phase 2: High, Medium and Low Recyclers: Attitudes, Behaviours and Needs*, Resource Recovery Forum, Skipton, UK

Schwartz, S. (1977) 'Normative influences on altruism', *Advances in Experimental Social Psychology*, vol 10, pp222–279

Shove, E. (2003) *Comfort, Cleanliness and Convenience – The Social Organisation of Normality*, Routledge, London

Sorrell, S., Schleich, J., Scott, S., O'Malley, E., Trace, F., Boede, U., Ostertag, K. and Radgen, P. (2000) *Barriers to Energy Efficiency in Public and Private Organisations*, Final report, project JOS3CT970022, European Commission, Brussels

Stern, P. and Aronson, E. (1984) *Energy Use: The Human Dimension*, Freeman, New York

Tajfel, H. (ed) (1982) *Social Identity and Intergroup Relations*, Cambridge University Press, Cambridge

Triandis, H. (1977) *Interpersonal Behaviour*, Brooks/Cole, Monterey, CA

Tversky, A. and Kahneman, D. (1974) 'Judgement under uncertainty: Heuristics and biases', *Science*, vol 185, pp1124–1131

Weber, M. (1930) *The Protestant Ethic and the Spirit of Capitalism* (reprinted 1992, 2004), Routledge, London

Part 2

Resisting Consumerism

8

The Dubious Rewards of Consumption

Alan Durning

'The avarice of mankind is insatiable', wrote Aristotle 23 centuries ago, describing the way that as each desire is satisfied, a new one seems to appear in its place. That observation forms the first precept of economic theory, and is confirmed by much of human experience. A century before Christ, the Roman philosopher Lucretius wrote:

> We have lost our taste for acorns. So [too] we have abandoned those couches littered with herbage and heaped with leaves. So the wearing of wild beasts' skins has gone out of fashion ... Skins yesterday, purple and gold today – such are the baubles that embitter human life with resentment.[1]

Nearly 2000 years later, Leo Tolstoy echoed Lucretius:

> Seek among men, from beggar to millionaire, one who is contented with his lot, and you will not find one such in a thousand ... Today we must buy an overcoat and galoshes, tomorrow, a watch and a chain; the next day we must install ourselves in an apartment with a sofa and a bronze lamp; then we must have car pets and velvet gowns; then a house, horses and carriages, paintings and decorations.[2]

Contemporary chroniclers of wealth concur. For decades Lewis Lapham, born into an oil fortune, has been asking people how much money they would need to be happy. 'No matter what their income,' he reports, 'a depressing number of Americans believe that if only they had twice as much, they would inherit the estate of happiness promised them in the Declaration of Independence. The man who receives $15,000 a year is sure that he could relieve his sorrow if he had only $30,000 a year; the man with $1 million a year knows that all would be well if he had $2 million a year... Nobody,' he concludes, 'ever has enough' (Lapham, 1988).

If human desires are in fact infinitely expandable, consumption is ultimately incapable of providing fulfilment – a logical consequence ignored by economic theory. Indeed, social scientists have found striking evidence that high-consumption societies, just as high-living individuals, consume ever more without achieving satisfaction. The allure of the consumer society is powerful, even irresistible, but it is shallow nonetheless.

Measured in constant dollars, the world's people have consumed as many goods and services since 1950 as all previous generations put together. Since 1940, Americans alone have used up as large a share of the earth's mineral resources as did everyone before them combined. Yet this historical epoch of titanic consumption appears to have failed to make the consumer class any happier. Regular surveys by the National Opinion

Research Center of the University of Chicago reveal, for example, that no more Americans report they are 'very happy' now than in 1957. The 'very happy' share of the population has fluctuated around one-third since the mid-1950s, despite near-doublings in both gross national product and personal consumption expenditures per capita.[3]

A landmark study in 1974 revealed that Nigerians, Filipinos, Panamanians, Yugoslavians, Japanese, Israelis, and West Germans all ranked themselves near the middle on a happiness scale. Confounding any attempt to correlate material prosperity with happiness, low-income Cubans and affluent Americans both reported themselves considerably happier than the norm, and citizens of India and the Dominican Republic, less so. As psychologist Michael Argyle writes, 'There is very little difference in the levels of reported happiness found in rich and very poor countries.'[4]

Any relationship that does exist between income and happiness is relative rather than absolute. The happiness that people derive from consumption is based on whether they consume more than their neighbours and more than they did in the past. Thus, psychological data from diverse societies such as the US, the UK, Israel, Brazil, and India show that the top income strata tend to be slightly happier than the middle strata, and the bottom group tends to be least happy. The upper classes in any society are more satisfied with their lives than the lower classes are, but they are no more satisfied than the upper classes of much poorer countries – nor than the upper classes were in the less affluent past. Consumption is thus a treadmill, with everyone judging their status by who is ahead and who is behind (Argyle, 1987).

That treadmill yields some absurd results. During the casino years of the mid-1980s, for example, many New York investment bankers who earned 'only' US$600,000 a year felt poor, suffering anxiety and self-doubt. On less than US$600,000, they simply were unable to keep up with the Joneses. One despondent dealmaker lamented, 'I'm nothing. You understand that, nothing. I earn US$250,000 a year, but it's nothing, and I'm nobody.'[5]

From afar, such sentiments appear to reflect unadulterated greed. But on closer inspection they look more like evidence of humans' social nature. We are beings who need to belong. In the consumer society, that need to be valued and respected by others is acted out through consumption. As one Wall Street banker put it to the *New York Times,* 'Net worth equals self-worth.' Buying things becomes both a proof of self-esteem ('I'm worth it', chants one shampoo advertisement) and a means to social acceptance – a token of what turn-of-the-century economist Thorstein Veblen termed 'pecuniary decency'. Much consumption is motivated by this desire for approval: wearing the right clothes, driving the right car, and living in the right quarters are all simply ways of saying, 'I'm OK. I'm in the group.'[6]

In much the same way that the satisfaction of consumption derives from matching or outdoing others, it also comes from outdoing last year. Thus individual happiness is more a function of rising consumption than of high consumption as such. The reason, argues Stanford University economist Tibor Scitovsky, is that consumption is addictive: each luxury quickly becomes a necessity, and a new luxury must be found. This is as true for the young Chinese factory worker exchanging a radio for a black-and-white television as it is for the German junior executive trading in a BMW for a Mercedes (Argyle, 1987; Scitovsky, 1976).

Luxuries become necessities between generations as well. People measure their current material comforts against the benchmark set in their own childhood. So each generation needs more than the previous did to be satisfied. Over a few generations, this process can redefine prosperity as poverty. The ghettos of the US and Europe have things such as televisions that would have awed the richest neighbourhoods of centuries past, but that does not diminish the scorn the consumer class heaps on slum dwellers, nor the bitterness felt by the modernized poor.[7]

With consumption standards perpetually rising, society is literally insatiable. The definition of a 'decent' standard of living – the necessities of life for a member in good standing in the consumer society – endlessly shifts upward. The child whose parents have not purchased the latest video game feels ashamed to invite friends home. Teenagers without an automobile do not feel equal to their peers. In the clipped formulation of economists, 'Needs are socially defined, and escalate with the rate of economic progress.'[8]

The relationships between consumption and satisfaction are thus subtle, involving comparisons over time and with social norms. Yet studies on happiness indicate a far less subtle fact as well. The main determinants of happiness in life are not related to consumption at all – prominent among them are satisfaction with family life, especially marriage, followed by satisfaction with work, leisure to develop talents, and friendships (Argyle, 1987).

These factors are all an order of magnitude more significant than income in determining happiness, with the ironic result that, for example, suddenly striking it rich can make people miserable. Million-dollar lottery winners commonly become isolated from their social networks, lose the structure and meaning that work formerly gave their lives, and find themselves estranged from even close friends and family. Similarly, analysts such as Scitovsky believe that reported happiness is higher at higher incomes largely because the skilled jobs of the well-off are more interesting than the routine labour of the working class. Managers, directors, engineers, consultants and the rest of the professional elite enjoy more challenging and creative pursuits, and therefore receive more psychological rewards, than those lower on the business hierarchy (Scitovsky, 1976).

Oxford University psychologist Michael Argyle's comprehensive work *The Psychology of Happiness* concludes: 'The conditions of life which really make a difference to happiness are those covered by three sources – social relations, work and leisure. And the establishment of a satisfying state of affairs in these spheres does not depend much on wealth, either absolute or relative.' Indeed, some evidence suggests that social relations, especially in households and communities, are neglected in the consumer society; leisure likewise fares worse among the consumer class than many assume (Argyle, 1987).

The fraying social fabric of the consumer society, though it cannot be measured, reveals itself poignantly in discussions with the elderly. In 1978, researcher Jeremy Seabrook interviewed scores of older people in the English working class about their experience of rising prosperity. Despite dramatic gains in consumption and material comforts their parents and grandparents could never have hoped for, they were more disillusioned than content. One man told Seabrook, 'People aren't satisfied, only they don't seem to know why they're not. The only chance of satisfaction we can imagine is getting more of what we've got now. But it's what we've got now that makes everybody dissatisfied. So what will more of it do, make us more satisfied, or more dissatisfied?' (Seabrook, 1978).

The elders Seabrook interviewed were afraid for their children, who they saw as adrift in a profoundly materialistic world. They were afraid of vandals, muggers and rapists, who seemed ruthless in a way they could not understand. They felt isolated from their neighbours and unconnected to their communities. Affluence, as they saw it, had broken the bonds of mutual assistance that adversity once forged. In the end, they were waiting out their days in their sitting rooms, each with his or her own television (Seabrook, 1978).

Mutual dependence for day-to-day sustenance – a basic characteristic of life for those who have not achieved the consumer class – bonds people as proximity never can. Yet those bonds have severed with the sweeping advance of the commercial mass market into realms once dominated by family members and local enterprise. Members of the consumer class enjoy a degree of personal independence unprecedented in human history, yet hand in hand comes a decline in our attachments to each other. Informal visits between neighbours and friends, family conversation, and time spent at family meals have all diminished in the US since mid-century.[9]

Indeed, the present generation of young Americans believes that being good parents is equivalent to providing lots of goodies. Raising a family remains an important life goal for them, but spending time with their children does not. According to the survey research of Eileen Crimmins and her colleagues at the University of California, Los Angeles, American high school seniors express a strong desire 'to give their children better opportunities than they have had,' but not to 'spend more time with their children'. In high schoolers' minds, 'better opportunities' apparently means 'more goods'. Writing in *Population and Development Review,* the researchers note, 'Who would have foreseen a decade ago that clothes with designer labels and computer video games would be "essential" inputs to a happy child?' (Crimmins et al, 1991).

Over the past century, the mass market has taken over an increasing number of the productive tasks once provided within the household, diminishing people's practical reliance on one another. More and more, flush with cash but pressed for time, we opt for the conveniences of prepared, packaged foods, miracle cleaning products and disposable everythings – from napkins to cameras.

Part of the reason for this transformation of the household economy is that as consumer-class women emancipated themselves from the most tedious types of housework, men did not step in to fill the gap. Instead, housework shifted into the mass market, paid for out of the proceeds of women's new jobs. As both men and women left the home, gutting the household economy, housework was shunted to the money economy.

The sexual imbalance in housework persists, and, if anything, women's total workload has grown as the household changed from a unit of joint production and consumption into a passive, consuming entity. American women in the early 1960s, for example, did as many hours of housework as their grandmothers had done in the 1920s, despite dozens of 'labour-saving' devices. And while American women, on average, have reduced their hours of housework somewhat since 1965, most of them have also taken jobs outside the home. American men's hours of housework, meanwhile, have barely increased at all since 1965. Data from the UK suggest a similar trend there.[10]

The commercialization of the household economy has cost the natural world dearly. Chores that shift out of the house take more resources to perform. Shirts pressed in commercial establishments require two trips, often by car, to the laundry. Meals from the take-out restaurant or the frozen foods section multiply the pack aging materials and transport energy used to nourish a family.

In the ideal household in the consumer society, people do little for themselves. We do not cook our food from scratch (55 per cent of America's consumer food budget is spent on restaurant meals and ready-to-eat convenience foods). We neither mend nor press nor make our own clothes. We neither bake nor build nor do repairs for ourselves. We produce little besides children, and once we have done that, we have a diminishing role. Day-care franchises are more expedient for watching youngsters than the old-fashioned, now dispersed, extended family. Disposable diapers (typically 3000 of them in the first year, at a cost of US$570) have displaced cloth ones.[11]

The evolution of the household from producer to consumer is evident in housing designs in affluent nations. Older houses had pantries, workshops, sewing rooms, built-in clothes hampers, and laundry chutes. New homes have compact kitchens equipped for little more than heating prepared foods. Laundry rooms and root cellars gave way to hot tubs and home entertainment centres. Basement workshops were compressed into utility closets, to make room for pool tables and large-screen televisions. Even garden-ing, one of the vestigial forms of household production still popular among the con-sumer class, is gradually turning into a form of consumption, as purchased inputs replace backyard resources. Britons, for example, spent about US$3 billion on their gardens and lawns in 1991, up from US$1 billion a decade earlier.[12]

Like the household, the community economy has atrophied – or been dismembered – under the blind force of the money economy. Shopping malls, superhighways, and 'strips' have replaced corner stores, local restaurants, and neighbourhood theaters – the things that help create a sense of common identity and community in an area. Tra-ditional communities are all but extinct in some nations. In the US, where the demise of local economies is furthest advanced, many neighbourhoods are little more than a place to sleep, where neighbours share only a video rental franchise and a convenience store. Americans move, on average, every five years, and develop little attachment to those who live near them.[13]

The transformation of retailing is a leading cause of the decline of traditional com-munity in the global consumer society (see Chapter 9). British researchers Carl Gardner and Julie Shepard describe the way civic and collective identity erode with the dwindling of local merchants. 'The town centre, once the natural focus for the people who live and work there, has ... lost its individual characteristics and any reference to its unique past. Now it is merely a cloned version of dozens of others up and down the country. Outside shopping hours ... many town and city centres have, as a result of the retail monocul-ture, become shuttered, barren, lifeless spaces' (Gardner and Shepard, 1990).

Another human cost of the consumer society appears to be an acceleration of the pace of life. Psychologist Robert Levine of California State University, Fresno, measured everything from the average walking speed on city streets to the average talking speed of postal clerks in six countries to show that the pace of life accelerates as countries indus-trialize and commercialize. Japanese urbanites moved fastest, followed by Americans, English, Taiwanese and Italians. Indonesians moved most slowly of all. As nations get richer, in other words, they hurry up (Levine, 1990).

Renegade economist E. F. Schumacher proposed an economic law canonizing that observation in 1978: 'The amount of genuine leisure available in a society is generally in inverse proportion to the amount of labor-saving machinery it employs.' The more people value time – and therefore take pains to save it – the less able they are to relax and enjoy it. Leisure time becomes too valuable to 'waste' in idleness, and even physical exercise becomes a form of consumption. In 1989, Americans devoted the wages of 1 billion working hours to buying such sports clothing as Day-Glo Lycra body suits, wind-tunnel-tested bicycling shoes, rain jackets woven from space-age polymers, and designer hiking shorts. Leisurewear has replaced leisure as the reward for labour. In Japan, meanwhile, a *reja bumu* (leisure boom) has combined with rising concern for nature to pump up sales of fuel-guzzling four-wheel-drive Range Rovers from England and cabins made of imported American logs (Schumacher, 1979; Watson, 1991; leisurewear from Rybczynski, 1991b; Linhart, 1988; Range Rovers from Reid, 1990; *Japan Economic Journal*, 1990).

Working hours in industrial countries, despite the reductions trade unionists have won in the past century, still exceed typical working hours before the Industrial Revolution. 'In medieval Europe,' observes Witold Rybczynski, a professor of architecture at McGill University in Montreal who studies leisure, 'religious festivals reduced the work year to well below the modern level of 2000 hours' (Rybczynski, 1991b).

The consumer society fails to deliver on its promise of fulfilment through material comforts because human wants are insatiable, human needs are socially defined, and the real sources of personal happiness are elsewhere. Indeed, the strength of social relations and the quality of leisure – both crucial psychological determinants of happiness in life – appear as much diminished as enhanced in the consumer class. The consumer society, it seems, has impoverished us by raising our income.

Notes

1 Aristotle, *Politics*, and Lucretius, *On the Nature of the Universe*, both quoted in Vanden Broeck (1978).
2 Tolstoy, *My Religion*, quoted in VandenBroeck (1978).
3 Worldwatch Institute estimate of consumption since 1950 based on gross world product data from Maddison (1989); minerals from Kirby and Prokopovitsh (1976); opinion surveys from Michael Worley (pers comm, 19 September 1990); gross national product per capita and personal consumption expenditures are adjusted for inflation from US Bureau of the Census (1991).
4 International comparison from R. A. Easterlin, 'Does economic growth improve the human lot? Some empirical evidence', cited in Argyle (1987); quote from Argyle (1987). Similar arguments are found in Campbell (1981), Wachtel (1989) and Trainer (1985).
5 Kroeger (1987); dealmaker quoted in Lapham (1988).
6 Banker quoted in Kroeger (1987); Veblen quoted in Lapham (1988).
7 Intergenerational rise of consumption standards from Crimmins et al (1991); redefining prosperity as poverty from Scitovsky (1976).
8 Endlessly shifting standard of decent living from Scitovsky (1976); quote from Crimmins et al (1991).
9 Time spent visiting and conversing from Robinson (1991); time at meals from Scitovsky (1976).
10 US women's housework before 1965 from Ross and Usher (1986) and from Daly and Cobb (1989); women's housework since 1965 from Robinson (1991); UK housework from Ross and Usher (1986).
11 US food budget from Berry (1990); diapers from Cutler (1990).
12 History from Strasser (1989), Rybczinski (1991a) and Lemann (1989); British gardens from Foote (1991).
13 History from Hayden (1984); frequency of moving from Reich (1988).

References

Argyle, M. (1987) *The Psychology of Happiness*, Methuen, New York

Berry, L. L. (1990) 'Market to the perception', *American Demographics,* February

Campbell, A. (1981) *The Sense of Well-Being in America: Recent Patterns and Trends,* McGraw-Hill, New York

Crimmins, E. M., Easterlin, R. A. and Saito, Y. (1991) 'Preference changes among American youth: Family, work, and goods aspirations, 1976–1986', *Population and Development Review,* March

Cutler, B. (1990) 'Rock-a-buy baby', *American Demographics,* January

Daly, H. E. and Cobb, J. B. Jr (1989) *For the Common Good: Redirecting the Economy Toward Community, the Environment, and a Sustainable Future*, Beacon Press, Boston

Foote, J. (1991) 'How does the garden grow?', *Newsweek,* 15 July

Gardner, C. and Shepard, J. (1990) *Consuming Passion: The Rise of Retail Culture,* Unwin Hyman, London

Hayden, D. (1984) *Redesigning the American Dream: The Future of Housing, Work, and Family Life,* W. W. Norton and Co, New York

Japan Economic Journal (1990) 'With permit rules relaxed, log cabin sales are soaring', *Japan Economic Journal,* 4 August

Kirby, R. C. and Prokopovitsh, A. S. (1976) 'Technological insurance against shortages in minerals and metals', *Science,* 20 February

Kroeger, B. (1987) 'Feeling poor on $600,000 a year', *New York Times,* 26 April

Lapham, L. H. (1988) *Money and Class in America: Notes and Observations on Our Civil Religion,* Weidenfeld and Nicolson, New York

Lemann, N. (1989) 'Stressed out in suburbia', *Atlantic Monthly,* November

Levine, R. V. (1990) 'The pace of life', *American Scientist,* September/October

Linhart, S. (1988) 'From industrial to postindustrial society: Changes in Japanese leisure-related values and behavior', *Journal of Japanese Studies,* summer

Maddison, A. (1989) *The World Economy in the 20th Century*, Organisation for Economic Co-operation and Development, Paris

Reich, R. (1988) 'A question of geography,' *New Republic,* 9 May

Reid, T. R. (1990) 'US automakers grind gears in Japan', *Washington Post,* 23 September

Robinson, S. J. (1991) 'How Americans use time', *The Futurist,* September/October

Ross, D. P. and Usher, P. J. (1986) *From the Roots Up: Economic Development as if Community Mattered*, The Bootstrap Press, Croton-on-Hudson, NY

Rybczinski, W. (1991a) 'Living smaller,' *Atlantic Monthly,* February

Rybczynski, W. (1991b) 'Waiting for the weekend,' *Atlantic Monthly,* August

Schumacher, E. F. (1979) *Good Work,* Harper and Row Publishers, New York

Scitovsky, T. (1976) *The Joyless Economy*, Oxford University Press, New York

Seabrook, J. (1978) *What Went Wrong?*, Pantheon Books, New York

Strasser, S. (1989) *Satisfaction Guaranteed: The Making of the American Mass Market*, Pantheon Books, New York

Trainer, F. E. (1985) *Abandon Affluence*, Zed Books, Atlantic Highlands, NJ

US Bureau of the Census (1991) *Statistical Abstract of the United States: 1991*, US Government Printing Office, Washington, DC

VandenBroeck, G. (ed) (1978) *Less Is More: The Art of Voluntary Poverty,* Harper and Row, New York

Wachtel, P. (1989) *The Poverty of Affluence*, New Society Publishers, Philadelphia

Watson, G. (1991) 'The decay of idleness', *Wilson Quarterly,* spring

Worley, M. (1990) National Opinion Research Center, University of Chicago, Chicago, IL, personal communication, 19 September

9

The New Commodity Fetishism

Fred Hirsch

The way in which productivity growth in the material sector pulls the pattern of individual activities toward vain but costly attempts to achieve parallel growth in the positional sector has been discussed [in Part I of Hirsch's *Social Limits to Growth*, from which book this chapter is reprinted]. Chapter 5 of that book suggested that this tendency has contributed to the perceived shortage of time, which in turn has exacerbated the pressure of positional competition, so that these two tendencies have become self-reinforcing. The increasing premium that people have put on their time has intensified a number of problems in economic and social organization. Most important, it has eroded sociability. This erosion has been deepened by the influence of advertising and the self-interest ethos of the market, including the anti-market ethos of consumerism. The present chapter suggests that the upshot of these several connected influences have together created a bias to material commodities.

This bias is a commodity fetishism in the fundamental sense of excessive creation and absorption of commodities and not merely an undue conceptual preoccupation with them in the original sense of Marx – a masking of social relationships under capitalism by their mediation through commodity exchange (Marx, 1951). By 'commodity' I mean here goods, and also services, sold on a commercial basis through the market or its equivalent. The concept of a commodity bias, therefore, implies that an excessive proportion of individual activity is channelled through the market so that the commercialized sector of our lives is unduly large. A related concept which is suggested by this approach is a 'commercialization effect' – meaning the effect on satisfaction from any activity or transaction being undertaken on a commercial basis through market exchange or its equivalent, as compared with its being undertaken in some other way.

The increasing commercialization of life in advanced countries is a complex phenomenon. Its discussion in the present context implies no more than that positional competition, and the increase in material productivity that underlies it, have strengthened this tendency. Other factors such as the decay of traditional social ties and the great increase in geographical mobility have obviously also played an important contributory part. The phenomenon could be analysed fully only in terms of the interaction of these and other influences in the general process of what social scientists during the headier days of the 1950s and early 1960s liked to refer to as 'modernization'. The focus here is on the specific, contributory influence of positional competition and what goes along with it.

The commodity bias affects not only the development of the non-material sector, through its influence on sociability and on instrumental means to positional goods which create new needs, but also the satisfaction derived from the material goods themselves.

I

Consumers derive satisfaction not from goods as such, but from the various assortments of properties or characteristics that they embody. This common-sense concept has been formalized in a development of consumer theory by Kelvin Lancaster under the revealing rubric, 'Goods Aren't Goods'.[1] In this conception, 'consumption is an activity in which goods, singly or in combination, are inputs and in which the output is a collection of characteristics'. Particular goods may derive additional or changed characteristics when used in combination with other goods.[2]

By a simple extension of this concept, the utility derived from goods can be seen as emanating not only from their embodied characteristics but also from the environmental conditions in which they are used. The most obvious of such conditions are associated with direct interaction between use of goods or services by different individuals – conventionally analysed by economists as external costs or benefits. As has been seen, the spreading of car ownership, through congestion, affects the transportation service of a particular car; and the spreading of university education, through the impact on the information content of given credentials, affects the service of a degree as a career entry ticket. Other environmental conditions that may affect commodity characteristics are social friendship and mutual aid. Such conventions respond over time to changes in individual actions, but at any given time have an equal impact on all, irrespective of specific individual behaviour.

Social norms deriving from conventions and general standards of human relationship over time may also be associated with specific services. The services of a doctor may yield, besides a direct improvement in health, additional characteristics stemming from the patient's trust in the doctor's judgement, his assessment of the doctor's motivation, and his assurance or anxiety about his prospects of securing similar services in the future. These latter characteristics are likely to be influenced by the social basis under which medical services are supplied – whether in piecemeal market transactions, private insurance, or comprehensive public insurance – and perhaps also by the underlying social ethos as it affects obligations and entitlements to mutual aid in the society. The effect of commercialization of medicine in the US in weakening the doctor–patient relationship is a matter of common experience and wide spread comment. One striking example of the accompanying diminution in trust is contained in a survey of the American Medical Association in 1969 showing that one in five of all physicians in the US had been or was being sued for malpractice.[3] This, in turn, has stimulated the pursuit of 'legally defensive' professional practice, marking a further twist in the diminution of trust between doctor and patient.

The characteristics yielded by the provision of other services, such as educational instruction, political or administrative leadership, or companionship, also may be affected by the basis on which such services are provided. The product or service that is supplied solely under the motive of satisfying private wants – whether these wants are for money, power or a quiet life – can be seen as different from the product or service sup plied at least partly under the motive of satisfying the wants or needs of others, including society as a whole.[4]

This neglect of the social context in which individual acquisition of goods and services takes place comprises a central aspect of modern commodity fetishism. It involves an excess preoccupation with commodities – including for this purpose specific professional services – as instruments of satisfaction. Orthodox economic analysis is concerned with the commodities people have, not with the way they get them. Yet the relevance of this dimension is uncontroversial when applied to at least one activity – sex. 'Bought sex is not the same.' And this has a wider significance.

The effect on the characteristics of a product or activity of supplying it exclusively or predominantly on commercial terms rather than on some other basis – such as informal exchange, mutual obligation, altruism or love, or feelings of service or obligation – has been termed here the commercialization effect. Economists have recognized, however reluctantly, that something like this commercialization effect applies to sexual activity. Some would explain this influence by irrational social taboos or conventions that bar this activity from the market sector; others by a rational, but unique, assessment by the 'consumer' that the nature or quality of the product or relationship here depends on the basis on which it is provided: a commercialization effect specifically acknowledged in the concept of prostitution.

Yet sexual prostitution can be seen as merely the polar extreme of a continuum in the more general commercialization effect. Thus, in the sexual relationship itself, a more explicit basis of exchange involves a diminution of unspecified mutual obligation, which in turn lowers the quality of the product. The move toward an exchange basis may take a variety of forms short of open commercialization – from the one-off barter transaction of a dinner for a sexual favour to the lengthy marriage con tract recommended by the magazine *Ms.,* in which mutual obligations of both parties on household duties, sexual tolerance and a host of other matters are drawn up and specified in the explicit detail of a business con tract. Such barter exchanges or contractual commitments focus, in effect, on the narrow commodity aspect of the relationship – the sexual and other favours to be exchanged – to the neglect of the associated external conditions such as the spirit in which the exchange is undertaken.[5]

Whether or not the more commercial arrangements diminish the totality of mutual obligation and trust in the particular relationship involved, they will almost inevitably erode social expectations that mutual obligation and trust will be available without similar specification in other, future relationships of the same kind. The more that is in the contracts, the less can be expected without them; the more you write it down, the less is taken – or expected – on trust.[6]

II

By influencing social norms and expectations in this way, commercialization or its equivalent embodies its own dynamic. More specifically, the dynamic is that of privatization,[7] or internalization, of benefits that were earlier assumed to be available through the influence of conventional norms of give and take. A key social function of such simple yet pivotal norms is to restrain people from maximizing their individual satisfaction in every specific transaction where this would conflict with their long-term self-interest.

Social norms are not always necessary to induce people to take a long-term rather than a short-term view of their self-interest. Goodwill accumulated by an established firm; an individual's reputation for truth and honesty among continuing acquaintances; an expected lifelong friendship – these are all cases where the inducement to take a long-term view of self-interest, as a result of being internalized, is built-in. These are cases in which qualities such as trust, mutual support and reciprocity have the characteristics of private goods so that the benefits and costs of a particular pattern of behaviour fall on the individual concerned. The problem arises, as pointed out in the previous chapter, when the effects of individual behaviour are diffused and uncertain in their incidence.[8] It is then that social norms, or alternative inducements or coercion, are required to evoke socially directed action. And self-interest alone, even long-term self-interest, is then not sufficient to ensure compliance since the individual can take a free ride on compliance by others, while others can take a free ride on compliance by him. This 'public goods' problem is discussed further in Chapter 9.

It follows also that a weakening of social norms, where they serve to uphold public goods, is likely to become self-aggravating. Once such conventions can no longer be counted on as the typical basis of behaviour – that is to say, once the typical behaviour to be expected of partners is an attempt to capture maximum private benefit from specific transactions – then the change in behavioural norms will feed on itself.

There will then be a 'tipping' effect of the kind analysed by Schelling in the context of neighbourhood tipping in the housing market. In this process, individual behaviour on the basis of given preferences produces a chain of reactions that works itself out only after culminating in a pattern that no single individual would himself choose (Schelling, 1971). In Schelling's example, a moderate urge among residents to avoid being in a small minority of their race may cause a nearly integrated housing pattern to unravel and highly segregated neighbourhoods to form, although the only racial preference existing was to avoid being in a minority of one-third or less. In the present example, erosion of conventions about mutual obligations could extend a certain distance within society without setting off dynamic effects – people being prepared to take some risk that the reciprocity they expect for their own socialized behaviour may go by default. But beyond the point at which the risk looks too high, behaviour 'tips' to securing fair exchange within the individual transaction. Commercialization, in the sense of securing fair exchange in each specific transaction, then becomes general. It is the essence of such situations, grounded in their public goods aspects, that individuals are never faced with the effect of their own behaviour in influencing the social norm. The impact on themselves is usually infinitesimal and, in any case, dominated by the direct or private result of their actions.

Generally, market institutions are inefficient at any collective provision and may fail completely at collective provision of social norms. Correspondingly, they have a tendency to overproduce specific commodities or services at which they are efficient. The outcome is a commodity bias. Bars are for beer rather than for gossip; note the telling construction of the American bar, where customers sit facing the bottles and the barman rather than each other, and the natural pick-up technique is to say *to the barman*, 'buy the lady a drink.' In the modernized English pub, the infra-red grill replaces the dartboard.

More precisely, the market is inefficient at providing those collective goods for which limitation or exclusion is impractical or costly.[9] Where the turnstile or its equivalent can be used to limit access to those who are willing to pay, collective goods can be, and are, provided privately on a commercial basis. But in the approach taken in this chapter, the exclusion itself may change the characteristics of the collective goods provided. The market may supply the same narrow commodity or service, but with different characteristics in its environmental use. The most graphic illustration would perhaps be the pub dartboard screened by a turnstile – a facility differing so radically from the traditional open area that it has to my knowledge never been tried. If, then, the game of darts is inextricably bound up with open socializing, the market incentive and the market pressure will be to offer other things instead.

So there are tennis clubs for tennis; commercial dating services; country clubs and total living environments tied to rental or ownership of particular residences. In each case, the individual's demand is catered to in a package suitable for marketing, which may or may not be the package that the individual would himself choose if he were presented with the full potential choice. A full choice would include a municipal park and a town plaza, financed by local or national taxes; and perhaps tax-financed subsidies for private individuals, firms or groups that provided comfortable or attractive facilities for socializing without direct charge: a subsidy for the open-access club.

In practice, the individual is confronted with choices only on a piecemeal basis and has to take as a fixture the relevant conditions of use. Thus the choice is not between private motor transport and public transport, but between buying an auto and putting up with the existing bus service; not between relying on private or public recreational facilities, but between supplementing existing public facilities or making do. Moreover, each initial choice tips the balance towards itself. With a double lock on your door, private guards at the apartment gates, and the private bills all this involves, your enthusiasm for bearing additional taxes to pay for more public policemen is likely to wane. Personal security and access to country lakes are increasingly being bought in the US on an exclusive basis; in their traditional form as open to all citizens, they have ceased to be available in many areas as a direct result of those facilities becoming market commodities, that is, privatized.[10]

Those interested primarily in the narrow commodity or activity will be well served; those who place a positive value on exclusion or exclusiveness will find their social environmental preference satisfied. On the other side, those who prefer social contact focused on casual meetings and activities or relationships less specifically geared to particular forms of consumption will be neglected; so also will those who place a positive value on open access, on non-exclusion. Their bad luck is that they derive utility from environmental characteristics that are outside the capacity of the market to provide. Since people with the first two sets of preferences have the engine of internalization on their side – which is to say that they have tastes that commercial enterprises find it profitable to cater to – the balance of forces in the market will tend to swing increasingly in favour of commodities, exclusion and commercialization.

This phenomenon is the generalized bias of the market: to cater to those particular consumer demands that are amenable to commercialization.[11] It is a bias that operates through the wider extension of property rights and excluding devices, that is, gates and locks that to many tastes are unpleasant in themselves. The intense unpopularity of the introduction of museum charges in Britain by the Heath government in 1973 may have been directed at the symbol of the turnstile as much as at the modest charge. This charge removed not only 10 pence from the pocket but also the pleasure derived by some visitors from the existence of a part of the cultural heritage as common property available freely to all.

It is a paradox in the extension of choice through the market mechanism that the spread of restrictive laws and barriers takes place in the name of freedom. This paradox is lost sight of in the conventional focus on the narrow concept of a commodity or service. To advocates of greater internalization of benefits from collective goods, the more flexible property arrangements and additional excluding devices that are needed merely add to the efficiency of the market exchange. 'If the owner of a hunting preserve is allowed to prosecute poachers, then prospective poachers are much more likely to be willing to pay for the hunting permits in advance' (Buchanan, 1965). A specific commodity or service can always be produced more efficiently when property rights are strictly delineated. Public rights in use, without effective obligations on individuals to maintain and protect the facility, lead to the familiar tragedy of the commons. (Everyone benefits from the upkeep of the common, but no one has the motivation to tend it himself, so there develops the opposite and fatal incentive to graze and overgraze it before others complete its ruin.[12]) Yet a common facility can give satisfaction in itself. Its loss through commercialization involving exclusion both removes one item in the circle of economic choice and curtails personal liberty in various dimensions, for example, of movement. This restriction needs to be put in the scale against the increase in narrow efficiency, that is, in output in relation to input of commodities on their market valuation, and in choice *within* the commercial sphere that privatization will usually involve.[13] Privatization will also affect the distribution of income. Unless the system of tax or other form of finance supporting the public good is extremely regressive, privatization will be detrimental to the poor, by removing what to them (though not of course to society) was a free good.

In the ways described above, major changes in social patterns or social norms can take place without being willed by any individual and without being consistent with any summation of individual wishes. A 'tip-over' of activities from social to market provision is a neglected example of the social irrationality that can result from rational individual economic behaviour.

Irrationality in this sense, and indeed the economic significance of the commercialization effect itself, is denied, usually implicitly, in much of the extension of economic analysis into the realms of neighbouring social sciences.[14] This extension, characterized by exponents and critics alike as 'economics imperialism', was begun by Joseph Schumpeter in his classic work *Capitalism, Socialism and Democracy* in 1942[15] and developed by followers such as Anthony Downs, Gary S. Becker, Harry G. Johnson, and many others. The common assumption, almost always hidden, is that the commercialization process does not affect the product, so that the product, independent of the process by which it is acquired, sufficiently defines the objective. This again rests on the economist's traditional view, now beginning to be questioned, that consumption is the sole economic maximand, with consumption seen as a collection of outputs represented in specific commodities or services.

The validity of the so-called economic view of democracy has been questioned by some political scientists, particularly those who stress the functional role of participation.[16] In the Schumpeter-Downs model, democracy is essentially a choice exercised periodically by the mass of the people among alternative and open ruling elites, who in turn are induced by the force of competition (from rival elites) to offer policies tailored to attract electoral support. The political arena in this approach is akin to the market mode for fulfilment of personal wants. It is an extension of the department store – and the problem is to find the managers who can undersell the rest of the street.[17] The alternative view sees popular participation as embedded in the democratic process, and crucial for its outcome. Without it, insufficient support will be forthcoming to sustain the democratic method from a variety of potential threats. These threats range from jeopardy of procedural safeguards by governing elites seeking to perpetuate their power, to the pressing of popular demands that exceed what the system can provide.[18] The 'economic' approach to politics neglects both the conditions in which the end products of democracy, that is, policies resulting from the democratic process, are provided; and the influence of these conditions on people's behaviour. As a consequence, it misdefines the objective of the process and omits a constraint that helps determine whether the process keeps going. It could therefore more properly be called a commodity approach to politics.

Sociologists cast essentially similar doubts on the validity of ignoring the process by which social services are made available. Richard Titmuss, in a striking empirical investigation of the supply of blood under different arrangements in different countries, produced strongly suggestive, if not decisive, evidence that reliance on commercial motivation rather than on altruism and mutual obligation had negative effects on the quality of the product and the efficiency of its provision.[19]

For these various reasons, therefore, an extension of the process of commercialization in our economy, substituting explicit exchange for in formal exchange, is in some sectors not an efficient means of meeting individual preferences.[20] It represents not what people want, choosing among all potential alternatives, but merely what they get when inadequate special provision is made for satisfying individual demands that the market is technically unsuited to fulfil. Commercialization feeds on itself in a way that may retard rather than advance social welfare, meaning by this no more than some aggregate of the satisfactions of individuals.

Notes

1   In Ehrenberg and Pyatt (1971). The original article, 'A new approach to consumer theory', is in Ehrenberg and Pyatt (1966).

2   This gives the formal basis for complementarity between goods, in which more of one good enhances the utility derived from the other.

3   Cited in Titmuss (1970). The number and cost of malpractice suits have since risen sharply, and are now recognized as a major problem in US medical practice. The perverse effect of market incentives on transactions that depend upon mutual trust has been recognized in orthodox economic analysis as resulting from a difference in relevant information available to the two parties to the transaction.

4   By broadening the view of economic welfare from consumption in its narrow, direct sense to consumption in its social context, this approach responds to the modern Marxist criticism that neo-classical welfare theory 'considers objects as ends in themselves' (see Gintis, 1972). The criticism applies particularly to the burgeoning application of orthodox economic analysis to a range of social questions. While the relevant environmental conditions can also be treated more conventionally as externalities or public goods yielding utilities or disutilities, additional to the utilities derived from individual consumption, such treatment obscures the association that may exist between these externalities and certain structural forms of consumption; specifically, it obscures certain distinctive characteristics of market provision as such, or the 'commercialization effect'.

5   An alternative explanation of the inferior 'quality' of sex when it is for pay has been suggested to me, I believe seriously. For some men, their sexual partners may be, in my terms, 'positional goods'. Accordingly, the female suppliers of such goods must be careful to maintain their status value, which precludes general marketing: only inferior women, therefore, will be available on the market. This skilful combination of the new Chicago economic approach to social questions with the traditional male approach to sexual questions fails to explain why many men consider (for any given sexual partner) bought sex inferior in itself.

6   The commercialization effect in its sexual illustration is discussed in greater detail in the appendix to this chapter as originally published in *Social Limits to Growth* (Hirsch, 1976), omitted from this reprint.

7   See note 13.

8   The problem has therefore been heightened by increased geographical mobility, which has general effects similar to those noted in the context of sociability. The fact that modern property developers do not live in the neighbourhoods they remould, and often nowhere near them, has been widely cited as an explanation of the reduced weight that they have given to aesthetic and social considerations compared with their predecessors, at least in European cities. Similarly, the mobility of corporation executives has tended to make corporate decisions less sensitive to their impact on local communities, at least until checked by a political reaction. Professor Kenneth Boulding has suggested Pittsburgh as an example of the good effects of having people live in the nests that they foul.

9   For a full discussion, but one confined to the 'narrow' commodity view, see Buchanan (1968).

10 A typical 'total security environment' being developed in the San Francisco Bay Area offered the following (*Sunday Tribune*, 1973):

> Only residents with special keys can drive through the four entry gates. Once inside, private underground parking is available. Visitors park outside and enter through lobby doors which are controlled by intercoms to each apartment. The front door of each apartment is equipped with two locks, including a high-security deadbolt. Inside the complex, residents and their guests can enjoy nearly 4 acres of privacy. Islanded in the centre of the lake is a spacious recreation centre containing saunas, gym, steam room, tanning rooms, billiards, fireplace lounge, lockers, colour TV, stereo system and a kitchen.

A less blatant version of this phenomenon can be observed in new towns and suburbs in the UK. A clerk living in Bracknell remarks (Young and Willmott, 1973):

> A funny thing is that you're supposed to be in the country but there are hardly any parks around that you can go to. In London we had Hyde Park and Hampstead Heath on a Sunday. This is supposed to be the country but it's all private.

11 The same influence explains why externalities are biased to costs, rather than benefits, and cannot be expected to balance. In the production of goods and services, external economies are an oddity (the standard example is bee pollinate, and that has been disputed) because normal market forces provide an incentive for these economies to be internalized, and for external diseconomies not to be.

12 See, in particular, Hardin (1968).

13 Privatization is used here to denote a move away from the provision of goods or services on a communal or subsidized basis to provision on a commercial basis, in which revenue is raised by specific charges paid by the user rather than through a system of tax finance or other collective means (of which the most famous example was communal labour to maintain the medieval commons before their privatization through enclosure). Privatization is a prominent example of commercialization, although the latter term is used more widely to cover the substitution of commercial exchange for implicit barter arrangements and conventions about mutual support.

14 In the conventional treatment, a switch in an economic activity from outside to inside the market sector, or from partial to more complete exchange on market terms, normally represents an unqualified improvement in economic welfare, at least if it leaves the distribution of income unchanged. The improvement stems from the gain from trade voluntarily conducted. It makes at least one person better off without making anyone worse off, thereby yielding a 'Pareto improvement'. This Pareto improvement forms the basis of traditional support among neo-classical economists – and some who would reject that label – for a wide range of policy issues and, in particular, for redistributive measures to be in cash rather than in kind. The present focus on the environmental use-cum-provision characteristics of consumption is a reminder that commercialization has additional effects that also need to be brought into the reckoning. The crucial limitation in the conventional analysis is that it does not allow for a change in the nature of the product according to the method of provision.

15 See Schumpeter (1942). The characterization 'economics imperialism' was introduced by Kenneth Boulding. See, for example, his 'Economics as a moral science' in *American Economic Review* (Boulding, 1969).

16 It is notable that one of the first textbooks to apply the economic method to political science, the widely used *Politics, Economics and Welfare* (Dahl and Lindblom, 1953), still recognized a functional difference between the political and the market mode:

> On the whole, the process of making market choices tends to narrow one's identifications to the individual or, at the most, to the family. The process of voting, on the other hand, with all that it presupposes in the way of discussion and techniques of reciprocity, tends to broaden one's identifications beyond the individual and the family.

In the further development of this line of analysis, in *An Economic Theory of Democracy* (Downs, 1957) and *The Calculus of Consent* (Buchanan and Tullock, 1962), any such distinction had disappeared. The political arena was merely an alternative to the market mode for the satisfaction of private wants, and the problem was to find the areas in which, and methods through which, it was a superior mode in this respect.

17 More formally, 'parties formulate policies in order to win elections, rather than win elections in order to formulate policies' (Downs, 1957, p28). This follows from the primacy accorded to the self-interest axiom, under which both voters and politicians seek to maximize their own incomes, prestige and power.

18 See, in particular, Bachrach (1967). See also Bottomore (1964) and Plamenatz (1973).

19 See Titmuss (1970). See also Arrow's discussion, 'Gifts and exchanges,' in *Philosophy and Public Affairs* (Arrow, 1972). A less discerning and more combative reply to Titmuss is by Cooper and Culyer (1973). 20 When efficiency is related to the 'broad' concept of the characteristics of goods and services in their environmental conditions of use.

References

Arrow, K. J. (1972) 'Gifts and exchanges', *Philosophy and Public Affairs*, summer, pp343–362

Bachrach, P. (1967) *The Theory of Democratic Elitism*, University of London Press, London

Bottomore, T. B. (1964) *Elites and Society*, Penguin, Harmondsworth, UK, Chapter 6

Boulding, K. (1969) 'Economics as a moral science', *American Economic Review*, vol 59, no 1, March, pp1–12

Buchanan, J. M. (1965) 'An economic theory of clubs', *Economica*, February, p14

Buchanan, J. M. (1968) *The Demand and Supply of Public Goods*, Rand McNally, Chicago

Buchanan, J. M. and Tullock, G. (1962) *The Calculus of Consent*, University of Michigan Press, Ann Arbor

Cooper, M. H. and Culyer, A. J. (1973) 'The economics of giving and selling blood', in A. A. Alchian, W. Allen, M. Cooper, A. Culyer, M. Ireland, T. Ireland, D. Johnson, J. Koch, A. Salsbury and G. Tullock (eds) *The Economics of Charity*, Institute of Economic Affairs, London, pp109– 143

Dahl, R. A. and Lindblom, C. E. (1953) *Politics, Economics and Welfare*, Harper and Row, New York

Downs, A. (1957) *An Economic Theory of Democracy*, Harper and Row, New York

Ehrenberg, A. S. C. and Pyatt, F. G. (1966) *Journal of Political Economy*, vol 74, pp132–157

Ehrenberg, A. S. C. and Pyatt, F. G. (eds) (1971) *Consumer Behavior*, Penguin, Harmondsworth, UK, pp340–360

Gintis, H. (1972) 'A radical analysis of welfare economics and individual development', *Quarterly Journal of Economics*, November, pp572–599

Hardin, G. (1968) 'The tragedy of the commons', *Science*, vol 162, pp1243–1248

Hirsch, F. (1976) *Social Limits to Growth*, Harvard University Press, Cambridge, MA

Marx, K. (1951) *Capital*, vol 1, Dent, London, Chapter 1, p84

Plamenatz, J. (1973) *Democracy and Illusion*, Longman, London, Chapters 4, 6

Schelling, T. (1971) 'On the ecology of micromotives', in *The Public Interest*, vol 25, pp61–98

Schumpeter, J. A. (1942) *Capitalism, Socialism and Democracy*, Harper and Row, New York

Sunday Tribune (1973) *Sunday Tribune*, Oakland, CA, 5 August

Titmuss, R. M. (1970) *The Gift Relationship*, Allen and Unwin, London, p166

Young, M. and Willmott, P. (1973) *The Symmetrical Family*, Routledge, London

10

False Connections

Alex Kotlowitz

A drive down Chicago's Madison Street, moving west from the lake, is a short lesson in America's fault lines of race and class. The first mile runs through the city's downtown – or the Loop, as it's called locally – past high-rises that house banks and law firms, advertising agencies and investment funds. The second mile, once lined by flophouses and greasy diners, has hitched on to its neighbour to the east, becoming a mecca for artists and new, hip restaurants, a more affordable appendage to the Loop. And west from there, past the United Center, home to the Chicago Bulls, the boulevard descends into the abyssal lows of neighbourhoods where work has disappeared. Buildings lean like punch-drunk boxers. Makers of plywood do big business here, patching those same buildings' open wounds. At dusk, the gangs claim ownership to the corners and hawk their wares, whatever is the craze of the moment, crack or smack or reefer. It's all for sale. Along one stretch, young women, their long, bare legs shimmering under the lamplight, smile and beckon and mumble short, pithy descriptions of the pleasures they promise to deliver.

Such is urban decay. Such are the remains of the seemingly intractable, distinctly American version of poverty, a poverty not only 'of the pocket' but also, as Mother Teresa said when she visited this section of the city, 'of the spirit'.

What is most striking about this drive down Madison, though, is that so few whites make it. Chicago's West Side, like other central-city neighbourhoods, sits apart from everything and everyone else. Its inhabitants have become geographically and spiritually isolated from all that surrounds them, islands unto themselves. Even the violence – which, myth has it, threatens us all – is contained within its borders. Drug dealers shoot drug dealers. Gang members maul gang members. And the innocents, the passers-by who get caught in the crossfire, are their neighbours and friends. It was that isolation which so struck me when I first began to spend time at the Henry Horner Homes, a Chicago public housing complex that sits along that Madison Street corridor. Lafayette and Pharoah, the two boys I wrote about in my book *There Are No Children Here,* had never been to the Loop, one mile away. They'd never walked the halls of the Art Institute of Chicago or felt the spray from the Buckingham Fountain. They'd never ogled the sharks at the John G. Shedd Aquarium or stood in the shadow of the stuffed pachyderms at the Field Museum. They'd never been to the suburbs. They'd never been to the countryside. In fact, until we stayed at a hotel one summer on their first fishing trip, they'd never felt the steady stream of a shower. (Henry Homer's apartments had only bathtubs.) At one point, the boys, so certain that their way of life was the only way of life, insisted that my neighbourhood, a gentrified community on the city's North Side, had to be controlled by gangs. They knew nothing different.

And yet children like Lafeyette and Pharoah do have a connection to the American mainstream: it is as consumers that inner-city children, otherwise so disconnected from the world around them, identify themselves not as ghetto kids or project kids but as Americans or just plain kids. And they are as much consumers as they are the consumed; that is, they mimic white America while white America mimics them. 'Inner-city kids will embrace a fashion item as their own that shows they have a connection, and then you'll see the prep school kids reinvent it, trying to look hip-hop,' says Sarah Young, a consultant to businesses interested in tapping the urban market. 'It's a cycle.' A friend, a black 19-year-old from the city's West Side, suggests that this dynamic occurs because the inner-city poor equate classiness with suburban whites while those same suburban whites equate hipness with the inner-city poor. If he's right, it suggests that commercialism may be our most powerful link, one that in the end only accentuates and prolongs the myths we have built up about each other.

Along Madison Street, halfway between the Loop and the city's boundary, sits an old, worn-out shopping strip containing small, transient stores. They open and close almost seasonally – balloons mark the openings; 'Close-Out Sale' banners mark the closings – as the African American and Middle Eastern immigrant owners ride the ebb and flow of unpredictable fashion tastes: GQ Sports; Dress to Impress; Best Fit; Chic Classics; Dream Team. On weekend afternoons, the makeshift mall is thronged with customers blithely unaware that store ownership and names may have changed since their last visit. Young mothers guiding their children by the shoulders and older women seeking a specific purchase pick their way through packs of teenagers who laugh and clown, pulling and pushing one another into the stores. Their whimsical tastes are the subject of intense curiosity, longing, and marketing surveys on the part of store owners and corporate planners.

On a recent spring afternoon, as I made my way down Madison Street toward Tops and Bottoms, one of the area's more popular shops, I detected the unmistakable sweet odour of marijuana. Along the building's side, two teenage boys toked away at cigar-sized joints, called blunts. The store is long and narrow; its walls are lined with shoes and caps and its centre is packed with shirts, jeans and leather jackets. The owner of the store, a Palestinian immigrant, recognized me from my previous visits there with Lafeyette and Pharoah. 'You're a probation officer, right?' he asked. I told him what my connection was with the boys. He completed a sale of a black Starter skullcap and then beckoned me toward the back of the store, where we could talk without distraction.

Behind him, an array of nearly 200 assorted shoes and sneakers lined the wall from floor to ceiling. There were the predictable brands: Nike, Fila and Reebok, the shoes that have come to define (and nearly bankrupt) a generation. There were the heavy boots by Timberland and Lugz that have become popular among urban teens. But it was the arrangement of shoes directly in front of me that the proprietor pointed to, a collection of Hush Puppies. 'See that?' he asked. 'It's totally white-bread.' Indeed, Hush Puppies, once of earth tones and worn by preppies, have caught on among urban black teens – and the company has responded in kind, producing the shoes in outrageous, gotta-look-at-me colours such as crayon orange and fire-engine red. I remember the first time Pharoah appeared in a pair of lime green Hush Puppies loafers – I was dumbfounded.

But then I thought of his other passions: Tommy Hilfiger shirts, Coach wallets, Guess? jeans. They were the fashions of the economically well heeled, templates of those who had 'made it'. Pharoah, who is now off at college, ultimately found his path. But for those who are left be hind, these fashions are their 'in'. They give them cachet. They link them to a more secure, more prosperous world, a world in which they have not been able to participate – except as consumers.

Sarah Young, whose clients include the company that manufactures Hush Puppies, suggests that 'for a lot of these kids, what they wear is who they are because that's all they have to connect them to the rest of the larger community. It marks their status because there's not a lot else.'

It's a false status, of course. They hold on to the idea that to 'make it' means to consume at will, to buy a US$100 Coach wallet or an US$80 Tommy Hilfiger shirt. And these brand-name companies, knowing they have a good thing going, capitalize on their popularity among the urban poor, a group that despite its economic difficulties represents a surprisingly lucrative market. The companies gear their advertising to this market segment. People such as Sarah Young nurture relationships with rap artists, who they lure into wearing certain clothing items. When the company that makes Hush Puppies was looking to increase their presence in the urban market, Young helped persuade Wyclef Jean, a singer with the Fugees, to wear powder blue Bridgeport chukkas, which bear a sneaking resemblance to the Wallabee shoes familiar to members of my generation. In a recent issue of *Vibe*, a magazine aimed at the hip-hop market, rappers Beenie Man and Bounty Killer are pictured posing in Ralph Lauren hats and Armani sweaters, sandwiched between photographs of other rappers decked out in Calvin Klein sunglasses and Kenneth Cole shoes. The first three full-page advertisements in that same issue are for Hilfiger's athletic line, Coach handbags (with jazz singer Cassandra Wilson joyfully walking along with her Coach bag slung over her shoulder), and Perry Ellis casual wear (with a black man and three young boys lounging on the beach). This, as Pharoah told me, represents class – and, as Young suggested, the one connection that children growing up amid the ruins of the inner city have to a more prosperous, more secure world. It is as consumers that they claim citizenship. And yet that Coach hand bag or that Tommy Hilfiger or Perry Ellis shirt changes nothing of the cruel realities of growing up poor and black. It reminds me of the murals painted on abandoned buildings in the South Bronx: pictures of flowers, window shades and curtains, and the interiors of tidy rooms. As Jonathan Kozol observes in his book *Amazing Grace*, 'the pictures have been done so well that when you look, the first time, you imagine that you're seeing into people's homes – pleasant-looking homes, in fact, that have a distinctly middle-class appearance' (Kozol, 1996).

But the urban poor are more than just consumers. They help drive fashions as well. The Tommy Hilfiger clothing line, aimed initially at preppies, became hot in the inner city, pushed in large part by rap artists who took to the clothing maker's stylish, colourful vestments. A 1997 article in *Forbes* magazine suggests that Hilfiger's 47 per cent rise in earnings over the first nine months of its fiscal year 1996–1997 had much to do with the clothing line's popularity among the kinds of kids who shop in Chicago's Madison Street (Levine, 1997). Suddenly, Tommy Hilfiger became cool, not only among the urban teens but also among their counterparts in the suburbs. 'That gives them a sense of pride, that they're bringing a style to a new height,' Sarah Young suggests. Thus, those who don't have much control over other aspects of their life find comfort in having at least some control over something – style.

There's another facet to this as well: the romanticization of urban poverty by some white teens. In St Joseph, Michigan, a nearly all-white town of 9000 in the state's south-western corner, a group of teens mimicked the mannerisms and fashions of their neigh-bours across the river in Benton Harbor, Michigan, a nearly all-black town that has been economically devastated by the closing of the local factories and foundries. This cadre of kids called themselves 'wiggers'. A few white boys identified themselves with one of the Benton Harbor gangs, and one small band was caught carrying out hold-ups with a BB gun. A local police detective laughingly called them 'wannabes'. At St Joseph High School, the wiggers greeted one another in the hallways with a high five or a twitch of the head. 'Hey, Nigger, wha's up?' they'd enquire. 'Man, just chillin'.'

But it was through fashions – as consumers – that they most clearly identified them-selves with their peers across the way. They dressed in the hip-hop fashion made popular by M. C. Hammer and other rap artists, wearing blue jeans big enough for two, the crotch down at their knees. (The beltless, pants-falling-off-hips style originated, many believe, in prison, where inmates must forgo belts.) The guys wore Starter jackets and hats, the style at the time. The girls hung braided gold necklaces around their necks and styled their hair in finger waves or braids. For these teens, the life of ghetto kids is edgy, gutsy, risky – all that adolescents crave. But do they know how edgy, how gutsy, how risky? They have never had to comfort a dying friend, bleeding from the head because he was on the wrong turf. They have never sat in a classroom where the desks are arranged so that no student will be hit by falling plaster. They have never had to say 'Yes, Sir' and 'No, Sir,' as a police officer, dripping with sarcasm, asks, 'Nigger, where'd you get the money for such a nice car?' From a safe distance – as consumers – they can believe they are hip, hip being defined as what they see in their urban counterparts. With their jeans sagging off their boxer shorts, with their baseball caps worn to the side, with their high-tops unlaced, they find some connection, though in the end it is a false bond.

It is as consumers that poor black children claim membership to the larger com-munity. It is as purchasers of the talismans of success that they can believe they've tran-scended their otherwise miserable situation. In the late 1980s, as the drug trade began to flourish in neighbourhoods such as Chicago's West Side, the vehicle of choice for these big-time entrepreneurs was the Chevrolet Blazer, an icon of suburban stability. As their communities were unravelling, in part because of their trade, they sought a connection to an otherwise stable life. And they sought it in the only way they knew how, the only way available to them: as consumers. Inner-city teens are eager to partici-pate in society; they want to belong.

And for the white teens like those in St Joseph, who, like all adolescents, want to feel that they're on the edge, what better way than to build some connection – however manufactured – to their contemporaries across the river who must negotiate that vertical drop every day? By purchasing, in complete safety, all the accoutrements associated with skirting that fall, they can believe that they've been there, that they've experienced the horrors and pains of growing up black and poor. Nothing, of course, could be further from the truth. They know nothing of the struggles their neighbours endure.

On the other hand, fashions in the end are just that – fashions. Sometimes kids yearn for baggy jeans or a Tommy Hilfiger shirt not because of what it represents but because it is the style of their peers. Those 'wiggers', for example, may equate the sagging pants with their neighbours across the river, but kids a few years younger are mimicking them as much as their black counterparts. Fashions grow long limbs that, in the end, are only distantly connected to their roots.

Take that excursion down Madison Street – and the fault lines will become abundantly clear. One can't help but marvel at the spiritual distance between those shopping at Tops and Bottoms on the blighted West Side and those browsing the pricey department stores in the robust downtown. And yet many of the children have one eye trained down Madison Street, those on each side watching their counterparts and thinking they know the others' lives. Their style of dress mimics that of the others. But they're being cheated. They don't know. They have no idea. Those checking out the array of Hush Puppies at Tops and Bottoms think they have the key to making it, to becoming full members of this prosperous nation. And those trying on the jeans wide enough for two think they know what it means to be hip, to live on the edge. And so, in lieu of building real connections – by providing opportunities or rebuilding communities – we have found some common ground as purchasers of each other's trademarks. At best, that link is tenuous; at worst, it's false. It lets us believe that we are connected when the distance, in fact, is much farther than anyone cares to admit.

References

Kozol, J. (1996) *Amazing Grace: The Lives of Children and the Conscience of a Nation,* Harper Perennial, New York
Levine, J. (1997) 'Baad sells', *Forbes,* vol 159, no 8, 21 April, p142

11

Living More Simply

Duane Elgin

It makes an enormous difference whether greater simplicity is voluntarily chosen or involuntarily imposed. For example, consider two persons, both of whom ride a bicycle to work in order to save gasoline.[1] The first person voluntarily chooses to ride a bicycle and derives great satisfaction from the physical exercise, the contact with the outdoors, and the knowledge that he or she is conserving energy. The second person bikes to work because of the force of circumstances – this may be financial necessity or stringent gasoline rationing. In stead of delighting in the ride, the second individual is filled with resentment with each push of the pedals. This person yearns for the comfort and speed of an automobile and is indifferent to the social benefit derived from the energy savings.

In outward appearances both persons are engaged in identical activities. Yet the attitudes and experiences of each are quite different. These differences are crucial in determining whether or not bicycling would prove to be a workable and satisfying response to energy shortages. For the first person it would. For the second person this is clearly not a satisfying solution and perhaps not even a workable one (to the extent that he or she, along with many others, tries to circumvent the laws and secure his or her own personal advantage). This example illustrates how important it is whether our simplicity is consciously chosen or externally imposed. *Voluntary* simplicity, then, involves not only what we do (the outer world) but also the intention with which we do it (the inner world).

The nature of simplicity that I will focus on in this chapter is that of a consciously chosen simplicity. This is not to ignore a majority of the human family that lives in involuntary material simplicity – poverty. Rather it is to acknowledge that much of the solution to that poverty lies in the voluntary actions of those who live in relative abundance and thereby have the real opportunity consciously to simplify their lives and assist others.

The Nature of Simplicity

The dictionary defines *simplicity* as being 'direct, clear; free of pretense or dishonesty; free of vanity, ostentation, and undue display; free of secondary complications and distractions'. In living more simply we encounter life more directly – in a first-hand and immediate manner. We need little when we are directly in touch with life. It is when we remove ourselves from direct and wholehearted participation in life that emptiness and boredom creep in. It is then that we begin our search for something or someone that will alleviate our gnawing dissatisfaction. Yet the search is endless to the extent that we are continually led away from ourselves and our experience in the moment. If we fully appreciate the learning and love that life offers us in each moment, then we feel less desire for material luxuries that contribute little to our well-being and that deprive those in genuine need of scarce resources. When we live with simplicity, we give ourselves and others a gift of life.

We both seek and fear immediacy of contact with life. We search for aliveness, yet we mask our magnificence in a shell of material ostentation and display. We seek genuineness in our encounters with others and yet allow pretence and dishonesty to infuse our relationships. We look for authenticity in the world about us and find that we have covered our miraculous existence with layer upon layer of fashions, cosmetics, fads, trivial technological conveniences, throwaway products, bureaucratic red tape and stylish junk. How are we to penetrate through these obscuring layers?

If you were to choose death as an ally (as a reminder of the preciousness of each moment), and if you were to choose the universe as your home (as a reminder of the awesome dimensions of our existence), then wouldn't a quality of aliveness, immediacy and poignancy naturally infuse your moment-to-moment living? If you knew that you would die within several hours or days, wouldn't the simplest things acquire a luminous and penetrating significance? Wouldn't each moment be come precious beyond all previous measure? Wouldn't each flower, each person, each crack in the sidewalk, each tree become a wonder? Wouldn't each experience become a fleeting and never-to-be-repeated miracle? Simplicity of living helps to bring this kind of clarity and appreciation into our lives.

An old Eastern saying states, 'Simplicity reveals the master.' As we gradually master the art of living, a consciously chosen simplicity emerges as the expression of that mastery. Simplicity allows the true character of our lives to show through – like stripping, sanding and waxing a fine piece of wood that had long been painted over. To further explore the broad relevance of simplicity, I will examine its worldly expression in three different areas: consumption, communications and work.

Simplicity and Consumption

To bring the quality of simplicity into our levels and patterns of consumption, we must learn to live between the extremes of poverty and excess. Simplicity is a double-edged sword in this regard: living with either too little or too much will diminish our capacity to realize our potentials. Bringing simplicity into our lives requires that we discover the ways in which our consumption either supports or entangles our existence.

Balance occurs when there is sufficiency – when there is neither material excess nor deficit. To find this balance in our everyday lives requires that we understand the difference between our personal 'needs' and our 'wants'. Needs are those things that are essential to our survival and our growth. Wants are those things that are extra – that gratify our psychological desires. For ex ample, we *need* shelter in order to survive. We may *want* a huge house with many extra rooms that are seldom used. We *need* basic medical care. We may *want* cosmetic plastic surgery to disguise the fact that we are getting older. We *need* functional clothing. We may *want* frequent changes in clothing style to reflect the latest fashion. We *need* a nutritious and well-balanced diet. We may *want* to eat at expensive restaurants. We *need* transportation. We may *want* a new Mercedes.

Only when we are clear about what we need and what we want can we begin to pare away the excess and find a middle path between extremes. No one else can find this balance for us. This is a task that we each must do for ourselves.

The hallmark of a balanced simplicity is that our lives become clearer, more direct, less pretentious and less complicated. We are then empowered by our material circumstances rather than enfeebled or distracted. Excess in either direction – too much or too little – is complicating. If we are totally absorbed in the struggle for subsistence or, conversely, if we are totally absorbed in the struggle to accumulate, then our capacity to participate wholeheartedly and enthusiastically in life is diminished.

Four consumption criteria, developed by a group in San Francisco while exploring a life of conscious simplicity, go to the very heart of the issue of balanced consumption:

- Does what I own or buy promote activity, self-reliance and involvement, or does it induce passivity and dependence?
- Are my consumption patterns basically satisfying, or do I buy much that serves no real need?
- How tied are my present job and lifestyle to instalment payments, maintenance and repair costs, and the expectations of others?
- Do I consider the impact of my consumption patterns on other people and on the Earth?[2]

This compassionate approach to consumption stands in stark contrast to the industrial-era view, which assumes that if we increase our consumption, we will increase our happiness. However, when we equate our identity with that which we consume – when we engage in 'identity consumption' – we become possessed by our possessions. We are consumed by that which we consume. Our identity becomes not a free-standing, authentic expression in the moment, but a material mask that we have constructed so as to present a more appealing image for others to see. The vastness of who we are is then compressed into an ill-fitting shell that obscures our uniqueness and natural beauty. When we believe the advertiser's fiction that 'you are what you consume', we begin a misdirected search for a satisfying experience of identity. We look beyond ourselves for the next thing that will make us happy: a new car, a new wardrobe, a new job, a new hairstyle, a new house and so on. Instead of lasting satisfaction, we find only temporary gratification. After the initial gratification subsides, we must begin again – looking for the next thing that, this time, we hope will bring some measure of enduring satisfaction. Yet the search is both endless and hopeless because it is continually directed away from the 'self' that is doing the searching. If we were to pause in our search and begin to discover that our true identity is much larger than any that can be fashioned through even the most opulent levels of material consumption, then the entire driving force behind our attempts at 'identity consumption' would be fundamentally transformed.

It is transformative to withdraw voluntarily from the preoccupations with the material rat race of accumulation and instead accept our natural experience – unadorned by superfluous goods – as sufficient unto itself. It is a radical simplicity to affirm that our happiness cannot be purchased, no matter how desperately the advertiser may want us to believe the fiction that we will never be happy or adequate without his or her product. It is a radical simplicity when we accept our bodies as they are – when we affirm that each of us is endowed with a dignity, beauty, and character whose natural expression is infinitely more interesting and engaging than any imagined identity we might construct with layers of stylish clothes and cosmetics.

A conscious simplicity, then, is not self-denying but life-affirming. Voluntary simplicity is not an 'ascetic simplicity' (of strict austerity); rather it is an 'aesthetic simplicity' where each person considers whether his or her level and pattern of consumption fits with grace and integrity into the practical art of daily living on this planet. The possessions that seemed so important and appealing during the industrial era would gradually lose much of their allure. The individual or family who, in the past, was admired for a large and luxurious home would find that the mainstream culture increasingly admired those who had learned how to combine functional simplicity and beauty in a smaller home. The person who was previously envied for his or her expensive car would find that a growing number of people were uninterested in displays of conspicuous consumption. The person who was previously recognized for always wearing the latest in clothing styles would find that more and more people viewed high fashion as tasteless ostentation that was no longer fitting in a world of great human need. This does not mean that people would turn away from the material side of life; rather, they would place a premium on living ever more lightly and aesthetically.

Some are concerned that ecological ways of living will undermine economic activity and produce high unemployment. This seems unfounded. Most of those choosing ecological ways of living are very intent upon leading purposeful lives that respond to the real needs of others. When we look around at the condition of the world, we see a huge number of unmet needs: urban renewal, environmental restoration, education of illiterate and unskilled youth, repair of decaying roads and bridges, provision of child care and health care, and many more. Because there are an enormous number of unmet needs, there are an equally large number of purposeful and satisfying jobs waiting to get done. The difficulty is that in many industrialized nations there is such an overwhelming emphasis placed on individual consumption that it has resulted in the neglect of work that promotes the public welfare. There will be no shortage of employment opportunities in an ecologically oriented economy. In moving toward simpler ways of living and a needs-oriented economy that does not artificially inflate consumer wants, an abundance of meaningful and satisfying jobs will become available along with the additional resources needed to pay for them.

The Earth does not have sufficient resources and environmental carrying capacity to allow all of the people in the world to consume at the levels, and in the forms, that have characterized industrial growth in the West. We need much more efficient forms of development – marked by frugality and ecological integrity. Food production, housing, transportation, energy production and many more areas of our lives will have to be diversely and creatively adapted if we are to sustain the process of global development in the 21st century. We must choose levels and patterns of consumption that are globally sustainable – that use the world's resources wisely and do not overstress the world's ecology. Simplicity of living has enormous relevance for meeting these challenges.

Simplicity and Interpersonal Communications

The ability to communicate is at the very heart of human life and civilization. If we cannot communicate effectively, then civilization itself is threatened. If we apply the principle of simplicity to our communications, then they will tend to be more direct, clear and honest. In this respect consider five areas where simplicity can enhance the quality of communication.

First, to communicate more simply means to communicate more honestly – it is to connect our inner experience with our outer expressions. Integrity, authenticity and honesty encourage the development of trust. With trust there is a basis for cooperation, even when there remain disagreements. With cooperation there is a foundation for mutually helpful living. Simplicity of communication, then, is vital for building a sustainable future.

Second, simplicity of communication implies that we will let go of wasteful speech and idle gossip. Wasteful speech can assume many forms: distracted chatter about people and places that have little relevance to what is happening in the moment; name-dropping to build social status; using unnecessarily complex language or overly coarse language; and so on. When we simplify our communications by eliminating the irrelevant, we infuse what we do communicate with greater importance, dignity and intention.

Third, simplicity is also manifest in communication by valuing silence. The revered Indian sage Ramana Maharshi said that silence speaks with 'unceasing eloquence' (Maharshi, 1972). When we appreciate the power and eloquence of silence, our exchanges with others come into sharper focus. The sometimes painful or awkward quality that silence brings in social settings is, I think, a measure of the mismatch between our social facades and our more authentic sense of self. Once we are comfortable in allowing silence its place in communication, there is the opportunity to express ourselves more fully and authentically. The simplicity of silence fosters dignity, depth and directness in communication.

Fourth, simplicity is also expressed in communication as greater eye contact with others. Because the eyes have been called the seat of the soul, it is not surprising that more direct eye contact with others tends to cultivate more soulful communication. This does not mean engaging others with a tight, hard and demanding gaze; rather, we can approach others with 'soft eyes' that are gentle and accepting. When we directly 'see' another in this way, there is often a mutual flash of recognition. The source of that shared awareness resides not in the pigmented portion of the eyes, but within the darkness of the interior centre – therein is the place that yields the spark of conscious recognition. It is the dancing and brilliant darkness of the interior eye that reveals that the essence of 'self' and 'other' arise from the same source. Emerson spoke eloquently of how poverty, riches, status, power and sex are all forms whose veil yields to our knowing eyes. What is seen goes beyond all of these forms and labels to reveal the very essence of who we are.

Fifth, simplicity can also be expressed in our communications as greater openness to non-sexual physical contact. Hugging and touching that is free from disguised sexual manipulation is a powerful way of more fully and directly communicating with another. Studies have shown that a strong correlation exists between acceptance of physical touching and a tendency toward gentleness (Prescott, 1975). If we are to learn to live together as a global family, then we must learn to touch one another with less physical and psychological violence.

Simplicity and Work

A third major example of the relevance of simplicity is how it can transform our approach to work. Our relationship with our work is enhanced greatly when our liveli-hood makes a genuine contribution both to ourselves and to the human family. It is through our work that we develop our skills, relate with others in shared tasks, and contribute to the larger society. Thomas Aquinas said, 'There can be no joy of life with-out joy of work.' Our joy of work and life can flourish when we move from an inten-tion of 'making a killing' for ourselves to that of 'earning a living' in a way that contributes to the well-being of all. In sensing and responding to the needs of the world, our work acquires a natural focus and intention that brings clarity and satisfac-tion into our lives.

Simplicity is also manifest in more human-sized places of employment. Many per-sons work within massive bureaucracies: huge corporations, vast government agencies, enormous educational institutions, sprawling medical complexes and so on. These work places have grown so large and so complex that they are virtually incomprehensible, both to those who work within them and to those who are served by them. Not surpris-ingly the occupations that often emerge from these massive organizations tend to be routinized, specialized and stress-producing. Simplicity in this setting implies a change in favor of more human-sized work places. This does not mean abandonment of the institutions that have arisen during the industrial era; instead, it means that we would redesign organizations in such a way that they are of more comprehensible size and manageable complexity. By consciously creating work places of a size that encourages meaningful involvement and personal responsibility, the rampant alienation, boredom and emptiness of work would be greatly reduced.

The quality of simplicity can also be expressed as more direct and meaningful par-ticipation in decisions about work – for example, direct participation in decisions about what to produce; direct involvement in organizing the work process; and direct partici-pation in deciding the structure of working arrangements (such as flexible hours, job sharing, job swapping, team assembly and other innovations).

In looking at three very different areas – consumption, communications and work – it is evident that simplicity has pervasive relevance that can touch and transform every facet of our lives.

Voluntary Simplicity: An Integrated Path for Living

To live more voluntarily is to live more consciously. To live more consciously is to live in a 'life-sensing' manner. It is to 'taste' our experience of life directly as we move through the world. It is to open consciously – as fully, patiently and lovingly as we are able – to the unceasing miracle of our 'ordinary' existence.

To live more simply is to live in harmony with the vast ecology of all life. It is to live with balance – taking no more than we require and, at the same time, giving fully of ourselves. To live with simplicity is by its very nature a 'life-serving' intention. Yet, in serving life, we serve ourselves as well. We are each an inseparable part of the life whose well-being we are serving. In participating in life in this manner, we do not disperse our energy frivolously but employ our unique capacities in ways that are helpful to the rest of life.

Voluntary simplicity, as a life-sensing and life-serving path, is neither remote nor unapproachable. This way of life is always available to the fortunate minority of the world who live in relative affluence. All that is required is our conscious choosing. This path is no farther from us than we are from ourselves. To discover our unique understanding and expression of this path does not require us to start from anywhere other than where we already are. This path is not the completion of a journey but its continual beginning anew. Our task is to open freshly to the reality of our situation as it already is and then to respond wholeheartedly to what we experience. The learning that unfolds along the path of our life-sensing and life-serving participation in the world is itself the journey. The path itself is the goal. Ends and means are inseparable.

A self-reinforcing spiral of growth begins to unfold for those who choose to participate in the world in a life-sensing and life-serving manner. As we live more consciously, we feel less identified with our material possessions and thereby are enabled to live more simply. As we live more simply and our lives become less filled with unnecessary distractions, we find it easier to bring our undivided attention into our passage through life, and thereby we are enabled to live more consciously.

Each aspect – living more voluntarily and living more simply – builds upon the other and promotes the progressive refinement of each. Voluntary simplicity fosters:

- A progressive refinement of the social and *material* aspects of life – learning to touch the Earth ever more lightly with our material demands; learning to touch others ever more gently and responsively with our social institutions; and learning to live our daily lives with ever less complexity and clutter.
- A progressive refinement of the *spiritual* or consciousness aspects of life – learning the skills of touching the world ever more lightly by progressively releasing habitual patterns of thinking and behaving that make our passage through life weighty and cloudy rather than light and spacious; learning how to 'touch and go' – to not hold on – but to allow each moment to arise with newness and freshness; and learning to be in the world with a quiet mind and open heart.

By simultaneously evolving the material and the spiritual aspects of life in balance with one another – allowing each to inform the other synergistically – we pull ourselves up by our own bootstraps. Gradually the experience of being infuses the process of doing.

Life-sensing and life-serving action become one integrated flow of experience. We become whole. Nothing is left out. Nothing is denied. All faculties, all experience, all potentials are available in the moment. And the path ceaselessly unfolds.

Notes

1   I am grateful to Arnold Mitchell for suggesting this illuminating example.
2   These questions were taken from an early version of the book *Taking Charge* (Simple Living Collective of San Francisco, 1977).

References

Maharshi, R. (1972) *The Spiritual Teaching of Ramana Maharshi*, Shambala Press, Berkeley, California, p56

Prescott, J. (1975) 'Body pleasure and the origins of violence', *Bulletin of Atomic Scientists*, November, pp10–20

Simple Living Collective of San Francisco (1977) *Taking Charge*, Bantam Books, New York

Voluntary Simplicity: Characterization, Select Psychological Implications and Societal Consequences

Amitai Etzioni

Voluntary Simplicity Characterization

Introduction

The idea that the overarching goal of capitalist economies needs to be changed and that achieving ever-higher levels of consumption of products and services is a vacuous goal, has been with us from the attractive life of the much poorer, pre-industrial artisan to that of the drudgeries of the more endowed industrial assembly-line worker.

In more recent times, criticism of consumerism was common among the followers of the counter-culture. They sought a lifestyle that both consumed and produced little, at least in terms of marketable objects, and sought to derive satisfaction, meaning and a sense of purpose from contemplation, communion with nature, bonding, mood-altering substances, sex and inexpensive products (Musgrove, 1974). Interestingly, Musgrove also notes the paradox that although the counter-culture is, 'marked by frugality and low consumption', it arises specifically in wealthy societies.

Over the years that followed, a significant number of members of Western societies embraced an attenuated version of the values and mores of the counter-culture. For example, studies by Ronald Inglehart beginning in the early 1970s found that, 'The values of Western publics have been shifting from an overwhelming emphasis on material well-being and physical security toward greater emphasis on the quality of life' (Inglehart, 1977). These 'quality of life' factors form what Inglehart calls 'post-materialist values', and include the desire for more freedom, a stronger sense of community, more say in government and so on. The percentage of survey respondents with clear post-materialist values doubled, from 9 per cent in 1972, to 18 per cent in 1991; those with clear materialist values fell more than half from 35 per cent to 16 per cent; those with mixed commitments moved more slowly, from 55 per cent to 65 per cent (Abramson and Inglehart, 1995). These trends were reported for most West European countries and, indeed, similar shifts occurred in most developed nations.

Personal consumption, however, continued to grow. For example, in the US between 1980 and 1990, per capita consumer spending (in inflation-adjusted dollars) rose by

21.4 per cent. The proportion of consumer spending devoted to dispensable ('luxury') items, such as jewellery, toys, video and audio equipment, rose in the same period from 6.78 per cent to 8.63 per cent (Lebergott, 1993). Meanwhile, the personal savings rate of Americans fell from 7.9 per cent in 1980, to 4.2 per cent in 1990 and has remained near this level ever since (US Department of Commerce, 1994).

Still, the search for alternatives to consumerism as the goal of capitalism continues to attract people. I focus here on one such alternative, referred to as 'voluntary simplicity'. Among those who have employed this term, or have done relevant studies, are Paehlke (1989), a professor of environmental and resource studies at Trent University in Ontario, Canada; Schor (1991), a professor of economics at Harvard University; and Leonard-Barton (1980), of the Harvard University Business School. Voluntary simplicity refers to the choice out of free will – rather than by being coerced by poverty, government austerity programmes or being imprisoned – to limit expenditures on consumer goods and services, and to cultivate non-materialistic sources of satisfaction and meaning.

As I have already suggested, the criticisms of consumerism and the quest for alternatives are as old as capitalism itself. However, the issue needs revisiting for several reasons. The collapse of non-capitalist economic systems has led many to assume that capitalism is the superior system and therefore to refrain from critically examining its goals, but capitalism does have defects of its own. Recent developments in former communist countries raise numerous concerns. Many in the East and West find that capitalism does not address spiritual concerns – such as the quest for transcendental connections and meanings – that they believe all people have (Handy, 1998). Furthermore, as so many societies with rapidly rising populations now seek affluence as their primary domestic goal, the environmental, psychological and other issues raised by consumerism are being faced on a scale not previously considered. For instance, the undesirable side effects of intensive consumer ism that used to concern chiefly highly industrialized societies, are now faced by hundreds of millions of Chinese, Indians and Koreans, among others. Finally, the transition from consumption tied to the satisfaction of what are perceived to be basic needs (secure shelter, food, clothing and so on) to consumerism (the preoccupation with gaining ever-higher levels of consumption, including a considerable measure of conspicuous consumption of status goods), seems to be more pronounced as societies become wealthier. Hence, a re-examination of this aspect of mature capitalism is particularly timely and needed. Indeed, the current environment of rising and spreading wealth might be particularly hospitable to moderate forms of voluntary simplicity.

This examination proceeds first by providing a description of voluntary simplicity, exploring its different manifestations and its relationship to competitiveness as the need and urge to gain higher levels of income is curbed. It then considers whether higher income and the greater consumption it enables produces higher contentment. This is a crucial issue because it makes a world of difference to the sustainability of voluntary simplicity: if voluntary simplicity is deprivational, it would require strong motivational forces for it to spread and persevere; on the other hand, if consumerism were found to be obsessive and maybe even addictive, then voluntary simplicity would be liberating and much more self-propelling and sustaining. The answer to the preceding question, and hence to the future of voluntary simplicity as a major cultural factor, is found in an application of Abraham Maslow's theory (Maslow, 1968) of human needs. It finds further reinforcement by examining the 'consumption' of a sub-category of goods whose supply and demand is not governed by the condition of scarcity in the postmodern era. The essay closes with a discussion of the societal consequences of voluntary simplicity.

Voluntary simplicity: Three variations

Voluntary simplicity is observable at different levels of intensity. It ranges from moderate levels (in which people downshift their consumptive rich lifestyle, but not necessarily into a low gear), to strong simplification (in which they significantly restructure their lives), to holistic simplification.

Downshifters

One, rather moderate, form of voluntary simplicity is practised by economically well off and secure people who voluntarily give up some consumer goods (often considered luxuries) they could readily afford, but basically maintain their rather rich and consumption-oriented lifestyle. For example, they 'dress down' in one way or another: wearing T-shirts, jeans and inexpensive loafers, and driving beat-up cars. The difference should be noted between people who voluntarily tone down their consumption (as measured by the amounts they spend on current consumption or save for future consumption) and those who exchange one set of goods for another, whose style is 'simple' but is actually just as (or even more) costly. Bruce Springsteen, for example, dresses in worn boots, faded jeans, and a battered leather jacket, and is said to drive a Ford (*New York Times Magazine*, 1996) and Urbach (1997) reports that:

> ... there has been a turn away from ... the 'overdesign' of the 1980s toward a world of 'simple' things. Instead of snazzy plates designed by architects, we have white dinnerware from Pottery Barn. In place of Christian Lacroix poufs and Manolo Blahnik pumps, we want Gap T-shirts, and Prada penny loafers. We like sport-utility vehicles, stain less-steel Sub-Zero refrigerators, Venetian blinds, retro electric fans, sturdy wooden tables – anything plain. Extravagance has surrendered to a look that is straightforward, blunt, unadorned.

Similarly, Viladas (1997) writes:

> In architecture and design today, less is more again. Houses, rooms and furnishings are less ornate, less complicated and less ostentatious than they were 10 years ago. Rather than putting their money on display, people seem to be investing in a quieter brand of luxury, based on comfort and quality.

Often this pattern is inconsistent and limited in scope, in that a person adhering to the norms of voluntary simplicity in some areas does not do so in many others. This moderate form of voluntary simplicity is symbolized by those who wear an expensive blazer with a pair of jeans, or drive a jalopy to their 50-foot yacht.

Brooks (1997) notes that, to those who are wealthy, rejecting the symbols of success is acceptable only, 'so long as you can display the objects of poverty in a way that makes it clear you are just rolling in dough'. This should not be surprising, for there are no widely recognized symbols of voluntary simplicity, and most people still desire to be recognized as successful by their community.

While downshifting is moderate in scope, and perhaps because it is moderate, it is not limited to the very wealthy. Some professionals and other members of the middle classes are replacing elaborate dinner parties with simple meals, pot-luck dinners, take-out food, or social events built around desserts only. Some lawyers are reported to have cut back on the billing hours race that drives many of their colleagues to work late hours and weekends in order to gain more income, a higher year-end bonus, and to incur the favour of the firms for which they work (Henley-Jensen, 1996). Some businesses have encouraged limited degrees of voluntary simplicity. For instance, in several work places there is one day (often Friday) in which employees are expected to 'dress down'. In some work places, especially on the West coast, employees may dress down any workday of the week. Asked 'days per week I can dress casually at my job', 52 per cent of Americans answered 'any day'; 18 per cent at least said 'one day a week' and only 27 per cent agreed with the statement 'can't dress casually at work', in *Public Perspective* (1997).

There seems to be no evidence that social scientists would find satisfactory, to show that downshifting is widely practised in some affluent societies, or that it has risen. There are some scraps of data but they, at best, can be said only to point in these directions. A study by the Merck Family Fund (1995) found that 28 per cent of a national sample of Americans, (and 10 per cent of the executives and professionals sampled – *NPR*, 1997), reported having 'downshifted' or voluntarily made life changes resulting in a lower income to reflect a change in their priorities, in the preceding five years. The most common changes were reducing work hours, switching to lower-paying jobs, and quitting work to stay at home (*New York Times*, 1995), which may – but do not necessarily – correlate with downshifting.

The same survey also found that 82 per cent of Americans felt that people buy and consume more than they need, suggesting that voluntary simplicity is viewed as commendable but not widely followed. Another survey, which also focused on sentiments rather than on changes in behaviour, found that three out of four working Americans would like 'to see our country return to a simpler lifestyle, with less emphasis on material success' (*Fortune*, 1989).

Strong simplifiers

This group includes people who have given up high-paying, high-stress jobs as lawyers, business people, investment bankers and so on, to live on less, often much less income. These people give up high levels of income and socio-economic status – one former Wall Street analyst restricts his spending to US$6000 a year. In another case, both members of a couple quit their jobs as high-paid executives in the telecommunications industry, and now live only on their savings – about US$25,000 per year – and spend their time writing and doing volunteer work (*NPR*, 1997). The *New York Times* (1995) reports,

> Choosing to buy and earn less – to give up income and fast-track success for more free time and a lower-stress life – involves a quiet revolt against the dominant culture of getting and spending. Enough small revolts are now taking place, researchers say, to make [the] phenomenon ... a major and growing trend of the '90s.

Strong simplifiers also include a large number of employees who voluntarily choose to retire before they are required to do so, accepting less income and lower pension payouts in order to have more leisure. It was reported that among men aged between fifty-five and sixty-four, 85.2 per cent were employed in 1960, while only 67.7 per cent were employed in 1990. Overall, the number of men and women who had retired by the age of sixty-three doubled between 1960 and 1990 from one-quarter to a half (*Boston Globe*, 1995). So, while it is clear that the aggregate number of people who retire early is increasing, some of this increase may well be involuntary as a result of forced retirement and downsizing and it is not known what the proportion of voluntary versus involuntary retirement is. Informal interviewing, including among the author's colleagues, suggests that a significant proportion of this increase is voluntary.

Ideas associated with voluntary simplicity are ideologically compelling, if not necessarily reflected in actual behaviour. In 1989, a majority of working Americans rated 'a happy family life' as a much more important indicator of success than 'earning a lot of money' – by an unusually wide margin of 62 to 10 per cent (*Fortune*, 1989). Also, numerous women and some men prefer part-time jobs or jobs that allow them to work at home, even if better paying full-time jobs are open to them, because they are willing to reconcile themselves to earning a lower income with being able to dedicate more time to their children and be at home when their children are there (*Boston Globe*, 1994). People who switch to new careers that are more personally meaningful but less lucrative also fall into this category. For instance, *Wall Street Journal* (1997) reports that 'a growing wave of engineers, military officers, lawyers, and business people ... are switching careers and becoming teachers'.

People who voluntarily and significantly curtail their income tend to be stronger simplifiers than those who only moderate their lifestyle, because a significant reduction of income often leads to a much more encompassing 'simplification' of lifestyle than selective downshifting of select items of consumption. While it is possible both for an affluent person to cease working altogether and still lead an affluent lifestyle, and for someone who does not reduce his or her income to cut spending drastically, one must expect that those who significantly curtail their income will simplify more than those who only moderate their consumption. Once people reduce their income, unless they have large savings, a new inheritance or some other such non-work related income, they must adjust their consumption once they choose to cut their income-producing labour.

People who adjust their lifestyle only or mainly because of economic pressures (having lost their main or second job, or for any other reason) do not qualify as voluntary simplifiers on the simple ground that their shift is not voluntary. One can argue that some poor people freely choose not to earn more and keep their consumption level meagre. To what extent such a choice is truly voluntary and how widespread this phenomenon is, are questions not addressed in this chapter. The discussion here focuses on people who had an affluent lifestyle and chose to give it up, for reasons that will become evident toward the end of the discussion.

In contrast, people who could earn more but are motivated by pressures – such as time squeeze – to reduce their income and consumption, do qualify because they could have responded to the said pressure by means other than simplifying – for instance, hiring more help (Schor, 1991). Moreover, there seems to be some pent-up demand for voluntary simplicity among people who report they would prefer to embrace such a lifestyle but feel that they cannot do so. *Gallup Poll Monthly*, reports that 45 per cent of Americans feel they have too little time for friends and other personal relationships, and 54 per cent feel they have too little time to spend with their children (Saad, 1995). Twenty-six per cent of Americans polled said they would take a 20 per cent pay cut if it meant they could work fewer hours (Gallup Organization, 1994). Presumably, these people face, or at least feel they face, only two choices: keep their current jobs or possibly face prolonged unemployment.

The simple living movement
The most dedicated, holistic simplifiers adjust their whole life patterns according to the ethos of voluntary simplicity. They often move from affluent suburbs or gentrified parts of major cities to smaller towns, the countryside, farms and less affluent or urbanized parts of the country – the Pacific Northwest is especially popular – with the explicit goal of leading a 'simpler' life. A small, loosely connected social movement, sometimes called the 'simple living' movement, has developed – complete with its own how-to books, nine-step programmes and newsletters – though Elgin (1981) suggests that, 'many persons experimenting with simpler ways of living said they did not view themselves as part of a conscious social movement'.

This group differs from the downshifters and even strong simplifiers not only in the scope of change in their conduct but also in that it is motivated by a coherently articulated philosophy. One source of inspiration is *Voluntary Simplicity*, originally written in 1981 by Duane Elgin, which draws on the traditions of the Quakers, the Puritans, transcendentalists such as Emerson and Thoreau, and various world religions to provide philosophical underpinnings to living a simple life. This philosophy is often explicitly anticonsumerist. Elgin (1981), for example, calls for 'dramatic changes in the overall levels and patterns of consumption in developed nations', adding that 'this will require dramatic changes in the consumerist messages we give ourselves through the mass media'. In 1997, The Public Broadcasting Corporation ran a special called 'Affluenza'. It was said to provide a treatment for an 'epidemic' whose symptoms are 'shopping fever, a rash of personal debt, chronic stress, overwork and exhaustion of natural resources'. It promised a follow-up on 'better living for less'. The Center for a New American Dream publishes a quarterly report on the same issues called simply 'Enough!'.

While one can readily profile the various kinds of simplifiers, there are no reliable measurements that enable one to establish the number of simplifiers of the three kinds or to determine whether their ranks are growing. One recent publication, though, estimates that nearly one out of four adult Americans (44 millions) are 'cultural creatives', who rank voluntary simplicity high among their values (Ray, 1997).

A comparative note

Voluntary simplicity is not a phenomenon limited to the contemporary American society. Indeed, while there seem to be no relevant comparative quantitative data, voluntary simplicity is somewhat more widespread in Western Europe, especially on the continent, than in the US. (Britain in this sense is somewhere between Western Europe and the US.) Many Europeans seem to be more inclined than Americans to sacrifice some income for more leisure time, longer vacations, visits to spas, coffee shops and pubs.

This is reflected in these countries' labour laws (which in turn reflect not merely power politics but are also an expression of widely held values), which provide for extensive paid vacation times, early closing hours for shops, closing of shops on Sundays and parts of Saturdays, subsidies allowing thousands to hang on to student life for many years, as well as extensive support for cultural activities (Schor, 1991). The collective result is that Western European societies produce less and consume less per capita than the American society in terms of typical consumer goods and services, but have more time for leisure, educational and cultural activities that are more compatible with voluntary simplicity than American society.

By contrast, consumerism seems to be powerful and gaining in many developing countries and former communist societies where consumerism is a much more recent phenomenon. In these societies the pursuit of washing machines, sexy lingerie and other luxury goods seems to be all the rage. *Chicago Tribune* (1994) reports that in China, 'Westernization and consumerism are rushing in so rapidly that even the Chinese ... are amazed... American democracy is nowhere present, but American consumerism is everywhere.' Similarly, *Boston Globe* (1996) reports that in Russia, 'a new wave of commercialism [is] sweeping the Russian capital'; and that one popular store in Moscow had brisk sales of US$1290 gold and silver seraphim, US$529 music boxes, and US$1590 plastic yule trees during the Christmas shopping season. 'Consumerism is thriving in Vietnam' (*Wall Street Journal*, 1994), where Honda motorbikes, mobile phones, fax machines and TVs are now popular in the cities. 'You can buy and rent laser discs..., young people drive sports cars, jewellery shops are bustling', these days in the once backward country of Burma (*Wall Street Journal*, 1996). And 'Despite their obvious affinity for Americana ... Israelis increasingly are questioning whether the dizzying construction of US-style shopping malls and American franchise shops is right for Israel', (*Los Angeles Times*, 1995), though they have long lost most of their pioneering spirit and have picked consumerism with a vengeance. In short, there seem to be very strong differences in the extent to which voluntary simplicity is embraced in various societies, affected by a myriad of economic, cultural and social factors not explored here.

Psychological Implications

Whatever the cultural differences, the ultimate question of whether or not voluntary simplicity can be sustained, and, moreover, greatly expand its reach among the citizens of various societies depends, to a significant extent, on the question of whether voluntary simplicity constitutes a sacrifice that people must be constantly motivated to make, or whether it is in itself a major source of satisfaction, and hence is self-motivating. To examine this issue the discussion next examines to what extent the opposite of voluntary simplicity – higher income and consumption – is a source of contentment. It then expands the answer by drawing on Maslow's observations about the hierarchy of needs.

Income and contentment

Consumerism is justified largely in terms of the notion that the more goods and services a person uses, the more satisfied a person will be. Early economists thought that people had a fixed set of needs, and they worried what would motivate people to work and save once their income allowed them to satisfy their needs. Subsequently, however, it was widely agreed that people's needs can be artificially enhanced through advertising and social pressures, and hence they are said to have, if not unlimited, at least very expandable consumeristic needs.

In contrast, critics have argued that the cult of consumer goods (of objects) has become a fetish that stands between people and contentment, one that prevents people from experiencing authentic expressions of affection and appreciation by others. Western popular culture is replete with narratives about fathers (in early ages), and recently of mothers as well, who slaved to bring home consumer goods – but far from being appreciated by their children and spouses found, often only late in their life, that their families would have preferred if the 'bread' winners would have spend more time with them and granted them affection and appreciation (or expressed their affection and appreciation directly, through attention and attendance, hugs and pats on the back, rather than mediate that expression by working hard and long to buy things). Arthur Miller's *The Death of a Salesman* is a telling example of this genre and, in 1997, Neil Simon was still belabouring this story in his play *Proposals*.

Social science findings, which do not all run in the same direction and have other well-known limitations, *in toto* seem to support the notion that income does not significantly affect people's contentment, with the important exception of the poor. For instance, Andrews and Withey (1976), found that the level of one's socio-economic status had meagre effects on one's 'sense of well-being' and no significant effect on 'satisfaction with life as a whole'. Similarly, Freedman (1978) discovered that levels of reported happiness did not vary greatly among the members of different economic classes, with the exception of the very poor who tended to be less happy than others. In a longitudinal study, Diener et al (1993) conducted interviews of the same individuals between 1971 and 1975 and again between 1981 and 1984. They found that at low incomes the amount of income does correlate strongly with happiness, but this correlation levels off soon after a comfortable level of income is attained. Second, that during the decade that passed between the interviews, the individual's income rose dramatically but the levels of happiness did not. These data emphasize the point that voluntary simplicity is an issue for those whose basic needs are met, and not for the poor or near poor.

Studies of the collective well-being of a country show that economic growth does not significantly affect happiness (though at any given time the people of poor countries are generally less happy than those of wealthy ones). Myers (1995) reports that in spite of the persistent belief among many Americans that more income will make them happier, this does not appear to be the case: while per capita disposable (after-tax) income in inflation-adjusted dollars almost exactly doubled between 1960 and 1990, 32 per cent of Americans reported that they were 'very happy' in 1993, almost the same proportion as did in 1957 (35 per cent). Although economic growth slowed since the mid-1970s, Americans' reported happiness was remarkably stable (nearly always between 30 and 35 per cent) across both high-growth and low-growth periods. Moreover in the same period, rates of depression, violent crime, divorce and teen suicide have all risen dramatically.

Recent psychological studies have made even stronger claims: that the more concerned people are with their financial well-being, the less likely they are to be happy. Kasser and Ryan (1993) found that, 'Highly central financial success aspirations ... were associated with less self-actualization, less vitality, more depression, and more anxiety.'

Lane (1993) summarizes the results of several studies as follows:

> ... [M]ost studies agree that a satisfying family life is the most important contributor to well-being... [T]he joys of friendship often rank second. Indeed, according to one study, an individual's number of friends is a better predictor of his well-being than is the size of his income. Satisfying work and leisure often rank third or fourth but, strangely, neither is closely related to actual income.

Lane (1993) reports that increases in individual income briefly boost happiness, but the additional happiness is not sustainable because higher income level becomes the standard against which people measure their future achievements.

These and other such findings raise the following question: if higher levels of income do not buy happiness, why do people work hard to gain higher income? The answer is complex. In part, high income in capitalistic consumeristic societies 'buys' prestige; others find purpose, meaning and contentment in the income-producing work per se. There is, however, also good reason to suggest that the combination of artificial fanning of needs and cultural pressures maintain people in consumeristic roles when these are not truly or deeply satisfying.

Voluntary simplicity works precisely because consuming less, once one's basic creature-comfort needs are taken care of, is not a source of deprivation, so long as one is freed from the culture of consumerism. Voluntary simplicity represents a new culture, one that respects work (even if it generates only low or moderate income) and appreciates modest rather than conspicuous or lavish consumption, but does not advocate a life of sacrifice or service (and in this sense is rather different from ascetic religious orders or some socialist expressions as in Kibbutzim). Voluntary simplicity suggests that there is a declining marginal satisfaction in the pursuit of ever-higher levels of consumption. It also points to sources of satisfaction in deliberately and voluntarily avoiding the quest for ever-higher levels of affluence and consumption, and instead making one's personal and social project the pursuit of other purposes. These purposes are not specifically defined other than that they are not materialistic. Indeed, just as some intrinsically find satisfaction in work and savings, rather than in purchasing power, so some voluntary simplicity followers find satisfaction in the very fact that they chose (and have not been forced to choose) a simpler lifestyle, and are proud of their choice. Moreover, as they learn to cultivate other pursuits, simplifiers gain more satisfaction out of life-long learning, public life, volunteering, community participation, surfing the internet, sports, cultural activities and observing or communing with nature. Often, as Elgin (1981) puts it: 'Voluntary simplicity [is] a manner of living that is more outwardly simple and inwardly rich.'

In each of these areas, some downshifters and even full-blown simplifiers slip back into consumerism, forever promoted by marketeers. Thus, internet surfers may feel that they 'need' to update their computer every other year or purchase various bells and whistles; and those engaged in sports feel they 'need' a large variety of expensive, ever-changing, fashionable clothing and equipment to enjoy their sport of choice. But a considerable number of members of the affluent classes in affluent societies – especially, it seems, societies that have been affluent for a while – find that they can keep consumerism under control and truly learn to cultivate lower cost sources of contentment and meaning. They enjoy touch football, a well-worn pair of sneakers, or take pride in their beat-up car.

An area that needs further study is the tendency of consumerism, when restrained, to leave a psychological vacuum which needs to be filled (the addiction of consumption is discussed, however, by Scitovsky, 1992; Schwartz, 1994). Those who try to wean themselves off consumerism often need support, mainly in the form of approval of significant others and membership in voluntary simplicity groups and sub-cultures. For instance, they may need to learn gradually to replace shopping with other activities that are more satisfying and meaningful. While some find shopping a chore, among the affluent, shopping is a major recreational activity, often done with peers – if not for actual consumption, then for collection and display purposes, anything from expensive knick-knacks to antiques. Numerous teenagers and many tourists also shop as a major recreational activity. Indeed, one must expect that for people who draw satisfaction from shopping per se, to curtail this activity may initially evoke an anxiety of unoccupied time that needs to be treated by developing a taste for and commitment to other activities.

The obsessive nature of at least some consumerism is evident in that there are people who seek to curb it but find it difficult to do so. Many people purchase things they later realize they neither need nor desire, or stop shopping only after they have exhausted all their sources of credit. (Reference is not to the poor, but to those who have several credit cards and who constantly 'max' them out.) In short, one expects that to convert a large number of people to voluntary simplicity requires taking into account that constant consumption cannot be simply stopped, that transitional help may be required, and that conversion is best achieved when consumerism it re placed with other sources of satisfaction and meaning.

Maslow, the haves and the have nots, and voluntary simplicity

Thus far, I have asked how difficult it is to sustain voluntary simplicity, given that it is common to assume that a high level of materialistic consumption is the main source of satisfaction driving people to work in capitalist societies. I suggested that evidence, while not all of one kind, tends to suggest that higher income does not lead to higher levels of satisfaction. Indeed, there is reason to suggest that the continued psychological investment in ever-higher levels of consumption has an addictive quality. People seek to purchase and amass ever more goods whether they need them (in any sense of the term) or not. It follows that voluntary simplicity, far from being a source of stress, is a source of a more profound satisfaction. This point is further supported by examining the implications of Maslow's theory to these points.

The rise of voluntary simplicity in advanced (or late) stages of capitalism, and for the privileged members of these societies, can be explained by a psychological theory of

Maslow (1968), who suggests that human needs are organized in a hierarchy. At the base of the hierarchy are basic creature comforts, such as the need for food, shelter and clothing. Higher up is the need for love and esteem. The hierarchy is crowned with self-expression. Maslow theorized that people seek to satisfy lower needs before they turn to higher ones, although he does not deal with the question of the extent to which lower needs have to be satiated before people move to deal with higher-level needs, or the extent to which they can become fixated on lower-level needs. He also does not draw a distinction between pro-social self-expression, for example arts, and antisocial self-expression, for instance abuse of narcotics. Some even suggest that Maslow's theory has been disproven because people do not seek to satisfy their needs in the sequence he stipulated. This may well be the case, but the only issue relevant here is whether people continue to invest heavily in the quest for 'creature comforts' long after they are quite richly endowed in such goods, and whether in the process their other needs are not well sated (even if they are not completely ignored). Western culture leaves little doubt that Maslow's thesis, if formulated in this way, is a valid one.

Maslow's thesis is compatible with the suggestion that voluntary simplicity may appeal to people after their basic needs are satisfied: once they feel secure that these needs will be attended to in the future, they may then objectively feel ready to turn more attention to their higher needs – although their consumeristic addiction may prevent them from noting that they may shift upwards, so to speak. Voluntary simplicity is thus a choice a successful corporate lawyer, not a homeless person, faces; Singapore, not Rwanda. Indeed, to urge the poor or near poor to draw satisfaction from consuming less is to ignore the profound connection between the hierarchy of human needs and consumption. It becomes an obsession that can be overcome only after basic creature-comfort needs are sated.

Consumerism has one, often observed, feature that is particularly relevant here. Consumerism sustains itself, in part, because it is visible. People who are 'successful' in traditional capitalist terms need to signal their achievements in ways that are readily visible to others in order to gain their appreciation, approval and respect. They do so by displaying their income by buying for themselves (or, in earlier days, for their wives) expensive status goods, as Vance Packard demonstrated several decades ago.

People who are well socialized into the capitalistic system often believe that they need income to buy things they 'need' (or that without additional in come they 'cannot make ends meet'). But examinations of the purchases of those who are not poor or near poor shows purchases of numerous items not needed in the strict sense ('could not survive', 'would end up in the street', 'would starve') but needed to meet status needs ('could not show my face'). This is the sociological role of Nike sneakers, leather jackets, fur coats, jewellery, fancy watches, expensive cars and numerous other such goods, all items that are highly visible to people who are not members of one's community, who do not know one personally. These goods allow people to display the size of their income and wealth without attaching their accountant's statement to their lapels.

In such a culture, if people choose a job or career pattern that is not in come-maximizing and voluntarily simplistic, they have no established means of signalling that they have chosen such a course rather than having been forced into it, and that they have not failed by the mores of the capitalist society. There are no lapel pins stating 'I could have, but preferred not to.' Voluntary simplicity responds to this need for status recognition without expensive conspicuous consumption by choosing lower-cost, but visible, consumer goods that enable one to signal that one has chosen, rather than been coerced into, a less affluent lifestyle.

This is achieved by using select consumer goods that are clearly associated with a simpler life pattern and are as visible as the traditional status symbols and/or cannot be afforded by those who reduced consumption merely be cause their income fell. For instance, those who dress-down as part of their voluntary simplicity, often wear some expensive items (a costly blazer with jeans and sneakers) or stylistic and far from inexpensive dress-down items (designer jeans), as if to broadcast their voluntary choice of this lifestyle. (Which specific consumption items signal voluntary simplicity versus coerced simplicity changes over time and from one sub-culture to another.) Brooks (1997) refers to this practice as 'conspicuous non-consumption'. In this way, voluntary simplifiers can satisfy what Maslow considers another basic human need, that of gaining the appreciation of others, without using a high – and ever escalating – level of consumption as their principle means of gaining positive feedback.

This idea is of considerable import when voluntary simplicity is examined not merely as an empirical phenomenon, as a pattern for social science to observe and dissect, but also as a set of values that has advocates and that may be judged in terms of the values' moral appropriateness. As I see it, the advocacy of voluntary simplicity addresses those who are in the higher reaches of income, those who are privileged but who are fixated on the creature-comfort level; it may help them free themselves from the artificial fanning of these basic needs and assist them in moving to higher levels of satisfaction. The same advocacy addressed to the poor or near poor (or disadvantaged groups or the 'have not' countries) might correctly be seen as an attempt to deny them the satisfaction of basic human needs. Consumerism, not consumption, is the target for voluntary simplicity.

Oddly, a major development being brought about by technological innovations makes it more likely that voluntary simplicity may be expanded, and that the less privileged and have-nots may gain in the process. In considering this development, I first discuss the nature of non-scarce objects and then turn to their implications for the reallocation of wealth.

Voluntary simplicity in the age of knowledge

Developed societies, it has been argued for decades, are moving from economies that rely heavily on the industrial sector to economies that increasingly draw upon the knowledge industry (Toffler, 1970; Bell, 1973). The scope of this transition and its implications are often compared to that which those societies experienced as they moved from farming to manufacturing. One should note that there is a measure of overblown rhetoric in such generalizations. Computers are, for instance, classified as a major item of the rising knowledge industry rather than traditional manufacturing. However, once a specific computer is programmed and designed, a prototype tested and debugged, the routine fastening of millions of chip-boards into millions of boxes to make PCs is not significantly different from, say, the manufacturing of toasters. And while publishers of books are now often classified as part of the knowledge industry and computers are widely used to manufacture books, books are still objects that are made, shipped and sold like other non-knowledge industry products. Acknowledging these examples of overblown claims is not to deny that a major transformation is taking place, only that its growth and scope are much slower and less dramatic than was originally expected. Indeed, given this slower rate of change, societies are able to face the ramifications in a more orderly manner.

The main significance of the rise of the knowledge age is that the resulting shrinking of scarcity enhances the possibility for the expansion of voluntary simplicity. This particularly important point is surprisingly rarely noted. Unlike the consumer objects that dominated the manufacturing age – cars, washers, bikes, televisions, houses (and computers) – many knowledge 'objects' can be consumed, possessed and still be had by numerous others, that is shared, at minimal loss or cost. Hence, in this basic sense, knowledge defies scarcity, thus reducing scarcity, which is a major driving principle behind industrial capitalist economies. Compare, for instance, a Porsche to Beethoven's *Ninth* (or a mini-van to a folk song). If an affluent citizen buys a particular Porsche (and all other billions of traditional consumer objects), this Porsche – and the resources that were invested in making it – are unavailable to any others (if one disregards friends and family). Once the Porsche is 'consumed', little of value remains. By contrast, the *Ninth* (and a rising number of other such knowledge objects) can be copied millions of times, enjoyed by millions at one and the same time, and it is still available in its full, original glory.

A commentator on a previous draft of this essay suggested that there is a measure of snobbism in showing a preference for the *Ninth* over a Porsche. But this is hardly the issue here; the same advantage is found when one compares an obscene rap song over a Volkswagen Beetle, or pornographic image on the internet to a low-income housing project. The criterion at issue is the difference between the resources that go into making each item and the extent to which it can be copied, consumed, and still be 'possessed' and shared.

True, even knowledge objects have some minimal costs – they need some non-knowledge 'carrier', have some limited material base, a disk, a tape or some paper, and most need an instrument – a radio for instance – to access them. However, typically, the costs of these material carriers are minimal compared to those of most consumer goods. While many perishable goods (consumer objects such as food or gasoline) are low in cost per item, one needs to buy many of them repeatedly to keep consuming them. In contrast, 'knowledge' objects such as music tapes or movie CDs can be enjoyed numerous times and are not 'consumed' (eaten up, so to speak). In that sense, knowledge objects have the miraculous quality of the bush Moses saw in Sinai: it burned but was not consumed.

What is said for music also holds for books and art. Shakespeare, in a 99-cent paperback edition issued in India is no less Shakespeare than in an expensive leather-bound edition, and above all, millions can read Shakespeare, and his writings are still available, undiminished, for millions of others. Millions of students can read Kafka's short stories, solve geographical puzzles, and study Plato, without any diminution of these items. That is, these sources of satiation are governed by laws that are the mirror opposite of those laws of economics that govern oil, steel and other traditional consumer objects from cellular phones to lasers.

Numerous games, but not all, are based on symbolic patterns and hence, like knowledge, objects are learned but not consumed and have only minimal costs. Children play checkers (and other games) with discarded bottle caps. Chess played by inmates, using figures made of stale bread, is not less enjoyable than a game played with rare, ivory hand-carved pieces. (One may gain a secondary satisfaction from the aesthetic beauty of the set and from owning such an expensive set, but these satisfactions have nothing to do with the game of chess per se.)

Similarly, bonding, love, intimacy, friendship, contemplation, communion with nature, certain forms of exercise (Tai Chi for instance, as distinct from the StairMaster), all can free one, to a large extent, from key laws of capitalistic economies. In effect, these sources of satisfaction, relationship based, are superior from this viewpoint to knowledge objects, because in the kind of relationships just enumerated, when one gives more, one often receives more and thus both sides (or, in larger social entities such as communities, all sides) are 'enriched' by the same 'transactions'. Thus, when two individuals who are learning to know one another as persons and become 'in vested' in one another during the ritual known as dating, neither is lacking as a result and often both are richer for it. (This important point is often overlooked by those who coined the term 'social capital' to claim that relations are akin to transactions.) Similarly, parents who are more involved with their children, often (although by no means always) find that their children are more involved with them, and both draw more satisfaction from the relationship. Excesses are far from unknown – for example, when some parents attempt to draw most of their satisfaction from their children, and sharply asymmetrical relations are also known in which one side exploits the other's dedication or love. Nonetheless, mutual 'enrichment' seems much more common.

The various sources of non-materialistic satisfaction listed here were celebrated by the counter-culture. However, voluntary simplicity differs from the counter-culture in that, even those highly dedicated to voluntary simplicity, seek to combine a reasonable level of work and consumption to attend to creature-comfort needs, with satisfaction from higher sources. The counter-culture tried to minimize work and consumption, denying attention to basic needs, and hence became unsustainable. To put it more charitably, it provided an extreme, path-blazing version for the voluntary simplicity that followed. Voluntary simplicity, while much more moderate than the lifestyle advocated by the counter-culture, reduces the need to work and shop as a result of fostering satisfaction from knowledge rather than consumer objects. As a result, it frees time and other scarce resources for further cultivation of non-materialistic sources of satisfaction, from acquiring music appreciation to visiting museums, from slowing down to enjoy nature to relearning the reading of challenging books to watching a rerun of a classical movie on television.

One should note that none of the specific sources of non-materialistic satisfaction are necessarily tied to voluntary simplicity. One can engage in a voluntarily simple life without enjoying music or nature, being a bonding person or a consumed chess player, an internet buff or a domino aficionado. However, voluntary simplicity does point to the quest for some sources of satisfaction other than the consumption of goods and services. This statement is based on the elementary assumption that people prefer higher levels of satisfaction over lower ones; hence if higher satisfaction is not derived from ever-higher levels of consumption, their 'excess' quest, that which is not to be invested in pursuit of unnecessary creature comforts, seeks to be invested elsewhere. It follows that while the specific activities that serve as the sources of non-materialistic satisfaction will vary, some such must be cultivated or voluntary simplicity may not be sustainable.

Social Consequences of Voluntary Simplicity

The shift to voluntary simplicity has significant consequences for society at large, above and beyond the lives of the individuals that are involved. A promising way to think about them is to ask what the societal consequences would be if more and more members of society, possibly an overwhelming majority, engage in one kind or another of voluntary simplicity. These consequences are quite self-evident for environmental concerns and hence need to be only briefly indicated; they are much less self-evident for social justice and thus warrant further attention.

Voluntary simplicity and environmentalism

There can be little doubt that voluntary simplicity, if constituted on a large scale, would significantly enhance society's ability to protect the environment. Moreover, if a significant number of people recast their lives according to the tenets of voluntary simplicity, even if they merely downshift rather than deeply recast their consumption, they are still likely to conduct them selves in ways that are more congenial to their environment than they were when they followed a life of conspicuous consumption.

First of all, voluntary simplifiers use far fewer resources than individuals engaged in conspicuous consumption. Simple means of transportation, such as bicycles, walking, public transportation, and even cars that are functional but not ostentatious, use significantly less energy, steel, rubber and other scarce resources than the cars that are currently often favoured. People who choose to restore old buildings or move to the countryside, tend, with notable exceptions, to use fewer scarce resources than those who build for themselves ostentatious residences, with expansive living rooms and extensive gardens even in hostile environments (for instance, green lawns next to the sea) and so on. And, of course, the more one purchases fashionable clothing, the more often it is discarded while still fully functional, which again 'burns up' scarce resources. From using fewer wrappings to simplifying gifts (especially during the Christmas season), simplifiers act in ways that are environmentally friendly, on the face of it.

In addition, voluntary simplifiers are more likely than others to recycle, build compost heaps and engage in other civic activities that indicate stewardship toward the environment, because simplifiers draw more of their satisfaction out of such activities than out of conspicuous consumption. Indeed, Stern (1984) shows that being committed to voluntary simplicity strongly correlates with being most apt to install insulation, buy solar heating equipment and engage in other energy-saving behaviours.

Elgin's *Voluntary Simplicity* (Elgin, 1981) is rife with environmental concerns; frequently he uses the terms 'voluntary simplicity' and 'ecological living' interchangeably. Other books on simple living also stress the connection between cutting back on consumption and helping the environment, including Alan Durning's *How Much is Enough?* (Durning, 1992), and Lester W. Milbrath's *Envisioning a Sustainable Society* (Milbrath, 1989).

The converse correlation holds as well. As people become more environmentally conscious and committed, they are more likely to find voluntary simplicity a lifestyle and ideology compatible with their environmental concerns. It should be noted, though, that while the values and motives of environmentalists and voluntary simpliflers are highly compatible, they are not identical. Voluntary simplifiers bow out of conspicuous consumption because they find other pursuits more compatible with their psychological needs, so long as their basic creature comfort needs are well sated. Environmentalists are motivated by concerns for nature and the ill effects of the growing use of scarce resources. Despite these different motivational and ideological profiles, often one and the same person is both a simplifier and an environmentalist. At least, those who have one inclination are supportive of those who have the other.

Voluntary simplicity and equality

The more broadly and deeply voluntary simplicity is embraced as a life style by a given population, the greater the potential for realization of a basic element of social justice, that of basic socio-economic equality. Before this claim is justified, a few words are needed on the meaning of the term equality, a complex and much-contested notion.

While conservatives tend to favour limiting equality to legal and political statutes, both those who are politically left and liberal favour various degrees of redistribution of wealth in ways that would enhance socio-economic equality. Various members of the left-liberal camp differ significantly in the extent of equality they seek. Some favour far-reaching, if not total, socio-economic equality in which all persons would share alike in whatever assets, income, and consumption are available, an idea championed by the early kibbutz movements. Others limit their quest for equality to ensuring that all members of society will at least have their basic creature comforts equally provided, a position championed by many liberals. The following discussion focuses on this quest for socio-economic, and not just legal and political, equality and on basic, creature-comfort equality rather than on a more comprehensive equality. (The debate about whether or not holistic equality is virtuous, and if it entails undercutting both liberty and the level of economic performance on which the provision of creature comforts depends is an important subject. However, this subject need not be addressed until basic socio-economic equality is achieved, and this has proven so far to be an elusive goal.)

If one seeks to advance basic socio-economic equality, one must identify sources that will propel the desired change. Social science findings and recent historical experience leave little doubt that ideological arguments (such as pointing to the injustices of inequalities, fanning guilt, introducing various other liberal and socialist arguments that favour greater economic equality), organizing labour unions and left-leaning political parties, and introducing various items of legislation (such as estate taxes and progressive income tax), ultimately do not have the desired result – namely significant wealth redistribution – in democratic societies. The most that can be said for them is that in the past they helped prevent inequality from growing bigger (Pechman, 1987). Moreover, in recent years, many of the measures, arguments and organizations that championed these limited, rather ineffectual efforts to advance equality could not be sustained, neither could they be successful after they have been greatly scaled back (for instance, note the changes in the Labour Party in the UK and the Democratic Party in the US in the mid-1990s). Moreover, for these and other reasons that need not be explored here, economic inequalities seem to have increased in many parts of the world. The former communist countries, including the USSR and China, where once a sacrifice of liberties was associated with a minimal but usually reliable provision of creature comforts, has moved to a socio-economic system that tolerates, indeed is built upon, a much higher level of inequality, one in which millions have no reliable source of creature comforts. Numerous other countries, which had measures of socialist policies, from India to Mexico, have been moving in the same direction. And in many Western countries social safety nets are under attack, being shredded in some countries and merely lowered in others. All said and done, it seems clear that if basic socio-economic equality is to be significantly advanced, it will need to be helped by some new or additional force.

Voluntary simplicity, if more widely embraced, might well be the best new source to help create the societal conditions under which the limited reallocation of wealth – needed to ensure the basic needs of all – could become politically possible. The reason is as basic and simple as it is essential: to the extent that the privileged (those whose basic creature comforts are well sated and who are engaging in conspicuous consumption) will find value, meaning and satisfaction in other pursuits, those that are not labour or capital intensive can be expected to be more willing to give up some consumer goods and some income. The 'freed' resources, in turn, can be shifted to those whose basic needs have not been sated, without undue political resistance or backlash.

The merit of enhancing basic equality in a society in which voluntary simplicity is spreading diverges from those that are based on one measure or another of coercion in several ways. First, those who are economically privileged are often those who are in power, who command political skills, or who can afford to buy support. Hence, to force them to yield significant parts of their wealth has often proven impractical, whether or not it is just or theoretically correct. Second, even if the privileged can somehow be made to yield a significant part of their wealth, such forced concessions leave in their wake strong feelings of resentment that have often led the wealthy to nullify or circumvent programmes such as progressive income taxes and inheritance taxes, or to support political parties or regimes that oppose wealth reallocation.

Finally, the record shows that when people are strongly and positively motivated by non-consumeristic values and sources of satisfaction, they are less inclined to exceed their basic consumption needs and more willing to share their 'excess' resources. Voluntary simplicity provides a culturally fashioned expression for such inclinations and helps enforce them, and it provides a socially approved and supported lifestyle that is both psycho logically sustainable and compatible with basic socio-economic equality.

A variety of public policies that seek to transfer some wealth and income from the privileged to those who do not have the resources needed to meet their basic needs, have been recently introduced. A major category of such policies are those that concern the distribution of labour, especially in countries in which unemployment is high, by curbing overtime, shortening the working week and allowing more part-time work.

Another batch of policies which seek to ensure that all members of society will have sufficient income to be able to satisfy at least some of their basic needs, approach the matter from the income rather than the work side. These include increases in the minimum wage, the introduction of the earned in come tax credit, and attempts at establishing universal health insurance, as well as housing allowances for the deserving poor.

In short, if voluntary simplicity is more and more extensively embraced as a combined result of changes in culture and public policies, by those whose basic creature comforts have been sated, it might provide the foundations for a society that accommodates basic socio-economic equality much more readily than societies in which conspicuous consumption is rampant.

Acknowledgements

The author would like to acknowledge Frank Lovett for his help with the research for this paper, and David Karp and Barbara Fusco for their editorial comments. I am particularly indebted to comments made by Professor Edward F. Deiner and David Myers.

References

Abramson, P. R. and Inglehart, R. (1995) *Value Change in Global Perspective*, University of Michigan Press, Ann Arbor

Andrews, F. M. and Withey, S. B. (1976) *Social Indicators of Well-Being: Americans' Perceptions of Life Quality*, Plenum Press, New York, pp254–255

Bell, D. (1973) *The Coming of Post-Industrial Society: A Venture in Social Forecasting*, Basic Books, New York

Boston Globe (1994) 'More mothers staying at home', *Boston Globe*, 18 December

Boston Globe (1995) 'To many, early retirement only a dream', *Boston Globe*, 29 October

Boston Globe (1996) 'Tinsel? Moscow buys that', *Boston Globe*, 25 December

Brooks, D. (1997) 'Inconspicuous consumption', *New York Times Magazine*, 13 April, p25

Chicago Tribune (1994) 'West meets East, with a vengeance', *Chicago Tribune*, 25 September, p13:2

Diener, E., Sandvik, E., Seidlitz, L. and Diener, M. (1993) 'The relationship between income and subjective well-being: Relative or absolute?', *Social Indicators Research*, vol 28, pp195–223

Durning, A. (1992) *How Much Is Enough? The Consumer Society and the Future of the Earth*, W. W. Norton, New York

Elgin, D. (1981) *Voluntary Simplicity*, William Morrow, New York

Fortune (1989) 'Is greed dead?', *Fortune*, 14 August

Freedman, J. L. (1978) *Happy People: What Happiness Is, Who Has It, and Why*, Harcourt Brace Jovanovich, New York

Gallup Organization (1994) *Telephone Survey of 1011 Americans*, 19–30 January

Handy, C. (1998) *The Hungry Spirit: Beyond Capitalism – A Quest For Purpose in the Modern World*, Broadway Books, New York

Henley-Jensen, R. (1996) 'Recycling the American dream', *ABA Journal*, American Bar Association, vol 82, April, pp68–72

Inglehart, R. (1977) *The Silent Revolution: Changing Values and Political Styles among Western Publics*, Princeton University Press, Princeton

Kasser, T. and Ryan, R. M. (1993) 'A dark side of the American dream: Correlates of financial success as a central life aspiration', *Journal of Personality and Social Psychology*, vol 65, p420

Lane, R. E. (1993) 'Does money buy happiness?', *Public Interest*, fall, p58

Lebergott, S. (1993) *Pursuing Happiness: American Consumers in the Twentieth Century*, Princeton University Press, Princeton, pp147–163, Appendix A

Leonard-Barton, D. (1980) 'Living lightly can mean greater independence, richer lives', *The Christian Science Monitor*, 21 October, p20

Los Angeles Times (1995) 'Ugly Americanization', Los Angeles Times, 2 September

Maslow, A. H. (1968) *Toward a Psychology of Being*, Von Nostrand, Princeton

Merck Family Fund (1995) *Yearning for a Balance: Views of Americans on Consumption, Materialism, and the Environment*, Merck Family Fund, Takoma Park, MD

Milbrath, L. W. (1989) *Envisioning a Sustainable Society: Learning Our Way Out*, State University of New York Press, Albany

Musgrove, F. (1974) *Ecstasy and Holiness: Counter-Culture and the Open Society*, Indiana University Press, Bloomington

Myers, D. G. (1995) 'Money won't buy you happiness', *Addiction Letter*, October, pp1, 3

New York Times (1995) 'Choosing the joys of a simplified life', *New York Times*, 21 September

New York Times Magazine (1996) 'The pop populist', *New York Times Magazine*, 26 January

NPR (1997) 'Voluntary simplicity', *NPR: Morning Edition*, 26 February

Paehlke, R. (1989) *Environmentalism and the Future of Progressive Politics*, Yale University Press, New Haven

Pechman, J. A. (1987) *Federal Tax Policy*, The Brookings Institute, Washington, DC

Public Perspective (1997) *Public Perspective*, August/September, p59

Ray, P. H. (1997) 'The emerging culture', *American Demographics*, February, pp29, 31

Saad, L. (1995) 'Children, hard work taking their toll on baby boomers', *Gallup Poll Monthly*, April, p22

Schor, J. B. (1991) *The Overworked American: The Unexpected Decline of Leisure*, Basic Books, New York

Schwartz, B. (1994) *The Costs of Living: How Market Freedom Erodes the Best Things in Life*, W. W. Norton, New York, pp154–162

Scitovsky, T. (1992) *The Joyless Economy: The Psychology of Human Satisfaction*, Oxford University Press, New York

Stern, P. (1984) *Energy Use: The Human Dimension*, Freeman, New York, pp71–72

Toffler, A. (1970) *Future Shock*, Random House, New York

Urbach, H. (1997) 'Hide the money', *New York Times Magazine*, 13 April, p25

US Department of Commerce (1994) *Statistical Abstract of the United States*, US Department of Commerce, Washington, DC, Tables 615, 619, 695.

Viladas, P. (1997) 'Inconspicuous consumption', *New York Times Magazine*, 13 April, p25

Wall Street Journal (1994) 'Consumerism is thriving in Vietnam, luring US companies despite poverty', *Wall Street Journal*, 13 May

Wall Street Journal (1996) 'Burma has healthy, up-to-date taste for consumer goods, survey shows', *Wall Street Journal*, 2 August

Wall Street Journal (1997) 'More career-switchers declare: "Those who can, teach"', *Wall Street Journal*, 8 April

Learning Diderot's Lesson: Stopping the Upward Creep of Desire

Juliet Schor

In the 18th century, the French philosopher Denis Diderot wrote an essay entitled *Regrets on Parting with My Old Dressing Gown*. Diderot's regrets were prompted by a gift of a beautiful scarlet dressing gown. Delighted with his new acquisition, Diderot quickly discarded his old gown. But in a short time, his pleasure turned sour as he began to sense that the surroundings within which the gown was worn did not properly reflect the garment's elegance. He grew dissatisfied with his study, with its threadbare tapestry, the desk, his chairs and even the room's bookshelves. One by one, the familiar but well-worn furnishings of the study were replaced. In the end, Diderot found himself seated uncomfortably in the stylish formality of his new surroundings, regretting the work of this 'imperious scarlet robe [that] forced everything else to conform with its own elegant tone'.

Today consumer researchers call such striving for conformity the 'Diderot effect'. And, while Diderot effects can be constraining (some people foresee the problem and refuse the initial upgrading), in a world of growing income the pressures to enter and follow the cycle are overwhelming. The purchase of a new home is the impetus for replacing old furniture; a new jacket makes little sense without the right skirt to match; an upgrade in china can't really be enjoyed without a corresponding upgrade in glassware. This need for unity and conformity in our lifestyle choices is part of what keeps the consumer escalator moving ever upward. And escalator is the operative metaphor: when the acquisition of each item on a wish list adds another item, and more, to our 'must-have' list, the pressure to upgrade our stock of stuff is relentlessly unidirectional, always ascending.

To avoid the pitfalls of Diderot, and the new consumerism more generally, requires a new consumer consciousness and behaviour. In this chapter, I outline nine principles to help individuals, and the nation, get off the consumer escalator. They are intended as remedies to the problems of too little saving, a harried lifestyle, a deteriorating environment, the growth of competitive spending and a lack of consumer control. I anchor my principles in the values of social equity and solidarity, environmental sustainability, financial security, and the need for more family and free time.

Principle 1: Controlling Desire

The first step in avoiding the Diderot effect is to become conscious of the process and the insidious ways it ensnares us. The second step is to rein in desire. Simple livers do it by creating more time and mental space in their lives, by simplifying and concentrating on what really matters to them. Religious leaders, knowing the weakness of the human will in resisting ever-present temptation, advise us to avoid 'occasions of sin'. Down-shifters stay away from malls and upscale shops, knowing that such exposure inevitably creates desire. They stop reading catalogues that come in the mail, chucking them directly into the recycle bin; consciously do less socializing with their shopaholic friends; and learn generally to recognize those first consumption stirrings so as to cut them off before they gain a full head of steam.

Another strategy is to emphasize product durability rather than novelty. If the things you buy last long enough for you to become emotionally attached to them, it will be easier to avoid buying new things. To succeed at this, you need to search for products that will continue to serve you well, both because they will not go out of fashion and because they are physically durable. Are the manufacturers stable, in case repairs are necessary? Is the fabric long-lasting? Will it age well as you age, becoming over time a comfortable and comforting friend, like Diderot's well-worn furnishings? Similarly, it is important to think through the long-term consequences of all significant purchases. If you buy the digital tape deck, will you be led into replacing your tape library with new versions that more fully exploit the capabilities of the new system? If you upgrade the computer, how much of your old software will be usable? If you buy your child a starter set for a Brio train, are you willing to pay for all those expensive add-on pieces? If you start a new sport, ask yourself how much you'll eventually pay out for equipment, lessons and fees. (And why has it become so imperative to take expensive lessons when picking up a new sport? Maybe a programme of relaxation might improve your tennis game more than paying for time with the club pro.) Doing without a contemplated purchase for a certain time may be a good test of whether in fact you need it. Will you really be different from almost everyone else and use that exercise machine for more than the first few months?

Martha Evans, a former accountant, describes her own version of the consumer escalator. 'There was a point where I was making a little more money at work, and I was very excited that it was coming. And then it came, and I could hear myself doing this mental tick-tick-tick: I can get this, this, this, and this, this, this. I'm sure it had to do with clothing, with maybe a trip, probably with some household improvements. I really need a kitchen, luxury things that I didn't have.' But before too long, Martha learned to control these thoughts. 'I would go through a mental exercise where I would say, "I simply have to stop wanting this, because I know that if I get this, that that's not going to be the end of it." I could tell where I was getting carried away wanting things, and there was not going to be any end to this wanting.'

Principle 2: Creating a New Consumer Symbolism: Making Exclusivity Uncool

Integral to the upward creep is the upscale itself. The new consumerism has taught affluent Americans to covet, and then buy, the Jil Sander suit, the Stickley chair, the SubZero fridge and the Coach briefcase (with a Montblanc and Filofax to go inside). When they display these products, they project taste, individuality and exclusivity. But isn't it odd that we must have the things certain others have to establish our credentials as a distinctive person – to avoid being seen as just like everybody else?

Some consumer symbols have become fair game for public scrutiny. Politicians and the media have attacked heroin chic and the anorexic images prevalent in fashion photography. But the symbolism of exclusivity and luxury is still off-limits. No one challenges the *New York Times* for devoting its second page to ads for extraordinarily expensive items affordable to only the top few per cent of society. There is as yet no social stigma associated with owning or displaying exclusive products. Indeed, it is rarely even noticed that companies advertise these commodities to a mass consumer audience, large numbers of whom cannot afford them and will go into debt, sacrifice everyday needs or turn to crime in order to obtain them. When we stop to think about it, what message are we sending here? That being middle class isn't good enough? That it's okay to wreck your personal or family finances to confirm your social acceptability? That if you are a low-wage earner, you are condemned to a life of inadequacy?

What if public attitudes to status consumption started changing, so that people saw as tacky attempts to buy their way into a personal image of exclusivity? What if a pattern of upscale purchasing became not something to aspire to but something 'uncool' in its inegalitarianism? What if wearing the US$2500 Jil Sander suit was no longer looked upon as power dressing but as overkill? What if, when we looked at a pair of Air Jordans, we thought, not of a magnificent basketball player, but of the company's deliberate strategy to hook poor inner-city kids into an expensive fashion cycle? What if more people began thinking like Jennifer Lawson's son, who thinks new clothing is socially ostentatious?

Awareness is the first step in breaking down these associations and immunizing ourselves against symbolic spending triggers. As marketers know full well, these symbols are powerful precisely because they reside partly in the realm of the unconscious. The see-want-borrow-and-buy sequence often does not survive the bright light of day. Denial also helps us live with our ambivalent (sometimes guilty) feelings about consuming exclusively or striving for distinction.

If there's something you really want but don't actually need, there's a good chance that a recurring symbolic fantasy is attached to it. A faster computer? The dream of getting more work done. A remodelled kitchen? The hope of eating proper family dinners. A luxury car? Making vice-president. Laying bare the fantasy illuminates the often tenuous link between the product and the dream, thereby reducing the power of the object. When identity and consumption are linked, getting too deliberate spoils the symbolism. After doing the cosmetics research, I found myself unable to buy designer-brand cosmetics, not only because I knew I was wasting my money but also because it made me feel foolish.

Not that these symbolic meanings are easy to break down. They are woven deeply into the fabric of our everyday lives. We have profound, if often unrecognized, emotional connections to commodities. On the other hand, Americans will not gain control over their spending habits until they begin to confront that symbolism head on. As the number of prestigious products grows, the financial pressures on people increase. Less and less of what we have remains mere background – things valued for their function, for what having them to use adds to our daily lives, rather than for what they convey about us as quality human beings. The classic pantheon of house, car and wardrobe has been joined by all manner of new status symbols: stoves come in restaurant quality to signal the requisite level of commitment to good cooking (for the really upscale, there's the US$10,000+ Aga, the model favoured by the Queen of England); wooden swing sets become an aesthetic (class) item that status-conscious association trustees are ready to go to court over; water (once a free, abundantly available non-commodity) has become classed into brand names, with a select few becoming status symbols; and a recent ad suggests that if no one has mentioned the distinctiveness of your garage door lately, it's time to have it redone. It is only by becoming aware of the thousand and one little ways that consumption is connected to distinction and status that we can begin to break down those barriers and consume in less socially exclusive (and expensive) ways.

Principle 3: Controlling Ourselves: Voluntary Restraints on Competitive Consumption

Imagine the following. A community group in your town organizes parents to sign a pledge agreeing to spend no more than US$50 on athletic shoes for their children. The staff at your child's day-care centre requests a US$75 limit on spending for birthday parties. The local school board rallies community support behind a switch to school uniforms. The PTA gets 80 per cent of parents to agree to limit their children's television watching to no more than one hour per day.

Do you wish someone in your community or at your children's school would take the lead in these or similar efforts? I think millions of American parents do. Television, shoes, clothes, birthday parties, athletic uniforms – these are areas where many parents feel pressured into allowing their children to consume at a level beyond what they think is best, want to spend, or can comfortably afford. In contrast to the fashionable ideology that a 'free market' is the best response to society's needs because it allows the freest expression of the public will, in these examples the self-control of a group of people leads to a better outcome for everyone. Voluntary restrictions on individual liberty can make sense. Giving up your right to spend US$100 on athletic shoes *may* make you – and your child – better off.

The foregoing examples are the obvious, and easy, ones, in part because they involve adult spending on children. But if the argument of this book is correct – that America suffers from too much competitive consumption – there should be plenty of other areas where collective restrictions would work.

What about adults spending on themselves? Situations in which people spend together come readily to mind. Everyone agrees that it's reasonable to put limits on the office Christmas gift exchange. Why not do the same for holiday spending within families? While some families already explicitly set limits, many do not but would appreciate the chance to reduce the value of both what they spend and receive. Voluntary agreements to limit the amounts spent almost certainly make people better off on other occasions as well: weddings, birthdays, baby showers. So too with various types of clubs. How many book club members would prefer to put new hardbacks off-limits and confine their choices to paperbacks? Isn't it better when a wine-tasting group operates with spending guidelines?

Other areas of social spending are also ripe for collective restraints. Do you have a group of friends with whom you regularly get together? What about keeping expenditures for an evening below a certain level? Try second- rather than first-run movies, or patronizing only restaurants where the entrees are below a certain price. Sometimes these customs evolve naturally, particularly when only a few people are involved and they know each other's financial situations. But at other times, restraint fails and spending can gradually escalate. It can be embarrassing to raise the issue; we fear we may be signalling that we are petty, cheap, or in an inferior economic position. If it were customary to be explicit about spending limits, the pressure on the individual would be lifted. Frugality could become a socially acceptable consideration.

The most difficult type of situation arises when private spending supports a previously developed social need for the product. I would prefer not to get a cell phone, an answering machine or a home-based fax. But as these products become universal, I can be seen as refusing to contribute my share to the new scheme of things if I resist adding them to my own stock of stuff.

I believe there are now many middle-class Americans who would welcome a deceleration or even a decline in the consumption standards of their reference groups. They don't want to give up their friends. They don't want to risk being seen as not 'one of us'. But they would like more financial leeway. Would you prefer that your associates not replace their cars too frequently? Or that your friends not remodel their kitchens, so you don't become ashamed of your own? Would you like to travel in circles in which it is normal not to have a house with a downstairs bathroom for guests? Do you wish that your neighbours dressed their children in hand-me-downs or with patches on the knees of their jeans? Do you wish you didn't feel like your child needs the latest computer software at home?

In these kinds of examples – cell phones, clothing standards, kitchen remodelling – explicit collective agreements are less workable. But more subtle shifts in the culture of consumption can achieve similar results. Steering the dinner party conversation around to these questions might get your friends thinking. Devoting your annual Christmas letter to issues of 'stabilizing' consumption might start a conversation among your correspondents. Organizing a clothing swap among your friends is a perfect opportunity for an initial discussion about spending on clothes. Getting the PTA to organize forums about lifestyles and values allows the community to work through the issues together.

In the past, collective limitations on spending were much more powerful. In traditional societies, various spending taboos and invocations of the 'evil eye' restrained competitive consumption. In Europe and North America, dress, housing and other types of consumption have been restricted. And throughout history, religious ideology has served as an additional brake: nearly all the world's religions have stressed the sacredness of simplicity and moderation. Coveting our neighbour's belongings was so important a no-no that it qualified as one of the Ten Commandments; when in the movie *Wall*

Street the antagonist announces that 'greed is good', he is talking about one of the seven deadly sins. But by the early 20th century, these restraints had been largely lifted. The notion of sufficiency, which long had regulated consumption, was discarded in the face of the promise of mass prosperity. Spending, even spending to excess, was extolled as good for the ego, if not for the soul. Consumerism became the new, therapeutic belief system. Religious, folk and legal impediments to consumption declined markedly. Most insidious of all, aggressive spending was made patriotic. It spread the wealth, we were told, creating jobs for the unemployed as well as profits for American industry. The movies contributed to the shift in values. An inclination to spend too much was cast as an attractive trait. If it was a fault, it was the fault of an open, honest, generous person; frugality was portrayed as the proclivity of a small, pinched personality. The result, at the century's end, is that almost half the population of the world's richest country say that they have just enough income to get by.

The hallmark of the kinds of controls I have been talking about is that they are mainly voluntary. If people don't welcome them, they won't work. They also need to be instituted collectively. While individuals *can* buck the system, few of us are so inclined. Because consuming is a social act, so too is consuming differently. This is one lesson we can learn from the Pacific Northwest, where simple living is going mainstream. Feeling like a part of a trend is a lot more comfortable than being an oddball. The social support possible in places like Seattle makes a world of difference. While the Northwest may have a culture and history more conducive to downshifting than, say, the culture of New York City, the initiatives I am suggesting are possible anywhere. Within the space of a few short years, millions of Americans joined a movement to turn off their televisions for a week in April. Pledging to limit purchases of athletic shoes, or Christmas gift giving, or birthday party competitions is equally possible.

Principle 4: Learning to Share: Both a Borrower and a Lender Be

The latest trend in lawn mowers is big and expensive – the riding mower. Here the dynamics are pretty clear. You saw your neighbour roll out his last summer. He first got the idea from his cousin, who was crowing about it. Of course, you really *need* the riding mower. You wouldn't have bought it otherwise, right? The question is, do you really need it 24 hours a day, seven days a week? Or could you be satisfied just having it when you want to mow?

Instead of joining the stampede for expensive riding mowers, what if you and a dozen of the families on the street got together and bought a couple of mowers for everyone's use? Call it a product 'library'. Set up on the model of the public library, it gives people the functional benefits of products without having to purchase them privately. How about a toy exchange? Your children could get the variety in toys they need, and you wouldn't have to be continually buying new ones. Or an athletic equipment library: you could try out cross-country skiing for a season *before* investing in your own skis. Lending libraries make sense for products that are not in use all the time (mowers, snow blowers, boats, athletic equipment) and for relatively inexpensive products that may be of limited usefulness to the individual but do not wear out quickly (books, toys, videos, CDs, clothes). The specifics of the library would vary with the product. With expensive items like mowers, a common fund would purchase the products. Members of the programme would be responsible for keeping the mower in good shape and returning it on time (or be fined). Reservations could be required for popular times. Mowers could be kept in private garages, to make access easy. For smaller products, like toys, donations may be sufficient to get the programme going.

Why not just rely on rentals or secondhand shops for these products? For some products, rental and secondhand markets do work. But for others, a lending library approach is better. Because people pay into the common fund and are part owners, they take better care of the products. This is especially important for expensive equipment, such as mowers, snow blowers, boats and some athletic equipment. Plus, there's the added savings of forgoing the rental chain's profit. For inexpensive products such as toys or CDs, an exchange (housed for convenience at the local library, the town hall, or another public building) allows frequent trading, avoids the cumbersome steps of selling and buying, and allows you to use popular items again and again.

The fact that such initiatives have been very limited suggests they need a jump-start. Public libraries, which have already branched out into videos and CDs, might begin by extending the repertoire of products they provide. Local governments could provide technical assistance for neighbourhood groups to get going. In low-income communities, government monies could justifiably be used for the initial purchase of some products.

Would lending libraries for products other than books actually work? They would naturally be susceptible to the tensions that can come with cooperative efforts, such as squabbling and freeloading. Moreover, Americans tend to be highly possessive, preferring to own above all else. But the success of libraries suggests that this mentality does not extend to all commodities and that cooperative efforts can succeed. Lending libraries would help people save money, use fewer environmental resources, and free up closet and garage space. They may also increase neighbourliness – sharing a mower with your neighbours is likely to lead to other kinds of social interaction. They're at least worth a try.

Principle 5: Deconstruct the Commercial System: Becoming an Educated Consumer

The next time you watch TV, try an experiment. Instead of zapping the commercials, or watching them mindlessly, try to deconstruct them. Watch the Jeep drive out to the edge of the Grand Canyon. What do you see? A chance to get closer to nature? Freedom and individuality? Or a gas-guzzling commodity that fills the air with smog, helps turn wilderness into cement, and is a leading cause of accidental death? As the Swoosh swooshes by, consider whether Nike really stands for women's power, independence and hipness, as it wants us to believe. Or is the US$2 million a day it spends promoting women in sports a sham in light of the US$1.60 a day it gives its female Vietnamese workers? As you look closely at the ad, ask yourself whether you really want to join a fashion trend that hooks lower-income youth into products that their parents cannot possibly afford. Or would you rather join an international community of people who are urging us to 'Just Do It' – 'it' being a boycott of Nike? When De Beers's diamond ads come on, with the beautiful musical backdrop of violins, think hard about what the imperative of a 'carat or more' ('so rare it will be worn by fewer than 1 per cent of women') really means. If you, along with the rest of the 99 per cent, haven't yet received one from your spouse, are you really unloved? And if you do wear that dazzling rock, how is it making your friends feel?

Once you've learned to 'read' a commercial, to anaesthetize yourself to its subtle messages, move on to other aspects of the commercial system. Investigate the commodities that you buy and use. Learn what they didn't teach you in school. And figure out what you *did* learn.

Even in the days before schools became adjunct marketing arms of corporations (with Channel One and force-feeding of commercials, educational materials produced by corporations, and school buses covered with ads), students were absorbing an apparently upscale consumer attitude. Indeed, one of the ironic results of our educational system is that the people with the highest degrees are the most susceptible to paying extra for designer names, status and prestige. They shop more, are more influenced by their reference groups, and feel more pressure to keep up. Perhaps that's because school has taught us more about how to want things than about how to choose wisely. But what if that started to change? What if we became interested in new kinds of consumer education, learning about a product's 'total package' and not just the price and the fancy features? To become good consumers, we need to know more about how products are produced and what tax the manufacturing process levies on the planet, as well as about the health, safety and environmental impacts of a product and its true long-term costs. We need to get beyond the seductive but superficial appearance of the commodities on the airwaves and the shelves.

Americans love Gap. We load up on Gap jeans, pocket-Ts, and accessories and aspire to the Gap look. In many circles, BabyGap gets as many oohs and aahs at a shower as frilly embroidered dresses did in an earlier era. Even that bastion of conservative dress, the New York Stock Exchange, donned khakis for its first-ever casual Friday. How many of us stop to consider, before buying these fashionable products, where and how they are made? We prefer not to think about the fact that they are produced by women (and even children) slaving away for nearly nothing in sweatshops where unions are often outlawed and work-place control is draconian. The Nike employees who make the products we just 'have to have' cannot even properly feed themselves, much less buy the shoes they produce. The globalization of the world economy has produced, in industry after industry, a proliferation of low-wage sweatshops, far out of view of the final consumer. Clothes, shoes, toys, knick-knacks, furniture – you name it, sweatshops are fuelling our consumer boom. These issues have attracted some public attention, and some companies are making efforts to police conditions in the sweatshops with which they contract. They are more interested in PR, however, than lasting change. The companies' rationalization that, no matter how low the wages the workers are better off than they would be having no job at all, is just not the point. What the employees need, and deserve, is a job *and* a pay cheque that supports them. Companies and consumers alike need to wean themselves off low wages and cheap production costs.

The ways in which consumption degrades the environment is another area we need to educate ourselves about. Americans know very little about the ecological impacts of their lifestyles beyond the obvious (cars are bad, recycling is good, excessive packaging is bad). We are oblivious to some of our most damaging consumer habits: air-conditioning, jet travel, meat, household toxins and the sheer volume of resources consumed each day (120 pounds). We are unaware that even seemingly innocuous products like coffee (new growing methods are reducing species diversity) and hamburgers (cattle grazing is causing desertification, and pesticides for corn feed are damaging human reproductive systems) have significant impacts. A necessary first step toward becoming an educated consumer is to learn about the impact your consumption has on the environment. Only then can you make responsible and informed choices.

To become educated, you cannot rely solely on the information that manufacturers provide. As I am writing this, a jury has found Dow Corning guilty of withholding information about the adverse health effects of breast implants. The tobacco and asbestos companies have done the same thing. In other industries (chemical, pharmaceutical, bioengineering, agribusiness, furniture and automobiles, to name only a few), health and safety studies are sometimes faulty, incomplete or non-existent. With the exception of a few federally mandated measures (gas mileage, energy-use information on appliances), environmental impacts are rarely revealed to the consumer. Companies do not want to uncover or publicize negative information about the products they sell.

How can consumers get the facts without time-consuming searches through literature that is often too technical for the layperson? Historically, consumers have become informed by creating consumer organizations and movements. By banding together and putting public pressure on manufacturers and retailers, consumer organizations help protect people from dangerous products, unscrupulous selling practices and insufficient information. But the few familiar examples (Ralph Nader's fight for auto safety in the 1960s, Consumers Union's *Consumer Reports)* point up how rare independent consumer organizations are today. Most of the product information we have is sponsored indirectly by the manufacturers, through magazines that review products (autos, computers, home furnishings, fashion) but are supported by industry ad revenues.

Americans also need to learn how *not* to spend – how to budget, plan their finances, be patient and save. Most American households don't have a family budget, and those who do tend not to follow them. The saving ethic has become so alien that many of us think of it in terms only of paying less than full price – as 'getting a good deal'. Financial management is neglected by the US education system. My Dutch students were shocked to find that their American counterparts are not taught in school how to save. While we've got the energy for a raging controversy about sex education, we have paid almost no attention to the ignorance of our youth when it comes to practising 'safe spending'. All schools should offer a basic course in money and spending. In addition to straightforward material such as the economics of compound interest and how to evaluate the long-term consequences of different savings patterns, young people also need to be taught about basic monthly expenses, how to make and stick to a budget, how to calculate what it takes to rent an apartment, and the true costs of owning a car. They need to learn long-term planning, how to prepare for education expenses, home-ownership, and the costs of raising children. They need to be exposed to basic facts about the finances of retirement, life insurance and disability.

We must also teach our kids to be savvy consumers, forewarning them especially about the risks of credit cards. They must know that when they buy on credit, they may end up paying two, three or four times the sticker price. They need to be able to figure out, *in the store,* how much more. Other important lessons include learning to arm themselves against the temptations of easy money, delaying gratification, and – because young people have been shown to be particularly vulnerable to the pitches of ad men – deconstructing the powerful symbolism that the commercial culture throws at them every day.

For the generations of adults who missed this course, remedial education is in order. Many of us, and especially women, entered adulthood knowing little or nothing about the value of money or how to manage it. We failed to realize that our understanding about how and when to use money can make or break our lives. We need to become conscious of the financial costs of the work-and-spend lifestyle: job-related expenses, beyond the obvious costs of child care and transportation; of the ways in which time and money substitute for each other; and of how stress and exhaustion almost inevitably lead to spending pressures.

Principle 6: Avoid 'Retail Therapy': Spending Is Addictive

Millions of Americans use consuming as a way to fight the blues, to savour a happy moment, to reward themselves, to enhance self-esteem or to escape from boredom. Indeed, consumerism is so pervasive that 'retail therapy' is a response to just about *any* mood state or psychological problem. But it carries considerable risk. As with consumption of drugs, alcohol and food, millions of Americans are experiencing spending control problems. Some have developed a psychological disorder called 'compulsive buying tendency'. While reports of oniomania, or buying mania, can be found in psychiatric texts in the early part of the 20th century, experts believe its prevalence has increased markedly in recent years, although no hard numbers exist.

Conforming to the stereotype, the paradigmatic case of compulsive buying tendency is a 36-year-old educated woman whose problem developed in her late teens. (Not a likely reader of this book, by the way, because books are at the bottom of the acquisition chain, and even if she bought it, she probably wouldn't read it: it's the act of acquiring that matters.) Compulsives prefer clothes, and after clothes, shoes, jewellry, and make-up – classic appearance- or identity-related items. By the time the typical sufferer comes in for help, she is using half her household income to pay the bills and a variety of severe personal problems have surfaced.

No one knows exactly how many Americans suffer from compulsive buying tendency. Ronald Faber of the University of Minnesota classified between 1.8 and 6 per cent of his sample (or up to 15 million) as suffering or at serious risk (Faber and O'Guinn, 1992). Using the same test on a group of mostly college students in Arizona, Allison Magee estimated 15–16 per cent (Magee, 1994). (We know the tendency is greater among youth.) On the other hand, clinically defined compulsives may not be fundamentally different from 'normal' consumers. They're just the extreme cases. Millions of ordinary people also exhibit high 'generalized urges to buy'. Indeed, an innocuous form of compulsive buying appears to afflict one-quarter of us. This should probably come as no surprise in a country where 41 per cent of the population age 22–61 (and nearly half of all young adults) say that 'shopping makes me feel good'.

The downshifter Patty Fuller fit the innocuous buyer profile. Because her buying was well within the limits of her substantial income, she never faced financial difficulties. 'I used to go mall shopping,' she says. 'My husband called it "medicinal spending." It used to take up a lot of my time. Everybody knew I was a shopaholic. It was the joke, when Patty comes to visit, you take her shopping. I loved it. It was my hobby.' Like the clinical cases, Patty could lose interest in what she bought. Sometimes she'd buy clothes she never wore. 'Or I'd wear them once. I gave a lot of stuff away to friends, just take it, take it. And I'd buy gifts for relatives and friends.' Eventually the combination of overwork and shopping led her to a radical change of lifestyle. 'I don't go into malls anymore.' And she doesn't give Christmas gifts. 'Because it just doesn't feel right anymore. When you sit down and think about the meaning of life, it's just not mainstream America, it's not what we purport in this country.'

How to avoid even the appearance of a problem? First, *analyse* your personal habits. People who score high on the compulsive spending scale also score high on the see-want-borrow-and-buy sequence. They are more oriented to fantasy and daydreaming. They are more materialist. And they tend to believe that consuming is a mark of social status. Figure out what kind of consumer you are. Second, avoid excessive exposure to tempting situations. New York, the nation's fashion capital, is known as a breeding ground for compulsive buyers. (Of course, with the country turning into one enormous shopping arcade, open 24 hours a day, avoidance is getting harder.) Finally, avoid impulse buying. It's a common habit, and not just for potato chips and Twinkies. Try locking up the plastic for six months and use only cash so that the costs of purchases will seem real. Don't use cards over the phone or on the internet; send a cheque instead. If you desperately want something, force yourself to sleep on it for a night, or, if it's a major item, a week. Buy only from lists thoughtfully constructed before going to stores. Make yourself wait for things so that you appreciate them. Participate in Buy Nothing Day, the annual day-after-Thanksgiving ritual of zero shopping that is fast becoming an international movement. Take the money you would have spent and put it in the bank. Or better yet, commit yourself to an automatic withdrawal savings plan – the method that, for most people, is the only way to ensure that saving actually happens. Then make sure your best friend has done the same.

Of course, the vast majority of us are not in danger of becoming compulsive consumers with a stash of cubic zirconia necklaces in the basement. (Television shopping is a magnet for problem over-consumers.) Nor are we likely to receive, as Patty Fuller did, a cautionary newspaper clipping from her mother-in-law with the headline 'Woman loses husband while shopping in the mall'. But we can all learn from the experiences of compulsive buyers. Spending can be addictive. It can absorb your consciousness, become a substitute for other activities and start to take over your life.

Principle 7: Decommercialize the Rituals

Even for the most determined among us, holidays and life rituals represent a formidable challenge to frugality. In an era when bar and bat mitzvahs cost as much as weddings, and weddings require practically a trust fund to manage, control can seem out of reach. Even families who want something simple and shun ostentation find themselves almost inexplicably shelling out thousands, or tens of thousands. There's a built-in upward creep to the process that catering managers put to work for themselves.

Large numbers of Americans express support for downscaling and decommercializing our ritual celebrations. A recent poll conducted by the Center for a New American Dream found that 39 per cent of Americans would 'welcome lower holiday spending and less emphasis on gift giving a lot'. But many find it hard to do on an individual basis. When John and Louise Mattson tried to limit their family's Christmas giving, John's stressed-out sister resisted, despite the fact that the overtime she worked to buy her gifts was making her sick. Arguments ensued, and in the end John and Louise dropped the idea and went along, against their better judgement.

Like many, the Mattsons feel that Christmas has become unacceptably commercialized, an orgy of shopping and spending. Even Halloween, once a simple holiday, now gobbles up US$2.5 billion in soft drink, candy, costume, decoration and beer spending. Many Americans yearn for holidays that feel authentic and true to earlier, non-commercial traditions. But what they, and many Americans, don't realize is the extent to which many of our most cherished holiday traditions have been commercialized for quite some time. And therein lies much of the difficulty of creating another way. Rudolph the Red-Nosed Reindeer was invented by an ad man for Montgomery Ward. Even Thanksgiving, arguably our most authentic holiday, was moved a week earlier by Franklin Roosevelt in 1939 at the urging of a department store owner hoping to lengthen the shopping season.

The first step in downsizing a holiday is to recognize the ways in which commercial interests have shaped our rituals and habits. Once you realize that large inventories of toys for children are a recent phenomenon, or that our ancestors didn't wrap gifts, it's easier to do things differently. Diamond engagement rings are not a time-honoured tradition but a product of recent vintage, brought to us by – who else – the diamond manufacturer. So too the knowledge that bridal registries were not the usual practice of the turn of the 20th century rich; they're also relatively new. Bride magazines, wedding consultants, wear-it-once dresses – new, new, new. When you know how weddings used to be celebrated, it's easier to close *Bride* magazine and be satisfied with an inexpensive affair. Learning the histories of holidays and then sharing the information with friends and family may help to take away some of the imperative of costly 'traditions'. Various simple-living groups and manuals suggest alternative, non-commercial ways to celebrate the holidays. They propose spending limits on gifts, limiting the number of gifts, spending time together as an alternative to gifts, making rather than buying tree ornaments and giving gifts of time and labour. Reorienting celebrations around home-prepared food rather than store-bought commodities is one way to get back to authentic holiday experiences, because food and drink have been at the centre of most historical traditions. Such a shift is likely to bring more creative satisfaction, less stress on the pocketbook and more social togetherness. (Thanksgiving has always been my favourite holiday – just food and family.) But, of course, such a change takes more time. To figure that one out, read on.

Principle 8: Making Time: Is Work-and-Spend Working?

As most people who have thought seriously about how to reduce their spending know, spending less requires time. It requires not only shopping more carefully or doing research, but acknowledging that the cheaper way to do something is usually more time-consuming. What's true in cooking (preparing dried beans, baking homemade bread, making a cake from scratch) is also true in general: cheaper transport is usually slower, making a Halloween costume takes more time, and ordering by mail (to avoid shopping) incurs shipping costs. While there are certainly exceptions, the principle is that you pay for convenience. People who work in stressful, time-consuming jobs know the drill well. It's hard to reduce spending because they need to 'buy' time – by getting others to do their housework, gardening, food preparation, chauffeuring, even shopping. And then they need to earn the pay cheque to pay for all those services.

For some of us, spending less requires breaking out of this harried, convenience-oriented lifestyle. It requires taking control of our lives on a daily basis, so that shifting to a more time-intensive but cheaper (and incidentally, more ecologically sound) lifestyle is possible. Of course, that is not easy to do. Most jobs do not offer 'downward flexibility' in hours, allowing the employee to work a little less, with a little loss in pay. Many, particularly the better-remunerated ones, are all-or-nothing propositions. At Telecom, 85 per cent of all respondents said that reducing hours in their job would be either impossible or fairly difficult.

However, it can be done. Millions of downshifters are finding ways. If you find yourself working long hours but spending everything you make, if you are stressed out and not even enjoying the consumer goodies you do have, then the work-and-spend cycle is not working for you. Start thinking seriously about a change that may entail earning less but will give you back control of your time and your life.

Principle 9: The Need for a Coordinated Intervention

A central argument of [the book from which this chapter is reprinted], is that competitive consumption creates a 'prisoners' dilemma' – both prisoners would be better off if neither one talked, but only the one who talks first gets a good deal from the prosecutor. The well-being of everyone could be improved if there were a way to harmonize individual behaviour and minimize the competitive incentives. If the Joneses could be induced not to upgrade their car or house or whatever, then the Smiths wouldn't have to either, and both would be happier. But central to the prisoners' dilemma is the inability of the two prisoners to bring about the best outcome because they are not allowed to confer and devise a common position. One way to make that happen is with a central coordinating entity – like the government.

The traditional route has been taxation. Consider the sport utility vehicle. As it has become the latest status symbol, individuals feel pressure to acquire one. While some people truly benefit from owning such a vehicle, others who never go camping or hunting or embark on off-road journeys end up on the bandwagon because that's what the with-it people are now buying. And it's not all image. Who wants to be in the car-sized

Corolla that Land Cruiser just ploughed into? Who wants to be the only parent in the class who can't accommodate the kids after the soccer game? For an individual, it's sometimes hard to escape the logic. But for the public, the trend is a definite negative.

If large vehicles were taxed more heavily than lighter, energy-efficient cars (instead of the other way around), the competitive spiral leading to the acquisition of more and more Land Cruisers, Explorers and Suburbans might slow down. If individuals were forced to be accountable for the effect of their vehicles on others' safety, they might be less likely to choose the 5000-pound gorilla. The roads would be safer, the environment cleaner and many families' bank accounts larger.

Lest luxury taxes sound intrusive, unfair, or even un-American, remember that we already do a tremendous amount of 'social engineering' through subsidizing and taxing specific commodities, including items designated as luxuries. In my state, a piece of clothing that costs above US$175 incurs sales tax, but less expensive items do not. There is also an extensive network of subsidies for tobacco and sugar farmers, energy conservation, military production, home-ownership, child care, charitable giving and the like. Consider also that higher taxes on some items could be counterbalanced by lower levies on others. If you bought the small, energy-efficient car, the sales tax could be waived altogether. When insurance companies raised the liability insurance rates for owners of sport utility vehicles, they implied that the rates on cars that do not do so much damage in collisions would be lowered.

The principle would be that the high-end, status versions of certain commodities would pay a high tax, the mid-range models would pay mid-range taxes, and low-end versions would be exempt. Property taxes could also be progressively structured, so that if you opt for a living room, family room, library, and glassed-in porch to go with the seven bedrooms and bathrooms in your new dream house, you'll face a higher tax rate than a family whose house is of median square footage.

Consumption taxes are a start. But mitigating the factors that give rise to competitive spending in the first place is also important. That starts with reversing 30 years of growing inequality in the distribution of income and wealth. It's not surprising that the upper-middle class has become 'the one to watch' (as NBC touts about itself): its members receive almost half of the nation's annual income and use it to create a compelling consumer lifestyle. What if tax and other government policies improved the distribution of income so that wealth and income were more fairly shared? The gap between aspirations and incomes would narrow, and people might choose to work less, borrow less and slow down their daily lives. (Government policies can also affect these choices.) They'd also have to worry less about protecting their possessions, since fewer individuals would steal the things the culture tells them they must have to be whole. Competitive spending pressures would ease – a rarely recognized side benefit of a more equal distribution of income.

A final area is advertising. Ad expenditures have skyrocketed in recent years and now stand at more than US$2000 per family. These expenditures are fully subsidized by taxpayers: advertising costs are deductible from corporate profits. If this write-off were revoked, it's likely there would be fewer ads, which nearly everyone but Madison Avenue probably agrees would be a good thing. (Sixty-five per cent of the public already agree with such an idea, and 80 per cent believe that prime-time advertising should be limited.) It's time to get this give-away on the congressional docket.

Filling the Void

The message children used to get from their bedtime stories was that money doesn't buy happiness. Though the new governess for our children, Miss Television, has a more modern message, an accumulating body of economic literature supports the old notion. Being poor, or devoid of possessions, does greatly impair one's well-being, but *beyond a certain point,* having more stuff doesn't seem to help. A fivefold increase in Japan's average income made its citizens no better off in terms of happiness. The post-war threefold increase in American incomes had the same result. On average, we're long past the point where additional income, or consumption, yields much psychic benefit. In large part, it is this evidence that makes me feel comfortable advocating the changes I do. Our history shows that the extra spending won't be missed.

On the other hand, a serious turning away from consumerism, as an ideology and a way of life, raises a whole set of issues that scholarly research has not really addressed. While it may be true that reorienting our emotional lives away from the symbolism of products would be liberating (I for one would welcome less pressure about the fabric I choose for my couch, or whether I'm keeping up technologically), such a shift would probably leave a void. James Twitchell (1996) overstates the case when he asserts that 'getting and spending is what gives our lives order and meaning'. But he does have a point. If we aren't flipping through catalogues or daydreaming about the perfect living room, what will we be doing?

The cynical answer is: watching television. Perhaps. But then again, television yields relatively low satisfaction and is often used by adults as a way to unwind after a stressful and exhausting day at work. It is often background, or company, a sort of white noise and light show. (Even now, 39 per cent of the population say they watch too much TV.) If we had more time off from working and could plan more satisfying recreation, we might well spend less time in front of the tube. The experiences of downshifters suggest there are plenty of satisfying ways to fill the void. They have the time to do the things the rest of us keep putting off, such as gardening, cooking, quilting, writing books, mountain biking, opening bed and breakfasts, socializing, playing music, joining book clubs, exercising, learning a language, taking care of their children and spending lots of time volunteering. Yes, yes, I know what you're thinking. Some of these activities, like gardening, can be terribly expensive. But remember, you don't need to be fully outfitted by Smith and Hawken, and maybe you could even get a garden tool library started. There really are cheap ways to do most things. Besides, with all the money you're saving, you can afford to splurge on something you really love.

Another option is civic re-engagement. Many of the people I interviewed have connected up with others who are also trying to live differently. There is now an expanding movement for new, less consumerist lifestyles, fuelled by organizations such as the Center for a New American Dream, the New Road Map Foundation, the Northwest Earth Institute, the Cultural Environment Movement, the Center for the Study of Commercialism, Unplug, TV Turn-Off Week and the Media Foundation. These groups are addressing the environmental, cultural and social effects of the old American dream and trying to devise a new one. They organize discussion groups, public forums, newsletters and community events. They are eager for new recruits.

I remain optimistic that we *can* fill the void. It can hardly be possible that the dumbing-down of America has proceeded so far that it's either consumerism or nothing.

We remain a creative, resourceful and caring nation. There's still time left to find our way out of the mall.

References

Faber, R. and O'Guinn, T. (1992) 'A clinical screener for compulsive buying', *Journal of Consumer Research*, vol 19, December, pp459–469

Magee, A. (1994) 'Compulsive buying tendency as a predictor of attitudes and perceptions', *Association for Consumer Research*, vol 21, pp590–594

Twitchell, J. (1996) *Adcult USA: The Triumph of Advertising in American Culture*, Columbia University Press, New York, p253

Part 3

Resisting Simplicity

The Politics of Sustainable Consumption: The Case of the Netherlands

Susan Martens and Gert Spaargaren

Introduction

As early as 1972, the Dutch government introduced the concept of 'ecologically adjusted behaviour'. The country's environment minister at the time declared, 'In a society as we know it, economic growth has to be controlled; it is not just about production, but also about critical consumption and responsible living.' Since the first upsurge of ecological awareness in the early 1970s, environmental considerations have become a regular feature of everyday life and the consumption practices attached to it. Dutch consumers have become accustomed to paying ecological taxes on gasoline, to separating their organic wastes, and to subscribing to a wide array of 'green electricity' schemes. From these observations, we might conclude that environmental considerations have gained a degree of independence from traditional aspects of consumer decision-making that are inspired by economic comparisons, comfort and convenience. Nonetheless, the domestic environmental pressures attributable to consumption remain high.

Consumption politics in the Netherlands during the 1970s and 1980s were organized around information campaigns to educate people about topical environmental problems and their personal responsibilities in helping to ameliorate them. Often, the government delegated these tasks to environmental education centres and non-governmental organizations (NGOs) that issued – usually with public financial support – moral appeals for critical and 'correct' consumption behaviour. During this period, discussion focused on limiting overall consumption as the solution to environmental problems, with substantially less attention to alternatives that could lessen harmful household practices. Policy-makers devoted considerable rhetorical energy to sustainable consumption during these years, but they often failed to produce tangible programmes.

The first Netherlands Environmental Policy Plan (NEPP), published in 1989, marks the beginning of more comprehensive consumption policy-making (VROM, 1989). The NEPP identified households as one of its environmental policy target groups, particularly with respect to their vital position in production–consumption chains. The 1989 document treated consumers as independent and potentially critical actors, with power to influence production. Moreover, the NEPP acknowledged that consumers were 'not [an] easily accessible target group'. While environmental policy-makers in the Netherlands have come to accept that consumption requires special attention, and that they should tailor initiatives to consumer requirements, the issue remains highly problematic. By the time the Dutch government released its third version of the NEPP a decade later, consumers were no longer treated as one of the target groups; instead, more sustainable consumption is to be achieved on the basis of ongoing product innovations (VROM, 1998). These circumstances suggest that politicians and policy-makers cannot decide whether to approach sustainable consumption from a consumer- or a producer-led perspective (Vermeulen, 2000).

Contentions that the future success of Dutch environmental policy depends on how these initiatives ultimately address the everyday practices of citizen–consumers are (once more) gaining ground (Beckers et al, 2000). If consumption is indeed a social phenomenon, then we need to take a fresh look at how to accomplish social transformation and what the major consequences will be. In other words, how will the Dutch style of environmental policy-making be affected by an emphasis on sustainable consumption? How will an invigorated politics of sustainable consumption influence the routines of everyday life, the levels of personal comfort, and the features of contemporary life that citizen–consumers in the Netherlands regard as indispensable?

By analysing past and present initiatives, we hope to arrive at a set of insights that might guide the country's future efforts in this area. In seeking to understand the current political status of sustainable consumption in the Dutch context, we draw on the theory of ecological modernization, which appears at present to be informing the activities of many of the relevant actors (see, for example, van Driel et al, 1993; Mol and Spaargaren, 1993; Duyvendak et al, 1999). The recommendations we present for the development of a politics of sustainable consumption are also embedded in this view.

We argue that policy-makers should not confront the issue of consumption from a one-sided perspective informed exclusively by environmental scientists and commitments to limit aggregate consumption. In this sense, we do not endorse efforts to 'tame the treadmill of consumption' as a narrow objective (see also Princen et al, 2002). Policy programmes that aim to lessen the environmental consequences of consumption by reducing (or radically restructuring) consumption will likely lead to questionable social and economic outcomes. These so-called de-modernization strategies tend to underestimate the potential to improve the environmental consequences of contemporary consumption by promoting more ecologically rational practices. Without taking a strong position on the desirability of limiting consumption in the absolute sense, we maintain the need to embed consumption in policy objectives developed by democratic environmental reform processes over the last several decades.

In addition, the involvement of citizen–consumers is indispensable in formulating environmental criteria that will steer the transformation of consumption practices. This participation is essential with respect to policies that emphasize the role of *consumers* (for instance, when considering the use of eco-labels), as well as in terms of the politics and policies that highlight the role of *citizens* (for instance, when reconfiguring the local or national water system or when formulating Agenda 21 activities). Both situations require a strong emphasis on active citizen–consumer contributions, and imply a need for strategies that privilege actors and institutions within civil society. Such a perspective suggests that a shift in governance – motivated by the development of new sustainable consumption policies – is the main driver behind several political changes presently under way in the Netherlands.

The next section discusses the factors that have prompted Dutch policy-makers to take a special interest in sustainable consumption and the conventional approaches that they have applied. We then assess the current state of environmental politics in the country and explain how developments in this sphere have contributed to the conceptualization of new strategies to green consumer behaviour. We then appraise several policy experiments carried out by NGOs and relevant government ministries to facilitate more sustainable consumption. The conclusion reflects on those initiatives that we deem to be most promising, describing how these pilot programmes can serve as useful building blocks for a future policy programme, as they combine a democratic environmental perspective with an equally strong focus on the everyday life of citizen–consumers.

Greening Consumption: The Dutch State of Affairs

Before describing some of the more striking features of Dutch consumption patterns and their related environmental effects, it is important to explain our conception of consumption practices. We refer to consumption not as isolated purchasing behaviours, but instead as a broad concept that encompasses the 'buying, using and disposal of products and services within the contexts of social practices, or consumption domains'. We use the terms 'consumption domain' and 'social practice' interchangeably when discussing the specific setting in which consumption occurs. There is, of course, a distinction between the two concepts. The notion of a social practice refers to clusters of everyday routines that are bound in space and time and are common among citizen–consumers – for example, dwelling or personal care. Social practices also include many types of activities that cannot be considered 'consumption' in the conventional sense. The term 'consumption domain', in its strictest usage, refers to a certain segment of consumer expenditure and excludes activities such as house cleaning. We consider it analytically preferable to refer to social practices when discussing the state of ecological modernization, since this includes a broader range of activities. However, consumption domain is currently the more widely used concept among the Netherlands policy-makers.

Per capita consumer expenditures in the Netherlands have approximately tripled during the second half of the 20th century. While there have been, during this period, some significant changes in provisioning patterns, the dematerialization anticipated by scholars and policy-makers has not occurred (RIVM, 2003). The adverse environmental impacts of consumption – the generation of toxic air emissions, the production of solid wastes, and the depletion of natural resources and energy – continue to increase. The third version of the NEPP estimated that consumption in the Netherlands was responsible for 10 per cent of the country's greenhouse gas emissions, 4 per cent of its releases associated with acidification, 19 per cent of its discharges contributing to eutrophication, and 14 per cent of overall solid wastes (see Table 14.1).

Recent debates also have emphasized the spatial dimensions of consumption, an outcome that is not especially surprising given the Netherlands' high population

Table 14.1 *Various consumption-related emissions*
in the Netherlands relative to total emissions

Emission category	Percentage
Greenhouse gas emissions	10
Acidification emissions	4
Eutrophication emissions	19
All wastes	14

Source: VROM (1998)

density. Within this context, the Dutch ecological footprint – particularly the landmass necessary for carbon dioxide sequestration – has been a frequent point of discussion. Of course, actual estimates vary depending on the method of calculation, but some local NGOs contend that citizen–consumers in the Netherlands occupy two to three times their 'fair share' of the Earth's surface. The National Strategy for Sustainable Development, released in 2002, assessed the country's ecological footprint in terms of average global productivity: the appropriated landmass was about 11 million hectares (approximately 0.2 per cent of the global total), while the Dutch population comprises 16 million people (0.26 per cent of the world total), and the country's land area is 33,943 square kilometres (0.026 per cent of the global total) (VROM, 2002a, 2002b; see also Postma, 2000 and Rood et al, 2001). Although commentators seem to agree that the Netherlands' ecological footprint needs to be reduced, few concrete policies have resulted.

Most technical studies that map the environmental effects of consumption focus on the so-called 'direct' and 'indirect' uses of energy. In this regard, the general trend among Dutch citizen–consumers is one of continued growth. The percentage increase in per capita energy use (from 35 GJ in 1946 to 120 GJ in 1995) exceeded even that of consumption in monetary terms. The largest expansion in energy use occurred between 1960 and 1980, largely due to the introduction of central heating and the expansion of personal automobile ownership. Efficiency improvements in the supply sectors somewhat offset this growth in energy consumption; in the absence of these advances, per capita energy use would have increased by a further 40 GJ by 1995 (Vringer et al, 2001; SCP, 2001).

Direct and indirect energy use among Dutch citizen–consumers is primarily attributable to a limited number of consumption domains (see Table 14.2).[1] The largest share of energy consumption in 1995 was assigned to three domains: home, food and housing (with leisure rapidly increasing).

The relative importance of these consumption domains is likely to change over time. For example, researchers suggest that by 2030 the amount of energy consumed for holidays will exceed that used for housing. Food and home energy consumption will also decrease, while that used for at-home and away-from-home leisure will rise sharply. On an aggregate level, the energy use is expected to grow. Notwithstanding the slow rate of dematerialization and efficiency improvements in the supply sectors, energy use among Dutch citizen–consumers is projected to increase between 56 and 74 per cent by 2030 (1995 base-line), making it difficult to meet both national and international targets. In terms of sustainable development, it becomes clear that consumer behaviour is an essential area for environmental politics and policy-making.

Table 14.2 *Energy consumption of the major consumption domains in the Netherlands as shares of national total*

Consumption domain	Energy consumption (percentage)	Definition of domain
Home	29	Maintenance, improvement and heating
Food	23	Obtaining, storing, preparing and eating
Dwelling	8	Cleaning, gardening and decorating
Indoor leisure	7	Reading, watching television, talking on the telephone and so forth
Outdoor leisure	5	Sports, cultural activities and so forth

Source: Vringer et al (2001)

Sustainable consumption initiatives: From alternative consumer culture to the creation of green-niche markets

As outlined earlier, environmental considerations have gained a certain degree of independence from the other factors that motivate Dutch citizen–consumers. On a more abstract level, the issue of sustainable consumption has become embedded in different initiatives involving individuals, social groups and industries. Over the last several decades, public discussions regarding the environmental implications of provisioning have developed in various directions. These deliberations have been framed in terms of the need to forge new styles and qualities of consumption, to interrogate the characteristics of consumption practices, and to involve different actors in the development of alternative practices.[2]

An interesting – though decidedly peripheral – manifestation of interest around sustainable consumption in the Netherlands is the so-called 'Platform True Prosperity'. This project is a joint initiative coordinated by more than two dozen organizations (NGOs, consumer groups, charities, religious organizations and trade unions). Proponents are seeking to foster a more balanced society and to link up with personal motivations to demonstrate that non-material values (such as silence and personal networks) can enhance quality of life. Organizations and individuals connect to the Platform by sharing ideas or by establishing small innovation projects – for example, regional non-monetary exchange economies and local community-garden projects. In some respects, the motivations that animate the True Prosperity discourse (an emphasis on the non-material qualities of life and a critical perspective on the culture of consumption) resemble those that informed the de-modernization strategies common in the Netherlands during the 1970s and 1980s.

Another campaign is the National Initiative for Sustainable Development (NIDO) that brings together industries, governments, civil-society groups and scientists to develop and implement thematic programmes promoting sustainable development. In contrast to True Prosperity, NIDO does not seek to bring about general changes in (consumption) culture, but the organization's adherents develop competencies in those social sectors that can promote sustainable-system innovations and transitions. One NIDO programme specifically designed to create market opportunities for sustainable products is the 'green products' initiative, which works to transform current sustainable consumer products and services niches into mainstream markets. To realize this goal, various associations of producers and consumers, research institutes and governments are working collaboratively on marketing strategies for green consumption alternatives.

In addition to these relatively large-scale initiatives, numerous smaller, independent activities in the Netherlands aim to develop tangible options for greening specific consumption aspects. Sponsored primarily by private companies, these projects are introducing green products and services. Prominent examples of environmentally sound products are solvent-free paints, biodegradable detergents, green-electricity schemes and a number of product groups categorized under other environmental labels. Less apparent examples of product innovations are the 'green savings' and 'green investment' programmes that the financial services industry and the national government have introduced since the mid-1990s (de Wit, 2002).[3]

Uneven development

Current social debates regarding sustainable consumption in the Netherlands are less intense and morally focused than they were during the 1970s. Both governmental and non-governmental actors today are more pragmatic, emphasizing practicable ways to organize emerging green markets and to promote sustainable consumption. These efforts have enlarged the number of sustainable alternatives and improved the overall quality of green products and services. However, the amount of innovation – or the extent of ecological modernization – differs greatly across consumption domains. Winsemius's (1986) policy life-cycle model provides an instructive approach for highlighting some of this variability, as well as the unequal rate of innovation in the different consumption domains (see Figure 14.1).

Figure 14.1 depicts the present position of several relevant consumption domains and illustrates their considerable differences in degree of ecological modernization to

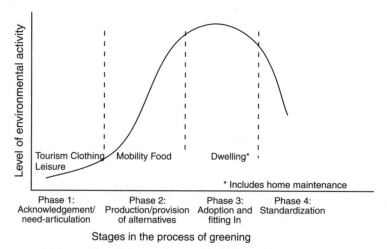

Figure 14.1 *Stages of ecological modernization for consumption domains in the Netherlands*

date. The availability of green products and services in tourism and leisure, for example, is still rather limited. The process of greening – as measured by the number of environmentally sound alternatives that are available, and the extent to which they have been incorporated into everyday routines – is substantially more advanced in housing and feeding.[4]

Regarding tourism, recent research has noted that efforts to facilitate more sustainable consumer choices are still in the initial stage. Initiatives to enable environmentally sound travel alternatives are confined to eco-accommodations in the Netherlands and abroad, programmes to facilitate sustainable tourism in the Alps, and an airline-ticketing scheme called Trees for Travel that allows consumers to purchase tree-planting certificates to compensate for airplane-generated carbon dioxide emissions. The slow pace at which tourism has been subjected to ecological modernization suggests that this consumption domain may be resistant to sustainability-enhancing changes (CEA, 1999). Holiday practices tend to be habitual, and are subject to change only as a result of new financial circumstances. Environmental considerations do not appear to play a significant role in consumers' holiday-planning decisions. The evidence suggests that, for at least the near to medium term, there is likely to be very little (articulated) consumer demand in the Netherlands for sustainable holiday alternatives.

If we now investigate a domain such as food, which is purportedly more environmentally advanced, the initial impression is that, at least in the Netherlands, a rather modest level of ecological modernization has been achieved. This impression is premised on the relatively small proportion – approximately 1 per cent in 1998 – of Dutch food consumption that consists of organic products (van der Grijp and den Hond, 1999). However, in assessing the potential for change here, a number of other indicators are important. The variety of retail outlets selling organic food products has increased significantly in recent years.[5] The number of supermarkets displaying over 15 organic items has expanded from 70 in 1995 to over 4000 in 1999.[6] Likewise, specialized organic groceries have become more prevalent, and their numbers throughout the country grew during this period from 280 to over 400. Moreover, a survey of Dutch consumers demonstrated that environmental concerns are an important motivation in the purchase of organic food products – 51 per cent of organic food consumers identified 'the environment' as their most important reason (Platform Biologica, 2001).

We can consider the choice of organic foods to be a 'dark green' expression of sustainable food-consumption practices. There are also several 'lighter green' possibilities, such as substituting meat with novel protein foods or purchasing seasonal products.[7] Major producers and retailers on the supply side of the food chain have become quite cognizant of these consumption changes. Growing consumer interest in organic produce is one of the key catalysts for a successful sustainability transition, because it prompts stakeholders to liberate more environmentally benign forms of food production from a counter-cultural typecast.[8]

The policy life-cycle model focuses attention on the undeniable fact that, over the past decade, producers and civil-society actors in the Netherlands have developed a significant number of innovations to facilitate sustainable consumption. However, not all of the alternatives have been unqualified market successes. For instance, the premature launch of the compact fluorescent light bulb led consumers to view energy-efficient lighting as inferior. Some researchers also draw attention to so-called rebound effects, especially with regard to energy use (Rood et al, 2001; Hofkes et al, 1998). Nonetheless, citizen–consumers have adopted numerous green products, and these items have become common features of everyday life. On balance, then, the situation concerning the ecological modernization of consumption is one in which several front-runner domains have reached a 'take-off phase', while others, because they are more resistant to environmental reform, are currently lagging behind.

Green Politics in the Netherlands: Negotiation and Consultation

We focus in this section on Dutch environmental politics in general, and consumption politics in particular, as part of sketching the political background for the greening of consumer behaviour. During the most recent elections in the Netherlands (May 2002 and January 2003), environmental concerns received only very modest attention, with little substantive discussion about the environment. The absence of timely and controversial issues may simply mean that the environment is not – at least for the time being – critical to the electoral fortunes of political parties. However, according to some analysts, the environment's relatively low salience is attributable to the non-adversarial positions that the main political parties take on these issues (Koopmans, 1995; Duyvendak, 1997). With the exception of the unequivocally green parties, it is in actual practice very difficult to distinguish Dutch political parties as either proponents or opponents of overtly green policies. If the entire political spectrum conveys a mildly green image and speaks to some extent a language of ecological modernization, the environment becomes less attractive as an arena for electoral contestation and more difficult to invoke for political benefit.

This political tendency to downplay environmental issues is further compounded by a strong systemic emphasis on communication and consensus. Many analysts attribute Dutch prosperity, social harmony and political stability to the so-called 'polder model', where unions of employers and employees seek to reach common agreement. During the second half of the 1990s, some commentators began to invoke the notion of a 'green polder model' to suggest that the country could only resolve conflicts over environmental policy if political parties, trade unions, environmental organizations, and other stakeholder groups cooperated (Duyvendak et al, 1999).

A commitment to communication and a consensual style of politics is not only emblematic of political debate in the Netherlands, but is particularly evident in the horizontal policy arrangements that characterize the environmental field. For example, 'policy networks' are regularly used to address circumscribed problems at the regional or local level and, as discussed above, the target-group approach has been in ascendancy. The target-group approach is a strategy, normally used at the national level, to bring together civil-society actors and government representatives to address specific environmental problems or policy areas. The relevant participants then enter into several rounds of negotiation on an ad hoc basis, with the aim of reaching voluntary accords for environmental performance standards and for instrument usage (Driessen and Glasbergen, 2000).

Although many Dutch politicians and government officials, as well as some members of the country's environmental movement, point to the benefits and accomplishments of the green polder model, less enthusiastic voices are also discernible. Critics maintain that the consensus model has the potential to create situations in which the negotiation table becomes the central stage, and political parties conveniently leave delicate environmental issues to other entities without much democratic legitimacy.[9] For opponents of the green polder model, corporatism and the surgical removal of the environment from the political agenda is a notable shortcoming.

Nevertheless, most analysts view the open and facilitative disposition that characterizes Dutch political parties as beneficial to environmental reform. Public debate does not typically frame environmental issues in oppositional, zero-sum terms, but rather as common problems for which everyone is responsible. However, this idea of collective obligation, especially concerning sustainable consumption, must be understood in its proper political context. Consumption demands delicate treatment because it is so closely intertwined with popular notions of individual freedom (Basset et al, 1994). Even in the Netherlands, it is extremely difficult for policy-makers to modify household consumption behaviour, even in circumstances when it is generally considered propitious to do so.

With time, it has become apparent that citizen–consumers are often beyond the reach of conventional environmental-policy interventions. There are several reasons for this inaccessibility. First, it is not feasible for the government to negotiate covenants with citizen–consumers, as it has with members of several prominent industrial sectors. Second, citizen–consumers comprise a heterogeneous target group that does not usually participate – collectively or through its individual members – in the neo-corporatist consultation circuits common in Dutch political life since the 1980s. Finally, consumers are not typically fluent in the highly specialized jargon that environmental professionals normally use to set objectives, to define approaches and to formulate instruments for change. In other words, conventional environmental policy frameworks are not compatible with a consumption-oriented approach (Spaargaren, 2003).

Modernizing consumption-oriented policies: The need for political innovation

The policy problems regarding sustainable consumption generate several questions. If the initiatives of the early 1990s did little to improve the environmental dimensions of consumer behaviour, how should the Dutch government approach consumers? What kinds of political innovations are prerequisites for a more effective consumption-oriented approach to environmental policy? What are the drawbacks associated with such an approach?

We begin with a discussion of the possible weaknesses inherent in more consumption-oriented environmental policies, and consider the 'individualization' of politics and political responsibilities as developed by Bauman (1993) and Princen et al (2002). Many environmental problems are ultimately rooted in the conduct of institutional actors, such as companies and governments. Under these circumstances, there is little merit imposing obligations on citizen–consumers, who not only lack the power to influence the organization of production and consumption, but also cannot – and arguably should not – be held responsible for issues that arise out of the 'treadmill of production and consumption' (Schnaiberg, 1980). It is likely to be unproductive, and above all illegitimate, to burden citizen–consumers with remedying such problems. If policy initiatives only advance individual solutions – and ignore institutional actors – socially regressive and environmentally ineffectual outcomes will be the result.

At the same time, it is equally important to avoid simply discharging citizen–consumers from responsibility for the impacts of their consumption practices. This is not intended as a moral statement; our point, rather, is that we cannot properly comprehend modern consumer societies by examining producers alone. As Rifkin (2002) terms it, we live in an 'age of access', and this implies – among many other things – that the secret to understanding the dynamics of production–consumption cycles resides in the practices of citizen–consumers, who participate as knowledgeable and capable agents in reproducing the basic institutions that facilitate their livelihoods. An appreciation of this feature of contemporary social life is essential for arriving at effective consumption-oriented policies that mediate between isolated individualism and one-sided structuralism (Giddens, 1991, 1998).

The Netherlands seems to need a 'new politics of consumption'. However, the Dutch experience thus far suggests that there are no easy solutions for such a project. The government has customarily addressed the environmental dimensions of consumer decision-making using social-psychological models that focus on individual attitudes. This approach has tended to exacerbate the risk of individualizing (or privatizing) environmental problems; it must be supplanted with perspectives sensitive to the contextual, structural characteristics of provisioning practices in modern societies. Table 14.3 tentatively compares the 'old' and the 'new' policy paradigms with respect to consumption.

While consumption politics in the Netherlands have conventionally been situated outside the mainstream of environmental politics, we can anticipate that this situation will change. The increasing relevance of policy initiatives aimed at citizen–consumers is rooted in features of modern societies that include shifting attention within production–consumption cycles to the 'modes of access'.

The following section moves beyond these general observations to describe several contemporary initiatives in sustainable consumption. Though some of these efforts are part of the pre-existing paradigm, others illustrate – at least on an experimental basis – the new mode of thinking about citizen–consumers.

Policy Initiatives to Facilitate Sustainable Consumption

This section provides an overview of the policy instruments that the Netherlands has developed to promote sustainable consumption. In addition to the Ministry of Housing, Spatial Planning and the Environment, several other arms of the Dutch government are highly involved in environmental policy-making and concern themselves, to varying degrees, with consumption's side effects. Moreover, a focus on citizen–consumers necessarily blurs the boundaries separating the various ministries, because the environmental consequences of provisioning transcend the limits of conventional policy domains.[10] Before describing the strategies of the different ministries, we highlight the role of Dutch NGOs in sustainable consumption.

Table 14.3 *Principles of consumption-oriented environmental policy-making: Old (or classical) and new policy perspectives*

Principle	Old (or classical) policy perspective	New policy perspective
Characterization of citizen–consumers	Citizen–consumers viewed as atomized actors performing isolated sequences of activities.	Citizen–consumers viewed as actors who participate in social practices that are shared with others and reproduced in time–space. Consumption involves the use of clusters of related goods and services.
Degree of citizen–consumer differentiation	Citizen–consumers treated as a homogeneous group with subgroups differentiated only with respect to levels of environmental awareness.	Citizen–consumers treated in terms of environmentally relevant social practices with focus on actual behaviours.
Procedures to promote greening	Greening of consumption analysed in terms of individual attitudes that guide conscious individual choices. Social structures are exogenous variables.	Greening of social practices analysed in terms of the duality of structure in interaction. Rationalization of behaviour investigated with respect to embedded social practices and connected to lifestyle choices in the context of life politics.
Relationship between citizen–consumer and life-world	Strong separation between consumer and producer rationality.	Emphasis on the interplay between consumer and producer rationality in different stages of the production–consumption cycle.
Perceived potential for improving the environmental performance of everyday consumption practices	Generally pessimistic.	High technical and social potential.
Conception of sustainable consumption	Reduced consumption in both quantitative and qualitative terms.	Potential to achieve comparable or even greater comfort, convenience and safety.

Dutch NGOs: Taking on a consumer perspective?

Dutch environmentalism has developed and diversified over the past three decades. In particular, large segments of the country's environmental movement have adopted eco-logical modernization as a central ideological tenet. As a result, the environmental agenda has shifted away from moral appeals of soberness and counter-cultural experi-mentation toward ecological rationality, emphasizing the search for strategies that improve the environmental performance of modern production and consumption (Spaargaren and Mol, 1992; Hajer, 1995). In general, Dutch environmentalism has come to perceive the establishment of environmentally sound consumption practices as the joint responsibility of multiple stakeholders – government, industry and citizen–consumers (Duyvendak, 1997; ADO, 1992).

Dutch NGOs – often, as part of collaborative efforts – have achieved some notable successes, fostering more sustainable production and consumption. For instance, by appealing to public opinion and negotiating with the government and the business sec-tor, they secured a ban on chlorofluorocarbons (CFCs) in spray cans. Other successes include stricter regulations governing the use of pesticides and chemical additives in food production, and the use of eco-labels. It is clear that many achievements of NGOs in the Netherlands regarding sustainable consumption are attributable to government lobbying and activities directed at industries. By approaching supply-side actors, these organizations have campaigned for the greening of policy and production processes (ADO, 1992).

Initially, NGO activities were not aimed specifically towards greening *consumption* practices, or towards expanding the scope of sustainable consumption by actively involv-ing citizen–consumers. However, for more sustainable consumption practices to become viable from a consumer standpoint, they will need to compete without sacrificing com-fort, convenience and overall product quality (van Vliet, 2002; Shove, 2003). The envi-ronmental movement in the Netherlands is becoming increasingly cognizant of this fact as they search for novel ways to link up with the everyday lives of citizen–consumers, and to facilitate more environmentally sound forms of consumption that correspond to extant expectations.

With these aims in mind, several Dutch NGOs have developed strategies to provide sustainable and high-quality consumption alternatives. For example, a 'green' automo-bile manual offers information on how to save energy – for instance, by regularly check-ing tyre pressure – without stigmatizing the actual ownership and use of an automobile. Another example is providing practical environmental advice for people moving to a new house through a CD-ROM that covers issues ranging from emptying the old premises and using a moving van to decorating a new home. NGOs in the Netherlands have also taken up the challenge of redefining and strengthening their relationship with citizen–consumers by forging new partnerships with public and private producers that facilitate more sustainable consumption.

The Ministry of Economic Affairs: Consumption politics within free-market conditions

The Ministry of Economic Affairs (Ministerie van Economische Zaken, or EZ) defines consumer policy as a separate policy domain, and is primarily concerned with developing initiatives that enable consumers to pursue their personal needs and norms without interference (subject to certain governmental prerogatives) (EZ, 2000). The EZ's outlook is based on the notion that consumers are sovereign market participants and it is the role of government to support them in their demand-side position. Specific policies are geared toward improving market access, promoting transparency of product information, and strengthening the legal position of consumers in disputes with producers. More broadly defined social concerns regarding consumption – such as sustainability – appear only when reliable information about a product's environmental dimensions is an issue. However, the degree to which the Ministry focuses on sustainability as a broader aspect of consumer policy is rather limited.

Nonetheless, the environmental aspects of consumption are central elements of other policy fields within the EZ's ambit, especially in terms of energy. Since the early 1970s, the Ministry has focused on citizen–consumers as users of domestic energy for home heating and hot water production. The approaches utilized in this context have been rather commonplace: establishing levies, imposing energy taxes, formulating subsidies for energy-efficient products and organizing information campaigns (often in cooperation with energy and installation companies). In its most recent campaigns, the EZ encouraged citizen–consumers to monitor their actual energy consumption, to become knowledgeable about their personal use and its environmental impacts. Additionally, the Ministry actively promotes the purchase of 'green energy' generated from renewable sources (Energie Ned, 2000).

The EZ, in collaboration with the Ministry of Spatial Planning, Housing and the Environment, is also responsible for developing and implementing integrated product policies (IPP). The primary aim of these initiatives is to stimulate all market parties – producers, consumers and retailers – to strive for reductions in the level of environmental pollution per product unit. Although IPPs are clearly connected to consumer practices, a goal of these programmes has been to avoid direct regulation of consumption. This is because, as SER (1994) explains, 'implementing policies to decrease the environmental pressure per product might prevent a situation in which the government is forced to influence the volume of consumption and/or the lifestyles of citizen–consumers'.

The EZ's overall policy style for handling issues at the interface between consumption and sustainability is best characterized as 'environmental policy within strict market relations'. The Ministry is normally reluctant to abandon a market approach for addressing the environmental side effects of material consumption. A guiding philosophy that the market is the most efficient way to distribute goods has remained largely unchallenged, and the EZ confines its interventions to the occasional imposition of ecological taxes to limit pollution. As such, the Ministry seeks to coordinate its activities with European-level regulations.

The Ministry of Agriculture, Nature Management and Fisheries: A citizen–consumer orientation in the making

The Ministry of Agriculture, Nature Management and Fisheries (Ministerie van Landbouw, Natuurbeheer en Visserij, or LNV) is a very broad and multifunctional arm of the Dutch government. The areas of its operations that impinge most closely upon material consumption and the environment are agriculture and nature management. The Ministry's responsibilities for agriculture are particularly interesting for current purposes, given recent developments regarding food production and safety. Citizen–consumers in the Netherlands have become highly critical of both conventional methods of producing food and of food quality. In recent years, considerable scrutiny has been devoted to the side effects of agro-industrial production – for example, the acidification of the landscape, the poor living conditions of livestock, and the use of chemical pesticides and hormones. LNV acknowledges these issues and refers to them as a turning point in the public discourse on agriculture. Ministerial officials have emphasized the need to increase organic production and to become more responsive to demand-driven approaches that consider the concerns of citizen–consumers in production decisions (LNV, 2000a). Such sentiments would seem to provide fertile ground for the development of agricultural policies that combine a strong commitment to both consumers and sustainability. However, recent statements have not actively articulated a demand-side approach to sustainable consumption.[11]

Within the area of nature conservation, a new orientation on consumption seems to be emerging in the Netherlands. A focus on citizen–consumers as vital actors is evident, for instance, in two recent series of policy reports entitled *People for Nature, Nature for People* and *Nature as a Living Environment*. The latter series aims to map the possibilities for linking nature policies with the needs and demands of Dutch society (Langers and Spinnenwijn, 1999). The Ministry, in particular, continues to search for new approaches that will increase its capacity for involving citizen–consumers (Kuindersma and Seines, 1999). In official formulations, then, nature conservation is experiencing a shift from top-down, centralized steering toward self-regulation by decentralized actors, most notably the local and provincial governments. At the same time, it is still unclear how the new discourse will influence actual decision-making, since the policy reports to date have served only exploratory purposes.

The Ministry of Transportation, Public Works and Water Management: Limited social and political margins for policies regarding sustainable mobility

From a sustainable consumption perspective, the most interesting initiatives of the Ministry of Transportation, Public Works and Water Management (Ministerie van Verkeer en Waterstaat, or V&W) are in terms of mobility. Because of the density of the Dutch transport system, the movement of goods and people has a large impact on the environment and the general quality of life. Dutch policy-makers have begun, in recent years, to devote increasing attention to personal mobility, partly because the largest growth has occurred with respect to so-called 'recreational' movements.

The general stance of the Ministry is that mobility is a central feature of modern society and it is a government responsibility to accommodate it, while at the same time ameliorating its negative side effects. The Ministry's National Traffic and Transportation Plan, 2001–2020, sketches its intended policy approach to achieve this combined goal: '[T]he needs of citizens are put centrally and will be respected, but as end users they will have to pay for their choices' (V&W, 2000). Consistent with this approach, the Ministry imposes regulatory taxes on automotive fuel, as well as hefty parking fees. Moreover, V&W has experimented over the last few years with systems of differentiated, electronic road pricing, but for the time being has postponed more widespread implementation because of political resistance. Transforming private automobile use, from a system that has never been subject to scarcity pricing into one that requires users to pay for their claims on available capacity, has been difficult in the Netherlands. A recent campaign statement by Wouter Bos, the leader of the Social Democratic Party (PvdA), highlights the lack of political enthusiasm for taking on the sensitive issue of excessive automobile use. Bos stressed that the days in which the party's policy in the field of mobility was premised on 'car pestering' were definitely over.

In addition to developing economic instruments, the Ministry aims to educate people about energy-efficient automobile use. Furthermore, automatic vehicle guidance (a generic term that refers to various technological means to support – and in some cases assume over the long term – the driver's tasks) is seen as an innovation that could improve automotive energy efficiency, and the Ministry has supported some pilot studies in this area. However, these initiatives have become mired in political wrangling over the appropriate role of government intervention in the lives of citizen–consumers and whether cars are part of the private realm.

The Ministry of Housing, Spatial Planning and the Environment: Exploring New Sustainable Consumption Policies

The Ministry of Housing, Spatial Planning and the Environment (Ministerie van Volkshuisvesting, Ruimtelijke Ordering en Milieubeheer, or VROM) is the core authority with respect to sustainable consumption policies in the Netherlands. In comparison to the other arms of the Dutch government, VROM focuses a great deal of effort on sustainability and the environmental dimensions of consumption. Moreover, since the mid-1990s, the ministry has actively considered the roles and responsibilities of citizen–consumers in fostering sustainable practices and has sought to involve them in developing sustainable consumption policies. Accordingly, the Ministry has launched several initiatives to analyse, evaluate, and stimulate more sustainable consumption practices. VROM has designed a number of pilot studies to catalyse internal discussions and to advance a consumption-oriented policy perspective that could become the basis for official guidance in a future iteration of the national environmental policy planning process. This section discusses some of these policy experiments and describes how VROM has begun to identify some building blocks for crafting a new policy style with which to address consumption as a central tenet of environmental policy-making.[12]

The Future Perspective Project: A little greener every day

VROM launched the Future Perspective Project to explore the potential for facilitating more energy-efficient lifestyles in the Netherlands. The scheme sought to generate insights regarding the roles of citizen–consumers as meaningful participants in Dutch climate policy and in the ability of the Netherlands to meet its greenhouse gas emission targets. The project's objective was to determine whether a small group of households could reduce their indirect energy consumption by 30 per cent and sustain this new level on a long-term basis.[13]

During a two-year study period, the participating households were encouraged to alter their lifestyles in ways that enabled them to achieve appreciable improvements in energy consumption. Since household incomes in the Netherlands were expected to rise during this time frame, participants received a 20 per cent supplement to their household budgets to see if they could successfully delink their increasing income from their energy use. For the length of the project, a 'sustainability coach' helped all of the households to monitor energy use and provided advice on energy-saving alternatives (CEA, 1999).

By the end of the study, most of the households had managed to reduce their energy consumption – on average by 31 per cent. One of the most interesting conclusions of the project is that energy efficiency gains were not equal in all consumption domains. An area that proved very resistant to improvement was long-distance transport, particularly in terms of summer-holiday travel. This sobering outcome is attributable to the limited number of energy-efficient travel modes, as well as to an unwillingness on the part of citizen–consumers to revise their vacation routines.

This policy experiment also offers valuable lessons about the longer-term implications of more energy-efficient lifestyle choices. Eighteen months after the formal conclusion of this project, researchers again measured the energy use of the study households. In most cases, direct energy consumption had increased, while indirect energy use was quite stable (especially with respect to food and leisure). The critical factors that limited the households' ability to sustain their improvements were the loss of the supplemental income and the lack of feedback that the sustainability coaches had previously provided. The high price and limited availability of energy-efficient products were related constraints. In contrast, some households managed over time to routinize their new energy-efficient practices by coming to view their new lifestyles as healthier, more relaxing and more economical.

The Future Perspective Project, because of its focus on citizen–consumers' actual daily behaviour, provides a useful starting point for exploring the prospects of more sustainable consumption. The study's insights regarding the practicability of energy improvements in different consumption domains, and the constraints imposed by the dearth of energy-efficient alternatives, are valuable. At the same time, the project did not consider the specific ways in which producers offer sustainable products and services. It also restricted consumption behaviour to 'green shopping', without looking into the social relations that accompany the purchase and use of items deemed environmentally preferable (Spaargaren, 2003).

The Domain Explorations Project:
Pinpointing environmental hotspots

In 1995, VROM launched the Domain Explorations Project, which aimed to identify opportunities for reducing the environmental side effects of consumer behaviour within five specific areas of everyday life relevant for consumption-oriented policy-making: feeding, clothing, housing, recreation and personal care (Schuttelaar and Partners, 2000; CREM, 2000; TNO-STB, 1999).

Within each of these domains, researchers assessed the environmental implications of various consumption practices, using life-cycle analysis (LCA) and other technical methods of evaluation. This quantitative mapping provided an overview of forms of consumption that required the most urgent attention, in other words, the areas of consumption that constitute environmental hotspots. The investigators then developed measures to address these major burdens, and to identify the best potential links in production–consumption chains. The project's next step calls for organizing so-called 'chain consultations' that will engage stakeholders from specific domains in discussions about strategies for achieving the proposed improvements.

This scheme reflects the pragmatic attitude prevalent in the Netherlands with respect to sustainable consumption, and serves as an important step toward creating the foundation for more consumption-oriented environmental policies. Rather than starting from a set of prefigured objectives, the conceptualization of carefully defined consumption domains serves as the point of departure for subsequent analysis and intervention. By mapping the areas that hold the greatest potential for improvement, it becomes possible to compare the resultant changes within (and among) the various consumption domains. These evaluations bolster the legitimacy of consumption-oriented environmental policies – at least in their technical form. However, this particular emphasis can also prove problematic. Citizen–consumers' experiences are tightly interwoven with their consumption choices, and these social aspects of provisioning do not lend themselves to the quantitative analysis inherent in LCA. Under such circumstances, it becomes difficult to assess the extent to which citizen–consumers have internalized the themes and terminology of specific policy interventions – for instance, reducing greenhouse gas emissions or protecting biodiversity.

The Citizen and the Environment Project:
A green 'consultation model'

VROM designed the Citizen and the Environment Project to foster meaningful relationships with citizen–consumers by abandoning the classical emphasis on technical system rationality. The scheme aimed to find potential linkages between government steering and the everyday life concerns of citizen–consumers. This initiative did not focus narrowly on provisioning practices, but also considered various relationships between citizen–consumers and the environment – for example, the ways in which environmental problems are defined and transportation choices are reconciled. The project was highly explorative and qualitative as it sought to provide input for a comprehensive reconsideration of environmental policy-making.

The researchers organized a series of small, independent projects to examine the impacts that a stronger consumption orientation would have on agenda-setting, policy-making, and the division of roles and responsibilities in environmental decision-making. The project employed a diverse array of methods and techniques, including workshops, expert sessions, panel meetings, interviews and focus groups, to study the environmental motives and concerns of citizen–consumers in different everyday life set-tings. For example, some respondents were interviewed while visiting an entertainment area or a day-care centre to identify how they encountered and experienced environ-mental issues in these places. They were also queried about their thoughts regarding how environmental policy-makers should address these issues (B&A Groep, 1997, 2000).

The researchers drew several conclusions regarding consumption-oriented environ-mental policy-making. This initiative suggested that VROM's current approach does not enable citizen–consumers to make connections between environmental goals and everyday life and that the Ministry needed to 'socialize' the environment (Spaargaren, 2003). In other words, to improve public uptake policy-makers should develop – as part of a dialogue with citizen–consumers – broader problem definitions that extend beyond the ecological context that is commonly used, and should formulate symbolic representa-tions of environmental problems that accord more closely with lived experiences. This study also made clear that the division between citizen–consumers and the government requires clearer delineation. Some environmental problems are the responsibility of individual citizen–consumers, while others require explicit governmental leadership.

The Warm Gulf Stream Project: A communication approach

The Warm Gulf Stream Project is a relatively new approach initiated under the aegis of VROM that starts from the idea that communication should be customized for differ-ent social groupings according to lifestyle characteristics and environmental perceptions. This strategy is predicated upon a categorization of Dutch citizens into eight ideal types: rational ecologists, passionate ecologists, conscious progressives, conservatives, techno-actives, contented citizens, materialists and indifferent citizens (Motivaction, 1999). For each of these classifications, VROM and other relevant government ministries sought to employ a specific style of environmental communication. For instance, the Dutch gov-ernment has utilized the Warm Gulf Stream approach to convey information about climate policy. Dutch citizen–consumers were asked to choose those measures for reduc-ing greenhouse gas emissions that conformed with their individual lifestyles – joining an ecoteam, purchasing green electricity, opting for public transportation, or buying 'trees for travel'.

This particular strategy is a specialized form of target-group segmentation. The search for targeted, tailor-made communications – instead of employing a universal approach – is a positive development that, to our minds, deserves encouragement. Nonetheless, we have concerns about the project's theoretical and methodological foun-dations. The particular clusters that this project employed are based on general patterns currently visible in Dutch society, and these values do not necessarily reflect actual con-sumption behaviour. We also have reservations about how suitable these categories are for predictive purposes, as lifestyle segmentations should be grounded in actual consump-tion practices (Ester, 1999). The social practices model we have formulated separately provides a more sociologically informed approach for developing this strategy (Beckers et al, 2000; Spaargaren et al, 2002).

Sustainable dwelling: A transitional policy field

The recently initiated Dutch policy field of 'sustainable dwelling, or home maintenance' is, in many respects, the consumption-oriented offspring of sustainable-building policies created three decades ago. Until the mid-1990s, sustainable building in the Netherlands was a technocratic endeavour that sought to close production loops, to promote the use of eco-efficient materials, and to increase energy efficiency. From 1995 onward, VROM has acknowledged the decidedly singular focus on the supply side of the housing market and sought to devote more attention to home-builders and citizen–consumers. To achieve this objective, the policy focus was broadened from merely sustainable building to the more expansive concept of sustainable home maintenance (VROM, 1997). As a result, the Ministry developed several policy initiatives to encourage environmentally friendly occupation and maintenance of buildings (Martens and Spaargaren, 2002).

One example of this approach is the Sustainable Do-It-Yourself (DIY) Project, jointly executed by four project partners: VROM, the Association of DIY Stores, the Consumer and Safety Foundation, and the Dutch Company for Energy and the Environment. Beginning in 1998 and lasting for two years, the aim of this scheme was to stimulate 'greener' DIY practices. This project was unique because it simultaneously paid attention to both the demand and supply sides of sustainable DIY. A training programme to increase the knowledge of store personnel about the environmental dimensions of different products is one example of a supply-side improvement. The primary strategy for greening the demand side was a mass media campaign to inform and educate consumers about possibilities for sustainable DIY. By employing an aggressive marketing approach – one that emphasized consumer rationality instead of a specific policy objective – this effort differed from traditional government information programmes.[14]

Policy-making in support of sustainable housing highlights the policy-style changes that VROM has made for addressing sustainable consumption. The Ministry has evolved away from its previously very limited emphasis on citizen–consumers toward a view that recognizes consumers as knowledgeable and capable actors. One of VROM's current goals – though it still remains to be seen how it will work out in practice – is to make citizen–consumers full-fledged policy-making partners in sustainable housing (VROM, 1999a, 1999b).

Conclusion

During the mid-1990s, Dutch NGOs and government ministries began to acknowledge the importance of citizen–consumers in fostering more sustainable consumption. During the past decade, the orientation of policy-makers has broadened from a rather narrow focus on meeting challenging targets, based on technical definitions of environmental problems, to a stronger commitment on consumer rationality. This shift is, to some extent, evident among all NGOs and relevant ministries. However, a wide variability exists regarding the actual application of these new policy discourses. By focusing on the different consumption domains (instead of on specific policy fields), this study makes it apparent that the process of change differs both qualitatively and quantitatively. Our analysis of the various participants involved in facilitating more sustainable consumption in the Netherlands prompts us to proffer a series of recommendations for improving the effectiveness of current interventions.

First, consumption-oriented environmental policy-making should be directed at 'policy units' that are both environmentally significant and connected to the everyday-life rationality of citizen–consumers. The Domain Explorations Project provides an effective foundation for defining the targets of specific policy initiatives. It is now necessary to elaborate upon and prioritize these domains. To prevent this process from devolving into a technocratic exercise that hides the social context of consumption, it is essential to create an active dialogue with citizen–consumers, as the Citizen and the Environment Project did.

Second, the selected policy units – or consumption domains – need to be analysed for prospective environmental hotspots that pose major environmental burdens (and concomitantly hold the potential for large-scale improvements). Government ministries should complete these investigations in cooperation with groups of citizen–consumers to develop appropriate environmental heuristics. Environmental heuristics are relatively simple and practicable principles that connect the predominantly technical rationale of environmentalism with the social rationale of the everyday life-world (Spaargaren et al, 2002). These rules of thumb should enable citizen–consumers to identify environmentally preferable alternatives, within a certain social context, that lead to improvements in the overall performance of the specific domains.

Third, an important issue related to developing environmental heuristics entails visualizing and framing environmental effects as objects of sustainable consumption policy. To date, policy-makers in the Netherlands have not developed many schemes that allow citizen–consumers to assess the environmental impacts of their consumption practices, either at an individual level or as they are embedded within a specific social setting or consumption domain. Researchers are now working – especially with respect to energy – to construct monitoring formats that are geared to consumer rationality and that employ the terminology and images of everyday life.

Fourth, we argue that environmental innovation progresses unevenly across the different consumption domains. Policy-makers need to consider the potential for reform in terms of creative public responses, as well as the available range of sustainable alternatives. In the past, policy objectives with respect to sustainable consumption were often overly ambitious, or did not mesh with improvements already achievable in everyday life. By first assessing capacity for additional ecological modernization in each consumption domain, policy-makers can better tune their interventions to the actual phase of the transition process.

Finally, consumption-oriented environmental policies suggest a need for the participation of citizen–consumers themselves. Active public involvement in shaping such initiatives demands novel approaches – focus groups, panel discussions and discussion forums. In addition, the description and analysis of different lifestyle groups deserves attention. Motivaction's (1999) differentiation of citizen–consumers into ideal types represents a good start, but this approach should be adapted in accordance with *actual* environmental dispositions and consumption practices. Lifestyle groups emerge from – and should be identified according to – the social practices that comprise everyday life.

Some of the building blocks described above are already available, while others still need to be developed. Reflecting upon the current state of knowledge and policy practice, we conclude that the success of efforts to encourage more sustainable consumption hinges on the extent to which they accord with consumer rationality. The social practices model we have described elsewhere strives to integrate several of these building blocks (Spaargaren, 2001; see also Giddens, 1984, 1991). This approach entails a primary focus on specific social practices within everyday life. Domains such as food, housing, leisure and clothing can usefully serve as new units of analysis for environmental policy-making and thus supplant the earlier emphasis on environmental consciousness or individual environmental attitudes. The model combines an emphasis on the everyday life-world with a strong emphasis on the social context in which behavioural routines are situated.

In recent years, we have tested the social practices model in several research and policy settings. On one hand, the model has been employed as an analytical tool to study the potential for sustainable transitions in certain segments of everyday life and to map the factors that could stimulate or impede progress. On the other hand, we have used it as a framework for reflecting upon and for evaluating existing policy initiatives with respect to sustainable consumption. As such, the social practices model has proven valuable in the search for more effective consumption-oriented environmental policies.

Most analysts contend that, since the late 1980s, the development of new horizontal policy arrangements in the Netherlands, as well as the turn towards market-based strategies and civil society actors, represents a major political renewal. The question, though, remains whether we can expect another equally embracing modernization of the environmental policy field in the near future, one characterized and inspired by an even stronger focus on citizen–consumers. We believe that such an approach is essential to prevent a loss of influence and legitimacy. At present, VROM and other relevant policy-making institutions in the Netherlands are pursuing a number of initiatives that influence the everyday life-world of citizen–consumers, but the scale of these efforts remains too limited and their scope overly fragmented. A more vigorous political debate regarding sustainable consumption and the role of citizen–consumers in environmental policy-making is required. An important step in promoting this public discussion entails expanding the pilot projects that various governmental ministries, private companies, NGOs and lifestyle groups have begun to pursue.

Notes

1 Refer to Vringer et al (2001) for a complete description of these consumption domains.
2 By the 1970s and 1980s, certain segments of Dutch society had already begun to turn their attention to the need for 'new lifestyles'. Initiatives consistent with this perspective were pursued primarily within the context of the ecumenical social movement that dedicated several newsletters and seminars to the topic.

3 There is an interesting distinction between 'dark' and 'light' green financial products in the Netherlands. The first generation of dark green investment funds was initiated in the 1970s and many of the rules governing these vehicles actively prohibit investments in heavily polluting industries. The financial products dating from the early 1990s are based on more flexible policies.

4 The relative positions of the consumption domains are predicated upon our own qualitative assessment, because well-defined sets of indicators and related quantitative analyses would require data that are not yet available. Most consumption figures in the Netherlands are expressed in terms of individual household expenditures on products and services in different domains. These data do not include, for example, the availability and accessibility of green alternatives or their overall quality in comparison with conventional substitutes.

5 This transformation includes alternative channels that make regular deliveries to individual subscribers' homes, such as farmers' markets and memberships in organic vegetable distribution networks.

6 One of the largest supermarket chains in the Netherlands – with more than 700 stores – routinely displays 250 organic products depending on the season (www.albertheijn.nl).

7 By 2002, meat alternatives captured a growing share (1 per cent) of Dutch consumers (Aurelia, 2002).

8 If we focus on the production (instead of the consumption) of food in the Netherlands, 1.7 per cent of all farmland in the country was used for organic agriculture in 2002. Official Dutch policy seeks to shift 10 per cent of all farmland to organic production by 2010. Present indications are that it will be quite difficult for the government – in collaboration with farmers and consumers – to achieve this goal (LNV, 2000b).

9 Because of concerns about co-optation, over-institutionalization and loss of public legitimacy, participation in horizontal policy arrangements has caused considerable internal debate within the Dutch environmental movement. Some NGOs have refused to engage in the proceedings – for example, in the contested case concerning the expansion of Schiphol Airport.

10 There have been appeals within Dutch political circles to create a new Ministry of Consumer Affairs. This debate is inspired, on one hand, by the success of such a ministry in Germany and, on the other hand, by uncertainty concerning the future of the current Ministry of Agriculture, Nature and Fisheries. The importance of fisheries and agriculture as policy fields is declining and nature conservation could be readily handled by the Ministry of Housing, Spatial Planning and the Environment. At the same time, the issue of food safety has become more important. Combined with other issues of public concern, it seems practicable to transform the current scheme for managing agricultural activities into a Ministry of Consumer Affairs.

11 The only concrete outcome that has emerged in this regard is a communication plan to attract and retain a new group of organic food consumers. According to official documentation, 'by informing the citizen about sustainable production, animal welfare and biodiversity, this same citizen will, in his or her capacity as a consumer, understand the real value of the organic product and therefore show more willingness to pay a higher price' (LNV, 2000c).

12 This section draws on Beckers et al (2000).

13 The focus was especially on households' indirect use of energy. In the Netherlands, this amounts to about 60 per cent of total domestic usage.

14 The design of the information campaign involved drafting a profile of the prototypical Dutch DIY enthusiast based on personal characteristics, preferences and 'DIY logic'. A typical home renovator in the Netherlands is a male homeowner who is between 25 and 59 years of age. He is married (or is living with a domestic companion), is the salaried member of the

household and has more than average interest in interior design. When choosing products and services the archetypal Dutch DIY aficionado considers quality to be a foremost criterion; subsequent considerations are safety and health, followed by price, environmental characteristics and convenience. Before undertaking a particular renovation task, he will solicit information from store personnel, as well as from brochures, product labels and promotional materials.

References

ADO (Alliantie voor Duurzame Ontwikkaling) (1992) *Duurzaam Gedragen: Strategieen voor gedragsverandering op weg naar een duurzame samenleving* (Sustainable Behaviour: Strategies for Behavioural Change on the Way to a Sustainable Society), ADO, Amsterdam

Aurelia (2002) *Congres vleesalternalieven 2002* (Conference on Meat Alternatives 2002), Den Bosch, Amsterdam

B&A Groep (1997) *Een herijking van da rol van de burger in het milieubeleid* (A Revision of the Role of Citizens in Environmental Policy), B&A Groep, the Hague

B&A Groep (2000) *Burger en Milieu. Verslag van een verkenning naar potentie en meerwaarde van 'burger en milieu'* (Citizen and Environment: Main Report), B&A Groep, the Hague

Basset, P., Berkelder, G., Kuipers, E., van Leeuwen, T. and van Ojik, B. (eds) (1994) *Een beter milieu begint bij de politiek* (A Better Environment Starts with Politics), Wetenschappelijk Bureau GroenLinks, Amsterdam

Bauman, Z. (1993) *Postmodern Ethics*, Blackwell, Oxford

Beckers, T., Spaargaren, G. and Bargeman, B. (2000) *Van Gedragspraktijk naar Beleidspraktijk* (From Social Practice to Policy Practice), Globus, Tilburg

CEA (1999) *Minder energiegebruik door een andere leefstijl?* (Reducing Energy Use by Changing Lifestyles?), CEA, the Hague

CREM (2000) *Domeinverkenning recreeren: Milieuanalyse recreatie en toerisme in Nederland* (Domain Exploration Recreation), CREM, Amsterdam

de Wit, K. (2002) *Green Investments in an Ecological Modernisation Perspective*, Institute of Environmental Studies, Amsterdam

Driessen. P. and Glasbergen, P. (eds) (2000) *Greening Society: The Paradigm Shift in Dutch Environmental Politics*, Kluwer, Boston

Duyvendak, J. (1997) *Waar blijft de politiek? Essays over paarse politiek, maalschappelijk, middenveld en sociale cohesie* (Where are Politics? Essays on Politics, Civil Society and Social Cohesion), Boom, Amsterdam

Duyvendak, J., Horstik, I. and Zagema, B. (eds) (1999) *Het Groene Poldermodel. Consensus en conflict in de milieupolitiek* (The Green Polder Model. Consensus and Conflict in Environmental Politics), Vereniging Milieudefensie, Amsterdam

Energie Ned (2000) *Environmental Action Plan of the Energy Distribution Sector*, Energie Ned, Arnhem

Ester, P. (1999) *Verklaringen van duurzame consumptie; Een spaurtocht naar nieuwe aanknopingspunten voor milieubeleid* (Explanations of Sustainable Consumption: A Search for New Starting Points for Environmental Policy), Publicatiereeks Mitieustrategie, the Hague

EZ (Ministerie van Economische Zaken) (2000) *Nota: Verslerking van de positie van de consument* (Report: Strengthening the Consumer's Position), Ministerie van Economische Zaken, the Hague

Giddens, A. (1984) *The Constitution of Society*, Polity Press, Cambridge

Giddens, A. (1991) *Modernity and Self Identity*, Polity Press, Cambridge

Giddens, A. (1998) *The Third Way: The Renewal of Social Democracy*, Polity Press, Cambridge

Hajer, M. (1995) *The Politics of Environmental Discourse: Ecological Modernization and the Policy Process*, Oxford University Press, New York

Hofkes, M., Idenburg, A. and Verbruggen, H. (1998) *Delinking Environment and Economy; The Necessity of Increased Eco-Efficiancy*, RIVM, Bilthoven, the Netherlands

Koopmans, R. (1995) *Democracy from Below: New Social Movements and the Political System in West Germany*, Westview Press, Boulder, CO

Kuindersma, W. and Seines, T. (1999) *Natuur in de zelfsturende samenleving: Een verkenning van de mogelijkheden* (Nature in the Self-Steering Society: An Exploration), Operatie Boomhut, the Hague

Langers, F. and Spinnenwijn, C. (1999) *Natuur als Leefomgeving: Natuur in de zelfsturende samenleving; inventarisatie van GIS-bestanden en natuurtypoliogieen voor een aanbod en vraagkaart natuur* (Nature as Living Environment), Operatie Boomhut, the Hague

LNV (Ministerie van Landbouw, Natuurbeheer en Visseritj) (2000a) *Voedsel en Groen, het Nederlandse Agro-foodcomplex in Perspectief* (Food and Environment: The Dutch Agrofood Complex), Ministerie van Landbouw, Natuur en Visserij, the Hague

LNV (2000b) *Natuur voor Mensen, Mensen voor Natuur* (Nature for People, People for Nature), Ministerie van Landbouw, Natuur en Visserij, the Hague

LNV (2000c) *Een biologische markt te winnen* (An Organic Market to Conquer), Ministerie van Landbouw, Natuur en Visserij, the Hague

Martens, S. and Spaargaren, G. (2002) *Gedragspraktijken in Transitie; de casus Duurzamer Wonen* (Social Practices in Transition: The Case of Sustainable Dwelling), Milieustrategie, the Hague

Mol, A. and Spaargaren, G. (1993) 'Environment, modernity and the risk society: The apocalyptic horizon of environmental reform', *International Sociology*, vol 8, no 4, pp431–459

Motivaction (1999) *Socioconsult; Milieubelevingsgroepen in Nederland: een kwanlitatief onderzoek naar drijfveren, profielen en mogelijkheden tot communicatie* (Environmental Perception Groups in the Netherlands: A Quantitative Research into Motives, Profiles and Communication Opportunities), Motivaction, Amsterdam

Platform Biologica (2001) *EkoMonitor: cijfers en trends. Jaarrapport 2001* (Ecological Monitoring: Figures and Trends – Annual Report 2001), Platform Biologica, Utrecht, the Netherlands

Postma, A. (2000) *Ecologische Voetafdruk, belekenis en bruikbaarheid* (Ecological Footprint, Meaning and Usefulness), Wetenschapswinkel voor Economic, Groningen, the Netherlands

Princen, T., Maniates, M. and Conca, K. (eds) (2002) *Confronting Consumption*, MIT Press, Cambridge, MA

Rifkin, J. (2002) *The Age of Access: How the Shift from Ownership to Access is Transforming Modern Life*, Penguin, London

RIVM (Rijksinstituut voor Volksgezondheid en Milieu) (2003) *Milieubalans 2003: Het Nederlandse milieu verklaard*, RIVM, Bilthoven, the Netherlands

Rood, G., Ros, J., Drissen, E., Vringer, K., Aalbers, T. and Speek, G. (2001) *Model Structure for Environmental Pressure Due to Consumption*, RIVM, Bilthoven, the Netherlands

Schnaiberg, A. (1980) *The Environment: From Surplus to Scarcity*, Oxford University Press, New York

Schuttelaar and Partners (2000) *Domeinverkenning Voeden: Ingredienten voor een gezond milieu* (Domain Exploration Feeding: Ingredients for a Healthy Environment), Schuttelaar and Partners, the Hague

SCP (Sociaal Cultureel Planbureau) (2001) *Het nieuwe consumeren, een vooruitblik vanuit demografie en individualisering* (The New Consumption: A Demographic Perspective), Social Culureel Planbureau, the Hague

SER (Sociaal Economische Raad) (1994) *Advies Produkt en Milieu* (Advisory Report Product and Environment), Sociall Economishe Raad, the Hague

Shove, E. (2003) *Comfort, Cleanliness, and Convenience: The Social Organization of Normality*, Berg, New York

Spaargaren, G. (2001) *Milieuverandering en het alledaagse leven* (Environmental Change and Everyday Life), Inaugural Address, Tilburg University, Tilburg, the Netherlands

Spaargaren, G. (2003) 'Sustainable consumption: A theoretical and environmental policy perspective', *Society and Natural Resources*, vol 16, no 8, pp687–701

Spaargaren, G. and Mol, A. (1992) 'Sociology, environment and modernity: Ecological modernity as a theory of social change', *Society and Natural Resources*, vol 5, no 4, pp323–344

Spaargaren, G., Beckers, T., Martens, S., Bargeman, B. and van Es, T. (2002) *Gedragspraktijken in Transitie* (Social Practices in Transition), Milieustrategie, the Hague

TNO-STB (TNO Strategy, Technology, and Policy) (1999) *Duurzame consumptie: Verkenning Kleding* (Domain Exploration Clothing), TNO-STB, Delft, the Netherlands

V&W (Ministerie van Verkeer en Waterstaat) (2000) *Van A naar Beter: Nationaal Verkeer – en Vervoersplan* (From A to Better: National Traffic and Transportation Plan 2001–2020), Ministerie van Verkeer en Waterstaat, the Hague

van der Grijp, N. and den Hond, F. (1999) *Green Supply Chain Initiatives in the European Food and Retailing Industry*, IVM Report R-99/07, Vrije Universiteit, Amsterdam

van Driel, P., Cramer, J., Crone, F., Hajer, M. and van Latesteijn, H. (1993) *Ecologische Modernisering*, Wiardi Beckman Stichting, Amsterdam

van Vliet, B. (2002) *Greening the Grid: The Ecological Modernisation of Network Bound Systems*, PhD thesis, Wageningen University, Wageningen, the Netherlands

Vermeulen, W. (2000) 'De weerbarstige consument' in P. Driessen and P. Glasbergen (eds) *Greening Society: The Paradigm Shift in Dutch Environmental Politics*, Kluwer, Boston, MA

Vringer, K., Aalbers, T., Drissen, E., Hoevenagel, R., Bertens, C., Rood, G., Ros, J. and Annema, J. (2001) *Nederlandse Consumptie en Energiegebruik in 2030* (Dutch Consumption and Energy Use in 2030), RIVM, Biithoven, the Netherlands

VROM (Ministerie van Volkshuisvesling, Ruimtelijke Ordening en Milieubeheer) (1989) *National Environmental Policy Programme*, 1988–1989, 21137, no 1–2, Tweede Kamer, VROM, the Hague

VROM (1997) *Tweede Plan van Aanpak Duurzaam Bouwen* (Second Action Plan Sustainable Building), VROM, the Hague

VROM (1998) *The Third Dutch National Environmental Policy Plan*, VROM, the Hague

VROM (1999a) *Diturzaam Bouwen Monitoring. Resultaten Plannen van Aanpak 1995–1999* (Sustainable Building Evaluation 1995–1999), VROM, the Hague

VROM (1999b) *Beleidsprogramma Duurzaam Bouwen 2000–2004* (Policy Programme Sustainable Building 2000–2004), VROM, the Hague

VROM (2000) *De Warme Golfstroom: Herorientatie op communicatie over milieu* (Warm Gulf Stream: A Reorientation on Communication about the Environment), VROM, the Hague

VROM (2002a) *The Fourth Dutch National Environmental Policy Plan*, VROM, the Hague

VROM (2002b) *Nationale Strategievoor Duurzame Ontwikkeling* (National Strategy for Sustainable Development), VROM, the Hague

Winsemius, P. (1986) *Gast in Eigen Huis: Beschouwingen over Milieumanagement* (Guest in Your Own Home: Reflections in Environmental Management), Samsom, Alphen aan den Rijn, the Netherlands

15

The Poverty of Morality

Daniel Miller

If 20 years ago the topic of consumption was unduly neglected across all the disciplines, today our problem seems as much constituted by a deluge of writing about our relationship with goods as by the flood of goods themselves. I want to argue, however, that this flood of writings may only amount to a trickle of insights into the nature of consumption, consumers and consumer culture. The discrepancy between the quantity and the quality of research is largely a result of the central role taken by morality within consumption research which has led to this branch of studies becoming largely a site where academics can demonstrate their stance towards the world, rather than a place where the world stands as a potential empirical critique of our assumptions about it.

I am going to write this in the form of a general commentary since I do not wish to cite any particular instances of that which I oppose. My excuse is that this case is unusual in that the people I most oppose are probably among the people I most admire and respect. I vastly prefer the overt moralists I critique here to the amoral or indeed immoral stances of those that they are critiquing. This is a plea to change style and direction, but I am trying not to lose too many friends as a result! My targets seem to be interdisciplinary including scholars in sociology, cultural studies, economics and consumer studies. My characterization seems to me largely untrue of history and I would have to confess to a bias that makes me think/hope that anthropology tends to be more nuanced. The stance I am critiquing seems to me more characteristic, though by no means confined, to US writing, where I would argue there has been considerable continuity in both the form of moralism and the beliefs about why people consume. Take, for example, the centrality of status competition and emulation to both Veblen and the recent work of Schor (1998), with the main difference being the degree to which Schor sees this factor as having spread through the population at large.

Is Consumption Materialistic?

My basic position is fairly simple. It seems to me that writings about consumption are saturated by a pervasive anxiety most acutely felt by fairly well-off academics, mainly in the US, about the possibility that they may be too materialistic. This is combined with a genuine desire to critique the inequalities and exploitation that follow various aspects of modern capitalism, and most recently a strident environmentalism. Put together, these have produced a veritable industry consisting of the critique of almost all aspects of consumption as a means to attack the triple-headed Cerberus of materialism, capitalism and planetary exploitation. This moral stance is so powerful that it refuses to be altered by exposure to the many actual studies of consumers and consumption in which they appear as other than that which this critique requires them to be for the purposes of expressing its moral position.

The result is an extraordinarily conservative vision of consumption. In a sense consumption has throughout history been seen as intrinsically evil. While production creates the world, consumption is the act whereby we use it up. Contemporary views perpetuate the historical sense of consumption as a wasting disease (Porter, 1993) whose diagnosis and prognosis are established; the only legitimate debate is about its cure. This is no great surprise since my argument follows closely the excellent history of this same moralism published by Horowitz (1985). Although he shows some changes in the nature of that moralism over time, it is the continuities in the basic ideological stance to the growth of consumerism that are striking. My case amounts to little more than the argument that this continues to be true today. That is, current writings about 'mega-malls' and 'virtual reality shopping' are recycling texts and arguments that may span millennia (e.g. Sekora, 1977). What all of this prevents is not only a proper encounter with actual studies of consumption and consumers but the emergence of an alternative critique based on that scholarly encounter, one that is sufficiently nuanced to be appropriately targeted at the complex and contradictory processes of consumption that can actually be observed (Miller, 1998b, 2001).

I consider all three of these assumptions: that consumption is materialistic, that it is capitalist and that it is incompatible with environmentalism. I also briefly tackle some other baggage that trails in the wake of this moralism, in particular the assumption that mass consumption is a form of Americanization of the world. But the central issue is that of materialism.

The critique of materialism is extraordinarily basic. There is an abiding sense in this literature that pure individuals or pure social relations are sullied by commodity culture. Indeed the central plank of the colloquial term 'materialism' is that this represents an attachment or devotion to objects that is at the expense of an attachment and devotion to persons. There may be people for whom the problem of materialism is genuine. I am sure we should all be deeply sympathetic to the dreadful plight of cosmopolitans who feel they have too many pairs of shoes and feel guilty because their cereal wasn't really organic, or that they bought their child a present instead of spending the requisite amount of 'quality time' with them. I guess there are many reasons why such people are appalled by the waste and quantity of consumer goods. But what is not acceptable is that the study of consumption, and any potential moral stance to it, be reduced to an expression of such people's guilt and anxieties. What this obviates is a quite different morality, an ethics based on a passionate desire to eliminate poverty. We live in a time when most human suffering is the direct result of the lack of goods. What most of humanity desperately needs is more consumption, more pharmaceuticals, more housing, more transport, more books, more computers. I would consider myself a hypocrite if I saw the aspiration of any other person to at least the same level of consumption that I enjoy with my family as anything other than reasonable. And I have never – and I really do mean never – met an academic carrying out research on the topic of consumption who appeared to practise for their own family this substantially lower level of consumption. So at a time when more than half the world does not have basic goods I find it hard to respect an approach to consumption whose only consideration is the superfluity of commodities.

Indeed I think we need to start with a fundamental question. Are most commodities of benefit to most people? Let us start with material culture itself. I do not believe in the pre-cultural human being stripped of the material world. Even Eastern philosophies that see enlightenment as the elimination of desire do not support the colloquial term 'materialism', since their aims are to eliminate desire in respect to persons as much as to things, while the contemporary critique of materialism is supposed to liberate people from things in order for them to engage in pure social relations. My upbringing in anthropology starts from the opposite concept of authenticity. Our bedrock for authentic social relations tends to be Mauss (1954) who in *The Gift* starts with the example of children exchanged as though they were things and then considers things exchanged as though they were persons. That is to say, the authenticity of non-capitalist society is seen in the inseparable nature of persons and things. It is the trajectory towards capitalist society that leads to the development of an ideology of pure personhood (e.g. Sennett, 1976) and an increasing distance from things that during the Enlightenment started to be seen as radically other to persons, as something that could detract from rather than enhance our humanity.

I do not wish to retrace my own steps to a philosophy of subject–object relations which is presented as a general theory of objectification and then culture in Miller (1987). Suffice to say I take a dialectical view. Humanity and social relations can only develop through the medium of objectification. Subjects are as much the product of objects as the other way around (exemplified in Bourdieu, 1977). It is possible for these objects to become oppressive when they are sundered from us, as Marx suggests, under capitalism or, as Simmel suggests, when we can no longer assimilate them within the growth of the subjective. As with all culture, material culture is contradictory in its consequences for humanity, but this should not detract from its centrality to the very possibility of our humanity. Clearly, however, this process is rather different in a society with a paucity of things from a society with an abundance. In our image of Australian Aboriginal material culture a very few objects and images form the basis of such a complex symbolic nexus that they become the medium of highly sophisticated cosmological and social projects (e.g. Munn, 1973; Myers, 1986). In our own society, however, the sheer plethora of things seem to make this impossible. We can certainly see the possibility, glimpsed by Simmel (1978), that we become superficially related to so many things that we are deeply involved in none, leading to what he saw as the blasé condition of some urban life. In addition the recent literature has assumed that the conditions under which we are led to desire, for example, branded goods through intense advertising are so problematic that any subsequent relationship of identity that we forge through them must be inauthentic.

What worries me is that this bogey of a deluded, superficial person who has become the mere mannequin to commodity culture is always someone other than ourselves. It is the common people, the vulgar herd, the mass consumer, a direct descendant of the older 'mass culture critique' of the 1960s. It is never the rounded person who is encountered within an ethno graphic engagement. If, however, we approach our own social relations and practice with the same level of respect, the same empathy and the same patience that a good ethnographer attempts to bring to the apparent authenticity of others, then we see something quite different – a world where a pair of Nike trainers or Gap jeans might be extraordinarily eloquent about the care a mother has for her child, or the aspirations of an asthmatic child to take part in sports.

We need to start with an acknowledgement that there are many things in the world that we see quite unproblematically as beneficial, and which we surely have in mind when we think in terms of the elimination of poverty, that is adequate housing, cheap pharmaceuticals, warm clothing, nutritious food. Why has all of this somehow become something other than consumption? Why is this not the foundation of consumer culture? Why, to use a title of a previous book, are we so afraid to acknowledge consumption? But it is not just objects. We see people whose possibilities in the world are constantly enhanced by huge quantities of knowledge: the library that supplies an endless possibility of books, the transport that allows them a diversity of places to experience, the development of information technology so that I can spend one hour correcting my (awful!) spelling instead of a week and use email to work with colleagues in Australia and not just in my department.

But what of the less obviously utilitarian things of the world? Do we really need a hundred styles of trousers to choose from, cuisines from every part of the world, an even faster computer? Again we can only consider such things from the basis of that same respectful encounter. After all we do not respect Australian Aboriginals for reducing their object world to the bare necessity of utility – even if they are not all original affluent societies (Sahlins, 1974). The idea that the people of Amazonia, or Melanesia or Aboriginal Australia either were or are people of simple or basic needs is such a bizarre distortion of a century of anthropology as to beggar belief. It is precisely the richness of their symbolism, the interpenetration of social and material relations, the way cosmology and morality is absorbed in and expressed through myth, material culture and other such media that makes up the core of anthropological teaching. Trobriand islanders are known for their huge piles of conspicuously long yams and the voyages of Kula to exchange armshells, not for their attachment to strict functionalism. It is often the poor who are most assertive about the centrality of symbolic consumption. It was those living in the worst slums of England that kept the best room of the house as a 'parlour' reserved almost exclusively for show (Roberts, 1973). Peasant villagers in India often get into debt not for basic land rights but by funding wedding feasts. It is the complexity of the symbolic systems of the peoples of the world, not some base utilitarianism, that anthropologists look for, expect to find and celebrate in their studies. So the question we ought to be asking of our own society is whether there is any similarly rich symbolic structure within our own material culture.

To answer this question I approach our material culture in the same spirit as I would that of Melanesia or Amazonia, that is through the nuance of ethnographic immersion. As examples I summarize two such ethnographic explorations. The first (Miller, 1998a) is concerned with a street of shoppers in North London. What do they do with the sheer quantity and diversity of goods? My argument in a nutshell is that we find a society that has seen a radical transformation over the last century in its ideals of love and care. Where once specific gestures based on social norms, such as flowers on Friday from husband to wife, were respected, today we feel that love is demonstrated only in the sensitivity shown by one individual for all that they have learned about the particular nature of the other. When a mother shops for her child she may feel that there are a hundred garments in that shop that would be fine for all her friends' children but she loves her own child enough that the exact balance between what his or her school friends will consider 'cool' and what her family will consider respectable matters hugely to her, enough for her to reject the lot and keep on searching until she finds the one article that satisfies this subtle and exacting need. A woman who feels her boyfriend has paid sufficient attention that he can successfully buy her a pair of suitable shoes while unaccompanied feels she really has a boyfriend to treasure. How this relates to commerce and capitalism I examine later; for now my only concern is to suggest that it is possible that people appropriate this plethora of goods in order to enhance and not to detract from our devotion to other people.

My second example is from Trinidad (Miller, 1994) where an oil boom turned this island from a developing region to a relatively wealthy one with access to large amounts of consumer goods. My argument is that Trinidadians, just like Australian Aborigines, are concerned to find a medium for objectifying their values and moral orders. Prior to the arrival of mass consumption the primary vehicle for this task was other people. In short, Trinidadians had strong and explicit views about what 'women are like', what 'Indians are like', what 'big shot people are like'. In my analysis I suggested that most of these dualistic and powerful stereotypes about gender, class, ethnicity and so forth are a result of the working out of a fundamental set of dualistic values that arose from their radical experience of modernity, particularly through the rupture of slavery and the subsequent centrality of freedom. In short, as in most societies, categories of persons become the objects that objectify our values. I then analysed the products of mass consumption, the cars, the clothes, the interior furnishings that have emerged with the oil boom and suggested that during that period there was a shift from the use of categories of persons to that of categories of things as the means to objectify these fundamental values and dualisms. Material culture presented several advantages over persons as vehicles for the expression of these symbolic systems. Furthermore, to some degree this released the burden on people as objects for the expression of value and led to a greater freedom to treat individuals more in terms of their particular character and less as mere tokens or stereotypes that stood for some particular value or moral position. So in this case the rise of material culture with the complex symbolism of mass consumer goods tended to lessen the treatment of people as stereotypes.

So in both these cases the mere desire to behave as a conventional anthropologist – by which I mean to empathetically consider the perspective of the people one is working with, whether Londoners or Trinidadians – creates the potential for exploring the appropriation of material culture in both settings in an analogous fashion to that of studying material culture in an Australian Aboriginal society. I do not wish to suggest that the postmodern perspective on rampant superficiality is impossible. For all I know if I carried out fieldwork in parts of Los Angeles I would finally encounter these, as it were, poor rich materialists, who have lost the capacity for anything other than superficial relationships with persons and things. But at the very least we need to consider the possibility that the sheer quantity of contemporary material culture might, among certain peoples and in certain circumstances, enhance their humanity and develop their sociality.

During my own fieldwork, the materialism that is being attacked has been actually found to be much more prevalent among the impoverished. It is when I work with the unemployed or those living on government housing estates that I find people who have sacrificed their concern for others, sometimes their own kin, because of sheer desire or a felt desperate need for things. It is people without education who tend to have difficulty appropriating the plethora of goods because it requires detailed knowledge and research to assimilate them. It was the people who found they could not relate to their kitchen furnishing who also had difficulty in establishing friendships and social lives (Miller, 1988). These experiences leave me feeling that I have the evidence to argue that increases in education, in wealth and in people's relationship with their material culture are also often the foundation for enhancing their social relations.

Instead it seems to me that research on consumption, especially that within the US, derives from something completely different than the desire to study actual consumption or consumers, something far removed from this commitment to ethnographic or equivalent experience based on an empathetic encounter with consumers. Rather, I see an astonishing continuity between the most recent discussions of consumption and the foundational work of Veblen and those that preceded him (see Horowitz, 1985). The mark of this 'Veblenesque' critique is that it always takes the most extreme examples of conspicuous consumption as its characterization of all consumption. So just as once it was the tiny sector of nouveau riche – those who could afford footmen and other such servants – that were Veblen's true consumers, so now it is always the evident excesses of wealthy consumers that come to stand for consumption in itself. As Veblen asserted the puritan value of labour and the priority of utility over display, so today symbolic expressions are never true 'needs' and are bound to express negative values such as status competition or insatiable greed. Consumption is still conspicuous consumption, and vicarious consumption based on emulation and the desire to deny labour. It's just that the examples used to illustrate the arguments have shifted by a century.

As I have written elsewhere (Miller, 1995) I have as much of a problem with the idea that consumption is an intrinsic good as that it is an intrinsic bad. I would not wish to generalize from the two instances I have just given to any version of a conclusion that suggested consumption must always be seen as a good thing. These are the two sides of a coin that seems only interested in consumption as a stance towards an often glib comment on the morality of the zeitgeist. In this respect there remains a considerable distinction between a material culture studies devoted to the ethnographic encounter with the dialectics of culture as social and material practice, and some cultural studies that seem to reduce the study of consumption to its potential contribution to what they call 'debates' and which contain many examples of consumption as a heroic struggle or act of resistance. I hope that my stance towards consumption has been consistently dialectical (Miller, 1987, 2001). I assume that there are both positive and negative elements to all such developments and it is the task of politics to accentuate the possibilities for human welfare and ameliorate the negative effects.

Is Consumption Capitalist?

The title of this chapter is intended to evoke the classic essay by E. P. Thompson, *The Poverty of Theory* (1978). Thompson is important in that, at the time he wrote his withering critique of Althusser, it might have been thought that theory – just like morality – is an intrinsically good thing for academics, and that to attack theory or morality is to profane the sacrosanct. In fact, his essay remains exemplary because I would argue that the problem with the critique of consumption as capitalist culture has a great deal in common with the critique of capitalism that characterized 1970s Western Marxism, and is making a series of rather similar misjudgements and mistakes.

On the one hand there was at that time a profound and necessary critique of inequality, which I hope most academics still support. Marxist ideas seemed to most academics in Western Europe to constitute the very essence of a moral critique, a feeling that social evils had to be exposed and opposed. Unfortunately several tendencies within that movement may have made it counter-productive to the critique of inequality in the longer term. The first was part of what Thompson called *The Poverty of Theory*. He argued that theory (today I would say morality) can become a form of closure. It recognizes the world only in as much as what it observes is generated by the stance it takes to the world. If consumption is capitalist, then only those consumption acts that are consistent with the dominant image of capitalism are recognized as true consumption. Second, it becomes abstracted from its relationship to the empirical. Althusser dismissed historical research as mere empiricism. By contrast, Thompson argues (pp199–200) that the cornerstone of historical research is the concept of experience that is a commitment to empathetically engage as closely as possible with people's experience of their time. While morality and theory seem to require no such encounter (they already know what they are against), the ethnographic enquiry I wish to promote, and the historical enquiry promoted by Thompson, represent a quest for an empathetic enquiry into experience. This is why I would argue today that the empirical encounter has actually become the proper source of contemporary radicalism as against the spurious claims to radicalism from theory and morality. Yet, rounded scholarship that is devoted to communicating the humanity of the consumer – not using them merely to test hypotheses – remains conspicuously rare in any of the disciplinary researches into consumption.

This is why it is equally important not to assume that consumption under capitalism is mere capitalist consumption. Thompson had no doubt that he was studying capitalism. But he never allowed his portrayal of the English working class to be merely a pawn in the game of critiquing capitalism. Indeed his primary task was to rescue the portrayal of the working people and return them to the flesh and blood humanity of experience. It was the theorists who had reduced the proletariat to simply a motif to be deployed within radical rhetoric. Similarly the task today is to rescue the humanity of the consumer from being reduced to a rhetorical trope in the critique of capitalism. The moralistic critique of consumption actually dehumanizes and fetishizes the consumer, and thereby serves the cause of the very capitalism it claims to critique.

Thompson's portrayal of the working class never denied the possibility of their own perspicacity and sense of struggle. In my first work on consumption (Miller, 1987) my aim was precisely to argue that it is not just a bunch of enlightened academics who feel alienated and cheated by the excesses of capitalism. Most people feel that they tend to be dehumanized and alienated from the vast scale and mechanized form of modern mass production. For this reason modern consumption should not be dismissed as merely the end point of a process which is used to characterize capitalism as a whole. Rather, I argued that consumption was the very means that people used to try and create the identity they feel they have lost as labourers for capitalism, using the mass of goods to counter the homogenization and massivity of capitalist production. Far from expressing capitalism, consumption is most commonly used by people to negate it. To merely critique it as the creature of capitalism is therefore to ignore the practice of actual consumers. But the moralists who need to use consumption for their critique of capitalism cannot understand that for ordinary people consumption is actually the way that they confront, on a day-to-day basis, their sense of alienation.

The conception of materialism held by Karl Marx, for example, could not have been more distinct from that employed within much critique of modern consumption. As recently pointed out by Stallybrass (1998), Marx saw that the problem for the proletariat was that they were sundered from people because they were sundered from things. Marx's enemy was poverty and the lack of possessions. He fully recognized the vital role of material culture within the development of social and cultural relations. The contemporary concept of materialism was quite alien to Marx himself, since even a cursory knowledge of his life suggests that he was very far from being any kind of an ascetic (Wheen, 1999).

By contrast the Western Marxism of the 1970s embraced a version of asceticism that assumed that contemporary material culture – because it is created by capitalism – is thereby tainted and will pollute those who live with it and through it. This asceticism proved its undoing. It allowed the political right wing to associate socialism with poverty. This ascetic left became deeply unpopular in a world where the actual proletariat still considered itself to be engaged in a struggle for a basic standard of living. This opened the way to the victory of the right-wing governments of Reagan, Thatcher and their ilk. More recently a reaction to this asceticism appeared in the form of a branch of cultural studies that seemed to celebrate modern consumerism as quite the opposite – a kind of heroic form of resistance or appropriation that was inevitably beneficial. The profundity of Thompson and Williams did not prevent a move whereby mass culture became popular culture and, merely because it was practised by working people, it was viewed as somehow authentic and noble.

Materialism in the sense employed by academics such as Thompson is precisely what we should embrace. It is a commitment to the unity of thought and experience, to our grounded existence (Thompson, 1978, p210). The problem with the critics of consumption is not that they are too materialist – what they see as the doomed condition of the world. To my mind the central problem of research on consumption is that most of the researchers are simply not materialist enough. They show little sense of the more profound kind of materialism that genuinely critical academic enquiry has tried to foster over the last century, as exemplified by researchers such as E. P. Thompson. They are insufficiently steeped in the materiality of ordinary experience and conduct insufficient fieldwork on social relations and material culture as human praxis. Much of what is developing in the contemporary critique of consumption is therefore replaying all that went wrong in the development of the European-based Western Marxist critique of capitalism of 20 years ago, with exactly the same danger that true moral effect will be lost under the overwhelming desire for moral affect.

The elimination of poverty depends on industrialization and mass production. Numerous little crafts are fine as a personal hobby, but as an economic foundation they are simply a recipe for increasing poverty. William Morris produced marvellous craft works, but I don't know many people who can afford to buy them. My own stance derives from the traditions of European social democracy. This tradition aims for higher taxation to fund increased welfare and redistribution and stronger state and international bureaucracy to curb the immoral effects of short-term competition-driven markets, such that, for example, pension funds run companies to provide long-term benefit to pensioners and not to syphon money from business to stock markets (Clark, 2000). But this social democratic tradition has established its complementarity to market economies and industrialization after seeing the destructive effects of the simplistic rejection of the 1970s (see Nove, 1983).

The social democratic programme fought for an increasing level of wealth based on redistribution as well as production. It recognized that even in affluent societies most people do not feel their needs have been fulfilled (e.g. Segal, 1998). It saw industrialization as having the potential for decreasing hours of work. The problem has been the decline in these developments as against the growing influence of a US model that is driven by the stock market and short-term financial goals (see Henwood, 1997; Hutton, 1996), and which has become associated with the increasing pressures on work described by Cross (1993) and Schor (1992). But this is a specific set of associations; it is not even intrinsic to capitalism, it is the particular combination of capitalism with liberalism that is characteristic of certain neo-liberal regimes. The social democratic alternative suggests there is nothing intrinsic to consumer societies that should lead to either inequality or higher pressures on work; what is required is a politics that remains consistent in regarding human welfare as its goal.

A Critique of the Americanization Critique

Imagine that we are carrying out a study of contemporary consumption among the middle class in Thailand (it could equally well be Nigeria or Sri Lanka). We have documented the involvement of this class in a wide range of modern consumer products. We have watched their kids watching Pokemon, we have seen the man in the family finally able to afford that Mercedes-Benz he has had his eyes on for some time. We observe a party well lubricated with bottles of whisky. After accumulating our evidence we write an academic article using this as a case study in Americanization.

We blithely ignore the evidence that neither Pokemon nor whisky nor Mercedes-Benz (any more than most of modern consumer culture) originate in the US. Contemporary consumer culture is actually produced throughout the world. Instead we focus upon the following features. First, the loss of what we see as authentic culture, which we imply is that which historically characterized the people of that particular region. We see this authentic culture as replaced by what we regard as an inauthentic culture that cannot really express the people of this region in the way the displaced material culture was able to do. Second, we focus upon the evidence for commodification and what we see as the rise of materialism, hedonism and individualism, all of which we associate with the same replacement of authentic by inauthentic material culture. Third, we focus on the evidence for globalization and the incorporation of these peoples in global commodity capitalism. Fourth, we draw attention to the development of class distinctions and status and other differences within that society as expressed by these consumption patterns. Finally, we conclude that the combination of all these factors is evidence for the continued spread of Americanization to the critique of which we believe we have now contributed.

Could it be that such apparently well-meaning, morally upright papers might at another level be largely self-serving, condescending, or even racist forms of academic production that primarily project the interests of middle-class American academics? I assume that the authors of such materials sincerely believe that these articles are an expression of their genuine concern with the welfare of other peoples and the damage they believe is being inflicted upon others by powerful forces they associate with their own society. So in no sense do I wish to impugn their motives. I simply want to suggest that they may misunderstand the implications of their own academic production. Indeed what such articles mainly serve to accomplish is the continued domination of a particular US stance on the topic of consumption itself – a stance that I criticized earlier – but here exported to the rest of the world. In a sense it may amount to an exploitation of the world for the benefit of one group's moral stance.

My argument rests on the degree to which the critique of Americanization makes the following assumptions. First, that the only population who have the right to claim an authentic relationship to modern consumer culture are US citizens. Second, that black people (with the possible exception of a home-grown US black middle class) cannot use such things as an expression of their own authenticity. Third, that the only place to have produced and to claim credit for the construction of this commodity culture is the US. Fourth, that only the US and its own form of capitalism can claim the 'blame' for the creation of class and social differences wherever they may be found. Fifth, that such wealth is in and of itself an inauthentic attribute for people from the developing world who therefore have less right to it than the 'naturally' wealthy of the first world. In effect wealthy black people of the developing world are an anomaly – they appear in academia like an ugly aberration in the purity of more authentic otherness. Sixth, that all relationships of the rest of the world to commodity culture can be characterized as one either of 'acceptance' – which is then symptomatic of colonial or post-colonial 'settlements' – or one of 'resistance' – which is when other people are deemed to have responded 'properly'. Finally, all other societies are deemed to be 'naturally' good, so if two tribal groups in Africa attempt to commit genocide, or a Korean government suppresses its people, this is not some expression of the complex history of that region but must be the side effect of either colonialism (now usually post-colonialism), capitalism or American influence. Under this condescending attitude only the US or Western Europe can be authentically bad.

Wolf (1982) wrote of the people without history, and Wolf was a passionate anthropologist deeply concerned with the welfare of peoples all around the world as well as the effects of colonialism and dependency. Yet curiously it is the mechanical application of blame/credit to the eponymous West (notwithstanding a sometimes contradictory employment of the term 'post-colonial') for whatever continues to happen wherever it continues to happen, that ensures that as far as we are concerned these continue to be peoples without history. The paradox of the critique of Americanization is that in essence it is itself a form of Americanization. The paradox is that by claiming all the blame for modern culture Americans can in effect take all the credit. Its starting point is that all consumer culture is in some respect deeply American. I have already noted that none of the goods in my admittedly fictional case were of US origin. The absurdity of this was brought home to me when I reviewed a book called *Re-Made in Japan* (Tobin, 1992). This was a series of studies about consumer culture in Japan. It makes clear that, notwithstanding the obviously huge contribution that the Japanese have made to the production of contemporary consumer goods, the Japanese had managed to convince themselves that consumer culture is actually something that had come to them from America and was a threat to authentic Japaneseness for this reason.

Potentially this denial of the contribution of the rest of the world to the production of modern culture is a disastrous state of affairs since as the people of each region of the world become users of commodity culture, they come to feel that they have become somehow less authentic, that this culture is not really theirs however much they possess it. I remember perceiving the pathology of this when talking to a Trinidadian who, during the oil boom, had purchased 25 pairs of jeans. However many pairs he purchased, he could never really possess them, since jeans would always remain American and he was not. What is being exported is the sense of alienation.

When studying in Trinidad, I took as my starting point the sentiments expressed in the novel *The Mimic Men* by V. S. Naipaul (1967). Naipaul appeared to be suggesting that without a deep history of their own, this mixture of displaced peoples have no hope of ever being other than mimics of the commodity culture and pretensions that are developed elsewhere. It is the relentless superficiality of this constant emulation that is ridiculed in his work. It is not that surprising that Naipaul later finds himself almost inexorably drawn to the region of Stonehenge – the wellspring of precisely the one culture he does regard as authentic, that of Britain. In an inspiring book, *The Enigma of Arrival* (1987), he starts to come to terms with his realization that he had in fact simply refused to countenance the authenticity of change and the fluidity of culture that was evident even around Stonehenge. Only then could he start to think of Trinidad itself as at least potentially authentic.

Much of my own fieldwork in Trinidad has been an attempt to demonstrate that consumption can be a process for the construction of inalienable and authentic culture from a regional and not just an individual perspective. I deliberately wrote about the most tainted and least likely examples of local culture: a soap opera produced in the US, Coca-Cola, the celebration of Christmas, the workings of capitalist firms and most recently the internet (Miller, 1994, 1997; Miller and Slater, 2000). In each case I emphasized what might be called *a posteriori* rather than *a priori* culture. That is, we have to allow culture to be the product of the subsequent localization of global forms, rather than only that which has some deep historical and local tradition. I argued that not only must Coca-Cola be understood in Trinidad as 'a black sweet drink' that comes from Trinidad itself (see also Watson, 1997), but that capitalism itself, as a system of production and distribution, is actively consumed and localized as much as the goods it produces. Even the latest example of evident globalization – the internet – turns into a powerful instrument for establishing the specific qualities of highly parochial and national cultural practices as well as objectifying a form of strident nationalism. By the same token I have tried to focus on the Trinidadian export not just of music and style but of company managers and web designers.

My conclusion is that the critique of Americanization has actually become one of the most pernicious examples of Americanization. I suspect peoples throughout the world are thoroughly oppressed by a critique of Americanization which constantly tells them that the culture they increasingly inhabit can never be theirs and denies any role they may have played in its production. Indeed we have reached the absurd stage when the only activity that is granted authenticity for most of the world is that of 'resistance'.

Conclusion: The Morality of Poverty Against the Poverty of Morality

Nothing in my experience of fieldwork, whether in peasant villages in India or state housing in London, suggests to me that there are social benefits to poverty. I cannot accept that the day-to-day struggle of most of the people of this world to increase their income is deluded. My problem is rather why the branch of academic enquiry I am concerned with seems to start from the premise that goods are to the detriment of their owners. I can only explain this by the following logic. First, that many of these academics belong to that tiny class that really do feel they have enough. Second, that many of them come from a historical tradition in which the entrepreneurial production of wealth developed in and through a protestant ideology of asceticism. That Weber remains the best foundation for analysing the dominant ideology of these academics is confirmed historically by Horowitz and remains evident today. Indeed there are yet older roots in the fear of consumption as an intrinsically destructive activity, the place where objects are used up. Third, it seems fair to add that the fear of materialism is shared by most people around the world even during their pursuit of possessions. What has been ignored are the measures most people take as consumers to counter the antisocial potential of their material culture (see Gell, 1986, and Wilk, 1989, on the role of the house in this regard). Instead I would argue that the proper starting point for the study of consumption is precisely this and several other contradictions that seem fundamental both to consumption and modern social relations. What wealth brings with it is not some simple good or bad effect but the clearer emergence of historical contradictions, for example, the incompatibility of a sense of freedom and the desire for social reciprocity, or the replacement of the interests of consumers by a host of 'virtual' consumers such as auditors, consultants, economists and litigious groups that claim to stand on behalf of consumers but usurp their interests. These contradictions are to my mind much closer to the actual struggles of contemporary consumers (see Miller, 2001).

In this chapter I have not dealt in any detail with environmentalists' critiques, basically because I accept them as a proper concern for the welfare of our descendants and our responsibility to our environment. But even this critique is weakened when it becomes a front for an ascetic repudiation of the need for goods per se. At this point it may become an enemy rather than an ally of the struggle over inequality and poverty, such as when the need to show how structural adjustment results in the removal of welfare provision for the poor is lost in a tide of green concerns about the World Trade Organization or when forest conservationists turn a blind eye to the needs of impoverished forest dwellers. There is no reason, however, for environmentalism merely to follow the ancient suspicion of consumption as that process which uses up resources and which thereby labels it an intrinsic evil. A genuine measure of sustainability that welcomes the ability of science to find methods to increase wealth without harming the planet is surely compatible. Similarly the desire to give credit to the way consumers consume and the authenticity of some of their desire for goods need not detract from the academic critique of the way companies attempt to sell goods and services, or exploit workers in doing so. I see nothing in this article that contradicts, for example, the recent critique launched by Klein (2001).

Finally, I certainly hope that there is nothing in this article which would suggest that I have any desire to reduce the centrality of morality to the academic analysis of consumption. My own starting point in seeking to become a professional academic was Habermas's (1972) argument against the illusion of such a morally neutral academia. What I have attacked in this article is the poverty of that morality that in its desire to attack materialism has increasingly separated itself from a consideration of the experience of poverty, the attack on inequality, the cry of injustice and the need to increase the standard of living. In short, an admission that among other things poverty is constituted by a lack of material resources. This may be properly tempered by environmentalist concerns, where these remain directed at the welfare of populations as well as that of the planet. What we learn from the academic study of consumption is not that material culture is good or bad for people. Rather we learn that people have to engage in a constant struggle to create relationships with things and with people, and there is much to be gained from an empathetic documentation of those struggles. In the meantime a literature that allows the anxieties of the rich to obscure the suffering of the poor and seems constantly to assume that goods are intrinsically bad for people is simply not my idea of a moral approach to the topic of consumption. It is rather a sign of an academic discipline that has lost touch with what it purports to study.

References

Bourdieu, P. (1977) *Outline of a Theory of Practice*, Cambridge University Press, Cambridge

Clark, G. (2000) *Pension Fund Capitalism*, Oxford University Press, Oxford

Cross, G. (1993) *Time and Money*, Routledge, London

Gell, A. (1986) 'Newcomers to the world of goods', in A. Appadurai (ed) *The Social Life of Things*, Cambridge University Press, Cambridge, pp110–138

Habermas, J. (1972) *Knowledge and Human Interests*, Heinemann, London

Henwood, D. (1997) *Wall Street*, Verso, New York

Horowitz, D. (1985) *The Morality of Spending*, Johns Hopkins University Press, Baltimore, MD

Hutton, W. (1996) *The State We're In*, Vintage, London

Klein, N. (2001) *No Logo*, Flamingo, London

Mauss, M. (1954) *The Gift*, Cohen and West, London

Miller, D. (1987) *Material Culture and Mass Consumption*, Blackwell, Oxford

Miller, D. (1988) 'Appropriating the state on the council estate', *Man*, vol 23, pp353–372

Miller, D. (1994) *Modernity: an Ethnographic Approach*, Berg, Oxford

Miller, D. (ed.) (1995) *Acknowledging Consumption*, Routledge, London

Miller, D. (1997) *Capitalism: An Ethnographic Approach*, Berg, Oxford

Miller, D. (1998a) *A Theory of Shopping*, Polity Press, Cambridge

Miller, D. (1998b) 'A theory of virtualism', in J. G. Carrier and D. Miller (eds) *Virtualism: A New Political Economy*, Berg, Oxford, pp187–215

Miller, D. (2001) *The Dialectics of Shopping*, University of Chicago Press, Chicago

Miller, D. and Slater, D. (2000) *The Internet: An Ethnographic Approach*, Berg, Oxford

Munn, N. (1973) *Walpiri Iconography*, Cornell University Press, Ithaca, NY

Myers, F. (1986) *Pintupi Country, Pintupi Self*, Smithsonian Institute Press, Washington, DC

Naipaul, V. S. (1967) *The Mimic Men*, Penguin, London

Naipaul, V. S. (1987) *The Enigma of Arrival*, Viking, London

Nove, A. (1983) *The Economics of Feasible Socialism*, George Allen and Unwin, London

Porter, R. (1993) 'Consumption: Disease of the consumer society', in J. Brewer and R. Porter (eds) *Consumption and the World of Goods*, Routledge, London, pp58–81

Roberts, R. (1973) *The Classic Slum*, Penguin, Harmondsworth

Sahlins, M. (1974) *Stone Age Economics*, Tavistock, London

Schor, J. (1992) *The Overworked American*, Basic Books, New York

Schor, J. (1998) *The Overspent American*, Harper Perennial, New York

Segal, J. (1998) 'Consumer expenditure and the growth of needs-required income', in D. Crocker and T. Linden (eds) *The Ethics of Consumption*, Rowman and Littlefield, Lanham, MD, pp176–197

Sekora, J. (1977) *Luxury: The Concept in Western Thought: Eden to Smollett*, Johns Hopkins University Press, Baltimore, MD

Sennett, R. (1976) *The Fall of Public Man*, Cambridge University Press, Cambridge

Simmel, G. (1978) *The Philosophy of Money*, Routledge and Kegan Paul, London

Stallybrass, P. (1998) 'Marx's coat', in P. Spyer (ed) *Border Fetishisms*, Routledge, London, pp183–207

Thompson, E.P. (1978) *The Poverty of Theory and Other Essays*, Merlin Press, London

Tobin, J. (ed.) (1992) *Re-Made in Japan*, Yale University Press, New Haven, CT

Watson, J. (1997) *Golden Arches East*, Stanford University Press, Stanford, CA

Wheen, F. (1999) *Karl Marx*, Fourth Estate, London

Wilk, R. (1989) 'Houses as consumer goods', in H. Rutz and B. Orlove (eds) *The Social Economy of Consumption*, University Press of America, Lanham, MD, pp297–322

Wolf, E. (1982) *Europe and the People without History*, University of California Press, Berkeley, CA

16

Relative Poverty – Relative Communication

Mary Douglas

No serious writer on the problems of poverty would defend a grossly materialistic view – either of the condition or of the remedy. Poverty is not merely due to lack of goods nor even to lack of money. It is much more a matter of personal dignity. So William Morris set the scene of his *News from Nowhere* in a society of beautiful people, who worked for the happiness of service and craftsmanship; material possessions were not important to dignity (Morris, 1890). Somehow, in our society, material goods do affect it, but it is not clear why personal degradation follows from their lack. Paradoxically an isolated tribe whose culture is poor in material goods but rich in spiritual ones does not excite our compassion until it has been debauched by desire for our kinds of goods. Obviously there are ways of keeping dignity intact without a vast array of material things. So the evidence of poverty in the midst of plenty is more than a deep reproach to our civilization – it is an unsolved problem. Two of the most common ways of posing it fail to clarify the issue; one is the materialist approach by way of comparisons of real income and levels of subsistence, the other by subjective assessment of relative deprivation. A third approach considers poverty primarily as restriction of choice. This opens up the most scope to anthropological analysis, so I shall return to it after saying more about the other two.

Let me start by making a distinction between destitution and poverty. The word destitution will here be used to refer to the state in which the main problems are subsistence problems and the main choices to be made are choices about purchases of food, drink and rent. The level of subsistence is always set by the particular technological conditions of the time. People may be actually subsisting, and likely to continue in such a condition, indefinitely, especially if relief is available to keep them alive at just that level. Private alms and public assistance are very properly channelled to the relief of destitution and for this purpose careful measures of real goods and the money income required for acquiring them have to be devised. But there is surely a complete break in the terms of the argument, a break in continuity between the problems of destitution and those of poverty. The questions have to be separated. The data relevant for the one have to be reconstrued to be made relevant to the other. Questions about subsistence are posed in material terms and physiological tests are applicable. When subsistence is at issue it is proper to consider levels of heating, intake of calories and proteins, the dampness of walls and ceilings. If it were not for speedy relief measures, those living near subsistence level would sink below it and die. Thus subsistence problems are not only physical problems, they are emergencies. Considerable confusion has arisen from taking the measures which are proper to this field of thought and applying them to broader problems, such as poverty: hence, indeed, many of the difficulties in defining the latter. For one reason it is unlikely that a physiological and material concept which is implicitly static can be used for a comparison of social relations which are essentially dynamic. Brian Abel-Smith and Peter Townsend (1965) wryly point out the absurdities in trying to update the standards of physical subsistence to match changing conditions:

> The subsistence standards used by earlier writers on poverty seem at first sight to lend themselves to comparisons over time. This approach allows a basket of foodstuffs and other goods to be defined as necessary to provide subsistence. The cost of purchasing these goods can be calculated for different years and the number of households with insufficient income to purchase the goods can be ascertained. Although the principle seems easy to state, there are problems in applying it in practice. For example, the goods on the market at the later period may not be the same as at the earlier period. The cumbrous garments which convention required women to wear at the beginning of this century were unlikely to be found on the market in the 1930s, let alone today. Electricity has replaced oil lamps and candles. Even food habits have changed. These are among the problems which face those who attempt to apply the same poverty line at different periods. Again, the choice of goods that are selected initially cannot be defined in narrowly 'physical' or 'nutritional' terms. In laying down what articles of clothing and items of food are necessary for physical efficiency, those in charge of the surveys have been unable to prevent judgments about what is conventional or customary from creeping in to their lists and definitions.

This quotation serves to reveal the muddle. It is fair enough, perhaps, to write as if somehow scientific, physical and nutritional judgements concerning poverty could be made more precise if they could be stripped of all the local conventional culture. For this is how the subsistence standards defined for national assistance purposes are intended. But how mad – there is a crucial difference according to whether the subsistence standards are to be applied by humans to pets or to other humans. For the first, the veterinary surgeons' criteria go. For the second, their own ideas about their own society must intervene. Our authors, after a little forehead-wrinkling, give up the task of devising a culture-free standard of living: 'Poverty is a relative concept. Saying who is in poverty is to make a relative statement rather like saying who is short or heavy' (Abel-Smith and Townsend, 1965).

The idea that poverty is to be measured by levels of physical subsistence goes back to Rowntree, of course, and has been made the main platform of our public policy for alleviating it. J. C. Kincaid (1973) soundly berates William Beveridge for using a standard of physical subsistence for the social security scheme which he pioneered. But what he dislikes is not the intrusion of physical subsistence, but that the standard was set too low. He trips on the same snag that catches everyone who takes a strictly material idea of the standard of living: 'Obviously even those at the very foot of society in contemporary Britain enjoy a standard of living that is somewhat higher than that of the poorest in Victorian society a hundred years ago and much higher than the norm in many underdeveloped societies today' (Kincaid, 1973, p75).

In saying this, Kincaid only echoes a widespread fallacy. The Report of the National Board for Prices and Incomes on the General Problems of Low Pay makes the same comment: 'Poverty is now accepted as being a relative concept. People who in this country are reckoned – or who reckon themselves – poor today are not necessarily so by the standards of twenty-five years ago or by the standards of other countries' (National Board for Prices and Incomes, 1971).

In the proper context, there is much to be said in favour of developing the concept of subsistence and material standard of living. Destitution is a grave problem and must be measured somehow, though the scale be imperfect. By comparison the relativist approach to poverty has flippant overtones. It implies that people feel poor because they see others richer than themselves. It tends to hang the weight of definition on subjective experience. By abdicating responsibility to define the condition the argument can only say that people feel poor because they see others richer than themselves. Poverty is then over-closely equated with jealousy, a feeling which intensifies with the widening of the reference group (Runciman, 1968). Since the poor cannot protect the view from their windows or preserve their garden plot from developers, their street from thundering traffic noise, their diet from monotony and so on, they must put up with increasing intrusion, narrowness and despoilment, and will do so all the more passively if unaware of persons that they can identify with who enjoy a better condition. Apart from trivializing a serious matter, the definition based on subjective jealousy can be soporific, while at least the subsistence approach leads to soup kitchens and doles. As Kincaid says: '... once a relative view of poverty is adopted, it follows that poverty cannot be abolished, since in any society where complete social inequality does not always prevail, the label of poor can always be given to the 10 per cent or 20 per cent of the population who come lowest in the hierarchy of income. If the absolutely poor need not be always with us, surely the relatively poor, by definition, cannot vanish' (Kincaid, 1973, p175). Like many others, his solution is to remove inequality of income. Whatever the merits of that policy (and it should of course apply to wealth as well as to income if it is to achieve its stated goal), the relativist definition of poverty on which it rests ought to be improved. Those who espouse it are right to reject a material standard and right to emphasize that personal dignity is at risk when market forces are uncontrolled. But they need not found their case on a negative sense of unfairness and jealousy. An anthropological approach would start from assuming that goods are used in a system of communication. It should be possible to be objective about the quantity of goods and the kind of goods needed for entering the system and catching the message necessary for participation. Deafness is a relative condition; a person can be more deaf or less deaf than another, but this does not mean that the experience of deafness is purely subjective, that it cannot be measured or defined, nor the effectiveness of deaf-aids be judged. Poverty should be regarded as a social defect equivalent to physical deafness. It is capable of definition and remedy. The difficulties of establishing this viewpoint lie largely in the history of economics.

For one thing, there is the over-narrowing of the problem to the individual's access to consumer goods. Since consumption is treated by economic theory as an individual matter, consumption goods being bought mainly to be consumed within the home, it is difficult to explain within that theory why one household's having more of them than another is damaging to the less well-provided – unless health is in danger. Hence the emphasis is on physical well-being. From this barren ground, Harold Watts (1968–1969) tried to establish a richer theoretical basis. He starts from the economist's central distinction between preferences and constraints: poverty is a property of the individual's situation, a severe constriction of the choice set. Second, he expands the time horizon for the choice set so as to include 'the value of the largest sustainable level of consumption, the sum of income flows from all sources evaluated at the normal rate they can be expected to maintain over the long run, instead of at the current level'. For purposes of calculating poverty he would convert net wealth (assets minus liabilities) into equivalent life annuities for purposes of measuring the capacity to sustain a level of consumption. 'So the unemployed dishwasher would be counted as poorer than the unemployed plumber even though both had the same zero level of current earnings.' Third, recognizing that poverty is not a discrete condition, he asserts that 'constriction of choice becomes progressively more damaging in a continuous manner'. The rest of his argument is concerned with working out a family's 'welfare ratio' as the ratio of its permanent sustainable income to an arbitrarily established 'poverty threshold'; a technical exercise of some ingenuity but difficult application. The first three definitional points (poverty as a constriction of choice, with lifetime implications and cumulative effects) make the best start to analysing the relation that is too often taken for granted between choice over goods and the protection of dignity. Poverty means constriction of choice: that is surely obvious. That the restriction has lifetime and cumulative effects may need some illumination. I take it that he is recognizing here that the move to a cheaper house means living in a poorer neighbourhood, sending children to less well-equipped schools, and so on, the familiar degeneration of circumstances which is summed up by 'lifetime cumulative effects'. To the layman this has the ring of truth, but the theoretical foundations for such a statement are hard to find in demand theory.

Consumption is a peculiar idea, embedded in the history of economic practice. It derives from the contrast with production, as the object or end product of the latter (Keynes, 1936). In this regard it has an analogy in accountancy as the net result when all costs of production have been subtracted and double counting eliminated. In systems analysis it has a general analogy with output when all input processes of transformation are reckoned. However, it also derives from its use in contrast with saving, since saving is that which might have been consumed but which is put aside for future consumption. In that case consumption counts as part of the costs of production and the only net gain is the saving. The concept arises as part of an equation. In the national aggregate consumption is equal to income minus savings; for the private individual it is his expenditure from income, part of that which the income has been earned to obtain. It is a concept which results from technical calculations. In the analysis of demand the assumptions about consumption have been so polished and refined that no false psychological ideas are entertained. In consequence there are no other ideas for why people should want goods at all. For lack of a formal theory, economics falls inadvertently into the materialist mode of thought. It is easy to see that physical subsistence is a basic need and measuring real income is one of the things that economics can do. Hence many economists' writings on needs give confidently a mixed list which starts with subsistence and includes such ill-assorted motives as benevolence and thrill (Knight, 1951).

For the anthropologist seeking a useful discussion of poverty the pitch is queered by lack of a systematic account of consumers' objectives. Hicks taught that the individual does not regard the commodities he buys as ends or objectives, as consumer theory would imply, but as means to the attainment of objectives. 'It would accordingly appear that we ought to think of the consumer as choosing, according to his preference, between certain *objectives;* and then deciding, more or less as the entrepreneur decides, between alternative means of reaching those objectives' (Hicks, 1956). Anthropology might be able to supply a systematic account of consumers' objectives, but hitherto none exists. If this first step were taken successfully, then two advantageous changes could be made in the present discussion of poverty. The first would be to treat subsistence as a cost, not as an output. The second would be to introduce some idea of scale or operations.

To treat subsistence as a means of obtaining other objectives makes some basic layman's good sense. For many of its practitioners, economic theory is primarily designed for under standing long-term stable conditions. The merits of adopting such an approach are described by G. L. S. Shackle (1968) in the introduction to a survey of theories concerning the rate of interest:

> ... in historical fact the cleavages between groups of theories have run along a few clear lines, which can for practical purposes be easily defined. These lines, of course, intersect each other and yield cross-classifications. One dichotomy is between equilibrium and development theories. Equilibrium is a test that selects for the economist one particular situation out of an infinity of situations and justifies his calling attention to it as something special. Just by the smallness of the ratio of what it accepts to what it rejects, no other test seems able to rival its selective power... on the most general grounds equilibrium has great claims as economiser of thought. To dispense with it has meant, in practice, to be reduced to mere factual enumeration...

Equilibrium theory does not claim that a sequence of actual economic states will terminate in an equilibrium state, but 'that no plausible sequence of economic state will terminate, if it does so at all, in a state which is not an equilibrium. The argument is straightforward; agents will not continue in actions in states in which preferred or more profitable ones are available to them nor will mutually inconsistent actions allow given prices to persist' (Hahn, 1973). If this branch of economics, central to the theory of demand, has been such a powerful organizer of thought, consumer theory would rightly expect to take advantage of these tools.

Equilibrium theory, being concerned with stable states, would be misapplied if it were to treat as stable a state which was in essence a crisis, a temporary emergency which must move either to stability or catastrophe. Whenever it is taken for granted that physical subsistence is the main and dominant objective of economic behaviour, the theory is being misapplied. Any one whose dominant concern is to survive is in a parlous state which cannot continue. If the whole society has to treat physical survival as a prior concern, again, it is in a mess. Its problems rightly come under those of destitution, not of poverty. The theory of demand needs some statement of a normal set of consumer's objectives, which can be assumed to be held under stable conditions. For any selected level of physical subsistence deemed a prior requirement for achieving this set of objectives, the economist can work out a production function. Such a two-level approach would ask for an account of consumer's objectives, and second an account of the prevailing technology creating the cost-structure within which they have to be achieved. Thus subsistence, instead of befogging the definition of poverty by its implausible status as one objective of consumption among others, would be relegated to the status of a cost.

By this route there is no need to look for a culture-free definition, either of human sub-sistence or of poverty: both have to be defined within the techno-cultural standards of the time. One last adjustment, consumer theory needs some concept of scale of opera-tions. So far the dimension is missing, so that there is no way of comparing consumers' operating on larger or smaller scale, or of thinking of how benefits of scale might help in achieving the consumers' objectives. Without taking account of benefits of scale, certain features of consumption behaviour go unrecorded, but if they are taken into account, we can bring strong arguments to support Harold Watts' view that restriction of choice may be cumulatively damaging. For we will be able to show that in the field of consumption alone, without regard to other aspects of the economy such as the labour market, there is a selective bias working in favour of some and against others. This is a serious problem concerning relative poverty which is lost to sight. The subjective experi-ence which looks like plain jealousy is partly due to fear of being unable to meet social commitments and partly due to the existence of a spiral on which the downhill run can seem disastrously fast to the consumer who finds the cost structure working against him. Whether the downward spiral leads to destitution or anywhere near it is a difficult mat-ter to demonstrate. But the existence of descending and ascending movements in the ability to command goods and services is worrying enough when the normal consump-tion project is recognized to be not an absorption into the household of more and improved goods wanted for their own sake, but the creation of a network of interper-sonal obligations.

Modern industrial man needs goods for the same reason as the tribesman. They need goods in order to commit other people to their projects. It is somewhat of an anachronism or solecism to use the words 'goods', 'consumption' and 'consumers' beyond the boundaries of capitalist industrial society. Yet something useful is served by doing so carefully. When I have developed an anthropological definition of consump-tion, the meanings will not be so stretched as they are now. Anticipating, the theory of needs should start by assuming that any individual needs goods in order to commit other people to his projects. He needs goods to involve others as fellow-consumers in his consumption rituals. Goods are for mobilizing other people. The fact that in the course of these rituals food gets consumed, flags waved and clothes worn is incidental. Subsist-ence is a fortunate by-product. Bodily subsistence happens to be served by some aspects of consumption activities, by the absorption of food, but the fading of cut flowers and the accumulation of dust on paintings, the dying chords of a song, these are other costs in consumption rituals which just don't happen to serve subsistence needs. For keeping the discussion on the right tracks, flowers might be a better favourite example to take of typical consumption goods than eggs and butter. In tribal society goods are used for paying compliments, for initiating marriages, establishing or ending them, for recogniz-ing relationships, for all celebrations, compensations and affirmations whatever. Every ethnography has an account of how the channels etched by gifts and counter-gifts con-stitute the social fabric.

The tribesmen also pass judgements on each other in respect of poverty. Most unusu-ally the man is reckoned poor who has everything he needs for subsistence for himself and his family but no more. The Turkana pastoralists of Uganda, for example, live on mixed herds of sheep, goats and cattle, with donkeys for transport. A family can live well enough with just sheep, camels and goats, and with less trouble, since cattle are delicate in this region and need special herding and watering care lavished on them. But without cattle a man has to accept inferior social status: cattle are needed for marriage payments and gifts to friends and allies (Gulliver, 1955). For us to think of poverty in terms of more or less real income is to be less intelligent as economists than the Turkana. They would never try to remedy a man's lack of cattle by giving him more sheep and goats. This is how we are tempted to think of remedying poverty, by subsidizing food and other things necessary for subsistence. Unless we know why people need luxuries and how they use them we are nowhere near taking the problems of inequality seriously.

An anthropological theory of consumption will require some new assumptions. The first aim would be to define consumption activity in a way that would be consistent with a communications theory of the use of goods. In the opening pages of *The Elementary Forms of Kinship* in 1949, Lévi-Strauss distinguishes three forms of transfers which uphold human society; the transfers of meanings, transfers of women and transfers of goods, thus giving three branches of anthropology, mythology, kinship and economics. The pity was to have kept them separate. The present essay is an attempt to incorporate the three branches into one theory of consumption.

The need to define and better understand consumption activity has been fully recognized by consumption theories (Lancaster, 1971; Muth, 1966). Their chosen examples often rise above the ingestion of vitamins to holidays and clothes and transport (Strotz, 1959; Gorman, 1959), and yet I fear that the following propositions will be unexpected and seem far-fetched.

First, let us assume that the ultimate object of consumption activity is to enter a social universe whose processes consist of matching goods to classes of social occasions. Second, for entry into such a universe, the individual needs the services of fellow-consumers. These services are either in the form of personal attendance at consumption events or of material contributions of goods (e.g. flowers) and their object is to create or confirm a grading of the occasion. For want of a better term, let me call these services offered by fellow-consumers 'marking'. This is in the spirit of the hallmarking of gold, silver and pewter, the signing and otherwise authenticating of work, the marking in the sense of judging and classing of performances in competitive/racing, dancing, music, and so on, or making in the sense of setting up milestones, boundaries and benchmarks of all kinds. Goods are endowed with value by the agreement of fellow-consumers. In marking events and grading categories, fellow-consumers uphold old judgements or make new fashions in the value of goods. Now it is mainly dry wine that is classed high, then gradually the place reserved for certain rare sweet ones is expanded; now it is only Beethoven, and then Vivaldi gets a better place; now it is either late 18th-century architecture or steel and concrete, nothing in between. The marking is spontaneous and unpredictable since it depends on the mobilization of fellow-consumers. But it is unmistakable. The women's magazine says 'Prints are being worn at the races': one only has to go to the races to see the profusion of printed silk dresses to know that the marking process is just so (Barthes, 1967). These matters of taste formation stand explicitly outside the scope of economics, but must be brought in somehow and made quantifiable for there to be a workable idea of consumption activities. Perhaps it is convincing that there can be no social universe without a system of discriminations in which goods are involved. Equally important for the individual is his dependence on fellow-consumers for his own point of entry into the classifications. He needs fellow-consumers not only to create the social universe around him but to assure himself a tolerable place in it. Their presence at his funerals and weddings and their regard for his birthdays established his significance and partly do so by the choice of goods used to mark the events. Thus it follows that the individual who can mobilize the largest number of fellow-consumers to join in marking his occasions has the best chance of a good place in the social scheme. It works both ways – if he has a good place, he can mobilize more people; if he can mobilize more, he will get a good place. We shall show later that there is inevitably a competitive element, since no one can be in two places at once and since grading activities are also selective.

These propositions will enable us to develop a concept of scale for consumption activities and an information theory of consumption which could supplement the information theories of market behaviour. Therefore it may be worth summarizing them:

1   All consumption activity is a ritual presentation and sharing of goods classified as appropriate to particular social categories which themselves get defined and graded in the process.
2   An individual's main objective in consumption is to help to create the social universe and to find in it a creditable place.
3   To achieve his main objective he needs to mobilize marking services from other consumers.
4   Successful consumption requires a deployment of goods in consumption rituals that will mobilize the maximum marking services from other consumers.

By this path, we can be free of the unintended materialist bias which clogs much discussion of poverty and free of the equally misleading over-spiritual outlook of some critics who suppose that all goods over and above subsistence are meaningless luxuries (Galbraith, 1974). Quite to the contrary, this approach allows meaning to all consumption activities and makes it easier to judge whether particular meanings are acceptable to any chosen ethical standpoint. We have now sketched an account of consumption that shows it to be essentially concerned with the creation and propagation of knowledge. It is admittedly a certain kind of knowledge, very different from scientific knowledge, very like aesthetic judgement when this is based on perceptions of fittingness. The marking services which create the knowledge categories and sustain them are free and unconstrained. True, there are rules of reciprocity, but they are not legally binding. We are in an area of social relationships of long-standing interest to anthropology – the sphere of the gift (Mauss, 1925). When one recipient of a gift, by a turn of bad fortune, cannot reciprocate, his partner has always the choice of applying the rules strictly, and so withdrawing from the relationship, or of lowering the rate. For example, it is well observed by Evans-Pritchard that the Nuer expected symmetry between the amount required for marriage payments and that required for blood-debts. But when rinderpest decimated their herds, they allowed the traditional 40 head of cattle to be paid by a prospective son-in-law to be considerably reduced – not so in the case of blood-debts, when every one of the 40 would be extracted from the enemy, by force if need be. I think it is safe to generalize and assert that there is no society known to anthropology so far which does not divide its transactions into at least two spheres, one which closely corresponds to our ideas of reciprocal gift giving, the other which is more strictly ruled by legally enforceable contract, which corresponds to our idea of commerce. These spheres are kept clearly apart. Usually the media of transactions are different in the two cases. It is incorrect for us to send fruit or flowers before an exam to one of the examiners, but correct to send them to a sick friend before an operation. The former gets his money fee in due course, the latter cannot have cash in lieu of a visit. Behaviour in each sphere is equally apt for transactional analysis. The principles of comparative advantage and benefits of scale apply to the gift sphere as well as to commerce. Even in Chicago where they say, 'There is no such thing as a free lunch', it is not permissible to send the dollar cost of a lunch in lieu of attending. There is a boundary, and arbitrage across it is resisted. Big discrepancies in prices on either side of the line are proof of this. For example, the lunch is low in cost compared with the deal that is to be negotiated across the table, or with the value of the information received. What we have said about the nature of consumption activity explains why. In essence, the sphere of reciprocal gifts and hospitality is the sphere in which goods mediate the forming of public judgements. The fellowship of consumers is by free invitation and free acceptance. Their rituals generate the categories of moral judgement on which society itself is constituted. If the owner of the biggest bag of shell money could move in and buy control of these rituals, enforce unwilling attendance of some and eject others from them at spear point, he would subvert the moral basis of society. Some things cannot be put up for sale; private integrity, political honour. Nor can they be legislated for; nor arranged by physical coercion. Gifts can never be under external compulsion, however compelling the internal rules of reciprocity for those involved in gift making.

Now we can consider the benefits of scale. It will be to the advantage of an individual to mobilize as many fellow-consumers as possible who can render him marking services. This is obvious in many ways. I will mention a few by way of illustration. For celebratory occasions there are intimate and public grades, the first needing only a few choice supporters. But the gamut between intimate and public gives full meaning to intimacy to the extent that a large force is mustered for the public events at the other end of the scale. Many people are needed for big celebrations. Meanings are reduced if support cannot be mobilized. Then again, the support of fellow-consumers is a source of information: the whole of consumption being defined as a knowledge system, some pieces of knowledge are disconnected and add nothing to each other; some overlap and reinforce, by eliminating uncertainty or by filling in gaps; the more varieties of knowledge over the widest horizon, the more the consumer is oriented confidently in his universe. This is one source of benefits of scale. A further one comes from the backing that the individual receives from fellow-consumers. If his backers are in a position to control the knowledge system which is the social scheme where he hopes to hold a respected place, the large scale of their operations is such that their approval of him guarantees his main objective. Whereas if his support comes from a quarter where only small corners of the map are known, people who themselves are isolated and can only muster a few supporters each, then his main objective of securing a good standing is endangered. There is yet another sense in which benefits of scale make an overwhelming difference to the success of the individual's main consumption project. To expand this needs some further thought about consumption as a cultural process.

Consumption is a process in which goods yield services in the course of which they are consumed – more or less immediately. Consumer durables, houses and pictures, and so on, yield these services over a long time; flowers and food more quickly. Consumption means nothing if it does not mean that some physical things in the end get consumed. But let us realize that the services they yield are of two kinds, one the enjoyment of physical consumption, the other the enjoyment of sharing names. Take football – some people actually play football; some go to all the football matches they can, others watch on television. The football fan internalizes inside his head a reel of names of historic matches, famous clubs, referees, inspiring captains and crafty managers, heroic goalies, great stadiums, good and bad grounds, good and bad years. Inside his heart, so to speak, are grades of passionate judgements passed upon them all. He has acquired this rich collection of names by investment of personal time and attention and some cash. When he meets an alleged fellow-consumer, a few sentences are enough to betray how much they really have in common and whether the joys of shared consumption will be released. Among these two kinds of satisfaction, the physical enjoyment is more in the nature of proving – as puddings much discussed are proven in the eating – proving, testing or demonstrating the reality which has been brought under control. In terms of time expended this is the minor side of enjoyment. By far the larger part of life is spent in sharing names that have been learned, distinguished and graded. Real consumption is the consumption that physically destroys goods. But there is further enjoyment to be had from a shared activity which is not subject to the process of depreciation or diminishing returns: the names are multiplied and revivified. Each consumption activity has its own field of names. Each field has three dimensions:

1   It can be broad or narrow in the geographical range over which its names are known, as between mother's apple pie and coq au vin, or peche melba.
2   It can be deep or shallow in the time depth in which the names can be placed chronologically in relation to one another.
3   It can be rich or poor according to the number and complexity of the criteria for grading the names.

By this approach we have laid underneath the process of consumption, as a prerequisite to satisfaction, something like a filing system inside the consumer's head. The consumer is actively scanning, judging and enjoying. Consumption has to be assimilated to culture in some such way as this to support the rest of what we have said about consumption activity as a ritual matching of goods to occasions. Some interesting comparisons arise now between the different aspects of consumption with respect to scale.

The physical testing or proving is limited as to the number of people who can share together. Fewer people can walk out and shoot a duck, or can sit down and eat a duck together than can sit down and talk about duck-shooting or eating. So at first sight it seems easier to share widely the enjoyment of names. But in practice names have heavy learning costs. The greater the historical depth, the more costly in time to learn the names. So the fields which afford the greatest number of discriminated names in relation to physical testing, instead of being the most open and democratic, are the most closed and elitist. Those fields which afford the least physical testing and the most discussion of names are appropriately said to be 'rich' in 'spiritual values' or to represent 'higher' or 'human values' contrasted with animal or physical satisfaction. In any consumption field there are a few top names and many smaller ones; a top name, such as

Shakespeare in the field of drama, is a constant point of reference and comparison for the rest of the field. Anyone who knows well a top name in a big field will know also and correctly grade a host of smaller ones connected with it, such as *The Merchant of Venice*, Shylock, and 'All that glitters'. So there are economics of effort in learning names. And economics of scale; for the most spiritual top names tend to overlap and offer reinforcing information. Top names travel farthest. They are the most widely known and so have big geographical as well as historical range. More Papuans and Africans know more names connected with Shakespeare than with Andrew Marvell. One definition we could put forward of poverty is to be poor in the spiritual enjoyments, for these are the costliest sort. Schools are right to strive to make children instant possessors of the costliest names; instant Shakespeare and instant history, subsidized ballet. This gives the children a chance to collect more names later. But they will never have incentive to do it unless they can see themselves entering a community of fellow-consumers who also share those very names. It could be a good investment; it could be sheer waste of time, depending on the other costs of shared consumption. For unless they are going to be able to transact allusions, jokes, quotations, reminiscences and reactions about the names they have got, they will not be able to use that source of enjoyment to further their main objectives.

So far I have said nothing about marriage or earning. So I have not connected up the transfers of meaning with economics and kinship. But it should not be difficult. Earnings are influenced by the scale of consumption. Since a wide network of beholden friends is a source of information about work, and of backing in creditworthiness and for jobs, there is a direct connection between work-seeking and income-maintaining through a well-deployed consumption programme. Marriages too: there are two kinds of impossible son-in-law, one who has no income, the other who has no manners. Essentially manners represent his past consumption experience: if the latter is appropriate, someone on the bride's side can put him in the way of an income. If he has enough money but no manners he may yet make the marriage. But to have no money and no manners is a hopeless barrier. Thus consumption patterns do more than result from economic distinctions: they reinforce them.

Now we have sketched in a dimension of scale in consumption. We can return to Harold Watts' assertion that poverty is cumulatively damaging. A consumption system which is closely related to earning capacity, in which consumers are selecting among one another for furthering each his own lifetime objective for acquiring more names and mobilizing more marking services has all the makings of a competitive system. The possibilities of big economics of scale generate further advantages for those who can use them, and increase disadvantages cumulatively. If this argument supports Harold Watts' thesis, and if learning costs constitute a further bar for those with an initial disadvantage, then the distinction I would like to see clarified between destitution and poverty becomes more important. Those who start in poverty may be afraid of ending in destitution. Subsistence measures will be needed, all the more because there is no mystery about the existence of poverty in the midst of plenty. Consumption is itself an activity which generates cumulative inequalities and is by itself capable of driving some people down to destitution. This should be recognized by everyone who selects among his uncles and nephews and godchildren, to give personal services of backing or promotion to a well-placed favourite. As to policy, a spiral is only a spiral. It can suck some people up and it can suck others down. To determine what is the incidence of its force is a highly technical matter. To add the enjoyment of names to the theory of consumption gives it the chance of developing within information theory instead of looking to physiological needs for its base-line. With an information theory of consumption we would concentrate more than ever on the general network of social relations which support the specialized endeavour of educationalists. By itself school education only gives a start. The child who leaves school will need a means of acquiring a wide range of useful names, access to specialized information services, a habit of seeking professional advice and means to pay for it, above all, a continual means of updating information as the technological base changes and everything else with it. Relative deprivation is like relative deafness: someone who is outside one conversation misses the clues and can't adapt quick enough to get into the next conversation, so the chance of making sense and the chance of playing a respected role diminish.

This is the line of reasoning which makes me very doubtful about the puritanical streak in some economists, rather well paid, highly respected and often old, who draw a moral line between luxuries and necessities and who feel that we could all do with less material things. Unintentionally they condemn other people to the affliction of social deafness. When an earthquake rumbles or a typhoon starts to blow, those whose ears are attuned may escape in time. Let us start to think of luxuries as signalling devices, transmitting from person to person information about the social system. Then puritan judgements seem smug. Advocates of egalitarian policies should not be ignorant about the uses of goods. The prophets of anti-growth depend implicitly on the idea that goods are primarily needed for food and shelter. If that were all, we could cut them down to a healthy level. But as they are for communicating messages, highly discriminated ones, their use is like a balloon: press it down here and it will billow out there, new goods and new names will be invented, especially new names. Whoever heard of the anthropology of consumption before now? The creation of totally new lists of highly discriminated names can be achieved in a few months. New clienteles with new centres of power and influence can shoot up and the possessors of lists of old names can find their value has leaked out overnight. Clearly more thought on the athropology of consumption is needed before we can apply it to practical issues but eventually it will supply an account of the main objectives of consumers and a better theoretical basis for understanding poverty. It starts from the lesson that human information systems cannot be stopped in their tracks, except at vast and arbitrary cost. Therefore it is better not to think of consumption as that part of the economic process which fits a worker to offer useful services in the labour market, but to try to understand what the transmission of goods does in establishing marriages and mythology.

References

Abel-Smith, B. and Townsend, P. (1965) *The Poor and the Poorest*, G. Bell and Sons, London, pp9–12, 57–67

Barthes, R. (1967) *Le Systeme de la Mode*, Seuil, Paris

Galbraith, J. H. (1974) *Economics and the Public Purpose*, Andre Deutsch, London

Gorman, W. M. (1959) 'Separable utility and aggregation', *Econometrica,* vol 27, pp469–481

Gulliver, P. (1955) *The Family Herds: A Study of Two Pastoral Tribes in East Africa, the Jie and the Turkana,* Routledge and Kegan Paul, London

Hahn, F. H. (1973) *On the Notion of Equilibrium in Economics,* Inaugural Lecture, Oxford University Press, Oxford, p7

Hicks, J. (1956) A *Revision of Demand Theory,* Oxford University Press, Oxford, p166

Keynes, J. M. (1936) *The General Theory of Employment, Interest and Money,* Macmillan, London

Kincaid, J. C. (1973) *Poverty and Equality in Britain: A Study of Social Security and Taxation,* Penguin, London

Knight, F. H. (1951) *The Economic Organization,* Kelly, New York

Lancaster, K. (1971) *Consumer Demand: A New Approach,* Columbia, New York

Lévi-Strauss, C. (1949) *Les Structures Élémentaires de la Parenté*, published in English as *The Elementary Structures of Kinship* (1969, tr. J. H. Bell, J. R. von Sturmer and R. Needham), Beacon, Boston, MA

Mauss, M. (1925) 'Essai sur le don: Forme et raison de l'échange dans les sociétés archaïques', *L'Année sociologique,* nouvelle série, vol I (1923–1924), pp30–186. English edition (1954, tr. Ian Cunnison) titled *The Gift* published by Cohen and West, London

Morris, W. (1890) *News from Nowhere,* serialized in *Commonweal* from January 11; first published in book form in 1891 by Reeves and Turner, London

Muth, R. F. (1966) 'Household production and consumer demand functions', *Econometrica,* vol 34, pp699–708

National Board for Prices and Incomes (1971) *Report 169: General Problems of Low Pay,* HMSO, London, p6

Runciman, W. (1968) *Readings in Reference Group Theory and Research*, The Free Press, New York

Shackle, G. L. S. (1968) 'Recent theories concerning the nature of interest in surveys of economic theory', *Money Interest and Welfare,* vol 1

Strotz, R. H. (1959) 'The unity tree – a correction and further appraisal', *Econometrica,* vol 27, no 3, pp482–488

Watts, H. W. (1968–1969) 'An economic definition of poverty', in D. P. Moynihan and C. S. Schelling (eds) *On Understanding Poverty,* American Academy of Arts and Science, New York

17

Two Alternative Economic Models of Why Enough Will Never Be Enough

Kjell Arne Brekke and Richard B. Howarth

> It is extraordinary to discover that no one knows why people want goods. Demand theory is at the very centre, even at the origin of economics as a discipline. Yet 200 years of thought on the subject has little to show on the question.
>
> DOUGLAS AND ISHERWOOD (1979, p3)

Per capita income in the affluent world grew by a factor of 15–20 between 1820 and 1990 (Maddison, 1995). At present, the citizens of industrial societies are richer than their ancestors could even dream of being. Yet while consumption has grown considerably, the amount of leisure has, at best, increased modestly. In addition, the evidence seems to suggest that the benefits from increased consumption have been rather disappointing. Self-reported happiness in rich societies has increased only slightly, if at all, during the last several decades (Easterlin, 1996). Non-economic factors seem to be more important than income in terms of their impact on life satisfaction. Blanchflower and Oswald (2000), for example, estimate that marriage has the same impact on life satisfaction as a US$100,000 increase in yearly income. So if social relationships are more important to well-being than income, why don't people spend more time building these relationships and less time in the labour market?

The level of labour supply has never been a paradox within economic theory, and this chapter will briefly present a standard model of consumer choice and how this theory explains the labour supply. The theory essentially sees labour supply as a choice between more leisure and more consumption. When people are observed working at a given level, this model suggests that their preferences for more consumption are sufficiently strong to justify that choice.

As an alternative to this, the paper will outline a second model in which consumption goods do not provide any direct benefits at all. In this model, consumers are concerned with maintaining a positive self-image. But personal characteristics are not perfectly observable, while consumption goods may be visible objects signifying success. Hence, to reinforce his or her self-image, an individual may put much effort into acquiring consumption goods.

The view that consumer goods are used to reinforce self-image is well known from other social sciences and is increasingly recognized in economics. Yet while this hypothesis does not in itself challenge the descriptive content of the traditional economic theory of consumer choice, the two frameworks differ considerably in terms of their policy implications. In particular, identity signalling – that is, using consumer goods to achieve a favourable self-image – can lead people to overvalue consumption goods while undervaluing collective goods such as environmental quality (Ng and Wang, 1993; Howarth, 1996). As we shall see, this argument is supported by a survey of some of the empirical studies that shed light on the relative importance of identity signalling.

Working Hard and Consuming Much

For the sake of simplicity we shall limit attention to models where the full set of consumption goods are aggregated into one good. Accordingly, the consumer faces only one trade-off, between consumption and leisure. The budget constraint then implies that total income equals total expenditure. While deviations are possible in the short run through savings or borrowing, saving (or borrowing) in the present will increase (or decrease) future consumption possibilities. It is also possible to spend less than total earning in the long run, through gift giving, but that would increase someone else's consumption. In national accounts, total income by definition equals spending on consumption, investment or foreign transfer. Foreign transfers are small, and investment equals savings that enhance future consumption. Hence, for simplicity we will invoke the long-term budget constraint even in the short run, assuming that total spending equals total income in the context of a simple static model.

Note that a consequence of this is that efforts such as a 'consume nothing day' will have no effect on total consumption unless people work and earn less. If individuals spend less on some commodities but earn the same income, money will accumulate in their bank accounts (or deficits may decrease more rapidly). Eventually, they will be able to spend more on some other product.

At a given wage, total income is determined by how many hours a person works each week, so that any explanation of the consumption level must account for the labour supply. And in the formal model of identity signalling described below, we shall assume that an individual's consumption is socially observable while labour effort and income are not. This assumption highlights how consumption is used to communicate identity. But since the levels of consumption and labour supply are two sides of the same coin, we will sometimes refer to how the results of hard work are used to anchor an individual's self-image.

Note also that in the following discussion we will consider the number of work hours per week as a matter of choice. At an individual level, this may not seem realistic since firms may not accept employees' demands for a shorter working week. Still, if most employees preferred lower payment in exchange for less work, firms should be able to attract workers even at a lower hourly wage by offering shorter working weeks. In sectors where wages are determined by bargaining between labour unions and firms, the labour union would fight for a shorter working week if that is what the workers really wanted. Thus we cannot explain the length of the working week by reference to the lack of individual choice.

Sustainable Consumption

There has been a rising concern about the links between economic growth, natural resource depletion and environmental degradation. Although the high level of consumption in affluent societies is not a problem in itself, authors such as Daly and Cobb (1989) and Meadows et al (1992) warn that today's consumption patterns may be unsustainable since they place excessive demands on the biophysical systems that support economic activity. In contrast with this view, advocates of the 'Environmental Kuznets Curve' hypothesis argue that economic growth may actually benefit the environment. Selden and Song (1994) and Grossman and Krueger (1995), for example, found that above a certain income level, some environmental health indicators improve as a society's income level increases. These results, however, are restricted to water quality and a set of pollutants emitted into the air. In other cases income and emissions are strongly correlated, as is illustrated by Durning's (1992) observation that the richest quintile of the world's population emits 35 times as much carbon dioxide as the poorest quintile. While the link between resource use and economic growth is not simply linear, environmental systems would clearly be profoundly stressed if the poor countries of the world adopted the lifestyles and technologies that currently prevail in industrialized societies. It is thus important to understand the forces that lie behind the consumption patterns observed in Western societies.

But the perspective presented here has consequences far beyond merely explaining aggregate consumption. At least as important for the debate over sustainability is the composition of consumption. It is possible to consume at a similar level but with far lower resource use and less environmental impact. A shift in the composition of consumption would come at a cost though. For instance, a policy to reduce greenhouse gas emissions would require firms to use less fossil fuel, which might reduce economic output (at least in the short run). Similarly, consumers would have to shift consumption away from energy-intensive products. There is thus a trade-off between such costs and improved environmental conditions. As will be discussed below, the motives behind our consumption have an important implication for the assessment of pollution abatement costs and hence for the optimal trade-off between consumption and environmental quality. We shall return to this important point below, after explaining the two alternative models.

Why are Modern People Overworked?
Two Alternative Views

Returning to the question we raised at the outset, why has the fraction of people's waking life spent working been more or less constant, while the income derived from this labour supply has increased by a factor of 15–20?

Whether the average number of working hours has increased or decreased is a subject of debate. Schor (1991) argues that the average number of weekly working hours prior to the industrial revolution was lower than the current average – an observation that contrasts interestingly with Sahlins' (1972) finding that the lifestyles of premodern hunter-gatherers were often dominated by high levels of leisure. On the other hand, Robinson and Godbey (1997) argue that leisure time increased somewhat in the late 1980s and early 1990s with the entire increment devoted to watching TV. There is also a substantial difference in the amount of leisure and the length of holidays between the US and Europe, with more vacation time and a lower labour supply in Europe. Thus, Schor's claim about the 'overworked American' does not fully extend to Europe.

While the exact number seems to be a matter of discussion, it seems clear that any reduction in working hours is at best small compared to the huge increase in affluence. The following sections provide two alternative explanations of why this might be so.

A traditional model

Suppose first that goods are valued for their practical use. In addition, we will adopt an assumption that is standard in applied economics, that is that working is considered an inconvenience and that people prefer as much leisure time as possible for a given income. Increased per capita income is reflected in the wage rate. The question is therefore how people's labour supply will respond to increased wages.

To understand the effect of an increased wage rate, it is convenient to decompose the effect into two components. Increasing the wage rate both changes the rate at which people can exchange leisure and consumption and at the same time augments total income. To isolate the effect of each of these components, it is useful to conduct a thought experiment. Suppose that wages increased, but that the government introduced a lump sum tax at the same time that was exactly equal to the amount that income would increase given a fixed labour supply. In this case, the individual would find that working the same number of hours kept income unchanged. To maintain affluence, the worker would thus have to work equally hard. On the other hand, an extra hour of work would now be better paid than before, providing an incentive to increase labour effort. This is called the substitution effect, which (all else equal) implies an increased labour supply in response to an increased wage.

Now suppose that the government removed the lump sum tax while wages remained at the new, higher level. Under these conditions, the return from an extra hour of work would be left unchanged, but the individual could afford both more consumption and more leisure at the same time. Under the standard assumption that leisure is a 'normal' good,[1] the individual would now work less due to what is termed the 'income effect'. Increased wages thus have two opposing effects: the substitution effect, which implies an increased labour supply; and the income effect, which implies a reduced labour supply. While the combined effect is theoretically ambiguous, empirical studies have found that the income and substitution effects roughly cancel each other out,[2] which implies that the labour supply should be largely independent of the prevailing wage.[3]

It is thus not a paradox within traditional theory that people in affluent societies work hard to maintain high and growing consumption levels, or that large increases in wages have not led to commensurate reductions in the labour supply.

Identity signalling

As noted above, Douglas and Isherwood (1979) argue that social scientists have been slow to develop a full understanding of the reasons that people demand goods and services. They offer quite a dramatic model: 'Forget that commodities are good for eating, clothing and shelter; forget their usefulness and try instead the idea that commodities are good for thinking; treat them as a nonverbal medium for the human creative faculty' (Douglas and Isherwood, 1979, pp40–41). In this section we will present a model that develops this perspective and its links to economic theory. In the model we shall consider, commodities do not provide direct utility but are instead only useful to communicate – that is, as a means of signalling one's identity to both oneself and to other members of society. Even in this stylized context, individuals can face incentives to work hard to acquire and display consumption goods. The argument presented here is a simplified version of a model explored in detail in Brekke and Howarth (2002).

Why do people use commodities to communicate, and what meanings do they convey? Consider the case in which people desire to achieve a favourable social position in comparison with other members of society and in which verbal assertions of relative position carry next to no information. As we know from academia, it does not suffice to simply argue 'I'm smarter than you!' if one's aim is to anchor one's identity as an intellectually gifted person. To reinforce a self-image as particularly gifted, it would be far more effective to publish many papers in highly accredited journals. If these papers were widely cited then all the better. The publication list and the number of citations are nonverbal means of communication. Why do these signals carry more information than straightforward verbal claims? The answer is that anyone can stake a verbal claim regardless of underlying ability, while it is in fact quite demanding to publish many papers that are widely cited, even for a gifted person.

Note that the non-verbal means of communication in this example extend beyond pure commodities to include (in this case) career achievements. Career achievements and consumption are highly related, however. Within a profession, income is clearly related to achievement. The best athletes have the highest market value, both in terms of the salaries that sports clubs will pay and the royalties they can earn through commercials and product endorsements. Similarly, promotion and salary decisions in most organizations are usually related to some conception of performance. The best research professors are typically offered positions at the best universities at the highest wages. The possessions an individual can afford are thus at least partly a signal of his or her career success.

This argument presumes that equal opportunities are available to persons with differing levels of inate ability. Otherwise success (financial or otherwise) might signal the head start provided by an advantaged background rather than a person's underlying effectiveness or diligence. In a world of unequal opportunities, people could and indeed do draw inferences concerning aptitude based on achievements, even though differences in initial opportunities will introduce noise to these observations. Moreover, individuals tend to compare themselves with others in their peer group. These are often people they meet at school, in the neighbourhood, at work, or through other shared activities. People in particular peer groups will thus be more equal in terms of opportunities than in randomly selected groups.

Among professional scholars, a person's publication list is a better signal of aptitude than his or her possessions. Individuals do not, however, limit their social contacts to professional colleagues who are able to directly assess their achievements. They also interact with people who do not know the relative rank of different journals or the amount of work required to write an influential paper. A similar argument applies to most professions (with some notable exceptions like professional sports). Outside of one's narrow peer group, one's publication list carries next to no information. In these contexts a person's possessions become important signals of his or her achievements, and hence of personal characteristics like aptitude in one's professional activities.

Possessions are also a signal of a person's talent in another area, that of spending money wisely. We all know of people who have wasted lots of money on reckless consumption and unwise investments. Typically, stories of such behaviour are seen as evidence of personal weakness that might well reduce a person's social acceptance. Hence even among close colleagues possessions convey some information about personal qualities.

To make the argument more formal, consider a model in which people have either high or low aptitude. Their career achievements depend on both their labour effort and their aptitude. Each person knows the amount of effort that she must expend to produce a certain output, but does not know how hard other people would need to work to achieve the same result. For a high-aptitude person, each unit of effort generates w units of income that are spent on consumption. A low-aptitude person, in contrast, earns just w units of income on each unit of effort. Here δ is a number between zero and unity that reflects the difference in productivity between the two groups. In this economy, consumption but not income is observable throughout one's social network. Accordingly, consumption provides a means of identity signalling.

In psychological terms, we assume that people derive an increment of utility (S) if they are able to maintain a self-image as possessing high aptitude. Since they do not directly know their relative aptitude, observable objects are required to create and reinforce their self-image. They thus obtain this benefit if and only if their consumption level is higher than the average in society.[4] To complete the model, we assume each unit of labour effort generates one unit of disutility. Accordingly, individuals view work as an undesirable activity to be undertaken only if it provides consumption goods that can be effectively used to establish a favourable self-image.

Using the tools of game theory, it can be shown that the model under discussion is characterized by a unique equilibrium in which:

1   High-aptitude people work at the level of effort δS that is independent of the amount of income that working provides. This generates the corresponding consumption level $w\delta S$ that increases in proportion to the effective wage (w).
2   Low-aptitude individuals choose not to work at all.

By an equilibrium, we mean a situation in which each person's behaviour is individually rational given the choices made by everyone else. In the equilibrium for this model, high-aptitude people will work so hard that people of low aptitude are unwilling to copy their consumption behaviour because the gain in terms of self-image would be fully offset by the disutility of working.

How does the signalling value of consumption relate to the prevailing level of affluence? In our model those with high aptitude have to work equally hard to achieve a favourable self-image irrespective of the level of affluence. To understand the intuition behind this result it is useful to consider the case of a manager for a manufacturing firm. The economic growth that has occurred since the industrial revolution is basically a product of increased productivity in the manufacturing sector. Thus, with economic growth the firm can produce much more per worker than 100 years ago. But even if the firm could produce much more than 100 years ago given the same number of employees, the firm's performance is not compared to the performance of firms 100 years ago. Instead, to prove that the firm is well managed, the firm must perform well compared to other contemporary firms. Thus, a manager cannot relax in the comfort of knowing that the firm is much more productive than similar firms 100 years ago. Similarly, an employee does not compare her consumption with that of an employee 100 years ago, but rather with the contemporary consumers that she encounters on a day-to-day basis.

Irrespective of profession, the amount of effort required to prove that a person is intellectually gifted, economically productive and so forth is no less now in our rich society than it was a century ago. As our modern economy is much more productive, we produce much more when we work equally hard. As a matter of simple accounting, increased consumption is a direct consequence. Total production as measured by gross domestic product is the sum of value added from all firms. Some of this value added is reinvested in the firm to increase future production. The rest is paid out as wages and dividends to workers and owners. Hence, when production increases, income increases, and as argued above, people would spend the income to reinforce identity even if goods had no direct benefits. Since people must work equally hard to show success even though productivity has increased, a higher level of consumption is required to signal success in an affluent society than in a poor one. The social meanings of goods are thus endogenously determined, giving the model a slight flavour of social constructivism.

For simplicity the model we have outlined incorporates only two classes of people, those with high and low aptitude. While this is obviously an oversimplification, our results may be extended directly to allow for a full spectrum of capability levels. Actual aptitudes are, of course, diverse in both level and type. A person may be highly capable in one area but patently inept in another, and it is not altogether obvious how these two fields of comparison should be aggregated and interpreted. Depending on definitions and prevailing social norms, the term 'high aptitude' might be applied to a small elite or conversely to a large majority of the population. In the interpretation as a small elite, the predictions of our model may resemble Veblen's (1899) analysis of 'conspicuous consumption', in which members of high social classes engage in the accumulation and display of wealth in an effort to stand apart. On the other hand, if we viewed the majority of persons as highly capable, social signalling might come to focus on the level of consumption required to appear in public without shame, to paraphrase a famous passage from Adam Smith (1776). The latter interpretation could be used to explain mass consumer culture, and not just the extravagance of a few. With a continuous distribution of aptitude, both effects would be present at the same time, and there would be pressure to consume more at all levels of aptitude as well as to distinguish oneself from lower categories.

This argument is somewhat extreme as we neglected 'that commodities are good for eating, clothing and shelter'. Still, we are able to explain continued consumption growth, and similar results arise in a model where goods and services provide both direct benefits and indirect benefits through identity signalling (see Brekke and Howarth, 2002, pp54–63). We do not claim that commodities have no use value; the point is rather that we can explain consumption growth without reference to these values.

Optimal Environmental Policy

The two alternative models discussed above each explain why the labour supply has shown little change despite large increases in material prosperity. These frameworks differ fundamentally, however, in terms of their policy implications. In applied economics, behavioural models are frequently employed to identify optimal trade-offs, not simply to describe or predict past or future economic trends. Since the total resources available to society are limited, it follows that increasing the supply of one good or service typically requires reductions in the availability of other goods. We can have better schools, more law enforcement, better public transportation and a cleaner environment if we accept less of something else such as private consumption. The two stories of what drives consumer behaviour give rise to widely different assessments of the welfare cost of reducing consumption.

The point here is related to Ng's (1987) argument that 'diamonds are government's best friend' since these are goods that can be taxed at no economic cost. The idea is that diamonds derive their usefulness as signals of social status because their high prices render them exclusive – that is unaffordable to people with comparatively low incomes. (See Bagwell and Bernheim (1996) for a formal model of why increased price may make a good more suitable for status signalling.) Developing this theme, Ng and Wang (1993; see also Howarth, 1996) present a model in which people's desire to achieve a high level of relative consumption implies that the standard measure of willingness-to-pay understates the social benefits of improving environmental quality. In this section we link this argument to the signalling model discussed above, showing that if goods are demanded for their symbolic meanings this will have significant impact on optimal environmental policy, and economic policy in general.

The crucial point is the following: if goods are used only for the direct services they provide – for eating, clothing, shelter and so forth – then the cost of reducing consumption should be counted in full. On the other hand, if goods are used only as a means of communication, there is no cost of reducing private consumption, provided that all consumers face the same reduction. We will focus on the last and least intuitive of these claims.

Leather shoes and a linen shirt were required in England to appear in public without shame when Adam Smith wrote *Wealth of Nations* in 1776. Today a decent house, a nice car and perhaps particular brands of clothing are required to send essentially the same message. While the required modern commodity bundle is much more expensive, the service it provides is essentially the same: to prove that a person possesses the characteristics that allow him to appear in public without shame, although we would use other words. Thus, in this model the total benefits a person derives from private consumption are the same irrespective of the general level of affluence, although in any society the rich enjoy greater benefits than the poor.

The implication of the different assessment of the cost of reducing private consumption becomes even more evident when we introduce a trade-off with some other good such as environmental quality. For concreteness, consider the case of climate change. The level and rate of climate change cannot be used as a signal of anything since we all live in the same climatic system. The cost of climate change is thus purely the direct cost in terms of more extreme weather conditions and even loss of life. But since our resources are restricted, reductions in greenhouse gas emissions will have a cost in terms of reduced private consumption. We thus have to consider the benefits of less global warming against the potential cost of reduced private consumption. But if commodities are used only to communicate, we just argued that there is no cost of reducing private consumption. We can thus get a benefit at no cost, and hence optimal emissions will be almost zero. This is in stark contrast to traditional climate models, in which the optimal policy implies only a rather modest abatement (Nordhaus and Boyer, 2000).

Climate change is just one example where the two models give rise to very different policy prescriptions. The same result would appear for all types of environmental quality and for the optimal provision of collective goods like public transport, public schools, etc. Obviously, goods are not only used for their symbolic meaning, so the claim that there is no cost of reducing private consumption is exaggerated. On the other hand, goods in fact *are* used in part for their symbolic meaning, which indicates that the cost of reduced private consumption is less than standard economic theory suggests. The question of exactly why people demand goods is thus essential to a large range of policy assessments. To determine optimal policy we thus need to know the relative importance of the two motives for consumption.

In our book *Status, Growth and the Environment* (Brekke and Howarth, 2002), we develop an intermediate model in which goods are used both in identity signalling and for their practical use value. In this model, goods do contribute directly to well-being but at the same time are used to communicate. To give an indication of the logic of this model, suppose that environmental taxes on fossil fuels led consumers to buy smaller and more energy-efficient cars. This would have a real cost in terms of the lower comfort and performance of a smaller car. But when smaller cars are common, a smaller car will be sufficient to signal the same degree of aptitude. While individuals will value cars both for direct benefits and for the purposes of identity signalling, from a social perspective only the former is relevant in evaluating the welfare effects that arise when everybody switches to a smaller car.

Using evidence from a variety of empirical studies, we calibrated this model and in order to determine the relative importance of identity signalling, we then applied the calibrated model to a range of policy issues. The results provide mixed support for Frank's (1999) claim that real-world tax systems should be reformed to shift the tax burden from income to consumption. On the other hand, they support the claim that considerable taxes on income or consumption are optimal. With respect to greenhouse gas emissions, we found that optimal emissions are significantly lower than in a model where goods have only direct use values. In addition, we found that it makes a huge difference for economic growth whether people use consumption or wealth in identity signalling. Viewed as a whole, these findings confirm the claim that it is decidedly important for policy analysis to know why people want goods.

Empirical Evidence on the Relative Importance of Social Identity

As we have seen, Adam Smith was aware of the role that identity signalling plays in motivating consumer behaviour, and this topic has recurred repeatedly in the development of economic thought. For a historical overview, see Mason (1998). Nonetheless, the dominant view among economists holds that working with models that account for the interdependent nature of preferences is overly complex and unnecessary to understanding and predicting the workings of economic systems, the objections of other social scientists notwithstanding.

As we have seen, each of the models discussed in this paper is consistent with the observation that the aggregate labour supply has remained roughly constant despite large increases in wages and affluence. This represents an example of a more general problem that arises in empirical tests of alternative theories of consumer behaviour. The two theories tell different stories about the basis for preferences but yield similar predictions regarding the influence of changing prices and incomes on aggregate economic variables. To distinguish between the models, analysts must employ different types of data than those used in traditional consumer econometrics.

Fortunately, there is empirical evidence that can be used to shed some light on the question. This evidence suggests that one may safely reject models that provide no account of how commodities are used to signal identity. Bolton and Ockenfels (2000), for example, show that much of observed behaviour in experimental games may be explained using models that include a concern for relative payoffs, although this outcome may relate more strongly to issues of fairness and reciprocity than to the symbolic meaning of consumption. In addition, several studies have demonstrated that a person's possessions indeed do convey social meanings that are readily interpreted by other members of society. In one such study, Sadalla et al (1987) found that a group of students were able to describe core aspects of an individual's personality after merely viewing pictures of the person's living room. The inferred characteristics correlated strongly with the individual's self-perception. This outcome could not arise unless the commodities to some extent were chosen to reflect the person's perceived identity (see also Tajfel, 1981; Bourdieu, 1984; McCracken, 1991; Dittmar, 1992). On the other hand, human beings obviously need to eat and dress warmly on cold days, so the claim that commodities are *only* used to communicate can obviously be rejected.

The interesting question is thus not which one of the two models is correct, but rather the relative importance of identity signalling and direct use value in models that integrate these effects. While achieving this aim is by no means easy, there is fortunately some available evidence. More reasonable is a model in which commodities are used both to signal aptitude and for strictly practical purposes. In our own previous work (Brekke and Howarth, 2002), we concluded that for the purposes of applied welfare analysis, such a model is equivalent to a model in which people care about both their absolute and relative levels of consumption. The question is thus to determine the importance of relative economic status in comparison with absolute consumption.

Solnick and Hemenway (1998) conducted an experimental study that asked 257 members of the faculty, staff and student body at the Harvard School of Public Health to evaluate two alternative states of the world. In one state the respondent would earn an annual income of US$50,000 in a society with an average income of US$25,000. In the other state the respondent would earn US$100,000 in a society in which a typical person earned US$200,000. The survey stipulated that prices would remain fixed at 1995 levels in both scenarios. In this study, equal numbers of respondents chose each state, indicating that a typical person would be indifferent between these options. The study therefore suggests that a quadrupling of average income would offset a doubling of one's own income, leaving the person in question no better off than the initial state of affairs.

Admittedly, this one study constitutes a meagre basis for determining the relative importance of absolute versus relative consumption. Interestingly, however, other authors have used a variety of approaches to obtain similar estimates. Johansson-Stenman et al (2002) use methods that are closely similar to those of Solnick and Hemenway (1998) to derive nearly identical conclusions. A different approach is taken by Frank (1984) and Frank and Sunstein (2000), who argue that a concern for local status makes it attractive for workers to accept a wage that is high relative to their colleagues but possibly lower than in other available jobs where local status is less. Frank (1984) estimates a model of wage differences between and within firms and compares this with a standard measure of the marginal productivity of labour, finding that the data support the local status theory. Frank and Sunstein (2000) use the results from Frank (1984) to estimate the importance of relative economic status by comparing the importance of local status in different occupations. They argue that in occupations with much social contact between workers, colleagues are likely to be an important part of the peer group and hence local status will be more important. The importance of relative income is then derived by comparing local wage dispersion in occupations with a high degree of social contact versus those with less. Through this approach, Frank and Sunstein find that relative income is somewhat more important than the Solnick and Hemenway study indicates.

The empirical evidence we have discussed relies either on untested assumptions or on survey responses as opposed to observed consumer behaviour. These facts run foul of the behaviourist and positivist epistemological stance adopted by many economists, according to which only observed behaviour can be used as the basis for empirical research. Still, the empirical evidence that is available suggests that identity signalling and hence relative consumption is too important to be ignored. For a more extensive survey of the empirical evidence, see Brekke and Howarth (2002).

Conclusion

Judged by their ancestors' standards, the citizens of contemporary industrial societies have become exceedingly rich. This growth was caused by major increases in labour productivity that allow each person to produce more output given the same degree of effort due to factors such as better capital equipment and better organization of production. With increased production it would be possible to work much less than before and still enjoy a much higher standard of living. However, authors such as Schor (1991) conclude that people work almost as hard as their ancestors. While this claim has mixed empirical support, we have argued above that it would constitute no paradox. In particular, we have offered two very different models that each explain this stylized fact. But while the two models explain the same observation, there is much additional evidence that is very hard to explain unless one accepts the hypothesis that commodities are used to signal a person's identity based on their symbolic meanings.

Of the two models presented above, the first provides the basis for the great majority of applied economic research, which seldom considers issues such as identity signalling and social status. A possible reason for this neglect is the problem of testing the theories against each other, since both explain the same basic observations. While it is hard to give a solid empirical estimate of the weight that individuals attach to relative consumption, we have argued that the available evidence does not support the neglect. The neglect of the symbolic meaning of goods is even more difficult to defend once one recognizes that the two models have substantially different policy implications.

The signalling model presented above gives only a very crude representation of the symbolic importance of goods, as it assumes that goods are only used to communicate one particular personal characteristic and that all comparisons are based on the average consumption level in society as a whole. In reality, the symbolic meanings of goods are much more complex, and people form groups and classes within which relative performance is judged. Schor (1998), for example, argues that due to the emergence of the modern media, people more commonly compare themselves with the super-rich than with the Joneses next-door (see also Frank, 1999.) In a similar vein, Falk and Knell (2000) present a model of optimal peer group choices. Such issues are ignored above.

There is also an issue of being normal versus standing apart, where the latter may be more related to the signalling model presented above. To take just one example, when a person's consumption behaviour conforms with the typical pattern of the group with which he or she identifies, that may be a statement of commitment to the group, and not a signal of personal characteristics. Such issues are not represented by the simple model described in this paper. There is thus much work left to be done in understanding why people want goods. In our view, integrating that understanding into economic theory and applied economic welfare analysis is an interesting and indeed crucial challenge.

Notes

1   A good is denoted 'normal' if the demand for the good is increases with income when the price of the good is held constant.
2   The empirical literature of course reveals a far more complex picture, with substantial heterogeneity in labour supply depending on age, sex, marital status, education and so on, and at least for some groups, the income effect does seem to dominate. See Røed and Strøm (2002) and the references therein.

3   In analytical terms, the labour supply $l = \alpha c/(\alpha c + \alpha l)$ is independent of the prevailing wage (w) for an individual who seeks to maximize the utility function $u = \alpha c \ln(c) + \alpha l \ln(1 - l)$. Here $c = wl$ is the individual's consumption level, $1 - l$ is the proportion of time she devotes to leisure, and αc and αl are parameters that determine the utility she derives from consumption and leisure. For a technical treatment of the substitution and income effects, look for a discussion of the 'Slutsky equation' in any micro-economics textbook.

4   Note that this concern about self-image is based on introspection and does not involve convincing other people that one has a particular set of characteristics. In this respect the model differs from the well-known work of Spence (1973), in which individuals must expend effort on education in order to signal their aptitude to potential employers. Our analysis, in contrast, is inspired by Mead's (1913) philosophical argument that people derive their social identities by viewing themselves from the perspective of others.

References

Bagwell, L. S. and Bernheim, D. B. (1996) 'Veblen effects in a theory of conspicuous consumption', *The American Economic Review*, vol 86, pp349–373

Blanchflower, D. and Oswald, A. (2000) 'Well-being over time in Britain and the USA', Working Papers 7487 2000, NBER, Cambridge, MA

Bolton, G. E. and Ockenfels, A. (2000) 'ERC: A theory of equity, reciprocity and competition', *American Economic Review*, vol 90, pp166–193

Bourdieu, P. (1984) *Distinction: A Social Critique of the Judgement of Taste* (translated by Richard Nice), Routledge and Kegan Paul, London

Brekke, K. A. and Howarth, R. B. (2002) *Social Identity and Material Goods*, Edward Elgar, Cheltenham

Daly, H. E. and Cobb, J. B. (1989) *For the Common Good*, Beacon Press, Boston

Dittmar, H. (1992) *The Social Psychology of Material Possessions, To Have Is to Be*, Harvester Wheatsheaf, Hemel Hempstead, UK

Douglas, M. and Isherwood, B. (1979) *The World of Goods: Towards an Anthropology of Consumption*, Penguin, Harmondsworth

Durning, A. T. (1992) *How Much Is Enough? The Consumer Society and the Future of the Earth*, Norton, New York

Easterlin, R. (1996) *Growth Triumphant: The Twenty-First Century in Historical Perspective*, University of Michigan Press, Ann Arbor, MI

Falk, A. and Knell, M. (2000) 'Choosing the Joneses: On the endogeneity of reference groups', unpublished manuscript, University of Zurich, Switzerland

Frank, R. H. (1984) 'Are workers paid their marginal product?' *American Economic Review*, vol 74, pp549–571

Frank, R. H. (1999) *Luxury Fever: Why Money Fails to Satisfy in an Era of Excess*, Free Press, New York

Frank, R. H. and Sunstein, C. R. (2000) 'Cost–benefit analysis and relative position', Working Paper No. 00-5, AEI/Brookings Joint Center for Regulatory Studies, Washington, DC

Grossman, G. M. and Krueger, A. B. (1995) 'Economic growth and the environment', *Quarterly Journal of Economics*, vol 110, pp353–357

Howarth, R. B. (1996) 'Status effects and environmental externalities', *Ecological Economics*, vol 16, pp25–34

Johansson-Stenman, O., Carlsson, F. and Daruvala, D. (2002) 'Measuring future grandparents' preferences for equality and relative standing', *Economic Journal*, vol 112, pp362–383

Maddison, A. (1995) *Monitoring the World Economy 1820–1992*, Organisation for Economic Co-operation and Development, Paris

Mason, R. (1998) *The Economics of Conspicuous Consumption, Theory and Thought since 1700*, Edward Elgar, Cheltenham

McCracken, G. (1991) *Culture and Consumption: New Approaches to the Symbolic Character of Consumer Goods and Activities*, Indiana University Press, Bloomington, IN

Mead, G. H. (1913) 'The social self', *Journal of Philosophy*, vol 10, pp374–380

Meadows, D. H., Meadows, D. L. and Randers, J. (1992) *Beyond the Limits*, Chelsea Green Publishing, Post Mills, VT

Ng, Y. K. (1987) 'Diamonds are a government's best friend: Burden-free taxes on goods valued for their values', *American Economic Review*, vol 77, pp186–91

Ng, Y. K. and Wang, J. (1993) 'Relative income, aspiration, environmental quality, individual and political myopia: Why may the rat-race for material growth be welfare reducing?' *Mathematical Social Sciences*, vol 26, pp3–23

Nordhaus, W. D. and Boyer, J. (2000) *Warming the World: Economic Models of Global Warming*, MIT Press, Cambridge, MA

Robinson, J. P. and Godbey, G. (1997) *Time for Life: The Surprising Ways American Use their Time*, Penn State University Press, University Park, PA

Røed, K. and Strøm, S. (2002) 'Progressive taxes and the labour market: Is the trade-off between equality and efficiency inevitable?' *Journal of Economic Surveys*, vol 16, pp77–110

Sadalla, E. K., Vershure, B. and Burroughs, J. (1987) 'Identity symbolism in housing', *Environment and Behaviour*, vol 19, pp569–587

Sahlins, M. (1972) *Stone Age Economics*, Aldine de Gruyter, New York

Schor, J. (1991) *The Overworked American: The Unexpected Decline in Leisure*, Basic Books, New York

Schor, J. (1998) *The Overspent American: Upscaling, Downshifting and the New Consumer*, Basic Books, New York

Selden, T. M. and Song, D. (1994) 'Environmental quality and development: Is there a Kuznets Curve for air pollution emissions?' *Journal of Environmental Economics and Management*, vol 27, pp147–162

Smith, A. (1776) *An Inquiry into the Nature and Causes of the Wealth of Nations*, Strahan and Cadell, London

Solnick, S. J. and Hemenway, D. (1998) 'Is more always better? A survey on positional concerns', *Journal of Economic Behavior and Organization*, vol 37, pp373–383

Spence, M. (1973) 'Job market signaling', *Quarterly Journal of Economics*, vol 87, pp355–374

Tajfel, H. (1981) *Human Groups and Social Categories: Studies in Social Psychology*. Cambridge University Press, Cambridge

Veblen, T. (1899) *The Theory of the Leisure Class*, Macmillan, New York

18

The Evocative Power of Things: Consumer Goods and the Preservation of Hopes and Ideals

Grant McCracken

This chapter examines another pragmatic use of consumer goods. In this case, we are concerned not with the redefinition of gender but with the cultivation of hopes and ideals. Consumer goods are bridges to these hopes and ideals. We use them to recover this displaced cultural meaning, to cultivate what is otherwise beyond our grasp. In this capacity, consumer goods are also a way of perpetually renewing our consumer expectations. The dark side of this aspect of consumption is that it helps to enlarge our consumer appetites so that we can never reach a 'sufficiency' of goods and declare 'I have enough.' This aspect of consumption also helps illuminate some of the irrational, fantastic, escapist attachments we have to consumer goods. Treating goods as bridges to displaced meaning helps to make these issues more intelligible.

Displaced Meaning and Consumer Goods

This chapter gives a theoretical account of a little-studied category of cultural meaning.[1] This category is here called 'displaced meaning' because it consists in cultural meaning that has deliberately been removed from the daily life of a community and relocated in a distant cultural domain. The chapter also seeks to give a theoretical account of the role of consumption in the evocation of this meaning. Consumption is one of the means by which a culture re-establishes access to the cultural meaning it has displaced. In sum, this chapter is designed to show what 'displaced meaning' is and how this meaning is represented and manipulated through the consumer system.

The topic of 'displaced meaning' has not been widely studied in the social sciences. The topics of 'ideals' and 'values' have been considered (e.g. Kluckhohn, 1962; Rokeach, 1979; Silverman, 1969) but these studies do not treat the strategic 'displaced' nature of this kind of cultural meaning. This is so common and useful a practice for human communities that it is odd that there should be so few theoretical concepts to deal with it. It is the purpose of this chapter to supply such a concept.

If the study of displaced meaning has not been abundant, the role of inanimate objects in the representation and recovery of cultural meaning is much better understood. In anthropology, the subdisciplines of structuralism and material culture have both examined this topic (Sahlins, 1976; Douglas and Isherwood, 1978; McCracken, 1986a, 1986b; Reynolds and Stott, 1986). American studies, a field that also uses the title 'material culture', has made this topic the object of intense and sophisticated research (Quimby, 1978; Prown, 1982; Schlereth, 1982). In the field of consumer behaviour, a long-standing interest in the topic has been sharpened by new approaches to its study (Holman, 1980; Hirschman and Holbrook, 1981; Levy, 1981; Mason, 1981, 1984; Belk, 1982; Solomon, 1983). Psychology is also the host of new research in this area (Graumann, 1974–1975; Furby, 1978; Csikszentmihalyi and Rochberg-Halton, 1981). Sociology, following a period of intense interest in the 1950s (e.g. Goffman, 1951; J. Davis, 1956, 1958) appears to be returning to this topic (Lauman and House, 1970; Nicosia and Mayer, 1976; F. Davis, 1985). The field of history is also beginning to devote itself to this question (Jackson Lears, 1981; McKendrick et al, 1982; Fox and Jackson Lears, 1983; McCracken, 1985). For all of its breadth and penetration, this work has also failed to consider the category of meaning here called 'displaced meaning'.[2]

A clearer understanding of the role of consumer goods in the representation and recovery of displaced meaning promises several contributions to scholarship. First, it will help clarify one of the ways in which objects carry meaning. This in turn will help advance the present effort in the social sciences to understand how objects serve as a medium of non-linguistic communication. To glimpse the role of goods in the recovery of displaced meaning is also to gain new insight into the systematic properties of consumption that are now dismissed as 'irrational', 'fantastic' or 'escapist'. When goods serve as bridges to displaced meaning they help perpetually to enlarge the individual's tastes and preferences and prevent the attainment of a 'sufficiency' of goods. They are, to this extent, an essential part of the Western consumer system and the reluctance of this system ever to allow that 'enough is enough'. A proper understanding of displaced meaning promises insight into aspects of consumption now obscure.

Displaced Meaning

The gap between the 'real' and the 'ideal' in social life is one of the most pressing problems a culture must deal with. There is no simple solution. Those who retreat into naive optimism must eventually accept that the gap is a permanent feature of social life. Those who move, instead, to open cynicism and a formal acceptance of the gap must contend with the unmanageable prospect of a life without larger goals and hope. The discrepancy between the realities and the moral imperatives of a community has no obvious remedy.

There are, however, several strategies at the disposal of a culture in its treatment of this chronic aspect of social life. This chapter is concerned with only one of them. It is concerned with what may be called the 'displaced meaning' strategy. Confronted with the recognition that reality is impervious to cultural ideals, a community may displace these ideals. It will remove them from daily life and transport them to another cultural universe, there to be kept within reach but out of danger. The 'displaced meaning' strategy allows a culture to remove its ideals from harm's way.

But the strategy does more than shelter cultural ideals. It also helps to give them a sort of empirical demonstration. When they are transported to a distant cultural domain, ideals are made to seem practicable realities. What is otherwise unsubstantiated and potentially improbable in the present world is now validated, somehow 'proven', by its existence in another, distant one. With ideals displaced, the gap between the real and the ideal can be put down to particular, local difficulties. It reflects contingent rather than necessary circumstances. The strategy of displaced meaning contends with the discrepancy between the real and the ideal by the clever expedient of removing the ideal from the fray.

Locations for Displaced Meaning

The culture that resorts to the 'displaced meaning' strategy must find a place for its ideals. There are many alternatives here. Ideals can be removed to an almost infinite number of locations on the continua of time and place. The continuum of time is, for instance, often made the location of a 'golden age'. Putatively, this golden age is always a historical period for which documentation and evidence exists in reassuring abundance. In fact, the period is a largely fictional moment in which social life is imagined to have conformed perfectly to cultural ideals. A version of this notion appears in Ovid's *Metamorphoses* (1960, p9):

> Golden was that first age, which, with no one to compel, without a law, of its own will, kept faith and did the right. There was no fear of punishment, no threatening words were to be read on brazen tablets; no suppliant throng gazed fearfully upon its judge's face; but without judges lived secure.

The 'golden age' tradition is especially active in the West where from Hesiodic and Platonic origins it has proven itself continually useful as a safe haven for cherished ideals (Nisbet, 1969, p51). Von Grunebaum called this confidence in a perfect past 'cultural classicism'. He makes it plain that this strategy of meaning displacement has existed not only in the West but in several oriental traditions as well (1964).[3]

Sometimes it is not a glorious past that becomes the location of unfulfilled ideals but a glorious future. The Western tradition has given ample demonstration of this location as well. Christian theologians have posited 'the other world' as a fundamental tenet of faith. Even the 18th-century philosophers who took issue with this Christian concept of the future created their own version of it in order to have a place to keep tenets safe from empirical test (Becker, 1932, p150). The future is a versatile location with many alternative possibilities: an anarchist's commune that has no law and no property, the perfect democracy in which all people are fully equal and free, the perfect socialist state that advances a common good over individual interest, the perfect laissez-faire society in which economic individualism decides all collective matters. Some of these may be realistic possibilities. They are, more important, also temporal locations in which ideals can find protection from the possibility of contradiction.

The future is, in some respects, more accommodating than the past as a refuge for displaced meaning. It is, after all, more unconstrained by historical record or demonstrable fact. The future has no limitation but the imagination that contemplates it. It is a tabula rasa while the past has certain, sometimes inconvenient, notation already in place. There is, as a result, perhaps some principle of meaning displacement here that says that the choice of the past and future as a location will be constrained by the degree of implausibility of the ideal to be displaced. The more extreme the degree of this implausibility the more likely is it to be transported to the future.

But the 'unspecified' character of the future is not only an advantage but also a weakness. A golden past can give credibility to cultural ideals by 'demonstrating' that these ideals were once extant. Future periods can establish no such illusion. They establish no grounds for the argument that ideals are practicable because once practised. Apparently, however, the 'true believer' still finds a future location of ideals compelling evidence for their plausibility. The utopian vision, apparently, has its own facticity. It exists in the mind of the believer with such vividness and authority that it has the force of demonstrable fact. Ideals displaced to a future location can be their own proof. They are validated by the imagination, verified in the act of thinking. The act of thinking can be an act of faith (Manuel and Manuel, 1979, p27). In sum, the future is a somewhat more accommodating location for displaced meaning than the past, but it is also marginally less authoritative.

It is also possible to transport one's ideals across the continuum of space. Somewhere in the present day, a society can be found that appears to live a life in which 'all keep faith and do the right'. Ideally, this society is sufficiently distant to ensure that thorough scrutiny is not easily undertaken, for this scrutiny is almost always disappointing. With this condition, displacement in space works just as effectively as displacement in time. The imperfections of a given society can now be dismissed as local aberrations. Ideals have found a place of safety.

There are some systematic properties to the displacement of ideal knowledge in space. Colonized countries tend to regard the 'mother country' or the 'fatherland' as the perfect fulfilment of local ideals. This misconception is encouraged especially by the propagandistic efforts in which all colonizers engage. It is also true that societies tend to favour their structural opposites when seeking out new locations. Industrial societies tend toward a certain fondness for pastoral societies. Pastoral societies look forward to the opportunities for perfection that development will bring. Similarly, traditional societies admire modern ones, and they, in turn, return the compliment. Somewhere on the spatial continuum there is always a perfect 'other' in terms of which locally unobtainable ideals can be cast.

The culture that seeks to contend with the discrepancy between real and ideal through the strategy of displaced meaning will never be disappointed. The continua of space and time are endlessly hospitable. They represent a vast ethnographic experiment in which recognizably human elements are combined and recombined in richly various configurations. Some one of these experiments must surely serve as a reasonable facsimile of what one wishes for one's own time and place. Thus can a culture protect itself from the gruelling possibility that local failure to realize ideals is a necessary and universal condition.

The displacement strategy is clearly more than an idle fiction, a game cultures play for their own amusement. It is indeed one of history's most powerful engines. Some significant part of the richness of the ethnographic and historical record follows precisely from the effort to realize distant ideals in the 'here and now'. The 'displaced mean-ing' strategy is therefore a vital source of historical transformation. Whatever success has been enjoyed in this pursuit of displaced ideals, it is also true that it has given rise to an astonishing collection of misadventures and calamities. It is a measure of the essential strength of the displacement strategy that this catalogue of disaster has not discouraged it. That the recovery of displaced meaning has brought tragedy and despair to virtually every culture has done nothing to discredit the strategy and nothing at all to dim the enthusiasm with which it is still pursued. Of all of the strategies with which a culture may contend with the discrepancy between the real and the ideal, displaced meaning should perhaps be regarded as a characteristically reckless 'species favourite'.

Displaced Meaning Writ Small

What occurs on this grand scale, for nations and cultures, also occurs on a much smaller one, for individuals. Like cultures, individuals display a characteristic refusal to attribute the failure of ideals to the ideals themselves. Like cultures, individuals prefer to displace their ideals, removing them from the 'here and now' to the relative safety of another time or place. Individuals, like cultures, find the 'displaced meaning' strategy a useful sleight of hand, one that sustains hope in the face of impressive grounds for pessimism.

The strategies evoked by individuals resemble those evoked by cultures. They seek out locations on the continua of time and place for their ideals. They 'discover' a per-sonal 'golden age' in which life conformed to their fondest expectations or noblest ide-als: the happy years of childhood or perhaps merely a single summer holiday. With ideals displaced to this largely fictional location, present difficulties and disappointments are rendered inert and hope allowed to sustain itself.

For individuals who cannot find a satisfactory location in the past, the future proves more accommodating. As noted above, the future is unspecified and therefore without constraints. What kind of future will prove a satisfactory location for ideals is often specified by convention. Conventional locations include 'when I get married ...', 'when I finally have my degree ...', 'when opportunity comes a-knockin' ...'. These desirable futures are collective inventions and subject to changing fashion. A favourite Victorian future began 'when I am acknowledged ...' and was especially popular among domestic servants who awaited the discovery that they were the illegitimate offspring of ancient, childless and staggeringly rich aristocrats.

Again, it is apparently true that the unspecified nature of the future does not pre-vent it from having great powers of persuasion. The individual believer can make a future location just as convincing a source of optimism as a past location. The fact that it has never been extant does not diminish it as a source of validation for ideals.

What cannot be found in a personal past or future can be sought out on the con-tinuum of space. Individuals are constantly engaged in the study of the lives of others for proof that their personal ideals have been realized. This tendency is exploited for political purposes in 'cults of personality' and for commercial ones in the Hollywood 'star system'. In both cases the willingness to transport one's ideals to a location outside of one's own life is used to persuasive effect. This phenomenon has been well studied under 'distant reference group', 'status emulation' and 'diffusion' theories in several of the social sciences without the recognition of the displacement process.

For both groups and individuals, quite astonishingly unhappy situations can be made tolerable through the judicious displacement of certain hopes and ideals. The displacement strategy has enabled both individuals and groups to suffer circumstances created by poverty, racism and dispossessed statuses of all kinds. So important is the role of displaced meaning in these lives that it cannot be forsaken without dramatic consequences. The individuals and groups who give up their displaced meaning are promptly moved either to consuming despair or fierce rebellion. It is, however, a measure of displaced meaning's terrible power that it can prevail unchallenged and unforsaken through generations of unhappiness.

The Evocative Power of Objects

It has been suggested that each culture must contend with a universal discrepancy between the real and the ideal and that one of the ways of doing so is the strategy of displaced meaning. It must now be observed that this strategy creates a difficulty. How does the culture re-establish access to the meaning it has displaced? This section of the chapter will argue that it is partly through inanimate objects and consumer goods that this problem is addressed. Goods serve both individuals and cultures as bridges to displaced meaning. They are one of the devices that can be used to help in the recovery of this meaning.

The question of recovery is a delicate one. The process of meaning displacement is undertaken in the first place in order to establish a kind of epistemological immunity for ideas. When an attempt is made to recover this meaning, care must be taken to see that this immunity is not compromised. Recovery must be accomplished in such a way that displaced meaning is brought into the 'here and now' without having to take up all of the responsibilities of full residence. When displaced meaning is recovered from its temporal or spatial location, it must not be exposed to the possibility of disproof. In other words, access must not be allowed to undo the work of displacement.

Let us examine just how consumer goods help to accomplish this delicate task. The discussion to follow is divided into two parts. The first part will examine how goods can serve as bridges before the act of purchase when they are no more than a gleam in the individual's eye. The second part will consider how goods serve as bridges when they have entered the individual's possession.

Goods serve as bridges when they are not yet owned but merely coveted. Well before purchase an object can serve to connect the would-be owner with displaced meaning. The individual anticipates the possession of the good and, with this good, the possession of certain ideal circumstances that exist now only in a distant location.

In this case, goods help the individual contemplate the possession of an emotional condition, a social circumstance, even an entire style of life, by somehow concretizing these things in themselves. They become a bridge to displaced meaning and an idealized version of life as it should be lived. When called to mind, these objects allow the individual to rehearse a much larger set of possessions, attitudes, circumstances and opportunities. A simple example of this is the use of a 'rose-covered cottage'. The individual reflects on the eventual possession of such a cottage and in the process reflects upon the possession of an entire way of life that specifies more or less explicitly a certain kind of livelihood, spouse, domestic arrangement and so on. The cottage becomes the 'objective correlative' of this diverse package of displaced meaning.[4] How goods serve as the correlatives of displaced meaning will be discussed in greater detail below.

The striking thing about the use of goods as bridges is their ability to establish access without undoing the work of displacement. They can accomplish both halves of the displacement strategy without compromising either. When goods become the 'objective correlative' of certain cultural meanings, they give the individual a kind of access to displaced meaning that would otherwise be inaccessible to them. They allow the individual to participate in this meaning, even in a sense to take possession of it. But goods accomplish this semiotic miracle without actually bringing displaced meaning into the withering light of the real world. In this capacity, the good makes displaced meaning accessible without also making it vulnerable to empirical test or compromising its diplomatic status.

Objects can be future-oriented as in the case of the 'rose-covered cottage', or they can be past-oriented as when an object comes to represent a happier time. Here, too, an object comes to concretize a much larger set of attitudes, relationships and circumstances, all of which are summoned to memory and rehearsed in fantasy when the individual calls the object to mind.

A good example here is the 'rosebud' insignia that adorns a childhood sledge in the movie *Citizen Kane*. This movie may be taken as a study in displaced meaning and consumption. The picture deliberately exploits the tragic and ironic implications of the protagonist's failure to see that it is his past (real or imagined) that he seeks so desperately and that the word 'rosebud' that so powerfully evokes this state of happiness is indeed the name of his childhood sledge. This object, a potential bridge to displaced meaning, has got lost in Kane's priceless collection of objects, no one of which can serve as the bridge he seeks so urgently.

The tragedy of *Citizen Kane* follows from the fact that its protagonist has lost touch not only with his past but also with the bridge that allowed him to gain access to this past. A popular interpretation of the movie finds an 'anti-materialistic' message in the movie. Poor, misguided Kane seeks his happiness in things, in a pathology of consumption. But the real nature of Kane's difficulty is not that he seeks his happiness in things. The displacement strategy moves all of us to similiar attempts. The real nature of his difficulty is that he is unable to determine in which of his possessions this happiness is really (or apparently) resident.

These two examples illustrate the use of objects as a bridge to displaced meaning in personal terms only. It is also true that groups make objects the 'objective correlative' of ideals that have been transposed to the past and future. These objects can be the flags of courts in exile, the national costume of a subjugated country, the sacred objects of a religion that awaits the millennium, or the emblem of any group that looks forward to the realization of ideals that are now unfulfilled (Firth, 1973). The 'log cabin', as the symbol of former civic virtues, serves one nation as a place to keep certain of its political ideals. The examples here are endless. Collective displaced meanings can be got to through consumer goods just as readily as private ones.

Thus far we have discussed objects that are coveted, not owned, by the individual. But ownership is not incompatible with the use of a good as a bridge to displaced meaning. Individuals can take possession of objects without destroying their strategic value. Normally, however, when the individual chooses a good to be a bridge to displaced meaning, he chooses something that is well beyond his purchasing power. There is no point in longing for what is readily within one's reach. Or, more accurately, desire rarely matures into longing when the object of desire is at hand. In most cases, then, the bridge to meaning is as inaccessible as the meaning itself. It does not admit of ready purchase. So when the individual does buy the good it is almost always as an exceptional purchase. It outstrips in value and/or character the scale of the consumer package presently in the consumer's possession.

The motivation for the exceptional purchase is usually anticipatory. It arrives as a 'front runner'. The good is purchased in anticipation of the eventual purchase of a much larger package of goods, attitudes and circumstances of which it is a piece. These purchases are long contemplated and looked forward to. Usually they include 'high involvement' goods such as a car, a watch, an article of clothing, a perfume, a special foodstuff.[5] Individuals buy them in order to take possession of a small concrete part of the style of life to which they aspire. These bridges serve as proof of the existence of this style of life and even as proof of the individual's ability to lay claim to it.

Normally the purchase of the good does not violate the displacement rule. It does not summon the larger system of which it is a part and so expose it to empirical scrutiny and proof. What is being bought is not the whole bridge but a small part of it. Indeed the purchase has a quality of rehearsal to it. It is consumption in training. The individual clearly understands that he or she is not laying claim to the whole parcel of displaced meaning that has been transported to another time and place, but merely a small, anticipatory part of it. This gives another virtue for the concrete and discrete nature of the good. It can be broken off and used to anticipate the larger purchase.

But when the purchase does evoke the displaced system of meaning, there is another solution. The individual simply discredits the object obtained as a bridge to displaced meaning and transfers this role to an object not yet in his or her possession. The consumer looks forward to a life that is, finally, fulfilled, satisfied, replete. But no sooner is this purchase made than the consumer transfers anticipation to another object. What has been long sought is swiftly devalued and the individual moves on to another bridge, so that displaced meaning can remain displaced. The process of 'trading up' is often driven in just this manner.

There is another solution to this problem. It takes the form of simple avoidance It has been suggested that living rooms are the sites of a family 'on its best behaviour'. Living rooms are places where a family lives to a higher standard, according to more exacting ideals. Having invested the living room with this displaced meaning, the family fastidiously avoids it. In the words of Kron (1983, pp93–94):

> Decorating folklore brims with tales of velvet ropes across the doorways of middle-class living rooms; sofas protected between social calls with clear plastic slipcovers, families spending evenings in living-room avoidance, and silent agreement among middle-class consumers that certain objects are inappropriate in the living room – TV sets, telephones, recliners, trophies. Some people even feel books don't belong there. All to pro-

tect the immaculate concept of the living room, an ironic name for a room no one lives in.

But the possession of objects that serve as bridges to displaced meaning is perilous. Once possessed, these objects can begin to collapse the distance between an individual and his or her ideals. When a 'bridge' is purchased, the owner has begun to run the risk of putting the displaced meaning to empirical test. Once the car that has for so long stood as a representative of 'what my life will be like some day' is in fact part of the individual's life, then displaced meaning is no longer fully displaced. It is now an incipient part of the 'here and now' and to this extent vulnerable to contradiction. The possession of an object that has served as a bridge to displaced meaning presents a clear and present danger to the individual's ideals.

The most striking illustration of this occurs from time to time when individuals unexpectedly receive wealth sufficient to buy any and every object they have ever used as a bridge. Purchase behaviour of this order effectively makes every bridge and every location suddenly accessible. One's displaced meaning is no longer safely out of reach. A Canadian woman recently won $900,000 in a provincial lottery and then succeeded in spending nearly half of this amount in a three-week period. A reporter talked to her toward the end of this riot of consumer activity, and she confided in him: 'A lot of fun is taken out of life when you just go out and buy whatever you want. It is not as wonderful as you think it will be before you win. I don't think you can ever get back to the way it was before' (Rickwood, 1984, pA14).

Indeed when one purchases all of the things that have served as bridges to displaced meaning and discovers that one's ideals remain unrealized, life is changed irrevocably.

The difficulty faced by the lottery winner is faced by any individual who enjoys great wealth. Great wealth enables the individual to buy virtually any and every thing he or she might want. As a result, the consumer devalues the purchase and transfers 'bridge' status to another object not yet owned. When anything can be bought on whim, there can be no location in space or time that can be used as a refuge of personal ideals. Never can they say, 'If I could only have a rose-covered cottage, then …' There are no happiness or fulfilment contingencies in the lives of the very rich.

There is, however, a way out of this dilemma as well. It is to buy what is scarce and rare; it is to collect. The virtue of pursuing collectibles rather than merely consumer goods is precisely that they have their own special scarcity. Collectibles are not available to any one with means. Their availability is constrained by the fact that they are no longer made (as in the case of antiques) or that they are not the products of mass manufacture and can therefore claim to be unique (as in the case of art). Not even a vast purchasing power will bring these objects into reach. Collectibles, unique or very rare, must be hunted down, brought out of hiding, won away from other collectors. When goods have this special elusiveness, they can once again become bridges. It is now possible for the individual to treat them as things to which certain displaced meanings adhere. They have the all-important quality of being beyond one's grasp and can therefore serve as bridges to displaced meaning. The individual can now pretend that there is a distant location for his or her personal ideals and that these ideals will be realized when the bridge to them is obtained. In short, collectibles make it possible once again to dream. One can look forward to that magic day in which one owns every Renoir outside of public collection.[6]

Let us now take up the precise mechanics of the process by which goods serve as bridges. How do they succeed in giving us conditional access to our displaced meaning? The answer to this question rests in the physical, economic and structural characteristics of goods and the contribution these characteristics make to non-linguistic communication. There are four aspects of goods that give them special efficacy in the expression of displaced meaning.

First, unlike the signs of other media of communication (e.g. spoken language, music), these signs are concrete and enduring.[7] This gives them a special advantage in the representation and recovery of displaced meaning. Displaced meaning is by its very nature insubstantial. It has been very deliberately removed from the 'here and now' and made remote. As a result, access is established best when this displaced meaning can be given substance and facticity. Goods have the virtue of suggesting, even demonstrating, this substance, through their own substance. In more theoretical terms, it may be suggested that the property of concreteness passes from the signifying object to the signified meaning. The rose-covered cottage, for instance, gives to the abstract conditions, circumstances and opportunities for which it stands something of its own squat, colourful, immovable substance. Suddenly the abstract notion of a perfectly happy life, spent with the perfect spouse, engaged in perfect circumstances, takes on a substance. In the peculiar epistemology of common sense, this substance has several striking implications. It suggests with new force the plausibility of the imagined circumstance. It suggests with new plausibility the possession of these circumstances. Finally, it stands as a kind of experiential proof of the existence of displaced meaning. These concrete signs help encourage the fiction that the intangibles for which they stand are indeed substantial and that they can be possessed concretely. They create a kind of concreteness that stands emotionally as a kind of 'proof' of the displaced meaning.

Second, these signs have the advantage of appearing to exploit a rhetoric trope well known for its persuasive powers. This trope is the 'synecdoche', a figure of speech in which a part is used to represent the whole (Sapir, 1977). The classic synecdoche appears in the expression 'all hands on deck', in which part 'hands' stands for the whole 'sailors'. When an object represents displaced meaning, it appears to do so in precisely this part-for-whole manner. The individual's concept of his or her future somehow comes to centre on a material piece of this future. To return to our example, it is the 'rose-covered cottage' that represents a large and diverse bundle of emotional conditions and social circumstances. Similarly, it is the imagined wedding ring that becomes the symbol of the perfect bliss of matrimony the individual looks forward to. The part represents the whole.

Third, the economic value of these objects helps give them symbolic value. The desired object stands beyond the individual's purchasing power as this is conventionally deployed. It is nearly or entirely unobtainable. It is to this extent scarce and to this extent desirable. But these, interestingly, are precisely the properties of displaced meaning. This meaning is itself scarce and desirable. For its own somewhat different reasons, it has been put beyond the individual's grasp and made correspondingly more desirable. In other words, the economic character of the desired objects makes them peculiarly well suited to stand for displaced meaning. The logical similarity between them makes for a special bond between signifier and signified.

The fourth quality that gives goods a special efficacy in the representation of displaced meaning is their plenitude. Goods in modern consumer cultures make up a vast array of objects which show a very considerable and finely differentiated range in their scarcity and cost. As a result, for most consumers there is always another, higher level of consumption to which they might aspire. These higher levels serve as a guarantee of safe refuge for displaced meaning. Should one level eventually be achieved by the individual, there will always be a still-greater one to which ideal meaning can be displaced.

In sum, when ideals have been removed to new locations in time and space, goods can serve as bridges to them. The goods enable individuals and groups to recover displaced meaning without bringing it fully into the demanding circumstances of the 'here and now'. Goods serve so well in this capacity because they succeed in making abstract and disembodied meaning extant, plausible, possessable and, above all, concrete. They represent displaced meaning by serving as synecdoches of this meaning. They represent this meaning by reproducing its value and scarcity through their own. Finally, they represent this meaning by creating a series of almost infinitely expandable locations through finely articulated diversity.

'Bridge' goods normally serve in this capacity when they are merely anticipated purchases. Inevitably some of them find their way into the individual's possession. When this occurs the individual must swiftly transfer 'bridge' status from the purchased object to one that is not now owned. Thus does displaced meaning remain displaced. Great wealth, however, frustrates this strategy by putting any and all objects within one's reach. The appropriate substitute strategy here is collecting. The uniqueness or great scarcity of collectibles allow them to serve as objects beyond one's reach and bridges to the displaced meaning.

Implications of the Displacement Effect

The use of goods to recover displaced meaning is one of the engines of consumption in modern society. It helps perpetuate consumer appetite. It helps declare certain purchases obsolete (when they can no longer serve as bridges) and demands the purchase of new goods. The pursuit of displaced meaning through goods makes the consumer sharply attentive to luxury categories of goods and to product innovation. It induces a willingness to violate the normal constraints of income and to make the exceptional purchase. It works constantly to whet appetite and to enlarge demand.

All of these things are plainly good for a sound economy. They are, just as plainly, serious impediments to the creation of a society in which tastes and preferences have internal limits, in which a sufficiency of goods becomes a consumer reality. Without these limits, without this sufficiency, there can be no reapportionment of resources within Western economies nor between the economies of the first and third worlds. The use of goods to recover displaced meaning commits us to consumption that exceeds physical and most ordinary cultural needs. It commits us to a consumer system in which the individual always achieves sufficiency as a temporary condition, no sooner established than repudiated. The displacement effect prevents Western economies from controlling the impulses that drive them and from taking control of the motive forces from which they draw their social energy. Hitherto, these aspects of consumption have been dismissed as simple greed and irrationality. According to the usual account, consumers buy luxury goods because they are the prisoners of extravagance. They are the captives of irrational appetites.

Thus speaks the traditional view. In point of fact, the matter is more complicated and, perhaps, somewhat less unworthy. Our taste for luxuries or goods beyond our conventional buying power, is not simply greed, not only self-indulgence. It is also attributable to our need, as groups and as individuals, to re-establish access to the ideals we have displaced to distant locations in time or space. This cultural and psychological phenomenon has its own peculiar rationality. It is at once more complicated, more systematic and more curious than we have previously recognized.

The account of displaced meaning proposed here will perhaps also help us to understand certain less macroscopic issues in the field of consumer behaviour. For instance, to know that goods are bridges to displaced meaning helps illuminate certain instances of 'consumer pathology' as Schlereth (1982) calls them. An individual's moments of compulsive, irrational, insupportable consumption may spring from a desperate effort to lay claim to certain meanings that they have displaced. It is also easy to see that a nasty, self-perpetuating logic can establish itself in which the desperate individual buys an exceptional good in search of displaced meaning, finds it incapable of delivering this meaning, and is then forced to buy another, still more expensive, good. More common and straightforward consumer actions may also be illuminated. Might the 'post-purchase dissonance' so often referred to in the literature (Cummings and Venkatesan, 1976) follow in some cases from precisely the unhappy discovery that the purchase of a 'bridge' does not indeed give one access to displaced meaning? Might the use of goods as a way of altering moods (as in the case of a purchase to 'cheer one up') also find explanation here? Certainly, the notion of goods as bridges to displaced meaning has been thoroughly domesticated and exploited by advertising professionals. This group consistently suggests through its advertisements that goods are bridges and that their purchases will give the consumer access to displaced ideals.

Displaced Meaning and the Nature of Hope in a Consumer Society

One of the things this chapter means to bring to light is the intimate connection between consumer goods and hope in consumer societies. Displaced meaning helps us to resist the pessimistic conclusions that unhappy personal or collective affairs threaten to force upon us. It allows us to suppose that while things may not presently conform to ideal expectations, there is a time or a place in which they do. The displacement of meaning allows us to take heart, to sustain hope. Goods also help to sustain hope by suggesting that displaced meaning can be recovered and realized in the 'here and now'. It is, however, absolutely essential for us never to receive what it is we want. It is necessary for us always to be denied the goods that would give us access to distant ideals. This requires the constant expansion of our wants. The things we want must always be beyond us, always just out of reach. For goods to serve the cause of hope, they must be inexhaustible in supply. We must always have new goods to make our bridges if hope is to spring eternal.

Conclusion

Hannah Arendt (1958) suggested that meaningful objects prevent the 'drift' and deterioration of our ideas of self and world. They help in this chief mnemonic capacity to remind us of who and what we are. This chapter has made another, contrary claim. It has suggested that goods are bridges to displaced meaning and to this extent objects that tell us not who we are, but who we wish we were. It has suggested that the displacement of meaning is a fundamental strategy cultures and individuals use to deal with discrepancy between the 'real' and the 'ideal'. When meaning is relocated in space or time, it is protected from empirical test but also removed from ready access. Consumer goods are bridges that allow groups and individuals to re-establish a limited kind of access to this meaning. Through goods we are able to entertain the eventual possession of ideals that present circumstances now deny us. Of all the kinds of meaning that consumer goods carry, displaced meaning is perhaps the least understood. This chapter has suggested one of the ways in which we might begin our study of it.

Notes

1   This paper originated in research funded by the Killam Trust and the Social Sciences and Humanities Research Council of Canada. Their assistance is gratefully acknowledged here. The paper has profited from comments by Russell Belk, Mary Ellen Roach Higgins, and my colleagues at the University of Guelph, Victor Roth and Montrose Sommers.
2   Indeed the present author's own effort to account for the meaning possessed by goods (McCracken, 1986a) fails to take account of this category of cultural meaning.
3   The practice of inventing the past to serve the needs of the present has a long and distinguished history; see Handler and Linnekin (1984) and Hobsbawm and Ranger (1983).
4   A striking example of this kind of meaning-bridge emerged in research conducted at the University of Guelph in the summer of 1985. One respondent spoke of the Caribbean sailing boat he was sure he would own one day. The purchase of this boat held for him the promise of certain qualities that were now missing from his life. The long and detailed interview demonstrated, however, that these were qualities that the respondent was not, realistically, likely ever to realize in his life. 'Transported to a boat in the Caribbean, these meanings (of autonomy, self-reliance, complete mobility and merciful isolation) are now within his grasp but well beyond his reach' (McCracken, 1986a, p63).
5   The term 'high involvement' is taken from the consumer behaviour literature and applies to possessions which have marked cultural significance as well as utilitarian value. This definition conforms roughly to the one defined as 'ego involvement' in Muncy and Hunt (1984, p193).
6   Collecting is a topic of new interest in the social sciences and consumption; see Belk (1982), Benjamin (1969) and Danet (1986).
7   The importance of an object's concreteness to its ability to serve as a symbol has been observed in several places in the literature: Basso (1984, pp44–45), Forty (1986, p66) and Richardson (1974, p4), to name a few.

References

Arendt, H. (1958) *The Human Condition*, University of Chicago Press, Chicago
Basso, K. (1984) 'Stalking with stories: Names, places and moral narratives among the Western Apache', in S. Plattner and E. Bruner (eds) *Text, Play and Story: The Construction and*

Reconstruction of Self and Society, American Ethnological Society, Washington, DC, pp19–55

Becker, C. (1932) *The Heavenly City of the Eighteenth Century Philosophers*, University Press, New Haven

Belk, R. (1982) 'Acquiring, possessing and collecting: Fundamental processes in consumer behavior', in R. Bush and S. Hunt (eds) *Marketing Theory: Philosophy of Science Perspectives*, American Marketing Association, Chicago, pp185–190

Benjamin, W. (1969) *Illuminations: Essays and Reflections*, Schocken Books, New York

Csikszentmihalyi, M. and Rochberg-Halton, E. (1981) *The Meaning of Things: Domestic Symbols and the Self*, Cambridge University Press, New York

Cummings, W. and Venkatesan, M. (1976) 'Cognitive dissonance and consumer behavior: A review of the evidence', *Journal of Marketing*, vol 13, pp303–308

Danet, B. (1986) 'Books, butterflies, Botticellis: A sociological analysis of the "madness" of collecting', Paper given at the Sixth International Conference on Culture and Communication, Temple University, Philadelphia, 9 October 1986

Davis, F. (1985) 'Clothing and fashion as communication', in M. Solomon (ed) *The Psychology of Fashion*, Lexington Books, Lexington, MA, pp15–27

Davis, J. (1956) 'Status symbols and the measurement of status perception', *Sociometry*, vol 19, pp154–165

Davis, J. (1958) 'Cultural factors in the perception of status symbols', *The Midwest Sociologist*, vol 21, pp1–11

Douglas, M. and Isherwood, B. (1978) *The World of Goods: Towards an Anthropology of Consumption*, W. W. Norton and Co, New York

Firth, R. (1973) *Symbols: Public and Private*, Allen and Unwin, London

Forty, A. (1986) *Objects of Desire: Design and Society from Wedgwood to IBM*, Pantheon Books, New York

Fox, R. and Jackson Lears, T. J. (eds) (1983) *The Culture of Consumption: Critical Essays in American History, 1880–1980*, Pantheon Books, New York

Furby, L. (1978) 'Possessions: Towards a theory of their meaning and function throughout the lifecycle', in P. Baltes (ed) *Lifespan Development and Behavior*, Academic Press, New York, pp297–336

Goffman, E. (1951) 'Symbols of class status', *British Journal of Sociology*, vol 2, pp294–304

Graumann, C. (1974–1975) 'Psychology and the world of things', *Journal of Phenomenological Psychology*, vol 4, no 1, pp389–402

Handler, R. and Linnekin, J. (1984) 'Tradition, genuine or spurious', *Journal of American Folklore*, vol 97, no 385, pp273–290

Hirschman, E. and Holbrook, M. (eds) (1981) *Symbolic Consumer Behavior*, Association for Consumer Research, Ann Arbor, MI

Hobsbawm, E. and Ranger, T. (eds) (1983) *The Invention of Tradition*, Cambridge University Press, Cambridge

Holman, R. (1980) 'Product use as communication: A fresh appraisal of a venerable topic', in B. Enis and K. Roering (eds) *Review of Marketing*, American Marketing Association, Chicago, pp250–272

Jackson Lears, T. J. (1981) *No Place of Grace: Antimodernism and the Transformation of American Culture 1880–1920*, Pantheon Books, New York

Kluckhohn, C. (1962) 'Values and value-orientations in the theory of action', in T. Parsons and E. Shils (eds) *Towards a General Theory of Action*, Harvard University Press, Cambridge

Kron, J. (1983) *Home-Psych: The Social Psychology of Home and Decoration*, Clarkson N. Potter, Inc, New York

Laumann, E. and House, J. (1970) 'Living room styles and social attributes: The patterning of material artifacts in a modern urban community', *Sociology and Social Research*, vol 54, pp321–342

Levy, S. (1981) 'Interpreting consumer mythology: A structural approach to consumer behavior', *Journal of Marketing*, vol 45, pp49–61

Manuel, F. E. and Manuel, F. P. (1979) *Utopian Thought in the Western World*, Belknap Press, Cambridge, MA

Mason, R. (1981) *Conspicuous Consumption*, St Martin's Press, New York

Mason, R. (1984) 'Conspicuous consumption: A literature review', *European Journal of Marketing*, vol 18, no 3, pp26–39

McCracken, G. (1985) 'Dress colour at the Court of Elizabeth I: An essay in historical anthropology', *Canadian Review of Sociology and Anthropology*, vol 22, pp515–533

McCracken, G. (1986a) 'Culture and consumption: A theoretical account of the structure and movement of the cultural meaning of consumer goods', *Journal of Consumer Research*, vol 13, pp71–84

McCracken, G. (1986b) 'Upstairs/downstairs: The Canadian production', in J. W. Carwell and D. Saile (eds) *Purposes in Built Form: Proceedings of the 1986 Conference on Built Form and Culture Research*, University of Kansas, Lawrence, pp68–71

McKendrick, N., Brewer, J. and Plumb, J. (1982) *The Birth of the Consumer Society: The Commercialisation of Eighteenth Century England*, Indiana University Press, Bloomington

Muncy, J. and Hunt, S. (1984) 'Consumer involvement: Definitional issues and research directions', *Advances in Consumer Research*, vol 11, pp193–196

Nicosia, F. and Mayer, R. (1976) 'Toward a sociology of consumption', *Journal of Consumer Research*, vol 3, pp65–75

Nisbet, R. (1969) *Social Change and History*, Oxford University Press, New York

Ovidus Naso, P. (1960) *Metamorphoses* (translated by F. Miller), Harvard University Press, Cambridge

Prown, J. (1982) 'Mind in matter: An introduction to material culture theory and method', *Winterthur Portfolio*, vol 17, pp1–19

Quimby, I. (ed) (1978) *Material Culture and the Study of Material Life*, W. W. Norton and Co, New York

Reynolds, B. and Stott, M. (1986) *Material Anthropology: Contemporary Approaches in Material Culture*, University Press of America, New York

Richardson, M. (1974) 'Images, objects and the human story', in M. Richardson (ed) *The Human Mirror: Material and Spatial Images of Man*, Louisiana State University Press, Baton Rouge

Rickwood, P. (1984) 'Lottery win not all roses, woman finds', *The Toronto Sunday Star*, 29 April

Rokeach, M. (ed) (1979) *Understanding Human Values*, The Free Press, New York

Sahlins, M. (1976) *Stone Age Economics*, Aldine, Chicago, pp149–183

Sapir, J. D. (1977) 'The anatomy of metaphor', in J. D. Sapir and J. C. Crocker (eds) *The Social Use of Metaphor*, University of Pennsylvania Press, Philadelphia, pp3–32

Schlereth, T. (ed) (1982) *Material Culture Studies in America*, American Association for State and Local History, Nashville, TN

Silverman, M. (1969) 'Maximize your options: A study in values, symbols and social structure', in R. Spencer (ed) *Forms of Social Structure*, University of Washington Press, Seattle, pp97–115

Solomon, M. (1983) 'The role of products as social stimuli: A symbolic interactionism perspective', *Journal of Consumer Research*, vol 10, pp319–329

von Grunebaum, G. (1964) *Modern Islam: The Search for Cultural Identity*, Vintage Books, New York

19

Consuming Goods and the Good of Consuming

Colin Campbell

There has long been a tendency in both academic and intellectual circles to devalue, and often to denigrate, that field of human conduct which falls under the heading of 'consumption'. This is due to the existence of a powerful tradition of thought that generally regards consumption with some suspicion, inclining us to believe that, even if it is not exactly 'bad', it can have nothing whatever to do with that which is good, true, noble or beautiful.

Two factors can be identified as largely responsible for this attitude of suspicion. One is the discipline with which the term 'consumption' is most commonly associated: economics. For it is inherent in the basic paradigm adopted by economists that *production* is singled out as the activity that matters. Although in theory consumption is the sole end and justification for all production, it is quite clear that production, not consumption, is the more valued and morally justifiable activity. A second reason for the bias in favour of production is to be found in that Puritan inheritance which itself gave rise to modern economics (if indirectly, via utilitarianism), and that, more pertinently, also encouraged successive generations to place work above leisure, thrift above spending and deferred above immediate gratification. It is this generalized asceticism that is largely responsible for the contemporary denigration of consumption.[1]

However, even the Puritans did not condemn all consumption; what they accepted as legitimate was consumption directed at satisfying needs, while fiercely condemning any expenditure in excess of what was deemed necessary to meet these needs. In other words, it was luxury consumption which was roundly condemned, not consumption in general. One of the main reasons modern consumption has such a bad press is that it is generally seen to be mainly 'luxury' or 'want-based' in character. Consequently, even the little moral legitimacy consumption once possessed has today largely been swept away.[2]

In contemporary society, then, there are essentially two attitudes toward consumption. First, it may be viewed as a matter of satisfying 'genuine' needs (what we may call 'basic provisioning'), in which case, even if this is considered a mundane matter of routine, day-to-day decision-making and habit, it is at least seen as a legitimate activity by most intellectuals. Alternatively, consumption is viewed as largely a matter of gratifying wants and desires by means of goods and services that are viewed as non-essential (that is, luxuries), in which case it is typically regarded as an arena of superficial activity prompted by ethically dubious motives and directed toward trivial, ephemeral and essentially worthless goals.

Now there are two distinct yet closely associated points to note about this latter attitude. The first concerns the idea that want-driven consumption concerns the 'unnecessary' and hence the unimportant things in life; this leads to condemnations of consumption on the grounds that it involves people in superficial or frivolous activities. Consumption is thus contrasted with 'real', significant activities such as work, religion or politics. The second and related point is that involvement in trivial activities, and especially the tendency to take them seriously, is assumed to stem from questionable motives: no one guided by high-minded or noble concerns, it is assumed, would ever become involved in such dubious pursuits. Consequently, consumption is viewed as the realm in which the worst of human motives prevail – motives such as pride, greed and envy. Any social scientist who wishes to understand consumption is forced to confront both of these moral judgements, since they are central to most theories of consumption.[3]

The question, therefore, is whether our understanding of the activities of consumption does indeed justify the condemnation with which it generally meets. In short, is consumption bad for us? In addressing this question, one is not concerned with whether consuming is harmful in the literal sense that our health or well-being is threatened by the nature of the items we consume. Rather, the focus is on the claim that consuming is deleterious because it is an activity (or a set of activities) that 'brings out the worst in us'; that is to say, because it encourages us to behave in morally reprehensible ways. Does consumption lead us to be greedy, materialistic, avaricious or envious? The predominant concern is with the motives (and to a lesser extent the goals) that are presumed to underlie modern consumption behaviour.[4]

The thesis advanced here will be that the usual antipathy toward the motives of consumption is, if not entirely without justification, extremely one-sided, if only because the social science theories that buttress it are hardly plausible. Close attention to why people actually do consume goods suggests the presence of an idealistic, if not exactly ethical, dimension. Therefore, we must first outline a somewhat different view of the nature of consuming in contemporary industrial (or post-industrial) society from those which currently prevail.

Modern Consumption

Why people consume goods is understandably a central question for social science. Essentially, there have been two general answers to this question – one economic, the other sociological. The inadequacies of the economic paradigm (in which the origin of wants is simply not explored) have been well documented elsewhere and will not be pursued here. On the other hand, the sociological model, which in practice means Thorstein Veblen's model, is still widely employed and its inadequacies are rarely noted.

In essence, Veblen's model assumes that consumption is a form of communication in which 'signals' concerning the wealth (and thus, it is argued, the social status) of the consumer are telegraphed to others. In addition, it is assumed that individuals seek to use such 'conspicuous consumption' as a way of improving their social standing, aiming ultimately to 'emulate' that 'leisure class' which, it is claimed, stands at the pinnacle of the class system. This view of consumption links it directly with an ethically dubious activity, social climbing. In assuming that consumers' main interest in goods is as symbols of status, Veblen asserts that consumers are motivated by a mixture of anxiety (over how others may view them) and envy (of those in a superior position). It is hardly surprising that, with the widespread acceptance of such a theory, consuming is commonly viewed as ethically suspect.

There are, however, many problems with Veblen's model, which generally can be said to be theoretically incoherent where it is not empirically false.[5] The key deficiency is that it does not account for the dynamism that is so typical of modern consumption. Status competition through conspicuous display does not require novel products; it coexists happily with an unchanging, traditional way of life.[6] In this respect, both the economic and the sociological models have the same central failing: they attempt to provide an ahistorical general theory that fails to recognize crucial differences between traditional and modern consumption. The question is not, Why do people consume? Rather it is, Why do we consume as we do? That is to say, why do *modern* individuals consume as they do?

The Problem of Consumerism

It is a fundamental mistake to imagine that modern consumption, or consumerism, is simply traditional consumption writ large, as if all that separates the two phenomena was a question of scale. Therefore, it is misleading to assume that modern consumption equals mass consumption. Consumption in modern societies may well be consumption 'for the masses', something that could not occur until modern techniques made large-scale production possible; but what really distinguishes it is its dynamic character. The very high levels of consumption typical of modern societies do not stem primarily from the fact that large numbers of people consume; rather, they stem from the very high levels of individual consumption, which in turn stem from the apparent insatiability of consumers and the fact that their wants appear never to be exhausted. While technological innovation and planned obsolescence both have a part to play in keeping consumption levels high, the greatest contribution is consumers' almost magical ability to produce new wants immediately after old ones are satisfied. No sooner is one want satisfied than another appears, and subsequently another, in an apparently endless series. No modern consumer, no matter how privileged or wealthy, can honestly say that there is nothing that he or she wants. It is this capacity to continuously 'discover' new wants that requires explaining.

What makes consumerism even more puzzling is that we typically discover that we desire novel products, ones with which we are unfamiliar. We cannot possibly know what 'satisfaction' (if any) such products might yield when we desire them. Indeed, it would seem that it is principally this preference for novel goods and services that lies behind the apparent inexhaustibility of wants itself, as manifest, for example, in the central modern phenomenon of fashion.

These, then, are the features that distinguish the modern from the traditional consumer. The latter generally tends to have fixed needs rather than endless wants, and hence consumes the same products repeatedly, as and when these needs arise. This pattern of consumption does not, as economists often seem to imply, simply result from the lack of resources to consume more. Rather, the pattern represents all the consumption that the 'needs' dictated by traditional ways of life require.[7] The problem to be addressed when attempting to account for modern consumption, therefore, is how it is possible for inexhaustible wants – often wants for novel products and services – to appear with such regularity.

A Hedonistic Approach

It is possible to provide at least a partial solution to this problem by regarding modern consumption activity as the consequence of a form of hedonism. In saying this, it is important to recognize that what is meant by hedonism or pleasure-seeking has nothing in common with that theory of satisfaction-seeking, deriving from utilitarianism, which traditionally underlies most economic theories of consumption.

The latter model is built around the idea that human behaviour is concerned with the elimination of deprivation or need. Consequently, it assumes that individuals interact with objects so as to make use of their 'utility' to 'satisfy' these 'needs'. Such conduct may bring pleasure to the individual, but not only is this not guaranteed, it is not the reason the object was desired. Thus, economic theory is not centrally concerned with pleasure-seeking behaviour. The principal reason for this is that while utility is a real property of objects, pleasure is a judgement that individuals make about stimuli they experience. As such, pleasure is not necessarily connected with extracting utility from objects. Trying to satisfy needs usually requires engaging with real objects in order to discover the degree and kind of their utility in meeting pre-existing desires. Searching for pleasure means exposing oneself to certain stimuli in the hope that they will trigger an enjoyable response. Hence, while one typically needs to make use of objects in order to discover their potential for need satisfaction, one need only employ one's senses to experience pleasure. What is more, whereas an object's utility is dependent upon what it is, an object's pleasurable significance is a function of what it can be taken to be. Only reality can provide satisfaction, but both illusions and delusions can supply pleasure.

However, since the elimination of basic human needs is generally experienced as pleasurable (as in the experience of eating when one is attempting to eliminate the deprivation caused by hunger), pleasure-seeking has traditionally been perceived as bound up with efforts to meet needs. This perception becomes less valid as the advance of civilization causes fewer people to experience the frequent deprivation of their basic needs, so that the pleasure associated with need-fulfilment tends to become more and more elusive.[8] The traditional hedonist's response is to try to recreate the gratificatory cycle of need-satisfaction as often as possible.

Traditional hedonism hence involves a concern with 'pleasures' rather than with 'pleasure', there being a world of difference between valuing an experience because (among other things) it yields pleasure, and valuing the pleasure an experience can bring – that is, focusing upon a distinct aspect or quality of the experience. The former is the ancient pattern. Human beings in all cultures seem to agree on a basic list of activities that are 'pleasures' in this sense, such as eating, drinking, sexual intercourse, socializing, singing, dancing and playing games. But since pleasure is a quality of experience, it can, at least in principle, be judged to be present in all sensations. Hence the pursuit of pleasure in the abstract is potentially an ever-present possibility, provided that the individual's attention is directed to the skilful manipulation of sensation rather than to the conventionally identified sources of enjoyment.[9]

Modern Hedonism

All too often, then, it has been assumed that hedonistic theories of human conduct emphasize sensory pleasures. This, however, is not necessarily the case, for although all pleasure-seeking can be said to have a sensory base, there is no reason that hedonism should concentrate exclusively, or even primarily, on the 'baser' appetites. Indeed, while an emphasis on the sensory may have characterized traditional hedonism, it is not characteristic of its contemporary counterpart; modern hedonism focuses less on sensations than on emotions.

Emotions have the potential to serve as immensely powerful sources of pleasure, since they constitute states of high arousal. Any emotion – even the so-called negative ones, such as fear, anger, grief and jealousy – can provide pleasurable stimulation. However, for the stimulation associated with such emotions to be experienced as pleasant, the extent of the arousal must be adjustable: it must be possible for the individual to 'control' the emotion. An ability to self-regulate emotion is much more than a mere capacity to suppress (though this is its starting point), but extends to the 'creation' of a given emotion at will.

Such emotional cultivation is achieved largely through the manipulation of what an individual believes to be the nature of his or her condition or environment, particularly through adjustments in the degree to which certain things are held to be the case. For example, to the extent that people can convince themselves that they have been harshly treated by life and don't deserve their bad luck, they will be able to enjoy the 'pleasure' of self-pity. To a large extent, however, the deliberate cultivation of an emotion for the pleasure derived from experiencing it does not centre around efforts to reconstruct what is believed about the real environment in this way. Rather, it tends to focus on the somewhat easier task of conjuring up imaginary environments that are sufficiently realistic to prompt an associated emotion. This modern, autonomous, self-illusory hedonism is called, in everyday language, daydreaming.

Daydreaming

Daydreaming is an integral part of the psychic lives of modern men and women, yet there is a tendency either to ignore its presence and/or to deny its importance. Nearly everyone in modern society both daydreams and fantasizes; this is a regular, daily activity for both sexes and all ages.[10]

Yet there has been little recognition of the importance of this phenomenon or of the fact that it is characteristically a modern practice, largely dependent on the development of individualism, literacy (that is to say, silent reading) and the novel. There is little doubt that the impulse lying behind daydreaming is a hedonistic one, as individuals turn away from what they perceive as an unstimulating real world in order to dwell on the greater pleasures imaginative scenarios can offer. In this context, the individual can be seen as an artist of the imagination, someone who takes images from memory or the immediate environment and rearranges or otherwise improves them so as to render them more pleasing. Such daydreams are experienced as convincing; that is to say, individuals react subjectively to them as if they were real (thereby gaining an emotional response), even while realizing that they are not. This is the distinctly modern faculty to create an illusion that is known to be false but felt to be true.

Generally speaking, the way reality is typically adjusted by the daydreamer so as to give pleasure is by simply omitting life's little inconveniences, as well as by adding what, in reality, would be happy (if not extraordinarily unlikely) coincidences. In this way, imagined experience characteristically comes to represent a perfected vision of life, and from what are often quite small beginnings, individuals may develop daydreams that become 'alternative worlds' – that is, elaborate works of art – deviating more and more from what might reasonably be expected of reality.

Although daydreaming is commonly dismissed as an inconsequential phenomenon, there are grounds for believing that it has significant effects. For example, although daydreaming is typically prompted by boredom, the pleasures it supplies mean that daydreamers are likely to experience 'real life' as more boring than they did before, increasing the probability that further daydreaming will occur. Thus, like all forms of pleasure, daydreaming can easily become addictive and result in a certain tendency to withdraw from ordinary life.

However, daydreaming differs from straightforward fantasizing in that it concerns events and scenarios that might actually occur at some point in the future. Indeed, daydreams often begin with simple, anticipatory imaginings surrounding real, upcoming events, such as holidays. This makes it more or less inevitable that actuality is going to be compared – in terms of pleasure gained – against the standard set by the anticipatory daydream, and hence generally experienced as (quite literally) disillusioning. For no matter how pleasant the real-life experience turns out to be, it is impossible for it to resemble the perfection attained in imagination. Consequently, disillusionment is very likely to prompt still more daydreaming, and thus, inevitably, further disillusionment. This suggests that daydreaming creates certain permanent dispositions: a sense of dissatisfaction with real life and a generalized longing for 'something better'.

The Spirit of Modern Consumerism

Such an understanding of the dynamics of how dreams and experiences of real life interact may make it possible to explain those mysterious features of modern consumerism identified above. These include not simply the question of where wants come from (and indeed go to), but also how it is that consumers have an inexhaustible supply of them, and why it is that they have such a strong preference for novel, as opposed to familiar, goods. We can now suggest that modern consumers will desire a novel rather than a familiar product, largely because they believe its acquisition and use can supply them with pleasurable experiences that they have not so far encountered in reality. One may project on to the novel product some of the idealized pleasure that has already been experienced in daydreams, but that cannot be associated with products currently being consumed (as the limits to the pleasure they provide are already familiar). For new wants to be created, all that is required is the presence in the consumer's environment of products that are perceived to be new.[11] Hence, we can say that the basic motivation underlying consumerism is the desire to experience in reality that pleasurable experience the consumer has already enjoyed imaginatively.

Only new products are seen as offering any possibility of realizing this ambition. But since reality can never provide the perfected pleasures encountered in daydreams (or, if at all, only very occasionally and in part), each purchase naturally leads to disillusionment; this helps explain how wanting is extinguished so quickly, and why people disacquire goods almost as rapidly as they acquire them. What is not extinguished, however, is the fundamental longing that daydreaming itself generates. For the practice of daydreaming continues (and indeed may be strengthened), and hence there is as much determination as ever to find new products to serve as replacement objects of desire.

This dynamic interplay between illusion and reality is the key to an understanding of modern consumerism (and modern hedonism generally), for the tension between the two creates longing as a permanent mode, with the concomitant sense of dissatisfaction with what is and the yearning for something better. Daydreaming turns the future into a perfectly illusioned present. Hence, individuals do not so much repeat cycles of sensory pleasure-seeking (as in traditional hedonism) so much as they continually strive to close the gap between imagined and experienced pleasures. Yet this gap can never be closed, for whatever one experiences in reality can be adjusted in imagination so as to be even more pleasurable. Thus the illusion is always better than the reality, the promise more interesting than actuality.[12]

This theory of consumerism is inner-directed. It does not presume that consumption behaviour is either guided by, or oriented to, the actions of others. In that sense, it breaks with the long-standing sociological tradition that presents consumption as an essentially social practice.[13] On the other hand, this theory does not present consumption as driven by material considerations. The idea that contemporary consumers have a magpie-like desire to acquire as many material objects as possible (the acquisitive society thesis) represents a serious misunderstanding of the basic motivational structure that leads consumers to want goods. The acquisitive society thesis is particularly at odds with the facts, for modern consumer society is characterized as much by the extent to which individuals dispose of goods as the extent to which they acquire them. Consumerism involves a high *turnover* of goods, not merely a high level of their acquisition. This fact is consistent with the claim that the true focus of desire is less the object itself than the experience the consumer anticipates possessing it will bring.

Consumerism and the Counter-Culture

By extricating modern consumption from its presumed connection with other-directed status striving and envy on the one side, and crude materialism and acquisitiveness on the other, an understanding of this sphere of activity may be reached that does not automatically carry with it overtones of moral disapproval or condemnation. Unfortunately, this aim does not appear to have been achieved, since, by closely associating consumption with hedonism, it seems inevitable that consumerism will remain an object of moral disapproval. Indeed, one could claim that the present theory only makes matters worse, as, in some quarters at least, pleasure-seeking is even more objectionable than the consumption of 'luxury' goods. Certainly we can say that, on the whole, pleasure has been the one constant target of moralists over many generations, largely because of the hostile attitude originally taken by the early Christian fathers and typically still held in our own day by fundamentalists and other representatives of the religious right.[14]

There is, however, an alternative moral tradition that not only defends the pursuit of pleasure, but associates it directly with the highest moral and spiritual ideals. This tradition of thought was represented historically by Antinomianism and then, in more re cent times, by Romanticism. It is still very much alive, with its last significant efflorescence occurring in the 1960s in the form of the movement we know as the 'counter-culture'.[15]

Central to the Romantic creed is the belief that the true and the good are both subsumed under the beautiful, and consequently that they, too, are to be discerned by means of the imagination. It also follows that these ideals, like beauty itself, can be recognized by their capacity to give pleasure, with the natural consequence that the path to virtue and enlightenment is identical with the pursuit of pleasure. This is recognizable as the faith that inspired many of the young counter-culturalists of the 1960s; yet it is only fair to observe that they were hardly renowned for their defence of the consumer society. On the contrary, they launched the very critique of commercial and material values that has, to a large extent, laid the basis for much of our current unease about the state of modern life. While the counter-culturalists defended pleasure-seeking, they also attacked what they saw as the evil of consumerism. How is this paradox to be explained?

To some extent it can be accounted for by the fact that the counter-culturalists, like the spokespersons for the conventional morality they claimed to reject, held to that erroneous view of the nature of consumption mentioned above. Hence, they accepted the assumption that consumerism involved status envy, acquisitiveness and materialism, while being perhaps understandably reluctant to recognize that their own high valuation of pleasure might be connected in some way with their experience as the first generation to be reared in a climate of widespread affluence.

In contrast to this explanation of the paradox, what one might call the 'official' explanation is that the Romantic identification of pleasure with the ideal realm of virtue and beauty means that there is an understandable hostility to any trivialization or 'prostitution' of this central dimension of human experience – hostility, in other words, to any tendency to treat the pursuit of pleasure as a simple end in itself, a mere 'recreation' in which push-pin could be regarded as on a par with poetry. Thus, the Romantics' principal objection to consumption (it is said) was not that it was prompted by a search for pleasure (even less that it gave pleasure), but that pleasure-seeking was not being taken seriously enough. In other words, Romanticism gives the highest possible legitimation to the pursuit of pleasure, especially the pursuit of imaginatively mediated pleasure, while condemning not merely simple-minded and crass pleasure but hedonism itself, when it is not associated with a high moral purpose.

The Goods of Consumerism

However, to suggest that one can approve of pleasure-seeking when it is part and parcel of the pursuit of high ideals, yet disapprove of it when, separated from such ideals, it is engaged in simply for personal gratification, presumes that it is possible to tell which is which. Unfortunately, this is not so easy. For example, the practice of taking drugs, especially LSD, was defended by many in the 1960s on the grounds that it was an important means of attaining enhanced self-awareness and spiritual enlightenment. But for many hippies and quasi-hippies, drugs were probably used with no such end in view, but simply because of the 'high' they yielded. It is difficult to distinguish between these two positions because, in practice, they often merge into one another; or perhaps, more accurately, the one can easily become the other over time. Individuals may set out to take drugs merely to gain a high, only to find that their awareness is transformed; or, alternatively, those who take drugs because they hope to attain enlightenment might, on the contrary, merely develop an addiction to a particular form of in tense physical stimulation.

It might be objected that this is to make heavy weather of what is really a fairly simple matter, since as far as most consumption activity is concerned, purely selfish, or at least self-interested, motives are obviously at work. Unfortunately for this argument, the presence of selfish interests is not incompatible with more high-minded concerns. While some consumption is merely a matter of mundane provisioning, much of it is of considerably less prosaic interest to those involved. Obviously, buying a house, a car, a boat or a set of furniture is, for most people, an act of some moment, linked to what might be considered their 'life projects'. Understandably, then, major purchases of this kind often figure prominently in people's thoughts, where they play a crucial role as both incentives and rewards. In other words, such acts of consumption are critically interwoven into the motivational structures of individuals, providing the energy they need to carry through difficult tasks as well as the gratification necessary if they are to believe subsequently that their efforts were worthwhile. In this direct and obvious sense, not merely actual consuming, but also imaginary, 'anticipatory consuming' can indeed be said to be good for us, since without it, we might lack good reasons for doing anything at all.

It does not necessarily follow, however, that because purchasing goods plays such an important part in the reward system of individuals, there is no idealistic or ethical dimension present in those projects around which individuals organize their lives. After all, although people's daydreams differ, a common factor, apart from the quality of pleasure, is the representation of the dreamer in an idealized manner. Thus, the pleasure people derive from daydreaming is not separate from their moral life; it is intimately associated with it: doing good – or more accurately, perhaps, imagining one self doing good and being good – often constitute an important part of the pleasures of daydreaming.

In this respect, the pleasures associated with imagining perfect scenarios relate directly to imagining oneself as a perfect person, one who exemplifies certain ideals. This point can be illustrated by considering two important aspects of modern consumption: fashion and tourism.

The theory outlined above helps explain why modern consumers should be so eager to 'follow fashion', without, however, having to resort either to the implausible suggestion that they are forced to do so, or that they are merely striving to 'keep up with the Joneses'. Since fashion is an institution that guarantees the controlled introduction of a degree of novelty into goods with high aesthetic significance, the taste for novelty generated by the wide spread practice of self-illusory hedonism helps explain the importance and persistence of this institution.

Unfortunately, there has been a consistent tendency for intellectuals to decry fashion, to treat it as a trivial, insignificant, even worthless phenomenon. Yet if we use the term properly, to refer to a consistent process of changes in style (rather than simply a synonym for custom or practice), opprobrium is entirely inappropriate. For fashion necessarily involves an aesthetic ideal, and those who dedicate themselves to keeping up with fashion – or even more interestingly, perhaps, to 'taking the lead in fashion' – can be said, quite justifiably, to be striving to bring their lives into line with the ideal of beauty. That there may be an element of narcissism involved, or that the conduct in question may be strengthened by the presence of such motives as pride or vanity, does nothing to negate the ideal dimension of such behaviour, since all forms of moral conduct probably require the helping hand of self-interest. 'Following fashion' may indeed, in some instances, be little more than a mindless and morally worthless endeavour, but it can also be the high-minded pursuit of a serious ideal.

Much the same can be said of tourism, which is increasingly becoming a central component, not merely of modern consumerism, but of modern life. Tourism does not involve the purchase of products, but of experiences; yet, as with fashion, novelty is the most critical quality in defining the parameters of desire. Here, too, there has been a tendency in some circles to caricature and despise the 'tourist' while celebrating, by contrast, the genuine 'traveller'. But this bias is hard to justify, since the acquisition of valued experiences is crucial to the goals that find favour in modern society (and especially, perhaps, in the contemporary US). The human potential and encounter-group movements of the 1960s and 1970s, as well as their successors, the quasi-religious and psychotherapeutic movements of the 1990s, stressed the importance of critical 'experiences' in helping individuals to discover their 'true selves' and hence maximize their potential. Such phrases are also often to be found in statements defining the goals of education, therapy and art. If the acquisition of 'experiences', especially those of a highly novel kind, is accorded such critical importance in contexts such as these, how is it that it should be denied this status when occurring under the heading of 'tourism'?

Is Consumption Good for Us?

I do not know. Such a question suggests both that we can agree on what constitutes the good life and that we know exactly what effects our current consuming practices are having on ourselves and our society. In addition, it is difficult to speak of 'consumption' as if it were a single, undifferentiated activity. However, as I have tried to show, there is something distinctive about modern consumption. By elucidating this I have endeavoured to shed some light on whether the motives and goals embedded in such activity can be considered good. Obviously there is no simple answer, for consumerism is a complex phenomenon.

However, it is clear that both self-interested and idealistic concerns are involved in consumerism. Indeed, consumerism is prompted by concerns and guided by values that underpin many other modern institutions, yet which, in those other contexts, are usually regarded favourably. It is not as if the theory I have outlined applies only to consumption. It applies with equal force to all forms of behaviour in which imaginative pleasure-seeking or desire plays a significant role. Romantic love is one such phenomenon, so one could ask, with equal justification, whether love is good for us.[16]

Hence, it is delusory to imagine that one can cordon off consumption from the larger moral and idealistic framework of our lives and dub it 'bad' without, in the process, significantly affecting the total moral landscape of our world. Consumerism probably reflects the moral nature of contemporary human existence as much as any other widespread modern practice; significant change here would therefore require no minor adjustment to our way of life, but the transformation of our civilization.

Notes

1   Another moral dimension to this discussion is associated with gender. Much consumption activity (especially shopping) has long been seen as primarily 'women's work', while production has been judged 'men's work'. This can also be seen as a major influence on the ethical judgements passed on consumption.

2   It has often been suggested that a new 'ethic' has arisen that serves to legitimate consumerism: see Whyte (1957), Reisman et al (1966) and Bell (1976). Tellingly, such claims are made by writers who do not themselves endorse the new ethic, but, on the contrary, seek to condemn it, often from a perspective of apparent support for the old ascetic Protestant values. Consequently, an attitude of suspicion, if not hostility, towards consumerism still typifies academic and intellectual discussions in this field.

3   This view sometimes places the blame on individuals for engaging in such practices, while at other times it exonerates them by arguing that consumers are typically coerced or manipulated into this form of behaviour by others (usually manufacturers or advertisers). In either case, however, consumerism itself is judged to be bad, whether the source of the evil lies in individuals or in the organization of the society.

4   This extremely negative view of modern consumption is not typically shared by consumers themselves; indeed, one suspects that it is not actually shared by academics and intellectuals, either, when actually acting as consumers. In fact, there has recently been a movement among intellectuals and some academics to view consumerism as far more significant (see Connor, 1989; Harvey, 1989; Featherstone, 1991; and Jameson, 1991). Here, there is a tendency to

regard consumption as the central focus of the efforts of individuals to create and maintain their personal identity. However, despite this development, there is little evidence of any change in moral tone. Such conduct is still likely to be despised, if not actually condemned.

5   In the first place, the picture of a single leisured elite whom all other classes seek to emulate (either directly or indirectly) inaccurately portrays the complex stratification system of modern societies. Second, what determines the consumption habits of this elite remains a mystery, as *they* have no one to emulate. Third, new fashions in the consumption of goods do not always or even commonly originate with a social elite and then 'trickle down' the status ladder as a result of imitation and emulation by those in inferior positions. In fact, fashions 'trickle up' or even 'across' just as often as they trickle down (see Blumberg, 1974). Fourth, social standing is not determined simply by wealth (let alone only by conspicuously displayed wealth); other qualities, most obviously birth, can still be important. Finally, treating wealth and leisure as equivalents, both signifying 'waste', is seriously misleading given the important Protestant tendency to applaud the first while deploring the second, as well as the Bohemian inversion of this view. For a full account of the emulation model of consumption, see Veblen (1925); for a critique, see Campbell (1992, 1994).

6   See, for example, Herskovits (1960).

7   See Hoyt (1956) and Nair (1962).

8   See the argument in Scitovsky (1976).

9   These two orientations involve contrasting strategies. In the first, the basic concern is with increasing the number of times one is able to enjoy life's 'pleasures'; thus, the traditional hedonist tries to spend more and more time eating, drinking, having sex and dancing. The hedonistic index here is the incidence of pleasure per unit of life. In the second, the primary object is to squeeze as much of the quality of pleasure as one can out of all the sensations one actually experiences during one's life. All acts are, from this perspective, potential pleasures if only they can be approached or undertaken in the right manner; the hedonistic index here is the extent to which one is actually able to extract the fundamental pleasure that 'exists' in life itself.

10   See Singer (1966).

11   Products need not actually be new; they merely have to be presented or packaged in such a way that it is possible for consumers to believe they are new.

12   That there is a close relationship between people's daydreams and their selection, purchase, use and disposal of goods and services is revealed, for example, by the nature of advertisements. But one should not assume from this that advertising *creates* daydreaming, as the latter appears to be an intrinsic feature of the mental life of modern humans and does not depend upon external agencies to prompt or support it.

13   See Veblen (1925) and Riesman et al (1966).

14   To suggest that consumerism is driven by pleasure-seeking is to raise the possibility that ecological and anticonsumerist movements might have something in common with earlier Puritanical movements. Perhaps an important underlying (if not openly admitted) impulse behind such movements might, indeed, be a hostility to pleasure. Could such movements represent a new Puritanism in their calls for us to sacrifice our energy-expensive and 'wasteful' way of life?

15   See, for the Romantic nature of this movement, Musgrove (1974), Martin (1981) and Campbell (1987).

16   The question has, of course, been posed before, and the answer much debated. See Peele (1975), Sarsby (1983) and Spector Person (1989).

References

Bell, D. (1976) *The Cultural Contradictions of Capitalism*, Heinemann, London

Blumberg, P. (1974) 'The decline and fall of the status symbol: Some thoughts on status in a post-industrial society', *Social Problems*, vol 21, pp480–498

Campbell, C. (1987) *The Romantic Ethic and the Spirit of Modern Consumerism*, Blackwell, Oxford

Campbell, C. (1992) 'The desire for the new: Its nature and social location as presented in theories of fashion and "modern consumerism"', in R. Silverman and E. Hirsch (eds) *Consuming Technologies: Media and Information in Domestic Spaces,* Routledge, London

Campbell, C. (1994) 'Conspicuous confusion? A critique of Veblen's Theory 7 of conspicuous consumption', *Sociological Theory*, vol 12, no 2

Connor, S. (1989) *Postmodernist Culture: An Introduction to Theories of the Contemporary,* Blackwell, Oxford

Featherstone, M. (1991) *Consumer Culture and Postmodernism*, Sage, London

Harvey, D. (1989) *The Condition of Postmodernity*, Blackwell, Oxford

Herskovits, M. J. (1960) *Economic Anthropology: A Study in Comparative Economics*, Alfred A. Knopf, New York

Hoyt, E. E. (1956) 'The impact of a money economy upon consumption patterns', *Annals of the American Academy of Political and Social Science*, no 305, pp12–22

Jameson, F. (1991) *Postmodernism, Or the Cultural Logic of Late Capitalism*, Verso, London

Martin, B. (1981) *A Sociology of Contemporary Cultural Change*, Blackwell, London

Musgrove, F. (1974) *Ecstasy and Holiness: Counter-Culture and the Open Society*, Methuen, London

Nair, K. (1962) *Blossoms in the Dust: The Human Factor in Indian Development*, Frederick A. Praeger, New York

Peele, S. (1975) *Love and Addiction*, Taplinger, New York

Riesman, D. with Glazer, N. and Denney, R. (1966) *The Lonely Crowd: A Study in the Changing American Character*, Doubleday-Anchor, New York

Sarsby, J. (1983) *Romantic Love and Society*, Penguin, Harmondsworth, UK

Scitovsky, T. (1976) *The Joyless Economy: An Inquiry into Human Satisfaction and Consumer Dissatisfaction*, Oxford University Press, New York

Singer, J. L. (1966) *Daydreaming*, Random House, New York

Spector Person, E. (1989) *Love and Fateful Encounters: The Power of Romantic Passion*, Bloomsbury, London

Veblen, T. (1925) *The Theory of the Leisure Class*, George Allen and Unwin, London

Whyte, W. H. (1957) *The Organization Man*, Doubleday-Anchor Books, New York

Part 4

Reframing Sustainable Consumption

20

Efficiency and Consumption: Technology and Practice

Elizabeth Shove

Introduction

In their own terms, national and international programmes of energy labelling have been remarkably effective. In making energy visible, market-based instruments like labelling and standard-setting are designed to help consumers make informed choices. Perhaps more important, they have encouraged manufacturers to design and produce more efficient freezers, washing machines, dishwashers and homes. Consistent with this approach, the UK government is currently exploring the idea of setting performance standards for air-conditioning in anticipation of global warming. In pursuing this route, the government is tacitly accepting and in a way legitimizing a solution, the widespread adoption of which would lead to a significant *increase* in energy consumption.

This example touches upon important questions about how responsibility for sustainability is negotiated between state and market. In concentrating on *efficiency* rather than consumption, policy-makers stick close to a politically safe position, providing information and advice but not going so far as to tell consumers and decision-makers how to live their lives. Insights from social psychology and economics have been important in designing incentives and other initiatives, the aim of which is to persuade people to buy and use low-energy light bulbs or to pick a more efficient freezer, boiler or washing machine. But as others have argued, the result is a somewhat technocratic approach that fails to engage with the big questions of what our needs are and how they are constructed and reproduced. In effect, demand – including demand for air-conditioning – is taken for granted and so taken out of the equation (Redclift, 1996; Slater, 1997; Wilhite et al, 2000). The range of theoretical and conceptual resources on which energy and environmental policy draws is limited precisely because the problem is routinely framed as one of developing and promoting the adoption of more efficient and more sustainable technologies.[1] Other theories and methods are required if we are to understand, analyse and perhaps influence current patterns of *consumption*. The first part of the paper provides a brief review of potentially relevant intellectual resources.

Social theories of consumption have revolved around a number of central problems including the emergence of consumer society, the relation between consumption and production and the symbolic role of consumer goods. Partly because of this, much has been written about acquisition, novelty and the social significance of conspicuous consumption (Campbell, 1992). By comparison, relatively little attention has been paid to the dynamics of demand for electricity or for inconspicuous energy-consuming services (Shove and Warde, 2001). Such issues are of more central concern to those interested in the development of sociotechnical systems (Hughes, 1983; Chappells et al, 2000; Van Vliet, 2002; Chappells, 2003; Southerton et al, 2004). Drawing some of these threads together with the help of a conceptual model of practice, I go on to examine the relation between consumption and technology with reference to two examples: indoor environmental comfort, and the changing role of domestic appliances. In both cases, the core idea is that much (energy) consumption is occasioned by the routine accomplishment of what people taken to be normal and ordinary practice. Assuming that this is the case, it is important to know what people do as a matter of course, how these 'doings' co-evolve and with what implications for sustainability. This argues for an approach that reunites issues of technical and product design (efficiency) with questions of consumption in recognition of the fact that practices so often require the use of technologies and appliances, and that technologies and appliances are frequently implicated in the invention and reproduction of practice.

It is easy to argue that energy policy-makers' preoccupation with efficiency has blinded them to major transformations in what people take to be normal and ordinary yet increasingly resource-intensive ways of life. However, it is misleading to make too strong a distinction between efficiency/technological design, on the one hand, and consumption/use on the other. While more efficient technologies sometimes provide exactly the same services but with fewer resources, this is not always the case. Taking a broader view, what matters is the relation between (more or less efficient) technologies, systems and appliances, and the co-evolution of routines, habits and practices.

Consumption, Technology and Practice

Although the utilities account for a significant proportion of household expenditure, people do not really 'consume' energy. Instead, they consume the services – heating, lighting, showering, cooking, television watching, computer interaction – that infrastructures of gas, electricity and water make possible. If energy and environmental policy is to make use of social theories of consumption, technology and practice, a first necessary step is to reconceptualize the problem. Instead of trying to figure out why people select more or less efficient technologies, the longer-term challenge is one of understanding the collective transformation of convention and hence the dynamics of demand. For example, how is it that people expect to inhabit increasingly uniform indoor environments all year round and whatever the weather outside? Why is it that the average UK washing machine is run some 274 cycles per year (DETR, 2000), but at lower temperatures than ever before?

In an effort to engage with some of these questions, Spaargaren (1997) adapts and simplifies Giddens' (1984) theory of structuration, using it to describe the relation between knowledgeable actors on the one hand, and institutional – and indeed infrastructural – rules and resources on the other. In this analysis, social *practices* like cleaning, cooking, washing and so on are in the middle of the frame, being defined, maintained and reproduced by and through the interaction of *agency* and *structure*.

Technologies, appliances, and more and less efficient infrastructures have multiple roles in this analysis. As hinted at in Figure 20.1, 'structures' refer to organizational and institutional systems *and* to the hardware of wires, pipes and power plant into which households are quite literally plugged. As other writers have explained, the design and operation of such systems is of practical importance for the development (or otherwise) of associated practices and patterns of demand (Hughes, 1983; Nye, 1992). Forty (1986), for example, describes how important it was to develop and sell all manner of domestic appliances in order to produce a more balanced load profile for the first electricity companies. By means of mediating technologies like vacuum cleaners, washing machines, toasters and kettles, the day-to day *practices* of housework evolved alongside the *infrastructures* on which they depended. Meanwhile, routines, habits and conventions – that is, the fine detail of how people live their lives – shifts as new technologies are accommodated and appropriated. For example, different standards, skills and conventions have emerged around the practice of washing with a machine (Shove, 2003).

By implication, relations between technology and practice and between practice and consumption are of real consequence for energy demand. Understandings of normal and ordinary routines change in ways that are at least partly related to the systems and technologies through which they are defined, delivered and provided. Equally, models of practice and assumptions about demand are quite literally built into networks and infrastructures of provision and into the design and development of specific artefacts.

In environmental terms, this scheme has two important functions. First, it demonstrates the interdependence of technical systems and practices, levels of demand and patterns of consumption being the outcome of *both*. Second, and because of this

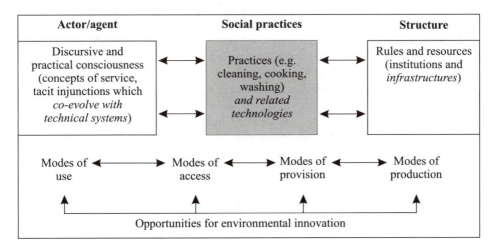

Source: adapted from Chappells et al, 2000, p23

Figure 20.1 *Actor–structure relationships and environmental innovations*

interdependence, it suggests that there are multiple possible points of intervention and environmental innovation. As illustrated below, policy-makers can intervene with respect to modes of production, provision, access and use. Critically, intervention at any one point in this integrated system is likely to influence the operation of the whole.

Although convincing in its own terms, it is not immediately obvious how this figure helps in understanding the relation between technological efficiency and energy consumption. Two further steps are required. One is to elaborate on the relation between practice and consumption. For purposes of this argument, consumption, including energy consumption, is best understood as the outcome of the routine accomplishment of ordinary practices. The second necessary step is to show how technologies, infrastructures and sociotechnical systems are implicated in the reproduction of practice. In the next section I consider two cases, first comfort and the indoor environment, and then the development and use of domestic freezers and washing machines in order to draw out some of the ways in which technology, practice and consumption intersect.

Technology, Practice and Consumption: The Case of Comfort

Looking back over the last century, comfort-related conventions and practices have changed dramatically. In the UK, few people now wake to traces of frost on the inside of their windows in winter. Meanwhile, the long lunchtime break is in decline in Southern Europe. Although people have reported being comfortable at temperatures ranging from 6 to 31°C. (Goldsmith, 1960, Nicol et al, 1999, p271), there is no doubt about it, indoor climates are converging. In environmental terms, the resources required to maintain uniform conditions indoors whatever the weather outside are considerable and increasing amounts of energy are consumed to this end. This, then, is an arena in which *consumption* is escalating fast, and in which it is doing so as a consequence of rapid and radical redefinitions of what indoor environments should be like.

In building design as in environmental policy, comfort is typically defined with reference to the purportedly universal properties and characteristics of human biology. From this point of view, the global convergence of indoor climates is normal, natural and something to be expected. Since the specification of comfort is not, in itself, in question, the only conceivable response is to develop and promote more *efficient* technologies for heating and cooling. Challenging 'need', for example, the 'need' for air-conditioning in the UK, is for the most part beyond the scope of policy-making as conventionally conceived. It is, in any event, a politically dangerous path to follow given the range of commercial interests at stake and the unpalatable consequences of advocating standards that fall short of 'comfort', however that is currently defined.

In this case the tension between consumption and efficiency is clear. The promotion of technical efficiency is by far the most common policy response, yet it is one that internalizes and takes for granted those features of indoor climate change that are the most problematic. Caught up in the flow – and arguably contributing to it – such efforts do nothing to challenge the institutionalization of lifestyles that depend upon standardized indoor environments, the maintenance of which is inevitably resource intensive.

But this is not the whole story. In practice, a number of the design professionals and clients interviewed as part of our research into the future of comfort in the UK[2] found themselves engaged in debates that were in essence about the cultural negotiability of comfort. This first extract reports on a discussion between a building services engineer and his client:

> The client said they wanted a non-air-conditioned building, and so we talked to them about what conditions would be like and what temperature they might achieve. And, they said 'what about comfort?', so we advised them that they must expect to make adjustments, to take jackets off or loosen ties, and they said 'oh well we can't do that, we're solicitors, actually we have a dress code...' And the engineer who was working on it said 'well if you really mean that it actually means you'd better have an air-conditioned building because otherwise it would be uncomfortable.'

It is through exchanges of this kind that conventions and technological solutions coevolve. This is a complex process and one in which images of modernity and Westernization can be as important as concepts of style and comfort. Hal Wilhite's study of the promotion of air-conditioning in Japan (Wilhite et al, 1996) suggests that, in the longer run, the symbolic relationship between the technologies of indoor climate control and emerging concepts of everyday practice are of defining importance for energy consumption. It is not just that there is status attached to having air-conditioning. In addition, its use challenges more traditional body-centred understandings of comfort and has further consequences for meanings and experience of health and well-being, for the clothing that people wear and for the design and use of the home. This work underlines the point that concepts of comfort and associated practices and ways of life are culturally and historically malleable. A building scientist interviewed as part of the Future Comforts project comments on the environmental policy implications of this observation:

> We know from studies across the world that if people don't have air-conditioning or if they don't have heating that they will dress appropriately and they will be comfortable in a very wide range of conditions, but we haven't quite brought that into play yet.

The practical question is how, and under what conditions, societies might (re)generate less resource-demanding interpretations and practices of comfort. In some cultures this might involve the reintroduction of the siesta. In others the waistcoat might come back into fashion. Alternatively, sensations of thermal variation might be valued in their own right. To go further here, and to put the insights of 'transition theory' (Geels, 2002; Elzen et al, 2004) into action implies a complete reversal of current methods. Rather than promoting efficient technology and the standardized assumptions of need and service associated with it, national and international agencies would have to encourage the proliferation of regional or at least climate-sensitive understandings of comfort and the development of a corresponding variety of localized sociotechnical regimes. Rather than inadvertently naturalizing the meaning of comfort, its definition could and perhaps should become the subject of explicit discussion and debate.

It is clearly a good idea to develop more efficient heating and cooling systems. Yet it remains the case that air-conditioned buildings generally consume more than those that are naturally ventilated. However, the more important issue is that their widespread development helps to standardize particularly demanding conventions of comfort. As this case demonstrates, technological strategies do not simply meet demand, they also help construct and sustain it. By implication, preferred technological solutions need not be especially efficient in their own terms. In the end what matters is whether their adoption and use supports the cultural persistence of more or less environmentally forgiving concepts of comfort.

Technology, Practice and Consumption: Domestic Appliances

The idea that domestic technologies 'script' and structure users' practices is potentially important for those interested in increasing efficiency and in reducing consumption. As Akrich (1992) explains, technologies frequently make demands of those who use them, permitting some actions and preventing others. In the two cases considered here – freezing and laundering – the exact nature of the relationship between user and appliance differs and does so in ways that have practical consequences for energy demand. As discussed below, the *size* of the domestic fridge-freezer is particularly important for total energy consumption. This begs the question: how do fridge-freezers come to be the shape they are today? Domestic washing machines are now considerably more efficient than they were even a few years ago. Some of this has to do with the fact that an increasing amount of washing is done at lower temperatures than ever before. In this case it seems that technological efficiency goes hand in hand with a transformation of practice, the net effect of which is to reduce consumption. Countering this tendency, the frequency with which people wash is on the rise. Whether we focus on efficiency or consumption, the process of laundering consists of a suite of interdependent practices, some of which entail more consumption, some less. As detailed below, these two cases suggest that efficiency and consumption are sometimes in tension, sometimes not. Which way this relation goes depends, at least in part, on the specific role that domestic appliances play in reproducing, contributing to and generating the images and meanings and the sets of competence and know-how of which ordinary practices are constituted.

Cold storage

European energy-labelling schemes are based on standardized tests conducted on different classes of appliance. Although a giant 'frost-free' freezer will undoubtedly consume more energy during the course of a year than a much smaller model, it may get an 'A' rating if it performs better than other appliances of a similar capacity. In terms of overall consumption, size is a critical issue yet there is no obvious answer to the question how big should a freezer be? A Consumers' Association *Which?* report from September 1970 advises consumers as follows:

You must first decide what size of freezer you want, which will depend on the size of your family, your house, your garden and your appetite, how often you want to shop, how often you entertain and so on.

There is no readily accessible estimate of the total volume of frozen and refrigerated space within British homes, but there is some evidence that larger 'American style' fridge-freezers are increasingly popular. According to a recent article (Pridham, 2004, p26) in *Kitchen and Bathroom Designer:*

> Never have fridges and freezers played such a major part in kitchen design. No longer hidden away behind a cupboard door, this once humble appliance has quite literally grown in stature and become a style statement to be shown off as a focal point in the kitchen.

The demand for more cold storage is, in part, related to the way in which freezers are used and what they are for. Are they devices with which to beat the seasons, are they justified in terms of bulk buying and economy, or is their value understood in terms of convenience (Shove and Southerton, 2000)? The relation between freezer and micro-wave is important in this equation as is the development of a commercial frozen food industry. More generally, the 'need' for a fridge-freezer relates to the nation's diet and to the type and quantity of food that people store in their homes. Few now have a dedi-cated larder or pantry. As the following respondent, interviewed as part of the 'Sustain-able domestic technologies' project,[3] explains, the list of what is kept in the fridge is extensive:

> One fridge contains lots of different chutneys, sauces, and jellies, jams that are ongoing, that really need to be refrigerated ... the potatoes live in the pantry but the other vegeta-bles like broccoli, leeks, carrots, all those kinds of things go in the bottom of the left-hand fridge. So all those vegetables to be cooked go in the left-hand fridge. All the salad things – fennel, tomatoes, celery etc. etc. – they all go in the bottom of the right-hand fridge.

A freezer of any size brings with it certain obligations. Households have to buy or pre-pare food for it, they have to remember what they have stored, and they have to plan ahead, defrosting and consuming according to a schedule that is partly imposed upon them. Several respondents viewed the freezer as a device with which to order and organ-ize the routines and rhythms of daily life. Interpreted positively, it allowed them to plan and prepare meals in advance and avoid making multiple shopping trips. More com-monly, this organizing imperative was experienced as a kind of pressure, as illustrated in this extract:

> When we're ordering the food, when we look at the frozen food section on the web, and we look, and often we buy things that we haven't thought about before, but we know we've got this wonderful freezer and we ought to use it. I think I just had a different idea altogether about the freezer and thought it was, er ... I know that she [mother in law] will often have cakes in her freezer, when we go and stay with her, I've noticed she buys

cakes from the local market and freezes them, and she will freeze milk and bread, and you see I wouldn't think about doing that ... so I'm trying to think that maybe this could save me time and I should think about this ... you know, we've got it, let's try and incorporate it into our daily lives.

The point here is that fridge-freezers have a dual role with respect to consumption and practice. They promise to help people live a more ordered and organized life. But how they are used in practice depends upon how personal injunctions and concepts of service (senses of how things should be done) intersect with changing institutions and infrastructures of provision. How big fridge-freezers are, what they contain, and to some extent how much energy domestic cold storage requires is, in a sense, the outcome of this interaction.

Laundering

Niall FitzGerald (1998), Chairman of Unilever PLC, summarizes his company's achievements over the last century as follows:

Our consumers can now machine-wash their clothes, with minimal effort, at much lower temperatures than ever before, using detergent powders, liquids – and now tablets. We have greatly reduced the grind and drudgery of household chores, and built a reliable and trusted range of brands. Clothes themselves can now be made out of dozens of different types of fabrics; coloured using an amazing range of some 200,000 dye combinations; and even finished with space age coatings, like Teflon.

The work involved in washing, and the meaning of washing well has changed dramatically over this period. Not so long ago, 'boiling was considered essential for getting the wash really clean and germ-free' (Zmroczek, 1992, p176). This is no longer the case. Although washing machines are likely to have a 'very hot' setting, the percentage of UK laundry washed at 90°C declined from 25 to 7 per cent between 1970 and 1998 and the average temperature of the washing water has dropped by half over the last 30 years (DETR, 2000). In environmental terms, this is good news, so how has this transformation come about?

One possible explanation is that there has been a net drop in dirtiness. The authors of a 1992 Consumers' Association *Which?* report conclude that 'we rarely have to deal with washing that is really dirty', and so advise consumers not to 'use 95°C unless you think you really need it' (Consumers' Association, 1992). Another is that detergent producers and domestic washing machine manufacturers have come to dominate the process and practice of cleaning clothes. Some 80 per cent of UK homeowners own an automatic washing machine (Mintel, 2003). While consumers and users decide which programme to use, it is the machine designers who determine just what it is that the appliance can do. There is some evidence that people have delegated responsibility for defining and producing appropriately laundered clothing to the machine and its detergents (Shove, 2003). In this situation, manufacturers have been able to reduce resource consumption because they are able to control what washing machines do, and hence what cleaning means.

In short, the story here is one in which concepts of cleanliness have changed and changed in such a way that new standards can be met with *fewer resources*. The resources required to do a 'normal' wash are less than they were before partly but not only because washing machines are increasingly efficient. At the same time, the frequency with which washing machines are run continues to rise. This hints at a different and more demanding interpretation of cleanliness. People might be washing at lower temperatures (and so more efficiently), but they are doing so, on average, 274 times a year per household in the UK. In this respect, concepts of cleanliness have changed but this time in ways that *increase consumption* of energy and water. Are people washing more often simply because each wash is less resource intensive than it used to be? Probably not. Instead we see the double-edged consequence of the practices and priorities that constitute laundering today. The ideal of always having freshly laundered clothing is one that justifies the frequent washing of garments that only 'need' a light wash because they have only been worn for just a day.

Discussion

Whether they are efficient or not, technologies are implicated in the organization and reproduction of practices like those of comfort, freezing and laundering and hence in the evolution of energy demand. Having said that, it is important not to overstate the extent to which technical systems structure conventions and concepts of need. The provision of comfort, cleanliness and food is frequently charged with moral and emotional significance. Gendered divisions of labour are often relevant and ideals of family life are rarely overturned by the arrival of a few new appliances. There are well-documented cases in which people hang on to 'traditional' skills and values that are of defining importance for national and personal identity (Parr, 1999) and, as others have explained, new technologies are adopted, rejected and appropriated with reference to existing complexes of routine, habit and practice (Lie and Sorensen, 1996). This is, in a way, the point. It is what people do that really matters, for it is this that organizes and also limits their consumption.

In concentrating so exclusively on improving efficiency, energy and environmental policy has arguably lost sight of the cumulative consequences of changing conventions of everyday life. In this article, I have suggested that we need to focus on the dynamics of practice – on how and why conventions and routines evolve as they do – if we are to figure out what lies behind increasing and sometimes also decreasing energy demand. As indicated in Figure 20.1. This means paying attention to the intersection of actors' definitions, understandings, competences and senses of obligation on the one hand, and to rules, resources, institutions and infrastructures on the other.

The three cases sketched above illustrate different aspects of this relation. I used the example of air-conditioning to show that efforts to increase efficiency may have the unintended consequence of supporting ultimately unsustainable conventions and expectations of comfort. Meanings of comfort have proved to be historically and culturally malleable. It is therefore possible to imagine alternative strategies in which efficiency takes second place to consumption and in which the long-term goal is to enrich and extend experiences and expectations and thereby avoid naturalizing standardized conditions of what Heschong (1979) refers to as thermal monotony. In writing about fridge-freezers, I drew attention to the many factors involved in determining their size and hence the energy consumption associated with domestic cold storage. Technical efficiency is part of this story, but so is the question of capacity. I took the freezer to be a more passive 'actor' in the construction of demand than the washing machine, for I suggested that the latter appliance has been influential in reconstructing the meaning of what it is to wash well. In this case, pressure to increase efficiency has helped reshape practices such that their successful accomplishment requires less energy consumption than it did before. On the other hand, concepts of freshness, which are an important part of this reconfiguration, also legitimize more frequent laundering and hence increase demand.

In conclusion, and as these various examples demonstrate, increased efficiency and reduced consumption do not always go hand in hand. One reason for this is that programmes designed to improve the technical efficiency of air-conditioning systems or freezers inevitably but perhaps inadvertently help maintain and sustain ways of life that include and increasingly depend upon artificial cooling. In this respect there is a close – but often problematic – connection between such initiatives and the dynamics of practice and escalating consumption. This view has a number of practical implications. First, if the real goal is to reduce *consumption,* increasing *efficiency* may not be the best way forward. Second, if we agree that people consume goods, services and resources not for their own sake but as part of the routine reproduction of what they take to be normal ways of life, then it is these ways and practices on which we should focus. At first sight such an argument takes us way beyond the normal reach and remit of energy and environmental policy. But on reflection, and by referring back to the row of opportunities for intervention identified in Figure 20.1, the upshot is to demonstrate how many *more* ways there might be of at least attempting to foster societies and sets of practices that can be reproduced sustainably.

Acknowledgements

This paper draws upon two Economic and Social Research Council (ESRC)-funded research projects: 'Future Comforts: Reconditioning Urban Environments', Award number 221 25 0005, with Dr Heather Chappells (Lancaster University), and 'Sustainable Domestic Technologies: Changing Practice, Technology and Convention', Award number 332 25 007, with Dr Dale Southerton and Professor Alan Warde (Manchester University) and with Dr Martin Hand (Queen's University, Canada).

Notes

1   Questions of demand sometimes reappear, for example, when increases in energy efficiency fail to have the anticipated effect. The so-called rebound effect refers to situations in which people exploit the results of efficiency by consuming more. Energy policy-makers have, for

instance, underestimated the extent to which the benefits of more insulation or a better boiler might be taken in the form of higher standards of service (i.e. a warmer home) rather than reduced consumption.

2   This research included interviews with a total of 13 building designers, engineers, clients and policy-makers, and a workshop in which a further 17 participants were involved.

3   Interviews were conducted with 40 households. The sample was structured so as to include people living in small terraced houses, in 1930s-style semi-detached homes and in new town houses.

References

Akrich, M. (1992) 'The de-scription of technical objects', in W. Bijker and J. Law (eds) *Shaping Technology/Building Society*, MIT Press, Cambridge, MA, pp205–225

Campbell, C. (1992) 'The desire for the new: Its nature and social location as presented in theories of fashion and modern consumption', in R. Silverstone and E. Hirsch (eds) *Consuming Technologies*, Routledge, London, pp48–66

Chappells, H. (2003) *Re-thinking Demand: Electricity and Water Networks in Transition*, PhD thesis, Department of Sociology, Lancaster University, UK

Chappells, H., Klintman, M., Linden, A., Shove, E., Spaargaren, G. and van Vliet, B. (2000) *Domestic Consumption, Utility Services and the Environment*, final report of an EU DGXII project, ENV-CT97-0467, University of Lancaster

Consumers' Association (1992) 'Washing Machines', *Which?*, January, pp44–48

Consumers' Association (1970) 'Freezers', *Which?*, September, p280

DETR (Department of the Environment, Transport and the Regions) (2000) *Washing Machines in the United Kingdom: A Sector Review Paper on Projected Energy Consumption for the Department of the Environment, Transport and the Regions*, WTWM4031, October, DETR, London

Elzen, B., Geels, F. W. and Green, K. (2004) *System Innovation and the Transition to Sustainability: Theory, Evidence and Policy*, Edward Elgar, Cheltenham

Fitzgerald, N. (1998) *Tomorrow's Wash: Challenges and Opportunities for the Detergents Industry in the 21st Century*, World Conference on Detergents, Montreux, 5 October, available at www.unilever.eom/ne/utj:s/wash.html

Forty, A. (1986) *Objects of Desire: Design and Society since 1750*, Thames and Hudson, London

Geels, F. (2002) 'Technological transitions as evolutionary reconfiguration processes: A multilevel perspective and a case study', *Research Policy*, vol 31, pp1257–1274

Giddens, A. (1984) *The Constitution of Society*, Polity Press, Cambridge

Goldsmith, R. (1960) 'Use of clothing records to demonstrate acclimatisation to cold in man', *Journal of Applied Physiology*, vol 15, no 5, pp776–780

Heschong L. (1979) *Thermal Delight in Architecture*, MIT Press, Cambridge, MA

Hughes, T. P. (1983) *Networks of Power: Electrification in Western society, 1880–1930*, Johns Hopkins University Press, Baltimore, MD

Lie, M. and Sorensen, K. (1996) *Making Technology our Own? Domesticating Technology into Everyday Life*, Scandinavian University Press, Oslo

Mintel (2003) *Laundry and Dishwasher Appliances: UK*, report by Mintel International Group, January, available to subscribers at http://reports.mintel.com/sinatra/reports/search/

Nicol, F., Raja, I., Allaudin, A. and Jamy, G. (1999) 'Climatic variations in comfortable temperatures: The Pakistan projects', *Energy and Buildings*, vol 30, pp261–279.

Nye, D. (1992) *Electrifying America: Social Meanings of a New Technology*, MIT Press, Cambridge, MA

Parr, J. (1999) *Domestic Goods: The Material, the Moral, and the Economic in the Post-War Years*, University of Toronto Press, Toronto, Canada

Pridham, E. (2004) 'Refrigeration', *Kitchen and Bathroom Designer*, vol 5, no 46, pp26–34

Redclift, M. (1996) *Wasted: Counting the Costs of Global Consumption*, Earthscan, London

Shove, E. (2003) *Comfort, Cleanliness and Convenience: The Social Organisation of Normality*, Berg, Oxford

Shove, E. and Southerton, D, (2000) 'Defrosting the freezer: From novelty to convenience', *Material Culture*, vol 5, no 3, pp301–319

Shove, E. and Warde, A. (2001) 'Inconspicuous consumption: The sociology of consumption, lifestyles, and the environment', in R. Dunlap, F. Buttel, P. Dickens, and A. Gijswijt (eds) *Sociological Theory and the Environment: Classical Foundations, Contemporary Insights*, Rowman and Littlefield, Lanham, MD, pp230–241

Slater, D. (1997) *Consumer Culture and Modernity*, Polity Press, Cambridge

Southerton, D., Chappells, H. and van Vliet, B. (eds) (2004) *Sustainable Consumption: The Implications of Changing Infrastructures of Provision*, Edward Elgar, Cheltenham

Spaargaren, G. (1997) *The Ecological Modernisation of Production and Consumption: Essays in Environmental Sociology*, Landbouw Universitiet, Wageningen, the Netherlands

Van Vliet, B. (2002) *Greening the Grid: The Ecological Modernisation of Network-Bound Systems*, PhD thesis, Wageningen University, the Netherlands

Wilhite, H., Nakagami, H. and Murakoshi, C. (1996) 'The dynamics of changing Japanese energy consumption patterns and their implications for sustainable consumption', in *1996 ACEEE Summer Study on Energy Efficiency in Buildings*, ACEEE, Washington, DC, pp8.231–8.238

Wilhite, H., Shove, E, Lutzenhiser, L. and Kempton, W. (2000) 'The legacy of twenty years of energy demand management: We know more about individual behaviour but next to nothing about demand', in E. Jochem, J. Sathaye and D. Bouille (eds) *Society, Behaviour, and Climate Change Mitigation*, Kluwer Academic Publishers, Dordrecht, the Netherlands, pp109–126

Zmroczek, C. (1992) 'Dirty linen: Women, class and washing machines, 1920s–1960s', *Women's Studies International Forum*, vol 15, no 2, pp173–185

21

Competing Discourses of Sustainable Consumption: Does the 'Rationalization of Lifestyles' Make Sense?

Kersty Hobson

Introduction

The past two decades have witnessed growing political and scientific acknowledgment that current levels of public and private consumption in high-income countries need to change for the sake of environmental sustainability. 'Consumption', along with 'production' and 'population', is now argued to be one of the main causes of global environmental change, and it has become a core concept in the sustainable development paradigm. For example, Agenda 21, the non-treaty action plan for achieving sustainable development (Grubb et al, 1993) clearly states the causal links between 'wasteful' and 'inefficient' post-industrial consumption patterns and global environmental change (UNCED, 1992; United Nations, 1998; United Nations Economic and Social Council, 1999).

Sustainable development is predominantly defined as economic and social development that meets human meets needs now without comprising future generations' ability to meet their needs (WCED, 1987; although for further discussion of definitions see McManus, 1996; O'Riordan and Voisey, 1997; Dobson, 1998; Sachs, 1999). In keeping with this framing, policy definitions of sustainable consumption can be loosely described as 'doing more with less' (as the Australian Department of the Environment has called their sustainable consumption initiative; see www.environment.gov.au). That is, individuals should be able meet their own consumption needs while also taking the environmental impacts of their actions into account. More specifically, the United Nations, which has emerged as a key player in the international sustainable development arena, defines it as 'The use of goods and services that respond to basic needs and bring a better quality of life, while minimizing the use of natural resources, toxic materials and emissions of waste and pollutants over the life cycle, so as not to jeopardize the needs of future generations' (IISD, 1999).

By this definition, sustainable consumption is the 'rationalization' of lifestyle practices (Smith, 1996; Sachs, 1993), which entails making them more efficient and shaping them according to the logic of instrumental rationality, as part of a prevailing ecological modernization paradigm. This paradigm posits that the 'scientization' of consumption practices necessitates the use of technologically driven and expert-led solutions (for further discussion see Cohen, 1998; Hajer, 1995, 1996). Such an approach has been also labelled 'weak sustainability' (Auty and Brown, 1997a), wherein scientific knowledge directs and feeds into rational policy debates that are then transferred into price adjustments, which are finally reflected in individual behavioural adjustments. Thus, to make sustainable consumption happen, this framing argues that consumers will have to learn about how toxic materials and waste emissions feature in the life cycles of the products they buy, and as a result of this new knowledge, individuals will change their consumption behaviour.

This framing of sustainable consumption is often presented in policy debates as a simple 'common-sense' approach to addressing problems in a world where resources are limited and getting scarcer. This article critically examines whether such a framing is indeed common sense. It considers the prevailing conceptual framing of sustainable consumption under the premise that no discourse tells us 'how it is', or is a neutral, free-floating entity that encompasses and defines all individuals' concerns and needs (Bourke and Meppem, 2000). Rather, discourses implicate sets of social, political and economic relations, forms of practice and power (Darier, 1999a, 1999b; Latour, 1993; Murdoch and Clark, 1994; Mills, 1998) and epistemological positions, which in turn inform policy approaches. Prevailing discourses of sustainability have become 'privileged narratives' (Bourke and Meppem, 2000) that tell one story about the causes and solutions to environmental problems. Are there other stories and less privileged narratives to be heard, which offer alternate framings of sustainable consumption?

This chapter positions policy discourses of sustainable consumption as founded upon neo-liberal ideas of international relations, the state and the individual. This is argued by examining how the rationalization discourse has been constructed within prevailing environmental policy structures and relations. Then the relevance of this discourse to its intended audience is considered. That is, how do individuals read and react to these sustainable consumption messages? This is an important question as ultimately the purpose of sustainable consumption is to affect changes in individuals' values, attitudes and actions (UNCED, 1992). This question is addressed by analysing interviews with participants of a sustainable lifestyle initiative in Britain, called Action at Home. The central argument to emerge is that not only does the rationalization discourse of sustainable consumption have little resonance with individuals who embrace other, 'alternate discourses of consumption', it also actively alienates them from the very causes it seeks to promote, thus reinforcing the status quo.

Forging the Sustainable Consumption Agenda: Trading Vested Interests in the Name of Common Good?

There now exists a general consensus within political communities that global environment problems can be linked directly to consumption practices of high-income countries. Figures abound to illustrate the grossly uneven geographical distribution of global populations in comparison to their resource use. For example, Agenda 21 states that developed countries have 24 per cent of world population, but use 75 per cent of its energy and 92 per cent of its cars (UNCED, 1992; also Jordan and Brown, 1997). Intuitively, it would seem that addressing this inequality is easy. High-income countries have to drastically cut consumption levels, by a factor of ten according to some research (IISD, 1999). Yet, understanding the causes of environmental problems does not necessarily lead to shared views on how to, and who should, address them (Conca et al, 1995). Nowhere is this more true than in international environmental policy forums, which have witnessed ongoing struggles over collective solutions to environmental problems.

These struggles partially stem from how the environment is conceptually framed from a policy perspective. Environmental problems have been recognized as requiring international cooperation and partnership (Tickell, 1977; UNCED, 1992), as their causes and effects cross international boundaries, making them truly global problems (Beck, 1992). Yet, sitting down at the negotiating table sees the translation of the 'environment' into a set of externalized resources or 'natural capital' (Pearce and Turner, 1990) whose ownership and entitlements require both bargaining and cooperation (Barrett, 1992) to secure national interests. This translation process can be seen in the framing of forests as 'carbon sinks' for one. Equally, environmental 'bads' are traced to their sources and framed as the responsibilities of particular nation states or regulated through international directives. The pragmatics of such an approach is easily arguable and is not debated here. Rather, this point is made to argue that this translation process – of the environment from ecology/nature to bundles of 'goods' and 'bads' to be managed in the name of risk mediation – is the first crucial step in the construction of prevailing rationalization approaches.

This is because, as these ownerships, entitlements and blames are negotiated in the name of common good, environmental regulation becomes mapped on to ongoing international policies, processes and allegiances. These have in turn shaped the international sustainable consumption agenda. For example, it is well documented that in the run-up to the Earth Summit conference, high-, transitional- and low-income countries all had different ideas about the main causes of global environmental problems, how obligations should be shared out, and which actions amounted to 'just' solutions (Barrett, 1992).

High-income countries pointed to population growth in the 'South' as being central to global environmental problems, arguing that continued economic growth was one way to alleviate the detrimental effects of poverty. To counter this, low-income countries argued that consumption levels in the 'North' were key, accusing some countries of attempting to practise forms of post-colonial control over Southern economic development and domestic policies (Kamieniecki, 1993; Grover et al, 2001). Thus, 'Rather than global partnership, there was mutual suspicion and deep controversies over very basic questions' (Jordan and Brown, 1997, p272). In the name of reaching a palatable form of consensus, the numerous discourses apparent at the start of negotiations were traded, distilled and rewritten to create the more moderate discourses that now prevail in Agenda 21, which have in turn been handed down to national governments to enact. These are 'sustainable livelihoods for the South', and 'sustainable production and consumption for the North'.

Through this process, high-income countries succeeded in constructing a sustainable consumption discourse that embodied their own interests, enabling them to remain part of, take leadership in, and hence have tangible controls over future international frameworks of environmental governance. Being a rich country negotiating with poor countries has distinct advantages, as the financing of sustainable development frameworks remain a vital and contested issue (Jordan and Brown, 1997). As a result, a discourse has been formed that does not threaten consumption as a form of practice but seeks to bind it to forms of knowledge – science, technology and efficiency – that embody the locus of power held by high-income countries in international relations. To paraphrase George Monbiot (2001), asking high-income countries what to do about over-consumption is like asking prison inmates what to do about crime.

The process whereby the sustainable consumption agenda was formed is important to this paper because its epistemological and ideological foundations have subsequently shaped national policy approaches. This includes how messages of sustainable consumption have been translated into public discourses intended to affect the practices of citizens. Also, it has partially shaped the meanings attached to being a good citizen in contemporary high-income societies, framing how individuals are normatively expected to respond to sustainable consumption messages, which is discussed further in the following section.

Why Sustainable Consumption Fits: The Neo-Liberal Discourse of Rationalizing the Citizen–Consumer

Any government in a high-income country that attempts to force its citizens to consume less would invariably find itself ousted come election time, except perhaps in times of war or other national crises. This is not only because any such enforcement is an affront to the tenets of liberal democracy (Achterberg, 1993), but also because these very tenets have emerged alongside the historical trajectory of consumption as a social and political project. This trajectory began in early modern Europe through the development of international markets, the subsequent growth in trade and the emergence of a new urban social class that valued forms of conspicuous consumption as identity and status markers (Chaney, 1996). By the 18th century, expansion in modes of production had given rise to a 'consumer culture' in countries such as England (Chaney, 1996). This 'culture' and the forms of governance relations that have co-evolved with it, have continued to evolve and to be transformed both culturally and politically over the centuries (e.g. Featherstone, 1991; Baudrillard, 1998; Slater, 1997), making consumption now 'the single most important objective of modern politics, more or less unquestioned right across the political spectrum' (Jacobs, 1997, p47).

With it has evolved a framing of social relationships and interactions between individuals and the state, which form part of the central tenets of neo-classical and neo-liberal theory (Booth, 1993). This 'evolution', however, has not been a gradual affair. Instead, decades of state protectionism in high-income countries gave way in the 1970s to avid free-market approaches strongly favoured by Margaret Thatcher in the UK and Ronald Reagan in the US (Smith, 1994), which have, arguably, remained the leading ideologies of these countries to date. These economic policies seek to, and have substantially succeeded in, 'rolling back the state'. This is the argument that regulation interferes with free-market operations. Environmental regulation has also been subject to this 'rolling back', illustrating how its form and existence is essentially a political outcome that is always in 'a state of dynamic tension with prevailing centres of economic and political power' (Gandy, 1999, p69).

An essential part of this ideology is the framing of individuals as consumers (Booth, 1993). The story goes that all individuals possess a utility function, which incorporates their tastes and preferences. The free market exists to satisfy the needs and wants of these autonomous consumers. Thus, a state of 'consumer sovereignty' exists, where freedom and consumption are inextricably linked (Smith, 1994; Walsh, 1994). If individuals care about the environment, it will be translated into preferences that are expressed through acts of consumption (Hackett, 1995).

This consumer sovereignty has subsequently been translated into a basis of citizenship – the citizen–consumer (Sagoff, 1988; Lunt and Livingstone, 1992; Abercrombie, 1994; Keat et al, 1994). As Aldridge (1994, p905) has noted, in prevailing neo-liberal economic policies 'the consumer is encouraged to feel a duty as a citizen to promote the cause of consumerism; the good consumer is a good citizen'. Indeed, the incorporation of environmental concern into preferences is considered the only way to forge a sustainable consumption agenda, as 'Ultimately the burden on the UK's environment is attributable to the choices and the actions of the consumers. To a great extent producers are, quite naturally, responding to meet the preferences of the customers' (DETR, 1998a, p4).

Criticisms of the assumptions implicit in the above statement have been heard from all corners of the academy. Questions have been raised about the legitimacy of 'consumer sovereignty' as a reflection of social and economic practices (Ciscel, 1984; Hansen and Schrader, 1997; Koritz and Koritz, 2001); whether acts of consumption can ever be considered 'rational' (Miller, 1998; Williams et al, 2001); along with debates over the moral foundations of capitalist systems (Harvey, 2000). Yet, the rationalization approach makes perfect 'neo-classical sense'. It does not threaten consumption but seeks to incorporate a new preference without impinging upon individual's (supposedly) sacred and deeply entrenched lifestyles (UNCED, 1992; Milton, 1996). Exactly how national governments have tried to make the environment part of individual's consumption preferences will be discussed below. Before this, however, it is important to note the emergence of another policy discourse that looks beyond consumption as the basis of environmental sustainability and thus potentially erodes the privileged place of the citizen–consumer nexus. This is the concept of environmental citizenship.

Environmental Citizenship: A Threat to Rationalization?

Environmental citizenship has become an internationally stated objective, which calls for individuals to know, care and act with care towards the environment (Hawthorne and Alabaster, 1999). This entails the emergence of an active citizen, mobilized by responsibility and duty, rather than the passive citizen, bounded by rights and privileges, as neo-classical theory tends to suggest (Pinkney-Baird, 1993; Selman and Parker, 1997; O'Riordan and Voisey, 1997; Myers and Macnaghten, 1998). Its emergence is indeed a move away from the language and framing of the citizen as merely a consumer, placing individuals as social actors who have key roles to play in making sustainable development work, as outlined in Agenda 21 (UNCED, 1992).

Thus, there initially appears to be two contradictory forces at play in sustainable development – the rationalization of the ecological sphere versus the transformation of society through cultural critiques and processes, often referred to as reflexive modernization (for further discussion see Giddens, 1991; Smith, 1996). Yet, it would be premature to suggest that in talking about personal and social values and responsibility, environmental citizenship presents a fundamental challenge to the privileged place that the rationalization discourse of sustainable consumption occupies in policy framings (although it may certainly be argued to have a great deal more resonance with bottom-up approaches to change: for example, see Pinkney-Baird, 1993). This is because both discourses share underlying themes, despite their inherent contradictions (Sagoff, 1988). For one, in neo-classical theory, increased public knowledge is believed to generate increased returns and stimulate growth (Langlois, 2001).

This idea has been applied to environmental problems, wherein growth in public and individual environmental knowledge creates a growth in pro-environmental awareness and behaviour (Ehrlich et al, 1999). This proposition applies to both the provision of consumer information – and hence the citizen–consumer rubric – and the creation of environmental citizenship, which is driven by the provision of information through formal education and public awareness initiatives (Hawthorne and Alabaster, 1999; UNCED, 1992). Thus, an environmental citizen is someone who has internalized information about environmental problems, creating a sense personal responsibility and duty that is then expressed through consumption and community actions. Even though environmental citizenship operates outside of the realms of consumption, being focused mostly on local spaces, it is still causally driven by the incorporation of an ethic into practices framed by the rationalization paradigm. In short, within policy discourses of sustainable consumption, morals and money are mixed together and overlap, to create a discourse coalition that pushes for individuals to bear the brunt of environmental 'bads'.

Whether this push is legitimate is a contentious issue. For example, research from the independent charity Waste Watch UK (1999) suggests that only 6 per cent of landfill waste comes from households. In Australia, just over half of energy use is used directly or indirectly by households, with the rest being used by manufacturing and export industries (Australian Bureau of Statistics, 2001), which have been criticized for side-stepping the sustainable development agenda and adopting, at best, ecological modernization, and at worst, 'business as usual' approaches (e.g. Welford, 1998). It has been argued that prevailing policy discourses are attempts to 'normalize' individual practices and to instil social norms without having to resort to unpopular regulation (Darier, 1999a). There is indeed strong support for this argument within this article's analysis of sustainable consumption. Its current framing represents a fine line between liberty and hegemony, with high-income countries attempting to create a value-free space in public discourse of sustainable consumption to avoid (being seen as) coming down on one side or the other.

Marketing the Environment through Information

The drive to provide individuals with information, either to 'create' responsibility or to affect consumption, underpins the choice of national policy mechanisms used to forward sustainable consumption issues in countries such as the UK. With few exceptions, initiatives have been based on voluntary, consumer information, such as the EU Eco-label scheme a green Claims Code to encourage more consumer information, and a series of public awareness initiatives (Geller, 1989; Hinchliffe, 1996; Staats et al, 1996; Blake, 1999).

The latter approach generally has two aims. First, to promote the overall goals of sustainable development by filling an alleged public information deficit on the causes and consequences of global environmental change (e.g. UK Sustainable Development Education Panel, 1999). Second, to tell individuals exactly what actions they should be taking, such as recycling or insulating their homes. Together, these initiatives represent the framing of consumption as being a public knowledge problem (Burgess et al, 1998; Eden, 1998; Ehrlich et al, 1999; Owens, 2000). An implicit assumption is that environmental problems have immediate resonance with individuals. Individuals either want to 'help' but do not know what to do, or simply learn environmental facts, which then awakens a latent sense of environmental responsibility (Lanthier and Olivier, 1999).

In the UK, campaigns have included the Conservative government's 'Helping the Earth Begins at Home' campaign (Eden, 1993; DOE, 1994; Hinchliffe, 1996) and their 'Going for Green' programme (Going for Green, 1996; Blake and Carter, 1997; Blake, 1999). Most recently, the current Labour government's 'Are you doing your bit?' campaign has used multi-media adverts to suggest that 'a few changes in what you do at home, at work, when shopping or getting about, is all that you need to do' (DETR, 1999a, p2).

However, despite these policy efforts, patterns of sustainable consumption have failed to emerge in the UK over the past decade. As Hawthorne and Alabaster argue, 'environmental citizens are not produced merely by programmes of education' (1999, p40). However, it is not the aim of this chapter to set up the 'straw man' of policy approaches, to simply knock them down. Ample research already exists to argue that 'shallow' approaches to promoting sustainable consumption practices, such as 'Are you doing your bit?' will be relatively ineffective in the face of the complexities and entrenched nature of individual consumption practices, positioned within contexts and infrastructures not conducive to living sustainably (Burningham and O'Brien, 1994; Harrison et al, 1996; Bulkeley, 1997; Macnaghten and Jacobs, 1997; Blake, 1999; Burgess et al, 1998; Myers and Macnaghten, 1998; Darier and Schule, 1999; Hobson, 2001a, 2001b). The question here is how the rationalization discourse of sustainable consumption, and its framing of the individual and consumption outlined above, are read and reacted to by individuals. In short, sustainable consumption is not happening. What role, if any, does this framing have in this lack of public uptake?

Other Voices, Other Concerns:
'Alternate Discourses' of Sustainable Consumption

A starting point to address this question is to consider other discourses of sustainable consumption or more broadly, sustainable living. Although it is not possible to discuss all the nuances of sustainability and consumption discourses here, the intention is to consider emergent strands or themes of some discourses. For example, some, which have arguably been around for many decades in various guises, focus on the nexus of consumption as a locus of power. Ethical consumption mobilizes consumer power to 'tread lightly on the Earth' (e.g. Bedford, 2000). Others turn away from consumption as a legitimate form of social practice and instead look towards 'voluntary simplicity' (Librova, 1999).

Another and more increasingly prevalent discourse broadens the focus away from consumption per se, and into ideas of 'sustainable societies'. This is not just about how resources are used but also about forms of social practice. It touches upon but still differs from the concept of environmental citizenship, as it is not about acting *for* the environment as an internalized norm. Rather the 'environment' is the context to, and an integral part of, a political project of social transformation. This transformation is ultimately founded upon the principle and ideal of social justice.

Some exponents look *towards* nature by focusing on caring for the Earth. This approach is often espoused by conservation non-government organizations, environmental philosophers (as in the journal *Environmental Values*) and spiritually orientated movements. For example, 'The guiding rules are that people must share with each other and care for the Earth' (IUCN/UNEP/WWF, 1991, p8). Others look *away* from nature as an ecological construct and towards social problems inherent in contemporary post-industrial societies. These discourses are voiced by social and environmental justice movements, women's groups, trade unions, and anti-capitalist protest groups such as Reclaim the Streets, who are 'A direct action network for global and local social-ecological revolution(s) to transcend hierarchical and authoritarian society (capitalism included), and still be home in time for tea' (http://rts.gn.apc.org).

These are experientially and politically focused discourses that introduce the concepts of fairness and justice into future-oriented perspectives. As Friends of the Earth (see www.foei.org/campaigns/SSP/indexssp.html) suggest:

> Making societies fairer has long been the object of social struggle. Making them sustainable – so that present and future generations can enjoy clean air, ample fresh water, healthy soil and the company of other species – is more recent. Yet it strikes at the heart of continued human survival. Deteriorating social and environmental trends make the need for *sustainable and fairer societies* the central challenge of our times [author's italics].

Thus, sustainable living is no longer just about consuming products but about how social and environmental resources of common good(s), spaces, networks, futures and relationships need to foster respect for each other and in turn, for the environment. In this sense, the environment is not (just) about 'nature', but about the total environment of lived spaces and daily experiences, the urban experience that is part of modern environmental histories (Castree and Braun, 1998).

It has been argued that environmental sustainability and social justice do not necessarily have mutually compatible aims (Dobson, 1998). Yet, these 'alternate' discourses appear to be formed along the same lines as Bookchin's argument that 'Social inequality feeds environmental degradation and resource overexploitation. Societies constructed upon hierarchies of race, class and gender are ... fundamentally based on exploitation' (Conca et al, 1995, p12). Thus, societies whose economic systems create and perpetuate inequality also create systems of environmental degradation.

An example how this discourse has been mobilized can be seen in the work of Women's Environment Network UK, which have linked health concerns with consumption practices, environmental degradation and social fairness (see www.wen.org.uk). Other women's groups have campaigned over 'sweatshop' conditions and pay, and outlined how the push for over-consumption detrimentally impacts on women, and as a result, families, communities and their environments (Klein, 2000; Grover et al, 2001). The UK Labour government has also recognized the need for 'joined-up thinking' in relation to sustainability issues. Their 1999 sustainable development strategy entitled 'A better quality of life' outlined the importance of tackling social exclusion and poverty in the quest for sustainable development (DETR, 1999b).

Another example is their 'Sustainable Communities for the 21st Century' programme launched in 1998, which acknowledged the importance of utilizing appropriate scales of action, stressing the role of local government in bringing about sustainable development.[2] In this way, discourses of sustainable societies that are increasingly prevalent in high-income countries have more in common with the 'sustainable livelihoods for the South' discourse of Agenda 21 than 'sustainable consumption for the North'. Rather than linking up efficiency, science and the consumer through voluntary market mechanisms, as the rationalization approach does, sustainable society discourses link up the moral citizen and personal experience with networked communities that range from global to local, through varied forms of overt and discrete social action.

Critical Social Sciences and the Environment: Alternate Discourses Reflected

These alternate discourses of sustainable consumption also partially reflect, and are reflected in, the work of critical social scientists, who have been asking questions about lay environmental perceptions, knowledges and concerns. This chapter is positioned within these literatures, as it is based upon the premise that valid contributions to changing how people think and behave – such as creating sustainable consumption patterns – require us to address values, beliefs, cultural assumptions and how these relate to cultural meanings (Reser, 1995).

To this end, researchers have been critically examining the environmental paradigm from the view of individuals who operate outside so-called 'expert' knowledge circles, to understand what they know and care about, and what forms of knowledge are implicated in environmental discourses (Murdoch and Clark, 1994). In doing so, it has been argued that environmental issues in high-income countries are inextricably linked to cultural and political practices (Beck, 1995; Burgess et al, 1998; Grove-White and Szerszynski, 1992). Individuals' environmental concern and perceptions are a collage of experiences and information, which are mobilized for political ends (Burningham, 2000), and whose moral impetus are often concerns about local and distanced procedural and distributive fairness (Owens, 2000; Hobson, 2001a).

This would suggest that the prevailing sustainable consumption discourse coalition has little resonance with lay publics. To examine this point further, this article presents empirical material drawn from qualitative research, to explore what happens when individuals are confronted with environmental information instructing them to rationalize their consumption practices. Does the information make sense to them and how do they react, not only to what is being said, but also the 'hidden messages' of the discourse? This research was undertaken with participants of a sustainable lifestyles programme called Action at Home, which is run by the charity Global Action Plan UK.

Global Action Plan: Origins and Aims

Global Action Plan began in the US in the late 1980s as a way of encouraging and empowering individuals to make changes in their attitudes towards the environment and in their household practices (Gershon and Gillman, 1992). A unique approach was developed, called the EcoTeam Programme, which entails a group of neighbouring households voluntarily joining forces to work through a set number of tasks outlined in the EcoTeam workbook. This workbook details step-by-step actions to take. Each group meets regularly to offer support to each other, to feed back progress, and to summarise the Team's behavioural changes, which are then reported back to a national Global Action Plan office (Harland et al, 1993; Staats and Herenius, 1995). Through these groups, it is hoped that households can share experiences and work through the numerous barriers to change. It is also hoped that the sustainable lifestyles message will then diffuse outwards through personal networks, into neighbourhoods and communities, creating widespread behavioural changes (Rogers 1995; Global Action Plan Nederland, 1998).

In the early 1990s, Global Action Plan UK (GAP) was founded. GAP reworked the original EcoTeam model, aiming not so much for group cohesion but for widespread participation (Global Action Plan UK, 1998a, 1998b, 1999). Along with programmes for school and work, they established the Action at Home programme, which is a 6 month voluntary scheme that aims to encourage changes in individuals' household consumption practices by providing information, support and feedback (Church and McHarry, 1992). It is not a nationwide information campaign but is instead targeted sequentially at specific geographical areas, to enable the establishment of local support and diffusion networks.

Participants in Action at Home sign up with GAP and pay a small fee. They receive a 'welcome' questionnaire that aims to establish a base-line of household environmental impact called a Greenscore, which is measured again at the end of the programme. They then receive monthly information packs with step-by-step suggestions for making small changes to their practices, along with 'money-off offers on various environmental products, and addresses for further information. The packs sequentially cover the topics of waste, water, transport, shopping and energy, ending with a 'next steps' pack about where to go once the six months is up. This makes Action at Home unique in terms of behaviour change programmes in the UK today, since its information sits within the rationalization framing of sustainable consumption and yet offers an intensive, rather than one-off, access to information over a set period of time, as well as facilitating local and national support networks.

To date, over 30,000 households have taken part in Action at Home (see www.globalactionplan.org.uk), which has affected behaviour changes in many households (for results see Global Action Plan UK, 1998b, 1998c). However, due to low returns of the questionnaires GAP have been uncertain about what is happening to individuals as they participated in Action at Home. To address this issue qualitative research was carried out, which focused on the processes and experiences of Action at Home participants over the six-month period.

Researching Action at Home: Methods and Case Studies

Fieldwork took place between October 1997 and May 1999, in two separate locations. The first location was Bournemouth, Dorset, where Action at Home was being publicized and distributed by the local authority. At the start of the programme (October 1997) and again at the end (April 1998), semi-structured single interviews took place with Action at Home households to talk about their experiences and thoughts on the programme (see Burgess et al, 1988a, 1988b; Crabtree et al, 1993; Kvale, 1996) for further method discussions). In total, 44 were carried out. To follow this, during 1998–1999, three companies[3] in the northwest of England purchased Action at Home as part of a pilot project, offering the programme to employees to encourage changes in their resource-use behaviours both at home and work. As part of the assessment of this project, one in-depth interview group was established at each work place. Each group met at the start of the programme (October 1998) and three months into Action at Home (January 1999). At the end of the six months (April 1999) group members was interviewed individually. All interviews were recorded and the following discussions are based upon analysis of the interview transcripts.

Emergent Debates and Moral Concerns: Action at Home as a Form of Discursive Practice

One possible assumption about Action at Home participants is that their involvement in the programme signalled an acceptance of the prevailing sustainable consumption messages, with them having internalized some norm of environmental responsibility (e.g. Eden, 1993; Finger, 1994). This could also possibly be reflected in the fact that just under half of the Action at Home participants interviewed made changes to one or more of their domestic practices as a result of taking part in the programme. These were all low-cost or no-cost behaviours, such as turning taps off when brushing teeth, which were easy to do and could be altered in an instant. However, the majority of practices detailed in the packs did not change. This is not surprising, as many of the changes recommended take time and/or money (Krause, 1993; Tanner, 1999), and there is only so much 'environmental space' in individual's lives to make behaviour or structural changes (Brandon and Lewis, 1999). This lack of scope for change resonated strongly in the interviews, especially in terms of complex and/or socially contentious actions, such as transport use and shopping choices. For example:

> Well I live in a rented flat, a first floor flat, no garden and although I totally agree with the objectives and sort of ideas of what you can do at home, it is very difficult for me to implement them and totally impractical in cases. I found it frustrating. (FEMALE, BOURNE-MOUTH, APRIL 1998)

As well as the many barriers to sustainable outcomes, why participants took part in Action at Home and how they reacted to the programme can help explain this behavioural inertia further. This challenges the assumption that these individuals have signed up to rationalization. That is, Action at Home participants' motivations were not focused on the environment per se, but more towards using the programme to ask themselves questions about how they were living and how they fitted in to ideas about 'right' ways to live. As one interviewee commented at the end of the programme:

> It was helpful for me to see where I stood. There was a few things that made me think, 'do I do it and if not, why don't I?' I was really glad to see there were a few things that I thought were important. (FEMALE, BOURNEMOUTH, APRIL 1998)

Rationalization framings of how individuals alter lifestyles to make them more sustainable suggest a process wherein new information is learned, weighed up against current practices, and then, contingent upon a number of factors, either accepted or rejected. What this framing misses are the emergent, and arguably most important, processes taking place when environmental information is read. Across all the interviews the information in the packs was constantly open to critique, argument and debate by participants. Interviewees asked questions about who is being (re)presented and given authority in the Action at Home information. Also, where does responsibility, both personal and social, lie for making the required consumption changes? How is it possible to live sustainably when society is not geared towards sustainable living? Whose vested interests are being represented? Who can you trust? Why is society structured so that the rich keep getting richer and the poor keep getting poorer?

In this sense, the discourses to emerge during the Action at Home interviews were about questions of personal and social rights and wrongs. Interviewees focused on their concerns about the distributions and abuses of equity, justice and power that they see in their everyday lives. This included loss of community, loss of respect for each other and the environment, social forces that promote over-consumption, the lack of fairness implicit in economic systems, loss of positive social spaces for interaction, the continuation of colonial attitudes towards developing countries and fear of 'where it is all going?'

(Grove-White and Szerszynski, 1992; Macnaghten and Urry, 1998). As an interviewee noted:

> At one time there were villages and towns and in the main, villages were a fairly close-knit community where there was inter-reaction and inter-cooperation in terms of how you managed things and how you do things. Now that has all been blown away on the basis that everybody lives a fairly insular life. Because of the way my life is, I know very few people who actually live where I live. (MALE, NORTHWEST, OCTOBER 1998)

This lack of interaction and respect was linked to lack of respect for the (often local) environment. For example, interviewees were disappointed about the state of their towns, where: 'There's litter all over the place, nobody gives a damn!' (male, Bournemouth, October 1997). Thus, they were not concerned with rationalizing their own lifestyles, but rather with how these lifestyles were part of, and made a contribution to, 'right' ways of living, encapsulated in debates about lack of community, interaction and mutual respect. Ultimately these debates concerned the sites and allocations of who is responsible for creating positive social change.

Arguing in Circles: The 'Discursive Trap' of Rationalizing Consumption Practices

With this in mind, it is clearer why so much behaviour is not 'rationalized' when individuals are exposed to new environmental information. There was little sign of an incorporation of an environmental preference or the awakening of a latent sense of environmental concern as framed by prevailing discourses. As participants became involved with Action at Home with the express purpose of being made to think, this is precisely what happened. That is, there were emergent inter- and intra-personal debates about what and why they can and cannot make consumption changes, which were inextricably bound up with broader arguments over social fairness and responsibility. As a result, not only did Action at Home fail to convince participants that it is dealing with what really matters to them, it also created a further distancing from the central messages of rationalization.

For one, this was because the broad range of social and moral concerns that underpinned Action at Home participants' involvement created a definite frustration at the static, limited and didactic nature of the environmental information provided in Action at Home. This was apparent through interviewees' many comments on how ineffective and downright frustrating it was having to chart their lives, choices and limitations in questionnaires:

> I must admit there were a few areas where I was a bit critical of it[4] and I've actually written hand-written notes on the forms as I was ticking the boxes. (MALE, BOURNEMOUTH, APRIL 1998)

> That sort of thing I feel you have to have a certain degree of your own autonomy over these things, you can't follow the letter. But when you're asked a straightforward question and then you are judged that you've got it wrong, you don't have any chance to explain how you do the things. (FEMALE, BOURNEMOUTH, APRIL 1998)

They also felt frustration at the way that the packs focused only on acts of consumption. Many felt that some recommended practices had no beneficial impacts on the environment while others felt they personally had no power whatsoever in the creating change in the market-place. Some pointed out how being told to consume less was quite insulting when so many people can hardly afford to consume enough (Macnaghten and Jacobs, 1997), especially seen as many of the interviewees in Bournemouth were retirees and those in the Northwest were sole earners in working-class households. Indeed, some felt that there were more than just a few practices at stake and that, as outlined above, the sustainable consumption discourse was an attempt to normalize individuals' practices. As one interviewee put it: 'I think its not that simple, even something like where you buy your milk from, you are being pushed into a different lifestyle almost' (male, Northwest, January 1999).

Thus, any idea that consumption is about instrumentally meeting individual needs was rendered meaningless in light of the multiple purposes that contextual forms of consumption served. For example, acts of consumption were linked to personal history and meanings, routine, servitude, social aspirations, finding spaces of leisure in modern urban settings, expressions of identity, as well as the creating and servicing of personal relationships (e.g. Appadurai, 1986; Livingstone, 1992; Jackson, 1993; Miller, 1995, 1998; Pred, 1996; Slater, 1997). Thus, trying to map a rationalization approach on to this complex and often partially obscured pattern of meanings and practices appeared a pointless exercise. Lifestyles formed through a multitude of personal and historical processes were being forced into a narrow, one-dimensional frame of reference that had little to do with the day-to-day experiences of interviewees.

These reactions call into question the prevailing approach of using the citizen–consumer or environmental citizenship as a means of encouraging social change. Participants did not feel like neo-liberal free marketeers whose exercise of preferences in the market-place is the embodiment of consumer sovereignty. Rather their concerns made them feel like 'semi-citizens' who viewed their own consumption practices as placing them in an ambiguous position of political power. That is, the importance and enjoyment of what they do and buy was openly and often proudly acknowledged. At the same time, there was a sense of entrapment and powerlessness through being defined politically by the project of consumption. For example:

> I think it's dreadful the way that supermarkets have taken over. When I go into a supermarket and ask for certain items, they say, 'oh there isn't the demand for it' and I say, 'well you haven't asked me have you?' You know I am always one of these consumers who has never been asked about anything. (FEMALE, BOURNEMOUTH, OCTOBER 1997)

On top of this, the narrow framing of the 'environment' alienated interviewees even further from the project of sustainable consumption. For one, information is often presented as definitive when interviewees were more than aware of its ambiguity: 'And also so many environmental things aren't so black and white' (male, Northwest, January 1999).

The 'environment as nature' had little resonance. The reality of sociostructural changes in society surpassed any ecological concerns, which were felt to have little relevance to urban existence:

> The sorts of changes within society, particularly the last five years, has meant that people's focus is totally different. I mean, this environment business is irrelevant. I've got far more important things to worry about than these things. (MALE, NORTHWEST, OCTOBER 1998)

As a result of these many discursive forces and counter-forces, Action at Home often had the opposite effect than intended. That is, not only did little behaviour change but also in the process of seeing the environment through the rationalization approach to sustainable consumption, interviewees felt distanced from and angered by the project. This created a 'discursive trap'. That is, through having their concerns and interests aroused by reading through and thinking about both the personal and social implications of the information contained in the packs, many realized it had 'little to do with them' and that it did not really address what was wrong with society. The vested interests embodied in the packs suddenly seemed more pernicious, and suspicions of hidden agendas were roused. Why were they being told what to do and how to live when governing institutions did little to address consumption issues? As one interviewee pointed out:

> Politicians are swayed by the money and industry. Look at that silly [ex-US president Bill] Clinton, you know he can't say boo to a goose. His environmental things are total rubbish because he's been taken by the short hairs by the car industry and the oil. (FEMALE, BOURNEMOUTH, APRIL 1998)

Thus, the discourse of rationalizing lifestyles presents itself to Action at Home participants like a form of social control through self-discipline (Darier, 1999a, 1999b) – ironically, the exact opposite of its neo-liberal foundations. In doing so, it does not address the 'bigger' and more pressing social concerns presented in interviewees' discourses, that talk about working towards, in policy and in practice, sustainable communities.

The Future of Sustainable Consumption: Reshaping Policy Perspectives and Enabling Spaces of Hope

The project of sustainable consumption, through its prevailing policy framing, appears to fundamentally misrepresent what matters to individuals in terms of social and environmental concerns. Instead of 'doing more with less', it appears that 'making the most of what we potentially can all share' is really at the heart of Action at Home participant's concerns. This suggests that in its current guise, sustainable consumption will not effect real changes in people's lives. Maybe this is the political intention. Even if it is not, relying on voluntary information and lifestyle initiatives will constantly create 'discursive traps' in individuals' lives, by using consumer-oriented information presented in impersonal media to ask highly contextualized and socially embedded questions.

Can anything be done to save the project of sustainable consumption? It would be overly simplistic to suggest a simple 'national governments should change their sustainable consumption discourses' solution, as that would ignore the structural and political contexts that the current discourse coalition has emerged from, and is embedded within. The rationalization of lifestyles can arguably be seen as embodying the state's position within the current environmental paradigm. That is, although governments are still looked towards providing solutions for all social ills, there are serious limitations to how effective national regulatory institutions can be in dealing with ever-increasing magnitudes of risk (Jordan and Brown, 1997; Gandy, 1999). For example, at the 'Rio Plus 5' review in 1997, the national results from Agenda 21 were considered 'meagre and inadequate' (Buck et al, 2000). This may be caused by lack of will and effort but also by the inherent difficulty of effecting subtle and often intangible social changes through unwieldy legislative and regulatory instruments.

Governments can be accused of side-stepping the real forces behind consumption issues, such as manufacturing, and using concepts of duty and responsibility to attempt to enforce obligations upon citizens. This was the overwhelming conclusion of Action at Home participants. Yet, placing sustainable consumption in its political context, it can also be argued that governments in high-income countries have been hoisted on their own petard and that of the global historicity of consumption and the rise of the nation state. They are, in effect, now attempting to (partially) close stable doors after the horses have bolted. With this is mind, it seems that an ecological modernization approach is the only reasonable path any high-income government can attempt to take in current political climes.

This does not mean that the alternate discourses of sustainable consumption should be ignored. Instead, the role of policy instruments should be reconsidered in relation to the concerns of individuals like Action at Home participants. As it stands, policy cannot legislate the subtleties of lifestyles, nor should it try. Instead, it could go some way to trying to breach the divide that exists between the disparate discourse of sustainability.

For example, there is no doubt that building strong and effective leadership can have positive effects on public perceptions of an issue, and if government were seen to be abiding by the principles of fairness and equity underlying alternate discourses of sustainable consumption, positive social capital could be built.

> I think if councils and governments – I'm not saying everybody because you always get people who just aren't bothered – but I think a lot of people would help them in return. If they saw that something was being done, it would stir your conscience and even if you were doing it for whatever reason, it doesn't matter. The fact that you're doing it, you're doing it, aren't you? But you've got to see people helping you. (MALE, NORTHWEST, OCTOBER 1998)

It has been argued elsewhere (Hobson, 2001b) that before government can tell people to do 'their bit' they have to be seen to be doing 'their own bit'. What exactly this 'bit' entails is perhaps what citizen's debates and on going discursive monitoring of governing institutions is concerned with (Sagoff, 1988). Some suggest that creating forms of public-regulatory interaction that are less expert driven and more inclusive would be one way to close the discourse divide between the governed and the governing (for further discussion see Healey, 1997; Owens, 2000; Rydin and Pennington, 2000). Another suggestion is to create and support institutions and organizations at the appropriate level of governance, to tackle sustainable society issues (Rydin and Greig, 1995; Blake, 1999; Stoll-Kleemann et al, 2001). That is, if current policy instruments alone cannot hope to address the complexities and contingencies inherent in the alternate discourses of sustainable consumption, they *can* offer support, financially and morally, for organizations trying to address some of the concerns manifest in the Action at Home interviews.

For one, organizations like GAP are working to improve and develop their programmes to make them more engaging and effective, and to focus on the contexts of consumption. Yet it remains woefully underfunded. Campaign groups like Friends of the Earth, who aim to engage in constructive dialogues about working towards sustainable communities, are often publicly labelled as subversive and essentially anti-government due to their non-mainstream agenda and approaches. Local or grass-roots organizations flounder due to lack of support, both politically and in their communities. In short, at all levels of governance, the potential, will and skills to address some of the issues that make up the 'alternate' discourse of sustainable consumption detailed in this paper exist. These span spatial and virtual networks that no longer fit simply into 'local' or 'national' spatial categories (Murdoch and Marsden, 1995; Silk, 1999) but cut across forms of communities that are constantly forming around public issues of justice and fairness.

One over-riding problem is that such communities are often viewed as essentially anti-government and thus, antisocial. Therefore, it is perhaps not only an issue of policy but also one of perspective. George Monbiot (2001) draws an interesting distinction between different forms of political action. Islamic activists describe enthusiastic but intelligent anger as *hammas* (a term that has been adopted by the Palestinian freedom movement but that does not essentially represent its chosen forms of conduct). This stands in opposition to uncontrolled, stupid anger called *hamoq*. When individuals voice social concerns that are grounded in wanting to see a fairer world they can be seen to be expressing *hammas*. Yet, when individuals start to question practices, such as consumption, as a legitimate moral basis for social practices, state and international actors treat them as if expressing *hamoq*. Individuals such as the Action at Home participants do not want revolution or anarchy. Rather, they are echoing age-old concerns about equity, privilege and justice. Their pathways towards sustainable societies have little to do with rationalizing consumption practices or with exercising their alleged citizen–consumer power. Rather, it is about creating 'spaces of hope' (to paraphrase Harvey, 2000) for a fairer future, spaces that governing institutions have the potential to help create and foster. Yet many feel these spaces are currently marginalized by prevailing approaches to issues such as sustainable consumption and thus, as social actors, they will continue to remain distanced from these projects.

Notes

1   However, this polarized distinction between North and South is now being reconsidered as multinational companies are increasingly turning their attention to capturing the emergent markets of the 4 billion poor of the world out of 'enlightened self-interest' (Slavin, 2001), with consumption levels in developing countries increasing. As a result it becomes more apparent that there needs to be constructive dialogue between North and South about how to achieve sustainable consumption at a global level (Grover et al, 2001).
2   This project still suggests that the role of local government in creating sustainable societies is to 'inform consumers about environmental issues' (DETR, 1998b). Added to this, the Labour government has been criticized by environmentalists, trade unionists and left wing commentators for doing very little concrete to combat social exclusion and poverty in the UK, which remains high by comparative European standards (Gordon, 2000).
3   These companies were the electricity company Norweb in Preston, Lancashire; North-West Water in Warrington, Chesire and British Aerospace in Warton, Lancashire.
4   He is talking about the 'welcome' questionnaire, received at the start of the Action at Home programme.

References

Abercrombie, N. (1994) 'Authority and consumer society', in R. Keat et al (eds) *The Authority of the Consumer,* Routledge, London, pp43–57

Achterberg, W. (1993) 'Can liberal democracy survive the environmental crisis?', in A. Dobson and P. Lucardie (eds) *The Politics of Nature,* Routledge, London, pp81–102

Aldridge, A. (1994) 'The construction of rational consumption in *Which* magazine: The more blobs the better', *Sociology,* vol 28, no 4, pp899–912

Appadurai, A. (1986) *The Social life of Things: Commodities in Cultural Perspective,* Cambridge University Press, Cambridge

Australian Bureau of Statistics (2001) *Energy and Greenhouse Gas Emissions Accounts, Australia, 1992–1993 to 1997–1998,* Australian Bureau of Statistics, Canberra

Auty, R. M. and Brown, K. (1997) 'Sustainable development: Taking stock', in R. M. Auty and K. Brown (eds) *Approaches to Sustainable Development,* Printer, London, pp296–302

Barrett, S. (1992) 'International environmental agreements as games', in R. Pethig (ed) *Conflicts and Cooperation in Managing Environmental Resources,* Springer-Verlag, New York, pp11–36

Baudrillard, J. (1998) *The Consumer Society: Myths and Structures,* Sage Publications, London

Beck, U. (1992) *Risk Society: Towards a New Modernity,* Sage Publications, London

Beck, U. (1995) *Ecological Politics in an Age of Risk,* Polity Press, Oxford

Bedford, T. M. (2000) *Ethical Consumerism: Everyday Negotiations in the Construction of an Ethical Self,* thesis, Department of Geography, University College London, London

Blake, J. (1999) 'Overcoming the "value–action gap" in environmental policy: Tensions between national policy and local experience', *Local Environment,* vol 4, no 3, pp257–278

Blake, J. and Carter, C. (1997) *Community and Environmental Attitudes and Actions in Huntingdonshire,* Committee for Interdisciplinary Environmental Studies, University of Cambridge, Cambridge

Booth, W. J. (1993) *Households: On the Moral Architecture of the Economy,* Cornell University Press, Ithaca, NY

Bourke, S. and Meppem, T. (2000) 'Privileged narratives and fictions of consent in environmental discourse', *Local Environment*, vol 5, no 3, pp299–310

Brandon, G. and Lewis, A. (1999) 'Reducing household energy consumption: A qualitative and quantitative field study', *Journal of Environmental Psychology*, vol 19, pp75–85

Buck, M., Kollman, K. and Carius, A. (2000) *International Environmental Policymaking and Transatlantic Co-operation: Setting the Agenda for Rio +10*, Report from Enhancing Prospects for Environmental Leadership: Challenges for Rio +10 Workshop, Lisbon, 10–12 February 2000, Ecologic, Berlin

Bulkeley, H. (1997) 'Global risk, local values? "Risk society" and the greenhouse issue in Newcastle, Australia', *Local Environment*, vol 2, no 3, pp261–274

Burgess, J., Harrison, C. and Filius, P. (1998) 'Environmental communication and the cultural politics of environmental citizenship', *Environment and Planning A*, vol 30, no 8, pp1445–1460

Burgess, J., Limb, M. and Harrison, C. (1988a) 'Exploring environmental values through the medium of small groups: 1. Theory and practice', *Environment and Planning A*, vol 20, no 3, pp309–326

Burgess, J., Limb, M. and Harrison, C. (1988b) 'Exploring environmental values through the medium of small groups: 2. Illustrations of a group at work', *Environment and Planning A*, vol 20, pp457–476

Burningham, K. (2000) 'Using the language of the NIMBY: A topic for research, not an activity for researchers', *Local Environment*, vol 5, no l, pp55–67

Burningham, K. and O'Brien, M. (1994) 'Global environmental values and local contexts of action', *Sociology*, vol 28, no 4, pp913–932

Castree, N. and Braun, B. (1998) 'The construction of nature and the nature of construction: Analytical and political tools for building survivable futures', in B. Braun and N. Castree (eds) *Remaking Reality: Nature at the Millenium*, Routledge, London, pp3–42

Chaney, D. (1996) *Lifestyles*, Routledge, London

Church, C. and McHarry, I. (1992) *The Household EcoTeam Workbook*, GAP UK/GAP International, London

Ciscel, D. H. (1984) 'Galbraith's planning system as a substitute for market theory', *Journal of Economic Issues*, vol 18, no 2, pp411–419

Cohen, M. J. (1998) 'Science and environment: Assessing cultural capacity for ecological modernization', *Public Understanding of Science*, vol 7, pp149–167

Conca, K., Alberty, M. and Dabelko, G. D. (eds) (1995) *Green Planet Blues*, Westview Press, Boulder, CO

Crabtree, B. F., Yanoshik, M. K., Miller, W. L. and O'Connor, P. J. (1993) 'Selecting individual or group interviews', in D. L. Morgan (ed) *Successful Focus Groups: Advancing the State of the Art*, Sage Publications, London, pp137–152

Darier, E. (1999a) 'Foucault and the environment: An introduction', in E. Darier (ed) *Discourses of the Environment*, Blackwell, Oxford, pp1–34

Darier, E. (1999b) 'Foucault against environmental ethics', in E. Darier (ed) *Discourses of the Environment*, Blackwell, Oxford, pp217–240

Darier, E. and Schule, R. (1999) 'Think globally, act locally? Climate change and public participation in Manchester and Frankfurt', *Local Environment*, vol 4, no 3, pp317–329

DETR (Department for Environment, Transport and the Regions) (1998a) *Consumer Products and the Environment*, DETR, London

DETR (1998b) *Sustainable Communities for the 21st Century*, DETR, London

DETR (1999a) *Every Little Bit Helps: Are You Doing Your Bit?*, DETR, London

DETR (1999b) *A Better Quality of Life*, DETR, London

Dobson, A. (1998) *Justice and the Environment*, Oxford University Press, Oxford

DOE (UK Department of the Environment) (1994) *Dos and Don'ts That Save You Money on Your Fuel Bills,* Energy Efficiency Office, DOE, London

Eden, S. E. (1993) 'Individual environmental responsibility and its role in public environmentalism', *Environment and Planning A,* vol 25, no 12, pp1743–1758

Eden, S. (1998) 'Environmental issues: Knowledge, uncertainty and the environment', *Progress in Human Geography,* vol 22, no 3, pp425–432

Ehrlich, P. R., Wolff, G., Daily, G. C., Hughes, J. B., Daily, S., Dalton, M. and Goulder, L. (1999) 'Knowledge and the environment', *Ecological Economics,* vol 30, no 2, pp267–284

Featherstone, M. (1991) *Consumer Culture and Postmodernism,* Sage Publications, London

Finger, M. (1994) 'From knowledge to action? Exploring the relationship between environmental experiences, learning and behavior', *Journal of Social Issues,* vol 50, no 3, pp141–160

Gandy, M. (1999) 'Rethinking the ecological Leviathan: Environmental regulation in an age of risk', *Global Environmental Change,* vol 9, no 1, pp59–69

Geller, E. S. (1989) 'Applied behavior analysis and social marketing: An integration for environmental preservation', *Journal of Social Issues,* vol 45, no 1, pp17–36

Gershon, D. and Gillman, R. (1992) *Household Ecoteam Workbook,* GAP, Woodstock, New York

Giddens, A. (1991) *Modernity and Self-Identity: Self and Society in the Late Modern Age,* Polity Press, Oxford

Global Action Plan Nederland (1998) *EcoTeam Programma,* Global Action Plan Nederland, the Hague, the Netherlands

Global Action Plan UK (1998a) *Action at Home: A Catalyst for Change,* GAP UK, London

Global Action Plan UK (1998b) *Action at Home National Report,* GAP UK, London

Global Action Plan UK (1998c) *Evaluation: A Global Action Plan Evaluation Report of the London Borough of Westminster Private Sector Home Energy Advice Campaign, October 1997–March 1998,* GAP UK, London

Global Action Plan UK (1999) *Action at Home in the UK: Barrier Report April 1999,* GAP UK, London

Going for Green (1996) *The Green Code,* Going for Green, Manchester

Gordon, D. (2000) *Poverty and Social Exclusion in Britain,* Joseph Rowntree Foundation, York

Grove-White, R. and Szerszynski, B. (1992) 'Getting behind environmental ethics', *Environmental Values,* vol 1, pp285–296

Grover, S., Flenley, C. and Hemmati, M. (2001) *Gender and Sustainable Consumption: Bridging Policy Gaps in the Context of Chapter 4, Agenda 21,* Report for the United Nations Commission on Sustainable Development, 7th Session, April 1999, www.earthsummit2002.org/toolkits/consumption/consumption.htm

Grubb, M., Koch, M., Thomson, K., Munson, A. and Sullivan, F. (1993) *The Earth Summit Agreements: A Guide and Assessment,* Earthscan, London

Hackett, P. (1995) *Conservation and the Consumer: Understanding Environmental Concern,* Routledge, London

Hajer, M. A. (1995) *The Politics of Environmental Discourse: Ecological Modernization and the Policy Process,* Clarendon Press, Oxford

Hajer, M. A. (1996) 'Ecological modernisation as cultural politics', in Lash, S., Szerszynski, B. and Wynne, B. (eds) *Risk Environment and Modernity: Towards a New Ecology,* Sage Publications, London, pp246–268

Hansen, U. and Schrader, U. (1997) 'A modern model of consumption for a sustainable society', *Journal of Consumer Policy,* vol 20, no 4, pp443–468

Harland, P., Langezaal, S., Staats, H. J. and Weenig, W. H. (1993) *The EcoTeam Program in The Netherlands: A Pilot Study of the Backgrounds and Experiences of the Global Action Plan,* Centre for Energy and Environmental Research, Leiden University, the Netherlands

Harrison, C. M., Burgess, J. and Filius, P. (1996) 'Rationalizing environmental responsibilities: A comparison of lay publics in the UK and Netherlands', *Global Environmental Change,* vol 6, no 3, pp215–234

Harvey, D. (2000) *Spaces of Hope,* University of California Press, Berkeley, CA

Hawthorne, M. and Alabaster, T. (1999) 'Citizen 2000: Development of a model of environmental citizenship', *Global Environmental Change,* vol 9, no 1, pp25–43

Healey, P. (1997) *Collaborative Planning: Shaping Places in Fragmented Societies,* Macmillan, London

Hinchliffe, S. (1996) 'Helping the Earth begins at home: The social construction of socio-environmental responsibilities', *Global Environmental Change,* vol 6, no 1, pp53–62

Hobson, K. (2001a) *Talking Habits into Action: An Investigation into Global Action Plan's Action at Home Programme,* PhD thesis, Department of Geography, University College London, London

Hobson, K. (2001b) 'Sustainable lifestyles: Rethinking barriers and behaviour change', in M. J. Cohen and J. Murphy (eds) *Exploring Sustainable Consumption: Environmental Policy and the Social Sciences,* Elsevier, Amsterdam

IISD (International Institute for Sustainable Development) (1999) *Instruments for Change: Making Production and Consumption More Sustainable,* website developed by IISD with support of the Government of Norway, www.iisd.ca/susprod (accessed 16 May 2006)

IUCN (World Conservation Union), UNEP (United Nations Environment Programme) and WWF (World Wide Fund for Nature) (1991) *Caring for the Earth,* IUCN/UNEP/WWF Gland, Switzerland, available at http://coombs.anu.edu.au/~vern/caring/caring.html

Jackson, P. (1993) 'Towards a cultural politics of consumption', in J. Bird, B. Curtis, T. Putnam and L. Ticker (eds) *Mapping the Futures: Local Cultures, Global Changes,* Routledge, London, pp207–228

Jacobs, M. (1997) 'The quality of life: Social goods and the politics of consumption', in M. Jacobs (ed) *Greening the Millennium? The New Politics of the Environment,* Blackwell Publishers, Oxford, pp47–61

Jordan, A. and Brown, K. (1997) 'The international dimensions of sustainable development: Rio reconsidered', in R. M. Auty and K. Brown (eds) *Approaches to Sustainable Development,* Printer, London, pp270–295

Kamieniecki, S. (ed) (1993) *Environmental Politics in the International Arena,* State University of New York Press, Albany, NY

Keat, R., Whiteley, N. and Abercombie, N. (1994) *The Authority of the Consumer,* Routledge, London, pp1–22

Klein, N. (2000) *No Logo,* Flamingo, London

Koritz, A. and Koritz, D. (2001) 'Checkmating the consumer: Passive consumption and the economic devaluation of culture', *Feminist Economics,* vol 7, no 1, pp45–62

Krause, D. (1993) 'Environmental consciousness: An empirical study', *Environment and Behavior,* vol 25, no 1, pp126–42

Kvale, S. (1996) *InterViews: An Introduction to Qualitative Research Interviewing,* Sage Publications, London

Langlois, R. N. (2001) 'Knowledge, consumption and endogenous growth', *Journal of Evolutionary Economics,* vol 11, no 1, pp77–94

Lanthier, I. and Olivier, L. (1999) 'The construction of environmental "awareness"', in E. Darier (ed) *Discourses of the Environment,* Blackwell, Oxford, pp63–78

Latour, B. (1993) *We Have Never Been Modern,* Harvester Wheatsheaf, Hemel Hempstead

Librova, H. (1999) 'The disparate roots of voluntary modesty', *Environmental Values,* vol 8, pp369–380

Livingstone, S. M. (1992) 'The meaning of domestic technologies: A personal construct analysis of familial gender relations', in R. Silverstone and E. Hirsch (eds) *Consuming Technologies: Media and Information in Domestic Spheres,* Routledge, London, pp113–130

Macnaghten, P. and Jacobs, M. (1997) 'Public identification with sustainable development: Investigating public barriers to participation', *Global Environmental Change,* vol 7, no 1, pp5–24

Macnaghten, P. and Urry, J. (1998) *Contested Natures,* Sage Publications, London

McManus, P. (1996) 'Contested terrains: Politics, stories and discourses of sustainability', *Environmental Politics,* vol 5, no 1, pp48–73

Miller, D. (1995) 'Consumption as the vanguard of history', in D. Miler (ed) *Acknowledging Consumption: A Review of New Studies,* Routledge, London, pp 1–57

Miller, D. (1998) A *Theory of Shopping,* Polity Press, Oxford

Mills, S. (1998) *Discourse,* Routledge, London

Milton, K. (1996) *Environmentalism and Cultural Theory: Exploring the Role of Anthropology in Environmental Discourse,* Routledge, London

Monbiot, G. (2001) 'Raising the temperature', *Guardian Weekly,* 26 July–1 August, p13

Murdoch, J. and Clark, J. (1994) 'Sustainable knowledge', *Geoforum,* vol 25, no 2, pp115–132

Murdoch, J. and Marsden, T. (1995) 'The spatialization of politics: Local and national actor-spaces in environmental conflict', *Transactions of Institute of British Geography,* vol 20, no 3, pp368–380

Myers, G. and Macnaghten, P. (1998) 'Rhetorics of environmental sustainability: Commonplaces and places', *Environment and Planning A,* vol 30, no 2, pp333–353

O'Riordan, T. and Voisey, H. (1997) 'The political economy of sustainable development', *Environmental Politics,* vol 6, no 1, pp1–23

Owens, S. (2000) 'Commentary', *Environment and Planning A,* vol 32, no 7, pp1141–1148

Pearce, D. and Turner, R. K. (1990) *Economics of Natural Resources and the Environment,* Harvester Wheatsheaf, Hemel Hempstead

Pinkney-Baird, J. (1993) *Agenda 21: Sustainable Development and Volunteering,* The Volunteer Centre UK, Berkhamsted, UK

Pred, A. (1996) 'Interfusions: Consumption, identity and the practices and power relations of everyday life', *Environment and Planning A,* vol 28, no 1, pp11–24

Reser, J. P. (1995) 'Whither environmental psychology? The Transpersonal ecopsychology crossroads', *Journal of Environmental Psychology,* vol 15, no 3, pp235–257

Rogers, E. M. (1995) *Diffusion of Innovations,* Free Press, New York

Rydin, Y. and Greig, A. (1995) 'Talking past each other: Local environmentalists in different organisational contexts', *Environmental Politics,* vol 4, no 2, pp271–294

Rydin, Y. and Pennington, M. (2000) 'Public participation and local environmental planning: The collective action problem and the potential of social capital', *Local Environment,* vol 5, no 2, pp153–169

Sachs, W. (1993) *Global Ecology: A New Arena of Political Conflict,* Zed Books, London

Sachs, W. (1999) 'Sustainable development and the crisis of nature: On the political anatomy of an oxymoron', in F. Fischer and M. A. Hajer (eds) *Living with Nature,* Oxford University Press, Oxford, pp23–42

Sagoff, M. (1988) *The Economy of the Earth,* Cambridge University Press, Cambridge

Selman, P. and Parker, J. (1997) 'Citizenship, civicness and social capital in Local Agenda 21', *Local Environment,* vol 2, no 2, pp171–184

Silk, J. (1999) 'Guest editorial: The dynamics of community, place and identity', *Environment and Planning A,* vol 31, no 1, pp5–17

Slater, D. (1997) *Consumer Culture and Modernity,* Polity Press, Cambridge

Slavin, T. (2001) 'The poor are consumers too', *Guardian Weekly,* 5–11 April, p27

Smith, D. M. (1994) 'Neoclassical economies', in R. J. Johnston, D. Gregory and D. M. Smith (eds) *The Dictionary of Human Geography*, Blackwell, Oxford, pp410–415

Smith, R. J. (1996) 'Sustainability and the rationalisation of the environment', *Environmental Politics*, vol 5, no 1, pp25–47

Staats, H. J. and Herenius, S. G. A. (1995) *The EcoTeam Program in The Netherlands, Study 3: The Effects of Written Information about the EcoTeam Program on the Attitude and Intention Towards Participation*, Centre for Energy and Environmental Research, Leiden University, the Netherlands

Staats, H. J., Wit, A. P. and Midden, C. Y. H. (1996) 'Communicating the greenhouse effect to the public: Evaluation of a mass media campaign from a social dilemma perspective', *Journal of Environmental Management*, vol 46, no 2, pp189–203

Stoll-Kleemann, S., O'Riordan, T. and Jaeger, C. C. (2001) 'The psychology of denial concerning climate change mitigation measures: Evidence from Swiss focus groups', *Global Environmental Change*, vol 11, no 2, pp107–117

Tanner, C. (1999) 'Constraints on environmental behaviour', *Journal of Environmental Psychology*, vol 19, no 2, pp145–157

Tickell, C. (1977) *Climatic Change and World Affairs*, Harvard Center for International Affairs, Cambridge, MA

UK Sustainable Development Education Panel (1999) *First Annual Report 1998*, Department of the Environment, Transport and the Regions, London

UNCED (United Nations Conference on Environment and Development) (1992) *Agenda 21 and the UNCED Proceedings*, Oceana Publications, Dobbs Ferry, NY

United Nations Department of Economic and Social Affairs (1998) *Workshop on Indicators for Changing Consumption and Production Patterns*, United Nations Headquarters, New York, 2–3 March 1998

United Nations Economic and Social Council (1999) *Comprehensive Review of Changing Consumption and Production Patterns*, Report of the Secretary-General, New York

Walsh, K. (1994) 'Citizens, charters and contracts', in R. Keat et al (eds) *The Authority of the Consumer*, Routledge, London, pp189–206

Waste Watch UK (1999) 'Information pages', www.wastewatch.org.uk

WCED (World Commission on Environment and Development) (1987) *Our Common Future (The Brundtland Report)*, Oxford University Press, Oxford

Welford, R. J. (1998) 'Corporate environmental management, technology and sustainable development: Postmodern perspectives and the need for a critical research agenda', *Business Strategy and the Environment*, vol 7, pp1–12

Williams, P., Hubbard, P., Clark, D. and Berkeley, N. (2001) 'Consumption, exclusion and emotion: The social geographies of shopping', *Social and Cultural Geography*, vol 2, no 2, pp203–220

22

Ethics of Consumption

Laurie Michaelis

Introduction

In the late 1990s, increasing efforts were made to resolve the many debates that surround the ethics of consumption (e.g. Crocker and Linden, 1998; Westra and Werhane, 1998). There remains a wide range of views on the rights and wrongs of modern consumption patterns and the best approaches to changing them. But if sustainable consumption is to be practically feasible, ways must be found to draw together some of the diverse perspectives and to translate concern into action.

This chapter considers, in the next section, the forces contributing to an increasing diversity of consumption in affluent societies. It explores the European cultural roots of the consumer society. It also explores some of the ethical tensions that shape current debates and may contribute to future social change.

In the following section, the chapter considers possible resources in traditions from around the world for an ethic of sustainable consumption. It notes how ideals of the good life and of the relationship between humanity and nature derive from different worldviews. It also briefly considers the role of social trends currently emerging.

The final section suggests a way forward, involving a variety of communities at different scales in developing their own ethics for sustainable consumption.

The Consumer Society

The modern consumer society represents a radical break from the past. The association of material consumption with the greater good contradicts the teachings of religions and philosophers over the last 3000 years. Yet, consumerism seems to have an irresistible attraction. This section begins by reviewing the forces behind the escalation of consumption. It then discusses the cultural foundations of consumerism, and of modern cosmopolitan society more generally, in the European Enlightenment and the Romantic movement. It goes on to explore some of the tensions that continue to threaten the stability of this new society.

Forces for the growth of consumption

Many mechanisms and forces contribute to the escalation of the consumption levels required to flourish in cosmopolitan society. Just five are considered here.

First, there seems to be an intrinsic human tendency towards the escalation of desire, through habituation to increasingly high-quality food, clothes and levels of comfort. Although we can also accustom ourselves to lower levels of quality and comfort, this seems to require considerable effort and strong motivation. This ratchet effect has been noted in numerous different cultures. References to the tendency can be found in the Bible, Taoist, Buddhist and Vedic writings, as well as in modern psychology.

Second, recent acceleration of the growth of consumption may be related to specific technological and institutional developments, in particular television and the car. Both of these technologies have contributed to the decline of local communities, potentially making conspicuous consumption more important as a means of indicating social status.

Third, the use of material consumption to meet social needs, especially for status display, leads to a competition to consume which has been extensively described by Veblen (1899), Hirsch (1976) and Schor (1998), among others. In a culture where income is an indicator of status, there is an incentive to earn and consume more to maintain and improve that status. While Inglehart (1990) finds from values surveys that this motive is fading in wealthy societies, our income relative to our peers does remain an important contributor to our self-reported happiness (Argyle, 1987). The spread of television amplifies this mechanism by leading people to compare themselves with celebrities and TV characters rather than their neighbours (Schor, 1998).

Fourth, within the competitive market system, there is continual pressure to increase and diversify the production of goods, to reduce their costs, and to increase the productivity of labour and increase wages. Hence, per capita income has risen tenfold since 1800, and labour productivity has increased twentyfold, while there is an increasing range of goods and services that can be purchased with the income. The new consumer credit industry has stimulated consumption through loan marketing, which has reduced the social stigma of debt in the last three to four decades.

Fifth, there is a general expectation that the material quality of life should improve continually. Citizens of modern countries are encouraged by politicians and the media to expect to have more disposable income and a better physical quality of life each year than the year before.

Cultural roots of mass consumerism

Human beings, like all animals, have to consume food to stay alive. We have always been consumers. There is also a long history of the use of material artefacts as a medium for displaying our identity and status to each other. Nor is there anything new in superfluous consumption by the wealthy. The court burials in the ancient Egyptian pyramids bear witness to this; so does the Romans' custom of using emetics to induce vomiting during banquets to be able to continue eating. Nevertheless, the consumerism of modern society represents a new cultural form: a tradition that brings together a set of values, practices, and understandings of the good life. It has several important characteristics which have been described and criticized in various ways (e.g. Galbraith, 1958; Fromm, 1976; Hirsch, 1976).

- Human well-being is largely equated with increasing material consumption, which is emphasized as a dominant goal in the consumer society. More consumption is generally taken to be a good in itself, and consumerist societies are committed to continually increasing consumption levels at a personal and at an aggregate level.
- Material consumption is a major route to belonging to a community and achieving status within that community.
- The culture is essentially competitive rather than cooperative – members of the community strive to be materially better off than others.
- The culture emphasizes individual rights (and just deserts) more than responsibilities to others.
- Individual freedom to own property and to consume is taken to be a fundamental right of all human beings: the only legitimate argument for limiting anyone's consumption is that it causes direct harm to somebody else.
- The natural world is viewed as a source of commodities which provide the basis for consumption, and is not valued in itself.

Although critics of modern society often talk as if the values of consumerism were almost universally shared, they are not. Modern societies also include large sub-cultures that adhere to more traditional community or religious value-systems with their own views on the good life. There are also sub-cultures that have rejected consumerism and are seeking to develop new principles to live by.

Consumerism, among other traditions, has evolved from the values, ethics and worldviews that developed in Europe during the early Enlightenment in the 16th to 17th century, and the Romantic movement in the 18th to 19th century (Taylor, 1989; Corrigan, 1997). Early Enlightenment thinkers were committed to progress, human rights, liberty, equality, the rational individual, and a utilitarian or instrumental view of nature. They adopted the Puritan idea that everyday life was valuable in itself – God was to be honoured through work as much as through prayer. The Industrial Revolution and the resulting increase in productivity could not have occurred without this way of thinking. The Enlightenment drew on the work of scientists such as Galileo and Newton, and philosophers such as Descartes, Locke and Hobbes. It is the foundation of the popular modern understanding of the individual (Taylor, 1989) and of modern economic and political institutions.

The Romantics brought an emphasis on aesthetic appreciation, emotional individualism, personal creativity and self-expression. The original movement was largely a reaction against the rational, instrumental worldview of early Enlightenment thinkers. While the instrumental worldview made modern production patterns possible, it is arguably the Romantic idea of an emotional, interior, expressive human being that is the cultural driver of consumption (Campbell, 1983). Consumption of goods becomes an important form of aesthetic appreciation and a means of self-expression. Perhaps more importantly, emotions, desires and wants are given a new validity. The Romantic movement made it respectable or even noble to succumb to both desire for, and enjoyment of, material goods. Consumerism, then, is partly a result of a somewhat uneasy marriage between Enlightenment science and the Romantic view of the individual.

To some extent, the two worldviews are represented in our society by different people, or at least by different roles. However, both are present to some extent, and are a source of internal conflict, in most Western individuals. The rational, instrumental worldview is dominant in bureaucratic management, whether in industry or government, and in markets. The Romantic worldview is more important in our home and recreational lives, in the world of art, and in the marketing and advertising industries.

Ethical tensions

Like any functioning cultural tradition, Consumerism is subject to tensions caused by internal inconsistencies and its continual dialogue with other traditions. Some of these tensions arise within the Enlightenment tradition, or between the Enlightenment and Romantic traditions. Others arise because of the persistence of older traditions in the West and because of the emergence of new reactions to consumerism.

Post-Enlightenment philosophers have developed a variety of ethical systems based on rational arguments starting from principles that are intended to be universal. Three major sets of principles have emerged:

1   Bentham's concept of utilitarianism (the idea that right action is that which leads to the greatest pleasure and the least pain for humanity as a whole);
2   Kant's idea of duties being universal rules (right action is that based on principles that could be universally recommended); and
3   the theory of the social contract, and in particular its recent development by Rawls (right action is that which would be endorsed by a social contract of a type which anyone would be prepared to enter, regardless of their race, creed, gender or position in society).

While philosophers have debated which of the principles should be applied, in practice they often function in combination, along with older ethical principles (such as scriptural revelation). Utilitarianism is perhaps the most influential principle in formal policy thinking, as it forms the ethical basis for most practical welfare economics. The theory of the social contract is also highly influential. It is grounded in, and provides formal expression of, the egalitarianism and the belief in human rights that lies at the heart of modern civic affairs. Kant's concept of duty is used less in formal economics and politics, but it is perhaps the dominant basis for our everyday perceptions of fairness.

None of these principles is fully consistent with most people's intuition about what is right. All of them claim to be founded on reason, but require *a priori* assumptions that are not generally accepted. In addition, the theories of Bentham and Rawls are founded on the modern concept of the individual, which underplays the complex social nature of human beings. Ethical debates in Western society are frequently impossible to resolve.

The tension between modern Western ethics and traditions from other parts of the world and other times may motivate future cultural changes. Indeed, some of those other traditions may contain important cultural resources for sustainable development. The tensions within modern culture will also help to determine its future. In some cases they may help to maintain equilibrium. In others, they may be the source of innovation or the cause of collapse.

The following sections will review some of the major sources of ethical tension in modern Western society, as well as those between the modern tradition and older value systems that persist in Europe and elsewhere.

Liberty v. equality

Without individual rights to liberty, property and the pursuit of happiness, capitalism would not function. It is a system that relies on individual self-interest to fuel innovation and drive the economy. One of the most fundamental commitments of the Enlightenment is that individuals should have these rights in equal measure. Yet the ideals of equality and liberty are in constant tension. In the 20th century the tension was highly visible – between East and West, political right and political left.

Recent political rhetoric in the West gives the impression that liberty has won out over equality. But the tension is now between those within the mainstream Western culture, and those who feel excluded from it. With continuing growth in the differences in wealth, income and material consumption, both between North and South, and within some industrial countries, the poor appear to have a diminishing voice in the international community. They are perceived increasingly by the rich as a force from outside society that must somehow be kept under control, through immigration controls and measures to remove beggars from the streets.

Thomas Hobbes argued that individuals are inherently selfish, and equal rights can only be achieved through the 'social contract' – constraints on liberty enforced by government. But liberty and equality can also be reconciled through fraternity, or solidarity. It may well be possible for people with a strong community orientation to find a balance between liberty and equality. Certainly the early success of capitalism seems to have been built on a more social model of the individual. The most successful early capitalists were devout Christians who were trusted by their clients and customers because they were known to follow an unselfish moral code. However, an increasing adherence to Hobbes' view may be one of the more self-destructive features of modern liberal democracies.

Individual v. community

The tension between the good of the individual and that of the community has also been a central theme in the political debates of the last two centuries. Bentham (1789) asserted that society is no more than the sum of the individuals that constitute it, a view more recently espoused by Margaret Thatcher. Others, most notably Marx, viewed society as an entity in itself and the individual as a product of, and role-player in, society.

Collectivist views are apparent in Plato's *Republic* and More's *Utopia*. On the whole, the pictures painted by these authors of ideal societies are unpalatable to modern Westerners, as they seem to involve strong bounds on individual liberty. Collectivist states were given a particularly bad name in the 20th century by Nazi Germany and the so-called Marxist regimes in the former Soviet Union, China and North Korea. Much of the modern commitment to individual liberty is a reaction against the experience of such regimes.

Political debate continues on the extent to which we should emphasize the liberty of the individual vis-à-vis the collective. But many, like Marx, have argued that individual freedom is at least partly illusory and that individual thought and action often derives from the collective (Commons, 1950; Dennett, 1993). If this is true, there is a need for better understanding of the mechanisms that shape our supposedly free choices and to explore ways of making collective choice more transparent.

Just deserts: rights v. needs

Weber credited the 'Protestant work ethic' as one of the main drivers of the Industrial Revolution and of capitalism on the European continent. Work was a duty for the glory of God and the good of the community. Taylor also notes the strength of this ethic in North America. But the work ethic has given way in Anglo-Saxon countries to an ethic of just deserts, which says that we have an obligation to work if we wish to live well, and that we have the right to enjoy what we have earned. According to this view, those without the means to support themselves cannot have worked hard enough.

For a time, from about 1950 to 1980, it appeared in Organisation for Economic Co-operation and Development (OECD) countries that liberty could be reconciled with meeting human needs through the Welfare State, where the government redistributed the wealth created through the liberal market to ensure that the needs of the poor were met. However, in the Anglo-Saxon world at least, taxation is increasingly seen as an infringement of the rights of the hard-working.

The rich do not generally see other people's needs as a reason to forgo their own rights, unless those needs are highly visible and urgent. Industrialized country citizens are prepared to contribute in response to TV pictures of starving and homeless people. However, bilateral aid for capacity-building is declining. While the rich might agree in theory that economic convergence is desirable, they do not see it as their obligation to facilitate that convergence. On the one hand, developing country economies might present some real or imagined competition to workers in the industrialized countries. On the other, there is a view that concessions do not work, and the poor must simply learn to help themselves and to compete in the real world of the market.

Humanity v. nature

The modern separation of most people from nature began with the land reforms that occurred throughout Europe during the 16th to 19th centuries. Increases in agricultural productivity (resulting in declining labour requirements) and rising wages in factories led many former peasants to seek work in manufacturing. Industrialization then led to the creation of a human world that is substantially separated from nature. Other profound changes have come from the development of electric light, food transport and storage technologies, and more recently central heating, air-conditioning and the car, which allow us to ignore the cycles of day and night, the weather and the seasons.

John Locke expounded a view, based on an interpretation of biblical sources, that nature exists essentially as a resource for humanity and should be developed (Locke, 1698); that there was more land on the Earth than the human population could wish to develop. There are two key issues here: one is the type of relationship people should have with nature; the other is the extent to which nature can accommodate human exploitation.

A counterpoint to Locke's instrumentalist view of nature came from the Romantic movement, which coincided with the Industrial Revolution in England and America.

Romantic artists and writers placed considerable emphasis on the appreciation of nature, rejecting the 'dark satanic mills' of the industrial world and creating a 'rural idyll', sentimentalizing rural life.

Romantic ideals continue to play a strong role in the modern environmental movement, in particular in its appeals to protect wildlife. This 200-year-old history of opposition between the business community and environmentalists probably continues to shape the current debate. The last decade has seen dramatic breakthroughs in mutual understanding as the protagonists in the debate have stopped arguing about principles. However, a fundamental disagreement remains and may become important again in the future. Does nature exist to give sustenance to humanity, or does humanity exist to act as steward to nature?

The Romantics were not the only critics of the Enlightenment ideal of progress. Thomas Malthus in 1798 believed that the human population, in England at least, had already expanded to the maximum level that the land could accommodate. Any improvements in land productivity would simply result in population growth, maintaining the level of poverty but increasing the level of crowding.

Malthus has not (so far) been vindicated, as agricultural productivity has outpaced population growth over the last two centuries, and most countries appear to be on the path to stable or falling birth rates. The predominant modern view is that the Earth's surface may be finite but human ingenuity is not. Technological and institutional innovation will continue to enable us to get more from less. Our experience suggests that we will continue to find ways of making agriculture and industry less wasteful of land and resources, and less polluting.

While it is true that technological progress has led to a cleaning up of industry, our economies still rely on growing extraction of fuel, water and materials from the environment. According to mainstream economic wisdom, we should not be concerned about this. If resources become scarce, their prices will rise, bringing demand under control and encouraging innovation to find more resource-efficient ways of living. However, scientists and some economists are concerned that the market mechanism does not take adequate account of the risk of irreversible damage to the environment; nor can it take account of potential catastrophes of a type that we have never experienced before and do not fully understand.

Ethical Resources for Sustainable Consumption

This section explores the resources that can be found in existing traditions from around the world, and considers how they might contribute either local or global ethics for sustainable consumption. It addresses three elements of the traditions:

- the way they explain our relationship with nature, and the implications for the way we should treat it;
- how they view the good life, and the implications for the attitude we should have to wealth and consumption; and

- how they view our relationships with each other, the basis for justice, and the implications for equity.

Table 22.1 provides an overview of the basic ethical principles of a number of traditions and the worldviews that underlie them. For reasons of space, it is not possible here to review all of the world's major traditions. The table includes three traditions that are current in modern Western society: the dominant Enlightenment tradition; the Romantic tradition, which has a symbiotic relationship with the Enlightenment tradition; and the Christian tradition (note that this has several different branches). Two other traditions, Hinduism and Buddhism, are included to provide a contrast with these European cultures.

Our relationship with nature

An ethic of sustainable consumption must address our link to nature, the impacts of our consumption choices on it, and the need and responsibility to nurture our environment.

Attitudes to nature in different cultures are shaped by beliefs about the nature and origin of the universe and of human beings, and by conceptions of God or the transcendent. The Western instrumental view of nature is often contrasted with perspectives from the East, from Africa, and from native Americans and Australians, among whom there seems to be a greater tendency to value nature more for itself. However, pre-Enlightenment Europe maintained many beliefs and practices that bore similarities to those of other regions. The modern disregard for the environment seems to stem mainly from shifts in worldview that began in about the 16th century.

Most agricultural societies, including those in Europe, have ancient traditions that emphasize the unity of human life with the rest of nature. Their creation myths often involve food plants having grown from the dismembered parts of the body of a primordial man (Campbell, 1959). The symbolism of the Green Man, disgorging vegetation from his mouth and sometimes other orifices, remains common both in the carvings on European churches and in similar iconography in other parts of the world. Much of the annual cycle of rituals of both Judaism and Christianity is bound up with nature.

The major traditions and religions – Buddhism, Christianity, Confucianism, Hinduism, Islam and Taoism – were developed in societies where cities were the centres of power. It is therefore unsurprising that the human link to nature is weaker than that in many of the more localized animist traditions.

The Judaeo-Christian view is somewhat ambiguous about the human relationship with nature, partly because of the different versions in *Genesis* of the creation story. In Chapter 1, God creates humanity to rule over nature and to make use of it. In Chapter 2, He makes a man to care for the Garden of Eden. In both cases, humanity is placed between God and nature, to carry out God's purpose for the world.

In Judaism, Christianity and Islam, the relationship with God is at least in some ways contractual. If we are good we will go to heaven; if we are bad we will be sent to hell. The model for the contract is God's covenant with Abraham and the Law (the *Torah*) given to Moses. Ethics are based, to a large extent, on interpretation of the scriptures and the duties they impose on us. These duties do include obligations to care for

Table 22.1 *Illustrative comparison of some major traditions and their ethics*

	Enlightenment science and economics	Romanticism	Christianity	Hinduism	Buddhism
Human origin	Darwinian evolution	Emergence from nature	Divine creation in image of God	Evolution out of primordial substance	Chain of causation; starts with ignorance
Human nature	Separate pleasure-seeking individuals. Rational mind + emotional body	Emotional individual, social, expressive, complex. Manifestation of archetypes (Jungian)	Individuals with immortal soul and mortal body	Multiple functions: thought, emotion, volition	Illusions of thought, knowing, emotion, volition, form
Nature of the world	Material, inanimate, infinite, non-anthropocentric	Organized around principles such as love, beauty, anthropocentric	Material, created by God	Material, created by God	Illusory
Ethical principles	Liberty, equality, maximizing happiness, rights and duties	Follow the voice within: return to nature as source; rights and needs of the individual	Development of the virtues (e.g. faith, hope, charity). Duty based on scripture	Duties and virtues	Duties and virtues; compassion
Relationship to nature	Use	Individual as part of nature	Dominion, stewardship, subduing	Common ground of being (Atman–Brahman)	Common illusory nature
The good life	Individually determined: the pursuit of happiness	Harmony with nature; following inner leadings	Obedience to God, development of virtue	Right action, knowledge of true nature, spiritual devotion	12-fold path to release from the illusion of ego and material existence. Right action, right knowledge, right concentration
Attitude to consumption and wealth	Support consumption in pursuit of happiness	Support consumption for aesthetic appreciation and expression	Wealth is a source of temptation and should be shared. Frugality is encouraged	*Upanishads* advocate non-attachment and sometimes asceticism	Non-attachment to possessions but asceticism also rejected
Societal goal	Progress	Harmony with nature	Universal practice of the true religion: God's kingdom; peace	Freedom from material existence	Universal release from suffering

nature, but this care is aimed more at increasing the usefulness of nature to humanity that at preserving its integrity.

In contrast, the *Vedas* and *Upanishads*, on which much Hindu philosophy is based and which are part of the cultural background of Buddhism, view humanity and the universe as manifestations of the same essence. Underlying the individual self is a universal Self or Atman, which is the same as Brahman, the universal ground of being. Spiritual practice leads to experience of this truth, with profound implications for the way we choose to treat other people and the world around us. Our relationship is one of a common identity and solidarity rather than a contract. Because of this, the principle of non-violence to all sentient life is a central theme in Hinduism, while compassion is central to Buddhism. Vegetarianism is widespread in both Hindu and Buddhist communities.

On the other hand, while Hinduism celebrates the joys of material existence, Buddhism views both the ego and the material world as illusory and the source of suffering. In both traditions, the highest goal of human life is to achieve release from the suffering of material existence. Hence, although there is a strong ethic of non-violence to avoid causing suffering to other sentient life, there is not necessarily any strong reason for positively caring for nature.

The philosophy of the *Upanishads* has parallels in Europe. Plato's philosophy, which found its way into Christianity through St Augustine, sees humanity and nature as expressions of the same 'Ideas' or essences. The medieval systems of Kabbalah, astrology and alchemy, as well as much popular belief, were founded on similar ideas and assumed a strong underlying connection between the individual and the universe. This view of the world was weakened with the translation of the Bible into the vernacular in the 15th century, and with the emergence of Protestantism. But it did not really decline until the industrial revolution led to the separation of most of the European population from the land.

There have been several efforts over the last 200 years to recreate the pre-industrial connection to the land, often linked to the aim of reviving the pre-urban sense of community. In recent years, there has been some revival in Europe of pre-Christian traditions that view humanity as part of nature and that equated nature with the divine, in the person of The Goddess (Campbell, 1959). The modern sciences of evolution and ecology also point us back towards a view of humanity as part of nature, as sharing a common identity. The 'bioregionalism' movement aims to bring people closer to the land and to encourage a more sustainable lifestyle based on consuming only local products, within the carrying capacity of the local ecosystem.

In conclusion, then, there does seem to be a widespread basis in many parts of the world for an ethical system that values nature in itself, but such traditions have not been able to compete effectively with modern culture. Progress in the continuing debate over the attitude we should have to nature depends on developing a better understanding of our various assumptions about the purposes of humanity and nature. We will return to the question of the purpose of humanity in the next section, which discusses conceptions of the good life.

The good life

The second section noted that human needs are context dependent. In particular, within a given culture, the capabilities an individual must possess in order to flourish depend on that culture's conception of the good life.

Modern Western society is unusual in its view on the good life. First, there is a commitment to making it attainable for all citizens. Conceptions of the good life in most other societies are only attainable for the minority who are able to step out of the normal life of working and maintaining a household. Second, modern society is reluctant to impose any one vision of the good life on its citizens. Rather, there is a commitment to the right of individuals to the freedom to pursue their own vision of happiness.

While this chapter is unlikely to achieve much by recommending any particular form of the Good, there is a great deal that can be learned from experience. First, we can draw on the various traditional views (while bearing in mind that these versions of the good life were intended for a minority). Second, there is a growing body of literature in the social sciences on the factors that make people happy. There are also numerous communities experimenting with alternative ways of living.

Traditional views on the good life

Often, the good life is defined as that which brings happiness, or that which satisfies. Plato and Aristotle, for example, saw happiness as the ultimate good. In the monotheistic religions, the good life is that which God would have us live.

While the good life is often intended to be a joyful one, the joy is supposed to be connected with being closer to God, rather than material well-being. In Christianity, Islam and Judaism, reward and punishment by God are important themes and are often portrayed as the primary motivation for living well.

In Hinduism and Buddhism the good life is portrayed more as a path that should be followed to achieve Moksa or Nirvana – release from the cycle of rebirth, or from the illusion of material existence.

Outside the consumer society there is widespread recognition that wealth does not in itself lead to happiness. In many cultures, wealth has been seen as a result of virtue or divine favour which is both part of, and a sign of, living the good life. Islam and Judaism view wealth in a positive light provided it is earned[1] and shared with the poor – although the book of Job represents an early questioning in Judaism of the link between wealth and virtue.

The pitfalls of wealth and acquisitiveness were widely recognized in the surge of philosophical and religious development during the five centuries from 800BC. At the beginning of this period, the Indian *Upanishads* proposed new ideals of austerity and non-attachment, which remain central values in Jainism and were strongly espoused by Mahatma Gandhi. Although non-attachment is usually portrayed as an Eastern value, it is also important in Greek philosophy and in Christianity. Hindu, Greek and Christian ascetics adopted extremes of self-denial and self-castigation.

Buddha (about 500BC) rejected both the extremities of over-consumption and asceticism as forms of striving and attachment, which lead to pain and suffering. Taoists also noted the addictive nature of wealth and advised moderation in consumption habits.

Many moral systems expound the virtues that form part of a good life and the vices that detract from it. The Hindu *Bhagavad Gita* lists the attributes of those of divine nature, which include fearlessness, purity of mind, charity, self-control, modesty, sacrifice and austerity; those of demonic nature are arrogant, conceited, give themselves up to insatiable desire, and strive to amass hoards of wealth. Taoist and Confucian writings are similarly concerned with virtues.

Plato's view of the good life was one that is ordered by the Idea of the Good. For him, the ultimate happiness was to be found in rational contemplation of the Good. The good life was open only to those able to engage in philosophical enquiry. His version of a utopia, described in *The Republic*, is a hierarchical society without private property, ruled by a corps of 'guardians', who are essentially philosophers and live the good life.

Aristotle's view of the good life has already been mentioned in the previous section. It involves the possession and exercise of a range of virtues, such as courage, moderation, justice, generosity, hospitality, truthfulness, perceptiveness, knowledge and practical wisdom. It also requires basic preconditions in the form of material well-being and stable family relationships. Aristotle, like Plato, saw the good life as something that could be achieved only by a minority – not, for example, by traders and artisans.

MacIntyre (1985) notes the link between the conception of the good life and the virtues required to achieve it. Plato's and Aristotle's ideas were adapted to Christianity by Augustine and Thomas Aquinas, respectively. For Augustine, the Good is God, and the good life is one of contemplation of God. The virtues required to live that life are faith, hope and love. Thomas Aquinas similarly defines the greatest good in life as the contemplation of God and argues that happiness does not lie in worldly pleasures, wealth, glory, or even in the exercise of the virtues. For both Augustine and Thomas Aquinas, the Good is to be achieved through life in the cloister: it is not available to the majority of the population.

The Reformation of the church in Europe, which forms the backdrop to the Enlightenment, was partly a reaction to the perceived elitism of the monastic system. With the invention of printing and the translation of the Bible, it became possible to imagine every citizen having a direct relationship with God in the 'priesthood of all believers'. A new conception of the good life arose. Instead of finding God in the silence of a monastery cell, He was to be found in everyday life and work.

The good life in modern society

In modern society, different traditions and hence rationales for the good life coexist. Many philosophers defend the individual's freedom to determine his or her own conception of the good (e.g. Nussbaum, 1993). Bentham (1825) argued that the societal Good is determined by whatever makes people happy. However, there are a number of drawbacks to this. The market economy contains structural incentives for businesses to market conceptions of the good life that support sales of their own products. Many other circumstances, including social norms, work culture and infrastructure constraints, provide strong pressures for individuals to adopt particular conceptions of the good life. Hence, by adopting a hands-off approach, governments may actually be failing to protect an important freedom. On the other hand, the freedom to choose a conception of the good may be unattainable in any case, to the extent that individual's wills are reflections of their social milieu.

For many people, having all of their needs met and having a full range of Nussbaum's 'capabilities', including the freedom (perhaps illusory) to choose their own goals, can be debilitating. Viktor Frankl (1984) describes how having a meaning, a purpose beyond ourselves, can bring happiness even in a life that is full of pain and suffering. He observes that the lack of meaning is a major cause of psychological problems in modern Western society.

MacIntyre (1985) has lamented the state of ethics in modern society, in particular the interminable debates over the ramifications of different ethical principles. He traces the problem to our reluctance to agree on a vision of the good life, and the decline in the cultivation of the virtues as means of achieving that vision. He argues that we need to revive the ideal of the good life in order to have a clear idea of how we should behave. If we knew how we wanted to live, it would be relatively straightforward to identify the virtues that we should cultivate in order to achieve that state. MacIntyre's thesis suggests that, if we wish to develop an ethic for sustainable consumption, we must first of all clarify our vision of the sustainable life: we need a compass to steer by.

The work of another contemporary philosopher, Charles Taylor (1989), suggests that Western society has not lost its ethical way but has created a new system of ethics. This system is motivated by:

- a defence of the 'ordinary life', and a suspicion of the 'higher goods' that have often been advocated by elites or by paternalistic or despotic rulers;
- strong principles of individual freedom;
- a general benevolence deriving from Christianity; and
- a desire for a universal basis for ethics.

Members of our society do not want to be told how to live, even for their own good. They are far more interested in entering into a dialogue through which they can work out their choices for themselves (Hobson, 2000). Such a dialogue needs to be informed by robust information on what works and what does not, and why. The work of Argyle, Inglehart and others (mentioned in the previous section) seems to confirm the message from the various traditions, that material consumption does not make us happy, and that we should devote more of our time to developing healthy family and community relationships. However, there is a difference between knowing what is good and being motivated to achieve it. Motivation appears to result as much from belonging to a community of people who share our conception of the good as it does from our own knowledge of the good.

Our relationship with other people: Justice and equity

Cultural traditions have widely differing views on the basis for, and nature of, social solidarity – that is, our relationships with others. Different societies have adopted particular forms of solidarity partly to fit with their demographic, economic and technological circumstances, but also emerging from their cultural traditions.

This section addresses two aspects of ethics that are important for sustainable development and relate to human relationships. The first is the principle of egalitarianism, which is central to Enlightenment thought and is reflected in much of the advocacy for sustainable development. The second is the question of supporting others, which must be addressed given that we start from a position of inequality.

Egalitarianism

Many cultural traditions assume some hierarchy of relationships. As described in the last section, there is often an elite group that is at the core of the tradition, eligible to participate in the good life. Others in society may fill a subservient role. This is the case in Plato's *Republic*, where the philosopher-guardians form the elite. In Hindu society the elite are the Brahmins. In Augustinian Christianity the elite was the priesthood and the fellowship of monks.

However, hierarchical relationships are not universal. Some Buddhist and Islamic cultures are egalitarian, and in India their ranks have been swelled by the conversion of lower-caste Hindus. In Buddhism the basis for equality is the Buddha-nature that exists in everyone, analogous to Luther's 'priesthood of all believers'.

It was also mentioned in the last section that the modern Western rejection of traditional concepts of the good life is closely linked to a rejection of elitist social structures. Taylor (1989) explains this rejection as emerging from the Reformation and the return to the Judaeo-Christian scriptures, which provide a more egalitarian basis for social solidarity. The Israelites were supposed to be a 'nation of priests'. There were many distinctions within that nation – in particular between men and women and between members of the tribe of Levy and others. However, the Law and the implied vision of the good were intended for all Israelites, and justice was even-handed between them. The important distinction was between Israelites, who had a covenant with God, and non-Israelites, who did not.

Early Protestant groups drew parallels between themselves and the Israelites, viewing themselves as a small group of the enlightened, surrounded by hostile papists. They were determinedly egalitarian in their treatment of each other, often describing themselves as 'brethren'.

Although modern society retains a commitment to egalitarianism, this often seems to conflict with other values. Part of the difficulty lies in the modern commitment to competitive individualism (deriving from the thought of Hobbes, Smith, Bentham, and others) and the rejection of communism as discussed in the following section. However, there may be more fundamental blocks to social solidarity in modern urban society, as it is very difficult for people to feel like 'brethren' in a community of several million.

Supporting others

Practically all cultural traditions include some encouragement for the rich to share with the poor. Some of the earliest records of such an ethic come from ancient Egypt, from advice apparently written for the education of the sons of the nobility. In the *The Instruction of Ptah-Hotep* (c. 2200BC) there are numerous injunctions for those who have bread to share it with those who do not, for 'the gift of affection is worth more than the provisions with which your back is covered'. Similarly the *Rig Veda* states that 'He is the liberal man who helps the beggar ... and ... immediately makes him a friend thereafter.'

Later philosophical and religious scriptures introduce additional reasons for generosity. In the *Torah* generosity to strangers is frequently encouraged 'for you were strangers in Egypt' – that is, apparently for reasons of empathy.

The concept of the reward in heaven (or a more pleasant future incarnation) for a righteous life brought new arguments for generosity. The *Koran* states that the 'truly righteous are those who believe in Allah ... and spend their wealth, for love of Him, on the kindred and the orphans and the needy and the wayfarer and those who ask, and for procuring the freedom of captives'. In Christianity, the message is even stronger: 'If thou wilt be perfect, go and sell that thou hast, and give to the poor, and thou shalt have treasure in heaven' (Matthew, 19:21).

Indian philosophy provides a rather different reason for sharing with the poor: that of a shared identity. The belief in reincarnation also provides a strong argument for kindness to other sentient beings – practised in an extreme form in Jainism.

There is clearly no shortage of reasons for sharing what we have. Giving money away can help to make friends, can be a source of satisfaction and can be of spiritual benefit to us (Argyle, 1998). However, it was noted above that generosity seems to have declined in the midst of a conflict of core values in modern society – in particular the principles of 'just deserts' and 'human rights'. While we have sympathy with the rights of the poor we increasingly believe that people deserve what they get.

If it is difficult to foster egalitarianism within a modern city, it is even harder on a global scale. This is especially true given the modern materialist conception of the good life: there is a profound fear that there is not enough to go around. Yet, with global communication and the plummeting cost of travel, the inequities are increasingly obvious to both rich and poor. The current response by the rich is to strengthen immigration controls. One way of escaping from this tension would be for the citizens of the North to rethink their conception of the good life so that it is based on ideals such as community and education, which are not limited by finite physical resources.

After Modernism

While the uneasy marriage between Enlightenment rationality and Romantic emotionalism remains the dominant culture in modern society, its foundations have been seriously eroded in the last half-century. The tensions described in this section are partly responsible, but forces for change have also emerged from developments in science, technology and human institutions. They take several forms:

- The 1960s saw a recognition in the West of the pointlessness of the modern drive for growth and consumption.
- Space travel is often credited with having given us a new perspective on the Earth as a finite, fragile and lonely planet which we must nurture if we are to survive.
- There is a growing awareness of the multiplicity of valid points of view, religions and forms of human flourishing. The new pluralism derives partly from the high levels of migration, travel, trade and communication that make up 'globalization'.
- New scientific approaches are emerging to deal with the complexity and interconnectedness of the real world, leading to a decline in the mechanistic worldview of the Enlightenment.
- Growing understanding of human psychology and consciousness is leading us towards a relational view of human nature: we increasingly view individuals as shaped by, and helping to shape, their social milieu.

These and other developments carry the potential seeds of an ethic of sustainability. Ronald Inglehart (1990) finds evidence from numerous surveys of values in different countries that there is a growing 'post-material' culture that emphasizes developing relationships rather than owning things. But the emerging worldview also presents a risk. We have recognized the emptiness of modern culture but we have no universal truths to replace it with. The Enlightenment ideal of society as a machine managed by a democratically elected government is giving way as we find it increasingly difficult to locate responsibility and influence in our society. Postmodern literature and art can be quite nihilistic. Modern culture has sought to find absolute and universal truth through science; the recognition that all truth is relative, filtered through individual perception, can leave us feeling as if we have no reference points. And without external sources of meaning, we have no motivation towards the good, or even for our own survival (McIntyre, 1985; Frankl, 1984).

Individuals in this postmodern society are confronted, therefore, with the need to construct or choose their own sources of meaning, and their own personal traditions to live by. They can, of course, buy into a ready-made package, in the form of an older cultural or religious tradition, but this now has to be a choice rather than an accident of birth.

Conclusions

The ethics of modern consumer societies seem to be, in many ways, at odds with the aim of achieving sustainable consumption. Modern conceptions of individual liberty and rights, property and just deserts, make it hard to imagine our society adopting controls on the type or volume of material consumption. There also seems little immediate prospect for a reversal of the trend towards greater disparity in consumption levels.

Yet, many people are dissatisfied with the morality of the market-place. They know from folklore and experience that consuming more will not make them happier, and they are conscious of the lack of purpose in modern life. They continue with their current lifestyles because they feel that they have no choice: material consumption is an integral part of functioning in our society.

Because of the social importance of much of our consumption, a shift to more sustainable consumption is unlikely to be readily achievable on an individual basis. It is likely to require a cultural change to which many different parts of society will have to contribute. It may involve deciding collectively how the good life should look, and to modify our behaviour accordingly.

There are many candidates for a vision of the good life and a related ethic of sustainable consumption, deriving from cultural traditions around the world. Practically all traditions, apart from that of the modern West, recommend that material consumption should be moderated. However, the consumer society is partly a reaction against these traditions. Sustainable consumption is unlikely to be achieved through the imposition of earlier ethical systems.

A more promising path might be to encourage dialogue on ways in which individuals and communities can address their social needs without material consumption, and to foster the grass-roots development of more sustainable ideals of the good life. A growing number of groups are exploring their visions of the good life and their views on the ethical principles that would support such a life. There is a need to draw together, evaluate and disseminate the experiences of those who have already made a decision to pursue their own version of the good life.

Notes

1   Both the *Torah* and the *Koran* contain prohibitions against charging interest on loans.

References

Argyle, M. (1987) *The Psychology of Happiness*, Methuen, London
Argyle, M. (1998) *The Psychology of Money*, Routledge, London
Bentham, J. (1789) *An Introduction to the Principles of Morals and Legislation*, reproduced in part in A. Ryan (ed) (1987) *Utilitarianism and Other Essays*, Penguin, London
Bentham, J. (1825) *The Rationale of Reward*, reproduced in J. Bowring (ed) *The Works of Jeremy Bentham*, Russell and Russell, New York
Campbell, C. (1983) 'Romanticism and the consumer ethic: Intimations of a Weber-style thesis', *Sociological Analysis*, vol 44, no 4, pp279–296
Campbell, J. (1959) *The Masks of God: Primitive Mythology* Volume 1 of 4, Arkana, Penguin Group, New York
Commons, J. R. (1950, posthumous) *The Economics of Collective Action*, Macmillan, New York
Corrigan, P. (1997) *The Sociology of Consumption*, Sage Publications, London
Crocker, D. A. and Linden, T. (eds) (1998) *Ethics of Consumption*, Rowman and Littlefield, Lanham, MD and Oxford
Dennett, D. (1993) *Consciousness Explained*, Penguin, London
Frankl, V. (1984) new postscript to *Man's Search for Meaning* (first published 1946), Washington Square Books, New York
Fromm, E. (1976) *To Have or To Be*, Jonathan Cape, London
Galbraith, J. K. (1958) *The Affluent Society* (3rd edn, 1979), Penguin, Harmondsworth
Hirsch, F. (1976) *Social Limits to Growth*, Harvard University Press, Cambridge, MA
Hobson, K. (2000) 'Sustainable lifestyles: Rethinking barriers and behaviour change', in M. Cohen and J. Murphy (eds) *Exploring Sustainable Consumption: Environmental Policy and the Social Sciences*, Oxford Centre for the Environment, Ethics and Society, Oxford
Inglehart, R. (1990) *Culture Shift in Advanced Industrial Society*, Princeton University Press, Princeton, NJ
Inglehart, R. (2000): 'Globalization and postmodern values', *The Washington Quarterly*, Winter 2000, pp215–228
Locke, J. (1982, original 1698) *Second Treatise of Government*, Harland Davidson, Inc., Wheeler, IL
MacIntyre, A. (1985) *After Virtue*, 2nd edn, Duckworth, London
Nussbaum, M. C. (1993) 'Non-relative virtues: An Aristotelian approach', in M. C. Nussbaum and A. Sen (eds) *The Quality of Life*, Oxford University Press, Oxford, pp242–269
Schor, J. (1998) *The Overspent American*, Basic Books, New York

Taylor, C. (1989) *Sources of the Self: The Making of the Modern Identity*, Cambridge University Press, Cambridge

Veblen, T. (1899) *The Theory of the Leisure Class: An Economic Study of Institutions*, Macmillan, New York

Westra, L. and Werhane, P. H. (eds) (1998) *The Business of Consumption: Environmental Ethics and the Global Economy*, Rowman and Littlefield, Lanham, MD and Oxford

23

Making Ends Meet – in the Household and on the Planet

Karl Dake and Michael Thompson

Introduction

Our predicament in relation to nearly all research on consumption and sustainability is much like that of the Dubliner who, chided by an American visitor for being unable to give directions in what was after all his native city, replied, 'Ah yes, but I wouldn't have started from here.' 'Here' in our case, is the I-PAT equation; the common-sense proposition that environmental impact (I) is some multiplication of population (P), affluence (A) and technology (T) (Ehrlich and Holdren, 1974).

The unquestioned assumption in the I-PAT equation is that the more money there is coming into a household the more stuff it will consume. Consumption, in other words, is a function of *disposable income*. And technology by making it easier and cheaper for us to get more of all those things that we want, simply compounds the consumptive excesses that inevitably result from our increased affluence. And, since this is going on in each and every household, we can move to the aggregate – the macro level – simply by multiplying household consumption by the total number of households – that is, by *population* (or, to be precise, by population divided by average household size). This leads to two important and widely relied-upon principles for making the I-PAT equation operational. First, we can use *top-down* modelling;[1] second, we can handle the micro level by means of the concept of *per capita* (or per household) *consumption*. Our argument, however, is that the I-PAT equation is profoundly wrong, that top-down modelling is wholly inappropriate for consumption behaviour, and that per capita (or per-household) consumption is a statistically invalid and seriously misleading concept.

So where would we start? And where is our starting point in relation to that from which the conventional approaches have set off? And, more constructively, how might these conventional approaches be modified so that they can set off from either of these starting points, thereby uncovering the surprises that lie in wait for those who choose one when they should have the other? In other words, how do we introduce some *reflexivity* into the whole consumption and sustainability debate (reflexivity being simply the self-conscious examination of the assumptions that underlie any analytical approach)?

Into Every Policy Analyst's Life
a Little Reflexivity Should Fall

The classic idea in economics generally, and in the I-PAT equation in particular, is that people make ends meet by prioritizing their needs in relation to their command over resources. Of course, this assumes that people's needs are always running way ahead of what is coming in – if you could have everything you wanted you wouldn't have to prioritize – and this realization leads to what is called the *non-satiety requirement.*

The non-satiety requirement does not insist that we can never have enough of something; only that we can never have enough of things in the plural. A person may become pig-sick of smoked salmon but he or she, economists assert, will always prefer a larger bundle of goods to a smaller one.[2] The result is what is sometimes called the 'colander theory of consumption': no matter how fast you pour the water (the resources) in, there are always plenty more holes (needs) for it to run out of!

Much of our work, over the years, has been concerned with seeking out instances where this requirement does not hold, and these instances have now accumulated to the point where we can say that the non-satiety requirement fits only a fraction of what is actually going on. People as members of households can, and often do, prefer a smaller bundle of goods to a larger one. 'How much is enough?' is a question that people often *do* ask, and answer (a recent, and best-selling, example being Dominguez and Robin, 1992), even though those who cling to the non-satiety requirement insist that they do not.[3]

A moment's reflection (reflexivity is just a fancy word for being reflective) will confirm that you can set about the vital business of reconciling your needs and resources – making ends meet – in a number of ways. You can try to bring your needs down inside the resources you command (like the fox who decided he didn't want the grapes he couldn't get), you can try to expand your resources to meet the needs you have (like Britain's Lord Gowrie resigning as Minister for the Arts because he couldn't live in London on £30,000 a year), you can let each spur the other onward and upward (like the apocryphal entrepreneur struggling to reconcile his gross habits with his net income), you can try to manage each relative to the other so as to maintain a comfortable overlap (rather in the way that a classical education is reputed to enable you to enjoy life without all the things it prevents you from getting) and so on.

There are, in fact, five permutational possibilities (the fifth being a Micawber-like resignation in which you just hope that 'something will turn up') and some people find their way to one, others to another and so on. To explain why it is that each of these possibilities is 'inhabited', and what it is that leads some people to one, others to another and so on, we need Cultural Theory: the theory that gives us the five distinct ways of reconciling needs and resources.

A brief outline of Cultural Theory

The basic proposition in Cultural Theory is that individuality, far from being something (like our fingerprints) that is inherent to each of us, is something that, to a considerable extent, we get from our involvement with others.[4] Where economists are struck dumb

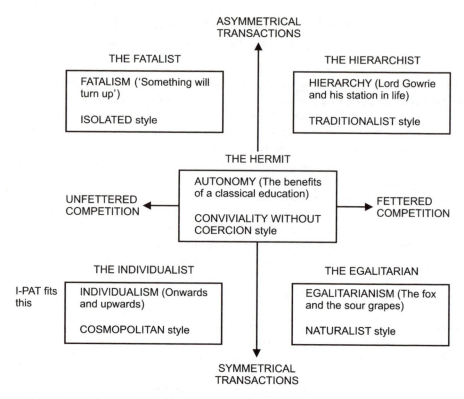

Figure 23.1 *Cultural Theory's five social beings, five forms of social solidarity and five consumption styles (ways of making ends meet)*

when asked 'Where do preferences come from?', the Cultural Theorist has a ready answer: people discover their preferences by establishing their social relations. Everything, therefore, comes down to the question of how many viable ways there are in which we can arrange our relationships (or find ourselves arranged into relationships or, more likely, a bit of both).

Cultural Theory's impossibility theorem states that there are five, and just five, ways. Two of these are the *markets* and *hierarchies* that have long been distinguished by social scientists, together with the observation that each induces in its constituent individuals (its *social beings*, as Durkheim has it) its distinctive rationality: the pursuit of the 'bottom line', for instance, by the individualistic characters who are committed to the market way of life, and the obsession with propriety (who has the right to do what and to whom) by those who uphold the hierarchy. Cultural Theory, by identifying the conditions that must be satisfied if these two familiar forms of *social solidarity* are to emerge and reproduce themselves, completes the typology, thereby introducing us to three less familiar solidarities (*egalitarianism, fatalism* and *autonomy*) each of which has its distinctive social being (the *egalitarian*, the *fatalist* and the *hermit*, respectively).

That each of these solidarities has implications for the consumption style of its constituent social beings becomes evident once we ask ourselves where the different ways of making ends meet fit, and do not fit, into this fivefold scheme (Figure 23.1):

- Distinguishing 'real' needs (those that Mother Nature can meet) from 'false' needs (those that, if we succumbed to them, would deprive future generations of the endowment we currently enjoy) goes with the *egalitarian* way of life.
- Lord Gowrie's fall from grace, and the sacrifice he must make if he is to regain his station in life, put him in the *hierarchical* solidarity.
- The entrepreneur's onward-and-upward struggle (which, alone among these five, is consistent with the non-satiety requirement, and with the I-PAT equation) reveals him as an upholder of the market way of life: the *individualistic* solidarity.
- The comfortable overlap between the inner resources that are opened up by a classical education and the somewhat limited needs that it gives rise to is something that only the hermit – the upholder of the *autonomous* solidarity – enjoys.
- Mr Micawber, with his fate entirely in the lap of the gods, has no active strategy for making ends meet (which each of the other four social beings, in his or her distinctive way, has). He is a *fatalist*: a member of a solidarity that coheres indirectly, through the actions of those – the egalitarians, the hierarchists, the individualists and the hermits – who are not themselves fatalists.

Different in a small number of ways

Let us now quickly run through these five consumption styles that, together, constitute our starting point:

- Back in the late 1960s, a reporter who visited the guitarist Eric ('Slow Hand') Clapton in his rural retreat was much impressed to find a discarded Afghan coat being used as a cover for the parrot's cage. It was the timing – Afghan coats being, that year, the very height of fashion – that proclaimed the style: the *cosmopolitan* style of the individualist, in which the world is his oyster and a thing of beauty a joy for a fortnight.
- *Dahlbaht* – a huge plateful of boiled rice with a few spoonfuls of watery lentils tipped over it – is something that the Western traveller in Nepal soon tires of. Yet, for the Nepalese, dahlbaht is like the roast beef of Old England.[5] A Nepalese friend, whose father happened to work in the royal stables, told us that the King and Queen of Nepal ate dahlbaht every day. Our friend found this piece of palace intelligence quietly satisfying: an indication that those at the very tip of the hierarchy were properly connected to those at the lower levels.

  Mushy peas in the North of England, cucumber sandwiches in the Home Counties, champagne at the wedding reception, syllabub[6] at the Reform Club, do much the same for their British consumers as does dahlbaht for the Nepalese. Hierarchists are *traditionalists*. They do not mess about with these dishes and drinks; they serve them as their parents and grandparents before them served them. They do not cut any corners; they do not get them out of packets, or pop them into microwaves, or serve them in those dishy glasses.
- Egalitarians are *naturalists,* so they would approve of dahlbaht, but not of its 'hallmarking' by the Nepalese royal family.[7] Mushy peas and cucumber sandwiches, similarly, are okay, but not if they come associated with badger-digging and the Male Breadwinner, on the one hand, and Henley Regattas and the Lady Bountiful

on the other. For egalitarians, consumption that upholds social differences, no matter how natural the ingredients may be, is artificial: as artificial as the chemicals that the multinationals put in their fizzy drinks and as unnatural as the conversion of rain forest to grassland to keep the world's fattest people in hamburgers. Champagne, too, is suspect because it is special. The individualist who quaffs it as a matter of course is guilty of excess, and the hierarchist who serves it when the occasion demands that it be served is similarly putting social expectations (pretensions, the egalitarian would say) before the over-riding human obligation: to stay within Mother Nature's fixed and finite limits.

- Fatalists have an *isolated* consumption style: a style that reflects their marginality vis-à-vis the richly patterned relationships enjoyed by the individualists, the hierarchists and the egalitarians. Fatalists will often claim to be traditionalists, and only careful observation will reveal that they are not, in fact, doing what their parents and grandparents did. Their conspicuous consumption, similarly, may look like that of the individualist. However, the items they consume so conspicuously (pints of lager, for instance) will tend to be undifferentiated (their labels, as it were, not being a vital part of the parade). And, even when the items *are* differentiated, the chances are they will no longer be at the height of their fashion (the dynamics of that process being determined largely by those who are not fatalists) (Thompson, 1979; Douglas, 1996). There will, as likely as not, be no occasion to rise to (as there usually is in the hierarchist's case), no potential followers to impress (as there usually are in the individualist's case) and no awareness of nature's limits (as there usually is in the egalitarian's case). The fatalist's blow-out, like the aesthete's art, is for its own sake, and, unlike the consumption activities of the individualist, the hierarchist and the egalitarian, does not support any preferred pattern of social relationships.
- *Conviviality* without coercion is the hermit style: a style that includes elements from all the others yet manages to distance itself from each of them. The hermit, unlike the fatalist, is not socially isolated, but he or she does have to be careful to avoid the sort of mutual expectations that come with the consumption styles of the individualist, the hierarchist and the egalitarian. Hermits embrace novelty but not emulation, and there is something timeless (rather than traditional) about the unchanging elements in their consumption. And, though they are certainly in favour of naturalness (the celebrated Tibetan hermit, Milarepa, ended up living on boiled nettles), they manage to avoid the sort of moral righteousness that comes so easily to the egalitarian. Hermits may be holy, but they're not holier than thou!

This fivefold scheme, though it may look like the most preposterous thing ever to come down the pike (especially to those who go along with the non-satiety requirement), has now been subjected to some rigorous empirical testing. A study of 220 British households has confirmed that these basic consumption units (some of which, of course, are comprised of just one individual) do indeed fall into these five styles, that each style is quite thick on the ground, and that these styles work their way through into markedly different 'purchasing preferences' (shopping baskets with systematically different contents). And, since manufacturers soon learn not to produce things that people do not want (or cannot be persuaded to want), these purchasing preferences quickly work their way through into markedly different physical flows within the economy (and the ecosystem) as a whole. And *changes* in these purchasing preferences quickly work their way through into *changes* in these physical flows.

A move away from red meat, for instance, or towards 'designer water', or to spending the weekend pottering in the garden instead of sitting in a traffic jam somewhere between that garden and the countryside, if taken up by a large proportion of households, soon translates into major changes in land-use patterns, refuse collection and recycling, oil consumption, car ownership and so on. But, and this is the whole point of not starting from where the I-PAT equation would have us start, there is seldom just one trend. Each style will be generating its own trend, usually (but not always) in a different direction to those that are being generated by the other styles and, to complicate these dynamics still further, there are always some households that (for discoverable reasons) are on the move from one consumption style to another.

However, it *is* possible to map these styles, at any particular moment, and to pinpoint the various items that are constituting those styles at that particular moment. And, if this mapping is repeated at regular intervals, then we can begin to see how the styles themselves are ebbing and flowing, and we can start to track the various changes in the repertoires of items that constitute those ebbing and flowing styles. Figure 23.2 provides an illustration of how this can be done, and it provides a graphic demonstration of all this rich patterning of consumption that is completely missed by the conventional per capita approach.

Those (like one of us) who are not skilled in the analysis and depiction of survey data will need some help in making sense of Figure 23.2. The five letters in the black boxes (I, F, H, E and A) mark the 'centres of gravity' of the households that were identified, by anthropological interview, as being individualist, fatalist, hierarchical, egalitarian and autonomous. The numbered dots that form the star-like arrangement are the households' responses to the questionnaire that was 'double-blinded' with the interviews. In other words, the interviewer (Michael Thompson) did not know how the households came out in the questionnaire, and the person who analysed the questionnaire results (Karl Dake) did not know how the households had come out in the interviews.[8] This star-like arrangement is produced by a computer program that is designed to secure, from the data it is fed, the maximum sense that can be displayed on just two dimensions.

The first thing to note is that the five 'centres of gravity' are well separated, with the four 'coercive' solidarities in fairly extreme and mutually polarized positions, and with the autonomous solidarity, as predicted, in the middle – carefully distanced from the other four.[9] Then, to read off the different consumption styles that accompany and support each of these solidarities, you should focus on those rays that lie roughly in the direction of the appropriate 'centre of gravity' *and* on those rays that lie in the diametrically opposed direction. For instance:

- *Individualists* are fashion conscious, like to look successful, prefer a tidy garden and don't join clubs (in the manner of Groucho Marx who wouldn't join any club that would have him as a member). They do not go in for vegetarianism, biodegradable products or informality, nor do they allot specific chores within the household or go out of their way to avoid fascist vegetables and the like – the products, as we coyly put it (we were doing this work for the Anglo-Dutch multinational, Unilever) of 'oppressive institutions'.

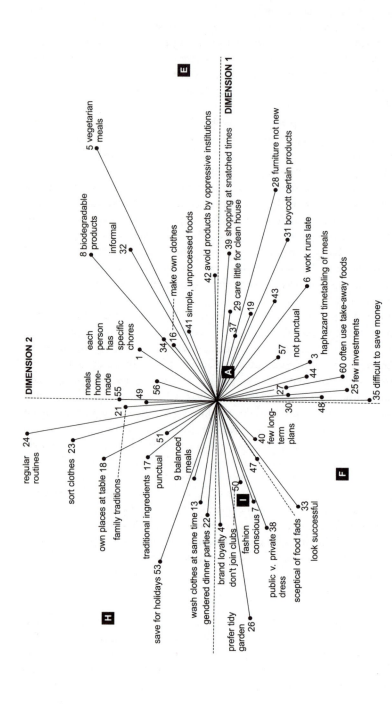

Note: $n = 77$ residents of London, Lancashire and Merseyside. Two discriminant functions show responses to 60 survey items describing household behaviour as well as the centroids for hierarchical (H), individualist (I), egalitarian (E), fatalist (F), and autonomous (A) households as classified by anthropological interview. The horizontal dimension accounts for 64.8% of the variance of self-reported behaviour; the vertical dimension accounts for an additional 17.7%. The interviews and the surveys were conducted double-blind. These findings therefore suggest a high degree of convergence for these two independent sources of information. Some points and some labels have been omitted for clarity.

Figure 23.2 *Consumption styles mapped by interview and questionnaire techniques.*

- *Hierarchists* gender their dinner parties (different wines for the ladies and the gentlemen, for instance). They use traditional ingredients, have their own places at table, are sticklers for punctuality and wash their clothes on 'wash-day', having first sorted them out according to colour and fabric. They do not boycott certain products, nor do they find that work often runs late, nor do they go in for take-away meals. They are not prepared to put up with old furniture,[10] nor are they comfortable with a house that is untidy.

- *Egalitarians* are about as opposed to both individualists and hierarchists as it is possible for them to get without disappearing off the diagram. Communality, together with unprocessed foods and biodegradable products (which, moreover, should be made by institutions that are not oppressive), is what they look for: an informal, joining, vegetarian sort of a life, in a pleasantly scruffy house filled with furniture that is not new and surrounded by a garden that is far from tidy. Egalitarians, unlike hierarchists and individualists, are not brand loyal, nor are they fashion conscious, nor do they wash their clothes on the same day each week, or sort them out into separate piles before they put them into the washing machine. Already, we can begin to see the power of this sort of approach. For instance, if you are thinking of siting a nuclear waste repository somewhere that is geologically ideal, and the people round about turn out not to sort their washing out into separate piles, forget it!

- *Fatalists* make few long-term plans, find it difficult to save money and are much addicted to take-away meals. They do not have regular routines or allotted household tasks or their own places at the table. Indeed, their take-away meals are likely to be eaten in front of that quintessentially fatalist piece of technology – the television set (Schmutzer, 1994; Putnam, 1995).

- We can say little about the *hermits,* because the questionnaire has not yet been developed to the point where it can tap into the autonomous solidarity. But the fact that the 'centre of gravity' of those households that were judged to be autonomous by the anthropological interviews falls very close to the 'absolute zero' of this two-dimensional scheme does provide some confirmation for the Cultural Theory predictions. Hermits, it suggests, do work hard to distance themselves from all the consumptive positions that the other four social beings dig themselves into, and so it should not be too difficult to design some questions that will capture this deliberate and carefully judged reticence.

All of the above brings us to the big question: so what?

The Theoretical and Practical Consequences of Rejecting the I-PAT Starting Point

Since most of the Cultural Theory effort, up until now, has been devoted to defining this new starting point and to providing some empirical support for its existence and validity, the various consequences of not starting from the I-PAT equation are not as well worked out as they will have to be. Even so, we can begin to see what some of them are:

- Consumption is never 'mindless'. In distinguishing the various ways in which some households do not comply with the non-satiety requirement we are able to see how it is that the various items (dahlbaht, champagne, old furniture and so on) are imbued with *shared* meanings within a consumption style that goes with a preferred way of living together: five consumption styles and five ways of living together – five kinds of social solidarity, each of which is all the time trying to strengthen itself and weaken the others.
- These different consumption styles, and the different forms of social solidarity that they support, are to be found in all societies – North and South, ancient and modern (and postmodern) – though in different proportions and patterns of interaction.
- Since it is the styles that really matter to people, and not the items that for the moment happen to be caught up in those styles, there is enormous scope (especially in the high-consuming North) for shifting the contents of each style in an environmentally desirable direction without in any way changing the style itself; without, therefore, changing the form of social solidarity that goes with each style. In other words, a 'whole new relationship with nature' is not essential (though those who believe it, as our final point explains, are a vital part of this process by which an entire population can achieve what might be called its *consumptive transition*[11]).
- All the constructive possibilities are in the *interactions between the styles*. It was egalitarian influence, for instance, that led to the individualists removing fur coats from their list of status symbols. And you now have to travel to places like Norway and the Faroe Islands to find anyone – individualist, hierarchist, egalitarian, fatalist or hermit – who is in favour of whale-killing.

Those who are wedded to the non-satiety requirement, and those who go around making accusations of mindlessness, will of course point to the statistics that show that consumption – environmentally harmful consumption – is everywhere on the increase. We do not deny this. Our objection is not that those statistics are false but that they are undiscerning and unhelpful. They hide the 'populations' within each country that is going the other way: egalitarian Northerners, for instance, who have embraced voluntary simplicity, and their individualistic compatriots who, in their pursuit of healthy living and personal success, are now eating much lower on the food chain. And in insisting that we are all the same – that we all want more and more – they diminish our humanity, treating us as one vast homogenized lump and throwing away the wonderful possibility that some of us (all of us, in fact, except for the poor old fatalists) may be the leaven within the lump.

Afterword

We should be careful not to blame the fatalists for being unleavened. Fatalists are fatalistic because the decisions that rule their lives are made for them by those – the constituents of the other four forms of solidarity – who are not themselves fatalists.[12] Treating people as synonymous with population – no different from cattle, in having fixed needs that have to be met from a fixed resource base: the ranges – is a pretty sure way of increasing the level of fatalism in a community. That, of course, is what policy-makers who rely on the I-PAT equation are doing. The more you treat people as cattle, the more likely they are to behave like cattle, and the more the policy-maker will come to be confirmed in his or her original assumption that that is how people are.[13] That is why it is so vital that the policy-maker becomes reflexive.

Notes

1   Policy-making in every area of sustainability (transport, energy, technology, etc.) is massively underpinned with computer models that purport to provide quite accurate, and predictive, descriptions of the key physical flows, their impacts, their social 'drivers' and so on. At the heart of these models is a single, often unquestioned, set of assumptions about human needs and wants: the rational utility-maximizing individual. The totality, therefore, is just the aggregation of these homogenized micro-level responses, and vice versa. But if the responses are not homogeneous this straightforward analysis – aggregation up, disaggregation down – will not work; micro and macro have to be seen each as the cause of the other, and top-down modelling is no longer valid. (For a more thorough exposition of this argument see Thompson, 1997a; for ways in which existing modelling can move itself away from these invalid assumptions, and from claims to prediction, see van Asselt and Rotmans, 1996, and de Vries and Rotmans, 1997).

2   An assertion that features in every economics textbook. See, for example Awh (1976), p42.

3   They insist because their theory would not work if people did not have to prioritize. It is the theory, therefore, that requires that people be insatiable!

4   See, for instance, Thompson et al (1990) and Schwarz and Thompson (1990).

5   This was written before the 'mad cow disease' crisis of March 1996.

6   The recipe for this dessert, made from fresh cream and soft fruit, is reputedly unchanged since Elizabethan days.

7   For an explanation of 'hallmarking', positional goods, etc., see Douglas and Isherwood (1978).

8   For more details of this study see Dake and Thompson (1993).

9   In other words, what we have here are five different consumption populations: *heterogeneity*. The per capita approach, however, assumes a single population: *homogeneity*. Statisticians are (or, at any rate, are supposed to be) scrupulous about sorting out their subject matter into homogeneous populations before applying their various techniques.

10   Furniture that would be regarded as 'secondhand', that is. 'Antique' is a different matter.

11   The levelling off, or the stabilizing at a lower level, of the currently increasing material consumption in most countries.

12   In order to simplify our presentation, we have spoken of 'fatalists', 'individualists', 'hierarchists' and so on as if an individual was always and everywhere just one of these ways. However, this is not what Cultural Theory says (nor, since our entire discussion is set within a single context – household consumption – is it what we are saying). There is no reason why a person cannot be a constituent part of more than one solidarity: hierarchist in the home (say), individualist at work, egalitarian in the sports club and so on.

13   The relationship, however, is *curvilinear*: self-fulfilling to begin with and then, as the surprises accumulate, becoming self-defeating (see Thompson, 1997b, 1998).

References

Awh, R. Y. (1976) *Microeconomics: Theory and Applications*, John Wiley, Santa Barbara

Dake, K. and Thompson, M. (1993) 'The meanings of sustainable development: Household strategies for managing needs and resources', in S. D. Wright, T. Dietz, R. Borden, G. Young and G. Guagnano (eds) *Human Ecology: Crossing Boundaries*, Society for Human Ecology, Fort Collins, CO, pp421–436

de Vries, B. and Rotmans, J. (1997) *Perspectives on Global Change*, Cambridge University Press, Cambridge

Dominguez, J. and Robin, V. (1992) *Your Money or Your Life*, Viking Penguin, New York

Douglas, M. (1996) *Thought Styles*, Sage, London

Douglas, M. and Isherwood, B. (1978) *The World of Goods*, Basic Books, New York

Ehrlich, P. and Holdren, J. (1974) 'Impact of population growth', *Science*, vol 171, pp1212–1217

Putnam, R. D. (1995) 'Tuning in, turning out: The strange disappearance of social capital in America', *Political Science and Politics*, December, pp664–683

Schmutzer, M. E. A. (1994) *Ingenium und Individuum: Eine sozialwissenschqftliche Theorie von Wissenschqft und Technik*, Springer, Vienna and New York

Schwarz, M. and Thompson, M. (1990) *Divided We Stand: Redefining Politics, Technology and Social Choice*, Harvester Wheatsheaf and University of Pennsylvania Press, London and Philadelphia

Thompson, M. (1979) *Rubbish Theory: The Creation and Destruction of Value*, Oxford University Press, Oxford

Thompson, M. (1997a) 'Cultural theory and integrated assessment', *Environmental Modelling and Assessment*, vol 2, pp139–150

Thompson, M. (1997b) 'Security and solidarity: An anti-reductionist framework for thinking about the relationship between us and the rest of nature', *Geographical Journal*, vol 163, no 2, pp141–149

Thompson, M. (1998) 'The new world disorder: Is environmental security the cure?', *Mountain Research and Development*, vol 18, no 2, pp117–122

Thompson, M., Ellis, R. and Wildavsky, A. (1990) *Cultural Theory*, West View, Boulder, CO, and Oxford

van Asselt, M. B. A. and Rotmans, J. (1996) 'Uncertainty in perspective', *Global Environmental Change*, vol 6, no 2, pp121–157

24

The Costs and Benefits of Consuming

Mihaly Csikszentmihalyi

Almost half a century ago. the social philosopher Hannah Arendt warned that advances in technology and the increase in free time were providing humankind with the opportunity to consume the whole world. 'That ... consumption is no longer restricted to the necessities but, on the contrary, mainly concentrates on the superfluities of life ... harbors the grave danger that eventually no object of the world will be safe from consumption and annihilation through consumption' (Arendt, 1958). At the time these lines may have sounded like hyperbole. But recent calculations suggest that if the rest of the world's population was to develop a lifestyle approaching that of the US or of Western Europe, at least two additional planets such as ours would have to be harnessed to provide the required energy and materials. Humans now consume 40 per cent of all the net photosynthesized biomass produced on the planet, with the developed countries consuming at rates that are often tenfold those of countries with less developed economies (Henderson, 1999). Since at this time we have no access to two spare planets to exploit, we should look more closely at what leads us to consume, in order to better understand what motivates this behaviour. It is no exaggeration to say that the future of the world may depend on it.

There are many ways to define 'consuming', depending on what aspect of the phenomenon one wishes to highlight. In the present case, I wish to bring attention to the most inclusive context in which consuming could be viewed: that of the physical consequences of the process in terms of energy exchange. From this point of view, a definition might run as follows: *consuming consists of energy expended to improve the quality of life by means of increasing entropy.* In other words, consuming entails an exchange of psychic energy (usually in its symbolic form, that is, money) for objects or services that satisfy some human need. These objects are relatively high in potential energy to begin with, but through the process of consuming they are broken down into useless things with low potential energy.

This definition seems paradoxical in that entropy – or the decay of ordered systems and objects to more random states with less potential energy – is a natural process for which no energy input is usually needed. The Second Law of Thermodynamics specifies that with time entropy must increase in all closed systems. So why are we willing to pay for something that would happen anyway? Why do we go to great lengths hastening the onset of disorder in the universe? The answer is, of course, that we expect to benefit in certain ways from increasing entropy.

For example, the steer that produced the rare steak one buys at the supermarket took a great deal of effort and energy to raise, feed, butcher and transport. It contains a relatively high number of calories, proteins and other substances that can be transformed into work. Because of this, it has a certain value. After the steak is consumed, however, its materials are broken down into waste with low potential energy and no value.

But as the food is transformed into waste, energy is liberated and transferred to the consumer. So the process of eating is not wasteful because the energy that went into the production of the steak goes to increase the diner's energy (however, one might point out that compared to eating other foods, eating steaks is relatively more wasteful). By contrast, most consumption provides little or no return of this kind to the consumer. Let us imagine, for instance, a father who feels the need to demonstrate his love for his small son by buying an expensive electric car for his birthday. Building the car took some raw materials, manufacturing effort, a great deal of marketing, salesmanship and transportation costs. The price tag took a not indifferent bite out of the father's pocketbook. For a few hours the boy plays with the car, and father and son have some mildly pleasant time out of it. But soon the novelty wears off. The car does not run well on the carpet or the sidewalk, so the boy takes it out more and more rarely. Now it sits in the basement, a useless hulk slowly turning to rust, taking up space. Is the result of such consumer behaviour a net increase in entropy or not?

Of course if one took into account the entire cycle of production and consumption we might see a different picture. Production entails a negentropic activity – one that takes raw materials and turns them into useful goods. Yet production also creates disorder in the planetary system: agrobusiness leaves dangerous chemical residues and washes away fertile topsoil; manufacture creates pollutants and exhausts limited natural resources. So to calculate the net effect of consumption one first needs to add up the positive outcomes: the increase in order due to productive processes, and the improvement in the quality of life. Then one should subtract from this the negative outcomes: the entropy caused by the processes of production, and the entropy caused by using up the goods produced. If the result is negative, it means that consumption is accelerating the rate of decay; if positive, it suggests that it helps the evolution of order in the universe. In the present essay, I am going to focus only on one term of this equation: how does consumption improve the quality of life?

How Consumer Behaviour Meets Existential Needs

Because consumer behaviour is largely driven by the desire to satisfy needs that have been programmed in our minds either by the genes we inherit or the memes[1] we learn from the culture in which we live, it is useful to start the analysis with a consideration of human needs. Of the many taxonomies developed by psychologists, the one by Abraham Maslow (1968, 1971) is one of the most succinct, and one that is familiar to students of consumer behaviour (Kilbourne, 1987). The model involves only five factors or levels, and it is reasonably comprehensive. We might, therefore, use it to help with a preliminary classification of what motivates consumer behaviour.

The 'lower' needs: Survival and safety

According to Maslow's theory, the most basic needs that motivate a person are physio-logical survival needs: to eat, drink, have sex, breathe, sleep, be warm and eliminate. When these needs are not met, the person will turn all of his or her psychic energy to the task of satisfying them. But as soon as these needs are met, a 'higher' set of needs will usually attract a person's attention. A great deal of consumer behaviour is directed to satisfy survival needs: food, clothing and shelter being paramount. However, as we shall see later, rarely does a product or service satisfy only basic needs; it is more usual for a whole range of lower and higher needs to be involved in every consumer exchange.

Next on Maslow's hierarchy are safety needs: to live in a stable, predictable environ-ment and to be free of anxiety. Many consumer decisions are prompted by safety needs, from buying a house in a 'good' neighbourhood to buying a handgun or antidepressant drugs. Other exchanges, including paying to get an advanced academic degree, or in vesting in retirement annuities, are also prompted at least in part by the desire to achieve security.

Love and belonging

The mid-point in Maslow's scheme, the need for love and belonging, is rooted in our fear of isolation and loneliness. Social animals like humans are genetically programmed to seek out the company of other members of the species. When alone (and especially when no pressing task demands attention), the quality of experience for most people declines; depression and bad mood take over (Csikszentmihalyi, 1991). In addition to this generic need for human company, human beings have also evolved a more specific desire to be close and to share the experiences of one or a few other persons, usually of the opposite sex. Thus, a need for affection, to love and be loved, is also fundamental to human motivation.

The implications of this set of needs for consumer behaviour are many and diverse. For example, bars, restaurants, sport arenas, museums and concert halls provide opportu-nities to mix with others, to see and be seen. The entire entertainment industry is pred-icated on experiencing good times vicariously in the company of virtual fellow-revellers. The psychic energy of consumers is targeted with ads that show masses of young people partying on beaches or in bars. If you buy this product, the subtext says, you will not have to be alone ever again.

The need to belong is also served by conformity. When we dress according to fash-ion, use the latest kitchen appliance, or take a vacation at the 'in' resort we feel that we are part of a group we aspire to belong to, and that we are accepted by its members. Again, advertising builds heavily on this need that once was known as 'keeping up with the Joneses', but which is apparently as old and universal as anything is in human nature.

Consuming relates to the need to love and be loved by providing opportunities to demonstrate one's feelings through gifts. From extravagant baby showers to elaborate funeral arrangements, through graduation presents and diamond rings, we express our feelings for each other by allowing the loved one to own things that took a great deal of energy to make or bring about, so that he or she can dispose of it and preside over its disintegration.

Goods used to express belonging or love have symbolic value. It is generally assumed that the more expensive the gift, the greater the appreciation or love felt by the giver, and thus the greater the obligation the recipient should feel in return. Thus, the energy expended on the gift is returned as goodwill. Objects that convey love and belonging need not be valuable in economic terms, however. The most cherished things in people's homes are rarely items that were bought, but rather things that embody the psychic energy of a loved one, like a quilt sewn by one's grandmother, or an athletic trophy won by one's child (Csikszentmihalyi and Rochberg-Halton, 1980). Thus gifts cannot be reduced to lower-order needs involving instrumental goals and calculation of exchange; at least occasionally they are expressions of relatively selfless agapic love (Belk and Coon, 1993).

The higher needs: Esteem and self-actualization

The need for self-esteem – to feel competent, respected and superior – is present already in children, and is presumably active even when the lower-order needs are not entirely met. But they become fully active after survival, safety and belongingness needs are more or less taken care of. At that point we can indulge in purchasing goods that show our uniqueness and separate us from the rest of the crowd. As Belk (1988) notes, 'Evidence supporting the general premise that possessions contribute to sense of self is found in a broad array of investigations.'

Goods that fulfil esteem needs are symbolic in nature, even though they often serve other motives as well. For instance, one's car could be used to drive to work and thus satisfies survival needs; it could also have been purchased because it is safe and reliable. But if we pay extra for status attributes, the car will then become a symbol indicating our superiority and social worth.

Not all objects consumed for esteem reasons are competitive status symbols. Many are acquired because they allow the person to practise and perfect a special skill which is important to his or her identity, such as musical instruments, tools, photo equipment, books that reflect the person's interests, sports and gardening equipment, and so forth. In our study of the meaning that household objects had for their owner, reasons dealing with self-esteem were among the most frequently mentioned, sharing first place with goods that were cherished for reasons of belongingness and love (Csikszentmihalyi and Rochberg-Halton, 1980).

The need for self-actualization, according to Maslow, be comes pre-eminent after the other four more basic needs are satisfied. It would seem that of all the needs, self-actualization has the least predictable impact on consumer behaviour. A person driven to achieve personal growth is more likely to lead a frugal life, perhaps to retire to an ashram or monastery, than to invest heavily in goods. The kind of persons Maslow used as models of self-actualization – Thomas Jefferson, Eleanor Roosevelt, Albert Einstein, Albert Schweitzer – were not big spenders, and in many ways strove to become independent of the market. Yet it has been argued that certain features usually associated with the sacred realms of life, such as ritual, mystery and *communitas*. can also accompany mundane consumer behaviour (Belk et al, 1989).

In fact, on a closer look it seems that many consumer decisions may be driven by the need for self-actualization. After all, travelling to sit at the feet of a genuine Buddhist guru entails buying at least a round-trip airfare ticket to India. The scholar in his study consumes esoteric knowledge that is expensive to produce and to preserve. Art, music and the appreciation of luxury items may also produce transcendent experiences. Perhaps only a few extremely dedicated altruistic individuals, such as Albert Schweitzer, Mother Theresa, and the saintly moral exemplars described by Colby and Damon (1992) can be said to have pursued self-actualization without increasing entropy in their environment.

A yardstick such as Maslow's model suggests that it may be possible to measure the value of consumer behaviour in terms of how various choices satisfy basic existential needs. It may be possible to answer such questions as, How expensive, in terms of energy expended, is it to satisfy security needs? Or esteem needs? For person X or Y? For a given community or nation? Having such information would allow us to make rational decisions about the value of consumer choices that currently are made without conscious awareness of the real costs and benefits involved.

This would be possible if consumer behaviour were driven solely by the predictable, universal needs that Maslow and others have identified. Unfortunately, consumer choices are made for a variety of other reasons that are even less clearly understood and that may place just as great a burden on planetary resources. We might designate this other class of needs as experiential needs, to distinguish them from the existential needs discussed thus far.

How Consumer Behaviour Meets Experiential Needs

The Maslowian model suggests that individuals are always motivated by some discrete, specific need for survival, safety and so on. In reality this is not the case. In everyday life, people often find themselves in an existential vacuum where no clear need suggesting a specific goal presents itself to consciousness. Normal American teenagers, for instance, when they are paged at random moments of the day, report 30 per cent of the time that what they are doing is not what they want to do, and that they cannot think of anything else they would rather be doing instead. Although this pattern is strongest when teenagers are in school, it is also typical of responses at home (Csikszentmihalyi and Schneider, 2000). While we have fewer data from adults, what there is suggests that they also spend quite a large part of their days in a state where, as far as they are concerned, 'there is nothing to do'.

This pattern is significant because when a person feels that there is nothing to do. the quality of experience tends to decline. One feels less alert, active, strong, happy and creative. Self-esteem declines. Contrary to what one might expect, such a negative experiential state is more likely to occur at home in free time and less often at work, where goals are usually clear and attention is more readily engaged (Csikszentmihalyi and LeFevre, 1989).

What this suggests is that in addition to the existential needs described by Maslow and others, we also have a need – perhaps peculiar to human beings – to keep consciousness in an organized state, focused on some activity that requires attention. When there is nothing to do and attention starts to turn inward, we begin to ruminate, and this generally leads to depression. By and large, when we start thinking about ourselves rather than about what we need to accomplish, attention turns to deficits. We are getting old and fat, we are losing our hair, our children don't worship us as they should, or we haven't accomplished much in life. As a result, our mood begins to turn sour (Csikszentmihalyi, 1993, 1997; Csikszentmihalyi and Figurski, 1982). The downward spiral of rumination is interrupted only when attention is again engaged by some need that suggests a goal: preparing dinner, taking the dog for a walk, or, if all else fails, watching the news on TV. Yet trying to fill unstructured time with passive entertainment does not work well; the quality of experience while watching TV is barely more positive than that of the slough of despond that awaits the unfocused mind (Kubey and Csikszentmihalyi, 1990).

The experiential need to keep consciousness tuned is responsible for a great deal of consumer behaviour. It could be said of shopping, as MacLuhan said of television, 'the medium is the message'. In other words, it often does not matter what we are shopping for – the point is to shop for anything, regardless. It is a goal-directed activity, and thus it fills the experiential vacuum that leads to depression and despair. The fact that we have to pay, that is, expend the equivalent of psychic energy, for what we acquire lends an additional importance to the activity. If we spend money, it must be worthwhile. As Linder (1971) pointed out, the value of the goods we consume in leisure becomes a measure of the value of our time. If in one hour's time I drink US$20 worth of a single-malt Scotch, while listening to a stereo that depreciates at the rate of US$5 an hour, in an apartment where rent prorates at US$10 an hour, then it means that my time is worth at least US$35 an hour – even without counting the cost of clothing, furniture and so forth that may also be contributing to the value of my time.

Thus, consuming is one of the ways we respond to the void that pervades consciousness when there is nothing else to do. Shopping and surrounding ourselves with possessions is a relatively easy way to forestall the dread of non-being, even though it may have serious consequences in terms of increasing entropy.

Yet consuming, beyond a certain point, seems to contribute little to a positive experience. Contrary to popular opinion, things that can be bought do not enhance happiness by much. The evidence for this statement, while circumstantial, is quite convincing. A number of studies show that beyond a rather low threshold, material well-being does not correlate with subjective well-being (Csikszentmihalyi, 1999; Diener, 2000; Myers, 2000). For instance, while the average American's income measured in constant dollars has doubled in the last 40 years, the level of happiness they report has not changed. Winning the lottery creates a small blip of happiness that lasts a few months, after which the lucky winner's happiness returns to what it was before. In a current longitudinal study tracking over 800 American teenagers through high school and beyond, we find that teens from the most affluent suburbs tend to be less happy and have lower self-esteem than those from middle-class communities, and even than those living in inner-city slums (Csikszentmihalyi and Schneider, 2000). Several researchers have shown that excessive concern with financial success and material values is associated with lower levels of life satisfaction and self-esteem, presumably because such concerns reflect a sense of 'contingent worth' predicated on *having* rather than *being* (Kasser and Ryan, 1993; Richins and Dawson, 1992).

In one study we correlated the happiness that American adults reported experiencing in their free time with the amount of fossil and electrical energy that the activity they were doing at the time consumed (Graef et al, 1981). If a person was reading a magazine when the pager signalled, for example, more energy was expended than if he or she had been reading a book, since producing a magazine (in terms of manufacturing paper, printing, sales, distribution and so on) requires more BTUs of energy per unit of reading time than it takes to produce a book. Thus if there were a direct relationship between energy consumption and quality of experience, a person should be happier when reading a magazine than when reading a book. Instead, we found the opposite: a slight but significant negative relationship between the average BTU load of activities and the happiness people experienced while doing them. There was an interesting gender difference: for men BTUs did not relate to happiness at all, whereas for women the relationship was quite strong in the negative direction. According to the Department of Energy, about 7 per cent of all the energy consumed in the US is spent on discretionary leisure activities, from travelling to snowmobiling, from skiing to TV watching. It is important to realize, therefore, that a substantial amount of this energy could be saved without impairing the quality of life, and perhaps actually improving it.

Why is there a negative relationship between energy consumed and happiness? The answer to this question may suggest a new way of thinking about consuming, one that maximizes the quality of experience while minimizing the amount of entropy produced as a result. The reason activities with low external physical energy requirements result in greater happiness is that they usually require greater inputs of *psychic* energy. Having a good conversation makes very little demands on environmental energy, but it demands concentrated attention and mental activity, and can be very enjoyable. So are activities such as reading, gardening, painting, working on crafts, writing poetry or doing mathematics. In general, people report being happier when they are actively involved with a challenging task, and less happy when they are passively consuming goods or entertainment (Csikszentmihalyi, 1997, 1999).

Consuming in the Third Millennium

Ever since Adam Smith, we have learned to say that production is justified by consumption; that the needs of the consumer dictate what the economy should provide (Borgmann, 2000; Smith, [1985] 1776). This relationship was so obvious to Smith that he did not believe it was worth arguing; ever since, it has become a mantra of economics. In reality, however, the situation has turned out to be exactly the opposite: it is the imperative to produce that is dictating the need to consume. Economic forecasts are based on in creasing demands: unless people buy more houses, more cars, more sporting equipment and clothes, the economy will falter. To buy – even if one does not have the means and has to fall ever deeper in debt – is a patriotic act. To refrain from consuming is antisocial; it is seen as a threat to the community. We have locked ourselves into a vicious cycle that forces us to increase entropy in the environment without providing commensurate value.

Is there a way to break out of this cycle? Obviously, we could not simply reduce consuming to the level appropriate to satisfy Maslow's survival and safety needs – even if we wanted to – without weakening the productive sector and causing unemployment to run rampant. But it might be possible to reinvent consumption in such a way that it would satisfy both existential and experiential needs at minimal energetic costs while at the same time preserving the economy.

The first step in this direction involves a clear accounting of the real costs of different consumer choices. Eventually this should lead to a new sense of good and bad beautiful and ugly. If the true entropic costs of a sport utility vehicle were kept in mind, for instance, even the most attractive vehicle of that sort would seem indecently coarse. Instead we would marvel at the beauty of a car made of bamboo and powered by sunlight. But to facilitate this transformation in taste, it will probably be necessary to legislate a new fiscal policy – one that taxed goods in proportion to the amount of entropy their production and consumption entailed.

Craftspersons, chefs, athletes, musicians, dancers, teachers, gardeners, artists, healers, poets – these are the workers creating goods that increase human well-being without degrading the complexity of the world. Is it impossible to develop an economy based on a majority of workers of this kind? Where consumption involves the processing of ideas, symbols and emotional experiences rather than the break down of matter? Let us hope this transition is not impossible, because otherwise the future looks grim indeed. And if the transition does come about, the *Journal of Consumer Research* will be filled with articles about music, art, poetry and dance – the creative energy of the new economy.

In the meantime, what suggestions does this perspective provide to those doing research in the field? Perhaps the main message is that ignoring the causes and consequences of consumer behaviour is dangerous. It would be unacceptable for neurologists to study an addictive drug without taking into account the pros and cons of its use. Similarly, research that deals with consumer behaviour without considering the context in which it is embedded cannot claim to contribute to basic knowledge, and remains little more than applied market research.

Science proceeds by developing an agreed-upon set of measurements and definitions. For consumer research to advance in the direction foreshadowed here, it seems that agreement on the following dimensions should be useful.

What are the costs of a specific unit of consumer behaviour, in terms of the consumer? The social network of which the consumer is a part? The ecological network? Such costs may best be expressed in the common language of entropy. Even though entropy is manifested differently in psychological, social and biological systems, at each of these levels it refers to an increase in disorder and loss of capacity to do work.

To balance the costs of consumption we should be able to measure accurately its benefits. These tend to be of a negentropic kind, that is, they involve greater order and greater disposable energy at the levels of the person, the social system and the environment. These benefits are not always congruent with each other. For instance, the purchase of a Ferrari may help the self-esteem of an executive pushing 50, but cause conflict with his wife.

Also, it is important to keep in mind that the relation between costs and benefits is usually quadratic rather than linear. Up to a certain point, material resources add greatly to the quality of life. But where is the point of inflection after which the relationship may no longer exist, or actually become negative?

We already know that material possessions alone do not improve the quality of life. We know that excessive concern for material goals is a sign of dissatisfaction with life. We know that trying to avoid the mental chaos of everyday life by resorting to acquisitions and passive entertainment does not work very well. Yet we insist in the vain hope that we can achieve happiness through consumption – regardless of consequences. Certainly one of the greatest services that consumer research can do for humankind is to document these realities, and diffuse them to as wide a public as possible.

Vague as these concepts are at this point, the progress of scholarship in the field will greatly benefit from taking them seriously. Eventually it should be possible to develop reasonably convincing cost–benefit analyses for different options, to allow consumers to make choices at a much higher level of rationality than is possible with current criteria.

Note

1   A 'meme' is a concept introduced by the British biologist Richard Dawkins (1976) to refer to programmed behavioural units that are learned, rather than inherited genetically. It is derived from the Greek word for imitation: mimesis. Several writers have found the concept useful for describing the production, selection and transmission of cultural information (e.g. Blackmore, 1999; Csikszentmihalyi, 1993; Wright, 2000).

References

Arendt, H. (1958) *The Human Condition,* University of Chicago Press, Chicago

Belk, R. (1988) 'Possessions and the extended self', *Journal of Consumer Research,* vol 15, September, pp139–168

Belk, R., Wallendorf, M. and Sherry, J. Jr (1989) 'The sacred and the profane in consumer behavior: Theodicy on the Odyssey,' *Journal of Consumer Behavior,* vol 16, no 1, pp1–38

Belk, R. and Coon, G. S. (1993) 'Gift giving as agapic love: An alternative to the exchange paradigm based on dating experiences,' *Journal of Consumer Research,* vol 20, December, pp393–417

Blackmore, S. (1999) *The Meme Machine,* Oxford University Press, Oxford

Borgmann, A. (2000) 'The moral complexion of consumption,' *Journal of Consumer Research,* vol 26, March, pp419–424

Colby, A. and Damon, W. (1992) *Some Do Care: Contemporary Lives in Moral Commitment,* Free Press, New York

Csikszentmihalyi, M. (1991) 'Reflections on the "spiral of silence"', *Communication Yearbook,* vol 14, pp288–297

Csikszentmihalyi, M. (1993) *The Envolving Self,* HarperCollins, New York

Csikszentmihalyi, M. (1997) *Finding Flow,* Basic, New York

Csikszentmihalyi, M. (1999) 'If we are so rich, why aren't we happy?', *American Psychologist,* vol 54, no 10, pp821–827

Csikszentmihalyi, M. and Figurski, T. (1982) 'Self awareness and aversive experience in everyday life', *Journal of Personality,* vol 50, no 1, pp15–28

Csikszentmihalyi, M. and LeFevre, J. (1989) 'Optimal experience in work and leisure', *Journal of Personality and Social Psychology,* vol 56, no 5, pp815–822

Csikszentmihalyi, M. and Rochberg-Halton, E. (1980) *The Meaning of Things: Domestic Symbols and the Self,* Cam bridge University Press, New York

Csikszentmihalyi, M. and Schneider, B. (2000) *Becoming Adults,* Basic, New York

Dawkins, R. (1976) *The Selfish Gene,* Oxford University Press, Oxford

Diener, E. (2000) 'Subjective well-being: The science of happiness', *American Psychologist,* vol 55, no 1, pp34–43

Graef, R., McManama Gianinno, S. and Csikszentmihalyi, M. (1981) 'Energy consumption in leisure and perceived happiness', in J. D. Claxton (ed) *Consumers and Energy Conservation,* Praeger, New York

Henderson, H. (1999) *Beyond Globalization,* Kumarian, West Hartford, CT

Kasser, T. and Ryan, R. M. (1993) 'A dark side of the American dream: Correlates of financial success as a central life aspiration', *Journal of Personality and Social Psychology,* vol 65, no 2, pp410–422

Kilbourne, W. E. (1987) 'Self-actualization and the consumption process: Can you get there from here?' in A. F. Firat, N. Dholakia and R. Bagozzi (eds) *Philosophical and Radical Thought in Marketing,* D. C. Heath, Lexington, MA, pp217–234

Kubey, R. and Csikszentmihalyi, M. (1990) *Television and the Quality of Life,* Erlbaum, Mahwah, NJ

Linder, S. (1971) *The Harried Leisure Class,* Columbia University Press, New York

Maslow, A. (1968) *Toward a Psychology of Being,* Van Nostrand, New York

Maslow, A. (1971) *The Farther Reaches of Human Nature,* Viking, New York

Myers, D. (2000) 'The funds, friends and faith of happy people', *American Psychologist,* vol 55, no 1, pp56–68

Richins, M. L. and Dawson, S. (1992) 'A consumer values orientation for materialism and its measurement: Scale development and validation', *Journal of Consumer Research,* vol 19, December, pp303–316

Smith, A. (1985 [1776]) *An Inquiry into the Nature and Causes of the Wealth of Nations,* Modern Library, New York

Wright, R. (2000) *Non-Zero: The Logic of Human Destiny,* Pantheon, New York

25

Consuming Paradise?
Towards a Social and Cultural
Psychology of Sustainable Consumption

Tim Jackson

An individual's main objective in consumption is to help to create the social universe and to find in it a creditable place.

MARY DOUGLAS (1976)

Behind the Consumer Society:
Commonality and Difference

We are living in a consumer society. To say this, is not just to make obvious points about the massive expansion in the availability of consumer goods and services in developed economies over the last 50 years. It is not just to point to the structural reliance of those economies on consumption growth, or even to highlight the extensive commercialization of previously public goods. All these things are important. But almost certainly there is more going on. Fundamental aspects of our cultural identity are different now than they were 150 or 200 years ago. Modern consumer society has its own logics, its own epistemologies and ethics, its own myths and cosmologies. And all of these are identifiably different from those of other times and places.[1]

None of this is very surprising. What defines culture is difference. Anthropologists and sociologists would be surprised – and worse still out of a job – if different societies at different times were all found to operate in pretty much the same way, under the same logics and the same narratives. At the same time, most social sciences – including anthropology and sociology, and almost certainly psychology – would founder if it were not possible to regard at least some aspects of human functioning as common across even quite striking cultural differences. At the very least, these sciences would be absolutely useless to us in understanding either society or human motivation if it were not possible to identify some features of both that could be regarded if not as strictly constant, then at least as evolving rather slowly over time.

A part of the aim of this chapter is to illustrate how this ability to negotiate between commonality and difference is vital to an understanding of (unsustainable) consumer society. It is also, as I shall argue, extremely useful in helping us to develop policies for a sustainable society. The substantive part of this chapter, however, is to argue in favour of five inter-related social-psychological 'propositions'. My hope is that these propositions will help us to understand better the unsustainable patterns of consumption with which we are now faced. More importantly, of course, I am hoping to improve our understanding of what needs to be done to deliver sustainable consumption.

The Naming of Names

Before elaborating these propositions, let me illustrate the balance between commonality and difference with two specific examples, whose relevance will, I hope, become clear later on.

The first example comes from anthropology. Anthropologists have always placed a good deal of importance on the existence and functioning of exchange rituals. Gift-giving, barter, trade, betrothal, slavery, dowry, the 'droit de seigneur', human sacrifice and the swapping of football cards among (usually male) teenagers: these are all examples of exchange rituals. There are often striking differences between the particular kinds of ritual which predominate and the forms these exchanges take in different cultural groups. Indeed, these operational differences can be as profound as whether private property rights are or are not recognized within a particular group; whether the rights of the individual are more or less important than the rights of the group; or, more spectacularly, whether one cultural group recognizes the basic rights of another cultural group at all – as for example in the case of slavery. But the importance of exchange, its relevance to kin relations within the family, to social relations within the group and to the defining of similarities and differences with other groups is taken as read. In other words, exchange is regarded as a necessary prerequisite for certain kinds of social functioning – in all societies.[2]

A second example of the balance between commonality and difference is provided by the concept of social or psychological 'anomie' – a potentially catastrophic 'loss of meaning' that can threaten the stability both of society and of individuals within society.[3] Sociologists and social philosophers have paid considerable attention to this phenomenon ever since Durkheim's work on suicide. But they have also emphasized the counterveiling force of 'nomization' – a continuing social process of meaning creation and maintenance that is essential to keep anomie at bay – both at the personal and at the social level. Meaning is created, maintained and sometimes destroyed through a variety of different kinds of social and institutional processes and relations, including personal and social identity, nationalism, communalism, kin relations, governance, cultural narratives and various forms of religious structure and organization.[4]

The specific forms of these processes again differ widely in different societies. In one society, organized religion plays a key role. In another society, anomie may be kept at bay through strong nationalism and binding institutions. In yet another, meaning is negotiated via myths, storytelling and forms of folk religion. What these societies hold in common is their aim of negotiating meaning and staving off anomie.

The two examples are connected. One of the key avenues of nomization – as the etymological roots of the word indicate – is the 'exchange of names'. When male teenagers (and sometimes grown men) exchange pictures of their favourite football players, or engage in hours of banter regarding the latest exploits of their favourite team, they are – to use Mary Douglas's evocative phrase – enjoying a 'conversation of names' (Douglas, 1976, p206). When a whole nation unites behind a particularly skilful fly-half who has dramatically clinched victory in a world cup competition by kicking a spectacular drop goal in the dying minutes of extra time, they are engaging in a process of nomization – the maintenance of social and cultural meaning – pursued through the collective recognition and repetition of a name: in this case, Jonny Wilkinson.[5]

And just in case we find ourselves tempted to dismiss this particular example as puerile and beneath contempt, we should perhaps pause to recognize that 'sustainable consumption' is itself – if nothing else – a name. There is a sense in which, when we convene workshops, publish papers and compile books on sustainable consumption, we are also engaged in a kind of exchange ritual. And much of what we exchange, in addition to erudite views, constructive criticism and the occasional acerbic barb, can be construed as a process of nomization. As a research community, we define ourselves around a name, and a set of ideas expressed in a common language which for us provides a framework of meaning within which communication is possible. And if you think carefully about this name, 'sustainable consumption', you will find that it only really makes sense within a particular context, at a certain place and time in history: specifically of course the context of a policy dialogue around human development that emerged in the late 20th and early 21st centuries (mainly in Western Europe).

But my point here is not to deconstruct the anthropological underpinnings of the sustainable consumption debate. It is rather to illustrate how anthropology and sociology and psychology continually negotiate between commonality and difference, between underlying psychological, sociological or anthropological concepts and processes (for example: exchange, anomie, nomization) and historically and culturally contingent social phenomena (such as football cards, rugby matches and papers on sustainable consumption). To be more precise, what these sciences help us do is to understand contingent phenomena in terms of underlying processes. And that, as I take it, is precisely the task implicit in establishing a credible social psychology of sustainable consumption.

A Proposition about Motivation and Functioning

But let me proceed straight to the first of my propositions about these underlying processes. This is something I have in a sense already primed you for. In my 'naming of names' example, I suggested that both anthropologists and sociologists recognize the importance of exchange rituals to certain kinds of social and psychological functionings. My first proposition argues that such functionings provide a useful basis for approaching the question of human motivations.

Proposition 1: Human motivations can be understood in terms of a set of underlying human 'functionings'.

Strange though it may seem, this innocuous-sounding proposition is an attempt to negotiate an extraordinary minefield of disagreements in the social sciences. You might perhaps recognize the source of these disagreements if I were to replace the word 'functionings' with 'needs'. In fact, in this latter form, Proposition 1 would look very much like something that characterized the development of social psychology for around the first 60 or 70 years of the 20th century. From William McDougall's (1908) early characterization of instincts to Abraham Maslow's (1954) hierarchy of needs, social psychology has made a series of concerted efforts to understand human motivation in terms of common (universal) underlying needs. And it might have made a lot of sense for me to phrase my proposition in terms of needs, precisely because the discourse of needs is something with which sustainable development is broadly familiar.[6]

Unfortunately, that discourse attracts as much criticism as it does praise, particularly among anthropologists and sociologists (whom I would like, for the moment at least, to keep onside). Critics accuse the needs theorists of a variety of crimes. Baudrillard, for example, argues that the whole needs discourse is a 'naïve and absurd moralism' (Baudrillard, 1968, pp24–5). Campbell (1998) suggests that the use of the word need is a purely rhetorical device whose aim is to impute moral legitimacy to the object of the alleged need. The claim 'I need a pair of Nike trainers' appears to carry more moral weight than the statement 'I want a pair of Nike trainers' or 'I desire a pair of Nike trainers' and to offer greater moral legitimacy to (alleged) sweatshop labour in the process!

As Wander Jager, Sigrid Stagl and I have pointed out in a recent paper (Jackson et al, 2004), there is a sense in which these arguments are missing a critical distinction (highlighted by later needs theorists such as Carlos Mallmann (1980) and Manfred Max-Neef (1991)) between needs and satisfiers; between the underlying motivations for subsistence, identity and so on, and the objects and artefacts which are employed in meeting (or attempting to meet) these needs; between the peer credibility that cements our teenage relationships and the particular brand of trainers that facilitates this. But for the sake of avoiding this by-now almost intractable argument, I prefer to couch Proposition 1 in terms of functionings.[7]

Interestingly, the language of 'functionings' was first offered to the debate about human progress by the economist, Amartya Sen. In a seminal paper written in 1984, the Nobel laureate suggested that conventional concepts of the 'living standard', based on measures of utility or opulence, fail to capture the complexity of human well-being. Instead, argued Sen, we should place a primary value on people's freedom or 'capability' to function without deficiency in a given context. The policy implications of this are significant. 'If, for example, we value a person's ability to function without nutritional deficiency', he wrote, 'we would favour arrangements in which the person has adequate food with those nutritional characteristics, but that is not the same thing as valuing the possession of a given amount of food as such' (Sen, 1984, p294).

Echoing, at a different level, the distinction made by Mallman and Max-Neef between (underlying, universal) needs and (culturally specific) satisfiers, Sen drives a wedge between the arrangements that make it possible to function effectively, and the bundle of economics goods required in that situation.[8] This turns out to be an absolutely critical distinction for sustainable consumption, as we shall see. And at one level it is, quite precisely the distinction between (functional) commonality and (cultural) difference on which I have predicated this chapter.

Of course, 'functioning without deficiency' is not entirely dissimilar in meaning to the idea of 'meeting needs'. To function without nutritional deficiency, for example, might be construed as meeting a need for subsistence. And I have already spoken of certain social and psychological functionings in ways that are reminiscent of Maslow's concept of 'social needs'. Participation and belonging are means of social functioning, if you like, just as nutrition is a means of physiological functioning. It is impossible to function socially without participating in the social group, just as it is impossible to function physiologically without adequate nutrition.[9]

I want to resist being overly prescriptive about specific types of functioning because I am keen to avoid the charges of moralism that social scientists raise, with some justification, against needs theorists. Sen himself evades this pitfall by never getting as far as articulating specific functionings, except as exemplars. His collaborator, Martha Nussbaum, is more prescriptive and has come up with a set of ten or so 'central human functional capabilities' that bears some resemblance to some typologies of human needs (Nussbaum, 1998). Personally, I would be quite happy to allow that the functionings we choose to defend as an appropriate basis for the 'good life' be negotiated openly in each individual cultural or social context.

I would, however, like to suggest that we pay attention to several broad kinds of functioning in pursuit of our understanding of human motivations. And it should be clear already that the range of functionings in which we might be interested includes more than purely physical or physiological functioning. Healthy physical functioning is essential to survival of the organism. Certain minimal nutritional inputs are required to maintain physiological health, and a number of other material inputs are needed for physical protection – clothing, houses and so on. But all the evidence suggests that social and psychological functioning is as important for proper development and healthy functioning as physical or physiological factors are. So for the purposes of this discussion, I want to propose five inter-related kinds of functioning in which we might be interested. These are illustrated in Figure 25.1.

It will immediately be noticed that some of these categories (physiological, psychological, sociological) express, at a very broad level, the kinds of things that are also captured by the typologies of needs theories. Interestingly, however, not all of the functionings in Figure 25.1 find a corresponding category in existing needs theoretic frameworks. Reproductive functioning is not echoed in either Maslow's hierarchy or in Max Neef's categorization. And yet, one of the key lessons from evolutionary psychology is that reproductive functioning offers some explanation for motivations, and in particular for consumer motivations, which often have the character and flavour of sexual desire.[10] In fact, no one who has been living on planet Earth for any length of time could doubt that we are motivated – for much of our lives, in no small measure – by reproductive functioning!

The fifth element in my framework – spiritual functioning – may also look a little unfamiliar, if not uncomfortable, to the Western eye. It is probably questionable to some whether human motivations have anything to do with spiritual functioning – or indeed whether there is any such thing as spiritual functioning, as distinct from psychological

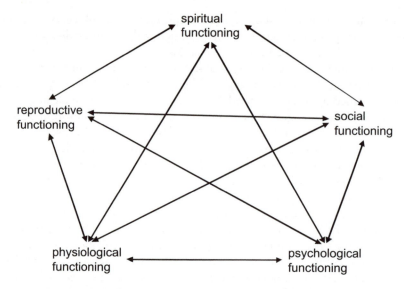

Figure 25.1 *Five inter-related forms of human functioning*

or social functioning, at all. On the other hand, the self-actualization need – in Maslow's terminology – and transcendence – offered as a possible tenth need in Max Neef 's framework – clearly have some suggestion of functioning that transcends social-psychological boundaries. And there are whole belief systems, lying a little outside the modern Western mould, within which spiritual functioning appears to offer an independent reality. So, for the moment at least, I would like to retain the possibility that spiritual functioning is an identifiably distinct component in the mix.[11]

It might be tempting to suggest that some of these kinds of functioning are more important in terms of underlying motivations than others. After all if we do not get enough food, we die. If we do not reproduce, the species dies. So we should expect these functionings to provide pretty fundamental motivational forces in our lives. But, as we have already noted, good social and psychological functioning is also key to survival and continuance. One of the key reasons for the sociological interest in anomie was to begin to understand why apparently healthy individuals would commit suicide in spite of good physiological health. Lessons from evolutionary psychology on social positioning indicate that higher social status is allied with increased chances of bearing healthy progeny, and increased chances of them surviving. Recent work on the relationship between health and inequality has suggested that those in lower income groups suffer higher health risks not simply because they have worse access to basic services but also because of the psychological stresses associated with being in a lower position in the 'pecking order'.[12] So it is not clear that a hierarchical ordering of functionings is appropriate.

This kind of evidence also illustrates another important aspect of functioning: namely that the different types of functioning are all strongly inter-related. The link between social-psychological functioning and physiological functioning is increasingly acknowledged by health science. Stress is known to be a generic mechanism which links social and psychological factors to physiological symptoms.[13] Anthropological evidence also suggests a key role for social relations in providing resilience in the face of physical shocks.[14] In the case of an emergency – the lights go out, unemployment looms, a loved one dies – the strength of our social relationships can make the difference between a successful transition to a secure new support base and a potentially disastrous collapse of the support mechanisms that guarantee full physiological functioning. Resilience to the tricks and turns life constantly throws at us is constructed from the gossamer threads which link our individual well-being to the social group. Little wonder that identity and social status hold such sway over us.

In summary, therefore, my suggested typology of functionings is non-hierarchical and highly interdependent. Figure 25.1 is certainly not intended to either prescribe or proscribe specific cultural 'arrangements' for 'functioning without deficiency' or to suggest preferences for or against any given set of economic goods. But I would like to claim that it does a decent job of dividing up the territory when it comes to identifying the kinds of things that motivate human behaviour.[15]

A Life without Shame

At this juncture, and before proceeding to my second proposition, I want to pause briefly to explore the relation between functioning and 'materiality'. It is, after all, the material requirements for functioning that are most relevant to us from the point of view of sustainability. We would clearly like to know how much or how little material consumption we can get away within seeking to achieve healthy functioning in various categories. And in particular, it is vital to contemplate how we might get away with less material consumption without impairing the level of different kinds of functioning.

At first glance it would appear that only one kind of functioning – physiological – demands, *a priori*, specific levels and types of material input. In particular, as I have already intimated, we must expect to have to meet certain minimum requirements for food, water, clothing and shelter. There seems no *a priori* reason to suppose that social, psychological or spiritual functionings impose such minimum requirements. Belongingness, affection, transcendence, for example, do not obviously need to be mediated by material goods and services – although clearly in our society they often are.

Perhaps more interestingly, there is now an intriguing body of evidence to suggest that psychological and social functioning may actually be impaired by high levels of materialism.[16] Far from being necessary to our survival, materialism threatens our environment, engenders inequality and does not even make us happy, according to this view. If this were the whole story, it would be a very happy state of affairs for sustainable consumption. Reducing material consumption would not only protect the environment it would also make us all happier. We really could all 'live better by consuming less'.[17]

Unfortunately, as Sen himself has pointed out, things are not quite so simple. Forgoing consumption is particularly problematic in a richer society, according to Sen. In a passage harking back to something Adam Smith once said,[18] Sen (1984, p298) argues that:

> To lead a life without shame, to be able to visit and entertain one's friends, to keep track
> of what is going on and what others are talking about, and so on, requires a more expen-

sive bundle of goods and services in a society that is generally richer and in which most people have, say, means of transport, affluent clothing, radios or television sets, and so on... The same absolute level of capabilities may thus have a greater relative need for incomes (and commodities).

Sen is clearly saying something recognizable about modern consumer society: namely that in this particular society we do appear to require a more expensive bundle of goods and services in order to 'function without deficiency'. And we could certainly at this stage agree – provided that we accept Proposition 1 – that these functionings are themselves fundamental aspects of human motivation, something from which ordinary mortals would be hard pressed to escape. At the same time there is something unsatisfactory in Sen's explanation. Or rather, it is not really an explanation at all, merely a description of a contingent state of affairs: we behave this way in rich societies, because this is what rich societies are like, Sen seems to be saying.

The clue to us getting beyond this, I contend, lies in the word 'shame'. Shame is a powerful emotion. In fact, it is both an emotion – an affective construct – and an intellectual response – a cognitive construct – stimulated by a particular kind of social situation. Certainly we *feel* shame personally – and most of us would go a long way to avoid the feeling. Equally importantly, however, the 'shameful' situation is always an interpersonal one. In feeling shame, an individual is responding to a relationship between his or her individual actions and the actions or expectations of others. Shame defines itself as a relationship *between* the individual and the group.

Shame is also, crucially, a signifier of the boundary between meaning and anomie – a point to which I return below. The apparently innocuous appeal to 'a life without shame' thus points us to an absolutely vital element in the search for an understanding of unsustainable consumption: the relationship between self and other.

A Proposition about Self and Other

The injunction to 'a life without shame' is one that demands that we look to our relationships with others in pursuit of healthy functioning. A little reflection shows that shame is not unique in this sense. Pride, approval, disapproval, loyalty, envy, belonging, affection, self-esteem, even disaffection and hate: these are all negotiations between self and other, between the individual and the group. We are driven, in other words, towards an undeniable overlap between psychological and social functioning, and to a second key proposition in support of our understanding of consumer society.

Proposition 2: Self is a social construct.

This overlap between social and psychological functioning is, once again, a key contribution from the field of social psychology. One of the earliest and most influential writers to make this relationship explicit was George Herbert Mead. For Mead, both the mind and the concept of self arise out of a fundamentally social process: communication. He distinguished two evolutionary phases in the communicational processes of species. The first phase is characterized by what Mead, (1934, p151) called the 'conversation of gestures' – illustrated through the now-famous analogy of a dog-fight:

> Dogs approaching each other in hostile attitude carry on such a language of gestures. They walk around each other, growling and snapping, and waiting for the opportunity to attack… The act of each dog becomes the stimulus to the other dog for his response. There is then a relationship between these two; and as an act is responded to by the other dog, it, in turn, undergoes change. The very fact that the dog is ready to attack another becomes a stimulus to the other dog to change his position or his own attitude. He has no sooner done this than the change of attitude in the second dog in turn causes the first dog to change his attitude. We have here a conversation of gestures.

This essentially unconscious process – prosecuted through gestures that are recognized only implicitly by the participants in the conversation – is to be distinguished from what Mead called the 'conversation of significant gestures' in which participants in the conversation remain not only fully aware that they are participating in a conversation, but must also gain familiarity with the 'significant symbols' (i.e. language) through which communication occurs. This transition from the conversation of gestures to the conversation of significant gestures is, in Mead's view, an evolutionary one. Only in humans, according to Mead, is a conversation of significant gestures possible.

It is clear from his writing that Mead is thinking of the conversation of significant gestures mainly in terms of language itself. However, it is in principle possible to envisage linguistic processes that are not carried out in full consciousness or awareness. The concept of cognitive 'scripts' that facilitate more or less habitual communicational responses – even in language – blurs the distinction between significant and non-significant gestures. Likewise, we can, in principle, conceive of non-linguistic 'conversations' in which it is possible to retain a level of awareness or reflexivity on the process itself. For example, clever use of 'body language' is not always unconscious. Just ask a cat-walk model!

Aside from these subtleties, however, Mead's concept of a conversation of gestures remains a useful one for understanding processes of social communication. In humans, according to Mead, the conversation of significant gestures (i.e. conscious or aware communication) supplements – although it never entirely supplants – the unconscious conversation of gestures. That we communicate both consciously and unconsciously through these social conversations has some important implications for sustainable consumption policy, which I shall return to later.

The most important aspect of Mead's ideas about communication is their implication for self and for identity. For Mead (1934, p135), the self only exists as a result of conversations of significant gestures:

> The self is something which has a development; it is not there at birth, but arises in the process of social experience and activity, that is, develops in the given individual as a result of his [sic] relations to that process as a whole and to other individuals in that process.

The self exists only in relation to social conversation. Even individual personal identity is an emergent property of inherently social relations. In Mead's view this emergent self plays an essentially evolutionary role. It is there to support the cohesion of the group. And it is able to achieve this precisely because it is a result of social conversations.[19] These social conversations provide the mechanism both for negotiating and for internalizing (in personal identity) the values, attitudes, beliefs and norms of the social group. At the same time, it is clear that the concept of the self also plays a key role in negotiating and perpetuating culture. Cultural norms are internalized in individuals by way of social conversations. But the relationship is a dialectical one. Some of those conversations, subtly and over relatively long periods of time, shift, mould and fashion cultural beliefs themselves. Without this dialectic, culture itself would remain essentially static. The individual is not without influence on his or her cultural milieu. But by the same token, the process of cultural transition can never be one that is entirely within the gift of any single individual.

Indeed, at the individual level – and sometimes even at the societal level – cultural transition is an inherently violent process. To question the belief system that constitutes one's own culture is to threaten meaning-structure at the social level. For an individual to challenge this, as many a would-be revolutionary has discovered to their cost, is to invite a resounding punishment. The more successful the challenge the more resounding the punishment.

There is a clear link here to the conversation of names alluded to above. Indeed, the retribution inflicted on dissenters and revolutionaries has something in common with the violence inflicted by one set of football fans on another. The conversation of names defines a social territory. To know and to applaud a particular name or set of names defines allegiance to a territory and membership of a social group. To challenge those names is to invite hostility from the group. What appears at one level puerile is, at another level, a powerful mechanism for social stability and the repression of dissent – as Bourdieu has pointed out.[20]

A Proposition about Agency and Structure

If the self exists only in relation to social conversation, then what are we to make of the concept of subjective agency? How is it possible, as human beings, to make subjective choices about specific courses of action? Are we capable of autonomous choice at all? Or are we simply social automatons, guided and cajoled through life by the norms and expectations of our peers? All the evidence from social psychology reinforces the vital importance of social norms, social identities, social learning in mediating and moderating individual attitudes and behaviours.[21] To ignore this evidence would lead us down a blind alley in any project to achieve sustainable consumption. Exhorting attitude and behavioural change at the individual level just will not wash.

Social psychology stops short, however, of insisting that our lives are devoid of agency. On the contrary, the concept of individual agency is almost a prerequisite for a workable psychology. It is not so for all social scientists. For decades, sociologists have been fascinated by the relationship between agency and what they call social structure:

the set of rules, norms, routines, institutions and meanings that constitute the 'objective reality' of society.

Some startling questions have characterized this debate. The first is the question of whether human beings are capable of exerting autonomous, directed social action at all; or whether they are rather locked into routine behaviours through historical and social processes over which there is no possibility of individual or even collective control. If each individual is capable of autonomous action, then how is it that social structures appear so resilient over time? How do we account for the prevalence of routine and habit in our everyday lives? Why do we not observe instead a continual chaotic anarchy of social behaviour, pushed this way and that by subjective agency with very little sense of normality or routine? On the other hand, if individual agents have little or no influence over social structures, then how is it that these structures change at all?

Few social theorists now espouse a view in which subjective agency is entirely absent from the world. For the most part, the debates have been resolved in favour of various 'structuration theories': models of how agency and social structure interact. The most famous of these was proposed by Anthony Giddens, who coined the term 'structuration'. Giddens' structuration theory attempts to model the interconnection between ordinary, everyday, routine action and the long-term, large-scale evolution of social structures. Specifically, his theory suggests that individual and collective agency provides for the continuous production and reproduction of complex patterns of social interaction – or in other words for the 'constitution of society'. But this kind of agency is only possible because actors have access to the 'transformative capacity' of historical social structures: language, norms, rules, meanings and power.[22]

This relationship clearly mirrors the dialectical relationship between individuality and culture discussed in the previous section. But what, if anything, does it offer us in the way of understanding the underlying processes governing consumer society?

Two specific things emerge. The first is that, in addition to being constrained by social norms and expectations, we also constantly find our actions constrained by the wider social structures which regulate our lives. Nor is this just an obvious point about physical infrastructure. We know full well that it is much more difficult to recycle in the absence of kerbside recycling facilities. Or to take public transport in the absence of reliable services. But the constraints of social structure are more pervasive, more deeply engrained and more subtle than this. The role of social structure, according to this view, is to continuously create and recreate a set of routine practices – accepted ways of doing things that are encoded in social institutions – which change only slowly over time, over which no individual has complete control and which become so much a feature of 'normal behaviour' that they go largely unquestioned in our lives.

The second important lesson follows from this. The ability to carry out these routine practices is encoded in what Giddens calls 'practical consciousness' – the everyday knowledge that people carry with them about 'how things are (supposed to be) done'. This kind of common knowledge operates at an almost subconscious level, allowing us to process routine tasks with little conscious thought or deliberation. And here, in spite of its origins in a sociological debate which has verged on dispensing with individual agency, is an insight strongly supported by psychology. Modern cognitive psychology recognizes a spectrum of cognitive modes, from automaticity to full control.[23] At one end of the spectrum, in unfamiliar situations that require the careful application of newly acquired skills, a good deal of cognitive effort is required. At the other are behaviours that are reproduced over and again on a routine basis with very little conscious thought at all. Habit appears to bypass cognitive thought altogether; and in doing so perpetuates the social structures around us. 'Habit is thus the enormous flywheel of society,' wrote William James in 1890, 'its most precious conservative agent.'

Where all this comes out is in a very strong suggestion that, in spite of Proposition 1, we cannot entirely think about personal motivations as guiding individual functioning in a conscious, deliberative way. Rather our behaviour is constantly framed in the context of wider social structures and through our routine responses to these. Or in other words, we are led to argue that:

Proposition 3: Human behaviour is framed and 'routinized' by social structure.

The Boundaries of Rationality

The implications of Propositions 2 and 3 for understanding consumer society (and for changing consumer behaviour) are quite profound. In the first place, of course, taken together they appear to undermine key principles of modernity, such as the centrality of individuality and individual choice. The suggestion implicit in Proposition 2 is that individualism is in some sense a kind of myth. Methodological individualism – which holds that it is individuals operating as more or less unilateral agents under the influence of largely free choice who determine behavioural patterns – looks almost entirely untenable under these Propositions.

Instead we must look to social influences and to underlying social and institutional structures as being absolutely vital influences (and constraints) on behaviour – and on behavioural change – at both individual and societal level. None of this is to deny the existence of individual cognitive deliberation, nor of personal tastes and preferences. But it does point to the vital importance of social norms and expectations, institutional structures, cultural signals and the sheer force of routine and habit as guiding forces in our lives.

An immediate casualty of this position is the rational choice model that lies behind most economic analyses of consumer choice (see Jackson, 2005b). The economic model suggests that people make choices on the basis of a cognitive deliberation over private costs and benefits. Provided that certain conditions hold – in particular the availability of 'perfect' information – then such choices are assumed to be in the best interest of the individuals (i.e. 'rational') and therefore to be a robust guide to 'optimal' behaviour. The failure of the model in real life – people rarely behave as economists might wish them to – is usually attributed either to a lack of information, or else to the existence of a series of 'hidden' costs and benefits that act as barriers or perverse incentives at the individual level.

The policy prescriptions that flow from the rational choice model tend to be relatively few and relatively straightforward. Typically, policy-makers are enjoined either to improve information flows (e.g. through labelling, information campaigns and so on) or else to use financial incentives and disincentives to shift the balance between individual costs and benefits to reflect the existence of hidden social costs and benefits.

The limited success of such interventions is one of the reasons for a recent resurgence of interest in understandings of consumer behaviour and public attitudes.[24] From the perspective outlined here, limited success is only to be expected. The individual is constrained in becoming more sustainable by a variety of important factors. In addition to the price and information constraints that are conventionally acknowledged, the individual must negotiate his or her own conflicting motivations in the context of a variety of cognitive, social and structural constraints. And in negotiating these, he or she is bound as much by the 'social fabric' in which self is constructed as by 'objective' institutions and infrastructures. A more sophisticated policy framework is needed to address this complexity.

A Proposition about the Symbolic Role of Artefacts

Again, it is worth pausing here briefly to raise the question of materiality. What do these conceptions of agency and self tell us about our relationship to material goods? Interestingly, they do not yet tell us much. Of course, the fact that our identities are socially constructed and our actions constrained by structure points once more to the vital importance of social and psychological functioning and leads to some understanding of the interaction between these two.

We also know, from experience, that identity is a key driver of material consumption – at least in our society. Indeed, identity – according to Gabriel and Lang – is the 'Rome to which all discussions of modern Western consumption lead' (Gabriel and Lang, 1995, p81). But this observation appears on the surface to be only a contingent fact about modern Western society. It does not quite expose the driving forces which gave rise to it. We cannot yet understand this key feature of modern consumer society in terms of any underlying process common to all societies. To begin to make sense of the way in which the social construction of modern identity relies so heavily on material goods we need a fourth key proposition, namely that:

Proposition 4: Material artefacts carry symbolic meanings.

This insight has become a defining feature of sociological debates about consumption and consumer society.[25] The hypothesis itself arose from the confluence of some rather diverse intellectual influences including the semiotics of Charles Morris, the structuralism of Roland Barthes, the social philosophy of Baudrillard, the social anthropology of Marshall Sahlins and Mary Douglas, the 'motivation research' of Ernest Dichter and the consumer research of Elizabeth Hirschmann and Morris Holbrook, Russell Belk and others.[26]

It would be impossible to do justice to the breadth and scope of this literature here. But the most important lesson from this huge body of work is very clear. Material commodities are important to us, not just for what they do, but for what they signify: about us, about our lives, our loves, our desires, about our successes and failings, about our hopes and our dreams. Material goods and services are not just functional artefacts. They derive their importance, in part at least, from their symbolic role in mediating and communicating personal, social, and cultural meaning not only to others but also to ourselves.

There are few places where the symbolic character of material consumption is more naked to the popular scrutiny than in the case of the automobile, which has long been recognized as far more than a means of getting from one place to another. In spite of an equally popular disdain for the fact – cars have come to symbolize (for their owners at least) a wide variety of cultural 'goods': social status, sexual prowess, personal power, freedom and creativity.[27] Like many other material artefacts, they are now deeply imbued with cultural symbolism, as the New York columnist Benjamin Stein (1985, p30) illustrates colourfully:

> Sometimes I test myself. We have an ancient, battered Peugeot, and I drive it for a week.
> It rarely breaks, and it gets great mileage. But when I pull up next to a beautiful woman,
> I am still the geek with the glasses. Then I get back into the Porsche. It roars and it tugs
> to get moving. It accelerates even going uphill at 80… It makes me feel like a tomcat on
> the prowl … with the girls I shall never see again pulling up next to me, giving the car
> a once-over, and looking at me as if I were a cool guy, not a worried, over-extended,
> 40-year-old schnook writer.

This example also points very clearly to the link between motivation (to drive a Porsche, for example) and reproductive functioning. But we would be entirely wrong to limit the symbolic importance of goods to sexual display, personal power and individual greed. Proposition 2 should already warn us against taking such an individualist position on the nature and function of symbolic goods. In fact, the evidence from anthropology insists that the symbolic role of goods is vital to social functioning at both personal and collective levels. In particular, it transpires that goods play key symbolic roles in exchange rituals, and have done for many millennia, as Lévi-Strauss first pointed out. Mary Douglas (1976, p208) highlights their role in the provision of what she calls 'marking services':

> First, let us assume that the ultimate object of consumption activity is to enter a social
> universe whose processes consist of matching goods to classes of social occasions. Second, for entry into such a universe, the individual needs the services of fellow consumers. These services are either in the form of personal attendance at consumption events
> or of material contributions of goods (e.g. flowers) and their object is to create or confirm
> a grading of the occasion.

Douglas's description of this process reveals an apparent arbitrariness in the way symbolic values are associated with particular goods, and the ways these goods are graded in and confer grades on social activities. At one point it might be a particular brand of fine wine, at another a particular musical composition, at another a type of cut flowers that signals and embodies the value assigned to a given social situation. These values both determine and are determined by social exchanges. In a sense the exchange of goods (and values) achieved in providing and receiving marking services is quite precisely a conversation of gestures. The symbolic role attributed by human beings to material artefacts creates a new 'language of goods' which becomes the subject and the object of whole new social conversations.

Whether these conversations are significant – in Mead's sense – is a very interesting question. Given that material goods and services operate as symbols, and that the formation of symbols appears to require creative faculties that belong within the realm of awareness, then presumably Mead would have answered this question in the affirmative. However, there is also plenty of evidence to suggest that our everyday responses to symbolic signals occur at a sub- or semi-conscious level. We may be fully aware, at some level, that – as one respondent in Belk's lovely study on consumer desire pointed out – 'no-one's gonna spot you across a crowded room and say, "wow! nice personality!"' (Belk et al, 2003). But that doesn't mean that we literally and consciously 'clock' every visual signal carried by material objects at every moment of our waking lives.

Sometimes our sense of whether or where we fit in a given social situation is nothing more than the presence or absence of an uncomfortable feeling of displacement. In all probability, it swept over us almost instantly upon entering the room, conveyed by a myriad subtle but undeniable visual signals: the clothes we were wearing, the clothes others were wearing, their demeanour, their haircuts, the way they tied their shoes, the shade of wallpaper on the walls, the kind of pictures hanging there, the fabric of the upholstery on the chairs.

The conversation of gestures opened up to us through the symbolic role of material goods is one that is neither fully aware, nor fully unconscious. As such it protects itself with a peculiarly powerful veil of 'collective misrecognition' (to use Bourdieu's phrase). We may be aware, intellectually, that the symbolic nature of goods plays an important role in social conversations. But we do not carry this awareness into every such conversation with us. And we seldom articulate it in a fully conscious conversation of ideas. And it is for this reason that the conversation of gestures encoded in acquiring, using, exchanging and disposing of material goods presents us with an incredibly difficult domain for policy intervention. I shall return to this difficulty in the final section of the chapter.

The key point here is this: that in facilitating an entire 'new' realm of social conversation (i.e. separate from the realm of animal gestures and separate from the 'significance' of the linguistic realm), the symbolic language of material artefacts fits them perfectly for an absolutely vital role in mediating social and psychological functioning. Material goods in this characterization form part of the social glue that allows people to interact and society to function.

We would be wrong however to construe the symbolic role of goods as an entirely modern pathology – a disease of consumer society. The insights from anthropology quite clearly contradict this. Anthropological evidence for the cultural role of artefacts as symbols can be found in every society for which we have any evidence over a very long period of time. This is not a defining feature of modernity. Things were ever thus.

Symbolic Self-Completion

The task of constructing and maintaining symbolic value – like the task of constructing and maintaining an identity – is a fundamentally social one. The value attached to symbols is constantly negotiated and renegotiated through social interactions in a given cultural context.[28] In the hands of certain sociologists and social philosophers, this insight has become the basis for a quite specific view of consumer society in which the individual is locked into a continual process of constructing and reconstructing personal identity in the context of a continually renegotiated universe of social and cultural symbols.

Giddens (1991) points to the 'dilemmas of the self' confronting individuals in modern society, when faced with the opportunity to reinvent ourselves through the continually enlarging choice of consumer goods. Baumann points to the convenient resonances between the process of perpetual reconstruction of identity, and the impermanent, transient nature of modern consumer goods. 'Aggregate identities, loosely arranged of the purchasable, not-too-lasting, easily detachable and utterly replaceable tokens currently available in the shops,' he writes, 'seem to be exactly what one needs to meet the challenges of contemporary living' (Baumann, 1998, p29). Cushman postulates that this 'empty self' which is constantly in need of 'filling up' is a cultural artefact generated quite explicitly by and for the commercialism of modern society (Cushman, 1990).

Elliott and Wattanasuwan (1998, and see Figure 25.2) offer a model in which two kinds of resources (material and symbolic) and two kinds of processes (individual and social) each play dual roles in the construction of identity. The basis for my self-concept at any one point in time includes my broad life history and situation, for example: 'I am a white forty-something British male, married and with three children, living in the south of England'. But that broad history is also coloured by a myriad of details about the precise nature of my life, and that detailed picture is constantly changing. As it changes, my self-concept changes with it. I am encouraged (by social norms and cultural signals) to think of myself as successful if I have access to certain kinds of material

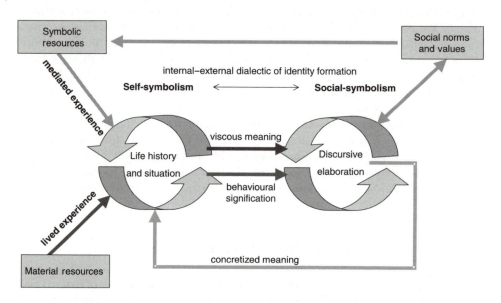

Source: Adapted from Elliott and Wattanasuwan (1998)

Figure 25.2 *The symbolic project of the self*

resources: a nice house, a smart car, decent clothes and so on. My lived experience of these material resources becomes a part of my self-concept. If they are ripped suddenly from my life, through tragedy or unemployment or disaster, I am disabled not just functionally but psychologically and socially as well. These material resources are a part of the 'lived experience' that creates and maintains my self-concept. But my relationship to these material resources is in part a 'mediated experience'. I know how to think about my car, my house, my clothes, my wife and my children, in part at least, because of the social symbolism which these elements of my life convey (to me and to others). These symbolic resources are as important to the negotiation of my self-concept as the material resources on which I rely functionally.[29]

Even more importantly, my lived and mediated experience of these material and symbolic resources is part of a social process. At best I am able to attribute what Elliott and Wattanasuwan call 'viscous' meaning to my experience at the personal level. I must then test out this unsolidified meaning through a process of 'discursive elaboration' in which I describe, discuss, argue about, laugh at and otherwise explore the mediated experiences I glean from the symbolic resources around me. And it is only in the social realm, that these meanings become 'solidified' and allow me to 'complete' the symbolic project of the self.

One of the interesting questions arising from this model is the extent to which it is or is not a common feature of all societies. Giddens appears to suggest that it is a characteristic of modernity. But as I have already pointed out, the association of symbolic meanings with material artefacts is common across all societies. In a seminal thesis on the subject, written in 1982, Wicklund and Gollwitzer argue that symbolic self-completion is a common project for all human beings, in all societies. A similar view is proposed by narrative identity theory.[30] Symbolic self-completion appears to be a part of the human condition. We are born, in some sense incomplete. We are faced as human beings with the project of social-symbolic self-completion. We use whatever resources are available to us for this project.

Clearly, however, the precise nature of those resources may differ from one society to another. In one society, symbolic self-completion may occur primarily through the social-symbolic importance attached to particular trades and capabilities. In another, it might be pursued mainly through the exchange of mythical social roles and narratives. What characterizes modern Western society, in the eyes of Baumann, Giddens, Cushman and a good many others is that the symbolic project of the self is mainly pursued through the consumption of material goods imbued with symbolic meaning. But the project itself is common across all societies.

A Proposition about Culture and Meaning

My final proposition is one that in some sense I have been building up to throughout this chapter, and should come as little or no surprise to the reader, although it operates at a slightly different level than the other propositions. It is a proposition about the nature of consumer society.

Proposition 5: Consumer society is a cultural defence against anomie.

In one sense, this is a fairly empty proposition. Or rather, it is derivative from a much more general proposition about society and meaning. As we have already seen, and has been argued with enormous cogence by Berger in particular, *every* society must defend itself against anomie. 'Every society is engaged in the never completed enterprise of building a humanly meaningful world,' he wrote in 1967 (Berger, 1967, p27). '[L]egitimations in the face of death are decisive requirements in any society' (pp43–4). The evolutionary role of social structure is precisely to provide the social rules and institutions that preserve the 'plausibility structure' of the society in question and defend it against shocks and intrusions. Perhaps most importantly, these institutions must provide for nomization – the continual creation and protection of meaning – and defend against anomie – the ever-present threat of loss of meaning.

These threats to meaning occur in a variety of ways. They can arise through the external influence of another cultural group. But they can also occur through rogue elements – the disenfranchised, dispossessed and occasionally the purely sociopathic elements – within the given group or society itself. They occur as a matter of course both at the individual level and at the social level through disaster, loss, bereavement and the prospect of personal mortality.

Individual loss threatens personal meaning. Collective loss threatens collective meaning. The Asian tsunami on Boxing Day in 2004, the earthquake that devastated Kashmir in October 2005, the hurricanes which lashed New Orleans, the attack on the World Trade towers in 2001: there is a sense in which such events can be thought of as the polar opposite of Jonny Wilkinson's last minute drop goal in the rugby world cup. A sense of helplessness, panic and deep-seated anxiety pervades our responses to these crises. All the collective meanings that we hold dear – our nationhood, our sense of cultural pride, our belief in progress, our adherence to the stability of global markets, our faith in humanity, our faith in the divine – tremble and shake under the influence of such tragedies. That such catastrophes are less common in modern society (at least in the West) does not for a moment reduce the threat they pose, nor the efforts we take to create meaning structures with which to defend ourselves from them.

The same is true at the personal level, where interestingly there is only a rather marginal diminution in the frequency and severity of devastating loss. There is less infant mortality. There are, in the West at least, fewer apocalyptic wars. Children seldom die in infancy now. Parents do not generally outlast their children. But the ever-present prospect of our own mortality and, perhaps more importantly, that of our relatives and friends still confronts our meaning-structures with a formidable task: how to ensure healthy functioning in the face of personal and social loss.

In modern society, there is very little in the way of open discussion about the social significance of this kind of meaning-threat outside the remnants of religious discourse, and the reflections of a few isolated social philosophers.[31] Fortunately, however, the rather lengthy history of the concept of anomie within sociology, and the equally impressive exploration of ritual within anthropology provide us with a rich source of evidence on the importance of these issues to the structure and nature of society. And the insights from these sources suggest that every culture is engaged, as a matter of course, in processes of meaning creation and maintenance – nomization – that allow society to continue to function – even when confronted by continual threats to meaning both from outside and within. As Berger (1967, p23) describes it:

> Every socially defined reality remains threatened by lurking 'irrealities'. Every socially constructed nomos must face the constant possibility of its collapse into anomy. Seen in the perspective of society, every nomos is an area of meaning carved out of a vast mass of meaninglessness, a small clearing of lucidity in a formless, dark, always ominous jungle.

The function of world maintenance is fulfilled in different ways in different societies. The cultural myths and narratives which provide for a sense of continuity and meaning are as varied as the cultures that devise them. In many earlier societies, the task was assigned to religious institutions and structures. These institutions engaged in often rather complex cultural 'theodicies' in defence of meaning: attempts to defend the central propositions of the religious order (the benevolence and omnipotence of deities, for example) in the face of personal and collective loss. 'Why should a caring God allow the innocent to suffer?' is far more than idle religious speculation about the nature of deity. It is a cry for meaning in a social world constantly staving off chaos.

Although originating in theological thought, theodicy has a profoundly secular function. Confronted with persistent injustice, the prosperity of ill-doers, the persecution of the righteous, how should we seek to live? Faced with the death of a loved one, the suffering of innocents, the sorrow of bereavement, where should we turn for solace? How are we to protect the authority of compassion and the promise of love? Where, in short, are we to find meaning in our lives? Construed in these terms, theodicy is the core task of world maintenance, as Berger himself recognized.[32] The form of these theodicies may differ from culture to culture. But the project of world maintenance is common across every culture. It is – like the project of self-completion – a feature of the human condition.

The Sacred Canopy: Consumer Culture as Theodicy

We may seem at this point a long way from the day-to-day business of sustainable consumption. What, after all, has the sociology of religion to do with energy efficiency, public transport, recycling rates, ethical investment or fair trade goods? Let me try to defend what might otherwise be seen as an elaborate diversion from the matter in hand by connecting two of my previous propositions to this final one.

Proposition 2 highlighted the importance of social conversation to some of our most basic psychological and social functionings. Conversation is also, according to Berger and others, one of the key avenues of world maintenance. 'The subjective reality of the world hangs on the thin thread of conversation…' he writes in *The Sacred Canopy*. 'The world begins to shake in the very instant its sustaining conversation begins to falter' (Berger, 1967, p22). It is not just our concepts of self and identity that are negotiated through social conversation. The reality and stability of the social world also depends on it; and with that reality, our sense of meaning and ontological security.

Proposition 4 introduced us to the idea that material artefacts themselves enter into social conversation as a 'language of goods'. We have seen how they facilitate a realm of conversation that appears to be vital to some key social and psychological functionings. Could it be that – by integrating themselves so thoroughly (and almost imperceptibly) in our social conversations – material artefacts are also implicated in the vital task of world maintenance? Could it be that in addition to their role in providing the physical stuff of our material world, consumer goods also constitute a vital part of the social fabric? 'An individual's main objective in consumption is to help to create the social universe and to find in it a creditable place,' claimed Mary Douglas (1976), in the quote with which this chapter opened. If taken seriously, this claim places the onus for world maintenance – in part at least – in the hands of our complex relationship to consumer goods.

In defence of this hypothesis, there are a number of places we might look for evidence and, perhaps remarkably, a number of places where we find it. The anthropology of religious iconography suggests that material objects have played a crucial role in religious belief in every society that we know of. Sacred artefacts have routinely been used to symbolize and concretize the religious order, communicate with divinity, connect us to the cosmos, separate what is precious or 'numinous' from what is profane, and remind religious devotees of shared meanings and beliefs.[33]

Perhaps even more striking is the evidence from consumer research, marketing studies and psychology that this kind of role for material artefacts is not confined to religious icons. Even in our largely secular world, the evidence suggests, consumer goods are implicated in a variety of quasi-religious functions. Csikszentmihalyi and Rochberg-Halton (1981) examined the role of ordinary household goods and found they were woven inextricably into shared and personal meanings. Belk and his colleagues (1989) have shown how the symbolic role of consumer goods is constantly employed in negotiating and defending boundaries between the sacred and the profane. Campbell (1987, 2004) has developed a view of consumer society in which material goods allow us to explore the ontological basis of the world and address fundamental questions about our place in it. Sheldon and his colleagues (2003) have marshalled psychological evidence to show how consumption plays a vital role in 'terror management' in the consumer society.

Of particular relevance to my argument here is a suggestion by McCracken (1990) that consumer goods play a role in negotiating what he calls 'displaced meaning'. Following Durkheim and others, McCracken argues that one of the most pressing problems a culture must deal with is the 'gap between the "real" and the "ideal" in social life': the distance between our aspirations – for ourselves, for our society, for our God, for human nature – and the reality with which we are daily confronted. Unconditional love, benevolence, compassion, forgiveness, altruism (for example) are neither pervasive realities in this world nor even particularly successful survival strategies. They must either perish as ideals or be protected in some way from the harsh light of day. The 'displacement of meaning' is, according to McCracken (1990, p106), one of the most effective ways of dealing with this gap:

> Confronted with the recognition that reality is impervious to cultural ideals, a community may displace those ideals. It will remove them from daily life and transport them to

another cultural universe, there to be kept within reach but out of danger... The strategy of displaced meaning contends with the discrepancy between the real and the ideal by the clever expedient of removing the ideal from the fray.

A culture that engages in the strategy of displaced meaning is faced with the need to establish a limited form of access to the displaced ideals. Ideals which remain forever inaccessible simply atrophy. Ideals which are too accessible become falsified by exposure to the withering light of reality. The recovery of displaced meaning is a delicate and potentially dangerous operation. It must provide the illusion of access to the displaced ideal without jeopardizing the 'epistemological immunity' of the ideal which displacement effects.

McCracken claims that material goods and services are ideally suited to this task for a number of reasons. In the first place, of course, their ability to carry symbolic meaning (Proposition 4) allows them to communicate our highest ideals. On the other hand, there is a clear distinction between the commodity (as physical object) and the ideal it symbolizes. One may possess the object; but possessing the object is not the same as possessing the ideal. Material consumption allows us to approach displaced ideals in a symbolic sense, and at the same time leave intact the displacement which protects the ideals themselves from too much scrutiny.

Finally, like Baumann and Giddens, McCracken points to the sheer volume of goods and services in the consumer society, which offer an almost infinite variety of strategies for approaching – and never quite recovering – displaced meaning. In a perverse kind of sense, the success of consumer goods as 'bridges' to meaning is quite precisely their continuing failure to recover displaced ideals. Since they approach displaced ideals without ever actually recovering them, consumer goods never quite foreclose the need for future bridges, never quite diminish the appetite for future consumption. Consumer culture perpetuates itself, in this view, precisely because it succeeds so well at failure!

The suggestion implicit in this discussion (and in the evidence base cited above) is that the consumer society is itself operating as a kind of secular theodicy.[34] The shared and negotiated meanings in consumer goods and services, the process of consumption itself, and the narratives of social progress inherent in consumerism all operate as what Berger calls a 'sacred canopy' – an intricate, overarching, set of cultural meanings through which we construct and defend social reality.

Clearly, consumer society could not hope to operate in this way were it not for the symbolic power of material artefacts, the fact that symbolic meanings are themselves negotiated through social conversation, and the fact that social conversations make a vital contribution to 'world maintenance'. Social and psychological functioning in the consumer society are subtly intertwined and mediated crucially through the evocative power of material goods. Meaning is negotiated and defended. Nomization is facilitated. And for most of us, for most of the time, these vital social conversations hold anomie at bay and allow society to function.

Beyond the Consumer Theodicy:
Towards Sustainable Consumption

There is, in the literature on sustainable consumption, an ongoing debate about the respective roles of internal, psychological factors – attitudes, values, beliefs – and external, situational factors – infrastructures, incentives, social norms – in influencing consumer behaviour. The emerging view is one which recognizes the need for a framework incorporating both internal and external factors. The attitude–behaviour–constraint model and value–belief–norm model of Stern and his colleagues are attempts to provide exactly that sort of framework for environmental policy-making (Stern, 2000; Stern et al, 1995; Stern et al, 1999). Elsewhere, I have teased out some of the policy lessons that might flow from this sort of framework, and some of these lessons have been incorporated in policy, for example, in the 2005 UK Sustainable Development Strategy.[35] A systematic approach to behaviour change, in this view, offers some hope of approaching sustainable consumption.

The arguments I have put forward in this chapter do not contradict that case. However, they add another – and rather considerable – level of complexity to it. What I have attempted to show here is that vital social and psychological functionings – identity creation, social cohesion, cultural defence against anomie – are all mediated through material consumption. This complexity should certainly warn us against any simplistic prescriptions for social change. Their embeddedness in social conversation, their vital role in negotiating meaning, and the depth of their engagement in cultural myths and narratives suggests that material consumption patterns might represent a sphere of resistance – potentially quite violent resistance – to social change. Indeed, if material goods and services play such vital roles in the creation of the social world, then it becomes extremely problematic for one set of people to suggest to another set of people – or to society at large – that their needs might better be served by forgoing those goods and services. Unfortunately, we are driven, by the same token, further away from the prospect of sustainable consumption.

So what exactly can we offer policy-makers from the understandings pursued in this chapter? Is it all just bad news for sustainable consumption? Or is there something positive we can take from it?

Certainly, in the first instance, we can make some quite useful recommendations about the way in which change is to be negotiated. Since identity and meaning are constructed socially, and since social norms and expectations constrain individual choice in quite fundamental ways, we can certainly make a good case for arguing that change must be seen as a social and cultural process. Behaviour change initiatives need to involve peer groups, local communities, society at large in a range of broadly discursive social processes, rather than attempting to effect change solely at the individual level through 'top-down' persuasion and exhortation.

We can also identify an absolutely key role played by symbolic resources, both in the social-symbolic construction of identity and also in the negotiation and defence of personal and cultural meaning. As Figure 25.2 illustrates and previous sections have discussed, these symbolic resources provide a vital link between self and other, between people and culture and are, in part, the medium for the social conversation on which the reality and stability of the social world depends.

A critical issue here (which must lie beyond the scope of this chapter to address in detail) is the question of who controls these symbolic resources. Do they lie within some kind of democratic control? Are they amenable to public policy intervention? Are they subject to control and influence by agents who seek to profit from their influence on others? Although it is clearly true that some social control over symbolic resources is possible, it remains almost self-evident that in modern consumer culture, much of this control has been handed over to the commercial interests of producers. Marketers, advertisers, designers and retailers not only have a vested interest in controlling symbolic resources, they also have a long and rather sophisticated experience in effecting this control to their own best advantage. To make matters worse, they also have at their disposal considerably more resources than those available to the public sector in its attempt to promote responsible or sustainable behaviour. It has to be asked whether this asymmetry in control over symbolic resources is appropriate or in the long-term best interests of society.[36]

Marketing standards are only one of a number of areas in which government policy determines not so much the precise nature of individual choice, but the social context in which symbolic value is created, identity and meaning are constructed, and agency is negotiated. There are a number of other such areas including trading standards, product standards, corporation law, social policies (such as family support and distributional policy), education, support for public sector broadcasting, and the frameworks within which religious institutions and other community groups operate. A key lesson from the analysis in this chapter is that government must seek to understand its own role and intervene more creatively in shaping this social context.[37]

Particular attention should perhaps be paid to the question of religious and community groups. If the analysis in this chapter is right, if a key function of the consumer society is the pursuit of meaning and the defence against anomie, then the transition to a sustainable society cannot hope to proceed without the emergence or re-emergence of meaning structures that lie outside the consumer realm. This is not to suggest, of course, that the route to sustainability lies in the revival of 18th-century theological utopianism. It does, however, highlight the importance of 'communities of meaning' capable of supporting the essential social, psychological and spiritual functionings that have been handed over, almost entirely in modern society, to the symbolic role of consumer goods.

Taken to their logical conclusion, the arguments in this chapter suggest that sustainable consumption cannot be achieved solely through policy intervention. On the contrary, it demands that we re-engage – as a culture – in some fundamental debates about human progress, about the basis for human well-being, and about meaning and value in human existence: debates which have haunted us for centuries but which in the consumer society have been chased from their central role in intellectual life by presumptions about economic progress and preoccupations with comfort and convenience.

It may sound facile to suggest that sustainable consumption is – at one level – about addressing our own mortality and confronting the anomie that has haunted every society throughout the ages. On the other hand, to proceed without attention to this kind of insight into the underlying processes of consumer society – processes that are held in common with just about every society we know of – is to invite a spectacular failure, not just in environmental terms, but in social terms as well.

By contrast, of course, a sophisticated approach to sustainable consumption, which recognizes some of these depths, may offer us our most realistic hope yet of re-visioning human progress and finding meaning and purpose in our lives.

Acknowledgements

An earlier version of this chapter was published as 'Consuming paradise? Unsustainable consumption in cultural and social-psychological context', in K. Hubacek, A. Inaba and S. Stagl (eds) *Driving Forces of and Barriers to Sustainable Consumption*, Proceedings of an International Workshop held in Leeds, UK, 5–6 March 2004. I am grateful to numerous participants in that workshop for an extremely lively discussion session which helped me enormously in revising the paper. I am grateful also for the intellectual generosity of several people who not only informed my perspective here but also spent time talking to me about ideas in this paper. They include Blake Alcott, Russell Belk, Colin Campbell, Ishani Erasmus, Tim Kasser, Grant McCracken, Laurie Michaelis, Miriam Pepper, Eivind Stø and David Uzzell. This work resulted from a Fellowship on the 'Social Psychology' of Sustainable Consumption supported by the Economic and Social Research Council (RES 332-27-001).

Notes

1 For more detailed elaborations of this point see, for example, Baudrillard (1970); Campbell (1987, 2004); Cushman (1990); Giddens (1991); Robbins (2002); Taylor (1989).
2 The point was made first by Lévi-Strauss (1949). See also Douglas (1976).
3 There are a number of slightly different definitions of the term 'anomie'. Durkheim defined it as a condition where moral norms are confused, unclear or simply not present. For Camus this was associated with a listless lack of moral direction. For Berger, the term is taken more to mean the failure of the processes of nomization – or in other words the collapse of normal personal, social or cultural meaning creation and maintenance functions. This is the sense in which I am adopting the term here.
4 A wonderfully clear exposition of this point can be found in Berger (1967). See also Camus (1942); Durkheim (1897); Giddens (1984); Weber (1922).
5 This example is very specific to the time and place in which this chapter is written. The original paper was written in early 2004, shortly after the English rugby team won the Rugby Union World Cup by the narrowest of margins against the host side (Australia). The win represented England's first major international sports trophy for several decades and the winning team was praised and feted by public and politicians alike. At the time, the BBC carried an online news story which spoke of politicians 'continuing to squabble over the Downing Street reception for England's World Cup-winning rugby team'. For a brief period the whole nation went rugby crazy. It turned out that the fly-half who kicked the winning goal, Jonny Wilkinson, had been injured quite badly in a previous match and has not since returned to international rugby. All the more reason perhaps to celebrate his moment of glory. I could of course equally have used another sporting triumph (for instance, the Greek football team's unexpected World Cup win in 2004) to illustrate the same point.

6   This is most obviously true of course in the Brundtland definition of sustainable development as development which 'meets the needs of the present without compromising the ability of future generations to meet their own needs' (WCED, 1987).

7   For a discussion of the relevance of human needs to sustainable consumption see Jackson et al (2004). See also Jackson and Marks (1999); Mallmann (1980); Max-Neef (1991).

8   Strictly speaking, Sen distinguishes between functioning itself, the capability to function, and economic goods that happen to be employed in the process. In Sen's schema it is the capability of functioning which is regarded as a good, rather than functioning itself, since an individual may choose – for a variety of reasons which lie beyond public judgement – not to employ that capability.

9   I should mention somewhere here that in adopting an approach that allies motivations to underlying functionings, I am also implicitly taking a very specific position in relation to the 'calculus of pleasure and pain' that occupied Enlightenment thinkers and behavioural psychologists for well over two centuries. Specifically, I do not accept here that motivation can be construed, simply, as the pursuit of pleasure or the avoidance of pain. Pleasure may well be related to healthy functioning (or needs satisfaction) and pain associated with 'disfunctioning'. Pleasure – or the promise of pleasure – may well be the 'proximal' cause of many behaviours – sexual promiscuity – but the one-dimensionality of the pleasure–pain calculus becomes deeply problematic when it comes to understanding the broad range of human behaviours, and offers little in the way of explanation. I am happy enough with the view in which pleasure and pain are evolutionary adaptations whose purpose is to signal and to signify 'successful' behaviours. But to me there is a distance between accepting the evolutionary role of pleasure and pain, and suggesting that this exhausts any discussion of the basis for human motivation. The evidence just does not support such a view.

10   For an overview of the relevance of evolutionary psychology to consumption see Jackson (2002a). For detailed discussions of the role of desire in modern consumer society see (amongst others): Baumann (1998); Belk et al (2003); Campbell (1994).

11   In defence of this inclusion I could also point to a wide literature both from Western counter-cultural writings on lifestyle (such as Elgin's writing on Voluntary Simplicity – reproduced as Chapter 11 in this volume) and also from Eastern philosophy, which suggest that there is a kind of human functioning which is not only different but sometimes at odds with material and psychological comfort, which indeed can only be approached through the negation of such desires; see for example, Bhikku (1956).

12   For useful surveys of the evolutionary psychology of human motivations see, for example, Wright (1994) and also Ridley (1994).

13   For a concise exploration of these points, see Wilkinson (2000).

14   This point is made succinctly by Mary Douglas and Baron Isherwood in their much-cited book *The World of Goods – Towards an anthropology of consumption* (1979).

15   This assertion was at least partly verified in a pilot survey carried out as part of a Masters dissertation at the University of Stirling by Ishani Erasmus (2005).

16   A useful overview of some of this evidence is provided in Kasser (2002); see also Lane (1994).

17   For an exploration of the various strands in this argument, see Jackson (2005a).

18   'A linen shirt, for example, is, strictly speaking, not a necessary of life… But in the present times, through the greater part of Europe, a creditable day labourer would be ashamed to appear in public without a linen shirt, the want of which would be supposed to denote that disgraceful degree of poverty which, it is presumed, no body can well fall into without extreme bad conduct' (Smith, 1776, p821–2).

19   To be honest, we are once again in a contentious domain here. Campbell, for instance, somewhat perversely for a sociologist, vigorously defends individuality against the incursions of social constructionism, and even argues that to construe Mead's concept of the self as a social

construction is mistaken (see Campbell, 1996). From my point of view, I am not sure this matters too much. I don't need to suggest that the self is purely a social construct – even if it appears that Mead really did see it in that way. All I need for my thesis is that the social influences on the self and on individual action are significant.

20 See, for example, Bourdieu (1984).

21 For further discussion of this see: Jackson (2005b).

22 Giddens (1984, pp28–29); for a useful overview of structuration as a social science concept see, Parker (2000).

23 See, for example, Bargh (1994, 1996).

24 See, for example, Chapter 2 in the UK government's 2005 Sustainable Development Strategy (Defra, 2005).

25 For a clear and compelling account of this relationship see Dittmar (1992, now sadly out of print). Equally compelling expositions are to be found in McCracken (1990, especially Chapter 7, reprinted as Chapter 18 in this volume); and in Csikszentmihalyi and Rochberg-Halton (1981).

26 A bibliography of sources discussing this issue would have to include: Barthes (1973); Baudrillard (1968, 1970); Belk (1988); Dichter (1964); Douglas (1976); Douglas and Isherwood (1979); Hirschman (1980); Miller (1995); Morris (1946); Sahlins (1976); Slater (1997).

27 See, for example, Haggett (2000).

28 This view is articulated particularly clearly in Elliott and Wattanasuwan (1998).

29 See, for example, Thompson (1990, 1995).

30 In addition to Wicklund and Gollwitzer (1982), see, Ricoeur (1984, 1992); Jenkins (1996).

31 Ernst Becker's extraordinary book *The Denial of Death* (1973) was a notable exception.

32 A substantial part of *The Sacred Canopy* (Berger, 1967) is given over to a discussion of various theodicies.

33 See, for example, Eliade (1959); Douglas (1969).

34 I have explored this hypothesis more extensively in another paper: Jackson (2002b). In particular, that paper attempted to show how the failure of the 18th- and 19th-century church to come up with a credible theodicy contributed to the conditions from which modern consumer society emerged. It also illustrated some of the mechanisms through which consumer society attempted to counter the theodical void left by secularization.

35 See Chapter 7 in this volume and also Jackson (2005b); Defra (2005, Chapter 2).

36 The commercial nature of this relationship is particularly problematic where children are concerned. From about the age of five onwards, social and developmental psychology suggests that the social community within which discursive elaboration of symbolic meanings occurs shifts gradually away from parental influence and towards the peer group. And yet it is clear that – at least until the early teens – this peer group lacks the critical faculties needed to resist, select or accommodate the complexities of the messages to which it is routinely exposed through advertising. It is precisely for this reason that some Nordic countries have banned advertising to children.

37 See also Chapter 7 in this volume for a fuller discussion of policy implications.

References

Bargh, J. (1994) 'The four horsemen of automaticity: Awareness, intention, efficiency, and control in social cognition', in R.Wyer and T. Skrull (eds) *Handbook of Social Cognition, Vol 1: Basic Processes* (2nd edn), Lawrence Erlbaum, Hillsdale, NJ

Bargh, J. (1996) 'Automaticity in social psychology', in E. Higgins and A. Kruglanski (eds) *Social Psychology: Handbook of Basic Principles*, The Guilford Press, New York/London

Barthes, R. (1973) *Mythologies*, Paladin, London

Baudrillard, J. (1968) *The System of Objects*, (extracted in *Selected Writings*, 1988), Polity Press, Cambridge

Baudrillard, J. (1970) *The Consumer Society: Myths and Structures*, (reprinted 1998), Sage Publications, London

Baumann, Z. (1998) *Work, Consumerism and the New Poor*, Open University Press, Milton Keynes

Becker, E. (1973) *The Denial of Death*, Polity Press, Cambridge

Belk R. (1988) 'Possessions and the extended self', *Journal of Consumer Research*, vol 15, pp139–168

Belk R., Wallendorf, M. and Sherry, J. (1989) 'Theodicy on the Odyssey: The sacred and the profane in consumer behaviour', *Journal of Consumer Research*, vol 16, pp1–38

Belk, R., Ger, G. and Askegaard, S. (2003) 'The fire of desire: A multi-sited inquiry into consumer passion', *Journal of Consumer Research*, vol 30, pp325–351

Berger, P. (1967) *The Sacred Canopy: Elements of a Sociological Theory of Religion*, Anchor Books, New York

Bhikku, A. (1956) *Handbook for Mankind*, Thammasapa, Bangkok

Bourdieu, P. (1984) *Distinction: A Social Critique of the Judgement of Taste*, Routledge, London

Campbell, C. (1987) *The Romantic Ethic and the Spirit of Modern Consumerism*, Blackwell, Oxford

Campbell, C. (1994) 'Consuming goods and the good of consuming', *Critical Review*, vol 8, no 4, pp503–520 (reprinted as Chapter 18 in this volume)

Campbell, C. (1996) *The Myth of Social Action*, Cambridge University Press, Cambridge

Campbell, C. (1998) 'Consumption and the rhetorics of need and want', *Journal of Design History*, vol 113, pp235–246

Campbell, C. (2004) 'I shop therefore I know that I am: The metaphysical basis of modern consumerism', in K. Ekström and H. Brembeck (eds) *Elusive Consumption*, Berg Publishers, New York

Camus, A. (1942) *Le Mythe de Sisyphe* (published in a new English translation, *The Myth of Sisyphus*, 2000, Penguin Classics, Harmondsworth)

Cushman, P. (1990) 'Why the self is empty: Toward a historically constituted psychology', *American Psychologist*, vol 45, no 5, pp599–611

Csikszentmihalyi, M. and Rochberg-Halton, E. (1981) *The Meaning of Things – Domestic Symbols and the Self*, Cambridge University Press, Cambridge

Defra (Department for Environment, Food and Rural Affairs) (2005) *Securing the Future – Developing UK Sustainable Development Strategy*, The Stationery Office, London

Dichter, E. (1964) *The Handbook of Consumer Motivations: The Psychology of Consumption*, McGraw Hill, New York

Dittmar, H. (1992) *The Social Psychology of Material Possessions: To Have is to Be*, St Martin's Press, New York

Douglas, M. (1969) *Purity and Danger*, Routledge, London

Douglas, M. (1976) 'Relative poverty, relative communication', in A. Halsey (ed) *Traditions of Social Policy*, Basil Blackwell, Oxford (reprinted as Chapter 15 in this volume)

Douglas, M. and Isherwood, B. (1979) *The World of Goods: Towards an Anthropology of Consumption* (reprinted 1996), Routledge, London

Durkheim, E. (1897) *Suicide* (reprinted in English translation, 2002), Routledge, London

Eliade, M. (1959) *Cosmos and History*, Harper, New York

Elliott, R. and Wattanasuwan, K. (1998) 'Brands as resources for the symbolic construction of identity', *International Journal of Advertising*, vol 17, no 2, pp131–145

Gabriel, Y. and Lang, T. (1995) *The Unmanageable Consumer*, Sage, London

Giddens, A. (1984) *The Constitution of Society – Outline of the Theory of Structuration*, University of California Press, Berkeley and Los Angeles, CA

Giddens, A. (1991) *Modernity and Self-Identity: Self and Society in the Late Modern Age*, Polity Press, Cambridge

Haggett, C. (2000) 'Control, risk and identity: The social ideology of the car', MSc Dissertation, University of Surrey

Hirschman, E. (1980) 'Comprehending symbolic consumption: Three theoretical issues', in E. C. Hirschman and M. B. Holbrook (eds) *Symbolic Consumer Behaviour, Proceedings of the Conference on Consumer Aesthetics and Symbolic Consumption*, Association for Consumer Research, New York

Jackson, T. (2002a) 'Evolutionary psychology and ecological economics: Consilience, consumption and contentment, *Ecological Economics*, vol 41, no 2, pp289–303

Jackson, T. (2002b) 'Consumer culture as a (failed) theodicy', in T. Cooper (ed) *Proceedings of the Conference 'Consumption, Christianity, Creation'*, Sheffield Hallam University, Sheffield, UK

Jackson, T. (2005a) 'Live better by consuming less? Is there a double dividend in sustainable consumption?' *Journal of Industrial Ecology*, vol 9, nos 1–2, pp19–36

Jackson, T. (2005b) *Motivating Sustainable Consumption: A Review of Evidence on Consumer Behaviour and Behavioural Change*, Sustainable Development Research Network, Policy Studies Institute, London

Jackson, T. and Marks, N. (1999) 'Consumption, sustainable welfare and human needs – with reference to UK expenditure patterns 1954–1994', *Ecological Economics*, vol 28, no 3, pp421–442

Jackson, T., Jager, W. and Stagl, S. (2004) 'Beyond insatiability: Needs theory, consumption and sustainability', in L. Reisch, and I. Røpke (eds) *The Ecological Economics of Consumption*, Edward Elgar, Cheltenham, pp79–110

James, W. (1890) *Principles of Psychology*, Dover Publications, Mineola, NY

Jenkins, R. (1996) *Social Identity*, Routledge, London

Kasser, T. (2002) *The High Price of Materialism*, MIT Press, Cambridge, MA

Lane, R. (1994) 'The road not taken: Friendship, consumerism and happiness', *Critical Review*, vol 8, no 4, pp521–554

Lévi-Strauss, C. (1949) *Les Structures Élémentaires de la Parenté*, published in England as *The Elementary Structures of Kinship* (1969, tr. J, H. Bell, J. R. von Sturmer and R. Needhon), Beacon, Boston, MA

McCracken, G. (1990) *Culture and Consumption*, Indiana University Press, Bloomington, IN, esp Chapter 7 (reprinted as Chapter 18 in this volume)

McDougall, W. (1908) *An Introduction to Social Psychology*, (reprinted in 18th edition, 1923), Methuen, London

Mallmann, C. (1980) 'Society, needs and rights', in K. Lederer (ed) *Human Needs: A Contribution to the Current Debate*, Oelgeschlager, Gunn and Hain, Cambridge, MA, pp37–54

Maslow, A. (1954) *Motivation and Personality*, Harper and Row, New York

Max-Neef, M. (1991) *Human-Scale Development: Conception, Application and Further Reflection*, Apex Press, London

Mead, G. (1934) *Mind Self and Society* (reprinted 1956), University of Chicago Press, Chicago, IL

Miller, D. (1995) *Acknowledging Consumption – A Review of New Studies*, London: Routledge

Morris, C. (1946) *Signs, Language and Behaviour*, George Braziller, New York

Nussbaum, M. (1998) 'The good as discipline, the good as freedom', in D. Crocker and T. Linden (eds) *The Ethics of Consumption: The Good Life, Justice and Global Stewardship*, Rowman and Littlefield, New York, pp312–341

Parker, J. (2000) *Structuration*, Open University Press, Milton Keynes

Ricoeur, P. (1984) *Time and Narrative*, University of Chicago Press, Chicago, IL

Ricoeur, P. (1992) *Oneself as Another*, University of Chicago Press, Chicago, IL

Ridley, M. (1994) *The Red Queen: Sex and the Evolution of Human Nature*, Penguin Books, Harmondsworth

Robbins, R. (2002) 'Capitalism and the making of the consumer', Chapter 1 in *Global Problems and the Culture of Capitalism*, Allyn and Bacon, Boston, MA

Sahlins, M. (1976) *Culture and Practical Reason*, University of Chicago Press, Chicago, IL

Sen, A. (1984) 'The Living Standard', reprinted in D. Crocker and T. Linden (eds) (1998) *The Ethics of Consumption: The Good Life, Justice and Global Stewardship*, Rowman and Littlefield, New York

Sheldon, S., Greenberg, J. and Pyszczynski, T. (2003) 'Lethal consumption: Death-denying materialism', in T. Kasser and A. Kanner (eds) *Psychology and Consumer Culture: The Struggle for a Good Life in a Materialistic World*, American Psychological Association, Washington, DC

Slater, D. (1997) *Consumer Culture and Modernity*, Polity Press, Cambridge

Smith, A. (1776) *An Inquiry into the Nature and Causes of the Wealth of Nations* (reprinted 1937), Modern Library, New York

Stein, B. (1985) 'The machine makes this man', *Wall Street Journal*, 13 June, p30

Stern, P. (2000) 'Toward a coherent theory of environmentally significant behavior', *Journal of Social Issues*, vol 56, no 3, pp407–424

Stern, P., Dietz, T. and Guagnano, G. (1995) 'The new ecological paradigm in social-psychological context', *Environment and Behavior*, vol 27, pp723–745

Stern, P., Dietz, T., Abel, T., Guagnano, G. and Kalof, L. (1999) 'A value–belief–norm theory of support for social movements: The case of environmental concern', *Human Ecology Review*, vol 6, pp81–97

Taylor, C. (1989) *Sources of the Self: The Making of the Modern Identity*, Cambridge University Press, Cambridge, MA

Thompson, J. (1990) *Ideology and Modern Culture*, Polity Press, Cambridge

Thompson, J. (1995) *The Media and Modernity: A Social Theory of the Media*, Polity Press, Cambridge

WCED (1987) *Our Common Future*, The report of the World Commission on Sustainable Development, Oxford University Press, Oxford

Weber, M. (1922) *The Sociology of Religion* (reprinted in English, 1993), Beacon Press, Boston, MA

Wicklund R. and Gollwitzer, P. (1982) *Symbolic Self-Completion*, Lawrence Erlbaum, Hillsdale, NJ

Wilkinson, R. (2000) *Mind the Gap: Hierarchies, Health and Human Evolution*, Wiedenfeld and Nicholson, London

Wright, R. (1994) *The Moral Animal – Why We Are the Way We Are: The New Science of Evolutionary Psychology*, Abacus, London

Index